MW00775224

MIRROR FOR GOTHAM

New York as seen by contemporaries from Dutch days to the present

THE NEW YORK PUBLIC LIBRARY
CHATHAM SQUARE BRANCH
33 EAST BROADWAY
NEW YORK, NEW YORK 10002

Fairchild Aerial Surveys, I

VERTICAL CITY

Visitors of the 1940's found New York "a vertical city . . . on the scale of the new times" (Le Corbusier). Here soaring Rockefeller Center dwarfs the spires of St. Patrick's Cathedral.

MIRROR FOR GOTHAM

New York as Seen by Contemporaries from Dutch Days to the Present

by
BAYRD STILL

With an Introduction by
JAMES F. RICHARDSON

THE NEW YORK PUBLIC LIBRARY
CHATHAM SQUARE BRANCH
33 EAST BROADWAY
NEW YORK, NEW YORK 10002

Fordham University Press
New York

Copyright © 1994 by Fordham University Press
All rights reserved
LC 94-17970
ISBN 0-8232-1528-8 (hardcover)
ISBN 0-8232-1529-6 (paperback)
Third printing 1995

Library of Congress Cataloging-in-Publication Date

Mirror for Gotham : New York as seen by contemporaries from Dutch days to the present / Bayrd Still ; with an introduction by James F. Richardson.
p. cm.
"First edition published by New York University Press, 1956"—T.p. verso.
Includes bibliographical references and index.
ISBN 0-8232-1528-8. — ISBN 0-8232-1529-6 (pbk.)
1. New York (N.Y.—Description and travel. 2. New York (N.Y.)—History. 3. New York (N.Y.)—In literature.
F128.3.S85 1994
974.7'1—dc20 94-17970
CIP

Printed in the United States of America

To

Mary Bayrd Colby

Millie Still Greenley

Carrie Still Floyd

CONTENTS

INTRODUCTION

The book you are about to read is fun.

Anyone who loves, cares about, or worries about New York City (and all Americans should be in one or more of these categories) will revel in this rich mixture of scholarly exposition and original source material on the nation's greatest city. Its author, Bayrd Still, late Professor of History at New York University, was one of the pioneers in systematic research and teaching on the urban experience in the United States. For this project he drew upon more than 600 accounts produced by travelers and residents from New Amsterdam's beginning as a fortified trading post in 1625 until the 1950s when the book was originally published. Each chapter opens with Professor Still's gracefully written exposition of the period under discussion, followed by selections from some of the sources. The introductory syntheses are based on material from the United States Census and whatever scholarly literature was available in the 1950s, as well as contemporary accounts.

Each of the source excerpts is preceded by a headnote identifying the author and the circumstances under which the comments were produced. More than half (forty-two of seventy-nine) of the writers chosen were British; there were also thirteen Americans, eight French, five Germans, and a scattering of other nationalities. Only eight women appear in the excerpts, although the author did note that women produced a considerable body of writing on the United States in the period from 1815 to 1845.[1] People who wrote for a living dominate the selections (at least sixty of seventy-nine); noted authors include James Fenimore Cooper, Frances Trollope, Charles Dickens, Walt Whitman, Mark Twain, Herbert Spencer, Rudyard Kipling, H. G. Wells, Arnold Bennett, and Ford Madox Ford. Other excerpts come from journalists famous in their time but now known only to specialists.

The book's focus is on Manhattan, with only a limited number of references to other boroughs. This concentration is justified because New York and Manhattan were coterminous until the late nineteenth century. Also, Manhattan is what makes New York special and significant. To this day, residents of other boroughs speak of going into the city when they travel to Manhattan.

Visitors commented most often on the visual impact of the city's core business, shopping, and entertainment areas and what one might glean from casual observation. A well-chosen group of photographs provide additional documentation and illustrate the sites most important to visitors.[2] Despite their limited knowledge and exposure, travelers felt free to offer their judgments of the city as a whole. Among the strengths of the expository portions of the book are Professor Still's assessments of when and why commentators were more or less impressed by the city. His command of the city's history enabled him to put in comparative context the comments of each writer and period.

Writers, whether travelers or residents, disproportionately came from elite backgrounds and usually avoided working-class areas of the city. For example, there are fifty-two index references to Broadway, the middle and upper class shopping and entertainment center, compared to four for The Bowery, which served the same functions for New York's workers. Some observers, including Charles Dickens, did seek out notorious areas such as the Five Points. On the whole, however, this is history from the top down, not the bottom up. This elite focus does not invalidate *Mirror for Gotham*; it does mean that readers should also consult the later work of such scholars as Raymond A. Mohl, Sean Wilentz, Christine Stansell, and Kathy Peiss to gain an understanding of the lives of working-class New Yorkers.[3]

One must remember the pioneering nature of Professor Still's achievement. For a variety of reasons historians came late to the study of cities in the United States, and it was not until the 1960s that the scholarly literature in urban history reached major proportions.[4] So it is not surprising that subsequent scholars have asked questions and used sources he did not. But as we learn new things we sometimes forget what is worth remembering. Bayrd Still always knew that each major city has its own personality, that each strikes visitors and natives alike as different from other cities, that this personality changes over time, and that it finds physical expression in the city's core.[5]

The personality of New York when *Mirror for Gotham* was produced was a generally positive one, and the tone of the book reflects that optimistic time. New York in the depressed 1930s did strike commentators as drab and declining, and Europeans during the war and immediate postwar period were somewhat bitter at how little the city was touched by the war. By the early 1950s, New York, home to the majority of Fortune 500 corporate headquarters, was clearly ascendant economically; with the United Nations headquarters it functioned as a world capital; its status as a cultural capital was enriched by the artists and intellectuals who had fled Nazi repression.

Whatever Cold War anxieties Americans felt had little impact on the book's contents. New York was the most important city in the world's most important country, and a wide variety of people wished to experience it first hand. Some critics might be appalled at what they considered its inhuman scale and pace, but most observers were impressed by its vitality and energy. Under the surface in the mid-1950s, economic and demographic trends were beginning to undermine some of the city's foundations, yet most observers focused on New York's strengths as business and financial center and art, entertainment, and publishing capital of the world.[6]

Reviewers received the book positively. Even when they criticized travelers for the superficiality of their comments, they commended Professor Still's judicious culling of these sources and the effective syntheses he provided at the beginning of each chapter.[7] Nelson Manfred Blake, in the *Mississippi Valley Historical Review,* considered the volume "a valuable contribution to the still sparse literature of American urban history." Blake's assessment reminds us how undeveloped the field of urban history was in the 1950s and how useful it was to have this collection of original source material, able scholarly synthesis, and illustrations on three centuries of the history of the nation's most important city.[8] New York City lovers simply reveled in the "range and variety" of the descriptions presented.[9] All reviewers praised the extensive notes, bibliography, and index, which remain valuable for those who wish to pursue particular periods or themes on the city's past.

This book looked backward on New York's past from the perspective of the 1950s. What can we say from the vantage point of the 1990s? How has New York City changed in the almost four decades since *Mirror for Gotham* was originally published? The short answer is: incredibly. Fortunately, we have evidence of what Bayrd Still thought of what was happening by the mid-1970s. In 1976 he published an essay entitled "Bicentennial New York, 1976" wherein he discussed demographic, economic, cultural, and political trends of the 1960s and early to mid-1970s. This piece drew upon a wide variety of sources, not just traveler's accounts.[10]

The perspective is much less positive than *Mirror for Gotham.* From the late 1950s onward (sometimes even earlier), contemporaries thought New York too big and too crowded. Areas that were formerly impressive now became oppressive—the result of a building boom in the 1960s and early 1970s that produced too many overly large and ugly office and apartment buildings. Crime and its companion, fear, is one of the major themes of the 1976 piece. In contrast, there are only two index references to crime in *Mirror for Gotham.*

From its earliest days New York experienced periods of slack trade, panics, and depressions as well as prosperity and booms. New York had no natural or artificial immunity from downturns in the national business cycle. What was different by the 1970s was that negative economic undercurrents perceptible from the 1950s had thrust upward to create economic and fiscal conditions in the city more severe than in the country as a whole. In 1951 the city reached its peak in manufacturing jobs with more than one million; by 1975 it had only 570,000. Manufacturing, which had provided one job in three, now made up only one in six. The garment industry alone had shrunk by 200,000 jobs. These losses were particularly distressing in view of the fact that manufacturing traditionally provided entry-level positions for those coming to the city with little formal education or training. Meanwhile, those who held desirable jobs in the city moved to the suburbs in ever-larger numbers. Retail trade followed affluent consumers, and there was a noticeable outmigration of corporate headquarters.

What did grow in the city were welfare rolls and municipal employees, whose number doubled between 1945 and 1975. Another budget-buster was the extension of open enrollment to the City University, with a corresponding increase in costs. (Professor Still's long connection with a private university as both faculty member and administrator made him particularly sensitive on this point.) The city's total spending grew more than fivefold between 1960 and 1975, and its per capita debt rose by 75 percent from 1970 to 1975 alone.[11] Municipal administrations dealt with these developments through various fiscal sleights of hand until 1975, when financial institutions refused to continue financing the city's short-term debt.

The city government, in effect, had to give over administration of its financial affairs to outsiders, headed by investment banker Felix Rohatyn, and seek aid from other levels of government in order to regain admittance to financial markets. To offset this humiliation, the city intensified its advertising campaign to promote itself as The Big Apple.

The use of this show-business term highlighted New York's persistent strength in the arts and entertainment, the most positive section of Professor Still's 1976 assessment. But even here there was a sour note with Broadway's shrinkage compared to its glory days in the late 1920s. Otherwise, this portion of the essay justly noted New York's reputation as the art and dance capital of world, its almost indigestible number of quality musical presentations, and its growing role as a center of book and magazine publication.

Throughout his career as a student of the American urban experience, Bayrd Still always paid particular attention to changes in the size and composition of a city's population and how contemporaries reacted to those changes. The most obvious demographic shifts of the years before 1976 were the outward movement of whites to the suburbs and the migration of African-Americans and Puerto Ricans into the city. These newcomers faced even more obstacles than previous European immigrants because of prejudice against their color and because of the decline of manufacturing.[12] Such economic and population shifts had serious financial implications for the city because of the loss of many substantial taxpayers and the increase of those needing extensive public services and assistance. Welfare is a particularly heavy burden for New York City because it pays a much larger share of the nonfederal portion than other cities.[13]

In 1965 the United States abandoned its long-standing policy of granting visas to potential immigrants on the basis of their national origins (a system which favored those from Northern and Western Europe) and substituted a series of preferences oriented toward the reuniting of families.[14] Still noted the early implications of the law in the rising numbers of Chinese and Cubans coming to New York, although in the mid- 1970s few could foresee the scale of changes coming in patterns of migration to the city.

In his 1976 discussion of government and politics (another subject largely ignored in *Mirror for Gotham* because it was beyond the scope of most travelers' interests), the author noted the proliferation of neighborhood associations in the late 1960s and early 1970s.

In addition to attempting to give local residents a voice in a heavily centralized and bureaucratized municipal government, these associations often sought to maintain the existing class and ethnic character of an area. Despite this institutionalization of territoriality and the bitter political conflicts between local African-American political activists and the teachers' union over control of schools, Still remained optimistic that most people thought of themselves as New Yorkers whose common interests outweighed differences of race, ethnicity, and class.[15]

Recent developments have shown even stronger tendencies toward separatism, most notably in Staten Island, the borough with the smallest population (378,977 out of a total city population of 7,322,564 in 1990) and the largest proportion of non-Hispanic whites (80 percent compared to 43 percent for the city). Staten Islanders have long complained of neglect and condescension from Manhattan elites, and they resent being the city's garbage dump (the Fresh Kills Landfill sounds more euphonious but smells just as bad). In many ways Staten Island is more like a suburb than the other boroughs, and its residents are no more eager than other suburbanites to bear the costs of urban problems. They are especially angry over recent changes in the structure of the city's government that have reduced the borough's relative weight in municipal affairs. Whatever the reasons, a majority of Staten Island's electorate voted in 1993 to secede from New York City. It will be up to the state legislature and the governor to determine whether or not that will happen.[16]

Journalist Chip Brown notes: "As Staten Islanders have made evident, it is getting harder and harder to find the connective tissue that holds New York together." He also reminds us that "Nothing said about the city is ever true for very long."[17] Felix Rohatyn has expressed his concern that fiscal crises will be more difficult to surmount in the 1990s than in the 1970s because "Today, the city is much more polarized along racial and class lines."[18] The unanswered question is whether New York City will be able to overcome the separatist tendencies now so prevalent both within its borders and around the world.

Unfortunately, Bayrd Still is no longer with us to offer his insights on New York in the 1990s.[19] What we can do is consult one of his favorite sources, the United States Census, to see what picture it offers. The following table is constructed from the *Census of*

Population and Housing for New York City for 1990. Some of the data is based on samples rather than the total population, and the census bureau has obvious difficulties in getting undocumented workers and others suspicious of authority to comply. With these caveats in mind, we can extract a valuable portrait of New York at the beginning of this decade.[20]

New York City: Population Profile 1990

Category	Number	% of total	% Foreign born	Fertility index	% of Group below poverty line
Total	7,322,564	100	28.4		
Whites (non-Hispanic origin)	3,163,125	43	19.4	772	9.6
Hispanic origin (any race)	1,763,511	24	34.9	1381	32.8
Blacks	2,102,521	28.7	26.6	1279	23
Asians and Pacific Islanders	512,719	7	79.1	964	16.1

Whatever their possible weaknesses, these statistics do indicate the dramatic demographic transformation of the city in recent years; if anything, they may understate it. Whites of European origin are less than half the total population, and almost one-fifth of this group is foreign born. More than one-quarter of the city's people of African origin were born outside the United States, increasingly from Africa and Latin America as well as the West Indies. Almost two in five New Yorkers five years of age or more do not speak English at home, and almost half of that group report that they do not speak English "very well." For the United States as a whole in the 1980s the largest numbers of immigrants came from Mexico, the Philippines, China, Vietnam, and Korea. In contrast, New York City received the most immigrants from the Dominican Republic, Jamaica, China, Guyana, and Haiti.[21]

The table also indicates the sharp disparities in poverty levels among different groups within the city. Non-Hispanic whites remain the dominant economic group, although they seem destined to be an ever-shrinking minority of total population. Asians, about four-fifths foreign born, show a mixed profile, with median incomes above the city's average but a poverty rate two-thirds higher than that of European-origin whites.

It is misleading to speak of both African-Americans and Hispanics, who can be of any race, as if they were undifferentiated, monolithic groups; with economic advances for some and continued immigration they become more internally diverse every year. What is striking is how poor they are as groups, and for many their condition has not improved with length of residence in New York. Those with above average incomes have often joined affluent whites in the trek to the suburbs. On the other hand, thousands of Puerto Ricans have given up on the city and moved back to the island. They are being replaced by people from the Dominican Republic and other Caribbean and Central American countries.[22] At the moment there seems to be more competition and resentment between Dominicans and Puerto Ricans than cooperation, so it is difficult for Hispanics to present a united front politically.[23]

Poorer New Yorkers have more children. The fertility index in the table is the number of children ever born to women ages fifteen to forty-four, and there is a direct correlation between the percentage of the group in poverty and its fertility. The city's children are thus more heavily minority and in poverty than its total population. The poorest of all are those being raised by single parents, who are overwhelmingly women, and the percentage of children in poverty has risen dramatically in recent decades. The census may underestimate poverty since poor households are less likely to return questionnaires. In a survey of 1990 household income, The Community Service Society of New York found 40 percent of the city's children living in poverty, compared to 20 percent nationally.[24]

These trends would be less worrisome if the city's economy were more robust. Of course, it is always difficult to distinguish between what might be a short-term cyclical downturn and a long-term structural decline. Whether cyclical or structural, there is no question that New York was hurting in the early 1990s. From December 1987 to December 1991 New York lost 135,000 jobs in financial services, which in turn triggered a loss of 32,000 jobs in construction.[25] The only bright spot was that the accompanying drop in office demand lowered rents to the point where firms that had considered leaving the city decided to stay.[26] On the down side, Felix Rohatyn thinks that the city is in a much more difficult economic and fiscal bind than in the mid 1970s. Costs have risen enormously because of the burdens associated with AIDS, the spread of crack cocaine, and homelessness.[27]

Well-paid jobs require more and more education and training while routine operations are computerized or moved elsewhere. The number of manufacturing jobs declined from 570,000 in 1975 to 320,000 in 1991. While New York firms continue to supply well-compensated advanced services to the world as a whole, only 55 percent of working-age New Yorkers are employed, compared to 66 percent nationally. Detroit is the only big city with a smaller percentage of working-age employed.[28]

Bayrd Still noted in 1976 that the number of public employees had grown much more rapidly than the city's population since the end of the Second World War. A similar phenomenon occurred in the flush times of the 1980s after the painful cuts of the late 1970s. One estimate is that municipal payrolls rose more than 23 percent between 1981 and 1991.[29] New medical and social problems like AIDS have put tremendous pressure on city services, and traditional responsibilities like police become ever more expensive. In 1990-91 the city spent $5,568 per capita, compared to $1,522 in 1974-75. Moreover, New York must spend so much to maintain its aging infrastructure that it is not able to compete with other cities in investing for the future with new capital projects.[30]

All of these difficulties are exacerbated by the fear of crime, which is even more pervasive in the 1990s than in 1976. Just before the mayoral election of 1993, *The New Yorker* noted that "In 1993, outrage about violence and lack of public safety is universal."[31] In a letter to *The New York Times*, the executive director of the Correctional Association of New York noted that the state's prison population (most of which comes from the city) has risen from 12,500 in 1973 to 64,500 in early 1994. He then asks, "But can anyone argue that the streets are safer, or that drug abuse and violence are less a threat to the quality of our lives?"[32]

More than 1,500 New Yorkers died from gunshots in 1993 compared to 44 fifty years earlier. Sociologist Nathan Glazer, in a review of a book on the history of Greenwich Village (where Bayrd Still lived and worked for four decades), wrote that the city is now suffering "a threatening social disorder that makes personal safety the first consideration of every New Yorker."[33]

With all its problems New York is still "The Big Apple," where people of talent, energy, and ambition come to test themselves and pursue their dreams. Immigrants bring vitality, imagination, and entrepreneurial zeal as well as languages other than English.[34] New York remains an incubator for art, ideas, and innovation as well as the nation's most well-developed advanced services sector. Heywood Broun once wrote of New York's great mayor, Fiorello La Guardia, "they have counted nine over Fiorello upon occasion but never ten." One can say the same for his city.[35]

Like so many who have contributed to New York's greatness, Bayrd Still was not a native. He was born in 1906 in Woodstock, Illinois, a small town about sixty miles northwest of Chicago. In his youth, going to the city meant Chicago, not New York. He entered the University of Wisconsin as an undergraduate to study journalism but switched to history under the influence of that strong department. He continued at Wisconsin as a graduate student, completing the Ph.D. in 1933 with a dissertation on the early constitutions of western states. Although Frederick Jackson Turner had left Wisconsin for Harvard in 1910, his influence remained strong in the department.[36]

For history as a discipline in the 1920s and early 1930s, cities seemed too contemporary and the history of cities too much the province of amateurs and antiquarians to interest professionals. Bayrd Still was one of the first academically trained historians to see the possibilities inherent in the study of the urban experience of the United States. He was much influenced by Bessie Louise Pierce's compilation of contemporary descriptions, *As Others See Chicago,* published in 1931. He began collecting contemporary accounts of cities and responses to changes in the size and composition of city populations. His research in contemporary materials convinced him that Americans had come to see the country's future as an urban one by the late 1860s. Notice that in *Mirror for Gotham,* a book covering more than three centuries, he devoted one chapter of ten to the single decade of the 1860s.

Meanwhile, he began teaching at the State Teachers College in Milwaukee, the forerunner of the current University of Wisconsin, Milwaukee. In 1941 he published a seminal article on the early history of five Great Lakes cities: Buffalo, Cleveland, Detroit, Chicago, and Milwaukee.[37] In addition to this important exercise in comparative urban history, he thought it possible to relate the history of a city as one would tell the story of an individual human life and so did research on Milwaukee in printed census materials, the city's newspapers, and its public records. He continued to work on the history of Milwaukee after moving to Duke University in 1938. After four years in military service during the Second World War, he returned to Duke and resumed work on *Milwaukee: The History of a City*, which was published in 1948 and issued in a revised edition in 1965.[38] It is a superb one-volume history of this important city, one often cited by subsequent scholars who have written more specialized studies on the city.[39]

Such general histories are known in the trade as "urban biographies," sometimes with a dismissive tone, but he made no apologies either for the descriptive term or the genre. Realizing by the 1970s that the field had so expanded in questions posed and sources used that no one person could attempt such a task, he continued to hope that groups of scholars working together could agree on scope and methodology to produce general histories of cities.[40]

In 1947, a year before *Milwaukee* was published, he moved to New York University to begin a program in teaching and research in urban history at the university's Washington Square center. Over the next three decades he directed some fifty-five Ph.D. dissertations, most on an aspect of New York City's history. Many of these dissertations were subsequently published in book form. While at NYU he also taught a popular undergraduate survey course in United States History at the Heights campus in the Bronx. He sometimes used the long subway rides back and forth to read graduate students' theses and dissertations. From 1955 to 1970 he served as head of the Department of History, and in a variety of other positions, including acting Dean of the College of Arts and Sciences and acting Dean of the Graduate School, while maintaining his other responsibilities. Upon his retirement as Professor of History in 1974 he accepted the position of University Archivist, an association he maintained for thirteen years. From 1962 to 1965 he was a member of the Landmarks Commission of New York City and served on the Mayor's Task Force on Municipal Archives. He also organized and led walking tours of Greenwich Village and the Washington Square campus.[41]

Bayrd Still was a consummate professional. No matter how busy, he always came to class prepared (and expected his students to follow his example); he gave all his graduate students the attention they needed to finish their theses and dissertations expeditiously; and he insisted on thorough research and clarity of thought and expression in their work. (His former students like to compare notes on how much red ink or blue pencil appeared on their dissertation drafts.) His definition of a professional was one engaged with the public, not dissociated from it. Therefore, in addition to his specialized work on the history of cities, he taught undergraduate pre-meds, gave a course on television, and introduced fellow walkers to the fascinations of the Village. In his view, historians should work to enhance public understanding, not teach and write solely for fellow historians.

It was partly for these reasons that in a 1977 interview published in the *Journal of Urban History* he said that he considered himself a historian of America's urban experience rather than an urban historian. The expansion of interest in America's urban past among younger scholars in the 1960s and 1970s brought with it new questions and new methodologies about which he had reservations. He said of himself that he was neither "quantitative" nor "conceptual"; therefore, he did not employ statistical techniques that went beyond numbers and percentages (he used census figures extensively in both his writing and his teaching) or social science concepts and theories.[42]

Bayrd Still's unease with these trends stemmed partly from having come of age in an earlier generation when training in quantification and social theory was rare among historians, but perhaps more importantly from a profound conviction that the historian's job was to produce coherent narratives and expositions of the past based upon materials contemporary to the period in question. The historian's findings should be presented in language accessible to members of the public so that interested citizens could read the history of their communities or the general history of cities in American society without becoming immersed in arcane formulae or an unfamiliar technical vocabulary.

In the 1950s this conviction had informed *Mirror for Gotham*, with its mixture of synthesis and excerpts from contemporary commentators on the history of New York City. In 1974 he expanded this technique to the nation as a whole in *Urban America: A History with*

Documents.[43] This volume's expository sections on the country's urban experience during various periods includes tables derived from the census on urban population size and composition. These tables were well known to his students (and to his students' students) in mimeographed form. This "extremely user-friendly" book also drew upon his decades of collecting contemporary comment, including material from the more troubled state of urban America in the late 1960s and 1970s compared to the 1950s.[44]

One of the shocks of my professional life has been meeting urbanists who do not like cities. That could never be said of Bayrd Still. He loved living in New York with its wealth of intellectual and cultural resources, and that love shows through in the following pages. His great interest outside of his work was music, especially vocal music. If you hadn't seen Bayrd for a while, just go to the opera, and he was always ready for a discussion on the relative merits of singers. Who could question the judgment and taste of a man who revered Victoria de los Angeles?

He once said that becoming autobiographical in print was a sign of intellectual decay,[45] but here the student feels impelled to deviate from the precepts of his teacher, and Bayrd was a fine teacher. One of his pedagogical strengths was the ability to walk into a classroom and put everyone at ease. In session after session he created an atmosphere that we were all friends engaged in a pleasant and rewarding enterprise. Among the students he put at ease in the 1956-57 academic year, when *Mirror for Gotham* appeared, were Marie Balfe and Jim Richardson, who met in his History of the American City course. When one of our children asked how did the girl from Rye and the boy from the Bronx ever get together, the answer was that Bayrd Still did it.

James F. Richardson

NOTES

1. Bayrd Still, *Mirror for Gotham: New York as Seen by Contemporaries from Dutch Days to the Present* (New York: New York University Press, 1956), p. 117.

2. Primarily pictoral books on New York include John A. Kouwenhoven, *The Columbia Historical Portrait of New York* (Garden City: Doubleday, 1953); Charles Lockwood, *Manhattan Moves Uptown: An Illustrated History* (Boston: Houghton Mifflin, 1976); Nathan Silver, *Lost New York* (Boston: Houghton Mifflin, 1967); and Benjamin Blom, *New York Photographs* 1850-1950 (New York: E. P. Dutton, 1982).

3. Raymond A. Mohl, *Poverty in New York, 1783-1825* (New York: Oxford University Press, 1971); Sean Wilentz, *Chants Democratic: New York City & the Rise of the American Working Class, 1788-1850* (New York: Oxford University Press, 1984); Christine Stansell, *City of Women: Sex and Class in New York, 1789-1860* (New York: Alfred A. Knopf, 1986); Kathy Peiss, *Cheap Amusements: Working Women and Leisure in Turn-of-the-Century New York* (Philadelphia: Temple University Press, 1986).

4. Raymond A. Mohl, "New Perspectives on American Urban History," *International Journal of Social Education*, 1 (Spring 1986), 69-97.

5. In addition to *Mirror for Gotham* see his articles "The Personality of New York City," *New York Folklore Quarterly*, 9 (Summer 1958), 83-92; and "The Essence of New York City," *New-York Historical Society Quarterly*, 43 (October 1959), 401-423. He also alluded to cities' personalities in Bruce Stave, "A Conversation with Bayrd Still," *Journal of Urban History*, 3 (May 1977), 341.

6. In addition to *Mirror for Gotham* see Stave, "Conversation," p. 353 and Bayrd Still, "Bicentennial New York, 1976" in Milton M. Klein, ed., *New York: The Centennial Years 1676-1976* (Port Washington, N.Y.: Kennikat, 1976), pp. 123-65.

7. John A. Krout in *American Historical Review*, 62 (July 1957), 930-31.

8. Blake, *MVHR*, 44 (June 1957), 121-23.

9. H. I. Brock, *The New York Times Book Review*, January 13, 1957, p. 10.

10. In Klein, ed., *New York*. The next several paragraphs are based on this essay.

11. U. S. Bureau of the Census, *County and City Data Book*, 1962, p. 545; U. S. Bureau of the Census, Statistical Abstract of the United States, 1977, pp. 302-304.

12. Oscar Handlin, *The Newcomers: Negroes and Puerto Ricans in a Changing Metropolis* (Cambridge: Harvard University Press, 1959); Nathan Glazer and Daniel Patrick Moynihan, *Beyond the Melting Pot: The Negroes, Puerto Ricans, Jews, Italians, and Irish of New York City*, 2nd edition (Cambridge: MIT Press, 1970).

13. See also Charles R. Morris, *The Cost of Good Intentions: New York City and the Liberal Experiment, 1960-1975* (New York: W. W. Norton, 1980) on the background of the fiscal crisis of 1975. Morris also cites health and hospitals as another service area where costs ballooned. Welfare expenses grew thirteenfold and health and hospitals tenfold during this fifteen-year period.

14. David Reimers, *Still the Golden Door: The Third World Comes to America* (New York: Columbia University Press, 1985); Roger Daniels, *Coming to America: A History of Immigration and Ethnicity in American Life* (New York: HarperCollns, 1990).

15. On the neighborhood asssociation movement since the 1960s see Robert Fisher, *Let the People Decide: Neighborhood Organizing in America* (Boston: Twayne Publishers, 1984).

16. Chip Brown, "Escape From New York," *The New York Times Magazine*, January 30, 1994, pp. 20ff. Robert D. Yaro, executive director of the Regional Plan Association, thinks Staten Island's secession vote more important than the mayoral election of 1993 and notes that some in Queens are now beginning to talk of going it alone. Not too many years ago other New Yorkers laughed at Staten Island's secessionists. See *The New Yorker*, November 15, 1993, p. 46.

17. Brown, "Escape," pp. 50, 60.

18. Rohatyn quoted in *The New Yorker*, November 29, 1993, p. 75. For an example of this polarization, see Richard Bernstein, "Wandering Jew," *The New Republic*, September 21, 1992, pp. 12-13 on the travails of Representative Stephen Solarz, whose congressional district became a "cartographic absurdity" spanning three boroughs in an effort to assure another Hispanic representative. The result is that "the politics of ethnic identity have reached a new stage of intensity in New York."

19. He died on November 19, 1992, in his hometown of Woodstock, Illinois.

20. U. S. Bureau of the Census, 1990 Census . . . Vols 1-6, passim.

21. *The New York Times,* July 1, 1992, B, 1:3, 2:1. For an analysis of migratory trends in and out of the city in the late 1980s and early 1990s see *The New York Times,* March 6, 1994, I, 1:1.

22. Alejandro Portes, "From South of the Border: Hispanic Minorities in the United States," in Virginia Yans-McLaughlin, ed., *Immigration Reconsidered: History, Sociology, and Politics* (New York: Oxford University Press, 1990), p. 171; The New York Times, July 1, 1992, B, 1:3, 2:1.

23. *The New York Times,* September 1, 1992, A, 1:2, B, 4:1.

24. *The New York Times,* June 10, 1992, B, 3:1. The survey was based on a relatively small sample, but given the compliance problems facing the census, it may still be more valid.

25. *The New York Times,* March 8, 1992, X, 1:1.

26. *The New York Times,* July 3,, 1992, A, 1:1.

27. *The New Yorker,* November 29, 1993, pp. 75-76.

28. *The New York Times* (National Edition), February 18, 1994, A, 12; Jason Epstein, "The Tragical History of New York," *The New York Review of Books,* April 9, 1992, p. 47.

29. Epstein, "Tragical History," p. 46.

30. U.S. Bureau of the Census, *Statistical Abstract of the United States,* 1977, p. 304; U.S. Bureau of the Census, *State and Local Government Finances,* 1992, p. 74; *The New York Times,* March 8, 1992, 36:1.

31. November 1, 1993, p. 7.

32. February 5, 1994, p. A10 (National Edition).

33. *Times Literary Supplement,* December 31, 1993, p. 5.

34. On immigrant entrepreneurship, see *The New York Times,* January. 20, 1992, I, 1, 20.

35. Broun quoted in Arthur Mann, *La Guardia: A Fighter Against His Times, 1882-1933* (Philadelphia: J. B. Lippincott, 1959), p. 332.

36. Bayrd thought historians should avoid autobiography. He gave these details, probably reluctantly, in Stave, "Conversation with Bayrd Still," pp. 323-25. This interview is the source for the next several paragraphs.

37. Bayrd Still, "Patterns of Mid-Nineteenth Century Urbanization in the Middle West," *Mississippi Valley Historical Review,* 28 (September 1941), 187-206.

38. Bayrd Still, *Milwaukee: The History of a City* (Madison: State Historical Society of Wisconsin, 1948; rev. ed. 1965). He was justifiably proud that both editions sold out.

39. Kathleen Neils Conzen, *Immigrant Milwaukee, 1836-1860: Accommodation and Community in a Frontier City* (Cambridge: Harvard University Press, 1976).

40. Stave, "Conversation with Bayrd Still," pp. 332-41. Encyclopedias of particular cities are either in print or in progress. David Van Tassel and John Grabowski, eds., *Encyclopedia of Cleveland History* (Bloomington: Indiana University Press, 1987); and Kenneth T. Jackson, ed., *Encyclopedia of New York City* (forthcoming).

41. For his obituary notice see *The New York Times,* November 25, 1992, D, 19:2; see also Raymond A. Mohl, "Bayrd Still, 1906-1992," *The Urban History Newsletter,* 9 (March 1993), 1-2.

42. Stave, "Conversation with Bayrd Still," pp. 338-46. I don't think he meant that these techniques were invalid, but he did want to go on record that they were not his way.

43. Bayrd Still, *Urban America: A History with Documents* (Boston: Little Brown, 1974).

44. His student Raymond Mohl offered this assessment of *Urban America* in his appreciation of Bayrd Still in *The Urban History Newsletter* (March 1993), pp. 1-2. This tribute is useful for biographical and bibliographical material and Still's impact on the field of urban history. Ray Mohl also served as a teaching assistant in Bayrd's undergraduate course and offers insightful comments on Bayrd in that role.

45. Stave, "Conversation with Bayrd Still," p. 323.

PREFACE

THIS IS A BOOK about New York City as contemporaries have described it through the years. There are many ways of taking the measure of the present-day metropolis. Aerial photography, the daily newspaper, the census, the city directory, and even the telephone book unveil virtually every facet of its form and life. For the New York of an earlier day, when evidence of this kind was less abundant, no source is more consistently rewarding than the accounts of contemporaries—visitors to the city or resident diarists and commentators—whose deliberate attempts to describe the local scene supply a substantial, if somewhat less objective, substitute for the reporter's or the camera's eye. And even for the modern city, such description has the advantage of being more manageable and more interpretative than the information that newspaper columns and official listings now so copiously provide.

Certainly no American city has been more often described, more written about, than New York. Foreigners have been discovering Gotham ever since news of a Western world excited European minds; and for Americans, whether professional writer or casual commentator, New York has been a constantly intriguing theme. A member of Henry Hudson's crew described the site of the future city more than a decade before the founding of the fortified trading post from which the modern metropolis was to rise; and in less than twenty years, particulars regarding the wilderness settlement were appearing in the European press. In succeeding generations an unceasing stream of contemporary comment mirrored the pattern of the city's growth and the behavior of the people who resided there. Today, the ever changing metropolis excites description and interpretation no less than did its colonial ancestor three centuries and more ago.

More than six hundred commentaries of this sort have been drawn upon in shaping the historical portrait of New York City which is presented in the pages that follow. Each constituted intentional description by way of book, article, letter, or diary entry written contemporaneously by an actual observer. Memoirs were ruled out for want of the contemporary touch, as were descriptions of the city in works of fiction and in guidebooks and gazetteers. In authorship, the widest range of nationality, occupation, and literary accomplishment prevails; in chronological terms, the coverage is also wide. Prior to the period of the Revolutionary War, there are some years for which no useful commentary of this type comes to hand, but for every year from 1774 to 1950 it has been possible to find one or more—and oftentimes many—contemporary accounts which shed revealing light upon the city of that day.

It goes without saying that some of these narratives mirror more faithfully than others the spirit and details of the urban scene. Some obviously were written on all too brief acquaintance with the city. Few writers were as intellectually humble as Lin Yutang who after ten years of residence in the United States contended that he did not know enough to write a book about Eighty-fourth Street, let alone all the "dark, fathomless, mysterious" city of New York. At times, language difficulties led to confusion for commentators who had to cope with a foreign tongue as well as a foreign scene. Not many were as frank in admitting this inadequacy as the Spanish visitor who entitled his book *New York: Impressions of a Nineteenth-Century Spaniard Who Does Not Know English.*

Bias inevitably affects the accuracy of some of the writing of this kind. The comments of visitors from Boston and Philadelphia now and again betray the rivalry with New York that prevailed among her urban competitors along the Atlantic coast; and observers of European origin were palpably not unaffected by the relations existing at the moment between their homelands and the United States. The resident commentator can be biased, too; yet local pride or nostalgia sometimes serves the historian when it prompts a reflective New Yorker to compare the existing city with the one he knew in bygone days. The resident's observations benefit from his closer acquaintance with the local scene; but his familiarity with it often results in the omission of details which the best of the foreign chroniclers do not overlook.

As might be expected, most commentators describe rather than assess. Although a tendency to interpret, as well as portray, has increased among observers of the last fifty years, the predominant contribution of their writing is in its description of the surface scene. In varying detail they delineate the physical appearance of the city and the urban amenities it afforded; the commercial activities which sustained its growth and largely set the pattern of its cultural and social life; the standard of living, attitudes, and day-to-day behavior of its varied population; and the ways in which the city exerted its ever widening influence in the national life.

But in the composite testimony of those who described New York there is more than simply a reflection of the passing parade. Amid the rhetoric, misinformation, plagiarism, and prejudice that are inevitable in writing of this kind, there becomes visible a portrait of the evolving city which has a lively reality no series of photographs, news articles, or census figures ever could provide. It is a portrait which, though it changes in detail almost from day to day, reveals the virtually constant fundamentals of the city's personality and growth: a port capable of accommodating a global commerce with access to an abundant hinterland; a cosmopolitan society drawn from every corner of the earth and with a flair for entertainment which produced in New York the great fun fair of the nation; and a dynamism in its daily activities, whether they take place amid "forests of masts" or "canyons of skyscrapers," which has made it, throughout most of its urban existence, one of the chief exhibits of the ever expanding potential of American life.

To amplify the picture of the metropolis which references to these narratives reveal, excerpts from the writing of representative commentators have been appended to each of the chapters. This has been done in part to make available accounts which, in some instances, are now almost inaccessible to the average reader. It has the additional advantage of permitting such personalities as Dickens, Whitman, Mark Twain, Kipling, Romulo, Le Corbusier, the controversial Mrs. Trollope, and a host of others to comment in their own words upon the New York scene, to add their individual and particular interpretation to this collective portrait of the Empire City in the successive stages of its phenomenal urban career.

Recourse to the linguistic talents of my obliging colleagues at New York University eased the problem of translation inherent in working with the many-tongued material on which this book is based. For assistance in this connection I am especially indebted to Professors Vincent P. Carosso, John E. Fagg, Minna R. Falk, Oscar J. Falnes, Seymour L. Flaxman, Robert A. Fowkes, Theodore F. Jones, and A. William Salomone, as well as to my graduate students,

Miss Sylvia Oberleitner and Miss Esther Larsen. In stylistic matters, I profited from the advice and counsel of Dean William B. Baer and Professor Henry Bamford Parkes of New York University and of Professor John Glaser of Ripon College. Acknowledgment should be made of the privilege of access to the rich resources of the New York Public Library and of the many services provided by members of its staff, particularly in the Reserve Book Room, the Print Room, and the departments of American history and local history. The same should be said of the Newberry Library, in Chicago, and of the New-York Historical Society, where Dr. James J. Heslin, Mr. Wayne Andrews, and Mrs. Meryle Evans were of especial help. In the selection of illustrations I had the good fortune to benefit from the wide and discriminating knowledge of Miss Grace Mayer, curator of prints at the Museum of the City of New York, as well as from the cooperation of her associate, Miss Patricia Pulling, of the Museum, Mr. A. B. Carlson, of the New-York Historical Society, and Messrs. Lowell Limpus and Maurice Symonds of the *Daily News*. In planning the picture pages I fortunately had recourse to the good taste and skill of Mr. Samuel Cauman, of New York University Press. Others to whom I am indebted for their willing cooperation and assistance are Mr. Lawrence Leder and Mr. Edward Spann, graduate students at New York University; Dr. John Frost, Miss Anne Corbitt, Miss Helen Cleverdon, Mr. William Finn, Mrs. Esther Levin, Mrs. Harold Butterfield, and Miss Margaret Daly, of the New York University libraries; and Miss Molly Foley and Miss Marian Vineberg of the secretarial staff. I am especially grateful to Miss Jeanette Ciangiola and Miss Patricia Fattibene for their loyal and capable assistance at all stages in the preparation of the manuscript and particularly in connection with reading proof and compiling the index. To all these, my sincere thanks.

Bayrd Still

New York, August 1956

ILLUSTRATIONS

EXCERPTS FROM CONTEMPORARY DESCRIPTIONS

MIRROR FOR GOTHAM

New York as seen by contemporaries
from Dutch days to the present

"Sights to which we are daily accustomed, make but little impression upon us, and therefore it is that New Yorkers frequently express an honest surprise at the discoveries . . . made by strangers." Alexander Mackay, *The Western World* (1850), I, 75.

1. *WHEN NEW YORK WAS NEW AMSTERDAM*

MANY A COMMENTATOR on New York has come to the city seeking opportunity for himself or others, and this was true of the two whose visits resulted in the first accounts of which we have knowledge describing the vicinity of the site upon which New York City was to stand. The first of these, the Florentine Giovanni da Verrazano, blundered upon New York Harbor in April 1524, as he sailed along the coast of the New World in search of a western waterway to China. Reporting his experiences to his sponsor, Francis I of France, he retraced the course of the "Dauphine" as it edged its way northward from the Cape Fear area.

"At the end of a hundred leagues," he wrote, describing their tentative entrance into the Lower Bay, "we found a very agreeable location situated within two prominent hills, in the midst of which flowed to the sea a very great river which was deep at the mouth." Ascending this "river," which must have been the Narrows, the voyagers found themselves in the Upper Bay. From its banks inquisitive natives, "clothed with the feathers of birds of various colors," rushed forward with a joyous welcome. But a "gale of unfavorable wind" discouraged venturing as far inward as Manhattan Island, and sent the explorers scurrying back to the "Dauphine" and away from New York Harbor. "We called it Angoulême," wrote Verrazano to his sponsor, "from the principality which Thou attaindest in a lesser fortune, and the bay which that land makes Sainte-Marguerite, from the name of Thy sister, who surpasses all other matrons in modesty and talent." [1]

History does not disclose the number of European adventurers who may have visited New York Harbor in the years immediately following Verrazano's tentative venture into this New World "Angoulême." Not until September 1609 was there another recorded contact, that of Henry Hudson, the English navigator, upon whose findings the first permanent European settlement in the area was based. Like Verrazano, Hudson was a symbol of Europe's quest for routes to the Far East. He was employed by the Dutch East India Company, under whose auspices he explored the great river which now bears his name. The day-by-day log of Robert Juet of Limehouse, a fellow Englishman in Hudson's command, is the authority for the details of this trip.

Approaching the harbor from the south, Hudson and his men, like Verrazano, skirted Sandy Hook and found themselves in the Lower Bay. Here, also like the Florentine traveler, they sensed the power of a river current pouring seaward. After exploring the Narrows, they nosed the "Half-Moon" cautiously into the Upper Bay. "The people of the Countrey came aboord of us," wrote Juet, "making shew of love, and gave us Tabacco and Indian Wheat." As the voyagers advanced up the Hudson they were approached, at a point possibly in the vicinity of what is now Forty-second Street, by "eight and twentie Canoes full of men women and children. . . . They brought Oysters and Beanes, whereof we bought some." After this and other similar transactions forecasting the future commercial activity of the region, Hudson sailed northward to a point beyond the site of Albany before turning homeward with the information upon which the Netherlands based its New World claims.[2]

Although Dutch traders and ship captains hastened to assert their nation's right to the area Hudson's voyage had revealed, more than fifteen years elapsed before the founding of the frontier outpost upon which New York City was to rise. In 1621 the Netherlands government chartered the Dutch West India Company and gave it a monopoly of trade in American waters. Settlements were planted at Fort Orange, now Albany, and at Fort Nassau, on the Delaware, by 1624; but it was not until 1625 or 1626 that the Company established New Amsterdam, progenitor of the Empire City of today.[3]

The Dutch village, like its populous successor, inspired description by both newly arriving residents and transient visitors; and some of them left accounts from which a picture of the frontier settlement that spawned a metropolis can be gained. Agents of the West India Company reported upon local conditions to their employers or to compatriots in the Fatherland; the accounts of now anonymous traders or mariners found their way into the pages of contemporary annals. A Jesuit missionary, touching the settlement, set down the details of his experience there; and visitors from British America, possibly with an eye to eventual conquest, took pains to describe the physical scene.

A fortified trading post was the nucleus of the future city. Passengers on the good ship "Arms of Amsterdam," which returned to Holland from America in November 1626, described the wilderness outpost not long after its founding. A fort had been staked out at the tip of the island, it was reported in Nicolaes van Wassenaer's annals for that year; and clustered nearby were some thirty small wooden dwellings which housed the Company's employees. In the vicinity stood a stone "counting-house," thatched with reeds; and a "horse-mill," then under construction close by, promised a supply of flour as well as a room, in its loft, for public meetings and worship.[4]

Activities connected with the fur trade and the processing of peltries, lumber, and wheat for export to the homeland mainly occupied the tiny trading establishment in its early years. Included in the cargo of the "Arms of Amsterdam" were "7246 beaver skins, 675 otter skins, 48 mink, 36 wild cat, and various other sorts," as well as samples of the lumber the vicinity afforded. The Dutch vessel carried, also, a letter from Isaack de Rasière, chief commercial agent of the Company since 1626, begging the "honorable gentlemen," his employers, to forward the cloth—"blue and standard gray," the beads, the mattocks, and the copper kettles necessary for supplying the Indian trade and for countering the already threatening attractions of rival French and English traders. He complained of the indifference of the Company's employees—"willing to draw their rations and pay in return for doing nothing"—and stressed the need for sober and industrious persons to develop outlying farms.[5]

The importance of farming to the welfare of the trading post was also apparent to Jonas Michaëlius, Manhattan's first ordained preacher. In 1628, the year of his arrival in the little settlement, he wrote a fellow pastor in old Amsterdam concerning the need for "ten or twelve more farmers with horses, cows, and laborers in proportion," to furnish the Company's personnel with "bread, milk products, and suitable fruit"—a plea that foreshadowed the dependence of the modern city upon its agricultural hinterland. But the abundance of the New World was already being sensed. With the makings of brick, salt, and lime, plenty of good quarry stone for constructing the fort, and a fruitful harvest in the barns, "God be praised," there were already signs that the rigors of pioneering would soon yield to easier times. "Affairs are beginning to go better and put on a different appearance," the optimistic dominie reported, "if only the Directors will send out good laborers and exercise all care that they be maintained as well as possible with what this country produces." [6]

The shortcomings, if not the policy, of the Company in this respect kept the community small for longer than one might imagine, considering the magnitude of its growth in years to come. As late as 1643—almost twenty years after its founding—Father Isaac Jogues, a Jesuit traveling southward from New France, saw what he called only the "commencement of a town" in the fort and the handful of mechanics' dwellings "ranged," as he wrote, under its insecure walls. At the moment, the gates and bastions of the stockade were being faced with stone, the French missionary reported; its garrison now numbered sixty men. Within the stockade stood the director's house, "quite neatly built of brick," storehouses, barracks, and a "pretty large stone church," replacing the "mean barn" in which services formerly were held. A brewery, a shed for boatbuilding with a sailmaker's loft, and houses for such essential persons as the baker, the midwife, the blacksmith, the corporal, and the barrelmaker had been completed by the later 1630's. Since 1642, a gabled inn on the bank of the East River, Manhattan's first hostelry, had accommodated transients such as English merchants engaged in the coastal trade.[7]

Despite their promotion of improvements of this type, the early directors of this New World trading establishment—Peter Minuit (1626–32), Wouter van Twiller (1633–37), and Willem Kieft (1637–47)—did little to foster its prosperity and growth. Kieft's high-handed policies toward the natives precipitated Indian warfare, and this took a serious toll of men and supplies between 1643 and 1645. Father Jogues reported that during his sojourn in the former year, "incursions of the natives . . . actually killed some two score Hollanders," in the vicinity, "and burnt many houses and barns full of wheat." So much grain had been destroyed that when "three large ships" came from Holland in that year, only two could find cargoes. Because of the negligence of the Company and the ineptitude of its local agents, the fort was periodically in disrepair and the equipment of the enterprise often unserviceable.[8]

The frontier settlement experienced a new vigor in the later 1640's. Midway in the decade, the Company inaugurated a more positive policy toward its New World dependency, and in 1647 it dispatched, as Kieft's successor, the irascible Peter Stuyvesant, former governor of Curaçao. The new director concerned himself with the appearance of the community as well as with the trade upon which it depended for its growth; and with the coming of new settlers it began to have the look of a town more than a trading post. The ever watchful British reported that although there had not been "six howses of free Burgers" in it in 1642, the Dutch had so much "emproued their buildings" about the fortified post "since the yeare 1647" that it had come to be known as "the ffort & Cittie of New Amsterdam." [9]

Under Stuyvesant's somewhat testy tutelage streets were straightened, fences repaired, and lots improved. By the early 1650's, a fairly compact flank of slim frame dwellings extended for some distance along the East River at the tip of the island; and occasional stone and brick structures, with ornamented gable ends facing the street and roofs of red or black pantile, fostered the impression that a Dutch town had been transplanted in New World soil. A wooden wharf, forerunner of the modern city's myriad facilities for shipping, was built in 1648 on the East River, where, according to an English visitor, "all ships usually ly at anchor, to lade and unlade goods, secure from hurt of any wind and weather." The construction of a wall or palisade, at the northern limits of the settlement, begun in 1653 and ultimately fortified with six partially armed bastions at equal distance, gave added defense as well as definition to the urban place.[10]

More specific recognition of urban status came in the same year when a grant of municipal government differentiated New Amsterdam legally from the province of which it had long been the administrative center and focal point. Possibly a thousand persons were dwelling in the fortified trading settlement by the mid-century. As the village community had matured, some of the citizenry, at least, had resented the lack of representative institutions and economic privileges enjoyed in Dutch towns of the Old World. Pressure exerted upon the States General and the West India Company, as early as 1649, finally brought results; and on February 2, 1653, Director Stuyvesant grudgingly proclaimed a grant of municipal government along lines similar to that in the Fatherland.

For the remainder of the Dutch period, local administration was vested in a schout, two burgomasters, and five schepens; their choice, however, unlike a more democratic situation in Holland, remained to a large extent in Stuyvesant's hands. With the grant of great and small burgher-right, in 1657, restricting trade to residents so endowed, the local citizens gained the monopolies and privileges customary in European municipalities at the time. These developments inevitably distinguished the emerging town from the pioneer fur-trading and agricultural economy of which it had been so integral a part.[11]

The growth of population had already presented other problems that were urban in character. Fire was then, as later, an ever present hazard, and the young settlement had to adopt methods to prevent and curtail the damage it might do. Fire wardens sought out defective chimneys in the hope of avoiding fire; and the municipality supplied leather buckets at suitable locations for public use when conflagrations should occur. The citizen watch, unable to cope with the nocturnal disorders of a port society, was replaced in 1658 by a "rattle watch," a paid police force which served from nine in the evening to drum beat at six the following morning. Sharing responsibility for public order was the militia, established in 1640. According to English estimates, it numbered two companies, by the early 1660's, in addition to the garrison of some seventy men attached to the fort. Improvement of the streets became an issue as early as 1657, and by 1661 cobblestone pavement had been laid on all the commonly used thoroughfares. A canal, or "gutte," as a British visitor called it in describing "Mannadens" in 1661, was constructed in Broad Street between the years 1657 and 1659. Extending "almost through the towne," it permitted the entrance of boats at high water and lent a suggestion of the water-laced Fatherland to this miniature Dutch capital in the New World.[12]

Although the population of New Amsterdam was small, contemporaries described a community whose social and economic patterns clearly foreshadowed the city of a later day. Its people, though meager in number, were already a motley group: company clerks, soldiers of the garrison, enterprising merchants, a few professional men, trappers from the wilderness or traders from other New World colonies, mechanics and artisans, apprentices, common laborers, sailors, and more than a few Negro slaves. By the middle 1640's, eighteen languages were spoken in the vicinity, the visiting Jesuit was told; and though the Reformed Dutch Church alone had official sanction, almost as many religious faiths as nationalities were represented in the already cosmopolitan urban scene. "No religion is publicly exercised but the Calvinist, and orders are to admit none but Calvinists, but this is not observed," Father Jogues reported in his account of "Novum Belgium," written after his visit in 1643; ". . . besides the Calvinists there are in the colony Catholics, English Puritans, Lutherans, Anabaptists, here called Mnistes [Mennonites], etc." The variety was increased when the first settlers espousing the Jewish faith arrived from Brazil and Holland in 1654.[13]

The vigor of its trading activity early stamped the community with the commercial tone that was to remain a distinguishing characteristic through the years. "The town is seated . . . commodiously for trades, and that is their chief employment for they plant and sow litle," wrote a now unknown English visitor, who described the commercial scene in 1661. From the Indians and settlers in the upcountry came "beaver, otter, musk, and other skins," according to his report; and from Long Island, beef, pork, wheat, butter, and some tobacco. From New England there were similar food products, as well as "flower" and "bisket," malt, fish, cider apples, iron, and tar; and from Virginia "store of tobacco, oxhides, dried, some beef, pork and fruit"—imports which suggest that the diminutive urban community was already to some extent dependent upon outside sources for its food.

In return, the traders or producers of such raw materials were supplied with "Holland and other linnen, canvage [canvas], tape, thrid, cordage, brasse, Hading cloth, stuffs, stockings, spices, fruit, . . . iron work, wine, Brandy, Annis, salt, and all usefull manufactures." "From Amsterdam come each year 7. or 8. big ships with passengers and all sorts of goods," the English visitor marveled, quite evidently not unimpressed with the flourishing commerce of the place, "and they lade back beaver and other skins, dry oxehides, and Virginia tobacco. Tis said that each year is carried from thence above 20000 sterl. value in beaver skins only." Such was the elaboration of trade which by the early 1660's had accompanied the transition of New Amsterdam from a wilderness trading post to an entrepôt of colonial commerce in the New World.[14]

In the convivial habits observed in New Amsterdam's "severall sorts of tradesmen and marchants and mariners" there was already an indication of the flair for entertainment that was to make New York an amusement center in years to come. It was a lusty, somewhat volatile society, enjoying the pastimes of both the town and the frontier, as befitted the nature of the environment: fishing, ice skating, horse racing, bowling on the green, and, most conspicuously, the enjoyments of the tavern. Such signs of good fellowship impressed Nicasius de Sille, who arrived in New Amsterdam in November 1653, after a seventy-three-day voyage from the Netherlands, and who served, before his removal to New Utrecht on Long Island, as a member of Stuyvesant's council, as provincial fiscal, and as schout of New Amsterdam. ". . . they all drink here, from the moment they are able to lick a spoon," de Sille confided to a friend in the Netherlands. "The women of the neighborhood entertain each other with a pipe and a brazier; young and old, they all smoke."

With an enthusiasm perhaps not entirely unrelated to the need for additional settlers, de Sille's letters to correspondents in the homeland attest to the abundance of a community in which life strongly reflected the bounty and flavor of the New World frontier. "The country suits me exceeding well. I shall not try to leave it as long as I live," he wrote in 1654, sentiments later echoed in trader Jacob Steendam's poetic paean to "New Netherland, thou noblest spot of earth." "The rivers are full of . . . good edible fish, which is very cheap, three large sea crabs for a stiver; also fruit," de Sille informed his friend Maximiliaen van Beeckerke. "Oysters we pick up here before our fort; among them are some so large that one must cut them in two or three pieces. . . . The Indians bring us wild geese, turkeys, partridges, wild pigeons, ducks, and various other birds and animals; in fine, one can live here and forget *Patria*. Beer is brewed here as good as in Holland, of barley and wheat. Wheaten bread is more common here than rye or buckwheat. . . . No gold or silver circulates here, but beads, which the Indians make and call seawant. . . . We can buy everything with it and gladly take it in payment. In short, once more, it is good here." [15]

Perhaps life was too good—it was too easy to "forget *Patria*"—as the frontier trading post grew into a flourishing and already cosmopolitan commercial town, numbering more than 1,500 persons by the early 1660's. The consequences of this attitude, as well as of the Company's neglect, became apparent in 1664, when, after less than forty years of Dutch dominion, New Amsterdam fell into English hands. The position of New Netherland made it naturally vulnerable to English attack; and the Hollanders' trading supremacy was a constant source of irritation to British merchants in both the

The J. Clarence Davies Collection, Museum of the City of New York

THE DUTCH VILLAGE

This earliest known view of New Amsterdam (above) is an approximation of the fortified trading post on the tip of Manhattan as it appeared to observers in the later 1620's. Presumably it was drawn by Cryn Fredericksz, who returned to Holland in 1626 after helping to lay out the original settlement and its fortification. A four-bastioned fort, rather than the one pictured here, was being constructed in 1628. The engraving was first published by Joost Hartgers in 1651. In the present reproduction it has been reversed to conform to the actual topography, with the East River in the foreground and the windmill on the west shore of Manhattan.

New Amsterdam as it looked on the eve of incorporation is pictured in the DeWit View (below) which dates to 1651 or 1652. In the center foreground is a small wooden wharf and to the left of it a crane and "gallows" for the weighing and display of merchandise. Fort Amsterdam stands at the left and beyond it the windmill. At the extreme right is the tavern which was built in 1642. In 1653 this became the Stadt Huys or city hall.

Museum of the City of New York

Museum of the City of New York

PROVINCIAL CAPITAL

Museum of the City of New York

The flourishing provincial capital as seen from Governor's Island on the eve of the American Revolution (above), a detail of the Ratzer Plan of the City of New York, published in 1776. The date depicted is 1767–1774. The British flag flies over Fort George, at the tip of the island; and the spire of Trinity Church rises above the trees to the right of it.

An early view of the interior of the city is William Burgis's representation of the New (later Middle) Dutch Church (left) erected between 1727 and 1731 at Nassau and Crown streets. Cobblestone pavement and coach travel testify to the increasing maturity of the urban society.

Fire fighting, eighteenth-century style, is depicted in the engraving below, which ornamented the meeting notice of the Hand-in-Hand Fire Company. Some of the members shoulder sacks for retrieving valuables, while others, forming a bucket brigade, convey water from a public well to a hand-pumped engine, from which it is directed upon the flames.

Stokes Collection, New York Public Library

New World and the Old. By the turn of the 1660's, England's merchants were taking aggressive action against the commercial supremacy of the Dutch; and by 1664 they had convinced the government of the importance of dislodging the "intruders" and consolidating Britain's holdings along the Atlantic coast.[16]

In mid-August of that year, four of His Majesty's frigates entered the Narrows and their commander demanded a surrender, offering favorable terms to the Dutch residents of Long Island and the burghers of New Amsterdam. Alarmed at rumors of a hostile fleet, the citizens hurried to improve the town's defenses; and the doughty director prepared to fight. But token resistance was all the burghers could—or cared to—offer; and as the British troops advanced to the ferry connecting Breuckelen and New Amsterdam, the citizens forced Stuyvesant to show them Britain's liberal surrender terms and compelled him to capitulate. On September 8, 1664, "the fort and town called New Amsterdam upon the island of Manhattoes" formally surrendered. Manhattan was then in British hands, and New Amsterdam became New York.[17]

NEW AMSTERDAM, FRONTIER TRADING POST: 1626

A graphic, if somewhat anticipatory, description of the wilderness trading post that became New York City appeared in 1626, soon after its founding, in Nicolaes van Wassenaer's *Historisch Verhael,* or, to translate its more complete title, *Historical narrative oj all the most memorable occurrences which have come to pass in Europe.* A Dutch scholar and physician, van Wassenaer published his annals or news-journal, one of the earliest to appear in Holland, semiannually from 1621 to 1631. In writing about New Amsterdam in 1626, van Wassenaer presumably relied upon information supplied by the crew or passengers of the vessel, "Arms of Amsterdam," which returned to Holland from the New World in November of that year. The following account appeared in the annals for that date, and coincides in detail with the later published Hartgers View of the settlement, supposedly the work of the engineer Cryn Fredericksz, one of the passengers on the "Arms of Amsterdam's" return voyage. It is reprinted, with the permission of Barnes and Noble, Inc., from *Narratives of New Netherland,* edited by J. Franklin Jameson.[18]

The colony is now established on the Manhates, where a fort has been staked out by Master Kryn Frederycks, an engineer. It is planned to be of large dimensions. The ship which has returned home this month [November] brings samples of all sorts of produce growing there. . . .

The counting-house there is kept in a stone building, thatched with reed; the other houses are of the bark of trees. Each has his own house. The Director and *Koopman* [commercial agent] live together; there are thirty ordinary houses on the east side of the river, which runs nearly north and south. The Honorable Pieter Minuit is Director there at present; Jan Lempou *schout* [sheriff]; Sebastiaen Jansz. Crol and Jan Huych, comforters of the sick, who, whilst awaiting a clergyman, read to the commonalty there, on Sundays, texts of Scripture and the commentaries. François Molemaecker is busy building a horse-mill, over which shall be constructed a spacious room sufficient to accommodate a large congregation, and then a tower is to be erected where the bells brought from Porto Rico will be hung.

The council there administers justice in criminal matters as far as imposing fines, but not as far as corporal punishment. Should it happen that anyone deserves that, he must be sent to Holland with his sentence. . . . Men work there as in Holland; one trades, upwards, southwards and northwards; another builds houses, the third farms. Each farmer has his farmstead on the land purchased by the Company [through the efforts of Peter Minuit, who purchased Manhattan Island from the Indians for sixty guilders, or about $24], which also owns the cows; but the milk remains to the profit of the farmer; he sells it to those of the people who receive their wages for work every week. The houses of the Hollanders now stand outside the fort, but when that is completed, they will all repair within, so as to garrison it and be secure from sudden attack.*

Those of the South River will abandon their fort [Fort Nassau], and come hither. At Fort Orange, the most northerly point at which the Hollanders traded, no more than fifteen or sixteen men will remain; the remainder will come down [to the Manhates]. . . .

* It apparently never became necessary to concentrate all the residents within the fort, if indeed the enclosure was ever either large enough or secure enough to make this advisable. According to the *Historisch Verhael,* under the date of October 1628, the population numbered 270. "They remained as yet without the fort, in no fear, as the natives live peaceably with them. . . . These strangers for the most part occupy their farms. Whatever they require is supplied by the Directors. . . . The cattle sent thither have thriven well, and everything promises increase, as soon as the land is improved, which is full of weeds and poor."

When the fort, staked out at the Manhates, will be completed, it is to be named Amsterdam.

MANHATTAN IN 1661

It is hard to escape the conclusion that the following precise description of the physical features and fortifications of New Amsterdam was designed to acquaint the English with the details of a community upon which by the turn of the 1660's they already had acquisitive designs. Called "Description of the Towne of Mannadens, 1661," it is of further interest because it indicates that the community was then already being called "Manhattan," a label derived from Manhates, which the Dutch called the island, and Manahata or Manhatoes, their names for its Indian inhabitants. The author of the description is unknown, but J. Franklin Jameson has suggested that it might have been written by a member of the party of the younger John Winthrop, Governor of Connecticut, who embarked for England from the Dutch port in July 1661. Significantly enough, when New Amsterdam fell to the British three years later, Governor Winthrop and his son, along with other New Englanders, were on hand to lend support. The excerpt is reprinted, with the permission of Barnes and Noble, Inc., from *Narratives of New Netherland,* edited by J. Franklin Jameson.[19]

The Easter-side of the Towne is from the North-East gate [at the eastern extremity of the wall] unto the point, whereon the Governors new house stands, and yt contains 490 yards. . . . On this side of the towne there is a gutte [canal], whereby at high water boats goe into the towne. Also on this side stands the Stat-house [originally the town tavern], before w[hi]ch is built a half moon of stone, where are mounted 3 smal bras guns. . . .

The Souther-side or roundhead of the Town [now the Battery] is bounded with the arm of the Sea. . . . Nearest the westerside of this head is a plot of ground, on w[hi]ch stands a windmill; and a Fort foursquare, 100 yards on each side, at each corner flanked out 26 yards. . . . In this Fort is the Church, the Governors house, and houses for soldiers, ammunition, etc.

The wester-side of the towne is from the windmill unto the North-west corner [the westernmost point of the wall] 480 yards. . . . The land side of the towne is from the Northwest corner unto the North E. gate 520 yards and lyeth neer N. W. and S. E. having six flankers [bastions] at equal distance, in four of w[hi]ch are mounted 8 guns. . . .

Within the towne, in the midway between the N. W. corner and N. E. gate, the ground hath a smal descent on each side much alike, and so continues through the town unto the arme of the water on the Easter-side of the Towne: by the help of this descent they have made a gut almost through the towne [Broad Street canal], keyed it on both sides with timber and boards as far in as the 3. small bridges; and near the coming into the gut they have built two firme timber bridges with railes on each side. At low water the gut is dry, at high water boats come into it, passing under the 2. bridges, and go as far as the 3. small bridges. . . .

The town . . . hath good air, and is healthy, inhabited with severall sorts of trades men and marchants and mariners.

2. NEW YORK UNDER BRITISH RULE

New York remained small by modern standards during the period of British rule. On the eve of the American Revolution—more than a century after England's acquisition of New Amsterdam—its population still did not exceed 25,000. At the time of the British conquest, fully a third of the available street-front space south of the "wall" remained unoccupied; and as late as 1775, the built-up portion of the city extended northeastward from the base of the island for little more than a mile. Yet to observers of the later eighteenth century, the burgeoning little seaport at the tip of Manhattan Island was a community of considerable consequence, the second largest in Britain's New World domain.[1]

The compactness of the place, with its "Brick and Stone" buildings, rising sometimes to five and six stories and roofed with red and black tile, impressed early visitors to the newly acquired British possession. Daniel Denton, a Long Islander, reported its "pleasing Aspect" in his *A Brief Description of New-York,* a promotional tract published for British consumption as early as 1670. Architectural novelties, reflecting the Dutch influence, intrigued two Bostonians who visited the city at the turn of the eighteenth century. Most of the brick houses bore the date of the year of construction, "contrived of Iron cramps to hold in ye timber to the walls," wrote Benjamin Bullivant, a visitor of 1697. The ornamentation of their narrow fronts, with brick of "divers Coullers and laid in Checkers," attracted the attention of his more widely quoted compatriot, schoolmistress Sarah Knight, who journeyed from Boston to New York on horseback in 1704. The interiors of the houses were "neat to admiration," she reported, "the wooden work . . . kept very white scowr'd . . . and the hearths . . . laid with the finest tile that I ever see."[2]

Dutch neatness was more agreeable to the average British visitor than the Dutch architectural practice of placing the gable end of the dwelling toward the street. Soon, however, the structural consequences of British rule began to bring changes in this respect. Trinity Church, designed in the "English style," was taking shape when Bullivant visited the city in 1697; and Abraham De Peyster's mansion impressed him as a "noble building of the newest English fashion." As late as the mid-eighteenth century, New York still had "the general appearance of a Dutch-town" to Thomas Pownall, arriving to become secretary to the governor in 1753. He nevertheless observed that the newest structures had been "built in a more modern taste, & many of the Gabel-ends of ye old houses, just as is done in Holland," had been "new fronted in the Italian stile." The adoption of English patterns was increasingly apparent by the eve of the Revolution. "Here is found Dutch neatness, combined with English taste and architecture," wrote the Frenchman Jean de Crèvecoeur in the early 1770's; "the houses are finished, planned, and painted with the greatest care. . . . Stone being scarce, nearly the whole town is built of brick." [3]

Shade trees and gardens softened the monotonous severity of the close packed streets, and lent the eighteenth-century city a somewhat rural tone. Two Labadist missionaries, Jasper Danckaerts and Peter Sluyter, visiting New York in 1679, saw trees "so laden with peaches and other fruit that one might doubt whether there were more leaves or fruit on them." The city still appeared "quite like a garden" some seventy years later, when New York was observed by Professor Peter Kalm, who visited America in 1748 under the auspices of the Swedish Royal Academy of Science. The Swedish naturalist took especial note of the variety of trees which gave the streets a fine appearance and afforded cooling shade. The water beech was the most numerous, and there were lime trees, elms, and locusts, with their lacy leaves and scented flowers; "one seldom met with trees of the same sort next to one another." Birds filled their branches, and to emphasize the bucolic note, "a kind of frogs," (locusts, perhaps), frequenting the trees in summer evenings, set up such a vibrant clamor that it was "difficult for a person to make himself heard." [4]

Mid-eighteenth century visitors admired the city's neat cobblestone pavements and the sidewalks of flat stone which had been laid on both sides of some of the streets. Unlike the travelers of later days, they universally attested to the cleanliness of these thoroughfares, a situation which was to change markedly for the worse in the nineteenth century. Lord Adam Gordon, a military visitor of 1765, attributed this salutary condition to the city's elevation, which permitted the streets to be "washed by every rain"; but Crèvecoeur was inclined to credit municipal and individual effort. Indeed, the city had hired a scavenger as early as 1695 and directed the inhabitants to sweep the streets in front of their homes; but real gains in municipal sanitation did not occur until the mid-eighteenth century. Thereafter, until the Revolution, the city's record in this respect was unusual for the time.[5]

By this date, the principal thoroughfares were Broadway, Broad Street, Water Street, and Hanover Street (now Pearl). "The Principal Street is a noble broad Street 100 feet wide called Broad Way," wrote Thomas Pownall in his topographical survey of Britain's dominions in the middle 1750's. "It commences at the north gate of the Fort by a kind of Square or Place formerly a Parade now a bowling green railed in, & runs directly in a strait line NE better than half a mile where it terminates by another intended square." On the west side of Broadway were "Several very handsome Spacious Houses of the principal Inhabitants," he reported, as well as "the Lutheran Church & the English Church called Trinity Church a very large plain brick Building, but within as spacious commodious & handsome a Place of Worship as I ever saw belonging to a private Parish." Broad Street, eighty feet wide, ran from the landing on the East River where the Exchange stood to the "Stadthouse or Townhouse," a distance of about a quarter mile. Water Street adjoined the "Vlys, Quays wharfs & docks on the eastern bank of the town." [6]

The city's docks and wharves betokened the maritime activity of the place. "A fine quay . . . reigns all round the town, built with stone and piles of wood outside," a Huguenot visitor observed in 1716. "There are small docks for cleaning and building small ships. At high-water, the vessels come up to the quay to lade and unlade." The practice of making artificial land to accommodate warehouses and wharves, which was in time to widen the toe of the island, had already begun when Crèvecoeur described New York of the early 1770's. In no American city had the "art of constructing wharves" been pushed to a farther extent, he reported. "I have seen them made in forty feet of water. This is done with the trunks of pines attached together, which they gradually sink, fill in with stone, and cover the surface with earth." [7]

The fort, nucleus of the original settlement, remained an imposing feature of the colonial capital, although contemporaries differed as to the degree of protection it might afford in time of attack.

Flying the emblem of the British nation, it symbolized England's authority over the New World city. Within its stone walls stood the governor's dwelling, barracks for the troops of the garrison, and a chapel, built, shortly before Dr. Bullivant's visit in 1697, with "a handsome Lantern or Cupulo, and a Large Bell." John Fontaine, who was entertained at the governor's house in 1716, thought the fort "a weak place and badly contrived"; but Peter Kalm, writing at the mid-century, judged it to be capable of defending the town "from a sudden attack on the sea side." The palisade, or wall, at the north was, however, "in a very bad state of defence," he reported, "since for a considerable time the people have had nothing to fear from an enemy." During the French and Indian War, the fortifications were improved both at the waterfront and along the line of the wall; but their condition was such as to win little praise from either a French observer or an English military visitor in 1765.[8]

Trade, upon which the settlement was founded, continued to be the main economic support of New York City in the era of British control; and here the testimony of the provincial governors, as well as of more transient newcomers, provides a contemporary view of the developing economy. "New York and Albany live wholly upon trade with the Indians England and the West Indies," observed Governor Dongan, in 1687, after he had been three and a half years in the colony. Like his predecessor, Sir Edmund Andros, who had become governor in 1674, he reported that "land provisions" constituted the principal exports from the city in the first generation of British rule. In Dongan's day, Manhattan's merchants shipped peltries, whale oil, and tobacco to England; to the West Indies, flour, bread, peas, pork, and sometimes horses. In return they received finished goods from England—"all sorts of English manufacture for Christians & blanketts, Duffells &c. for Indians," as Governor Andros had reported in 1678, and from the West Indies, rum and molasses, the last of which, according to Dongan, "serves the people to make drink and pays no custom." Vessels from England and New England and a few of local construction serviced this trade.[9]

From 1678 to 1694, the economy of the provincial city benefited from the exclusive privilege, granted by Governor Andros, of grinding and packing all the flour exported from the province. This mercantile regulation favoring the provincial "metropolis" so stimulated milling that in 1692 an English traveler observed that the city was "ye chief Grainary to most of ye West Indian Islands."

Bread and biscuit were also produced and meat packed, in quantity, for export.[10]

Peter Kalm's *Travels into North America,* as well as a report to the Lords of Trade and Plantations issued at the direction of Governor George Clinton, in 1749, reveals the proliferation of trade and commerce which had taken place by the mid-eighteenth century. Imports—"the Inward Trading," according to Clinton's inventory—now came from many parts of the globe: "from Great Britain, European Goods, & those [from] India with Silk Manufactures chiefly. From Ireland Linnen and Canvas. . . . From British Colonies, enumerated Commodities, Piemento, Sulphur, Strawplating, Lime juice, Coffee . . . , Hides, . . . Mahoganie, Plank, Ebonie, & Negros. From Europe and Africa, . . . Salt. From the African Coast . . . Negros: now less than formerly. From the Northern & Southern parts of this Continent; Fish, Oil, Bluber, Whale fins, Turpentine oil, Seal Skins, Hops, Cyder, Flax, Bricks, Cole, Lamp Black, certain wrought Iron, Tin & Braziery, Joinery, various Carriages and Chairs. From Plantations not under his Ma[jest]y's Dominions, Molasses, Sugar & Rum," as well as drugs, dyestuffs, indigo, coconuts, cotton wool, and snuff.[11]

Exports now flowed to London and its outports, to Ireland, to several ports in Europe, to Madeira and the Azores, to other British possessions on the North American continent, and to British and neutral ports in the West Indies. As earlier, the produce of the land constituted the bulk of the goods exported both to Europe and to American markets; but shipments to Europe were supplemented by products imported from other parts of the New World and by the prizes acquired by privateers and certified for sale in the local vice-admiralty courts. Peter Kalm reported that a three-cornered trade between New York, the West Indies, and England or Holland helped to finance the importation of manufactured goods by the provincial city. When cargoes were lacking for the westward journey, coals from Newcastle, taken on as ballast, sold in America "for a pretty good price."

Activity in the harbor mirrored the increasing business of the port. By contrast with the thirty-five vessels of Governor Dongan's day (1687), ninety-nine cleared the port in 1746 and seven hundred in 1772, with exports valued at £82,707. The value of imports had climbed from £54,900 in 1746 to £343,970 in 1772. A French traveler of 1765 reported that the city was the "metropolis of the province," and that because of its "Comodious situation" it commanded "all the trade of the western part of Connecticut and that of East Jersy." No season prevented "their shipin from going out and Coming into port," he asserted; and "pilot boats at the narows" were always "ready to Conduct them In on first sight." [12]

Retail merchandising, in which New York City was ultimately to excel, developed slowly in the eighteenth-century municipality. Merchants sold goods at their warehouses, as did the artisans, at their shops. Meat and produce could be bought in the public markets. Auctions, or vendues, were a popular method of merchandising at the turn of the eighteenth century. "They have Vendues very frequently," wrote Madam Knight after her visit in 1704, "and make their Earnings very well by them, for they treat with good Liquor Liberally, and the Customers Drink as Liberally and Generally pay for't as well, by paying for that which they Bidd up Briskly for, after the Sack has gone plentifully about, tho' sometimes good penny worths are got there." Shopkeepers became more numerous after 1730, and the retail trade began to flourish.[13]

Although Peter Kalm admittedly saw little evidence of manufacturing in 1748, the provincial governors had already begun to apprise the home government of tendencies in this direction. The prelude to manufacturing was the processing of foods, timber, and furs for export and the servicing of the ships engaged in trade, a need which early led to the establishment of rope walks at the outskirts of the city. In 1715, Governor Robert Hunter, writing to the Board of Trade, denied that the people of New York City were wearing clothing of their own manufacture, however much this might be the case among the "Planters and poorer sort of Country people." But by 1732, there was enough local production of beaver hats for export to neighboring colonies, the West Indies, and southern Europe to prompt Parliament to forbid their exportation. When Andrew Burnaby was in New York in 1759 and 1760, he reported the production of "a small quantity of cloth, some linen, hats, shoes, and other articles for wearing apparel." He added to this list glass manufacturing, sugar refining, and the distilling of rum. Several slitting mills had been erected for the purpose of making nails, he observed, but "this is now prohibited, and they are exceedingly dissatisfied at it." [14]

Sir Henry Moore, who arrived as governor in 1765, at the beginning of the Stamp Act controversy, minimized the extent of local manufacturing, despite what he called the "pompous" claims of the colonials in this regard. Reporting to the Lords of Trade early in January 1767, he admitted the existence of a small linen factory of no more than fourteen looms supported "chiefly by the Subscriptions of a set of men who call themselves the Society of Arts and Agriculture." Though coarse cloth was generally woven in the home, he denied that there was any "established Fabric of Broad Cloth" in the province. The output of a little foundry "lately set up near this Town for making Small Iron Potts," was as yet inconsiderable, in the governor's opinion. The production of hats, though quite extensive, was hindered by the high price of labor. Governor Moore believed that so long as land was readily available, the scarcity of labor would always obstruct the development of manufacturing in the New World. To support this contention, he cited the experience of a "Master of a Glass-house . . . set up here a few years ago," who was "now a Bankrupt," and who attributed his ruin "to no other cause than being deserted . . . by the Servants, which he had Imported at great expence." [15]

Within a decade, however, the letters of a Scottish visitor presented a picture of local industry which must have been less reassuring to the British manufacturer and which revealed one of the causes of the growing tension between the maturing colonies and the Mother Country. "They have several large roperies, distilleries, breweries, and a large iron work," wrote Patrick M'Robert, during his sojourn in the city in 1774. "They have plenty of mechanicks of all kinds, by whom almost every thing that is made with you in Britain is made to as great perfection here." [16]

Ethnic variety, already apparent in the days of Dutch dominion, characterized the city's population under British rule. Captain William Byrd, a visitor from Virginia in 1685, estimated the inhabitants to be "about six eighths Dutch, the remainder French and English." Two years later, Governor Dongan bemoaned the fact that foreigners were the "most prevailing part" of the population, an opinion echoed in 1692 when Charles Lodwick wrote members of the Royal Society that "Our chiefest unhappyness here is too great a mixture of Nations, & English ye least part." French travelers like Antoine de la Mothe Cadillac, the founder of Detroit, and the Huguenot John Fontaine were surprised to note the privileges Frenchmen enjoyed and their prominence in the government. Germans, Scots, and Irishmen in considerable number increased the variety as the years went on; and Negroes, engaged in the "laborious" occupations, became so numerous (about a sixth of the population in 1771) as to "hurt" the eyes of European visitors unaccustomed to slavery.

The Jewish community, which numbered such leading merchants as Jacob Franks, of German origin, and Louis Gomez, of Spanish-Portuguese background like most of the Jewish residents of colonial New York, had gained greatly in prestige since the seventeenth century. Peter Kalm noted that they worshiped in a synagogue (which had been built in 1728), owned their own dwelling houses, as well as large country seats, kept shops in town, and played an important role in the community's foreign trade. Actually, the city's Jewish ingredient suffered some civil disabilities, in law if not always in practice, as did the Catholic population; but for all that Kalm could see, they enjoyed "all the privileges common to the other inhabitants of this town and province." [17]

Despite the still frequent reminders of the city's Dutch origins, in customs as well as architecture, time and British contacts increasingly shaped the urban society to English ways. This was apparent to Dr. Alexander Hamilton, a Scottish-trained physician who had settled in Annapolis in 1739. Even though "Dutchmen" possessed the chief places in the government, their language and customs had begun "pritty much to wear out," he wrote after his visit to New York City in 1744. Indeed, they threatened to die but for "a parcell of Dutch domines" who were endeavoring to preserve the Dutch customs through the medium of church schools. In the opinion of Professor Kalm, the transformation was especially apparent in the town and its neighborhood. Most of the young people spoke English and would even take it amiss if they were called Dutchmen and not Englishmen, he wrote, after his visit in 1748. Other travelers noted the tendency, by the mid-century, for young people to "fall off" to the Anglican church from the Dutch churches and the French church, which in 1750 had but a small congregation. "There are still two Churches in which religious worship is performed in [the Dutch] language," a French visitor reported in 1765; "but the number that talk it Diminishes Daily." [18]

The variety of its churches emphasized the cosmopolitanism of the provincial city. With the assumption of English rule, the Anglican Church gained the official sanction that the Reformed Dutch Church had earlier enjoyed; but this development did not preclude open worship by other sects to an even greater degree than under the rule of the allegedly more tolerant Dutch. Governor Dongan, himself a Catholic, catalogued the denominations in 1687 when he wrote, "Here bee not many of the Church of England; few Roman Catholicks; abundance of Quakers preachers men and women especially; Singing Quakers, Ranting Quakers; Sabbatarians; Antisabbatarians; some Anabaptists some Independents; some Jews; in short of all sorts of opinions there are some, and the most part of none at all." Two years earlier, William Byrd had observed that there were as many sects at New as at Old Amsterdam—"all being tolerated, yet the people seem not concerned what religion their neighbour is of, or whether hee hath any or none." [19]

The Labadist missionary, Jasper Danckaerts, testified to the scarcity of Anglican communicants when he attended a service at the church within the fort, in 1679. It was conducted by the Reverend Charles Wolley, the first clergyman of the Church of England to be assigned to the province, who had arrived in the colonial city in August of 1678. Thirty communicants listened to Wolley's sermon, which he read out of "a little book." To Chaplain Wolley's surprise, the vaunted tolerance of the Hollanders did not characterize the two Dutch dominies who were his fellow ministers at the time. These two—one "a Lutheran a German or High-Dutch, the other a Calvinist an Hollander or Low-Dutchman"—"had not . . . spoken to each other with any respect for six years together," Wolley confided to his journal. In his opinion they "behav'd themselves one towards another so shily and uncharitably as if Luther and Calvin had bequeathed and entailed their virulent and bigotted spirits upon them and their heirs forever." [20]

The growth of population brought an increase in the number and variety of places of worship. Peter Kalm counted nine church edifices in 1748: Trinity, the Anglican church, which was opened for services in 1698; two Dutch churches, conspicuous for their lack of ornamentation; a German Lutheran church and one of the German Reformed faith; a Presbyterian church, recently built of stone, with a steeple and a bell; the Huguenot church; the Quaker meetinghouse; and the Jewish synagogue. The Anabaptists had been worshiping in a house on Broad Street since 1720. In 1774, when Patrick M'Robert visited the city, the number of churches had increased to sixteen. The Anglicans and Presbyterians now had three houses of worship, each, and there were churches for the Anabaptists, the Moravians, and the Methodists, as well as those earlier reported.[21]

Most novel, to Peter Kalm, was the service at the Jewish synagogue. Here, he wrote, a "young Rabbi read the divine service, which was partly in Hebrew, and partly in the Rabbinical dialect. Both men and women were dressed entirely in the English fashion; the former had all of them their hats on, and did not take them off during service. The galleries, I observed, were appropriated to the ladies, while the men sat below. During prayers the men spread a white cloth over their heads; which perhaps is to represent sack cloth. But I observed that the wealthier sort of people had a much richer cloth than the poorer ones. Many of the men had Hebrew books in which they sang and read alternately. The Rabbi stood in the middle of the synagogue, and read with his face turned towards the east: he spoke, however, so fast, as to make it almost impossible for anyone to understand what he said." [22]

Although outsiders rarely failed to mention the variety of New York's churches and the steeples which, in the eighteenth century, were beginning to accent its skyline, they do not leave the impression that piety was a generally pervasive characteristic of the social scene. An Anglican chaplain, John Miller, was offended by the "wickedness and irreligion" of the inhabitants in the decade of the 1690's. Frequenting taverns was their "daily practice," and carousing and gaming "their night employment," he complained, no doubt with special reference to the garrison which was his particular charge. Many were addicted to "cursing and swearing, . . . some doing it in that frequent, horrible, and dreadful manner as if they prided themselves both as to the number and invention of them." And not a few regarded fornication "rather to be chosen than lawful wedlock." Many couples lived together "without ever being married in any manner of way," or, once married by a justice of the peace, thought it "no great matter to divorce themselves, as they term it, and marry to others where they can best, and according to their own liking." [23]

Travelers of the eighteenth century continued to note the city's secular tone. Madam Knight, despite a manner somewhat more tolerant than that of the average Bostonian, remarked that New Yorkers of 1704 were "not strict in keeping the Sabbath as in Boston and other places." Dr. Hamilton found, some forty years later, that to "drink stoutly" was the "readiest way for a stranger to recommend himself" to the local society, and that to "talk bawdy" and to have a knack at punning passed among some for "good sterling wit." Writing in the 1770's, Crèvecoeur regretted that King's College, forerunner of Columbia University, then located between Barclay and Murray streets in what is now the lower city, had not been built in some "rural retreat, where the scholars could be kept from . . . the dissipations and pleasures always numerous in large cities," a point elaborated by a contemporary visitor who estimated that "500 ladies of pleasure" kept lodgings near St. Paul's, in the vicinity of the school.[24]

In other ways the society of the busy seaport mirrored the secular, mercantile spirit of the eighteenth-century provincial capital. It was apparent to the city's visitors that here amusement and entertainment flourished more than learning and the arts; and both the dress and the dwellings of the leading citizens exhibited the ostentation that accompanied increasing commercial wealth. "The English go very fasheonable in their dress," wrote Madam Knight, as early as 1704; in the apparel of the Dutch dowagers she noted "Jewells of large size and many in number." Dr. Hamilton found that the "women of fashion" appeared more in public in New York than in Philadelphia, at the time of his visit in 1744, and dressed "much gayer." The "handsome Spacious Houses of the principal Inhabitants," on lower Broadway, with their rich interiors, and numerous Negro servants, symbolized both the affluence of the wealthy merchant families and the growing distance between them and the more nondescript element in the urban community.[25]

Travelers agreed that New York City was the gayest of the British colonial towns. Already it had some of the flavor of a tourist attraction that was to characterize it in later years. Young Ezra Stiles, future president of Yale, reaching it via horseback in 1754, "took prospect of the city" from the steeple of the Middle Dutch Church in Nassau Street; inspected the market, the exchange, the various churches, and the fort and battery; "bot Curiosity"—in good tourist fashion—at Mr. Noel's shop; and enjoyed a round of teas, calls, collations, and other "elegant entertainment." [26]

Good food and drink were early available at the taverns within the city or at country resorts like Clapp's, "a kind of a pleasure garden." Here, in 1679, Governor Fletcher regaled his guests with "good Cyder & mead" or meals such as one that offered the diners "Soupe—a dish of Beanes and bacon—a dish of rosted Lamb and Sallad—a dish of young peas—a dish of rosted chicken a Dish of tarts—a Dish of curds & Creame—. . . a dish of mulberries & Currants." Local pastimes still reflected the informality of the frontier, but entertainment became somewhat more sophisticated with the advent of public balls, following the arrival of a dancing master in 1737. However, as late as 1759, when young Andrew Burnaby visited Manhattan, sleighing expeditions competed in the winter with indoor amusements, and summer entertainment included "going in parties upon the water, and fishing; or making excursions into the country." "Turtle feasts," or barbecues, occurred once or twice a week at houses, outside the city, "pleasantly situated on the East River." "Thirty or forty gentlemen and ladies meet and dine together, drink tea in the afternoon, fish and amuse themselves till evening, and then return home in Italian chaises," the future curate reported.[27]

Manhattan's man-about-town of the eighteenth century passed agreeable hours at the coffeehouses and taverns and in the company of the numerous clubs that flourished in that day. A Huguenot visitor, John Fontaine, was entertained in 1716 by both the Irish Club and the French Club. Dr. Hamilton, apparently bearing adequate references from Maryland in 1744, enjoyed the hospitality of the Hungarian Club, whose members, according to his report, were all good "bumper men." At establishments like the Exchange Coffee House or the Merchant's Coffee House he could count on "the best of company and conversation." [28]

Music and the drama did not have the continuous professional performance that prevails in the modern metropolis; hence contemporary comment may not reflect as much of this kind of entertainment as actually was available in eighteenth-century New York. To judge from visitors' accounts, music was frequently enjoyed in the home and increasingly performed by individuals or small groups in public places. The first public concert, of record, took place in 1736, when a harpsichord, violin, and German flute were played at Todd's Tavern. In 1744, Dr. Hamilton attended a similar performance at this local hostelry, at which he heard a "tollerable concerto of musick" performed by one violin and two flutes. When Ezra Stiles visited the city ten years later—in 1754—he was taken to call on a local musician who, with his host, played on the violin "most charmingly & on the spinet & organ." Professional performances increased in number in the sixties and seventies. A public concert attended by a visitor from Boston—in 1773—was "very full." Though the music was "indifferent," the ladies were sprightly, familiar, beautiful, and—of doubtful help to the performers—"loquacious." [29]

Professional drama had its beginning in the city in 1732 when a band of English players inaugurated regular performances that continued, under makeshift circumstances, for a period of two years. Not, however, until the arrival of Lewis Hallam and his repertory company, in 1753, and the construction of a playhouse, in 1758, was there real promise of the theatrical pre-eminence that New York was to attain in later years. The Boston Patriot, young Josiah Quincy, found the "playhouse" an almost irresistible temptation when he visited New York in May of 1773, on his return from a trip to Charleston in the interest of the colonial cause. He found such enjoyment in the acting of Hallam and his troupe as to conclude that if he "had stayed in town a month," he would have gone to the theatre "every acting night." [30]

Even his less corruptible compatriot, John Adams, appears to have been distracted by the tempo of the city's social life. So much "breakfasting, dining, drinking coffee, &c., about the city," prevented the visitor from exploring the more serious side of the community as much as he could have wished. "With all the opulence and splendor of this city, there is very little good breeding to be found," Adams complained, in the course of a month's sojourn in New York, en route to the Continental Congress, in the fall of 1774. "We have been treated with an assiduous respect; but I have not seen one real gentleman, one well-bred man, since I came to town. At their entertainments there is no conversation that is agreeable; there is no modesty, no attention to one another. They talk very loud, very fast, and altogether. If they ask you a question, before you can utter three words of your answer, they will break out upon you again, and talk away." [31]

The state of intellectual endeavor in the eighteenth-century city won only qualified acclaim from the few observers who saw fit to comment on that side of life in provincial New York. In the opinion of Andrew Burnaby, who visited the city in 1759, science and the arts had "made no greater progress here than in the other colonies." He nevertheless reported that "every one seems zealous to promote learning"—an attitude reflected in the opening of a subscription library in 1754 (members paid £5, principal, and an annual fee of ten shillings) and in the founding of King's College, the city's first institution of higher learning, in the same year. Only one wing of the college, consisting of twenty-four sets of apartments, was completed at the time of Burnaby's visit; in spite of a "great scarcity of professors," as well as of funds, about twenty-five students were in attendance, he wrote, and "seven gentlemen" had taken degrees in the recent commencement. Crèvecoeur, describing the college in the early 1770's, admired its beautiful architecture, good library, and "large number of mathematical instruments of great value." Harvard-trained John Adams was less impressed. The future President commented in 1774: "There is but one building at this college, and that is very far from full of scholars; they never have had forty scholars at a time." [32]

The resort to private subsidy for libraries and institutions of learning did not mean that the municipality had forsworn all responsibility for the welfare of its citizens. It simply took a limited view of its obligations along these lines. The eighteenth-century concept of municipal function implied less of service than control, however much the civic welfare was desired. In less than a year after the English conquest of New Amsterdam, Governor Richard Nicolls had reconstituted the Dutch municipal officialdom along English lines, with an appointive mayor, aldermen, and sheriff to replace the burgomasters, schepens, and schout of Dutch days. In 1683, Governor Dongan authorized popular election of the hitherto appointed aldermen, and this advance in representative government was confirmed in the charter of 1686. At the outbreak of the Revolution, the city was governed under the Montgomerie charter of 1731. According to its provisions, the governor annually appointed a mayor, recorder, town clerk, and treasurer, while the freeholders and freemen in each of the now seven wards annually elected an alderman, an assistant, and such minor officials as assessors, collectors, and constables.

These elements of popular control did not escape the attention of young John Adams, who found occasion, while breakfasting with the treasurer of the province, to discuss "the constitution of the city." "The aldermen are the magistrates of the city, and the only ones," he noted in his diary; "they have no justices of the peace in the city; so that the magistracy of the city are all the creatures of the people. The city cannot tax itself." The Council must ask the Assembly "every year to be empowered by law to assess the city for a certain sum." [33]

Most travelers of the period were, however, less interested in the form of the municipal government than in the services it provided;

and these were noticeably meager in colonial days. Drinking water was a matter of prime importance to the visitor, indeed to beast as well as man in a horse-borne age. Although there were municipal wells within the city limits, Peter Kalm spoke for most of the visitors when he contended that there was "no good water to be met with in the town itself." As a result, residents were in the habit of resorting to "a large spring of good water," at a short distance from the city, to obtain a supply "for their tea and for the use of the kitchen." Other travelers referred to the purchase of water from vendors who made their living by "carting of it into town where they sell it by the pale & Ca." [34]

The water supply was also important for its use in connection with the ever prevalent hazard of fire in the congested colonial community. As in the Dutch period, the municipality required periodic inspection of hearths and chimneys as a means of preventing fires and expected the aid of all the citizens when fires broke out. Jean de Crèvecoeur reported in 1772 that "all the inhabitants of the city" were required "to keep suspended in the halls of their houses a certain number of leather buckets and a certain number of sacks." They were "to carry these to fires with the greatest of speed, to help the pumpers, to maintain order, to carry water, and to save the belongings of the victims." The Volunteer Fire Department had its origins in December 1737 when the General Assembly of the colony passed an act instructing the Corporation to appoint "not more than 42 able, discreet, sober men as firemen." Thus was set a pattern of fire fighting that prevailed in the city until the mid-1860's. By 1772, these volunteer fire fighters numbered 163 men, organized into eleven companies, each commanded by a foreman. The members served without remuneration, but were exempted from certain other civic duties.

The city's first fire engines were imported from England in 1731, and their extended use prompted an increased concern for an adequate water supply. In 1774 there was discussion of a reservoir and pumping plant from which water could be conducted throughout the city. The reservoir and pump, powered by a steam engine capable of raising two hundred gallons fifty-two feet per minute, were apparently completed; but the outbreak of the American Revolution prevented the construction of the system of hollow logs by which the water was to be distributed to the consumer.[35]

The guardians of the law made much less impression on New

York's visitors than did its fire-fighting force, mainly because they were so much less apparent. Constables, the principal law enforcement officers, acted as policemen during the day. At night, the municipality resorted to various expedients depending on the danger of the times. Early in the eighteenth century the preservation of nocturnal order was the responsibility of four hired bellmen who made the rounds of the city announcing the state of the weather and the hour of the night. A citizen watch, constituted in 1731, enlisted the compulsory services of all inhabitants in turn, including women, although substitutes could be supplied.

In 1762, the common council decided to re-establish a paid standing force for nighttime protection; and on the eve of the American Revolution, the municipality was employing sixteen regular watchmen at an annual salary of £32 for duty every night, and eight others at £16 for duty on alternate nights. A system of street lighting, authorized in 1761, also contributed to the maintenance of public order. Although the police of colonial New York City was inadequate in times of serious emergency, Captain William Owen of the Royal Navy had cause to praise it after his visit in 1767. "I lost my gold Watch, one night, in a very extraordinary manner," he reported; "but through the assiduity of an old Dutch Alderman and his mirmidons, it was restored to me before sun-set the following Evening." [36]

In the form and function of its government, as in its physical appearance, New York of the later eighteenth century approximated the pattern of a British colonial city, yet with a New World flavor identifiably its own. The qualities of language, religion, and architecture which had made it seem foreign to British visitors at the outset of English rule had been tempered by time, by British contacts, and by the experiences attending its mercantile growth. To travelers of the later eighteenth century its predominantly English-speaking population, the prevalence of its Anglican and Presbyterian churches, and the English tone of its club life and its educational institutions marked it as another British city.

Yet in the ethnic variety of its people, the numerous reminders of its Dutch origins, and the "gayety and dissipation" with which its society was "tinctured," it reflected a personality peculiar to itself, and in its rising resistance to the restraints of Parliamentary regulation an identification with other American cities whose expanding economies were precipitating tension within the British Empire.

Moreover, its economy continued to exhibit a well-being and an abundance which especially in the eyes of European visitors differentiated it from the cities of the Old World. "I know of no place where food of every kind is cheaper or more abundant," wrote Jean de Crèvecoeur in 1772, reflecting in tone what was to be for many years the reaction of Europeans to the American standard of living as exemplified in New York City; "meat, pork, ham, mutton, butter, cheese, flour, fish, and oysters, all combine to render living wholesome and reasonable; thus everybody lives in comfort, everyone is nurtured on good food, the poorest laborer not excepted." [37] This was the provincial New York City that in the decades following 1763 was to challenge British rule.

NEW YORK IN 1697: EARLY EVIDENCE OF BRITISH RULE

By the close of the seventeenth century, New York was already beginning to show the effects of the British conquest. It was still a Dutch town, but with an increasingly English overlay. As the seat of the colonial governors, it was inevitably affected by British patterns of architecture, religion, government, and social conduct. The beginnings of this transformation are reflected in an account written by Dr. Benjamin Bullivant, a Boston physician and onetime attorney general of Massachusetts who fraternized with the city's leading citizens during a visit to New York in 1697. The original manuscript of Bullivant's journal is owned by the New-York Historical Society. The following excerpts from it, reprinted with the Society's permission, are from Wayne Andrews' edition of it entitled "A Glance at New York," which appeared in the *New-York Historical Society Quarterly* for January 1956.[38]

. . . his Exc. [Governor Benjamin Fletcher] was pleased to aske me, if I cared to see the fort & platformes. . . .

The fort stands upon a point, that hath a most lovely prospect. . . . The walls . . . are about 20 feet high from without & pallisaded besides. His Exc. is also makeing a Low Battery of 8 or 10 gunns without ye walls, next Hudsons River. There are besides sundry Batteries in the City, some of 12 or 14 great guns towards the harbour, others towards the land at ye passadge to the town gate. . . .

his Exc. honoured me . . . to shew me . . . the English church, new from the ground, of good brown square stone & brick exactly English fashion with a Large square steeple at the west end, not yet half carried up. . . . his Exc. hath beene pleased to give greate encouragement to this worke, and you see his armes upon the East end carved in stone and Coloured, at present ye English use the New Dutch Church once a Sabath. . . .

Having been now 4 dayes at N. Y. I have Learned to say something of its Constitutions, & fashions. it was made a city by a Charter in gouuernor Dungans time hath a Mayor Sheriff, Recorder, and a town clerck, nominated by ye Gouuernor and Councill. Six Aldermen, and six com̄on Councell men elected by the freemen, vizt, one Alderman & one Council man for each of the 6 wards in the City. The Mayors court is kept every Tuesday, he hath no ensigns of honour but the beareing a white staffe in his hand, Like ye Sherifs of London. . . .

They have many publique wells enclosed & Covered in ye Streetes I do not know I ever saw above one pump. . . .

I attended his Exc. from ye Fort about 11 of the clock to the Dutch church, he hath most of the gent in Com̄ission attending him on foot, & is followed by ½ a company of Musquetiers with the drum beateing to the church doore, he is mett by the Mayor & Sheriffe with theyr white staffes and so accompanied to Church In which his Excellency hath a stall on purpose, distinct & elevated, with a cloath of State & Cushion before him, on each side are Stalls for the mayor, Sheriff, & Aldermen & principall gentry. The Mayor & Sheriff have a Carpet of Turkie worke before them, Sermon ended we returned as we came & in the afternoon had prayers only. The Dutch seeme not very strict in Keepeing the Sabath, you should see some shelling peas at theyr doors children playing at theyr usuall games in the streetes & ye taverns filled.

A SWEDISH PROFESSOR REPORTS ON NEW YORK'S ECONOMY: 1748

Of all the travelers of the colonial period, the Swedish naturalist Peter Kalm left the most detailed exposition of the trading activities that supported New York's economy in the mid-eighteenth century. Kalm was Professor of Economy in the University of Åbo, in Swedish Finland, and a member of the Swedish Royal Academy of Science, which sponsored his trip. Actually he spent only five days in New York—from October 30 to November 3, 1748; hence some of his comments may have been based upon reading as well as experience. Nevertheless, his comprehensive account appears to benefit, at least in this portion of the work, from the scientist's capacity for objective and detailed observation. The following excerpt is taken from John R. Forster's translation of Kalm's *Travels into North America.*[39]

New York probably carries on a more extensive commerce, than any town in the English North American provinces; at least it may be said to equal them: Boston and Philadelphia however come very near up to it. The trade of New York extends to many places; and it is said they send more ships from thence to London, than they do from Philadelphia. They export to that capital all the various sorts of skins which they buy of the Indians, sugar, logwood, and other dying woods, rum, mahogany, and many other goods which are the produce of the West Indies; together with all the specie which they get in the course of trade. Every year they build several ships here, which are sent to London and there sold; and of late years they have shipped a quantity of iron to England. In return for these, they import from London stuffs, and every other article of English growth or manufacture, together with all sorts of foreign goods. . . .

New York sends many ships to the West Indies, with flour, corn, biscuit, timber, tuns, boards, flesh, fish, butter, and other provisions; together with some of the few fruits that grow here. Many ships go to Boston in New England, with corn and flour; and take in exchange, flesh, butter, timber, different sorts of fish, and other articles, which they carry further to the West Indies. They now and then take rum from thence, which is distilled there in great quantities, and sell it here with a considerable advantage. Sometimes they send yachts with goods from New York to Philadelphia, and at other times yachts are sent from Philadelphia to New York; which is only done, as appears from the gazettes, because certain articles are cheaper at one place than at the other. They send ships to Ireland every year, laden with all kinds of West India goods; but especially with linseed, which is reaped in this province. I have been assured, that in some years no less than ten ships have been sent to Ireland, laden with nothing but linseed; because it is said the flax in Ireland does not afford good seed. . . .

The goods which are shipped to the West Indies, are sometimes paid for with ready money, and sometimes with West India goods, which are either first brought to New York, or immediately sent to England or Holland. If a ship does not chuse to take in West India goods in its return to New York, or if no body will freight it, it often goes to Newcastle in England to take in coals for ballast, which when brought home sell for a pretty good price. In many parts of the town coals are made use of, both for kitchen fires, and in rooms, because they are reckoned cheaper than wood, which at present costs thirty shillings of New York currency per fathom. . . . New York has likewise some intercourse with South Carolina; to which it sends corn, flour, sugar, rum, and other goods, and takes rice in return, which is almost the only commodity exported from South Carolina.

NEW YORK CITY ON THE EVE OF THE REVOLUTION: 1774

For a concise, yet many-sided, picture of New York City which captures the vigor and variety of the urban scene on the eve of the Revolution, it would be hard to improve on letters "wrote on the Spot" by Patrick M'Robert, a Scotchman of some means who visited New York City in August 1774. M'Robert spent parts of 1774 and 1775 in America, perhaps with a view of settling there. His letters were written "for the amusement of a particular friend," without thought of publication, but they were ultimately published in pamphlet form in the hope of correcting some of the "misrepresentations and contradictory accounts received from that western world." The following excerpts from letters written in New York in August 1774 are drawn from Carl Bridenbaugh's edition of M'Robert's *A Tour Through Part of the North Provinces of America* . . . , and are reprinted here with the permission of the Historical Society of Pennsylvania.[40]

The city is large, and contains a great many neat buildings. The publick buildings, and places of worship, are generally very neat, and well finished, if not elegant. The college [King's College, now Columbia], tho' only one third of the plan is compleat, makes a fine appearance, on one of the finest situations perhaps of any college in the world. Here are taught divinity, mathematicks, the practice and theory of medicine, chymistry, surgery, and materia medica. One circumstance I think is a little unlucky, the enterance to this college is thro' one of the streets where the most noted prostitutes live. This is certainly a temptation to the youth that have occasion to pass so often that way.

The new hospital tho' not quite finished is another fine building upon the same plan as the Royal Infirmary at Edinburgh. . . .

They have three English churchs, three Presbyterian, two Dutch Lutherian, two Dutch Calvenists, all neat and well finished buildings, besides a French church, an Anabaptist, a Methodist, a Quaker meeting, a Moravian church, and a Jews synagogue. There are many other fine buildings belonging to private gentlemen and merchants; but the streets are in general ill paved, irregular, and too narrow. There are four market places, all well supplied with all kinds of provisions.

They are pretty well supplied with fresh water from pumps sunk at convenient distances in the streets. Their tea water they get at present brought in carts thro' the streets from the suburbs of the city; but they are now erecting a fire [steam] engine for raising the spring into a reservoir, from whence, by pipes, they can convey it to any part of the city. They are pretty well guarded against accidents from fire, by obliging every citizen to register their house, and for one shilling a vent yearly, to have them swept once a month. They have also a number of engines kept at convenient distances: to each of these is appointed a captain, and a certain number of men. And when a fire happens, a premium is always allowed to the captain and his men who can first make their engines play upon the fire. By this precaution fire seldom happens, and by the proper disposition of the engines, when it does happen, it is seldom allowed to spread farther than the house it brakes out in. . . .

Near the fort is an equestrian statue of king George the III. upon an elegant pedestial in the middle of a fine green rail'd in with iron. At the crossing of two public streets, stands at full length a marble statue of lord Chatham erected by the citizens in gratitude for his strenuous opposition to the stamp act in 1766. They have several large roperies, distilleries, breweries, and a large iron work carried on here. They have plenty of mechanicks of all kinds, by whom almost every thing that is made with you in Britain is made to as great perfection here. The inhabitants are in general brisk and lively, kind to strangers, dress very gay; the fair sex are in general handsome, and said to be very obliging. Above 500 ladies of pleasure keep lodgings contiguous within the consecreated liberties of St. Paul's. This part of the city belongs to the church, and has thence obtained the name of the *Holy Ground.* Here all the prostitutes reside, among whom are many fine well dressed women, and it is remarkable that they live in much greater cordiality one with another than any nests of that kind do in Britain or Ireland.

It rather hurts an Europian eye to see so many negro slaves upon the streets, tho' they are said to deminish yearly here. The city is governed by a mayor, and divided into seven different wards, over each of which an alderman and an assistant presides. They have generally the same laws and regulations as in England. There are computed between twenty-six and thirty thousand inhabitants in the city; in this number are, I believe, included the slaves, who make at least a fifth part of the number. . . .

Labourers have their three and four shillings a-day about New York; but at present they seem rather overstocked, owing to the arrival of so many adventurers from Britain and Ireland; . . . .

All necessaries of life are plenty, and reasonable; For example, beef at four and five pence the pound; good mutton the same; a good hen at a shilling, and pork and veal in proportion; butter sixteen pence the pound; the best flower, seventeen shillings the hundred weight; West India rum from three shillings and six pence, and three and nine pence the gallon. Rum distilled here, at two and six pence the gallon; beer, and all sorts of wine, about the same prices that you have them at; cyder, four pence the bottle. The only dear drink is London porter, which is two shillings the bottle. Observe, that in all the above rates and prices, I speak of the currency of the country, which is in proportion as seven pence sterling to a shilling.

3. *RESISTANCE, REVOLUTION, AND RECONSTRUCTION* (*1765–1789*)

Contemporary comment reflects the tension, the physical dislocation, and the efforts at reconstruction which in turn affected life in New York City during the generation in which the thirteen colonies won their freedom from Great Britain. In the course of these volatile years, New York was a seedbed of revolution, a Patriot bastion, an occupied city, a Tory haven, and finally the capital city of the newly emerging United States. Always a city of transients, New York was plagued in this period with a more fluctuating and transitory population than at any other time in its municipal career. Its population dropped from 25,000 to 5,000 as its residents fled in the face of the British occupation; rose to some 33,000 with the influx of Loyalist refugees, British soldiers, and the motley ingredient that attaches itself to a garrison town in time of war; and momentarily declined again as it changed from Tory refuge to American city. Commentators on this confused and ever changing scene included royal administrators, proponents of revolution, Patriot soldiers, resident Loyalists, Tory refugees, and, in time, visitors from the sister states and inquiring Europeans bent upon observing the transformations of the postwar years.[1]

Visitors of the early 1760's detected signs of the unrest that prevailed as a result of revenue measures passed by the British Parliament after 1763. The Sugar Act of 1764 threatened the profits of the merchants who trafficked in rum and molasses with the Dutch and French West Indies. The Stamp Act was especially offensive to the lawyers and newspapermen. Artisans, tradesmen, and mechanics, irked as much by local inequalities as by Parliamentary innovations, were easily encouraged to resist. The rising tension was observed by Lord Adam Gordon, Army officer and member of Parliament, who traveled in America and the West Indies in 1764 and 1765. "People here, live . . . very Comfortably, did they chuse to be contented," he reported, with some condescension. "It is hoped they will soon come to better temper, after Taxes become more familiar to them." A French observer of consequence, sojourning in the city in August 1765, found that nothing was talked of "but the spirited and patriotic behavior of the Inhabitants of the northern Colonies," who had surrounded the stamp officer's house and forced him to resign. The Patriots of New York, he reported, "all Declare Solemnly that when the Stamp papers Come over they'l set fire to the house wherein the[y] are lodged." [2]

As friction mounted, popular demonstrations and boycott agreements mirrored the local resistance to Parliament's attempt to raise "the Arm of Government by Revenue Laws." Upon the arrival of the detested stamps, patriotic New Yorkers lived up to their threats and burned the provincial governor in effigy. Later when an attempt was made to land a cargo of tea, after Parliament had taxed that popular commodity, the local Sons of Liberty staged their own "tea party," along lines similar to that of their fellow Patriots of Boston. In the opinion of Cadwallader Colden, provincial governor from 1761 to 1776, the city population was clearly instigating the resistance movement in the province. "The present political zeal and phrenzy is almost entirely confined to the City of New-York," he reported to Lord Dartmouth in July of 1774; "the people in the counties are no ways disposed to become active, or to bear any part in what is proposed by the citizens." [3]

Sentiment in the city was by no means unanimous, however, as the festering difficulties with the Mother Country came to a head. Many conservative merchants feared that the resistance movement, sparked by the Sons of Liberty, would get out of hand. War would interfere with trade; this conviction was always to affect the thinking of the merchant element when New York faced involvement in a war. The crosscurrents of local opinion were explained to John Adams by Alexander McDougall, one of the chief accelerators of revolutionary opinion in New York City. "Mr. McDougall gave a caution to avoid every expression here which looked like an allusion to the last appeal," the future President recorded in his diary in August 1774. "He says there is a powerful party here who are intimidated by fears of a civil war, and they have been induced to acquiesce by assurances that there was no danger, and that a peaceful cessation of commerce would effect relief. Another party, he says, are intimidated lest the levelling spirit of the New England Colonies should propagate itself into New York. Another party are prompted by Episcopalian prejudices against New England. Another party are merchants largely concerned in navigation, and therefore are afraid of non-importation, non-consumption, and non-exportation agreements. Another party are those who are looking up to Government for favors. . . ." [4]

Eight months later—on the eve of Lexington and Concord—the conflict of opinion was no less intense. "The People here are very much divided, & Party spirit is very high," wrote Dr. Robert Honyman, a Scotsman recently settled in Virginia, who visited New York in March of 1775. Handbills, advertisements, and extracts of letters on both sides were "daily & hourly printed, published, pasted up, & handed about." Men, women, and children—"all ranks & professions"—were "mad with Politics." In the week preceding the opening skirmishes in New England, the Liberty Party were "at their wits end" to prevent a "very large Transport" from taking on "Straw, Plank & other Stores" for the use of the British Army in Boston. On April 15, the Patriot faction, in procession, carried the Liberty flag through the New York streets, and after "many tumults & outrages" hoisted it on the Liberty pole. "I went & saw all the transactions of this Evening," Dr. Honyman reported, "& from the whole entertain a much more contemptible notion of the high faction than ever I did. I left them assaulting one Hardin's house; who alone defended it against them all, & bid them defiance. . . . bought the Crisis from Anderson the printer of it. This is by far the most treasonable & audacious piece that has yet been published." [5]

With the outbreak of hostilities in Massachusetts, real authority in New York City, as on the provincial level, fell into the hands of extralegal organizations. A Committee of One Hundred, or Committee of Safety, was elected on May 1, 1775. Early in February 1776 this was superseded by a Committee of Fifty, highly Patriot in tone, which remained in control until the British Army took possession of the city in the following September. The diary of Pastor Ewald G. Schaukirk of the Moravian Church reports the "commotion and confusion" that prevailed late in April 1775 as the Patriot element prepared for open resistance. "Trade and business was at a stand; soldiers were enlisted; the inhabitants seized the keys of the Custom House; and the arms and powder were taken from the Corporation," he wrote, alarmed at this revolutionary turn of events. Conservative Judge William Smith was similarly apprehensive. He wrote with some bitterness: "Armed Parties summon the Town publicly to come and take arms & learn the Manual Exercise. They are publicly delivered out and armed Individuals shew themselves at all Hours in the Streets—Consternation in the Faces of the Principal Inhabitants. . . . The Merchants are amazed & yet so humbled as only to sigh or complain in whispers." [6]

Confusion increased in February of the succeeding year when it became apparent that military action would, in time, shift from Boston to New York. General Lee's arrival on February 4, 1776, for the purpose of constructing fortifications, precipitated a mass exodus from the city. On the ensuing Sunday "People in almost every street were loading their carts with goods," making such a racket that the few who went to church "could scarcely hear the Preacher's voice." A New York paper reported on February 15 that the "greatest part of the inhabitants, with their movables," had "taken refuge in the country, particularly the women and children." [7]

In the months that followed, New York City was pretty much transformed into a Patriot camp. Soldiers from "New-England, Philadelphia, and Jersey" now replaced the earlier residents, and fortifications were erected in every part of the town. "General Lee is taking every necessary step to fortify and defend this city," wrote Frederick Rhinelander to Peter Van Schaack, on February 23. "To see the vast number of houses shut up, one would think the city almost evacuated. Women and children are scarcely to be seen in the streets. Troops are daily coming in; they break open and quarter themselves in the houses they find shut up. Necessity knows no law." [8] Lieutenant Isaac Bangs, arriving with the Revolutionary troops from New England, on April 17, "found every street leading from the Water almost stoped with Breast Works built by Genl Lee, to prevent the Enemy from landing to set fire to the town." The stone wall of the Battery was being reinforced with turf against an enemy assault.

The city surpassed the expectations of this young Harvard graduate, who had left the practice of medicine to enter the Patriot Army. Like many a soldier of a later day, he availed himself of the opportunity, which military service provided, to see new sights. He admired the "beautiful prospect" of the city from the fort, puzzled over the abortive waterworks, and inspected the "air furnace," where brass fieldpieces and iron cannon for the Patriot Army were being produced. He attended services in most of the city's churches and concluded, after the fashion of a good New England Patriot, that the

"Devout behaviour of the Dutch" was more agreeable than "all the Pomp, Equipage, & Majestick Expressions of the English Church." He visited the homes of hospitable local residents and found entertainment in the grog shops and public houses which offered a popular retreat for the Patriot soldiery, as did the "Holy Ground" in the vicinity of Trinity Church—the locale of the prostitutes—which Bangs called the "usual place of abode" of many of the men. He predicted that unless the General did something about "these horrid Wretches" he would soon have his army "greatly impaired," for they "not only destroy men by Sickness, but they sometimes inhumanly murder them; . . . since Monday last two Men were found inhumanly Murthered & concealed, besides one who was castrated in a barbarous manner." [9]

Opinions differed as to the behavior of the American soldiery who made up such a conspicuous part of New York's population in 1776. The author of a now anonymous letter, written in April of that year, expressed surprise that "so undisciplined a multitude, as our Provincials are represented to be," should be causing so little mischief. They had "the simplicity of ploughmen in their manners," and seemed "quite strangers to the vices of older soldiers." An opposing view was that of Nicholas Cresswell, who arrived in New York on September 7, 1776, in an unsuccessful attempt to escape to the British fleet, then riding at anchor two miles from the town. "Nothing to be got here," he despaired. "The town full of Soldiers . . . the nastiest Devils in creation. . . . If my countrymen are beaten by these ragamuffins I shall be much surprized." [10]

A week later, the forces Cresswell had tried to reach were in possession of the city. Engagements on Long Island late in August had gone against the Americans. On September 15, Howe's troops captured New York City; and with the fall of Fort Washington on the sixteenth of November, Manhattan Island was in British hands. Ambrose Serle, Lord Howe's secretary from May 1776 to June 18, 1778, recorded in his journal the climactic events of September 15—when the Patriots surrendered the city to the forces of the now repudiated Mother Country. The scene in the harbor was "awful & grand. . . . The Hills, the Woods, the River, the Town, the Ships, and Pillars of Smoke, all heightened by a most clear & delightful morning," excited Serle's romantic imagination. Fire from the fortifications on Manhattan was no match for the guns of the "Renown," the "Repulse," and the "Pearl," sailing sternly up the Hudson, nor for the concerted discharge of cannon from the fleet in the East River as well, which covered the landing of the troops. "So terrible and so incessant a Roar of Guns few even in the Army & Navy had ever heard before. . . . The Rebels were apparently frightened away by the horrid Din, and deserted the Town & all their Works in the utmost Precipitation," wrote Serle—an estimate of the situation which was confirmed, in his diary, by Archibald Robertson, lieutenant-general in the Royal Engineers.

"Nothing could equal the Expressions of Joy, shewn by the Inhabitants, upon the arrival of the King's officers," the admiral's secretary reported. Their happiness—at least that of those who put in an appearance—drove them about like "overjoyed Bedlamites." One woman pulled down the "Rebel Standard" from the fort and trampled it under foot. "They carried our officers, at their first Landing, in Chairs or upon their Shoulders up and down the Streets. They have felt so much of real Tyranny, since the New England & other Rebels came among them, that they are at a Loss how to enjoy their Release." By September 19, many of the loyal inhabitants were returning with their goods to the town; "as to the rebellious, the Quarter master General has marked G. R. upon the Doors of their Houses, which are to serve for Habitations to the Army."

That the "rebellious" were more numerous than Serle had originally thought becomes apparent from the comments in his journal during the weeks following the British occupation. A fire, probably not incendiary in origin, he laid to a "New England plot." With evident satisfaction he reported that one man, apprehended with matches, was "knocked down by a Grenadier & thrown into the Flames for his Reward: Another, who was found cutting off the Handles of the Water-Buckets to prevent their Use, was first hung up by the Neck till he was dead and afterwards by the Heels upon a Sign-Post by the Sailors." On October 31, he inveighed against the many "pretended Friends," who secretly injured or stole the horses brought over for the use of the Army and who communicated all they could to the enemy. "The People in general form the most impudent, base & hypocritical Characters, that can be met with out of Crete or Greece," he concluded. "The truest Idea that can be raised of the best I have seen among them, may be taken from some of our upstart, ill-bred Tradesmen, who have Meanness enough to be ostentatious or wrangle about any thing, but [are] capable of shewing the Spirit or using the Language of Gentlemen in nothing." [11]

NEW YORK IN REVOLT

The resistance of the Patriots of New York City was the theme of this mezzotint published in London in 1775. Based on an actual incident, it depicts a Patriot barber refusing to finish shaving the commander of a British transport, once the latter's identity is revealed. Wig boxes bearing the names of such New York Radicals as John Lamb, Isaac Sears, and Alexander McDougall identify the barber with the Patriot cause.

The appearance of the British fleet in the Upper Bay was the prelude to the British occupation of New York City on September 15, 1776. This water color, portraying the fleet at anchor between Long Island and Staten Island, in July, was one of a series painted during the war by the Scotsman Captain Archibald Robertson, who served as an engineer officer with the occupying forces.

Seven years of military occupation brought hardship and suffering to many New Yorkers and damage to whole sections of the city. Below is a sketch of Trinity Church, supposedly made by Lord Rawdon of Cornwallis's staff. It shows the ravages of a fire, on September 21, 1776, that left the church and its vicinity in ruins.

Picture Credits:
(*top*) Stokes Collection, New York Public Library
(*center*) Spencer Collection, New York Public Library
(*below*) Emmett Collection, New York Public Library

Stokes Collection, New York Public Library

The Edward W. C. Arnold Collection; photograph courtesy of Museum of the City of New York

NEW YORK IN THE EARLY FEDERAL PERIOD

By the close of the eighteenth century, the architecture of New York reflected the city's already cosmopolitan lineage. The water color (above) of Broad Street, painted by George (John Joseph?) Holland in 1797, shows dwellings in the Dutch style, with characteristic gabled fronts; others built or "new-fronted" after the English fashion; and the City Hall, previously Federal Hall, on the present site of the Subtreasury Building, decorated with the stars and eagle of the new Republic.

Federal Hall was the scene of Washington's first inauguration (left), April 30, 1789. Having served since 1704 as the City Hall, the structure was remodeled by Major L'Enfant in 1788–1789 for the use of the Congress of the young United States. When Congress moved to Philadelphia in 1790, the building was again the City Hall until 1811. This view—the only known contemporary representation of the inauguration—was drawn by Peter Lacour and engraved by Amos Doolittle, who published it in 1790.

Overcrowding, insecurity, and unnatural extremes of living characterized life in the occupied city. William Eddis, a Maryland Loyalist who stopped at an East River residence en route to London in 1777, professed a desire to avoid the "crowded city" whenever possible. The shortage of houses, already acute because of the troops, was immeasurably aggravated by the fire. "The destruction was very great," a resident Loyalist reported, following the conflagration; "between a third and a fourth of the City is burnt. All that is west of the New Exchange, along Broad Street to the North River, as high as the City Hall, and from thence along the Broad Way and North River to King's College, is in Ruins. . . . Our Distresses were great before, but this Calamity has encreased them tenfold. Thousands are hereby reduced to beggary." [12]

As the months went on, the commandeering of dwellings and other structures for the use of the British, the confiscation of rebel property, the arrival of additional troops, and the influx of Loyalist refugees, "come daily shivering in for protection," compounded the difficulty. "What a Pity it is to see such a fine City as this almost half Burned to ashes," wrote an unnamed Irishman, apparently from Dublin, who reached New York on the brig "Dash," on October 29, 1782, after having been chased for hours and fired on by a sloop, "and to see now nothing rem[ainin]g but the bare walls of fine Churches & other Public Buildings or to see those rem[ainin]g Converted into magaziens or other purposes for use of the army—as are some of their meeting houses—the College & the Exchange &ca. . . ." [13]

The insecurity of life in occupied New York sprang from a number of causes. Food and fuel were at times scarce and always costly. The occupying British rarely lacked provisions, at least at first, but, as Eddis reported in 1777, "every article bears an exorbitant price." On the other hand, British and Americans alike appear to have suffered for lack of fuel in the already dependent urban environment. "Wood often could not be purchased for money," wrote the wife of General Riedesel, commander of German troops; "if by chance a little was for sale, it cost ten pounds by the cord. . . . The poor were obliged to burn fat, in order to warm themselves and cook their meals." Serle, visiting the outskirts of the town in January 1777, reported that all the fences and most of the wooden houses in the environs were "destroyed for Fuel." In these disjointed times, robberies and assaults were a daily, or nightly, occurrence; a citizen watch of eighty men was reactivated upon rumors of plots and threatened incendiarism. Added to this were the frustrations attending government by martial law and the apprehensions of a people who realized that their future welfare depended upon the increasingly doubtful success of British arms.[14]

Despite the existence of want and misery, an appearance of almost feverish commercial activity and social gaiety often prevailed. The presence of the troops brought a demand for goods and services; and shippers found profitable opportunities at the chief port of supply for Britain's fighting force. War profiteers fattened on privateering, provisioning the British, and indulging in illicit trade with other American colonies. Their affluence contrasted sharply with the poverty of the residents of "canvas town," a shambles which had sprung up in the burnt-over area. A Hessian officer gained the impression that the war had made all the inhabitants of the city rich. Wood choppers, coachmen, and chimney sweeps earned what he considered phenomenal wages. One of his compatriots reported that the wives of cobblers, tailors, and day laborers went about in "chintz, muslin, and silk trains." "This display increases daily as they get money from the troops," he wrote in a letter to his homeland; "they need not give a grain of salt without pay." [15]

The extravagant and carefree behavior of the military brought criticism even from those who supported the British cause. Pastor Schaukirk frowned upon the desecration of the ruins of Trinity Church, when a promenade was constructed there in 1779 for the diversion of the military "gentlemen." "A house opposite is adapted to accommodate the ladies or officers' women, while many honest people, both of the inhabitants and Refugees cannot get a house or lodging to live in or get their living." Cricket, horse racing, bull-baiting, concerts, dancing assemblies, and theatrical productions occupied the time of officers from whom the resident Loyalists expected military action; and on the occasion of the King's and Queen's birthdays, there were costly demonstrations and fashionable balls such as the one, in 1780, over which "Fritschen" Riedesel, general's wife and darling of the officer society, presided. A British soldier, departing for England from New York late in 1781, reported that the landlord of a tavern in Brooklyn, "where parties are made to go and eat fish," had saved "an immense fortune" during the war.[16]

New York City remained in British hands for some time after the Americans had achieved their independence through the force of arms. A cessation of hostilities was announced to the troops on April 19, 1783, just eight years after military conflict had commenced at Lexington and Concord; and in the succeeding month, George Washington and Sir Guy Carleton began to make preparations for the evacuation of the British from New York City, an event which occurred on November 25. Meanwhile, thousands of Loyalists who had sought refuge there were fleeing the assumption of American control.

Many problems of reconstruction faced the war-abused and partially ruined seaport town. Popular government had to be restored; and a sizable portion of the city, ravaged by fire, stood in need of rebuilding and repair. Yet despite the destruction and dislocation of the war years, New York adjusted to independence with remarkable speed. Within four years after the evacuation of the British, visitors were remarking upon its "grand" buildings, the "abundance of shops and warehouses," the numerous shipping in its harbor, and the prevailing evidences of order in the municipal scene.[17]

Political reconstruction took place with the restoration of orderly government along popular lines. During the British occupation, the military, together with the Department of Police and the City Vestry, had supervised every detail of community existence. Now, with elections to the Common Council, on December 15, 1783, and the governor's appointment of James Duane, as mayor, in the following February, the traditional agencies of government by popular consent again appeared. Within a year after the evacuation, "good order and regularity" had taken the place of "anarchy and confusion," an anonymous "Citizen" proudly reported in *Loudon's New York Packet* in December 1784; and by the time the Reverend Manasseh Cutler observed the city, three years later, he could report that he knew of no other place of any considerable magnitude where such "perfect order" prevailed.

Since January 1785, New York City had been the capital of the newborn nation, which was now governed under the Articles of Confederation. Cutler, in New York to negotiate with the Congress regarding grants of western lands, was especially impressed with the streets of the young capital city. They "are kept in fine order, pavements entire and even," he wrote after a sojourn in July of 1787; "no teams drawn with more than one horse, or with iron-shod wheels, are allowed to pass the streets. The pavements gradually descend from the houses to the center of the streets, where the gutters are for carrying off the water." Within the hitching posts, sidewalks, laid with freestone, were wide enough for pedestrians to walk three abreast.[18]

European visitors to New York also attested to the speed with which the city had repaired the ravages of war. One of these was Luigi Castiglioni, a young Italian naturalist whose curiosity about the new Republic led to a sojourn in the United States from 1785 to 1787. To this Italian visitor, New York looked more like "a flourishing European city than the capital of a new country." Trade appeared to be languishing at the moment for lack of favorable commercial treaties with the major European powers; but he was nevertheless convinced that the city's advantages for trade and communication with Europe would prompt continued growth.

Castiglioni was struck with the luxury of taste and table that prevailed in the New World capital. Public dancing parties, theatrical performances, and travel in splendid coaches connoted the sophistication of the local society. According to his report, the young ladies "of the first class," though "less refined than those of Boston," were "given to much luxury of style and fashion." This opinion was seconded by Brissot de Warville, who came to the United States in 1788 as the agent of a French syndicate speculating in American lands and debts. The French reformer was shocked at the "ravages" luxury was making upon the republican society he had come to America to observe. "If there is a town on the American continent where the English luxury displays its follies, it is New-York," he complained. "You will find here the English fashions. In the dress of the women, you will see the most brilliant silks, gauzes, hats, and borrowed hair. Equipages are rare, but they are elegant. The men have more simplicity in their dress; they disdain gewgaws, but they take their revenge in the luxury of the table." [19]

Like Manasseh Cutler, European visitors detected a prevailing regard for social distinctions which seemed to belie the equalitarian philosophy of the American Revolution. Cutler observed that the "gentry" rode in coaches, chariots, and phaetons; the common people, in "open chairs." "The several classes of people mix very little," he wrote. At the same time, contemporary observers were of the opinion that New Yorkers exhibited a hospitality toward strangers that distinguished the city from Philadelphia where "an affectation of superiority in certain families" often offended the outsider.[20]

The promise of its port as well as its position as the administrative center of the young nation underwrote the speed with which New York was transformed from an occupied city to a prospering peacetime capital. With the exploitation of new markets in the Orient and increasing access to the ports of France, Spain, and even the West Indies came a revival of commerce that was further stimulated by the assurance of national regulation achieved in the framing of the Federal Constitution of 1787. The city doubled in population, between 1783 and 1786, to reach 23,614 in August of that year. Within ten years it had added nearly 10,000 more. By 1788, it had regained its prewar commercial position and looked to the future with all the optimism of expansive youth.

"Let those men who doubt the prodigious effects that liberty produces on man, and on his industry, transport themselves to America," wrote Brissot de Warville, after his arrival in New York in that year. "What miracles will they here behold! Whilst every-where in Europe the villages and towns are falling to ruin, rather than augmenting, new edifices are here rising on all sides. . . . the activity which reigns every-where, announces a rising posterity; . . . I walked out by the side of the North River; what a rapid change in the space of six weeks! . . . On all sides, houses are rising, and streets extending: I see nothing but busy workmen building and repairing." The process of transforming provincial New York into a full-fledged American city had begun; and the opening of the national era found the community undergoing the perennial change and growth that were to be one of its most conspicuous physical characteristics in succeeding years.[21]

A YANKEE SOLDIER IN NEW YORK CITY: 1776

A Patriot soldier's reaction to New York City, as its citizens undertook open resistance to England, is found in the *Journal of Lieutenant Isaac Bangs,* a Yankee officer who came to New York with the New England troops on April 17, 1776. Bangs, a native of Harwich, Massachusetts, and a graduate of Harvard College, was twenty-four years old when he interrupted the practice of medicine in his home town to join the Revolutionary Army. His *Journal,* covering the period from April 1 to July 29, 1776, provides a forthright picture of the American defenses in the city, the treatment of Tories at the hands of the local citizens, and the behavior of the Patriot soldiers who were stationed in New York City previous to its capture by the British on September 15, 1776.[22]

[April] 19th. I spent the greatest part of my Time in viewing the City, which I found vastly surpassing my Expectations. The City is nearly as populous as the Town of Boston; the Publick Edifices greater in number, yet not in general so grand & Magnificent as those of Boston. . . . On the South west part of the Town, which is a Point between the two Rivers, is a very strong & costly Fort built by the Kings Troops & many masons men for the Protection of the City from the Enemy.

On the outside of the Fort at the Edge of the wall was a Battery, erected at a vast Expence to the King, built of hewn stone, the outside about ten feet high, the inside filled up to form a plane that [at] the Wall was not more than a foot and a half high. Our people were busily employed in making a Turf Wall upon the stone Wall, & when we arrived had almost finished as compleat a Battery as ever I saw. Several other Fortifications were erected in this Town, which made it tolerably strong & safe against any attacks of the Enemy. From the above-mentioned Fort a spacious street runing east northerly in a right line, reached without the Town about 1 Mile. In this, near the Fort, is the Equestrian Statue of King George 3d. . . . The design was in imitation of one of the Roman Emperors on Horseback. . . .

June 4. I tarried in the Camp all Day. This Day is the Kings Birth Day. No Festivity, Joy, or Mirth were discovered on this Occasion. . . .

June 12. I mounted Guard at the N[orth] River in the City with the Hair Caps, i.e., York Tories who tho they have & are deserving of a Bad Character, yet they behaved very well by being kept in good Subjection. . . . There are very many in the City of York who have behaved in an inimical Manner to America, a large Mob this Day visited many of them, & treated them very inhumanly by carrying them on a Rail through the Streets, stripping them, &c. Many of the Officers endeavoured to suppress them [the mob], but were unable only to disperse them for a little time. Towards Night they [the mob] came nigh our Guard, & I desired the Capn. to turn out the Guard and disperse them, but he was unwilling; however, they did no Violence to the two Tories whom they were in pursuit of, but brought them to us & desired us to keep them, which we did out of compassion to the poor Men, but as no Crime was sent in against them, we dismissed them at relieving of the Guard. They were unwilling to quit the Guard House, which they thought a safe Asylum, & we left them but not as Prisoners. . . .

July 6. Have the News of the United Colonies being Declared free & independent States by the Congress; may they be able to support themselves free & Independent, and never again be brought under the Yoke of Bondage by Cunning & designing Men.

The whole Choir of our Officers, together with Col. Baldwin & the chief of his Officers, went to a Publick House to testify our Joy at the happy news of Independence. We spent the afternoon merily in playing at Bowles for Wine. . . .

July 9. This afternoon the Declaration of the Independence of the 13 American States was read to the Several Brigades. It was received with Joy, which they severally testified by three Cheers.

July 12. [Enemy fire from the harbor prompted a return from the Patriots, in which six Americans were killed from their own cannon fire.] It is said that several of the Company out of which they were killed were drunk, & neglected to Spunge, Worm, & stop the Vent, and the Cartridges took fire while they were raming them down.

The Cannon from the City did but very little execution, as not more than half the Number of the Men belonging to them were present. The others were at their Cups & at their usual place of abode, Viz., on the Holy Ground. . . .

Sunday [July] 14. Almost the whole Regt. are sick with the Camp Distemper. . . .

[July] 23d. . . . Saw the infamous Proclamation issued by Lord Howe & now made publick by order of the Congress, offering Pardon to those in any of the Colonies who will return to their Duty & acknowledge the Supremacy of Parliament. . . . But will Americans tamely submit to those merciless Tyrants who have already done their utmost to reduce them to a state of abject slavery? and will they acknowledge? What can they acknowledge? but that they have bravely stood forth in defence of those Rights & Priviledges which the God of Nature hath bestowed upon them, & which they may not give up (unless unable to support them) without affronting that being who delights in the Liberty & prosperity of all his Creatures?

NEW YORK UNDER MILITARY OCCUPATION: 1776–1783

A picture of daily life in New York City from the outbreak of hostilities in 1775 through the period of British occupation emerges from the outspoken comments in Pastor Schaukirk's diary. Ewald G. Schaukirk, minister of the Moravian Church, was a native of Stettin, Prussia. After filling positions on the Continent and in England, he was sent to New York in 1774, where he served as pastor of the Moravian Congregation from 1775 to 1784. His sympathies were with the Loyalists, but he was often critical of the Army that was sent to fight their cause. The following excerpt is quoted with the permission of the Historical Society of Pennsylvania.[23]

April 29th. [1775] Saturday. The past week has been one of commotion and confusion. . . . Fear and panic seized many of the people, who prepared to move into the country. . . .

August 28th. [1775] Monday. Moving out of the city continues, and some of the Streets look plague-stricken, so many houses are closed. The dividing of all men between 16 and 50 years into Ward companies, increases the movement.

September 18th. [1775] Monday. The Minute men paraded today, with their baggage and provisions. It was thought they were going on an expedition, but they marched but five miles out of the city and returned in the evening. Many of them got drunk, fought together where they had halted, and on their return the Doctors and Surgeons were kept busy. May the Lord have mercy on this poor City!

January 20th. [1777] Monday. It appears from the newspapers, that another attempt to destroy the city by fire would be made. The city watch was regulated anew, by which eighty men watched every night in the different wards; and the Light Horse patrol the streets. Today a beginning was made with the inhabitants to take the oath of allegiance to the King. Every day two wards are taken—the Governor, Mayor, and other officers being present.

November 29th. [1777] Saturday. A plot was discovered that many here (it is said there has been prepared a list of 300 to be arrested) had been enlisted for the rebel service, and intended to fall on the city within or set it on fire, when an attack was made on the island by the rebels. Several were arrested, one Mott and wife, in the Bowery; a shoemaker; a saddler; a milkman; and Skimmey, a tailor, who made his escape. . . .

August 19th. [1779] Thursday. . . . the military gentlemen amuse themselves with trifles and diversions. Recently the walk by the ruins of Trinity Church and its grave-yard has been railed in and painted green; benches placed there and many lamps fixed in the trees, for gentlemen and ladies to walk and sit there in the evening. A band plays while the commander is present, and a sentry is placed there, that none of the common people may intrude. A paltry affair! . . .

September 22d. [1780] Friday. It being the anniversary of His Majesty's, our dear Kings Coronation-Day, great rejoicings were made. Besides the usual firing at noon from the Battery, and 1 o'clock from the ships in the river, and at the Watering Place, in the afternoon all the City Militia, to a very great number, the volunteer companies, and a part of the regulars marched with flying colors out of town, and drew up in line from the East river to the North river, and in the evening a *Feu de Joie* was fired in respect to the day and in celebration of the brilliant victory obtained by Earl Cornwallis near Camden, in South Carolina. . . .

December 16th. [1780] Saturday. The year is near ended and nothing has been done by the troops here. . . . thro' idleness [they] fall into all manner of the worst of vices, contract illnesses, which take off many. Thus they dwindle away by that means, and by small excursions which answer no real purposes. . . . The general language even of the common soldiers is, that the war might and would have been ended long before now, if it was not for the great men, who only want to fill their purses; and indeed it is too apparent that this has been and is the ruling principle in all departments, only to seek their own private interest, and to make hay while the Sun shineth, and when they have got enough then to retreat or go home—let become of America what will! . . .

December 11th. [1781] Tuesday. Weather very cold; great distress for want of wood. . . .

February 1st. [1782] The rents of houses are again raised to extravagant figures. . . .

April 8th. [1783] Tuesday. At noon the King's Proclamation of the cessation of hostilities, was read at the City Hall, which had previously been done on board of the men-of-war and to the troops.

May 3d. [1783] Saturday. Many of those persons who left the city when the troubles began are returning. . . .

November 25th. [1783] Tuesday. Today all the British left New York, and General Washington with his troops marched in and took possession of the city. . . .

HESSIAN VIEWS OF NEW YORK CITY: 1777, 1780

The letters of Hessian soldiers written from New York are less significant for the accuracy of their observations than for what they reveal of the attitudes of the German mercenaries toward New Yorkers and their standard of living, even in wartime. Their comments suggest, by implication, what must have been the disdain of the Americans toward the "foreigners" who were aiding the British cause. The following excerpts are reprinted, through the courtesy of Houghton Mifflin Company, from Ray W. Pettengill's *Letters from America, 1776–1779.*[24]

From a Hessian in Rhode Island to his brother, June 24, 1777.

New York . . . is one of the prettiest, pleasantest harbor towns I have ever seen. For the houses are not only built fine and regular in English style, most of them like palaces, but they are all papered and most extensively furnished. For that reason it is too bad that this land, which is also very fertile, is inhabited by such people, who from luxury and sensuous pleasure didn't know what to do and so owe their fall to naught but their pride. Everyone at home who takes their part and thinks they had good cause for rebellion ought in punishment to spend some time among them and learn how things are here (for the meanest man here can, if he will only do something, live like the richest among us). . . . For though the majority are descended from runaway vagabonds expelled from other places, yet they are so stuck up and make such display, especially in New York, as perhaps nowhere else on earth. . . . The worst thing about it is that at the king's express command the troops must treat these folk most handsomely—though at heart they are all rebels. . . .

Letter from a German Officer in New York, September 11, 1780.

The sums which the army consumes here are incredible. . . . the price of foodstuffs, wages for labor and personal services, and all merchants' wares is dearer than in the East and West Indies, which used to be the most expensive places. You will not believe, I presume, that a wood-chopper earns daily six florin, Rhenish money, and more? or that a good coachman will not serve for less than four hundred florins, good board, and clothing? Perhaps you would like the chimney sweep's profession? There is a royal chimney-sweep here, who has to look after the quarters belonging to the army. He keeps a half-dozen negroes, each of whom can sweep at least twenty chimneys a day, and often must clean more; and for each chimney his master, who sits quietly at home, is paid two shillings York money (twenty-eight coppers). The negroes get nothing out of it save coarse food and rags.

4. *NEW YORK IN THE EARLY NATIONAL PERIOD*

IN THE LONG VIEW, the most dramatic development in the history of New York between the achievement of independence and the close of the War of 1812 was its supplanting of Philadelphia as the most populous city of the United States. When the French reformer La Rochefoucauld-Liancourt visited America in 1797, New York still had to yield first place to the Quaker City as "the largest and best town" in the young Republic. But by 1815, the situation had obviously changed. To his compatriot, the Baron de Montlezun, a visitor at the close of the war, New York had the "appearance of a large city more than Philadelphia." The latter appeared to have "reached the peak of its splendor," he reported in his *Souvenirs des Antilles,* an account of a trip to America in 1815 and 1816. New York's population had overtaken that of its Pennsylvania rival; and in the Frenchman's opinion the more northerly city was "evidently destined to become the most frequented port and most flourishing city of the New World." [1]

The records of visitors of the period are more helpful than those of the census takers in assessing the relative size and prestige of these two urban rivals of the Atlantic coast. In separating the population of Philadelphia city from the thickly populated "liberties" which adjoined it, the census leaves the impression that New York was the more populous city as early as 1790, with a count of 33,131 to Philadelphia's 28,522. But from contemporary comment, it is clear that Philadelphia and the contiguous liberties were regarded as an urban unit, and that, on this basis, it was not until shortly after 1810 that New York, to contemporaries, surpassed Philadelphia in size. The rivalry between the two neighboring cities was especially intense in these years. "New York and Philadelphia dislike one another with an indescribable hatred," wrote the German military authority, Dietrich von Bülow, who made two trips to America in the 1790's. "If Philadelphia should become extinct, everybody in New York would rejoice, and vice versa. New York is the vilest of cities, write the Philadelphia journalists. In New York they speak no better of Philadelphia."[2]

The superiority of its location for commerce was the factor to which most observers attributed the newly rising pre-eminence of New York City. The French statesman Talleyrand perceived this advantage as early as the mid-1790's, when, as a refugee of the French Revolution, he spent two years in the United States. Projecting a business venture involving trade with the West Indies, he recommended New York as the center of operations. "Its good and convenient harbor, which is never closed by ice [and] its central position to which large rivers bring the products of the whole country, appear to me to be decisive advantages," he wrote. "Philadelphia is too buried in the land and especially too inaccessible to wood of all sorts. . . . Boston is too much at the extremity of the country, does not have enough flour, and has not a large enough outlet for the commodities of the West Indies, except molasses." Often, during the winter, vessels bound for Philadelphia were forced to sail to New York, with resultant benefit to the merchants there, the Baron de Montlezun reported. Its location for trade with the interior made it, as one visitor wrote, "a sort of Mecca to the hungry backwoodsman, who was sure to make a pilgrimage once in his lifetime to yield his homage on its counters." And merchants from the South were already visiting its stores and warehouses to replenish their stocks.[3]

In the opinion of most foreign observers, the city, already so favored geographically by its port, gained immensely in this period from the unsettled conditions in Europe. "The Americans have benefited from the struggles of England and France," wrote François Marie Perrin du Lac, a French author and local administrator who visited New York in 1801; "and New York is particularly able to furnish provisions to the southern colonies of the belligerent powers. Sugar, cotton, coffee, indeed all the provisions that they receive in payment, are transported on their ships to Europe and exchanged for territorial products or manufactures, which they carry to the colonies or to the United States. . . ." Moreover, the drought from which England and France had been suffering had forced Europe to turn to the United States for raw materials, with a resultant flow of both manufactures and currency to the New World. "Everything in the city is in motion," Perrin du Lac romanticized; "everywhere the shops resound with the noise of workers, . . . one sees vessels arriving from every part of the world, or ready to depart, and . . .

one can not better describe the opulence of this still new city than to compare it to ancient Tyre, which contemporary authors called the queen of commerce and the sovereign of the seas." [4]

The view of Perrin du Lac was seconded, somewhat reluctantly, by a Bostonian visitor, Jonathan Mason, who had represented Massachusetts in the United States Senate from 1800 to 1803. Sojourning in New York, en route from Boston to Savannah, in November 1804, the former senator found the progress of the city, "as usual, beyond all calculation." The seven hundred buildings, "erected [in] the last twelve months," were signs of economic health which he failed to discover in Philadelphia, where, "though the citizens deny it, . . . they do not trade so much or so well as [in] New York." Young William Johnson of Newton, New Jersey, looking for a new business location, concluded late in 1805 that New York was "the London of America" and as such would surely "take the lead of business to any other place in the United States." [5]

The city's commerce continued to flourish until 1808, but then it began to show the damaging effects of the federal embargo of the previous year. The unfortunate results of this policy, as far as New York's business was concerned, were observed by John Lambert, a professional traveler from Britain, who came to North America in 1806 hoping, in the course of his travels, to promote the cultivation of hemp in Canada. When he first reached New York, in November of 1807, the city was a scene of prodigious activity. "Every thought, word, look, and action of the multitude seemed to be absorbed by commerce." But how different the face of affairs upon his return to the city in April of 1808! Gloomy looks had replaced the glow of prosperity, the streets near the waterside were "almost deserted, and *grass had begun to grow* upon the wharfs." Conditions must have been much improved, however, by 1811, for when Timothy Dwight, president of Yale University, visited the city in that year he was struck by the "busy hum" of its daily life: the "bustle in the streets; the perpetual activity of the carts; the noise and hurry at the docks . . . ; the sound of saws, axes, and hammers, at the shipyards"; and such a rapid increase of buildings as to make the city seem perpetually new.[6]

Physically, the city—for all its commercial vigor—was still a relatively unimposing place. American visitors, less used to sizable cities, were more likely to be impressed with the incipient metropolis than were the European travelers of the time. South Carolina's John

Drayton, who visited New York in 1793, was "enraptured with the scene"; but the novelist Chateaubriand, fleeing in 1791 the excesses of the French Revolution, was distressed with the "uniform level" of the city and the absence of "scarcely anything that rises above the mass of the walls and roofs." With a population no larger than 100,000, as late as 1815, it reminded English visitors of such British mercantile centers as Manchester, Bristol, or Liverpool.[7]

Broadway, now built up for a distance of two miles, was already the city's chief sight—that, and the City Hall, which Timothy Dwight called "the most superb building in the United States." At the foot of the street, in the vicinity of the Battery, were the dwellings of the leading merchants. Impressive, three-story, brick structures, built in the English style, with iron grill work in front and kitchens on the first floor, they were said to differ little from the residences in London's West End. Beyond these ranged commodious shops, stocked with merchandise "richer and more beautiful than that of Philadelphia," their windows presenting as "splendid and varied a show" as could be met with in the British capital. Poplar trees, planted along the sidewalks, lent an ornamental and somewhat suburban note to the city's principal thoroughfare. The City Hall, begun in 1803 and first occupied in 1811, stood at a right angle to Broadway and fronted upon the triangular plot known as City Hall Park. The white marble structure, distinguished for its grace and symmetry, was composed of two beautifully proportioned wings flanking a central portico surmounted by a cupola.[8]

Occupying a full block on Broadway, between Thames and Cedar streets, was the City Hotel, first of the great urban caravansaries which were to become so characteristic a feature of the Manhattan scene. Opened in 1794, it provided visitors with better accommodations than had been available in the lodging houses that catered to transients before that day. Its manager boasted in 1811 that a "new and elegant bar-room and coffee room" had recently been added. A similar establishment, the Washington Hall, built in 1809, rivaled the City Hotel when Baron de Montlezun visited the city in 1815. The cornerstone of Tammany Hall at Nassau and Frankfort streets was laid in 1811; and once completed, it served as a hotel as well as the headquarters of the Tammanyites.[9]

The cleanliness for which the city had been admired in the late colonial period appears to have prevailed until the mid-1790's, and perhaps later in some parts of the town; for Perrin du Lac reported, after a visit in 1801, that the streets and sidewalks were clean and regularly lighted at night. From about 1795, however, most visitors criticized the filthiness of the streets, especially in the vicinity of the wharves and docks. Moreau de St. Méry, another of the French refugees who sojourned in New York in the mid-1790's, reported that it was "not unusual to see animals of all sorts wandering about, chiefly cows and pigs." Windowpanes and sidewalks were washed on Saturdays, but nobody bothered "to remove the dead dogs, cats and rats from the streets." The quays and certain parts of the suburbs exceeded "in public and private nastiness" anything that the emigree French philosopher, the Count of Volney, had beheld, even in Turkey. The continuing lack of an adequate water supply was a contributory cause of these difficulties, to which the ravages of yellow fever periodically called the visitors', as well as the residents', attention.[10]

Political events on the turn of the 1790's tended to further the variety of New York's already cosmopolitan population. New York continued to be the capital of the young nation—now under the Federal Constitution—until August of 1790. This naturally attracted, as one traveler wrote, a "concourse of strangers." But the most novel element in the diversified society of this generation was the French emigrees, whose arrival was prompted by the changing course of the French Revolution and who lent a somewhat transient Gallic flavor to a society which had its roots primarily in New England, other parts of New York, and the British Isles, in addition to the original Anglo-Dutch ingredient. Henry Wansey, a retired English clothier who visited New York in 1794, found one of the tea houses "filled by Frenchmen," but he observed that the tricolored cockade was popular with all the residents, "whether aristocrats or democrats."

The French newcomers were themselves a varied group. An early migration in 1789 was followed, during the middle nineties, by a more numerous influx of members of the nobility and upper bourgeoisie. To these were added some 4,000 refugees of the 1793 Santo Domingo Negro uprising. Philadelphia was the principal haven for the French exiles, but New York drew so many that advertisements in French were printed in the newspapers, and a short-lived *French and American Gazette* appeared.[11]

New Yorkers were apparently of mixed minds with respect to supporting the French Revolution. The official representatives of the newly formed French Republic resented what they regarded as local indifference to their cause. "If there are men here who have produced a revolution, their appearance does not betray it," wrote the Comte d'Hauterive, French consul in New York in 1793. "If I had come through a revolution as these people have, and if I were dining with Frenchmen, I would not have time to eat or drink, so much would I have to say about their affairs and ours." His compatriot Ferdinand Bayard, a visitor of 1791, had already asserted that the pretensions to luxury and the passion for foreign merchandise in the "maritime cities" of the United States were destroying true republicanism in these quarters and predisposing the citizens toward England.[12]

At the same time, however, French exiles of a more conservative stamp frequently came under attack from New Yorkers with pro-Jacobin sympathies. Moreau de St. Méry described a Fourth of July procession which he witnessed from a house near Broadway where Talleyrand was staying. In the van of the local citizenry were numerous French Jacobins, marching two by two and singing the "Marseillaise" and other Republican songs. As they passed Talleyrand's dwelling, they "interrupted themselves to address invectives" to Talleyrand, Beaumetz, and other Frenchmen who were observing them from the windows. "The Minister of France to the United States, Genêt, . . . was in the procession, and sang and insulted us like all the others." [13]

If New Yorkers were divided in their sympathies toward the French, the latter exhibited a similar reaction toward the Americans. Indeed, despite a tradition to the contrary, French visitors were not unanimous in their approval of the United States, any more than were their neighbors across the English Channel. "The short time we spent in New York showed us the Americans in the best possible light," wrote Louis Ange Pitou, who visited New York in 1801, on his return to France, after having been deported earlier for writing couplets regarded as derogatory to the Jacobins and the Directory. "The French people who know them are divided in their opinion of them. . . . Their country has become the warehouse of the world during the Revolution in Europe. . . . The immense wealth they have possessed for several years has raised the price of labor enormously. . . . All they need to make them happy is to learn how to limit their desires." [14]

At the turn of the nineteenth century, as earlier, its expanding commercial prosperity conditioned the social and cultural life of New York City. One consequence of this was to continue, if not to accentuate, the gulf, already of long standing, between the city's fashionable society and the "inferior orders of the people." John Lambert asserted in 1807 that the society of New York consisted of "three distinct classes." In the first were the divines, lawyers, physicians of eminence, principal merchants, and people of independent property. The small merchants, retail dealers, clerks, subordinate officials, and members of the three professions made up the second class; and the "inferior orders of the people," the third. He noted that the Park and the Battery were no longer "much resorted to by the fashionable citizens of New York," for they had become "too common." Now, the "genteel lounge" was "in the Broadway, from eleven to three o'clock, during which time it is as much crowded as the Bond-street of London." There, among the strolling New York beauties, one could admire pretty Democrats "à la mode Française" and "sweet little Federalists à la mode Anglaise." Regardless of politics, however, popular preference favored the "light, various, and dashing drapery of the Parisian belles." [15]

In the opinion of the Honorable Jonathan Mason, who fraternized with such leading families as the Kings, Ogdens, and Livingstons, during his visit to New York, there was more "society" than "etiquette" in New York City in 1804. New Yorkers "live well and are hospitable," he reported, with proper Bostonian condescension. "They are wealthy; . . . feel conscious of all their advantages, and . . . rate them full high." For beauty and refinement, New York women suffered, in his opinion, when compared to their sisters in Philadelphia; New York had "a great many [more] young men," though, so far as he could see, they were "not disposed to matrimony." The professional facilities for amusement hardly impressed the Bostonian senator, even though, according to his fellow New Englander Timothy Dwight, they occupied "as much time, attention, and expense as would ordinarily be pleaded for by the veriest votary of pleasure"—more, in the opinion of this Yankee educator who visited New York in 1811, than could be justified by either religion or common sense.[16]

The theatre had had a considerable following since the middle 1780's, when stock companies began to appear for regular seasons; and by 1800 the city could boast two playhouses, one of them the

Park Theatre, built in 1798 at a cost of $130,000, and capable of seating an audience of 2,000. Another commercial amusement attraction was a mechanical panorama which represented the battle of Alexandria and the death of Abercrombie. The continuing fondness of New Yorkers for "music, dancing, and plays" was reported by young Francis Baily, ultimately to be president of the Royal Astronomical Society, who visited New York in 1796. Frequent musical societies and concerts promoted the residents' skill as performers, he contended; and as to dancing, there were two "assembly-rooms" in the city which were "pretty well frequented during the winter season," and private balls were "likewise not uncommon."

When John Lambert visited New York in 1807 and 1808 the course of entertainment moved at an even more accelerated pace. In the winter, there were "the theatre, public assemblies, philosophical and experimental lectures, concerts, balls, tea- and card-parties, cariole excursions out of town, etc." In summer, when all indoor entertainment save "tea-parties" appears to have ceased, there were hunting, shooting, fishing, horse racing, and excursions upon the water. Throughout the year, the New York Sunday was *triste* to a degree that surprised visitors used to Continental ways. "Shops closed, no newspapers, church going, sound of bells, Bible reading, retreat, general silence: that's the picture on the Sabbath," one visitor reported. For all its pretensions to urbanity, New York City of the early nineteenth century had much in common with a predominantly rural America.[17]

With the achievement of national independence, even more than earlier, parades, celebrations, and public events offered New Yorkers and their guests a kind of "free entertainment" that was to become a traditional aspect of the Manhattan scene. The framing of the Federal Constitution was signalized by two events: a procession which installed the "ship of state" on the pedestal, in the Bowling Green, which formerly supported the statue of George III and a dinner, in a field outside the city, attended by the inhabitants, members of the Congress, and the foreign ministers. The welcome accorded George Washington, arriving for his inauguration, on April 23, 1789, was prophetic of many another celebration with which future New Yorkers were to greet the visiting "great." Cheering thousands crowded the banks of the Harbor as the presumptive President approached the city in an elaborately decorated barge, manned by thirteen white-clad harbor pilots. According to one eyewitness, "you could see little else along the Shores . . . but Heads standing as thick as Ears of Corn before the Harvest. . . . The Streets were lined with the Inhabitants as thick as the People could stand, and it required all the Exertions of a numerous Train of City officers with their Staves, to make a Passage for the Company." In the evening, the city was "illuminated in a superb Manner." [18]

During the short period in which New York City was the national capital, visits to Federal Hall, at Wall and Broad streets, seat of the Congress, were a favored "tourist attraction." Annually, on the Fourth of July, the citizens were awakened by the "firing" of cannon and the ringing of bells; and processions of troops and public societies were the prelude to fireworks and "illuminations" in the evening. The evacuation by the British was memorialized by festivities on November 25—when the militia often marched in review before the mayor—and sometimes by services of thanksgiving on the succeeding day.[19]

That feasts and festivals were more to the New Yorker's taste than intellectual fare was the settled opinion of visitors to the city in these years. They agreed that the prevailing absorption with business left little opportunity for cultivating science and the arts, despite the existence of a public library, three or four reading rooms and subscription libraries, and a museum of natural curiosities (containing, as John Lambert said, "nothing worthy of particular notice"). Even before the Revolution, the demand for the services of portrait painters had brought such artists as West, Copley, and Peale at least temporarily to the city; but the collection at the Academy of Fine Arts, founded on a subscription basis in 1802, did not impress visitors with the city's resources in this field.

Jonathan Mason thought the casts at the Academy "showed talent," but in his opinion, too, the exhibits at the American Museum were "not worth mention." He anticipated Timothy Dwight's comment in 1811 that the "general attachment to learning" was "less vigorous" in New York than in Boston. "The education of the young men is simple and hardly designed to make scholars," the Frenchman Perrin du Lac had written in 1801. "All their studies are reduced to learning to read, write, and count. . . . Primarily these people are commercially-minded; all their thoughts are directed toward making a fortune, which almost always stifles the love of science and abstract learning." This opinion was supported as late as 1815 by his compatriot Baron de Montlezun. "New York . . . is uniquely a city of business," he asserted. "One finds nothing unusual there, in literature or the arts." [20]

The years from 1808 to 1816 are the most barren of available contemporary comment in all the annals of this much described city. Early in the period, the insecurity of ocean travel discouraged the visits of foreign commentators, and then from 1812 to 1815 the United States was again at war with England. Despite local opposition to involvement, the declaration of war—in June of 1812—brought a burst of effort to improve New York's meager defenses; but tension in the city relaxed as military activity appeared to be confined to the nation's frontiers.

Renewed British effort in the summer of 1814 and the capture of Washington, D. C., in August of that year, put another face on matters. Alarm became universal, and for a time, the city was virtually an armed camp. All available militiamen were called into service. Independent companies, dormant since the first year of the war, were reactivated. The Iron Greys, the New York Hussars, the Neptune Corps of Sea Fencibles marched and countermarched by night and day. Governor Tompkins and Adjutant General Van Rensselaer took up residence in the city. Upon the appeal of the Council of Defense, volunteers contributed a day's or a night's labor on earthworks at Brooklyn or Harlem Heights. On one occasion it was the master butchers, bearing their version of the prevailing slogan: "Free Trade and Butchers' Rights"; on others, the Patriotic Sons of Erin, or a group of free colored men, a thousand strong. Even a "company of ladies from New York City," led by the music of the Tammany Society, turned out for an hour's work on the fortifications. Fortunately, the attack failed to materialize. Early in 1815 came the welcome news of peace, the prelude to an era of expansion in which this "city of business"—by now the nation's first in size—was to experience truly phenomenal growth.[21]

NEW YORK, THE "LIVERPOOL OF AMERICA": 1793, 1794

By the close of the eighteenth century, New York already had the appearance and character of the larger towns of Great Britain. This was the testimony of Thomas Cooper, an English scientist and educator, who ultimately settled permanently in the United States and became president of South Carolina College. Cooper's sympathy for the democratic aspects of the French Revolution predisposed him to favor the American experiment. In the United States, he became an active Jeffersonian and was sentenced to six months in prison and a $400 fine for attacking the Sedition Law. The following excerpt is from *Some Information Respecting America*—his account of a preliminary visit to the United States in 1793 and 1794.[22]

America is a large place: and between the different states, there are strong shades of difference; nor does a large town furnish the same answer to your queries as the country.

In Boston, New York, Philadelphia, and Baltimore, the state of society is much the same as in the large towns of Great Britain, such as Birmingham, Bristol, Liverpool, and Manchester. The American towns I have just enumerated contain together about the same number of inhabitants as the English towns just mentioned; that is, about 200,000. . . . New York, for instance, is a perfect counterpart of Liverpool: the situation of the docks, the form of the streets, the state of the public buildings, the inside as well as the outside of the houses, the manners, the amusements, the mode of living among the expensive part of the inhabitants—all these circumstances are as nearly alike, in the towns last mentioned, as possible. In all the American towns above noticed, there are theatres and assemblies. They are, in short, precisely what the larger and more opulent provincial towns of Great Britain are. Hence also you may easily conceive, that European comforts and conveniences are not scarce. In fact, you may find in Philadelphia or New York, every article of that description usually kept in the shops in the English towns I have referred to, in equal plenty, but not indeed equally cheap. To the price of all articles of luxurious furniture (pictures, pier glasses, carpets, etc.) add one-third to the English price, and you have the full American price. House-rent is also much the same as in the places hitherto compared: if anything, somewhat dearer in America for houses of the same size and convenience. The houses in the one set of towns as in the other, are built of brick and stone.

Another Englishman who likened New York City to Liverpool was Henry Wansey, a retired clothier, who came to America for reasons of curiosity as well as business in 1794 and to New York in May of that year. His chatty narrative, published as *An Excursion to the United*

States of North America in the Summer of 1794, provides a picture of the day-by-day activities of the busy commercial city in the middle 1790's.[23]

We moored our vessel at Burling slip at four in the morning, and after a little refreshment I landed, and enquired out the Tontine coffee-house. New York is much more like a city than Boston, having broad footways paved, with a curb to separate them from the road. The streets are wider, and the houses in a better style. Boston is the Bristol, New York the Liverpool, and Philadelphia the London, of America. The Tontine tavern and coffee-house is a handsome large brick building; you ascend six or eight steps under a portico, into a large public room which is the Stock Exchange of New York, where all bargains are made. Here are two books kept, as at Lloyd's, of every ship's arrival and clearing out. This house was built for the accommodation of the merchants, by Tontine shares of two hundred pounds each. It is kept by Mr. Hyde, formerly a woollen-draper in London. You can lodge and board there at a common table, and you pay ten shillings currency a day, whether you dine out or not. No appearance of shop windows as in London; only stores, which make no shew till you enter the houses. House rent is very dear, a hundred pounds sterling a year is a very usual price for a common storekeeper. . . .

May 19, 1794. Dined with Mr. Jay [the ambassador's brother], and in the evening went to the theatre. . . . Mrs. Cowley's play, *A Bold Stroke for a Husband,* with the farce of *Hob in the Well;* the actors mostly from England: price of admittance to the boxes, one dollar. A very bad theatre; a new one is going to be built by subscription, under the direction of Hodgkinson, the present manager. Mrs. Wrighten, who used to sing at Vauxhall twenty years ago, and was afterwards an actress at Bristol, is one of their principal female performers; her voice is as clear and shrill as ever. I think them altogether far inferior to the Boston company. . . .

May 24, 1794. As I was getting up in the morning, I heard drums beating and fifes playing. I ran to the window, and saw a large body of people on the other side of the Governor's House, with flags flying, and marching two and two towards the water-side. . . . it was a procession of young tradesmen going in boats to Governor's Island, to give the state a day's work. Fortifications are there erecting for strengthening the entrance to New York harbour; it is a patriotic and general resolution of the inhabitants of this city, to work a day gratis, without any distinction of rank or condition, for the public advantage, on these fortifications. Today, the whole trade of carpenters and joiners; yesterday, the body of masons; before this, the grocers, school-masters, coopers, and barbers; next Monday, all the attorneys and men concerned in the law, handle the mattock and shovel, the whole day, and carry their provisions with them. How noble is this! How it cherishes unanimity and love for their country! How much does it tend to unite all ranks of people, and render the social compact firm and united. . . .

You cannot board in any good boarding house, for less than seven or eight dollars a week, finding your own wine. . . . New York is as healthy and pleasant a place to live in, as any city I ever saw. The price of provisions fluctuates here exceedingly, like Bath; and persons who know how to take opportunities, may furnish themselves very cheap; after refusing to buy at their prices, I was soon after asked by the same persons, *what would I give?*

A FRENCH EMIGREE DESCRIBES NEW YORK CITY: 1797

The commentary of Frenchmen on the New York scene—in books, letters, and journals—is especially illuminating for the period from 1787 to 1801. Some were French liberals, curious to observe the workings of America's republican experiment. Others were exiles of the French Revolution, some of whom remained in the city long enough to get more than a superficial view of its life. The refugee group included such well-known figures as Chateaubriand, Volney, Moreau de St. Méry, Talleyrand, Beaumetz, Saint-Mémin, Louis Philippe, and the Duke of La Rochefoucauld-Liancourt. The latter, a social reformer who cast his lot with the king, was forced to flee to England upon the suspension of Louis XVI in 1792. From there he journeyed to Philadelphia. Following is an excerpt from his *Travels,* published in 1799, in which he described his wanderings in the United States and Canada from 1795 to 1797.[24]

New York is, next to Philadelphia, the largest and best town in the United States. These two cities rival each other in almost every respect. Philadelphia has hitherto had the advantage, but from the fine situation of New York there is reason to expect that sooner or later it will gain the superiority.

It is calculated that this city contains at present upwards of fifty thousand inhabitants. There have been no less than four hundred and fifty new houses built here in this present year. It is increased and beautified with unheard of quickness; a circumstance owing, no doubt, in a great measure, to the immense benefit its trade has derived for these two or three years from the present state of Europe. But if peace diminish, as it certainly will, their excessive profits, the extension of the cultivated lands and settlements in this vast territory, the produce of which will find, directly or indirectly, a vent by Hudson's River, will insure a solid foundation, independently of all foreign circumstances, for the increasing prosperity of the trade of New York. To all these advantages New York adds that of lying more to the eastward, and nearer to the sea than any port in America, except Boston; and it is never choaked up with ice. . . .

The town had formerly been built without any regular plan, whence every where almost, except what has been rebuilt in consequence of the fire, the streets are small and crooked; the foot-paths, where there are any, narrow, and interrupted by the stairs from the houses, which makes the walking on them extremely inconvenient. Some good brick houses are situated in these narrow streets; but in general the houses are mean, small, and low, built of wood, and a great many of them yet bear the marks of Dutch taste. The new part of the city built adjoining to Hudson's River, and parallel with its course, is infinitely more handsome; the streets there being generally straight, broad, intersecting with each other at right angles, and the houses much better built. There is not in any city in the world a finer street than Broadway; it is near a mile in length, and is meant to be still farther extended: it is more than a hundred feet wide from one end to the other. Most part of the houses are of brick, and a number of them extremely handsome. From its elevated situation, its position on the river, and the elegance of the buildings, it is naturally the place of residence of the most opulent inhabitants.

AN ENGLISH ACTOR VIEWS THE URBAN SCENE: 1797

The diversity of New York's population impressed the English actor-manager John Bernard, who made his first American appearance at the Greenwich Street Theatre on August 25, 1797. He later played with a Philadelphia company and remained in the United States until 1819, becoming one of America's first traveling "stars." The middle states appeared to him to be the "epitome of Europe" and New York more "a large fair" than "an abiding city." The following excerpt from his *Retrospections of America, 1797–1811,* as edited by Mrs. Bayle Bernard, describes the daily activity of the New York merchant, as well as some of the boarding house "birds of passage" which he considered most of New York's population to be. It is quoted here by courtesy of Harper and Brothers.[25]

The house I stopped at gave me a tolerable specimen of the varieties of society now converging at this great exchange, and enabled me thereby to solve a mystery which had puzzled the heads of numerous travellers—the multifariousness of an American breakfast-table. Here was a French gentleman of *l'ancien régime* looking melancholy and mysterious, in a bag-wig and point-lace ruffles, who had two cards of address, the one styling him "Marquis," the other "Dancing-master." Here was an English agriculturist just arrived, a firm believer in the doctrine of ready-roasted pigs squeaking "Come, eat me." Here was a Kentucky land-owner, proving London to be the Babylon of the Apocalypse, and predicting England's downfall, in order to heighten the value of his disposable property. Here were major-generals from Vermont, walking encyclopaedias of the war, and planters from "Caroliny," who were alternately explaining the free principles of their "Constitution" and reading the description of runaway slaves. Here were Italians who had brought over Fantoccini to refine the taste of the infant country; Germans who had come to hunt out some distant relatives; lean and voracious Scotchmen looking as if they could swallow the continent; and Irish "jintlemen" of slender figures and fortunes, who having come to America to live cheaply, had spent a year's income in crossing the ocean. To meet such a variety of tastes it was necessary that the board should do something more than merely gratify the impulses of an American stomach. Each must be pleased, and we were accordingly provided with fish, ham, beef, boiled fowls, eggs, pigeons, pumpkin pies, lobsters, vegetables, tea, coffee, cider, sangaree, and cherry-brandy!

The habits of the New York merchants reminded me of my friends at Guernsey. They breakfasted at eight or half past, and by nine were in their counting-houses, laying out the business of the day; at ten they were on their wharves, with aprons round their waists, rolling hogsheads of rum and molasses; at twelve, at market, flying about as dirty and as diligent as porters; at two, back again to the rolling, heaving, hallooing, and scribbling. At four they went home to dress for dinner; at seven, to the play; at eleven, to supper, with a crew of lusty Bachanals who would smoke cigars, gulp down brandy, and sing, roar, and shout in the thickening clouds they created, like so many merry devils, till three in the morning. At eight, up again, to scribble, run, and roll hogsheads. What a day's work this would have been for a Carolinian! Thus the New-Yorker enjoyed his span of being to the full stretch of the tether, his violent exertions during the day counteracting the effects of his nocturnal relaxations, besides giving him a relish to return to them. Certainly few men throughout the Union worked harder for enjoyment.

NEW YORK IN GOOD TIMES AND BAD: 1807, 1808

The most conscientiously detailed travel description of New York City for the period immediately preceding the War of 1812 is the work of John Lambert, who traveled through Canada and the United States from 1806 to 1808. Apparently a professional traveler, Lambert came to America with the sanction of the Board of Trade, in the hope of fostering the cultivation of hemp in Canada. He remained in Lower Canada for a year and then proceeded to the United States, reaching New York City on November 24, 1807. His account of his travels, entitled *Travels through Canada, and the United States of North America, in the Years 1806, 1807, & 1808,* abounds in detail and is remarkably free of bias. It was widely read and speedily ran through three editions. In the following excerpts, Lambert comments on the physical appearance and social practices in the city in 1807 and 1808, a period which saw both prosperity and depression in the Empire City.[26]

About ten o'clock at night we arrived at New York; it was very dark, and as we sailed by the town, lighted lamps and windows sparkled everywhere, amidst the houses, in the streets, and along the water-side. The wharfs were crowded with shipping, whose tall masts mingled with the buildings, and together with the spires and cupolas of the churches, gave the city an appearance of magnificence, which the gloomy obscurity of the night served to increase. . . .

New York is the first city in the United States for wealth, commerce, and population; as it also is the finest for its situation and buildings. . . . New York has rapidly improved within the last twenty years; and land which then sold in that city for fifty dollars is now worth 1,500.

The Broadway and the Bowery Road are the two finest avenues in the city. . . . The houses in the Broadway are lofty and well built. . . . In the vicinity of the Battery, and for some distance up the Broadway, they are nearly all private houses, and occupied by the principal merchants and gentry of New York; after which the Broadway is lined with large commodious shops of every description. . . . There are several extensive book stores, print-shops, music-shops, jewellers, and silversmiths; hatters, linen-drapers, milliners, pastry-cooks, coachmakers, hotels, and coffee-houses. The street is well paved, and the foot-paths are chiefly bricked. . . .

The City Hotel is the most extensive building of that description in New York; and nearly resembles, in size and style of architecture, the London Tavern in Bishopsgate-street. The ground-floor of the hotel at New-York is, however, converted into shops, which have a very handsome appearance in the Broadway. . . . There are three churches in the Broadway: one of them called Grace Church, is a plain brick building, recently erected: the other two are St. Paul's and Trinity; both handsome structures, built with an intermixture of white and brown stone. The adjoining churchyards, which occupy a large space of ground, railed in from the street, and crowded with tomb-stones, are far from being agreeable spectacles in such a populous city. . . .

The Park, though not remarkable for its size, is, however, of service, by displaying the surrounding buildings to greater advantage; and is also a relief to the confined appearance of the streets in general. It consists of about four acres planted with elms, planes, willows, and catalpas; and the surrounding foot-walk is encompassed by rows of poplars: the whole is enclosed by a wooden paling. . . .

The Theatre is on the south-east side of the Park, and is a large commodious building. The outside is in an unfinished state; but the interior is handsomely decorated, and fitted up in as good style as the London theatres, upon a scale suitable to the population of the city. It contains a large coffee-room, and good sized lobbies, and is reckoned to hold about 1,200 persons. The scenes are well painted and numerous; and the machinery, dresses, and decorations, are elegant, and appropriate to the performances, which consist of all the new pieces that come out on the London boards, and several of Shakespeare's best plays. The only fault is, that they are too much curtailed, by which they often lose their effect; and the performances are sometimes over by half past ten, though they do not begin at an earlier hour than in London. The drama had been a favourite in New York before the Revolution. . . .

New York has its Vauxhall and Ranelagh; but they are poor imitations of those near London. They are, however, pleasant places of recreation for the inhabitants. The Vauxhall garden is situated in the Bowery Road about two miles from the City Hall. It is a neat plantation, with gravel walks adorned with shrubs, trees, busts, and statues. In the centre is a large equestrian statue of General Washington. Light musical pieces, interludes, etc. are performed in a small theatre situate in one corner of the gardens: the audience sit in what are called the pit and boxes, in the open air. The orchestra is built among the trees, and a large apparatus is constructed for the display of fireworks. The theatrical corps of New-York is chiefly engaged at Vauxhall during summer. . . .

Every day, except Sunday, is a market-day in New York. Meat is cut up and sold by the joint or in pieces, by the licensed butchers only, their agents, or servants. Each of these must sell at his own stall, and conclude his sales by one o'clock in the afternoon, between the 1st of May and the 1st of November, and [by] two [o'clock] between the 1st of November and the 1st of May. Butchers are licensed by the mayor, who is clerk of the market. He receives for every quarter of beef sold in the market six cents; for every hog, shoat, or pig above 14 lbs. weight, six cents; and for each calf, sheep, or lamb, four cents; to be paid by the butchers and other persons selling the same. To prevent engrossing, and to favour housekeepers, it is declared unlawful for persons to purchase articles to sell again in any market or other part of the city before noon of each day, except flour and meal, which must not be bought to be sold again until four in the afternoon: hucksters in the market are restricted to the sale of vegetables, with the exception of fruits. The sale of unwholesome and stale articles of provision; of blown and stuffed meat, and of measly pork, is expressly forbidden. Butter must be sold by the pound, and not by the roll or tub. Persons who are not licensed butchers, selling butchers' meat on commission, pay triple fees to the clerk of the market. . . .

The manufactures of America are yet in an infant state; but in

New York there are several excellent cabinet-makers, coach-makers, &c. who not only supply the country with household furniture and carriages, but also export very largely to the West-Indies, and to foreign possessions on the continent of America. Their workmanship would be considered elegant and modern in London; and they have the advantage of procuring mahogany and other wood much cheaper than we. . . .

There are upwards of twenty news-papers published in New York, nearly half of which are daily papers; besides several weekly and monthly magazines or essays. . . .

The booksellers and printers of New York are numerous, and in general men of property. . . .

A public library is established at New York, which consists of about ten thousand volumes, many of them rare and valuable books. The building which contains them is situated in Nassau-street, and the trustees are incorporated by an act of the legislature. There are also three or four public reading-rooms, and circulating libraries, which are supported by some of the principal booksellers, from the annual subscriptions of the inhabitants. There is a museum of natural curiosities in New York, but it contains nothing worthy of particular notice. . . .

Much has been said of the deficiency of the polite and liberal accomplishments among both sexes in the United States. Whatever truth there may have formerly been in this statement, I do not think there is any foundation for it at present, at least in New York, where there appears to be a great thirst after knowledge. The riches that have flowed into that city, for the last twenty years, have brought with them a taste for the refinements of polished society; and though the inhabitants cannot yet boast of having reached the standard of European perfection, they are not wanting in the solid and rational parts of education; nor in many of those accomplishments which ornament and embellish private life. It has become the fashion in New York to attend lectures on moral philosophy, chemistry, mineralogy, botany, mechanics, &c.; and the ladies in particular have made considerable progress in those studies. . . .

Dancing is an amusement that the New York ladies are passionately fond of, and they are said to excel those of every other city in the Union. I visited the *City Assembly*, which is held at the City Hotel in the Broadway, and considered as the best in New York. It was the first night of the season, and there were not more than one hundred and fifty persons present. I did not perceive any thing different from an English assembly, except the cotillons, which were danced in an admirable manner, alternately with the country dances. Several French gentlemen were present, and figured away in the cotillons with considerable taste and agility. The subscription is two dollars and a half for each night, and includes tea, coffee, and a cold collation. None but the first class of society can become subscribers to this assembly. Another has, however, been recently established, in which the genteel part of the second class are admitted, who were shut out from the City Assembly. A spirit of jealousy and pride has caused the subscribers of the *new assembly* to make their subscription three dollars, and to have their balls also at the City Hotel. It was so well conducted, that many of the subscribers of the City Assembly seceded, and joined the opposition one, or subscribed to both. . . .

The style of living in New York is fashionable and splendid; many of the principal merchants and people of property have elegant equipages, and those who have none of their own may be accommodated with handsome carriages and horses at the livery stables; for there are no coach stands. . . .

New York abounds with religious sects of various denominations; but the episcopalians and presbyterians seem to be the most numerous, at least they have more places of worship than any of the others. The quakers form but a small community in this city, and even that is decreasing; for the young people do not appear much inclined to follow up the strict ceremonials of their parents in point of dress and manners. . . .

There are several rich and respectable families of Jews in New York; and as they have equal rights with every other citizen in the United States, they suffer under no invidious distinctions. . . .

There are about 4,000 negroes and people of colour in New York, 1,700 of whom are slaves. These people are mostly of the Methodist persuasion, and have a chapel or two of their own with preachers of their colour; though some attend other places of worship according to their inclination.

Lambert's two visits to the city, in November 1807 and in April of the following year, gave him an opportunity to observe the contrast

between the normally vigorous commercial life of the seaport city and the drastic effects of Jefferson's Embargo.

When I arrived at New York in November, the port was filled with shipping, and the wharfs were crowded with commodities of every description. Bales of cotton, wool, and merchandize; barrels of potash, rice, flour, and salt provisions; hogsheads of sugar, chests of tea, puncheons of rum, and pipes of wine; boxes, cases, packs and packages of all sizes and denominations, were strewed upon the wharfs and landing-places, or upon the decks of the shipping. All was noise and bustle. The carters were driving in every direction; and the sailors and labourers upon the wharfs, and on board the vessels, were moving their ponderous burthens from place to place. The merchants and their clerks were busily engaged in their counting-houses, or upon the piers. The Tontine coffee-house was filled with underwriters, brokers, merchants, traders, and politicians; selling, purchasing, trafficking, or insuring; some reading, others eagerly inquiring the news. The steps and balcony of the coffee-house were crowded with people bidding, or listening to the several auctioneers, who had elevated themselves upon a hogshead of sugar, a puncheon of rum, or a bale of cotton; and with Stentorian voices were exclaiming, "Once, twice." "Once, twice." "Another cent." "Thank ye, gentlemen," or were knocking down the goods which took up one side of the street, to the best purchaser. The coffee-house slip, and the corners of Wall and Pearl-streets, were jammed up with carts, drays, and wheelbarrows; horses and men were huddled promiscuously together, leaving little or no room for passengers to pass. Such was the appearance of this part of the town when I arrived. Every thing was in motion; all was life, bustle, and activity. . . .

But on my return to New York the following April [1808], what a contrast was presented to my view! And how shall I describe the melancholy dejection that was painted upon the countenances of the people, who seemed to have taken leave of all their former gaiety and cheerfulness? The coffee-house slip, the wharfs and quays along South-street, presented no longer the bustle and activity that had prevailed there five months before. The port, indeed, was full of shipping; but they were dismantled and laid up. Their decks were cleared, their hatches fastened down, and scarcely a sailor was to be found on board. Not a box, bale, cask, barrel, or package, was to be

The J. Clarence Davies Collection, Museum of the City of New York

NEW YORK IN THE 1820's

The still somewhat rural flavor of New York City in the early 1820's is caught in this engraved view of Broadway and City Hall Park (above), after a painting by Baron Axel Klinkowström, a Swedish visitor of 1818–1819. Dogs and stray pigs mingle with promenading pedestrians on tree-shaded Broadway. To the right, in its three-cornered park, stands the imposing City Hall, first occupied in 1811 and completed in 1812. At the extreme left is the porch of St. Paul's Chapel, and at the curb a lamp post illustrative of the type of street lighting used before the introduction of gas in 1827. The second house beyond St. Paul's was that of John Jacob Astor.

A water color of the ornate interior of the Park Theatre, in 1822 (right), suggests New York's resources in the field of theatrical entertainment by that date. The play was "Monsieur Tonson." Charles Mathews and Miss Johnson are on the stage, and many distinguished New Yorkers are in the audience. The original Park Theatre, opened in 1798, was destroyed by fire in 1820 but immediately rebuilt.

Courtesy of The New-York Historical Society, New York City

The Edward W. C. Arnold Collection; photograph courtesy of Museum of the City of New York

THE COMMERCIAL SCENE IN JACKSONIAN TIMES

The "forest of masts" which impressed contemporaries with the commercial vigor of New York City by the turn of the 1830's is apparent in William J. Bennett's drawing of South Street from Maiden Lane in 1828. Here vessels from all parts of the world line the quays, their bowsprits overtopping the busy throng at the waterside.

The "Ice Cream Man" (left) was one of the personalities of the New York commercial scene described in a little book called *The Cries of New York,* published in the city in 1846. On the title page, its publisher, John Doggett, boasted that its fifteen illustrations were "Drawn from Life by a Distinguished Artist."

The "distinguished artist" of *The Cries of New York* may have been Nicolino V. Calyo who painted a series of water-color drawings of New York types, in about 1840. One of these was the oyster-man with his open stand, who, like the proprietors of the numerous oyster cellars, ministered to a prevailing taste of New Yorkers in the early nineteenth century.

Museum of the City of New York

THE CRIES OF NEW YORK. 29

ICE CREAM MAN.

"Ice Cream! Ice Cream!" *that* fact is very plain—
We *hear* you *scream*—don't tell us so again!

ell-known and agreeable luxury is particularly acceptable during the try weather in July and August; indeed it is esteemed by many as a le luxury at all seasons. Besides the numerous confectionaries and where it is sold, and which are much patronised by citizens in the evenings, some who are not particular as to the *quality* of this article, plied by colored men who take it round the city in covered pails. Gar- here Ice Cream is sold, have been known in this city for at least half ry.

h of the Ice Cream, however, sold in this city, is in truth Ice *Milk* which shows the difficulty of obtaining cream. How seldom is it New Yorker enjoys that luxury in either tea or coffee!

Museum of the City of New Y

seen upon the wharfs. Many of the counting-houses were shut up, or advertised to be let; and the few solitary merchants, clerks, porters, and labourers, that were to be seen, were walking about with their hands in their pockets. Instead of sixty or a hundred carts that used to stand in the street for hire, scarcely a dozen appeared, and they were unemployed; a few coasting sloops, and schooners, which were clearing out for some of the ports in the United States, were all that remained of that immense business which was carried on a few months before. The coffee-house was almost empty; or, if there happened to be a few people in it, it was merely to pass away the time which hung heavy on their hands, or to inquire anxiously after news from Europe, and from Washington: or to purchase a few bills, that were selling at ten or twelve per cent. above par. . . . In short, the scene was so gloomy and forlorn, that had it been the month of September instead of April, I should verily have thought that a malignant fever was raging in the place; so desolating were the effects of the embargo, which in the short space of five months had deprived the first commercial city in the States of all its life, bustle, and activity; caused above one hundred and twenty bankruptcies; and completely annihilated its foreign commerce! . . .

The embargo had a considerable effect upon the amusements of the people, and rendered the town gloomy and melancholy. The sailors, however, belonging to the shipping in port had a holiday, and, while their money lasted, amused themselves with fiddling, dancing, and carousing with their girls. . . .

Being anxious to return to Canada, I did not feel an inclination to make any stay at New York, particularly as there was little else to see but *gloomy looks* and *long faces.* Having therefore rested myself five or six days, to recover from the effects of the tossing and tumbling which I had sustained during the passage, I bade adieu to that elegant city, which I regretted to leave in such a melancholy state of dejection.

NEW YORK CITY IN THE SECOND WAR WITH BRITAIN: 1812–1815

Shortages, high prices, and unemployment resulting from the British blockade were the first effects of the War of 1812 upon New York City. But not until the last year of the conflict was there widespread fear of attack. The following contemporary accounts suggest the changing attitudes of wartime New York, and the local reaction to news of peace.

Washington Irving wrote, in January 1813: "This war has completely changed the face of things. You would scarcely recognize our old peaceful city. Nothing is talked of but armies, navies, battles, etc. . . . Had not the miserable accounts from our frontiers dampened in some measure the public zeal, I believe half our young men would have been military mad." [27]

At the news of the capture and burning of Washington, D. C., the columns of *The Columbian,* for August 27, 1814, carried the following alarm.[28]

Your capital is taken! 13,000 British troops may have marched for Baltimore, and before this hour it may have fallen. Six days ago the people at Washington were in perfect security. In six days the same enemy may be at the Hook, and if they assail your city with a powerful force by land and by water, what will be your fate? Arise from your slumbers! Let every citizen arise and enroll himself instantly and prepare to defend our city to the last extremity! This is no time to talk! We must act, and act with vigor, or we are lost.

Word of renewed British activity had already excited the citizenry to strengthen New York's defenses. The following notice appeared in the New York *Evening Post,* August 20, 1814.[29]

Notice from "A Citizen of Colour."

The committee of defence have assigned next Monday for the people of colour to contribute their services to work on the fortifications. On this occasion it becomes the duty of every coloured man, resident in this city, to volunteer. The state of New York has evinced a disposition to do us justice. . . . Under the protection of her laws we dwell in safety and pursue our honest callings, none daring to molest us, whatever his complexion or circumstances. And such has been the solicitude in our behalf, manifested from time to time by our legislature, that there is a fair prospect of a period not far distant, when this state will not contain a slave. Our country is now in danger. . . . we have now an opportunity of shewing that we are not ungrateful. . . . but are willing to exert ourselves . . . for the protection of our beloved state.—Let no man of colour, who is able to go, stay at home on Monday next; but let every one assemble at 5 o'clock, A. M. in the Park, to join with their brethren in their patriotic effort.

In 1846, the editor of the New York *Journal of Commerce* recalled early reactions to the news of peace.[30]

The evening of February 11, 1815, . . . [the *Gazette*] office was about being closed, when a pilot rushed in and stood for a moment, so entirely exhausted as to be unable to speak. . . . Presently the pilot, gasping for breath, whispered intelligibly, "Peace! peace! . . . An English sloop-of-war is below with news of a treaty of peace. . . ."

All hands rushed into Hanover Square, crying—"Peace! *Peace!* PEACE!" The windows flew up. . . . No sooner were the inmates sure of the sweet sound of peace than the windows began to glow with brilliant illuminations. The cry of "Peace! *Peace!* PEACE!" spread through the city at the top of all voices. No one stopped to inquire about "free trade and sailors' rights." No one inquired whether even the national honor had been preserved. The matters by which politicians had irritated the nation into the war had lost all their importance.—It was enough that the ruinous war was over. . . . Never was there such joy in the city. A few evenings after, there was a general illumination, and although the snow was a foot deep and soaked with rain, yet the streets were crowded with men and women, eager to see and partake of everything which had in it the sight or taste of peace.

5. *AMID A FOREST OF MASTS* (*1815–1845*)

In the generation following the close of the War of 1812, New York, like young America, entered upon a period of zestful growth, expanding to a degree that amazed visitor and resident alike. "I was not prepared to find such a large and populous city on a coast where two hundred years ago there was only an insignificant village," wrote Baron Axel Klinkowström, a Swedish naval officer who had his first glimpse of the city from the harbor in the fall of 1818. Less than thirty years later, a visiting historian from the University of Berlin recognized New York to be "next to London, . . . the first commercial city in the civilized world"; and Walt Whitman, already in love with the emerging metropolis, had called it "the great place of the western continent, the heart, the brain, the focus, the main spring, the pinnacle, the extremity, the no more beyond, of the New World." [1]

As its population swelled from less than 100,000 in 1815 to more than 371,000 in 1845, the youthful city quickened its relentless northward march. Greenwich Village and Houston Street were at its outward limits when Lieutenant Francis Hall, a visitor of 1816, observed its already rapid northerly advance. By the mid-forties, Fifth Avenue was built up "without any very great gaps," nearly to Twentieth Street, and according to the diarist George Templeton Strong, an "ambitious little row of houses" was "starting up" as far north as a once remotely projected Forty-second Street.[2]

Loaded carts, in continuous "procession up Broadway," symbolized the magnitude of the "tide of migration" that since the middle twenties was flowing "from the lower to the upper parts of the city"; and the inflated prosperity of the middle 1830's accelerated the "uptown" trend. As Philip Hone remarked, in 1836, the "old down town burgomasters" were "marching reluctantly north to pitch their tents in places which, in their [own] time, were orchards, cornfields, or morasses, a pretty smart distance from town." Hone, himself, similarly tempted by the high prices offered in connection with the "transmutation" of the lower city to business, moved from a house opposite City Hall Park to one, some eighteen blocks northward, just south of Astor Place. By 1845, Strong was confiding to his diary his family's intentions to "emigrate" still farther northward to the vicinity of Twentieth Street and Gramercy Park.[3]

The expansion of the mid-twenties found native commentators hard put to restrain their astonishment at the size and vigor of this "grand emporium of the western world." "We are rapidly becoming the London of America," wrote the veteran New Yorker, John Pintard, in 1826. "I myself am astonished & this city is the wonder of every stranger." James Fenimore Cooper, in the succeeding year, detected in New York's rapid growth the beginning of a movement of population toward the city rather than to the forested frontier. To the Alabaman visitor Mrs. Anne Royall, one of the earliest professional travel writers of native birth, life in New York—with its "thrice told multitude"—was such as to fill the "western stranger with amazement"; and Theodore Dwight, New York journalist and professional traveler, found it difficult to adjust to the idea that "240,000 people" could be residing "in one place!"[4]

European observers, too, arriving in increasing numbers in these more settled years, saw more to praise in New York City than in the other parts of the nation which they were at pains to describe. "Queen of the Atlantic Coast"—*"la reine du littoral"*—was the tribute of the French economist Michel Chevalier to New York in the mid-thirties; and even the average British visitor found less to criticize by this date than he had in the first decade or so after 1815, when war-created antipathies were strong. The otherwise vitriolic Mrs. Trollope could not praise New York enough; and Dickens, whose *American Notes* and *Martin Chuzzlewit* were hardly laudatory of American life, regretted upon his departure from the city, in 1842, having to leave the "generally polished and refined" society with which he had become acquainted there.[5]

Physically, in this generation, New York City suggested the carelessness of growing youth. Travelers of the 1820's—both native and foreign—complained of its unkempt and cluttered streets, its squalid, smelly slips, and its ever present pigs. Bales and boxes of merchants' wares, or sawyers preparing wood for the market, often blocked the pedestrian's way. "The streets of New York are not to be perambulated with impunity by either the lame, or the blind, or the exquisitely sensitive in their olfactory nerves," warned a Glasgow printer upon his return to Scotland in 1823; "to use an American phrase, a person must be 'wide-awake,' not to dislocate his ankles by the inequalities and gaps in the side-pavements, or break his legs by running foul of the numberless moveable and immoveable incumbrances with which they are occupied." What diarist Philip Hone called the "annual metamorphosis" of the city was in part responsible for the cluttered appearance it often had. "Brickbats, rafters, and slates are showering in every direction," he wrote of the lower city in 1839. "The spirit of pulling down and building up is abroad. The whole of New York is rebuilt about once in ten years."

If "overturn" was the "maxim of New York"—in Hone's opinion—there was also little in the way of public architecture at this time to suggest maturity or age. Apart from the white marble City Hall, with its classic portico, there was "scarcely a public building deserving of notice," and even the municipal edifice was criticized for its painted wooden dome and lack of "simplicity and grandeur." As for the churches, their lofty, but always wooden steeples, though an admired feature of the city's skyline, had "an air of paltriness and insecurity" to visitors "from the *old country*." [6]

By the turn of the thirties, the fast-growing city appears to have gained somewhat in physical appeal. Travelers praised the cheerful, yet substantial appearance of its residential architecture, "always kept painted . . . the colour of the red brick with white lime in the seams." To Carl Gosselman, a Swedish visitor of 1826, the "vertical" construction in the English fashion was preferable to the "horizontal" style common in his native land. Broadway, which Gosselman called "unforgettable," increasingly drew the attention that it was to receive for many years as the main focus of the visitor's interest. The length and breadth of the storied thoroughfare were at the moment its chief attractions, as well as the passing throng for which it was the fashionable promenade. Averaging eighty feet in width, it was built up for a distance of two and a half to three miles by the early thirties; but the impressiveness of its vista was marred by the wide diversity in elevation and type of structure—"from the wooden cottage of one story, to the massive brick edifice of five or six."

Americans of the period liked to compare Broadway with London's Regent Street; and although most Europeans refused to go this far, they did agree that it surpassed anything England's provincial cities had to offer. Its "handsome shops" impressed Mrs. Trollope in 1831; and a royal visitor of the succeeding year—Maximilian, prince of a small house of Rhenish Prussia—found them "but little inferior to those of London and Paris." By 1837, many of the stores had been fitted up with large plate glass fronts, similar to those in the English capital.[7]

Broadway's chief ornament, after 1836, was the Astor House—"a really magnificent hotel," in the opinion of Thomas Colley Grattan, British consul, who arrived in New York in 1839. An impressive pile of granite, six stories high, it overlooked City Hall Park from the west side of Broadway, and with its 600 beds dwarfed the largest hotels of London and Paris. The chief eyesores of the thoroughfare, according to contemporaries, were its wretched pavement and the clutter of awnings and advertising matter suspended on beams extending to the outer edge of the sidewalk, above the pedestrians' heads. On the pillars supporting these beams were pasted large printed placards announcing the bargains to be had inside; and show-boards with bills of every color, suspended by hooks or rings, gave the street the appearance of a carnival or fair. Its upper limits, between Sixteenth and Twenty-third streets, cut through a newer section, where "handsome streets and avenues" crossed each other at right angles, and where residents of the now congested lower city were building splendid homes.[8]

By the prosperous middle thirties, visitors were increasingly struck with the fevered tempo of the urban scene. The English traveler Charles Latrobe, contrasting American cities in 1832, called Philadelphia the most symmetrical, Baltimore the most picturesque, Washington the most bewildering, New York the most "bustling"; and his assessment, at least of Manhattan, was invariably echoed by other commentators in these years. The Swedish pioneer Gustav Unonius, stopping in New York on his way westward in 1841, was convinced that one had "need of a pair of eyes in the back of the neck and of an eye at each ear, in order to escape being run over or trampled down" by Broadway's "surging throng." [9]

"The hurry-scurry of the Broadway and Wall-Street," with their "driving, jostling, and elbowing," exasperated Andrew Bell, a British visitor of 1835. "Add to this the crashing noises of rapid omnibuses, flying in all directions, and carts (for even they are driven as fast as coaches are with us), and we have a jumble of sights and sounds easy to understand but hard to describe. The most crowded parts of London can scarce be compared with it." The noise was louder than that of London—for want of the wooden pavement used in Oxford

Street—in the opinion of Friedrich von Raumer, professor of history at the University of Berlin. Even Walt Whitman was disposed to criticize this aspect of the city. "What can New York—noisy, roaring, rumbling, tumbling, bustling, stormy, turbulent New York—have to do with *silence?*" he asked in 1842. "Amid the universal clatter, the incessant din of business, the all-swallowing vortex of the great money whirlpool, . . . who has any . . . idea . . . of silence?" [10]

The tumultuous liveliness of the business scene was a consequence of the city's undisputed leadership, by the thirties, as a center of American commerce and trade. It was a rare traveler who failed to mention, among his first impressions, the "forest of masts"—*"pépinière de navires,"* to quote the French—that screened the city from the harbor, or the bowsprits that spanned the footway at the waterside. To Karl Bernhard, duke of Saxe-Weimar-Eisenach, the city appeared in 1825 to be attracting "nearly the whole commerce of the country." The completion of the Erie Canal in this year made New York the terminus of the most efficient route into the interior, further suggesting, to local residents, the limitless future of the Empire City and its commercial superiority over "our carping sister, Philadelphia." But contemporaries noted evidences of other and equally important causes of the city's commercial supremacy: the availability of her port for the receipt of English goods, frequently sold at public auction; the regular sailings of the packet ships, which Dickens called "the finest in the world"; signs of a flourishing coastal trade; and the shipments of cotton which made New York a way station on the route by which the Southern staple was exported to Europe. Its lively communications gave the city the quality of a "large post office," wrote the Swedish visitor Carl Gosselman after his visit in 1826. With a "whole continent behind it" and "almost as active a connection with all parts of the globe," people and products as well as letters moved to and from it from all over the world.[11]

Manufacturing, in which Philadelphia—as in population—originally outclassed the Empire City, also contributed to New York's prosperity in the period following the War of 1812. In his *Description of the City of New-York* (1827), an early book of a promotional nature dealing with New York City, James Hardie reported that between 1812 and 1825 the annual output of cloth had increased from less than 3,000 yards to nearly 1,175,000. "Other factories have advanced in at least an equal ratio," he wrote, "and new ones are almost daily springing into existence." The French economist Chevalier emphasized the importance of the financial community in the city's growth. "In fifty years the population of New York has increased tenfold, its wealth probably an hundred fold; . . . the merit belongs chiefly to the industry, the capital, the intelligence, and the enterprise of that, numerically speaking, insignificant minority of Wall Street and Pearl Street," he wrote, in the course of his sojourn in the United States in the early 1830's.[12]

For all the growth in manufacturing and finance, it was business and commerce which set the tone of the urban scene and gave the city the "air of a town sacrificed to trade." "Many of their expressions are derived from their mercantile habits," asserted a young officer of the Royal Navy, who circulated in New York society in 1826. "A young lady, talking of the most eligible class of life from which to choose a husband, declared that, for her part she was all for the *commissions*. This elicited from my companion, the major, one of his best bows, in the fond presumption that she alluded to the military profession—not at all; the sequel of her conversation explained but too clearly, that *Commission Merchants* were the fortunate objects of her preference." [13]

By the 1820's, the effects of the "democratic ferment" in American life were increasingly noted by commentators on the New York scene. Beyond the prevailing absorption with business, the aspects of Jacksonian New York which impressed observers most forcibly were the general well-being of the working people, the democratic attitudes of the citizens as a whole, the expensiveness of feminine attire, and the unexpected number of Negroes in the urban population. Even the most critical commentators admitted the absence of beggars; and socially progressive Frances Wright claimed to have looked in vain for poor or uneducated persons when she visited New York in the fall of 1818. Baron Klinkowström, commenting upon conditions following the panic of 1819, reported that although there were supposed to be "a great number of poor," in New York, he had seen no one "lying starving on the streets" as was frequently the case "in the big cities of Europe." The English authoress Harriet Martineau marveled at the "spruce appearance of all the people," in the flourishing middle thirties; and the comfortable furnishings in the mechanics' homes led Francis J. Grund, a cosmopolitan visitor of 1836, to conclude that laborers in America were "really less removed from the wealthy merchants and professional men than they are in any part of Europe." [14]

This view was supported by the Swedish immigrant Unonius in challenging the unfavorable comments about the United States which his compatriot Carl Hauswolff had published in Sweden in 1835. In the New York of 1841 Unonius saw no sign of the wan and ragged newcomers whom Hauswolff had described with such telling pathos. Instead of Hauswolff's "pale and wan faces," full of homesickness for their native land, Unonius observed "wholesome and powerful-looking men, prepared to face whatever fate they may meet in the Far West." Those who had taken up residence in New York as artisans and laborers told him "almost without exception that they were doing well financially, in spite of the fact that many of them had big families to support." Most of them were "dressed in a way we are accustomed to see only among the gentry." [15]

Travelers at the turn of the thirties detected signs of the tension that was developing between employer and employee as new methods of production reduced the intimacy which formerly had existed between owners and workers. They described the public meetings of the "Workies" and supplied their readers with the arguments of the handbills in which the mechanics and workingmen proposed political action as a means of achieving desired reforms—a program which included more adequate compensation for their labor, the abolition of imprisonment for debt, an efficient lien law, and the exemption of mechanics' tools from sale by execution. Yet despite this evidence of unrest, the European observer appeared to be convinced that the condition of the "more humble classes, . . . tradesmen, shopkeepers, clerks, and artisans," was certainly more comfortable than that of the same classes in Europe. Even in the wake of the panic of 1837, visitors saw little evidence that the small folk of the city were "labouring under any visible want of the necessaries of life." [16]

Opportunities for speculation, in connection with the city's growth, helped to foment the economic crisis that occurred in 1837. James S. Buckingham, touring America following his defeat in the Parliamentary elections of that year, laid the collapse to the extravagant expenditures "of the trading classes"—in "furniture, in entertainment, in equipages, in dress, in servants"; but speculation in city real estate was an even more obvious cause. Visitor and resident alike reported the "rage for speculation" that struck the city in the middle thirties. "Everybody is speculating, and everything has become an object of speculation," wrote Michel Chevalier in August of 1835. The whole of Manhattan Island was laid out in building lots, and, according to the French economist, enough had been sold to accommodate a population of two million. "Everything in New York is at an exorbitant price," wrote Philip Hone in March of 1836. "Rents have risen 50 per cent for the next year." [17]

The effects of overtrading began to be noted in the late fall of 1836; and by the spring of 1837, the "card house" of speculation had collapsed. "Railroads and canals will not bring . . . more than half their value a year ago," the former mayor reported. "Lots . . . somewhere about One Hundredth Street . . . which cost last September $480 a lot have been sold within a few days at $50." The British novelist Frederick Marryat, arriving in May, found Broadway like "a new made widow." Perhaps with an element of creative license, he painted a lurid picture of pedestrians, with careworn faces, brooding over their departed affluence, and unemployed mechanics pacing up and down "with the air of famished wolves." Barter became common at the city's stores, and tickets for shaves and oyster dinners took the place of change. A section of unfinished buildings, whose construction was halted by the depression, looked "as if the work had been stopped by the enchanted ring of some evil spirit," when the French diplomat Adolphe de Bacourt visited the "extreme end" of New York in 1840. Some improvement was noted in the early forties, but as late as the fall of 1842, the Tory politician John Robert Godley reported that the value of New York real estate had declined more than one-half in the past five years and that tradesmen were still paying their workers in produce for want of currency.[18]

Abundant comment—not always complimentary—testifies to the many manifestations of democracy in the New York scene in Jacksonian days. Charles Henry Wilson, a sarcastically uncomplimentary English visitor of 1819, was repelled by the lack of dignity at the City Hall, where justice was "unwigged," the "segar" in "constant requisition," and the spectator "stupified with smoke, and *spit upon* as an especial mark of freedom." Thirty-one-year-old Richard Cobden, later champion of corn-law repeal, took a more tolerant view of the situation, in 1835, but he was nevertheless somewhat surprised to see "judges on the bench without badge of any kind and a barrister pleading in a claret colored coat with pepper & salt pants & white stockings." [19]

The most critical visitors invariably poked fun at the city militia for their unmilitary manner and motley attire. Travelers on the turn of the twenties observed the citizen army drilling in civilian clothes and led by storekeepers or tailors who counted a "military command" the acme of achievement. "Falstaff's ragged regiment was nothing in comparison" to the unshaven citizens in "long-tail blues, short jackets, and white and pink blouses" who drilled in the Park during Robert Collyer's visit in the early forties.[20]

In 1817, the acidulous Henry Fearon was shocked to find the pit of the city's best theatre filled with "none in dress, manners, appearance, or habits above the order of our Irish bricklayers." A similar situation was less offensive to the Spanish liberal Ramon de la Sagra, who visited New York in 1835. He nevertheless admitted that he found it unusual to see the parterre "filled with lightermen and market porters, with their hats on, eating pastry and gnawing apples." "Having bought their tickets, they exercised in all its fullness the right to listen, judge, applaud, what seemed good to them; but not a single person committed the least indecency," he reported, after attending a performance at the American Theatre in the Bowery. Indeed, when Patrick Shirreff attended a benefit for Frances Kemble in 1833, he was amused to see the operatives in the pit "enforcing chaste manners" on the more socially select members of the audience. When a number of gentlemen assumed what he called indelicate postures in one of the boxes, voices in the pit called out, " 'A Trollope, a trollope,' and a general hissing and hooting from the same quarter had the effect of inducing the offenders speedily to withdraw." [21]

Reformers like Frances Wright were, of course, impressed by the confidence with which the local artisans, in 1818 and 1819, identified themselves with the behavior of their government; and James Boardman, an English businessman who spent two years in the United States—from 1829 to 1831—admired the "independence of feeling" of workingmen who "looked like men who knew they were free; but who knew also how to enjoy freedom." The ready civility and extreme neatness of apparel of the Irish waiters at the Astor House in the 1840's gave Thomas Grattan "an instant notion of independence, in mind as well as circumstances." The British consul was "pleased to observe such an evident contrast between the condition of this class of men in America and that of their fellow-countrymen at home." On the other hand, many travelers supported Frances Kemble's contention that shopkeepers and servants were democratic to the point of insolence; and Alexis de Tocqueville, visiting New York City in 1831, predicted that the nation would have to resort to armed force to repress the excesses of urban democracy.[22]

Neither Tocqueville nor his companion Beaumont was much impressed with New York City. Like most French travelers of this period they missed the domes, clock towers, monuments, and handsome edifices which gave an air of age and elegance to European cities. To Tocqueville, the New World city had the appearance of a suburb. He saw the leveling effect of democracy in what he considered the mediocrity of manner and similarity of attire of its inhabitants. Both he and Beaumont were surprised to find so many Catholics and Catholic churches in the city; and Beaumont commented with some irony upon the pretensions to family tradition in this "democracy," which caused some of the older families to "put heraldic arms on their carriages and on their seals." [23]

Few travelers failed to describe the parade of female elegance—"a moving bed of tulips"—which was the chief attraction of Broadway in Jacksonian days. Paris was still the model for the New York belles, who dressed "to the very complexion and arrangement of their shoestrings *à la Française.*" A flippant young British officer marveled at seeing "Pink satin, bonnets & feather and boots to match of the same material at 10 o'clock in the morning" in Broadway. Less charitable was the view of Thomas Colley Grattan. "The flaunting air of these ladies, their streaming feathers and flowers, silks and satins of all colours" made them look "like so many nymphs of the *pavé,*" wrote the British consul; "and many awkward mistakes take place in consequence." Frances Kemble called the extravagance of the female wardrobe "quite extraordinary" and asserted that "twenty, forty, and sixty dollars [were] paid for a bonnet to wear in a morning saunter up Broadway." According to Mrs. Anne Royall, "a ten dollar hat, a thirty dollar shawl, with silk and lace" were common even among "the poorer class of females." [24]

Many British visitors noted the already characteristic New York "pallor," in both sexes, and, while confirming the reputed beauty of American women, commented, not always admiringly, upon the unrounded quality of the female figure. Young Richard Cobden was struck with the "pallid & unhealthy complexion of the American ladies," many of whom appeared "so pale & sickly that in Britain they would be regarded as consumptives." Hypercritical Thomas H. James, a visitor of 1845, remarked that the "prominent point of female loveliness which the whole English race so much excel in, is entirely wanting in the American ladies; they are as *flat* as their own horrid seacoast." "What they want in busts they make up in bustles," he reported, "and to an excess that . . . is so glaring and preposterous as to be downright indelicate." One Scotsman professed to have heard it whispered that the ladies carried "their complexions in their pockets," and adjusted them to the seasons by "applying the rouge in Spring & leaving the carmine to nature in August." Travelers who came in contact with the city's best society found its female ingredient amiable and attractive but with a sort of "Trans-atlanticism" which lacked the elegance and distinction customary in European social circles. Frances Wright was impressed by the fact that the "youth of both sexes" in New York enjoyed a "freedom of intercourse unknown in the older and more formal nations of Europe." [25]

Even before the turn of the 1820's, the first signs of the coming tide of European immigration excited comment on the part of local observers. To one of them (John Pintard), writing in the fall of 1819, "emigrants in sholes from Europe" seemed to be thronging the city's streets. Cooper, learning that 22,000 Irishmen had reached the city in one year, during the mid-twenties, asserted that the "extraordinary medley" of its people made New York the only city in the Union, except perhaps New Orleans, without the "air of a provincial town." In this point of view he was supported by Lafayette's secretary, Levasseur. The latter, after touring the United States in 1824 with the Revolutionary hero, wrote that immigration was already making New York less "national" in character than the other cities of the country. By 1835, visitors were describing sections of the city where "one might suppose that a slice of Cork or Dublin had been transferred to America—houses, people, dirt, and all." German-born Francis Lieber commented on the variety of languages heard in the city on the turn of the thirties; and by the mid-forties, Nathaniel P. Willis, a resident commentator on the passing scene, found the Battery, on Sundays, the "Champs-Elysées of foreigners," where nothing was heard but French and German, spoken by artisans "newly arrived in old country costume." [26]

Other parts of the British Isles were also represented, if less numerously, in the waves of immigration that were flowing toward New York and America. The city of the early thirties had no attraction for one Welsh immigrant who recorded his disillusionment with New York in a letter to the *Cymro America,* a Welsh weekly journal published in New York in 1832. He complained of the bad water, the high cost of fuel, the danger of losses by fire, the high taxes, and such urban noises as the shouts of the chimney sweeps—like "the yells of starving savages who had not savored human flesh for at least forty days." The proportion of aliens in the city's total population increased from 11 per cent in 1825 to 35 per cent twenty years later.[27]

More novel, however, to most European observers, were the relatively numerous New Yorkers of the Negro race. Less familiar to Europeans, than the immigrants, they accounted for what travelers like the Irish actor Tyrone Power considered the city's "foreign tone." In 1790, Negroes had constituted almost 10 per cent of New York's population; but although their number increased from 3,262 in that year to 16,358 in 1840, they comprised only 5 per cent of the total population at the latter count. There were no slaves in New York City after 1827, but even after that date, travelers continued to notice a segregation in church and theatre which they found it difficult to reconcile with the professed ideals of the new nation; and reformers like Charles Dickens wrote lurid descriptions of the squalor in which many Negroes lived. Evidence of existing discrimination is seen in the fact that when the Mexican legislator D. Lorenzo de Zavala (later Vice President of the Republic of Texas) visited New York in 1830, he was unable to procure a hotel room in New York and was forced to stay in the home of a Negro.[28]

The citizens of "sable cast" were in this period, as later, of unusual interest to the city's Scandinavian visitors. Baron Klinkowström, who visited New York while slavery existed there, was interested in the economic activities of the free colored people, who managed small stores, or ran oyster and fruit stands and barber shops. Already apparent to this commentator was the animosity of the Irish newcomers toward the free Negro, an attitude which was to cause serious trouble in the city during the Civil War. The Swedish novelist, Carl Arfwedson, a visitor of 1832, was fascinated by the multicolored finery of the colored people as they strolled, on Sundays, at the Battery, the women with bonnets "decorated with ribbons, plumes, and flowers, of a thousand different colours," the men with yellow gloves, jaunty hats, and waistcoats "all colours of the rainbow." Most travelers of the period leave the impression that the colored population, though generally employed in servile occupations, nevertheless constituted an established and accepted ingredient in the city's cosmopolitan society. Mrs. Trollope thought they wore more of an "air of consequence" in New York than in Philadelphia; and both she and Sarah Maury, another English visitor, remarked upon the self-assurance with which "smartly," if somewhat flamboyantly, dressed Negresses and their "gallant" beaux mingled with the promenading throng on Broadway.[29]

The "domestic manners" of New Yorkers of the twenties, thirties, and forties were naturally much affected by the rapid growth of the city and the pace of the commercial activity there. Houses were scarce, and rent was high. Servants were at a premium. Even the permanent residents—if anything was permanent in this fast-expanding city—resided in hotels and boarding houses to an extent not customary elsewhere. When Baron Klinkowström arrived in 1818, the leading hostelries were the City Hotel, the Mechanics Hall, and the Washington Hall. With the increase of people and business in the succeeding twenty years came the addition of such "spacious establishments" as the Waverley, the Mansion House, the American, the Carlton, the Clarendon, the Globe, the Athenaeum, Holt's—"a boundless labyrinth," and especially the Astor House, luxurious symbol of the city's commercial pre-eminence in the middle thirties. Opened in May of 1836, it filled the block from Vesey to Barclay Street. Stores occupied the lower floor along the street; and the main entrance, at the center of the Broadway front, was flanked by Doric columns and opened into a handsome vestibule.[30]

Guests at the City Hotel in the twenties could be served in their private apartments; but the prevailing practice at most hostelries of the period was to dine, *table d'hôte,* at fixed hours, in the hotel dining room. When Lieutenant De Roos stayed at the City Hotel in 1826 there was "a public breakfast at half past seven o'clock and a dinner at two." Businessmen of the neighborhood, as well as the regular residents of the hotel, sat down at tables accommodating fifty to a hundred people and disposed of their meals in silence with a directness and dispatch which amazed the European visitor.[31]

Supplementing the hotels were numerous boarding houses, suited to all levels of the population. Baron Klinkowström recommended this mode of living as preferable to hotel life. He liked the intimacy of the boarding house and the companionship of the paying guests. "Often there is a chance to make a good match in such houses, and decorum is observed," he reported, during his sojourn in New York from 1818 to 1820. And young newlyweds could avoid the expense of setting up a home by living in such places until they had two or three children. Among his fellow lodgers, during his visit, were "two refined women and their husbands and a few single women with their mothers." The host and hostess were "quality folk" who joined in the company and did the honors. Breakfast was served at nine and dinner at four or five, after which the guests gathered in the living room before a glowing fire and spent the evening in "card playing, games, or merriment." [32]

Some visitors deplored the lack of privacy and fashion which went along with boarding house life, but they admitted the compensation in the abundant food and inexpensive rates—three to four dollars a week on the average. Harriet Martineau, a traveler of the middle thirties, found "this method of living rather formidable the first day," and never became completely reconciled to it, despite all the good manners she professed to have witnessed at public tables; but Mrs. Felton, a wealthy Englishwoman who visited New York at about the same time, concluded that boarding house living had distinct merits and offered a sumptuous fare for the charges asked. Whatever one thought of it, the boarding house was a typical attribute of life in New York during the period. Walt Whitman asserted in 1842 that if he were called upon to describe the universal Yankee nation in laconic terms he would say that they were "a boarding people." "Perhaps the appelation will more particularly apply to the New Yorkers, and denizens of two or three other large cities," he wrote in an editorial for the New York *Aurora;* "but it holds good, to a certain degree, for every section of the republic." [33]

According to Mrs. Felton, it was the servant problem which drove so many New Yorkers to substitute the boarding house for the home. Irish immigrants provided the chief source of domestic workers, together with the colored element in the population; but employers complained that the Irish put on airs almost immediately upon their arrival, and that servants generally took the equalitarian philosophy of the time so seriously as to insist upon being called, not servants, but "helps," "helpers," or "hands." Salvatore Abbate e Migliore, an Italian who circulated intimately in the city's society during his visit in 1845, reported that "second rank society" usually had "two or three servant girls, boarding houses three to six," in the latter employed at from four to six dollars a month. Of the six servants in the boarding house at which he stayed, three were Irish, one Scotch, one Negro, and one mulatto.[34]

Contemporaries admired the rich interiors in the dwellings of New Yorkers who maintained their own homes; and fine furniture was always visible on the first of May, the city's already traditional "moving day," when the transfer of household goods amidst a confusion of "carts, waggons, and drays, ropes, canvas, and straw, packers, porters, and draymen" gave the city the appearance of "a population flying from the plague." The new home of William H. Aspinwall on University Place called forth the acclaim of both Hone and Strong, early in 1846. ". . . house and furniture both, are really magnificent," wrote the latter. "One can't make a satisfactory guess at the amount he's invested in rosewood and satin, mirrors, cabinets, and vertu. And they say that Langdon, William B. Astor, and Penniman go beyond him in display and costliness." Fine fittings of this kind were especially on view on New Year's Day, when it was the custom for the ladies of the fashionable households to be at home to their friends. "Every house is opened on the occasion," wrote James Boardman, after visiting the city on the turn of the thirties, "and the tables spread with all the variety which the confectioner and the vineyards of France and Madeira can supply." Philip Hone spent five hours making calls on the first of January in 1844; and his daughters prided themselves on having received 169 callers.[35]

Jacksonian New York City had an identifiable "Society"; but it is apparent from contemporary comment that there was now much less evidence of the "class" distinctions which had been so obvious to observers previous to the 1820's. The "first families" were recruited from the merchant group, both long-time New Yorkers and New Englanders who more recently had cast their lot with the city's commercial growth. Although contemporaries detected some pretensions to aristocracy in their behavior, they found this attitude nowhere nearly so prevalent as in Philadelphia, a condition which they laid to the greater fluidity of the New York commercial scene. "Rich men spring up like mushrooms," wrote Thomas Hamilton, after his visit in 1831 and 1832. "Fortunes are made and lost by a single speculation. . . . There is comparatively no settled and permanent body of leading capitalists, and consequently far less room for that sort of defensive league which naturally takes place among men of common interests and position in society."[36]

Two observers of the early 1840's contrasted the social tone of New York and Boston. N. P. Willis found the society of the Empire City less respectable but more individualistic in character than that of the Massachusetts capital. "Every man you meet with in our city walks with his countenance free of any sense of observation or any dread of his neighbor," Willis asserted. "Boston has the advantage in many things, but a man who has any taste for cosmopolitanism would very much prefer New York." To Charles Dickens, commerce made the difference. "The tone of the best society in this city is like that of Boston," the novelist wrote, after his sojourn in New York in 1842; "here and there, it may be, with a greater infusion of the mercantile spirit, but generally polished and refined, and always most hospitable. The houses and tables are elegant; the hours later and more rakish; and there is, perhaps, a greater spirit of contention in reference to appearances, and the display of wealth and costly living." [37]

The "infusion of the mercantile spirit" undoubtedly helps to explain the broad expansion of entertainment facilities in New York during the period. After a five months' sojourn in 1823, one British traveler reported that in no city of the same size in Europe was so much money expended for amusements as in New York, a situation not unrelated to his further reference to the "ten or twenty thousand strangers" resident in the city during most seasons of the year. The phrenologist George Combe reached a similar conclusion after a visit in 1838. "The condition of the population is precisely that in which places of public amusement may be expected to be most successful," he wrote. "The city, at all times, contains a large number of strangers, whose evenings are at their own disposal; of young men engaged in trade, who live in boarding houses and hotels, who have plenty of money and no domestic ties; and of rich merchants, and their families, whose tastes are, to a certain extent, intellectual, but whose mental resources are not very extensive: and these form a solid phalanx of play-going people." [38]

The dramatic fare which New York City offered both resident and stranger was already of a very high order, for, despite occasional crudities both before and beyond the footlights, the years from 1820 to 1840 marked a brilliant period in the history of the New York stage. The playbills of the day recall repeated performances by some of Europe's most distinguished actors, singers, and dancers, such as Kean, Macready, J. B. Booth, Mathews, Charles and Frances Kemble, Malibran, Forrest, Charlotte Cushman, Fanny Elssler, Ellen Tree, and many others. The Park Theatre, rebuilt to accommodate 2,500 persons, and reopened in 1821, was still the fashionable house; but in the course of the period others were added, some of them, in elegance of decoration, the equal of London's best. Frances Kemble, who accompanied her actor father to America in 1832, described the

Park Theatre as "well formed, . . . with plenty of gold carving and red silk about it, looking rich and warm." The Bowery Theatre, an even handsomer structure, was opened in 1826, and Niblo's Gardens in 1830, where, in 1832, there was "an excellent band of music, . . . a good display of fireworks," and a panorama depicting the "struggle of the Greeks for liberty and the battle of Navarino." The English journalist and politician James S. Buckingham, visiting the city in 1837, noted the existence of six theatres, "well-filled every night."

To visiting performers, the chief novelty in the playhouses of New York in the 1830's was the great predominance of men in the audience. Tyrone Power, who toured America from 1833 to 1835 and again in 1837 and 1838, reported that, though the house was crowded at his opening in 1833, there were not "twenty females in the dress circle; all men, and enduring, I should imagine, the heat of the black hole at Calcutta." Frances Kemble had a similar experience; and in both the dress circle and the private boxes she "saw men sitting with their hats on." Though the critical Mrs. Trollope was pleased with almost everything else about New York City, she found "more than usually revolting" the informalities at the theatre, especially the spitting of tobacco, which constituted a "running accompaniment" to the entertainment on the stage.[39]

The theatre suffered in popular appeal during the depressed early forties. The popular fancy was taking momentarily a more serious turn, and lectures were "all the vogue." "Regular courses have commenced at the Mercantile Library Association, the Mechanics' Institute, the Lyceum, and the Historical Society," Philip Hone reported in November of 1841. George Templeton Strong made a similar, if more flippant, comment, late in 1842. "I don't know but I'll turn popular lecturer—that's fashionable now—deliver a series of lectures before the Sixth Ward Library Association or the Communipaw Lyceum on the life and times of Sir John Snooks, the History of the Steam Engine during the fourteenth century or the peculiar features of the farthingales of the Elizabethan era." [40]

Opera and concerts were not as frequently performed as the spoken drama in the commerce-focused city of the thirties and forties. The first season of regular Italian opera was presented at the Park Theatre, beginning in November 1825, but such was the popular reaction that when the Duke of Saxe-Weimar-Eisenach attended a production of *Don Giovanni,* in the following spring, he concluded that this "exotic fruit" was not adapted to the public taste. Italian opera was performed sporadically in the mid-thirties and again in the early forties; by the mid-forties, however, it had gained a dependable audience. By 1847, there was such a "furor" on the subject, according to George Templeton Strong, as to prompt the construction of a new opera house, which was opened in Astor Place late in that year. In this period of the city's adolescence as a music center a number of choral societies provided a tolerable musical offering; but a real advance was evident in the founding of the Philharmonic Society in 1842, which performed concerts of standard symphonic fare. Musicians of distinction like Ole Bull were already performing to sold-out houses. Strong, who was an avid music lover, had to stand to hear the famous violinist in December 1843. "Such a jam I believe was never known before; 4,000 tickets were sold and the Tabernacle was as full as it could . . . be. Had to stand all the evening, though I was on the ground an hour and a quarter before the time. . . . Didn't regret it, though, for he is a most transcendent player." [41]

In the realm of the graphic arts, the city still offered little of which to boast—a result of the prevailing emphasis on commerce and industry, in the opinion of Tocqueville's companion Beaumont, in 1831. It nevertheless had a community of artists, however small in number by contrast with the group which was to give it distinction in later years. When James B. Longacre, the noted Philadelphia engraver, visited New York in 1825, he fraternized with Henry Pickering, George Catlin, Rembrandt Peale, Peter Maverick, Colonel John Trumbull, Asher Durand, and Samuel F. B. Morse, all artists or engravers of considerable repute. He thought the statues in the New York Academy of Fine Arts superior to those in the Pennsylvania Academy; called the panorama of Athens, then on display, the "largest and best" he had seen; and enjoyed a private collection of paintings which included a Rubens and two Rembrandts. Residents like George Templeton Strong made frequent visits to the city's several galleries; and by 1845 occasional Europeans were praising the "good copies from the European masters," as well as the paintings of such artists as Durand and Thomas Cole, on display at the New York Academy of Fine Arts, and were reporting that there were excellent collections in a number of private homes.[42]

New Yorkers themselves were somewhat on the defensive regarding the educational facilities which the city offered. John Pintard acknowledged "the contempt with wh[ich] we are regarded by our rival sisters B[oston] & P[hiladelphia]" in this respect, and hailed the founding of the University of the City of New York (now New York University) in 1831 as promising to "work wonders in rearing up a new generation whose superior education must change the present, in a degree, grovelling character of N[ew] Yorkers." In the opinion of Theodore Dwight, New York's public schools were the "best large ones in the country, excepting those of Boston," and in some departments far superior to those of the Massachusetts city. The vast majority of the private schools, on the other hand, particularly the fashionable ones, he called "miserably defective." He rated Columbia College and the University of the City of New York as "very respectable institutions for the higher branches of learning." Facilities for "self-instruction" included, among others, the Mercantile Library Association, the Apprentices' Library, the City Library, and the Athenaeum.[43]

As in the preceding generation, large receptions—or assemblies—now held at the best hotels, engaged "Society" in the winter months, as did panoramas, exhibitions, public lectures and forums, and such outdoor diversions as sleigh riding and promenading on Broadway. In summer, New Yorkers were already in the habit of escaping the congestion of the city by excursions to Coney Island, Hoboken, and "Rockaway bathing place." Robert Heywood, a British tourist, spent the night at a "large hotel" at Rockaway in August 1834. He set out by horse at five o'clock in the morning and arrived at ten. At half past two, music announced dinner, during which he was served an extensive bill of fare, including a bottle of claret and "a head of corn." In June of the following year, young Richard Cobden enjoyed an outing on Coney Island, where he ate clams and shellfish. In July he journeyed to Hoboken, "a country retreat used much for children to walk in during the morning & in the afternoon the resort of multitudes of cocknies from New York. On a Sunday tens of thousands of visitors sometimes cross in the Hoboken ferry boats—the view of the city from this promenade is the best I have yet seen." It was a two-hour trip to Rockaway by ferry, railroad, and six-horse omnibus in 1844.[44]

For all its commercial vigor and varied entertainment, there was still much that was crude and provincial about New York City in Jacksonian times; and despite their praise of its refined society, foreign travelers complained at length, and with reason, of the hazards and harassments of daily living there. Local criticism of the inefficiency of the police finally led to the establishment of a systematic police force in 1844. The existing watchmen and police officers were no match for "gangs of hardened wretches" who infested many parts of the city with their brawls and drunken frolics, wrote Philip Hone, in 1839. Yet many European visitors were surprised at the order which prevailed at public celebrations "without the aid of a single bayonet or uniform." Fires were often of great magnitude; and eager, but frequently contentious, volunteer firemen, using hand-stroked, goosenecked engines, offered little competition to the flames. So frequent were the conflagrations that some visitors regarded them as the most dependable of the city's entertainments. " 'When the fire breaks out tonight,' Carl said to me one night, 'we'll go out and take a look at it,' " Gustav Unonius reported after his visit in 1841. "It was like deciding to go to the theater to see a play that had been announced and that could be counted on with certainty to come off. And sure enough, we did not have long to wait for the spectacle." [45]

Until the completion of the Croton Water Works in the early forties, the city continued to suffer from the lack of good water. There had been agitation for a municipal works since the later eighteenth century, but until the 1840's New Yorkers had to rely on private enterprise to provide their water supply. The main source was the Manhattan Company, which had been chartered in 1799 and which piped the water to its customers through bored wooden logs. Baron Klinkowström found this water "poor and brackish" at the time of his visit in 1819—a situation which encouraged the widespread popular consumption of "an artificial soda water" which in summer he saw "for sale on every corner." It may have accounted, too, for the business enjoyed by the thousands of grog shops, which travelers continued to notice.[46]

The fast-expanding population led to continuous proposals, throughout the twenties and thirties, to improve the water supply, either through incorporating private concerns that would be more effective than the Manhattan Company or through building a municipal works, in imitation of the precedent earlier established in Philadelphia. Perhaps it was consistent with the philosophy of Jacksonian times that in 1835 the citizens voted to impose this responsibility on the city government. On the Fourth of July, 1842, New Yorkers celebrated the introduction of water—piped from the Croton River—into the Murray Hill Reservoir, on the present site of the New York Public Library. Political spouting for the moment gave way to water spouts, Philip Hone reported. "Nothing is talked of in New York but Croton water; fountains, aqueducts, hydrants, and hose attract our attention and impede our progress through the streets." Soon New Yorkers were installing bathrooms and enjoying the abundance of the newly acquired water supply.[47]

The lack of adequate water for most of the period, however, explained the generally filthy streets, of which the city's visitors complained, and in contemporary opinion was also responsible for the toll of death from yellow fever and cholera, which periodically cast a pall over the usually bustling city. Common sewers were lacking as late as the early forties, and pigs still served as scavengers for garbage. Broken pavements added to the hazards of urban transit as horse-drawn vehicles rattled in profusion along the crowded streets; and the duskiness of the thoroughfares, even after the introduction of gas lighting in the middle twenties, aggravated problems of both traffic and crime. Housing conditions for the poor, above all in the vice-ridden Five Points area—today's Chinatown—were deplorable; and many observers, especially those from Germany, pointed to the need for breathing spaces in the form of parks, squares, and public pleasure grounds.[48]

Yet despite these inadequacies in the physical and administrative aspects of the fast growing city, commentators of this generation, more than ever before, detected a dynamism in the life of New York that derived in part from the vitality of its fluid, effervescent society, in part from the rapidly accelerating vigor of its commercial life. As Theodore Dwight wrote in 1833, "Whoever visits New York feels as he does in a watchmaker's shop; everybody goes there for the true time, and feels on leaving it as if he had been wound up or regulated anew. . . . He hears a clicking, as it were, on all sides of him, and finds everything he looks at in movement, and not a nook or corner but what is brim-ful of business. Apparently there is no inactivity; that is, no person is quiescent both in body and mind at once. The reason of this is, that the lazy are excited by the perpetual motion of the busy, or at least compelled to bestir themselves to avoid being run over." [49]

But, for all such signs of progress and activity, there were a transiency and disorder in this Jacksonian urban scene which both the rapidity of the city's growth and the increasing participation of the average man in its politics help to explain. Asa Greene caught the undisciplined variety of its still adolescent character in the concluding paragraph of his *A Glance at New York* (1837): "New York is a very great city; a very populous city; a very expensive city; a very scarce-of-hotels city; a remarkably religious city; a sadly over-run-with-law-and-physic city; a surprisingly newspaperial city; a rather queerly governed city; an uncommon badly watered city; a very considerable of a rum city; a very full-of-fires city; a pretty tolerably well-hoaxed city: and, moreover, a city moderately abounding in foul streets, rogues, dandies, mobs, and several other things, concerning which it is not necessary to come to any specific conclusion." New York of the thirties reminded Frances Kemble of a fair, "an irregular collection of temporary buildings, erected for some casual purpose, full of life, animation, and variety, but not meant to endure for any length of time." And as late as the middle forties, as far as the amenities of urban living were concerned, it was still a city of fires and fevers, awaiting the attributes of urban maturity which only administrative experience and scientific progress could supply.[50]

NEW YORK IN 1817

The provincial, unkempt, yet self-assertive society that was New York City in the years immediately following the close of the War of 1812 is realistically portrayed in Henry B. Fearon's *Sketches of America,* published in London in 1819. Fearon arrived in New York on August 6, 1817. He toured the country for about ten months investigating conditions on behalf of thirty-nine English families who contemplated migration to the United States. Like most travelers of this postwar period he did not find it easy to praise American life.[51]

At one o'clock we anchored close to the city. A boy procured us two hackney coaches, from a distance of about a quarter of a mile. I offered him an English shilling, having no other small coin in my possession. He would not take so little; "For as how I guess it is not of value. I have been *slick* in going to the stand right away." This was said with a tone of independence, which, although displeasing to my pride, was not so to my judgment. Mr. Adams satisfied the young republican by giving him half-a-dollar. . . . There was no sense of having received a favour in the boy's countenance or manner. . . . A great number of people were on the wharf looking at us and our vessel. Many of them were of the labouring class. They were not better clothed than men in a similar condition in England; but they were more erect in their posture, less care-worn in their countenances; the thought of "the morrow" did not seem to form a part of their ideas; and among them there were no beggars. Intermixed with these were several of the mercantile and richer classes. Large straw hats prevailed; trowsers were universal. The general costume of these persons was inferior to men in the same rank of life in England. Their whole appearance was loose, slovenly, careless, and not remarkable for cleanliness. The wholesale stores which front the river, have not the most attractive appearance. The carts are long and narrow, drawn by one horse; the hackney coaches are open at the sides, being suited to this warm climate . . . : the charge 25 per cent. higher than in London. . . . The general mode of living for those who do not keep house, is at hotels, taverns, or private boarding-houses. My present residence is at one of the latter. Here are two public apartments, one for a sitting, the other a dining room. At present, about forty sit down to table. The lady of the house presides; the other ladies, who are boarders, being placed on her left. The hours are—breakfast, eight o'clock; dinner, half past three; tea, seven; supper, ten. American breakfasts are celebrated for their profusion: presenting eggs, meat of various kinds, fish, and fowls. . . . The hours of eating are attended by all with precision: charge, two dollars per diem, exclusive of wine. The entire expense is about 18 dollars per week. . . .

I have walked alone through the streets for the purpose of forming an independent judgment. Every object is new. I hardly dare trust myself in forming conclusions: one most cheering fact is indisputable, the absence of *irremediable* distress. The street population bears an aspect essentially different from that of London, or large English towns. One striking feature consists in the number of blacks, many of whom are *finely* dressed, the females very ludicrously so, showing a partiality to white muslin dresses, artificial flowers, and pink shoes. I saw but few well-dressed white ladies, but am informed that the greater part are at present at the springs of Balstan and Saratoga. The dress of the men is rather deficient in point of neatness and gentility. Their appearance, in common with that of the ladies and children, is sallow, and what we should call unhealthy. . . . In a British town of any importance, you cannot walk along a leading street for half an hour without meeting with almost every variety of size, dress, and appearance among the inhabitants; whilst, on the contrary, here they seem all of one family. . . . The young men are tall, thin, and solemn; their dress is universally trowsers, and very generally loose great coats. Old men, in our English idea of that phrase, appear very rare. . . .

The shops (or stores, as they are called) have nothing in their exterior to recommend them; there is not even an attempt at tasteful display. The linen and woollen drapers (dry good stores, as they are denominated) leave quantities of their goods loose on boxes in the street, without any precaution against theft. . . . A great number of excellent private dwellings are built of red painted brick, which gives them a peculiarly neat and clean appearance. In Broad-way and Wall-street trees are planted by the side of the pavement. . . . Most of the streets are dirty: in many of them sawyers are preparing wood for sale, and all are infested with pigs,—circumstances which indicate a lax police.

Upon the whole, a walk through New York will disappoint an Englishman: there is, on the surface of society, a carelessness, a laziness, an unsocial indifference, which freezes the blood and disgusts the judgment. An evening stroll along Broad-way, when the lamps are alight, will please more than one at noon-day. The shops then look rather better, though their proprietors, of course, remain the same: their cold indifference may, by themselves, be mistaken for independence, but no person of thought and observation will ever concede to them that they have selected a wise mode of exhibiting that dignified feeling. I disapprove most decidedly of the obsequious servility of many London shopkeepers, but I am not prepared to go the length of those in New York, who stand with their hats on, or sit or lie along their counters, smoking segars, and spitting in every direction, to a degree offensive to any man of decent feelings. . . .

Both wholesale and retail wine and spirit sellers are grocers: their establishments are called grocery stores. A great proportion of the retail are small chandlers' shops, and are often denominated grog-shops. They are usually at the corners of streets, and mostly owned by Irishmen. Their chief commodity is New England, or what is emphatically called "Yankee" rum. All spirits are commonly drunk mixed with cold water, without sugar. . . . It is estimated that there are 1500 spirit-shops in this city; a fact opposed to my first impressions of American habits, which, on the point of sobriety, were favourable, judging from the absence of broils and of drunkards in the streets: but more attentive observation, aided by the information of old residents, enables me to state that the quantity of malt-liquor and spirits drunk by the inhabitants of New York, much exceeds the amount consumed by the same extent of English population. The beastly drunkard is a character unknown here; yet but too many are throughout the day under the influence of liquor, or what is not inappropriately termed "half-and-half!" a state too prevalent among the labouring classes and the negroes. Many date the source of this to the *extremes* of the climate. Another and a leading cause is, that numbers of the lower orders are European emigrants. They bring their habits with them. They are here better employed and better paid than they were in the country which gave them birth; and they partake too largely of the infirmities of our nature to be provident during the sunshine of prosperity. . . .

Returned to New York, I visited the several public exhibitions. The first in order was the "Museum," the collection of which is small—in excellent condition, and displayed with much taste. . . .

"The Academy of Fine Arts," as it is called, is exhibited in the same building. The collection is small; and, upon the whole, very indifferent, with the exception of two or three rustic pieces. Among the casts, there are a Venus, an Apollo, and a fighting gladiator. . . .

Mr. Van Derlyn, an artist of considerable merit, has a small exhibition, in which is a well-executed copy of Lefebre's Napoleon. . . .

There is a mechanical Panorama, exhibiting much ingenious mechanism. The wax-work exhibition is tolerably good: the dresses are splendid. The figure of the Goddess of Liberty feeding the American eagle is beautiful and interesting.

The *Theatre* is about the size of the "Royal Circus," and as well fitted up as the second-rate London theatres. . . . I went to the pit, concluding that, with an allowance for the difference of country, it would resemble the same department in an English establishment; but found it consisted of none in dress, manners, appearance, or habits above the order of our Irish bricklayers;—a strong fact this to prove the good payment of labour. Here were men that, if in London, could hardly buy a pint of porter—and should they ever think of seeing a play, must take up their abode among the gods in the upper gallery: yet, in America, they can pay three-quarters of a dollar—free from care, and without feeling, on the following morning, that they must compensate, by deprivation or extraordinary labour, for their extravagance. Many wore their hats, and several stood up during the performance: there did not seem to be any power which could prevent either practice. The boxes were respectably filled: the female part of the audience made considerable display. Between the acts, gentlemen withdrew: indeed at this period the house, in every part, was deserted, except by the ladies. The cause of this practice is to indulge in the fatal habit of rum-drinking. A part of the gallery is allotted for negroes, they not being admitted into any other part of the house.

GREENWICH VILLAGE—HAVEN FROM YELLOW FEVER: 1822

The filthiness of parts of the city, which its critics noted, helped to cause the periodic epidemics of yellow fever and cholera which struck New York frequently between 1790 and the 1860's. Upon the first sign of the scourge, the city government encouraged the residents to leave the affected section, barricaded the streets, and instituted such countermeasures as spreading quicklime and coal dust in the gutters and setting fires to purify the air. Those of the residents who could do so fled to the neighboring village of Greenwich which until the 1820's was presumably remote enough from the city to provide reasonable safety from the disease. The consequences of these periodic flights to Greenwich were described by Peter Neilson, a Glasgow businessman who arrived in New York when the yellow fever epidemic of 1822 was at its height. The following excerpt is from his *Recollections of a Six Years' Residence in the United States of America,* published in Glasgow in 1833.[52]

We cast anchor opposite to a part of the town deemed sufficiently healthy, nearly three miles above the point which forms the southern boundary of the city. On going ashore, the bustle that prevailed was beyond description, nearly the whole of the business-part of the city being removed out to the fields which skirt the suburbs. An immense variety of temporary wooden buildings, such as may be seen at Glasgow during the fair, were speedily erected for the accommodation of the citizens; and the business transacted here during two months was prodigious; some of these buildings were fitted up as hotels, where 200 or 300 people were boarded, but the accommodation for beds, etc. at such a time, may easily be conceived to have been none of the best. For such accommodation, however, people were very happy to pay an extravagant price; and in many instances, in the first hurry of the business, until a sufficiency of booths were erected, respectable persons were obliged for nights to bivouac in the fields. This may give an idea of what formidable terrors the first appearance of the yellow fever creates. . . .

In this irregular and temporary city in the field, you might find in one groupe, banking-houses, insurance offices, coffee-houses, auctioneers' salesrooms, dry goods, hardware, and grocery stores, milliners' shops, barbers' shops, and last, though not least, a suitable proportion of grog and soda-water shops. . . .

This state of matters continued till nearly the end of October, when a slight black frost appeared, which instantly dissipated all fears on account of yellow fever, and the consequent numerous removals back to the city, resembled the breaking up of the camp of some great army.

JAMES FENIMORE COOPER TO THE DEFENSE: MID-1820'S

Although Cooper's censure of Americans is more often remembered than his praise of them, it was the hypercritics like Henry B. Fearon whose writings prompted the American novelist to come to a somewhat lukewarm defense of New York City and other parts of eastern America in his *America and the Americans,* a work which, when originally published in 1828, was entitled *Notions of the Americans. Picked up by a Travelling Bachelor.* Cooper had resided for some years in the vicinity of New York before moving to the city in 1822. In *America and the Americans* he describes New York as it was in 1826 when he went to France to serve as consul at Lyons. Written during 1827 and 1828, the book seems to have had a twofold purpose: to chronicle Lafayette's New World tour, which occurred in 1824, and at the same time to correct the impressions of America left by overly critical travelers of the preceding two decades. The book takes the form of a series of letters written by a fictitious European traveler who arrived in New York at the time Lafayette did. Despite this literary device, the work provides a perceptive, sane, and generally accurate account of the city which Cooper knew as a resident, the New York whose rapid growth confirmed his opinion that "a new era" was "about to dawn" upon a United States which had "ceased to creep" and had now begun "to walk erect among the powers of earth." In the following comment Cooper appears to be advising his readers that New York and its residents are not as crude as they have been painted, and that even though the leveling tendencies in the society do not enlist his entire approval, they are understandable consequences of the rapidity of change and "effervescence" in the New York scene.[53]

In construction, New York embraces every variety of house, between that of the second-rate English town residence, and those temporary wooden tenements that are seen in the skirts of most large cities. I do not think, however, that those absolutely miserable, filthy abodes which are often seen in Europe, abound here. The houses of the poor are not indeed large, like those in which families on the continent are piled on one another for six or seven stories, but they are rarely old and tottering; for the growth of the place . . . forces them out of existence before they have had time to decay. I have been told, and I think it probable, that there are not five hundred buildings in New York, that can date further back than the peace of '83. A few old Dutch dwellings yet remain. . . .

In outward appearance, New York, but for two things, would resemble a part of London that should include fair proportions of Westminster (without the great houses and recent improvements), the city, and Wapping. The points of difference are owing to the fact that, probably without an exception, the exterior of all the houses are painted, and that there is scarce a street in the place which is not more or less lined with trees. . . . The common practice is to deepen the colour of the bricks by a red paint, and then to interline them with white. . . . But, in many instances, I saw dwellings of a lively cream colour; and there are also several varieties of stone that seem to be getting much in use latterly. . . .

I have elsewhere said that the city of New York is composed of inhabitants from all the countries of Christendom. Beyond a doubt a very large majority, perhaps nine-tenths, are natives of the United States; but it is not probable that one-third who live here first saw the light on the island of Manhattan. It is computed that one in three are either natives of New England, or are descendants of those who have emigrated from that portion of the country. To these must be added the successors of the Dutch, the English, the French, the Scotch and the Irish, and not a few who came in their proper persons from the countries occupied by these several nations. In the midst of such a mélange of customs and people, it is exceedingly difficult to extract anything like a definite general character. . . .

As might be expected, the general society of New York bears a strong impression of its commercial character. In consequence of the rapid growth of the city, the number of families that may be properly classed among those which have long been distinguished in its history for their wealth and importance, bears a much smaller proportion to its entire population than that of most other places. . . . Still, a much larger class of what in Europe forms the *élite* of society exists here, than strangers commonly suppose. . . .

It strikes me that both a higher and a lower order of men mingle in commerce here, than is seen elsewhere, if, perhaps, the better sort of English merchants be excepted. Their intimate relations on " 'Change" bring them all, more or less, together in the saloons; nor can the associations well be avoided, until the place shall attain a size, which must leave every one the perfect master of his own manner of living. That hour is fast approaching for New York, and with it, I think, must come a corresponding change in the marshalling of its coteries. . . .

But it is not difficult to see that society in New York, in consequence of its extraordinary increase, is rather in a state of effervescence than settled, and, where that is the case, I presume you will not be surprised to know, that the lees sometimes get nearer to the surface than is desirable.

MEN AND MANNERS IN JACKSONIAN TIMES

Most observers of the New York scene in Jacksonian days had an eye for the behavior of those "average men" for whom Cooper showed some disdain. The undisciplined activity of the volunteer fire fighters, the perfunctory eating habits of New Yorkers, at the quick-lunch houses, and the hubbub and babel at the wharves of this "grand focus of American commerce" excited the interest of Captain Basil Hall, an articulate Scot who devoted himself to writing and travel after serving in the Napoleonic wars. Following are excerpts from his *Travels in North America in the Years 1827 and 1828,* the product of his first long tour, taken in company with his wife and child.[54]

As we passed along, many things recalled the seaports of England to my thoughts, although abundant indications of another country lay on all hands. The signs over the shop doors were written in English; but the language we heard spoken was different in tone from what we had been accustomed to. Still it was English. Yet there was more or less of a foreign air in all we saw, especially about the dress and gait of the men. Negroes and negresses also were seen

First day of May in New York.—A General Move.

The J. Clarence Davies Collection, Museum of the City of New York

NEW YORK DAY BY DAY

1830's AND 1840's

The demand for houses in New York of the 1830's encouraged the Gothamite's proclivity to change his residence. On February 1, landlords set the rents. Tenants who could not meet them had to move on the first of May. The resulting scene, as in this woodcut of Broadway near St. Paul's Chapel (above), presented the visitor with a "ludicrous spectacle"—streets "filled with carts laden with furniture, porters, servants, children, all carrying their respective movables."

Museum of the City of New York

The scarcity of houses also forced many New Yorkers to resort to living in boarding houses and hotels. Visitors were disturbed at this transient way of life, but many passed agreeable hours in settings such as the one depicted in this "Scene in a Fashionable Boarding House" (right), a lithograph issued by J. H. Bufford, in about 1840.

Retrenchment after the Panic of 1837 led to the popularity of serious entertainment, such as lyceum lectures, which were "all the vogue" in the 1840's. In the unsigned pen and ink drawing (*ca.* 1841) (below) the meteorologist James P. Espy is delivering a lyceum lecture to a generally responsive audience at Clinton Hall.

Museum of the City of New York

THE MID-NINETEENTH-CENTURY CITY

Bustle and activity set the tone of life in New York at the turn of the 1850's. Typically busy was this section of Broadway skirting City Hall Park (top), as portrayed in a lithograph by Deroy from a painting by August Köllner. At the right, the famous Astor House has replaced John Jacob Astor's dwelling; St. Paul's Chapel is next door; and the spire of Trinity Church looms in the distance. At the left, with its enticing posters, is Barnum's Museum.

By the fifties, the fashionable residential section had moved northward to the vicinity of Washington Square, shown here as painted by Major Otto Bötticher in 1851. In the foreground, members of the Seventh Regiment parade; on the east side of the Square are the Gothic edifice of the University of the City of New York (now New York University) and the Reformed Dutch Church.

The undisciplined behavior of the volunteer fire laddies provided an almost continuous show for visitors of the fifties. The companies vied to arrive first at a fire, as Volunteer Engineer Company 21 is seen doing in this lithograph by N. Currier, 1854. It is one of a series of four, entitled "The Life of a Fireman." A watchman, constantly on duty, rang the alarm bell on the roof of the City Hall at the right to indicate the location of the fire.

The J. Clarence Davies Collection, Museum of the City of New Y

The Edward W. C. Arnold Collection; photograph court of Museum of the City of New York

The J. Clarence Davies Collection, Museum of the City of New Y

in abundance on the wharfs. The form of most of the wheeled carriages was novel; and we encountered several covered vehicles, on which was written in large characters, ICE. . . .

At two o'clock in the morning . . . I was awakened by loud cries of Fire! fire! . . . In a few minutes the deep rumbling sound of the engines was heard, mingling in a most alarming way with the cheers of the firemen, the loud rapping of the watchmen at the doors and window-shutters of the sleeping citizens, and various other symptoms of momentous danger, and the necessity of hot haste. . . . A second and far more furious alarm brought all the world to the windows. The church bells were clanging violently on all hands. . . .

On the top of the City Hall, . . . a firewarden or watchman is constantly stationed, whose duty when the alarm is given, is to hoist a lantern at the extremity of a long arm attached to the steeple, and to direct it towards the fire, as a sort of beacon, to instruct the engines what course to steer. There was something singularly striking in this contrivance, which looked as if a great giant, with a blood-red finger, had been posted in the midst of the city, to warn the citizens of their danger.

I succeeded by quick running in getting abreast of a fire engine; but although it was a very ponderous affair, it was dragged along so smartly by its crew of some six-and-twenty men, aided by a whole legion of boys, all bawling as loud as they could, that I found it difficult to keep up with them. On reaching the focus of attraction, the crowd of curious persons like myself began to thicken, while the engines came dashing in amongst us from every avenue, in the most gallant and business-like style.

Four houses, built entirely of wood, were on fire from top to bottom, and sending up a flame that would have defied a thousand engines. But nothing could exceed the dauntless spirit with which the attempt was made. In the midst of a prodigious noise and confusion, the engines were placed along the streets in a line, at the distance of about two hundred feet from one another, and reaching to the bank of the East River, as that inland sea is called, which lies between Long Island and the main. The suction hose of the last engine in the line, or that next the stream, being plunged into the river, the water was drawn up, and then forced along a leathern hose or pipe to the next engine, and so on, till at the tenth link in this curious chain, it came within range of the fire. As more engines arrived, they were marshalled by the superintendent into a new string; and in about five minutes after the first stream of water had been brought to bear on the flames, another was sucked along in like manner, and found its way, leap by leap, to the seat of the mischief. . . .

The chief things to find fault with on this occasion, were the needless shouts and other uproarious noises, which obviously helped to exhaust the men at the engines, and the needless forwardness, or it may be called fool-hardiness, with which they entered houses on fire, or climbed upon them by means of ladders, when it must have been apparent to the least skilful person, that their exertions were utterly hopeless. A small amount of discipline, of which, by the way, there was not a particle, might have corrected the noise; and the other evil, I think, might have been removed, by a machine recently invented in Edinburgh, and found to be efficacious on like occasions. . . . I lost no time in writing home for a model of the whole apparatus, which I received just before leaving America, and left with a friend, to be presented to the Fire Department of New York. I hope they may find it useful in that city, which seems to be more plagued with fires than any town in the world. . . .

On the 21st of May [1827], I accompanied two gentlemen, about three o'clock, to a curious place called the Plate House, in the very centre of the business part of the busy town of New York.

We entered a long, narrow, and rather dark room, or gallery, fitted up like a coffeehouse, with a row of boxes on each side made just large enough to hold four persons, and divided into that number by fixed arms limiting the seats. Along the passage, or avenue, between the rows of boxes, which was not above four feet wide, were stationed sundry little boys, and two waiters, with their jackets off—and good need too, as will be seen. At the time we entered, all the compartments were filled except one, of which we took possession. There was an amazing clatter of knives and forks; but not a word audible to us was spoken by any of the guests. The silence, however, on the part of the company, was amply made up for by the rapid vociferations of the attendants, especially of the boys, who were gliding up and down, and across the passage, inclining their heads for an instant, first to one box, then to another, and receiving the whispered wishes of the company, which they straightway bawled out in a loud voice, to give notice of what fare was wanted. It quite baffled my comprehension to imagine how the people at the upper end of the room, by whom a communication was kept up in some magical way with the kitchen, could contrive to distinguish between one order and the other. . . .

We had been told by old stagers of the excellence of the corned beef, and said to the boy we should all three take that dish. Off the gnome glanced from us like a shot, to attend to the beck of another set of guests, on the opposite side of the room; but, in flying across the passage, turned his face towards the upper end of the apartment and called out, "Three beef, 8!" the last word of his sentence referring to the number of our box. In a trice we saw the waiters gliding down the avenue to us, with three sets of little covered dishes, each containing a plate, on which lay a large, piping hot slice of beef. Another plate was at the same time given, with a moderate proportion of mashed potatoes on it, together with a knife, and a fork on which was stuck a piece of bread. As the waiters passed along, they took occasion to incline their ears to the right and to the left, to receive fresh orders, and also to snatch up empty tumblers, plates, and knives and forks. The multiplicity and rapidity of these orders and movements made me giddy. Had there been one set to receive and forward the orders, and another to put them in execution, we might have seen better through the confusion; but all hands, little and big together, were screaming out with equal loudness and quickness—"Half plate beef, 4!"—"One potato, 5!"—"Two apple pie, one plum pudding, 8!" and so on.

There could not be, I should think, fewer than a dozen boxes, with four people in each; and as everyone seemed to be eating as fast as he could, the extraordinary bustle may be conceived. We were not in the house above twenty minutes, but we sat out two sets of company, at least. . . .

On the first day of every month throughout the year, a number of packet ships sail from this grand focus of American commerce, to various parts of the world; and as they all start about the same hour, no small bustle is the necessary consequence. Exactly as the clock strikes ten, a steam-boat with the passengers for the different packets, leaves the wharf, close to a beautiful public promenade called the Battery. We resolved to take a trip in this boat on the morning in question, as if we had been embarking for a voyage, but merely to see how things were managed. The crowd on the shore was immense. Troops of friends, assembled to take leave, were jostled by tradesmen, hotel keepers, and hackney coachmen, urging the payment of their accounts, and by newsmen disposing of papers wet from the printing press, squeezing amongst carts, waggons, and wheelbarrows, filled with luggage. Through this crowd of idle and busy folks, we elbowed our way, with some difficulty, and at last found ourselves on the deck of the steamer. Here a new description of confusion presented itself. There were no fewer, the captain assured us, than one hundred and sixty persons on board his boat at that moment, destined for the different packets; . . . the crush, therefore, may be imagined!

At length we put off, and paddled alongside of two packets for Havre, two for New Orleans, and one for each of the following ports, Charleston, London, and Liverpool. Every set of passengers was accompanied by a huge mountain of chests, portmanteaus, bags, writing-desks, bird-cages, bandboxes, cradles, and the whole family of great-coats, boat-cloaks, umbrellas, and parasols. The captains of the several packets were of course on board of the steamer, in charge of their monstrous letter bags; while close under their lee came the watch maker, with a regiment of chronometers, which he guarded and coddled with as much care as if they had been his children. The several stewards of the packets formed a material portion of our motley crew, each being surrounded, like the tenants of the ark, with every living thing, hens, ducks, turkeys, to say nothing of beef and mutton in joints, bags of greens, baskets of eggs, bread, and all the et caeteras of sea luxury. Slender clerks, belonging to the different mercantile houses, flitted about with bundles of letters, bills of lading, and so forth. . . .

At one end of the deck stood a very lively set of personages, chattering away at a most prodigious rate, as if the fate of mightiest monarchies, to say nothing of Republics, depended upon their volubility. This group consisted of a complete company of French players, with all their lap-dogs, black servants, helmets, swords, and draperies—the tinsel and glitter of their gay profession. They had been acting for some time at New York, and were now shifting the scene to New Orleans, as the sickly season had gone past. Our ears could also catch, at the same moment, the mingled sounds of no less than five different languages, French, Spanish, German, Italian, and English, all running on without the parties having the least apparent consciousness that there was anything remarkable in such a confusion of tongues.

The attitudes of servants and especially Negroes interested Karl Bernhard, Duke of Saxe-Weimar-Eisenach, whose trip to the United States in 1825 and 1826 was prompted by the thought that he might ultimately settle in the New World. He arrived in gaslit New York City in mid-September, 1825. In the following excerpt from his *Travels Through North America* he describes the Negro community of the period and a parade of the city's Negro residents celebrating the forthcoming abolition of slavery in the city and state.[55]

On returning home at night, I observed that the streets were not well lighted. I was afterwards informed, that the corporation of the city was just engaged in a quarrel with the gas-company relative to the lamps; this quarrel protracted the inconvenience, though it was somewhat lessened by the numerous stores, which are kept open till a late hour, and are very splendidly lighted with gas. The gas-lights burn in handsome figures; at a music-store, I saw one in form of a harp. . . .

The servants are generally negroes and mulattos; most of the white servants are Irish; the Americans have a great abhorrence of servitude. Liveries are not to be seen; the male servants wear frock coats. All the families complain of bad servants and their impudence, because the latter consider themselves on an equality with their employers. Of this insolence of servants I saw daily examples. Negroes and mulattos are abundant here, but they generally rank low, and are labourers. There are but a few slaves in the state of New York, and even these are to be freed in the year 1827, according to a law passed by senate of the state. There are public schools established for the instruction of coloured children and . . . there are several churches belonging to the coloured population; most of them are Methodists, some Episcopalians. A black minister, who was educated in an Episcopalian seminary, is said to be a good preacher. . . .

On the afternoon of the third of October, there was a great procession of negroes, some of them well dressed, parading through the streets, two by two, preceded by music and a flag. An African club, called the Wilberforce Society, thus celebrated the anniversary of the abolition of slavery in New York, and concluded the day by a dinner and ball. The coloured people of New York, belonging to this society, have a fund of their own, raised by weekly subscription, which is employed in assisting sick and unfortunate blacks. This fund, contained in a sky-blue box, was carried in the procession; the treasurer holding in his hand a large gilt key; the rest of the officers wore ribands of several colours, and badges like the officers of free masons; marshals with long staves walked outside of the procession. During a quarter of an hour, scarcely any but black faces were to be seen in Broadway.

The day-to-day behavior of the rank and file of New Yorkers on the turn of the 1830's finds colorful description in James Boardman's *America and the Americans.* Little is known about the author save that he described himself as an "independent 'business man.' " He arrived in New York in June of 1829 and stayed in the United States until May 1, 1831. His sympathies were clearly with America's "common men," whose "high character and appearance" he admired. He liked the country so well that he determined "to disabuse the British public of their prejudices" regarding it. The following excerpts describe the living conditions of the average man, his amusements and celebrations, and the "movable propensity" of New Yorkers as exhibited in their tendency to change their residence every year.[56]

My first impressions, on landing in New York,—and they were subsequently confirmed,—were the high character and appearance of the working classes; . . .

The carters, workmen, and others, who earn their bread by the sweat of their brow, appeared extremely well clothed; were intelligent; and, if addressed civilly, were civil in return; yet without any doffing, or even touching the hat, or making the slightest approaches to servility to those who, according to English phraseology, would be styled their betters.

All exhibited an independence of feeling not observable in the same classes of society in England; and yet nothing like insolent vulgarity was apparent. . . .

The boarding-houses of those numerous classes, the smaller shopkeepers and merchants' clerks, are in general miserably furnished. . . .

It is by no means uncommon to see four, or even five or six beds in the same room, and these are of the meanest description, without furniture even in the depth of winter: a chest of drawers is, indeed, a rara avis; each boarder making a general depository of his trunk or portmanteau, as poor Jack does of his chest in the forecastle of a ship. . . .

Oyster cellars abound; and immense quantities of these luxuries are likewise vended from small waggons in the streets; at which locomotive shops, the pedestrian may be supplied with biscuits, pepper, and ginger beer; in short, for a few pence, the carter or mechanic has a whet which might satisfy even a gourmand. . . .

July 4 celebration, 1830. Although the more intellectual part of the population, as the members of literary and scientific institutions, and the ministers of religion, might be content to celebrate the occasion by delivering patriotic odes and addresses, the joyful feelings of the bulk were expressed in a manner more congenial to their tastes; and a review of some thousand militia, cavalry, infantry, and artillery, with marchings and counter-marchings in close order, open order, and, perchance, disorder, together with a liberal expenditure of gunpowder, formed the grand attraction of the day. . . .

A military command is the acme of the ambition of an American store-keeper, and a hundred Major Sturgeons forgot their counters in the delights of pie-bald chargers, leopard-skin housings, and gay uniforms; each of whom, either by his apparent knowledge of tactics, or, what seemed to have more influence, his knowledge of holiday display, endeavoured to win a smile from the delighted fair who crowded the windows, or attract the admiration of the countless thousands who filled the streets. . . .

"The moment night with dusky mantle covered the skies," hundreds of illuminated booths, skirting the more open quarters of the city, displayed their attractions to the moving multitude, in the shape of fringed hams, pickled oysters, garnished lobsters, and roasted pigs, with lemons in their mouths; . . . all which good things might be washed down with Philadelphia porter, ginger beer, foaming mead, or other beverages, more exhilarating perhaps, but less innocent.

Although these places are the resort of the working population, a little excess in whom, at this joyous moment, might be forgiven, I did not, in a perambulation of several hours, witness a single instance of what could be termed disorderly conduct.

During the whole of this festival, every street and alley re-echoed with the reports of petty fireworks, of which quantities are brought from China, no less to the profit of the dealers than to the delight of all the boys, whose little savings banks are drained upon the occasion. . . .

In spite of the declaration of the venerable Franklin, . . . that "three removes are as bad as a fire," the inhabitants of New York are the most locomotive people on the face of the earth. This movable propensity appears to be partly caused by a progressive state of prosperity; for, as the value of property in this city has always been steadily increasing, the owners are unwilling to grant leases, hoping each successive year to add materially to their rent rolls.

In consequence of this encouraging state of things, an annual valuation takes place of every rented building in the city, and one day is appropriated to the letting of tenements and another for removals. These important seasons are the first of February and the first of May. On the former, the landlords, which term, curious enough, is still preserved by the republicans, visit their tenants; and unless arrangements have been previously entered upon, they state the rents they expect to receive for the ensuing year. If the occupier of a building assents to the proposals, the affair is ended; but if the reply is in the negative, the owner placards the walls with the words, "To Let," to which is sometimes added the rent demanded; and on the evening of this day it is common to see at least one third of the houses and stores thus ticketed, and these remain until tenants are found. At last comes the all-important first of May, which, to a stranger just arriving, presents the most singular and ludicrous spectacle imaginable,—nothing less than a whole city turned topsy-turvy, thousands of persons being in the act of removal, the streets filled with carts laden with furniture, porters, servants, children, all carrying their respective movables, from the candelabra of the drawing-room to the fish-kettle of the "foolish fat scullion," and the gingerbread wares of the nursery.

As the operations of entering upon and quitting the houses are simultaneous, the confusion within doors is in perfect keeping with the scene displayed in the streets, the whole affording no bad illustration of chaos.

To an Englishman, with his strong local attachments, this system of change would be an intolerable nuisance; but the New Yorker, no doubt from habit, not only looks upon it as a matter of course, but seems to feel an elevation of spirits at the anticipation of this agreeable variety in his social existence; and it is no uncommon circumstance to meet with individuals who have resided in a dozen different houses in as many years; and yet who speak of their wish to try the advantages of another quarter of the city when the proper season arrives.

The augmented transit facilities which implemented the northward thrust of the city in the 1820's and 1830's presented traffic hazards to which the old-time residents of New York were not accustomed. One of these was John Pintard, whose letters to his daughter provide a graphic picture of day-to-day developments in the Empire City from the close of the War of 1812 to the middle 1830's. Born in 1759, Pintard served his native city both as city inspector and as clerk of the Common Council. In his later years he was employed as secretary of the Mutual Insurance Company. The following comment on urban transit in New York's "omnibus era" is from the edition of his letters by Dorothy C. Barck, published in volumes 70 through 73 (1937–1940) of the New-York Historical Society *Collections*. It is reprinted with the permission of the New-York Historical Society, which owns the Pintard Manuscripts. The excerpt is from a letter dated March 1, 1833.[57]

[One] has only to step to the corner wh[ich] the B[roa]dway caravans pass every 5 minutes. From 8 to 10, they are crammed with business men, after 10 there is space eno[ugh]. Ladies going below or coming up at noon, take a seat in these accommodating vehicles, walk up for exercise & ride back or vice versa. 6 Tickets for 50 c[en]ts from Wall St[reet] to the upper part of B[roa]dway, 8 c[en]ts the ride. Indeed in the Greenwich carriages one may go a distance above 2 miles at the same rate. Take all these stages, West, No[rth] & East & they exceed 70, & from the cheapness of the Fare are always filled. These accommod[ation]s for intercourse have raised the value of Lots in the upper districts of our city & the number will increase with its growth. B[roa]dway is such a thoro'fare as to render it hazardous crossing the streets, to avoid wh[ich] I usually take a side st[reet] where I feel safe. . . .

The political assertiveness of the city's mechanics and artisans—a local manifestation of Jacksonian Democracy—was a subject of interest to foreign travelers on the turn of the 1830's. A meeting of mechanics and others in April 1829 resulted in the formation of a short-lived Workingmen's Party, which polled about 30 per cent of the New York City vote in that year. The ambitions of the "operative class" elicited comment from Thomas Hamilton, one of the most perceptive British visitors of the early thirties. Hamilton, a neighbor of Sir Walter Scott, had already attained some reputation as a novelist and writer for *Blackwood's* magazine, when he came to America late in 1831. The following comment on the demands of the "Workies" is from the book which resulted, *Men and Manners in America,* published in London in 1833.[58]

The operative class have already formed themselves into a society, under the name of *"The Workies,"* in direct opposition to those who, more favoured by nature or fortune, enjoy the luxuries of life without the necessity of manual labour. These people make no secret of their demands, which to do them justice are few and emphatic. They are published in the newspapers, and may be read on half the walls of New York. Their first postulate is "EQUAL AND UNIVERSAL EDUCATION." . . . They solemnly declare that they will not rest satisfied, till every citizen in the United States shall receive the same degree of education, and start fair in the competition for the honours and offices of the state. . . . There are others who go still further, and boldly advocate the introduction of an AGRARIAN LAW, and a periodical division of property. These unquestionably constitute the *extrême gauche* of the Worky Parliament, but still they only follow out the principles of their less violent neighbours, and eloquently dilate on the justice and propriety of every individual being equally supplied with food and clothing; on the monstrous iniquity of one man riding in his carriage while another walks on foot, and after his drive discussing [over] a bottle of Champagne, while many of his neighbours are shamefully compelled to be content with the pure element. Only equalize property, they say, and neither would drink Champagne or water, but both would have brandy, a consummation worthy of centuries of struggle to attain.

All this is nonsense undoubtedly, nor do I say that this party, though strong in New York, is yet so numerous or so widely diffused as to create immediate alarm. In the elections, however, for the civic offices of the city, their influence is strongly felt; and there can be no doubt that as population becomes more dense, and the supply of labour shall equal, or exceed the demand for it, the strength of this party must be enormously augmented. . . . It is nothing to say, that the immense extent of fertile territory yet to be occupied by an unborn population will delay the day of ruin. It will delay, but it cannot prevent it.

MRS. TROLLOPE PRAISES NEW YORK: 1831

An unprecedented number of women left a record of the New York scene in travel accounts published between 1815 and 1845. One of these was Mrs. Anne Royall, America's first professional woman travel writer, who published ten volumes of travels in America between 1826 and 1831. Most of the female commentators were, however, Europeans. Two had accompanied their husbands on trips to the New World: Mrs. Basil Hall, in 1827, and Clara von Gerstner, in 1838. Two were intellectuals: freethinking Frances Wright and Harriet Martineau, the "Malthusian old maid," who was lionized in the city because of her writing on religious and economic subjects. The actress Frances Kemble published her *Journal* after she married and settled in the United States; and in the case of two others, Mrs. Felton and Sarah M. Maury, travel books were by-products of trips made for recreation or health. The most notorious for her comments was Mrs. Trollope, whose book, *The Domestic Manners of the Americans,* was to make her the symbol of British prejudice toward American society. Actually, despite her reputation for criticizing the country, no woman traveler of the period, with the possible exception of Frances Wright, was more enthusiastic about most features of New York than Mrs. Trollope, as the following excerpts from her controversial book, reprinted by permission of Dodd, Mead and Company, will reveal.[59]

New York . . . appeared to us . . . a lovely and a noble city. To us who had been so long travelling through half-cleared forests, and sojourning among an "I'm-as-good-as-you" population, it seemed, perhaps, more beautiful, more splendid, and more refined than it might have done, had we arrived there directly from London; but making every allowance for this, I must still declare that I think New York one of the finest cities I ever saw, and as much superior to every other in the Union (Philadelphia not excepted), as London to Liverpool, or Paris to Rouen. . . .

I think it covers nearly as much ground as Paris, but is much less thickly peopled. The extreme point is fortified towards the sea by a battery, and forms an admirable point of defence; but in these piping days of peace, it is converted into a public promenade, and one more beautiful, I should suppose, no city could boast. From hence commences the splendid Broadway, as the fine avenue is called, which runs through the whole city. This noble street may vie with any I ever saw, for its length and breadth, its handsome shops, neat awnings, excellent *trottoir,* and well-dressed pedestrians. . . . were it not so very far from all the old-world things which cling about the heart of an European, I should say that I never saw a city more desirable as a residence.

The dwelling houses of the higher classes are extremely handsome, and very richly furnished. Silk or satin furniture is as often, or oftener, seen than chintz; the mirrors are as handsome as in London; the cheffoniers, slabs, and marble tables as elegant. . . . Every part of their houses is well carpeted, and the exterior finishings, such as steps, railings, and door frames, are very superior. Almost every house has handsome green blinds on the outside. . . . I saw many rooms decorated within, exactly like those of an European *petite maîtresse.* . . .

The great defect in the houses is their extreme uniformity. . . . Mixed dinner parties of ladies and gentlemen . . . are very rare.

. . . we saw enough to convince us that there is society to be met with in New York, which would be deemed delightful any where. Cards are very seldom used; and music, from their having very little professional aid at their parties, is seldom, I believe, as good as what is heard at private concerts in London. . . .

If it were not for the peculiar manner of walking, which distinguishes all American women, Broadway might be taken for a French street, where it was the fashion for very smart ladies to promenade. The dress is entirely French; not an article (except perhaps the cotton stockings) must be English, on pain of being stigmatised as out of the fashion. Everything English is decidedly *mauvais ton;* English materials, English fashions, English accent, English manner, are all terms of reproach; and to say that an unfortunate looks like an English woman, is the cruellest satire which can be uttered. . . .

The hackney coaches are the best in the world, but abominably dear, and it is necessary to be on the *qui vive* in making your bargain with the driver; if you do not, he has the power of charging immoderately. On my first experiment I neglected this, and was asked two dollars and a half for an excursion of twenty minutes. When I referred to the waiter of the hotel, he asked if I had made a bargain. "No." "Then I expect" (with the usual look of triumph) "that the Yankee has been too smart for you."

The private carriages of New York are infinitely handsomer and better appointed than any I saw elsewhere; the want of smart liveries destroys much of the gay effect; but, on the whole, a New

York summer equipage, with the pretty women and beautiful children it contains, looks extremely well in Broadway, and would not be much amiss anywhere.

. . . again we enjoyed the elegant hospitality of New York. . . . In truth, were all America like this fair city, and all, no, only a small proportion of its population like the friends we left there, I should say, that the land was the fairest in the world.

PROSPERITY AND PANIC IN THE 1830'S

The overexpansion of the prosperous middle thirties and the depressed conditions that followed the ensuing panic of 1837 were described by two European travelers, one a Spaniard and the other an Englishman. One could hardly find a more succinct description of New York's flourishing economy of the middle thirties than that of Ramon de la Sagra, Spanish botanist, economist, and historian, who visited New York in 1835. A political liberal, Sagra was on his way back to Spain after a twelve years' sojourn in Cuba, where he had served as director of the botanical garden at Havana and professor of botany in the university there. He was the author of numerous works in the fields of economics and Cuban history. The following excerpt is from his *Cinco meses en los Estados-Unidos de la América del Norte desde el 20 de abril al 23 de setiembre de 1835.*[60]

We arrived on Sunday the 19th. In spite of the bad weather, the docks were crowded with people; elegant and commodious vehicles were stationed at the foot of streets bordered with sidewalks and unusually neat. Broadway is magnificent, especially at night, when gas light brightens its fine stores. . . .

But what pleases me most here is neither the appearance of the city, the width of the streets, the neatness of the dwellings, nor other externals; it is instead the tremendous commercial activity that I see, the continual pursuit of industry, the progress of the population, the general affluence and a certain air of well being which prevails among all classes. Since my arrival, I have spent my time surveying the city, and I have been astonished at the extraordinary development which it is experiencing at the moment. Everywhere they are building houses, repairing whole sections, constructing superb hotels, opening large squares, and as if to second this activity, laying out new streets and embankments. If, turning away from the city, one observes the dock area, the picture is not less vigorous. The whole length of the wharves, there rises up a forest of masts belonging to the vessels of many nations, and steamships engaged in trade among the various states of the Union. On the North River [the Hudson], the bay and its eastern arm, magnificent steamboats cross and recross without ceasing, coming and going at all hours of the day and night, laden with passengers, merchandise, and raw materials. With these ships, which furrow the water in all directions, mingle many little craft.

The dislocations and social expedients resulting from the panic that was the sequel to these expansive times are detailed in Captain Frederick Marryat's *Diary in America*. Marryat had attained his lieutenancy in the British Navy in 1812, and in 1814 was fighting on the American coast. Upon resigning in 1830, he took to writing. He had an established reputation as a novelist when he arrived in New York City in May of 1837. His flair for narrative is evident in the following excerpt, in which he describes conditions shortly after the panic struck.[61]

My appearance at New York was very much like bursting into a friend's house with a merry face when there is a death in it. . . .

Two hundred and sixty houses have already failed, and no one knows where it is to end. Suspicion, fear, and misfortune have taken possession of the city. . . .

The militia are under arms, as riots are expected. . . .

Nobody refuses to take the paper of the New York banks, although they virtually have stopped payment;—they never refuse anything in New York;—but nobody will give specie in change, and great distress is occasioned by this want of a circulating medium. Some of the shopkeepers told me that they had been obliged to turn away a hundred dollars a-day, and many a southerner, who has come up with a large supply of southern notes, has found himself a pauper, and has been indebted to a friend for a few dollars in specie to get home again. . . .

The distress for change has produced a curious remedy. Every man is now his own banker. Go to the theatres and places of public amusement, and, instead of change, you receive an I.O.U. from the treasury. At the hotels and oyster-cellars it is the same thing. Call for a glass of brandy and water and the change is fifteen tickets, each "good for one glass of brandy and water." At an oyster shop, eat a plate of oysters, and you have in return seven tickets, good for one plate of oysters each. It is the same everywhere.—The barbers give you tickets, good for so many shaves; and were there beggars in the streets, I presume they would give you tickets in change, good for so much philanthropy. Dealers, in general, give out their own bank-notes, or as they are called here, *shin-plasters,* which are good for one dollar, and from that down to two and a-half cents, all of which are redeemable, and redeemable only upon a general return to cash payments.

Hence arises another variety of exchange in Wall street.

"Tom, do you want any oysters for lunch to-day?"

"Yes!"

"Then here's a ticket, and give me two *shaves* in return. . . ."

A mania [for speculation] . . . had infected the people of America for two or three years previous to the crash: it was that of speculating in land; and to show the extent to which it had been carried on, we may take the following examples:—

The city of New York, which is built upon a narrow island about ten miles in length, at present covers about three miles of that distance, and has a population of three hundred thousand inhabitants. Building lots were marked out for the other seven miles; and, by calculation, these lots when built upon, would contain an additional population of one million and three-quarters. They were first purchased at from one hundred to one hundred and fifty dollars each, but, as the epidemic raged, they rose to upwards of two thousand dollars. At Brooklyn, on Long Island, opposite to New York, and about half a mile distant from it, lots were marked out to the extent of fourteen miles, which would contain an extra population of one million, and these were as eagerly speculated in.

DICKENS DESCRIBES NEW YORK: 1842

Like his compatriot Mrs. Trollope, Charles Dickens found more to admire in New York City than he did in most of the America he visited in 1842. He was impressed with the commercial prowess of "the beautiful metropolis of America" and thought its best society generally polished, refined, and always hospitable. He was amused, more than flattered, by the huge ball, given in his honor on February 14, the night after his arrival, especially when one local newspaper asserted that "Dickens was never in such society in England as he has seen in New York, and . . . its high and striking tone cannot fail to make an indelible impression on his mind." It was, indeed, a stupendous occasion:

the Park Theatre magnificently decorated and a reception by the mayor and other dignitaries before 3,000 people in full-dress attire. The public's adulation, however, did not blind the English novelist to the seamier side of the metropolis which he viewed through a reformer's eyes. He was repelled by its penal institutions, "an ill-managed lunatic asylum, a bad jail, a dismal workhouse, and a perfectly intolerable place of police-imprisonment." And its Five Points area he found the squalid equal of London's Seven Dials. Dickens' disapproval of this aspect of the society as well as his admiration for the city's physical and cultural achievement stand out in the following excerpts from his *American Notes for General Circulation,* published as a result of his trip.[62]

There are many by-streets, almost as neutral in clean colors, and positive in dirty ones, as by-streets in London; and there is one quarter, commonly called the Five Points, which, in respect of filth and wretchedness, may be safely backed against Seven Dials, or any other part of famed St. Giles's.

The great promenade and thoroughfare, as most people know, is Broadway; a wide and bustling street, which, from the Battery Gardens to its opposite termination in a country road, may be four miles long. . . .

This narrow thoroughfare . . . is Wall Street: the Stock Exchange and Lombard Street of New York. . . . Below, here by the water-side, where the bowsprits of ships stretch across the footway, and almost thrust themselves into the windows, lie the noble American vessels which have made their Packet Service the finest in the world. They have brought hither the foreigners who abound in all the streets: not, perhaps, that there are more here than in other commercial cities; but elsewhere they have particular haunts, and you must find them out; here they pervade the town. . . .

Again across Broadway, and so—passing from the many-colored crowd and glittering shops—into another long main street, the Bowery. A railroad yonder, see, where two stout horses trot along, drawing a score or two of people and a great wooden ark with ease. The stores are poorer here, the passengers less gay. Clothes ready made, and meat ready cooked, are to be bought in these parts; and the lively whirl of carriages is exchanged for the deep rumble of carts and wagons. . . .

Once more in Broadway! Here are the same ladies in bright colors, walking to and fro, in pairs and singly. . . . We are going to cross here. Take care of the pigs. Two portly sows are trotting up behind this carriage, and a select party of half a dozen gentlemen hogs have just now turned the corner. . . . They are the city scavengers, these pigs.

The streets and shops are lighted now; and as the eye travels down the long thoroughfare, dotted with bright jets of gas, it is reminded of Oxford Street or Piccadilly. Here and there a flight of broad stone cellar steps appears, and a painted lamp directs you to the Bowling Saloon, or Ten-Pin alley. . . . At other downward flights of steps are other lamps, marking the whereabouts of oyster cellars. . . .

Let us go on again; and passing this wilderness of an hotel with stores about its base . . . plunge into the Five Points. . . . We have seen no beggars in the streets by night or day; but of other kinds of strollers plenty. Poverty, wretchedness, and vice are rife enough where we are going now.

This is the place, these narrow ways, diverging to the right and left, and reeking everywhere with dirt and filth. Such lives as are led here, bear the same fruits here as elsewhere. The coarse and bloated faces at the doors have counterparts at home, and all the wide world over. . . .

What place is this, to which the squalid street conducts us? A kind of square of leprous houses, some of which are attainable only by crazy wooden stairs without. . . .

Here, too, are lanes and alleys, paved with mud knee-deep: underground chambers, where they dance and game; the walls bedecked with rough designs of ships, and forts, and flags, and American Eagles out of number: ruined houses, open to the street, whence, through wide gaps in the walls, other ruins loom upon the eye, as though the world of vice and misery had nothing else to show: hideous tenements which take their name from robbery and murder; all that is loathsome, drooping, and decayed is here.

Our leader has his hand upon the latch of "Almack's," and calls to us from the bottom of the steps; for the assembly-room of the Five-Point fashionables is approached by a descent. . . . Heyday! the landlady of Almack's thrives! A buxom fat mulatto woman, with sparkling eyes, whose head is daintily ornamented with a handkerchief of many colors. Nor is the landlord much behind her in his finery, being attired in a smart blue jacket, like a ship's steward, with a thick gold ring upon his little finger, and round his neck a gleaming golden watch-guard. How glad he is to see us! What will we please to call for? A dance? It shall be done directly, sir: "a regular breakdown." . . .

Here are the Tombs once more. The city watch-house is part of the building. It follows naturally on the sights we have just left. . . . What! do you thrust your common offenders against the police discipline of the town into such holes as these? Do men and women, against whom no crime is proved, lie here all night in perfect darkness, surrounded by . . . noisome vapors . . . and breathing this filthy and offensive stench? Why, such indecent and disgusting dungeons as these cells would bring disgrace upon the most despotic empire in the world!

. . . there are, in New York, excellent hospitals and schools, literary institutions, and libraries; and an admirable fire department (as, indeed, it should be, having constant practice) and charities of every sort and kind. . . .

There are three principal theatres. Two of them, the Park and the Bowery, are large, elegant, and handsome buildings, and are, I grieve to write it, generally deserted. The third, the Olympic, is a tiny show-box for vaudeville and burlesques. It is singularly well conducted by Mr. Mitchell, a comic actor of great quiet humor and originality, who is well remembered and esteemed by London playgoers. I am happy to report of this deserving gentleman, that his benches are usually well filled, and that his theatre rings with merriment every night. I had almost forgotten a small summer theatre, called Niblo's, with gardens and open-air amusements attached; but I believe it is not exempt from the general depression under which Theatrical Property, or what is humorously called by that name, unfortunately labors.

6. *A BUSTLING CITY (1845–1860)*

EYEWITNESSES LEAVE NO DOUBT that growth was the keynote of New York's development between 1845 and 1860, a growth so "rank" and "luxuriant" as to eclipse the progress of the middle thirties and so solid and enduring as to underwrite the transition from city to metropolis that had occurred by the close of the Civil War. "This is a great city, and is daily becoming greater," wrote the Manchester journalist Archibald Prentice in 1848; and his astonishment at the size and animation of the potential metropolis was almost invariably echoed by commentators of the succeeding decade. Sir Charles Lyell, the eminent Scottish geologist, was struck by the progress which had taken place between his first visit in 1841 and his second, four years later. The city, at last recovered from the depression that had plagued it between 1837 and 1843, now seethed with a universal and everlasting "bustle"—a "rush of life," as Thackeray commented in 1852—which amazed its residents and impressed its guests.[1]

"The city is spreading north . . . out of all reason and measure," wrote George Templeton Strong, in the later forties; "ten years more of this growth will carry the city beyond the Lower Reservoir." Streets appeared to be *daily* extended northward in this "Jack the Giant-killer's beanstalk" of a city; and barricades and scaffoldings furthered the now traditional impression of ceaseless change and growth. A "continuous chain" of omnibuses crowded Broadway, creating such a "crush of traffic" that a visitor of 1850 reported that "you often have to wait ten minutes before you are able to cross the street." Gone was the condescension with which British travelers had viewed Broadway a generation earlier. By the fifties they were willing to admit that London could not provide its equal. Not even the cluttered and dirty condition of many of the city's streets and pavements, which most of the foreign visitors continued to criticize, or the obstructing festoons of telegraph wires overhead checked their admiration for a city whose "monster hotels," handsome shops, and "stately mansions" equaled, if not surpassed, Old World standards.[2]

By the fifties, most of Broadway no longer presented the alternation of "poor wooden structures and splendid edifices" observed by travelers a generation earlier. Once a thoroughfare of small frame dwellings and three-story brick buildings, it now offered a succession of imposing marble, stone, or cast-iron-faced structures rising five or six stories in height—"high growths of iron, slender, strong . . . splendidly uprising toward clear skies," as Walt Whitman wrote in his paean to "Mannahatta" at the turn of the sixties. William Chambers, a prominent Edinburgh publisher, who visited the city in 1853, found its stores and hotels "more like the palaces of kings than places for the transaction of business." A. T. Stewart's dry-goods store, "a huge building of white marble," was one of these, as was also the St. Nicholas Hotel, between Broome and Spring streets, which, since its opening in January 1853, had outclassed the much admired Astor House. James Robertson, a visiting English businessman, called the St. Nicholas "perhaps the largest [hotel] in the world" and certainly "the most comfortable, and the most elegantly furnished in the States." Its 600 rooms accommodated upwards of a thousand guests; and at the time of his visit, in 1854, there were 322 servants in the establishment. Young Sir John Acton, the future historian, an official representative to the New York Exhibition of 1853, was impressed with the mirrored dining room of the St. Nicholas where every dish had a spirit lamp under it and where forty waiters, "in a kind of uniform," performed everything "harmoniously and at the word of command." [3]

By the early fifties, Fifth Avenue was becoming a potential rival for Broadway in the interest of the visiting public, and promised to be what a local guidebook of 1853 called it, "the most magnificent street on this continent," if not yet "the finest [street] in the world." From Washington Square northward, this "Nabob-street of New York" was bordered by the imposing dwellings of the city's leading residents. According to the somewhat supercilious young Acton, the "great people" of the city no longer lived on Broadway, but on Fifth Avenue. Here impressive structures of brown sandstone, "of a richly decorated style of street architecture," lent "quietude and splendor" to this New World "Belgravia." Publisher Chambers was impressed with their plate-glass windows, silvered door handles, plates, and bellpulls, and "superb" furnishings and interiors. In one mansion "the spacious entrance hall was laid with tesselated marble pavement; the stair and balustrades were of dark walnut wood; one of the apartments was panelled in the old baronial fashion; and in a magnificent dining-room, the marble chimney-piece . . . cost . . . as much as 1500 dollars." These dwellings all had basement stories, and, as another British traveler wrote, owed "their stately appearance . . . to the massive staircases leading to the porches." [4]

Lower Manhattan was now increasingly relegated to business, as the former merchant-residents moved "uptown" or to the city's "suburbs." As Strong had predicted, by 1862 most of the island was built up as far north as Forty-second Street and in some parts beyond to Fiftieth. An index of the continuing northward progress of business and society was the opening in August 1859 of the Fifth Avenue Hotel, at the northwest corner of Fifth Avenue and Twenty-third Street, opposite Madison Square, then "the grandest part of New York." As the Astor House had been surpassed, with the advance of population, by the St. Nicholas, so now the latter was eclipsed in luxury, at least, by this latest hostelry, more than twenty blocks to the north of it. According to a visitor of 1861, the new hotel, with its accommodations for 800 guests and its passenger elevator, one of the first in the city, "majestically" held "superiority over all its brethren." A further indication of the city's northward trend was the laying of the cornerstone of St. Patrick's Cathedral at Fifth Avenue and Fiftieth Street in August of 1858.[5]

Observers already sensed the implications of the voracious advance of the city's business section. If New York should go on increasing and flourishing, asked Henry Philip Tappan, chancellor of the University of Michigan, would not "all the works of the present busy and prosperous generation sink into insignificance" and leave no trace behind? "The New York of to-day is not the New York of fifty years ago; and fifty years hence where will the New York of to-day be?" he queried in an address before the New York Geographical Society in March of 1855. "The city has not only advanced in magnitude, it has also been rebuilt. The palaces of the last generation were forsaken and turned into boarding-houses, then pulled down and replaced by warehouses. He who erects his magnificent palace on Fifth Avenue to-day, has only fitted out a future boarding-house, and probably occupied the site of a future warehouse." [6] His prediction was to be proved accurate before the century closed.

Visitors from abroad were more inclined than were the local residents to recognize the metropolitan character of the fast-growing community and to identify the central city with its ever expanding residential fringe. As early as 1844, a perceptive German scholar had asserted that "Hoboken on the Jersey side, and Brooklyn and Williamsburgh on the other side of the East River, considering their short distance," might properly be regarded "as portions of New York." By 1857, Charles Mackay, manager of the *Illustrated London News,* was describing New York as "the Queen of the Western World, with New Jersey on the one side, and Brooklyn on the other. The three form but one city in fact, though differing in name." An Englishwoman who visited the United States in 1854 reported that Brooklyn, Williamsburg, Hoboken, and Jersey City were the residences of a "very large portion of the merchants of New York," who had "deserted the old . . . part of the town," leaving it "merely an aggregate of offices." For their accommodation, steam ferries, "with space in the middle part for twelve or fourteen carriages and horses, and luxurious covered apartments, heated with steam-pipes on either side," plied to and fro every five minutes at a charge of one halfpenny a passenger.[7]

Even some resident observers were conscious of the metropolitan whole. To Walt Whitman, more spiritually attuned to the city than any other of its commentators, the Brooklyn ferry was the symbol of the oneness of Manhattan and its Long Island neighbor. Tying the "tall masts of Mannahatta" to the "beautiful hills of Brooklyn," it unified the "million-footed"

> City of hurried and sparkling water! city of spires and masts!
> City nested in bays! my city!

The author of a more prosaic description of the city, written in 1853, had already pointed out that it was "now no unusual thing for people to reside three, four, or five miles from their places of business" and that by cheap and speedy means of conveyance "regions round about the city, as far as ten miles from the center of business," were "brought into such intimate union with the city itself as to render them suitable and even economical places of residence for those who spend their hours of business in the densest part of the town." The writer was even so brash as to predict that by 1900 "a city of cottages . . . and villas . . . among cultivated fields and miniature groves" would cover a circular area of fifty miles diameter, centering upon the City Hall! [8]

Statistics of both population and business explain the pressure that was forcing New Yorkers northward on Manhattan and across the "bounding waters" for purposes of residence. The population of the central city more than doubled in the fifteen years between 1845 and 1860, swelling from 371,223 to 813,669 people; and across the river in Brooklyn there was more than a fivefold increase between 1840 and 1860. Thus, by the turn of the sixties, what was already recognized as the metropolitan area actually, as Whitman wrote, contained more than a million people. The immigrants who were pouring into the New York port by the hundred thousands yearly made up so large a part of this number that some commentators contended that Europe, not the United States, was responsible for the city's growth. But rural and small-town America were also contributing to the expanding size. "The crowd in Broadway . . . seems to have come from out of town," New York's George William Curtis commented in 1862. "It has a strange, wondering air. And the population of the city itself is so incessantly reinforced by those who come from the country that the city has always a little air of novelty to its own citizens." [9]

As the flood of immigrants—from Ireland and Germany, especially—swelled in unprecedented proportions, the newly added foreign-born ingredient attracted more comment from contemporary observers than it had before. Cosmopolitan New York, already regarded as less provincial than most of the cities of the United States, began now to be labeled as the least "American" of them. The wharves were daily crowded with bewildered newcomers—ruddy Germans, disheveled Irish, and anxious Englishmen; and Broadway swarmed with the "true sons of Erin" and the "noble offspring" of the Rhine. "The flood arrives without interruption," wrote Jean J. Ampère, professor of literature at the Collège de France, a visitor at the turn of the fifties. Actually, more than 319,000 immigrants reached the New York port in 1854 alone. By 1850, foreign-born persons constituted as much as 48 per cent of the city's population, and this was still the case on the eve of the Civil War. Of these, Irishmen were the most numerous. They numbered close to 204,000 in 1860, when there were nearly 120,000 New Yorkers of German birth and some 27,000 of English origin.[10]

Lack of resources compelled most of the newcomers to live in the deteriorated sections of the lower city—a "degenerate lodging-house population" which a traveler of the fifties observed to be crowded into tenement houses, "three or four stories high, containing from ten to twenty rooms, badly lighted and ventilated; often a family—mostly foreigners—in each room." By the fifties such depressed areas as the Five Points, which was centered at the intersection of Baxter, Worth, and Park streets, were a motley of foreign elements: Irish, German, Polish, Italian, and Chinese, together with impoverished white and Negro natives.[11]

Most distinctively European in this period was the city's *Kleindeutschland,* or "Little Germany," which by the forties extended from the Bowery into the Tenth Ward. German commentators reported that as one passed along the Bowery almost every sign was in German; and from their references to lager beer, singing societies, and celebrations of the *Maifest,* it is apparent that by the middle forties, the Germans of New York did not "lack their customary enjoyments." The German liberal, Karl T. Griesinger, who visited the section ten years later, wrote that one did not need to know English to make a living there; the German lending library, *Volkstheater,* churches, and beer gardens, where one could enjoy himself after the manner of the "continental Sunday," were proof that life in *Kleindeutschland* was "almost the same as in the Old Country." A German commentator at the turn of the sixties proudly reported that the habits of the once-despised "Dutchman" were permeating the American element and that New Yorkers had elected a mayor of German parentage in 1857.[12]

By the sixties, many of the poorer immigrants had migrated to the northern part of the city where they led a semirural existence as "squatters" at the outer limits of the built-up area. Impoverished German laborers occupied "Dutch Hill" at First Avenue and Fortieth Street; and a "shanty town" extended from Fortieth to Eightieth streets along the Hudson, inhabited by German and Irish immigrants who made a meager living as ragpickers and cinders gatherers or worked in the stables of the horse railway companies.[13]

The traditional animosity between the English and the Irish led British visitors to be particularly hard on this fast-increasing element in New York's population. They pointed to the disproportionate number of Irish-born inmates in the Alms House, prisons, and charity hospitals and asserted that "the scum and off-scourings of European cities"—obviously unfit for the farm or frontier—remained in

New York to swell its "pauper and criminal population." They laid the shortcomings of the existing municipal administration to the manipulation of the foreign vote in local politics, and especially to the influence of the Irish—by the mid-fifties "the best organized and strongest vote in the city of New York." Only in such a city as this did the unabsorbed immigrant threaten America's popular institutions, in the opinion of the now mature Richard Cobden. "It is only in places like New York, with its vast foreign sediment & froth, (German and Irish) where some Americans complain of the evil of universal suffrage," he wrote, after a second visit to the United States, this time in 1859.[14]

For their part, the Irish newcomers made no secret of their dislike for their former British masters. As early as 1848, they attempted to influence national policy on behalf of independence for their native land. "England is treated, . . . in the Irish meetings, in a manner that simply defies description. . . . The greater the lies, the greater the applause," wrote Ole Raeder, Norwegian consular official, who visited New York in 1848. The Irish were also markedly hostile toward the city's Negro residents, competing, in the opinion of most British observers, for the jobs as barbers, coachmen, and house servants which the colored citizens presently held. Such commentators predicted that the increase in immigration would further depress the occupational status of New York's Negro population, which, incidentally, declined in number from 16,358 in 1840 to 12,472 on the eve of the Civil War.[15]

Commerce, to which New York owed its rise, was still the mainstay of the city's growth. ". . . belted round by wharves as Indian isles by coral reefs—commerce surrounds it with her surf," wrote Herman Melville of his native city when he was creating *Moby-Dick* in 1850. The Manchester editor Archibald Prentice ventured the calculation that its bay would hold "all the navies of the world" and contended that its river was the "outlet for the best corn producing country in the world," its merchants probably "the most active in the world, native born or drawn from every country where there is commercial enterprise." A Scottish scientist expressed the prevailing reaction of the traveling public when he wrote in 1855: "One needs to come down to the river quays to see the greatness of New York." [16]

By 1860 no other American city could contest the commercial supremacy of the "New World Liverpool." Once recovered from the depression of the early forties, the business of the port expanded until, by 1860, in terms of value, New York's shippers were handling more than a third of the nation's exports and more than two thirds of its imports. Despite the aspirations of its Atlantic seaboard rivals, New York continued to benefit not only from its location but from the well-timed efforts of its citizens. Having triumphed earlier in the race for canal connections with the Middle West, it won a similar victory when the completion of both the Erie and the Hudson River railroads, in 1851, gave it continuous rail connections with the western market before either Philadelphia or Baltimore could achieve this goal. And the transfer of the Cunard Line's terminal from Boston to New York in 1848 gave the city an additional advantage over its Massachusetts competitor in both domestic and foreign trade. Moreover, by the middle fifties, as a British businessman observed, it was "*the* money market of the States" and therefore offered facilities to merchants in the transaction of their business which could not be afforded by any other city.[17]

As was true a hundred years later, it was commerce and business rather than other types of economic activity that caught the visitor's eye—not only at the wharves, but along the city's crowded streets. "New York, it seems, is celebrated for its extensive dealings in 'dry goods,' the common phrase for all kinds of clothing and haberdashery," wrote the Scottish publisher William Chambers, after his visit in 1853, "and its shops or stores for the retail of these articles are of most extraordinary dimensions." There was already apparent a degree of specialization in the city's merchandising activities that continued to impress newcomers in the ensuing years. Edward Watkin, a British visitor of 1851, was astounded at this aspect of the city's commercial streets. "Here, was a quarter of a mile of 'hardware' warehouses; here, as great a length of 'cassimeres and woollens goods stores'; here, a few hundred yards of 'straw-bonnet stores'; and there, a whole street devoted to 'leather stores' and 'leather findings.' It seemed as if almost every kind of supply had its chief quarter in the city. The notion given by all of this, especially in this busy season, when the buyers from a distance are in town making their 'fall' purchases, of the extent and energy of business is quite startling to a stranger accustomed to more quiet waters." [18]

Less was said about the manufacture of goods than of the sale of them, for only travelers with access to statistics, like the British businessman James Robertson, were aware of the part that manufacturing was already playing in the city's economic growth. "New York is not merely a commercial city," he wrote, following his visit in 1853 and 1854. "She is largely engaged in manufactures of various kinds,—indeed more so than any other city in America." The product of her manufacturing industries, despite their presumably "diminutive scale," had been valued at $105,218,308 in 1850, he reported. By 1860, when New York had moved even farther ahead as a manufacturing center, the value of the product had reached nearly $160,000,000. The garment industry was already making remarkable strides in these years, and New York's Hanford and Brother, a firm which employed more than 2,000 operatives in 1854, was the most extensive clothing factory in the country.[19]

Nevertheless it was commerce, as earlier, which gave the pre-Civil War community the social fluidity, the gaiety, the extravagance, and the transient ways of life which commentators had already begun to note in the generation following the close of the War of 1812. "The commercial spirit predominates over every other, and largely infuses itself into the society of the city," wrote Alexander Mackay, an English lawyer and journalist who visited New York in 1846. "There is a permanent class of wealthy residents, who form the centre of it; its great bulk being composed of those who, by themselves or friends, are still actively engaged in the pursuits of commerce. With a few exceptions it is, therefore, in a state of constant fluctuation, in accordance with the fluctuating fortunes of commercial life. Its doors are guarded," he admitted, "but they seem never to be closed, and you have a constant stream flowing in and out. The consequence is, that there is much more heart than refinement about it. It is gay to a degree, sprightly, and cordial, but far less conventional than the corresponding circle in Philadelphia." [20]

Others took a less charitable view of the prevailing preoccupation with business and success. William Bobo, of South Carolina, missed the neighborliness of his native section among a throng whose one "great object" was *"the penny;* upon *it* turns every action of their lives as well as motive of their natures." The tension of the race for business bothered the Polish revolutionary, Adam de Gurowski, who arrived in the United States in 1849. "The American seems always in a hurry and excited; at his meals, in his study, and at his counter," he complained, in the fifties. "For example, in the morning hours, when the New York business population, old and young—and all is business in New York—pours out into the main artery, in Broadway, and descends hurriedly 'down town,' nothing in the world could stop or divert the torrent. Even if Sebastopol had been in their way, those men would have run over it at one rush." [21]

As earlier, the conspicuously extravagant attire of female New Yorkers continued to symbolize the commercial affluence of the city. Still fashioned upon Parisian models, there was a uniformity of style which gave their costumes a "manufactured stamp." "The luxury of this city is prodigious," wrote William Makepeace Thackeray, who came to New York in December of 1852 to lecture on the chief authors of Queen Anne's reign; "surely Solomon in all his glory or the Queen of Sheba when she came to visit him in state was not arrayed so magnificently as these New York damsels. . . . I never saw such luxury and extravagance such tearing polkas such stupendous suppers and fine clothes. I watched one young lady at 4 balls in as many new dresses, and each dress of the most 'stunning' description." A woman visitor of the mid-fifties reported that the ladies of New York dressed beautifully and in very good taste. It offended her to see "costly silks and rich brocades sweeping the pavements of Broadway, with more effect than is produced by the dustmen"; but she contended that "more beautiful toilettes" were to be seen "in this celebrated thoroughfare, in one afternoon, than in Hyde Park in a week." [22]

As in the previous generation, the prevalence of hotel and boarding house living—even beyond the demands of the commercial and traveling public—continued to strike the city's visitors as odd. The English journalist Charles Mackay admitted that the large hostelries, with their uniform charge of $2.50 per day for bed and board, were "the finest, most convenient, and best administered establishments in the world"; yet, like many other travelers, he regretted the fact that half of the guests were permanent residents—husbands, wives, and children. "The reasons alleged for this custom," according to William E. Baxter, a British public figure who visited the city in 1846 and again in 1853–54, were "the difficulty of procuring good servants in a country where the labouring classes can employ their time much more profitably, the vexation and annoyance almost invariably given by the Irish girls who act in this capacity, the enormous rent demanded for apartments, and the high price of provisions." Baxter discovered that many of the handsomest mansions in the upper part of the city were boarding houses, and he was not a little amused by the interviews he had with "pompous dames" who received him in "elegantly furnished drawing rooms" before showing him "the dear and shabby apartments upstairs." [23]

Madame Marie Fontenay de Grandfort, a Frenchwoman who lectured on her country's literature in the middle fifties, contended that New York women enjoyed an undue freedom, that affluent New Yorkers did not know "the pleasures of the family circle," and that American children had an air of independence and maturity not customary in European youth. After observing the youngsters of New York, William Ferguson concurred in the last opinion. "Much amused this morning at the breakfast table with a specimen of Young America," wrote the Scottish scientist in his notes for March 8, 1855. "A little boy of six or seven came in alone, and sat gravely down, ordered, with the greatest self-possession, beef-steaks and potatoes, and awaited their coming with the utmost dignity. We saw this repeated often elsewhere. There are no children, in our sense of the term, in America—only little men and women. They seem born with all the responsibility of citizenship, and wear it with great gravity. . . . They address their parents as 'Sir,' and 'Madam'; and ere they are well out of the nursery, assume the airs and bearing of ripe manhood. . . . The merest boy will give his opinion upon the subject of conversation among his seniors; and he expects to be listened to, and is." [24]

Despite their generally unprecedented admiration for many aspects of the New York scene, the commentators noted with increasing frequency, during the late forties and fifties, the unfortunate concomitants of urban life: misery, destitution, vice, and crime. A French scholar, who visited New York in 1851, concluded that though the New World metropolis exhibited more "civilization, more of Europe," than he had expected, the disadvantages of large cities had also clearly begun to manifest themselves there. Homeless waifs and squalid housing, pickpockets and saloons, rowdies and houses of prostitution not only elicited increasing comment from the city's visitors, but caused its residents to admit that the larger the city the more likely the appearance of evil as well as of good.[25]

The diaries of both Philip Hone and George Templeton Strong suggest that local residents, too, recognized the social problems that attended the growth of New York City to metropolitan proportions. "Our good city of New York has already arrived at the state of society to be found in the large cities of Europe . . . where the two extremes of costly luxury . . . and improvident waste are presented in daily and hourly contrast with squalid misery and hopeless destitution," Hone wrote early in 1847. His fellow New Yorker Strong was also concerned about the "social diseases" which the growing city increasingly produced: the monotonous daily drudgery of "our swarms of seamstresses"; the haunting sight of troops of "ragged girls, from twelve years old down, brutalized already almost beyond redemption by premature vice"; and the rowdyism of young blackguards like the Dead Rabbit Club and the Bowery Boys, who made a joke of public order in the later fifties.[26]

This side of the city was also reflected in the rise of a kind of sensational "literature," exposing the "seamier" aspects of the New York scene, a type which was to become increasingly popular in the 1870's and 1880's as books about "life in the big city" attracted an ever widening audience. Two of the earliest examples of this shady genre were *New York in Slices by an experienced carver* (1849) and *New York by Gas-light: with here and there a streak of sunshine* (1850), the work of a local journalist, George G. Foster. In the former, the author sought to impress his readers with the fact that there was a seamy side behind the city's "pleasures and palaces." The latter dealt with such topics as "Broadway at evening: hooking a victim . . . midnight orgies," "Bowling and Billiard Saloons," "The Golden Gate of Hell—Prostitution in General—a Fashionable Brothel," "A Night Ramble—the Upstairs Drinking Saloons," "Five Points at Midnight," "The Dance House," "The Ice Creameries," "Mose and Lize—the b'hoys and g'hals of New York," and "The Dog Watch—Thieves, etc." [27]

Contemporaries at the same time took note of the hospitals, asylums, juvenile reformatories, prisons, and houses of refuge by which the community was attempting to keep the fast-multiplying social problems within bounds. "Bible and tract societies, and church missions, make extraordinary exertions," wrote William Chambers, after his visit in 1853; "and the industrious and affluent, moved by representations from the press, are uniting in efforts for social improvement." The accomplishments of the church in this respect were cited by the Reverend Georges Fisch, pastor of the French Evangelical Church of Paris, who visited New York on the eve of the Civil War. He detected signs that in some churches a preoccupation with professional singers and fashionable pastors was already excluding the working classes from "the privilege of hearing the gospel," but he praised the work of the church in regenerating the Five Points area and for the daily prayer meetings, held in Fulton Street since 1857, which reflected the concern of local businessmen for "Christian works." [28]

For all the misery which they observed—and which seemed to be more than ever shaping this New World city to the pattern of the Old—visitors of the period, at least until the panic of 1857 hit the city, continued to be of the opinion that the workingman of New York was better off than his European counterpart. Resident observers like George Templeton Strong contended that the effect of the crisis of 1857 on New York City was far more "sudden, acute, and prostrating than that of 1837." Unemployment mounted in the fall of 1857, and by 1858 about 130,000 persons, or one-seventh of the population, were receiving relief. "Walking down Broadway you pass great $200,000 buildings begun last spring or summer that have gone up two stories and stopped, and may stand unfinished and desolate for years," wrote the distinguished diarist in October of 1857. "Almost every shop has its placards (*written,* not *printed*) announcing a great sacrifice, vast reduction of prices, sales at less than cost. . . . In Wall Street every man carries Pressure, Anxiety, Loss, written on his forehead. . . . The financial crisis has thrown thousands of the working class out of employment and made it difficult matter enough to maintain peace and order in the city through the winter." Encouraged by that "archdemagogue [Mayor Fernando] Wood," the unemployed were "marching in procession—holding meetings in Wall Street—listening to seditious speeches—passing resolutions that they were entitled to work and the wages of work, and that if they were not provided with work they would take the means of subsistence *vi et armis.*" [29]

Contemporaries found little to praise in the services provided by the local government at a time when the problems of municipal administration were aggravated by political corruption as well as by economic crises and the rapid pace of city growth. The local residents were reported, in 1853, as calling their police "the worst in the world," although the force had been regularized in 1844 and put into formal uniform nine years later. James Robertson thought New York the dirtiest city he had ever seen and detected no improvement until, in the winter of 1853–1854, the merchants of Broadway voluntarily subscribed money "to pay for the performance of [street cleaning] duties which the authorities neglected." Fire fighting was still performed by citizen volunteers; and visitors were appalled at the confusion and hubbub that resulted from placing this crucial responsibility upon nonprofessionals, who served "more for love of excitement than from any praiseworthy desire for the preservation of property." [30]

The provision of urban transit—complicated by both the increase in population and the widening distance between work and residence—was left to private enterprise; but here, too, service was far from adequate, as well as much more democratic than some European visitors thought desirable. Horse railways were the newest solution to the problem. Since their "monster cars," drawn by four horses, could accommodate from twenty to thirty persons, they helped to meet the fast-broadening demand for public conveyance. Started abortively in the thirties, they were in operation by the fifties on a number of the avenues parallel to Broadway. There, as elsewhere, gaily painted, horse-drawn omnibuses continued to serve the traveling public; but contemporaries complained of the callousness with which riders were crammed like "live lumber" into the vehicles. In the winter of 1856 the condition of the streets led to the replacement of the omnibuses by "great crowded sleigh-caravans," half of whose suffering occupants had to "stand in the wet straw with their feet freezing, . . . their ears and noses tingling in the bitter wind, their hats always on the point of being blown off." For individual use, New Yorkers had to depend on cumbersome two-horse hackney coaches; and as late as 1857, travelers were surprised at the local lack of the low, two-wheeled, one-horse hansom cabs, then popular in England.[31]

In the expansion of amusement facilities to accommodate the increase of population in this period, New York anticipated its later fame as a pre-eminent center of entertainment. Travelers of the forties found New York the "gayest city in the United States" with the possible exception of New Orleans, and by the mid-fifties they could report that "Broadway and its neighborhood" contained "more places of amusement than perhaps any district of equal size in the world." It boasted three major theatres—already "deriving their chief support from strangers visiting the town, either for business or recreation." In addition there were the splendid gilt and white Academy of Music at Fourteenth Street and Irving Place, opened early in October of 1854, where wealth and fashion as well as seasons of Italian opera were on display, and also the popular houses where Wood's and Christy's minstrels performed to unwearied

The Edward W. C. Arnold Collection; photograph courtesy of Museum of the City of New York

THE CIVIL WAR SCENE

Marching troops mingled with busy pedestrians in wartime New York of the middle 1860's. Here columns of soldiers attract at least some attention as they cross Printing-House Square, at the intersection of Park Row (right) and Nassau Street. The Square gained its name around 1860 from the many newspaper and publishing offices in the vicinity. The *Tribune* and *Times* buildings fronted on the square, and southward on Park Row were the offices of the *World* and the *Scientific American*. Broadway omnibuses and the horsecars of the Third Avenue Railroad are in the foreground.

There is less of the picturesque and more of the modern in the postwar Broadway that comes increasingly to life in the photography of Mathew B. Brady. This view (to the right), looking north from Spring Street in 1867, shows the individualism of its now massive business blocks, with their ornate stone or cast iron fronts. Coaches, drays, and cabs crowd the streets with horse-drawn traffic. Its nighttime illumination is still confined to the light of the gas lamps seen in the foreground.

Museum of the City of New York

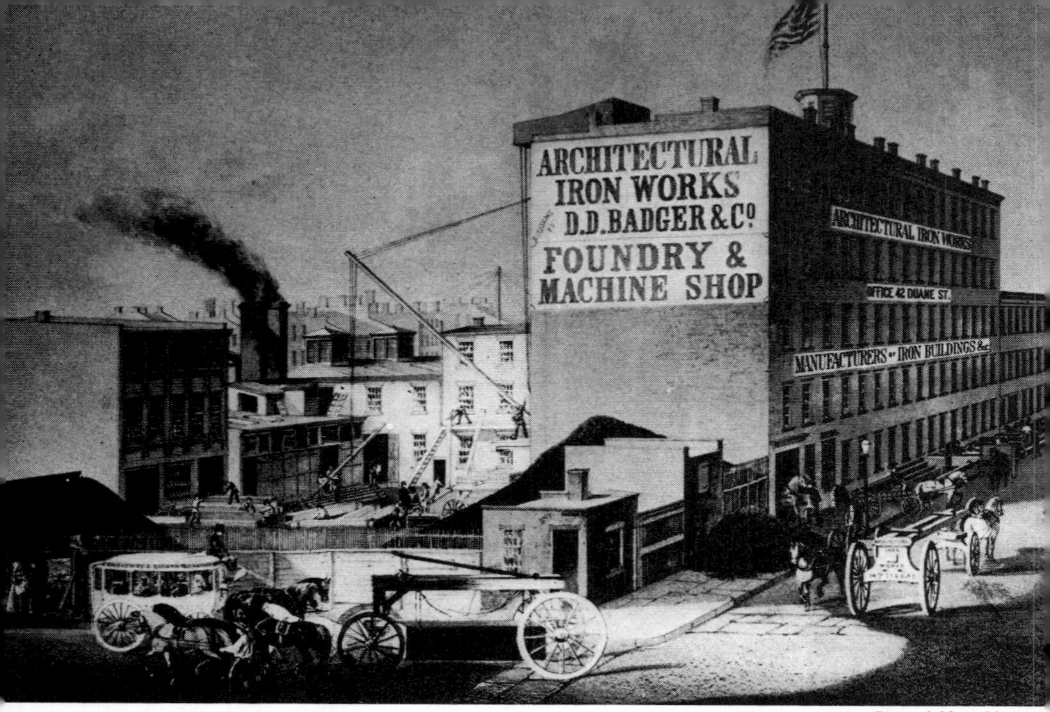

Museum of the City of New York

CIVIL WAR AFTERMATH

The expansion of industry during the decade of the Civil War was reflected in the prosperity of such enterprises as the Architectural Iron Works, one of the largest manufacturers of structural iron in the 1860's. The lithograph above, which appeared in the catalogue of the firm in 1865, shows the heavy horse-drawn carts used for delivering the iron columns and metal fronts that graced Broadway's newest commercial structures at the mid-century.

Evidences of war-made wealth were seen not only in ornate stores and mansions but also in the expensive "turn-outs" in Central Park. This was the subject of the Currier and Ives lithograph of 1869, reproduced below. George Templeton Strong was reminded of the profits of "Shoddy and petroleum" in observing the "sumptuous turn-outs, with liveried servants" whose occupants "looked as if they might have been cooks or chambermaids a few years ago."

The J. Clarence Davies Collection, Museum of the City of New York

audiences. Barnum's Museum, the city's best-known amusement attraction, was reaching the peak of its popularity on the eve of the Civil War. Established at Broadway and Ann Street in December 1841, its collection was assembled from a number of the city's earlier museums and supplemented as a result of the ingenuity of its resourceful manager. From the chained bear on its roof to the "What is it?" featured inside, on the turn of the sixties, Barnum's colossal humbug was a magnet to the city's visitors. The "Lindomania" in the fall of 1850—prompted by the arrival of Jenny Lind for concerts in Castle Garden—was attended by "such a spontaneous outbreak" of rushing, crowding, hurrahing, and serenading as the city had "never before seen." But by November a correspondent to the *Southern Literary Messenger* asserted that New York "had too many fresh sources of excitement every day to allow of any great constancy to one object." [32]

By the fifties the gustatory attractions of the city were already becoming associated with its entertainment appeal. Travelers had long extolled the virtues of the city's many handsomely fitted subterranean "Oyster Saloons." Added to these, by the fifties, were sumptuous restaurants catering to the *beau monde*. Two were outstanding: Thompson's and Taylor's. In the mirrored splendor of the latter, Isabella Bishop found fashionable patrons "regaling themselves upon ices and other elegancies in an atmosphere redolent with the perfume of orange-flowers and musical with the sound of trickling water, and the melody of musical snuff boxes." Meals at the great hotels were a continuing source of "wonder and interest." The Scotch scientist William Ferguson, who was a guest at the St. Nicholas in 1855, reported a choice of "two soups, two kinds of fish, ten boiled dishes, nine roast dishes, six relishes, seventeen entrees, three cold dishes, five varieties of game, thirteen varieties of vegetables, seven kinds of pastry, and seven fruits, with ice-cream and coffee." And there were always the delights of the hotel bars, where, according to Charles Mackay, "gin-sling, brandy-smash, whisky-skin, streak of lightning, cock-tail, and rum-salad" were "consumed . . . morning, noon, and night, by persons who in a similar rank of life in England would no more think of going into a gin-shop than of robbing the Bank." [33]

Like their predecessors, the commentators of this period agreed that New York provided more opportunity to gratify recreational than intellectual interests; along with most American cities of the time, it appeared to be "elevating utility above thought and beauty." In New York as elsewhere in the "reforming fifties," visitors found an eager interest in lectures. "Statesmen, clergymen, professors, authors, mechanics, ladies and gentlemen, everybody lectures," wrote Francis and Theresa Pulszky, who accompanied Louis Kossuth to America in the early fifties. But the existence of such permanent institutions as the New-York Society Library, the Athenaeum, the National Academy of Design, the New York Gallery of the Fine Arts, the Cooper Union, founded in 1857, and even the Astor Library, opened in Lafayette Place three years earlier, only partially disproved the accuracy of young Acton's comment, in 1853, that New Yorkers knew only the "beautiful in use." [34]

Among collegiate institutions, the University of the City of New York, now New York University, attracted more attention, for the moment, than Columbia University, although the enrollment of neither institution exceeded 150, in 1850, according to a British visitor of that year. Columbia had the larger library, but New York University impressed the city's visitors with its imposing marble structure, built in the English collegiate style, on Washington Square, and with the inventions of its scientific faculty, which, according to one English traveler, helped to make the city great. However, as late as 1855, Chancellor Tappan, of the University of Michigan, was arguing that a city of New York's size should afford more extensive facilities for higher education and "all the humanizing influences which the presence of works of art and public libraries, and institutions of art and learning, can exert over the population at large." [35]

In the New York that visitors described on the eve of the Civil War, the outlines of the modern city were coming more than faintly into view. Already its metropolitan limits encompassed at least a million people, and the city was admittedly the main doorway and mercantile showcase of the Western world. As the ever changing city pressed northward on Manhattan, Broadway and Fifth Avenue took on characteristics that were to distinguish them in later years; while crowded hotels, overburdened urban transit, and multiple housing foreshadowed the city of more recent days. With the increased size and variety of its fast-expanding population came social problems which Europe's older cities already knew, as well as requests for broadened urban services which anticipated the demands of modern times.

Rapidly increasing wealth widened the distance between the rich and poor, but there was as yet no numerous leisure or literary class; and though European city dwellers found New York "more like home" than other parts of the United States, there was still an untempered roughness in its society that suggested less the Old World than the New. But whatever their reservations with respect to its culture, resident and visitor were of one mind as to both the pulsating dynamism of the local scene and the influence of mercantile activity and leadership in every phase of its daily life. Walt Whitman's Manhattan teemed with "trottoirs throng'd, vehicles . . . houses of business . . . shops and shows." The desire to make money was "necessary to enable one to sympathize with the rest of mankind and be sure of his common humanity with the people about him," George Templeton Strong asserted in 1850. And this point of view was seconded by two English travelers who visited New York ten years later. "New Yorkers seem to live to make money and spend it," they reported, stating an opinion that was now by no means original. "Fortunes are not the rule, for money is seldom hoarded, but spent in the same reckless way in which it is made. There is little inducement to a man to put by money. To be much thought of, a New Yorker must be in trade. Merchants are thought more of than lawyers and medical men, while those who do nothing, be they rich as Croesus, are thought little of at all." [36]

MANHATTAN IN THE MID-FORTIES

One of the first travelers to note the rapid improvement in New York City following the depressed conditions of the early forties was the Scotsman Sir Charles Lyell, geologist and graduate of Oxford University. His two trips to the United States, made in 1841 and 1845–1846, at which time he was approaching 50 years of age, were primarily scientific in purpose. They resulted in two works, *Travels in North America* (1845) and *A Second Visit to the United States of America* (1849), from which the following comments on the city's newly acquired water supply, the elegance of its society, and the increase in its omnibus traffic are drawn.[37]

It is only three years since we were last in this city, yet in this short interval we see improvements equaling in importance the increase of the population, which now amounts in round numbers to 440,000; New York containing 361,000, and Brooklyn, which is connected with it by a ferry, together with Williamsburg 79,000. Among other novelties since 1841, we observe with pleasure the new fountains in the midst of the city supplied from the Croton waterworks, finer than any which I remember to have seen in the center of a city since I was last in Rome. Two of them are now, in spite of an intense frost, throwing up columns of water more than thirty feet high, one opposite the City Hall, and another in Hudson Square; but I am told that when we return in the summer we shall see many others in action. A work more akin in magnificence to the ancient and modern Roman aqueducts has not been achieved in our times; the water having been brought from the Croton river, a distance of about forty miles, at the expense of about three millions sterling. The health of the city is said to have already gained by greater cleanliness and more wholesome water for drinking. . . . The water can be carried to the attics of every house, and many are introducing baths and indulging in ornamental fountains in private gardens. The rate of insurance for fire has been lowered; and I could not help reflecting as I looked at the moving water, at a season when every pond is covered with ice, how much more security the city must now enjoy than during the great conflagration in the winter of 1835 when there was such a want of water to supply the engines. . . .

Next to the new churches and fountains, the most striking change observable in the streets of New York since 1841, is the introduction of the electric telegraph, the posts of which, about 30 feet high and 100 yards apart, traverse Broadway, and are certainly not ornamental. Occasionally, where the trees interfere, the wires are made to cross the street diagonally. . . .

Every fortnight the "Journal des Modes" is received from France, and the ladies conform strictly to the Parisian costume. Except at balls and large parties, they wear high dresses, and, as usual in mercantile communities, spare no expense. Embroidered muslin, of the finest and costliest kind, is much worn; and my wife learnt that sixteen guineas were not unfrequently given for a single pocket handkerchief. Extravagantly expensive fans, with ruby or emerald pins, are also common. I had heard it said in France that no orders sent to Lyons for the furnishing of private mansions, are on so grand a scale as some of those received from New York; and I can well believe it, for we saw many houses gorgeously fitted up with satin and velvet draperies, rich Axminster carpets, marble and inlaid tables, and large looking-glasses, the style in general being Parisian rather than English. It was much more rare here than at Boston to see a library forming part of a suite of reception-rooms, or even a single book-case in a drawing-room, nor are pictures so common here.

In the five months since we were last in this metropolis, whole streets had been built, and several squares finished in the northern or fashionable end of the town, to which the merchants are now resorting, leaving the business end, near the Battery, where they formerly lived. Hence there is a constant increase of omnibuses passing through Broadway, and other streets running north and south. Groups of twelve of these vehicles may be seen at once, each with a single driver, for wages are too high to support a cad. Each omnibus has an opening in the roof, through which the money is paid to the coachman. We observed, as one woman after another got out, any man sitting near the door, though a stranger, would jump down to hand her out, and, if it was raining, would hold an umbrella over her, frequently offering, in that case, to escort her to a shop, attentions which are commonly accepted and received by the women as matters of course.

All the streets which cross Broadway, run east and west, and are numbered, so that they have now arrived at 146th-street—a mode of designating the different parts of the metropolis worthy of imitation on both sides of the Atlantic.

THE "EMPRESS CITY" OF THE WEST: 1849

The "impetuous go-aheadness" of New York City on the turn of the fifties is reflected in the comments of Lady Emmeline Stuart-Wortley, who arrived in New York on May 16, 1849. Like most women travelers, this daughter of a duke and wife of a baron found much to admire in the "handsome," dynamic "Empress City" of the West, which bewildered the titled visitor with its "kaleidoscopical" variety, the "cosmopolitanism" of its citizenry, and the "extraordinary stir and bustle and tumult of business." The following comments on the city, reprinted from her *Travels in the United States, . . . during 1849 and 1850,* were made after Lady Emmeline had traveled along the Atlantic coast and visited the cities of the trans-Allegheny West.[38]

New York is certainly altogether the most bustling, cheerful, lifeful, restless city I have yet seen in the United States. Nothing and nobody seem to stand still for half a moment in New York; the multitudinous omnibuses, which drive like insane vehicles from morning till night, appear not to pause to take up their passengers, or it is so short a pause, you have hardly time to see the stoppage, like the instantaneousness of a flash of lightning. How on earth the people get in and out of them, I do not know: the man behind surely must sometimes shut a person half in and half out, and cut them in two, but neither he nor they have time to notice such trifles. . . .

From the cupola that surmounts the [City Hall], a view of the whole vast city is commanded; . . . and there is also an apartment constantly occupied, night and day, by a watchman, whose office it is to keep a perpetual look out for fires, and to give the alarm, by striking an enormous bell which hangs in a belfry in the rear of the cupola, and which is exclusively used for this purpose. . . . The sound can be heard from one end of the city to the other, and is almost instantaneously responded to by a hundred others in every direction. The number of strokes indicates the particular ward. . . .

The French appear to muster numerically stronger than any other people, but this arises from the fact, that nearly all the New Yorkers are accoutred in Parisian costume. Their very hair is cut and combed, and their beards trimmed and clipped strictly *à la Française,* which does not in general improve their personal appearance. Looking merely to the people, you might often fancy yourself in the Boulevards, instead of in Broadway. *Au reste,* Germans, Swedes, Poles, Italians, and hosts of others meet you at every turn. There are but few Russian visitors here it seems; but I am very much struck by the apparent *entente cordiale* that exists between Russia and the United States. There seems an inexplicable instinct of sympathy, some mysterious magnetism at work, which is drawing by degrees these two mighty nations into closer contact. Napoleon, we know, prophesied that the world, ere long, would be either Cossack or Republican. It seems as if it would first be pretty equally shared between these two giant powers. . . .

There are a great number of military companies in New York, and some of them are really very martial-looking indeed. I am told there is a company of Highlanders, formed by the sons of fa[i]r Caledonia; and there are German, French, Italian companies, &c. There are a number of target companies, each known by some particular name—usually, I believe, that of a favourite leader who is locally popular among them. Others take their appellation from some celebrated historical character, and others from anything that happens to occur to them, it would seem.

A few of them are "The Washington Market Chowder Guard" (chowder is a famous dish in the United States), "Bony Fusileers," "Peanut Guard," "Sweet's Epicurean Guard" (surely these must be confectioners), "George R. Jackson and Company's Guard," "Nobody's Guard," "Oregon Blues," "Tenth Ward Light Guard," "Carpenter Guard," "First Ward Magnetizers," "Tompkins' Butcher Association Guard," "Mustache Fusileers," "Henry Rose Light Guard," "Atlantic Light Guard," "Junior Independence Guard," and multitudes of others.

The militia numbers about one hundred companies, which comprise six thousand men. The Target Companies are said not to fall short of ten thousand men. . . .

I hear that some of the best and finest of their organizations are formed out of the fire companies, who thus take upon themselves a twofold responsibility. . . .

Often the lieutenants and captains of the Target Companies are artisans, labourers, clerks, and mechanics. The companies elect their officers, and constantly without the least favour . . . shown "to class, or rank, or wealth." The man who is most distinguished by these advantages, frequently shoulders his musket as a private; and yet he may most largely subscribe to the company's expenses for yearly "excursions," and other contingencies and needs.

THE SOCIAL SCENE IN 1853

The social contrasts which attended the growth of the metropolis in the early fifties were apparent to William Chambers, a prominent Edinburgh publisher, who visited the United States in 1853. A self-made man, Chambers had begun to write gazetteers and other books about Scotland as early as 1830. *Chambers's Edinburgh Journal* first appeared in 1832, and thereafter the budding publisher engaged in an extensive program, which included the publication of *Chambers's Encyclopaedia.* As lord provost of Edinburgh, he promoted the passage of the Edinburgh City Improvement Act in 1867. The future Edinburgh official reached New York City late in 1853, after having journeyed through Canada and the upper Middle West. He stayed at the Astor House, at which he had made a reservation in advance, for he had been forewarned of the "difficulty of procuring accommodation in any hotel in New York." His eye for the social problems of the city is reflected in the following excerpts from his perceptive volume, *Things as They Are in America*.[39]

At the first look, we see that New York very much resembles the more densely-built parts of London. The houses, tall, and principally of brick, are crowded into narrow streets, such as are seen in the neighbourhood of Cheapside, with the single difference, that many of the buildings are occupied in floors by different branches of business, with a profusion of large sign-boards in front. For the most part, the houses have sunk floors, accessible by a flight of steps from the foot-pavement; and these cellar-dwellings are very commonly used for some kind of small business, or as "oyster saloons," or "retreats"—the names considerately employed to signify taverns and groggeries. Wherever any of these older brick edifices have been removed, their place has been supplied by tenements built of brown sandstone; and it may be said that at present New York is in process of being renewed by this species of structure. . . . The more narrow thoroughfares are at the same time widened and paved according to modern taste. The more ancient, though much changed part of the city in which the throng of business chiefly prevails, is confined to the southern division, stretching from the Battery a mile northwards. . . .

Hampered as to space, New York has no room for villas; and in this respect there is a marked difference between it and our English cities. Those among the more affluent orders who dislike living in streets, require to proceed by ferry-steamers across either of the two bounding waters, and on the opposite shore find spots for ruralising. . . .

Interest is centered in Broadway, and mainly towards its southern extremity. Hereabouts are the handsomest public buildings, the finest stores, some of the largest hotels, and the greatest throng of passengers. At about half a mile from the Battery, we have on the line of Broadway an opening called the Park, which though only a railed-in patch of ground, with a few trees and footpaths through it, is a very acceptable breathing spot in the midst of everlasting bustle.

Some traveller speaks of the buildings of Broadway as being a mixture of poor wooden structures and splendid edifices. There may be a few houses of an antiquated class, but any such general description is totally inadmissible in the present day. We see for the greater part of its length, a series of high and handsome buildings, of brown sandstone or brick, with several of white marble and granite. Some of the stores and hotels astonish by their size and grandeur. . . .

Without a court, and not even the seat of the state legislature, New York cannot be described as the place of residence of a leisurely or a numerous literary class. Its more opulent inhabitants, connected some way or other with business, form, nevertheless, an aristocracy with refined tastes, and ample means for their gratification. Advancing northwards from the more busy parts of the town, the elegance and regularity of the houses become more conspicuous, and at last we find ourselves in the quietude and splendour of a Belgravia. Here the edifices are entirely of brown sandstone, and of a richly decorated style of street architecture. . . . The furnishings and interior ornaments of these dwellings, particularly those in Fifth Avenue, are of a superb kind; no expense being apparently spared as regards either comfort or elegance. . . .

Standing on the steps of the Astor House, we have the thoroughfare of Broadway right and left, with the Park in front—Barnum's theatre, covered with great gaudy paintings, across the way—and can here perhaps better than anywhere else, observe the concourse of passengers and vehicles. . . . That which appears most novel, is the running to and fro of railway-cars on East Broadway. . . . Permitted, for some mysterious reason, by the civic authorities, lines of rail are laid along several prominent thoroughfares. . . . The cars on these street-railways are hung low, seated like an omnibus, and will stop at any point to take up or set down passengers. The ordinary omnibuses of New York have no cad [conductor] behind. The door is held close by a cord or belt from the hand of the driver, who relaxes it to allow the entry or exit of the passengers. I was amused with the manner in which the fare is taken in these vehicles. The passenger who wishes to be set down, hands his money through a hole in the roof to the driver, who forthwith relaxes the cord, and the door flies open. As there appeared to be no check on two or more departing when only one had paid, I suppose the practice of shirking fares is not very common. . . . The drivers are . . . unconscionable in their reception of extra passengers, particularly if the applicants be ladies. In such cases, the gentlemen either stand, or take the ladies on their knee. . . .

The necessity for seeking vehicular conveyance arises not more from the extreme length of the city, than the condition of the principal thoroughfares. I am indeed sorry to hint that New York is, or at least *was* during my visit, not so cleanly as it might be. Statists assure us that it possesses 1500 dirt-carts, and in 1853 cost the sum of 250,000 dollars for cleaning. Where these carts were, and where all this money was expended, I cannot imagine. The mire was ankle-deep in Broadway, and the more narrow business streets were barely passable. The thing was really droll. All along the foot-pavements there stood, night and day, as if fixtures, boxes, buckets, lidless flour-barrels, baskets, decayed tea-chests, rusty iron pans, and earthenware jars full of coal-ashes. There they rested, some close to the houses, some leaning over into the gutter, some on the doorsteps, some knocked over and spilt, and to get forward you required to take constant care not to fall over them. . . . Passing up Broadway . . . and looking into a side-street, the scene of confused débris was of a kind not to be easily forgotten—ashes, vegetable refuse, old hats without crowns, worn-out shoes, and other household wreck, lay scattered about as a field of agreeable inquiry for a number of long-legged and industrious pigs. . . .

It was a delicate subject to touch upon, but I did venture to inquire into the cause of these phenomena. One uniform answer—maladministration in civic affairs; jobbing of members of the corporation into each other's hands. . . . You could not take up a newspaper without seeing accounts of unchecked disorders, or reading sarcasms on official delinquencies. . . .

As a great emporium of commerce, growing in size and importance, New York offers employment in a variety of pursuits to the skilful, the steady, and industrious, and on such terms of remuneration as leaves little room for complaint. It would, however, be a prodigious mistake to suppose that amidst this field for well-doing, poverty and wretchedness are unknown. In New York, there is a place called the Five Points, a kind of St. Giles's; and here, as in some other quarters of this great city, you see and hear of a sink of vice and misery resembling the more squalid and dissolute parts of Liverpool or Glasgow. . . .

In New York, the means of social improvement, through the agency of public libraries, lectures, and reading-rooms, are exceedingly conspicuous. One of the most munificent of these institutions, is the recently opened Astor Library, founded by an endowment of the late John Jacob Astor, who bequeathed a fund of 400,000 dollars to erect a handsome building and store it with books for the free use of the public. I went to see this library, and found that it consisted of a splendid collection of 100,000 volumes, a large proportion of which were works in the best European editions, properly classified, with every suitable accommodation for literary study. The New York Mercantile Library, and the Apprentices' Library, are institutions conducted with great spirit, and of much value to the community. A large and handsome building was in process of erection at a cost of 300,000 dollars, by a benevolent citizen, Mr. P. Cooper, for the purpose of a free reading-room and lectures.

THE ECONOMIC BASE IN THE FLOURISHING FIFTIES: 1853–1854

A comprehensive analysis of the commercial foundations of New York City's prosperity in the middle fifties is to be found in James Robertson's *A Few Months in America: containing remarks on some of its Industrial and Commercial Interests.* The author was a businessman, and the avowed aim of his book was to provide information on "the material interests of the country." In the following excerpts from it, from which most of the supporting figures have been deleted, he discusses the role of trade, transportation, and finance in the city's rapidly expanding economy.[40]

The sudden rise, and wonderful progress of the commerce of New York, have been unprecedented. At the end of the last century, its foreign trade was surpassed by that of Philadelphia; and at no very distant date, it was of no great magnitude; but within the last few years it has advanced with rapid strides.

. . . there is a wide difference between the value of the exports and imports. This arises from the largest portion of the exports of the States being sent abroad from the southern ports; while of the imports, the largest portion is received at New York. The imports seem to have gradually increased with the wealth and population of the country; but the exports from this and the other northern ports, received a new impulse by the relaxation of the commercial restrictions of Great Britain, and since 1847 have more rapidly increased.

The imports consist of dry goods, or manufactured articles of cotton, wool, silk, and flax; of iron, raw and manufactured; and of sugar, tea, coffee, fruits, &c. From this point they are distributed to other parts of the States, either directly, or through other cities of the seaboard.

The exports are composed of gold, breadstuffs, provision, &c. [including cotton], by far the greater portion of which is sent to Great Britain. . . .

The shipping belonging to the port has increased as rapidly as its commerce, and bears a larger proportion to the value of that commerce than in any other mercantile city of any magnitude. That arises from two causes. First, because the exports from New York are principally of raw produce, therefore bulky, and requiring a large amount of tonnage for their conveyance to foreign markets. Secondly, because much of the shipping that is employed in the southern ports, to convey their cotton and other produce to foreign markets, is owned by New York merchants.

The tonnage belonging to the city . . . amounts to more than a fourth part of the entire shipping of the States, and is more, I believe, than that belonging to any other port in the world. . . .

The proud position now occupied by New York as the first commercial city of the New World, insures it a still more rapid progress, and a yet higher pre-eminence. At an early period of its history, it had much to fear from the competition of its rivals, Boston and Philadelphia. Indeed, as I have already remarked, the latter surpassed it in the extent of its foreign commerce, at the end of the last century, and till 1810, was a-head of it in population. With a much richer State, and as convenient access to the west, it might, had its inhabitants been possessed of enterprise, have striven to maintain its superiority. But the favourable opportunity was allowed to slip, and never again presented itself. New York had taken the start, and has now so entirely outstripped it in population, wealth, enterprise, and foreign intercourse, that it can never hereafter fear any rival on the east coast.

That pre-eminence which New York now enjoys, it owes to several favourable circumstances,—to great natural advantages, and to those which it has derived from the enterprise of its inhabitants. It has a most magnificent harbour, twenty-five miles in circumference, and capable of containing the whole navies of the world. It lies close upon the sea; and by the Hudson river, it has convenient access to some distance in the interior. Those natural advantages alone, would have made it a port of much consequence, but they did not satisfy the inhabitants. A new world was opening up in the north and west, and with those regions it was desirable that New York should be brought into communication. In 1825 the Erie Canal was opened, connecting Lake Erie with the Hudson river. By this means New York was brought into communication, not only with the fertile valleys of the western part of the state, but also with the whole coast of the western lakes; an inland navigation of hundreds of miles was opened up for the enterprise of its merchants, and the whole produce of the west was directed to its harbour for distribution to the markets of the world. The cost of transportation from Buffalo to New York previous to the opening of the canal, was about $100 per ton, and the length of passage was twenty days. Now the cost of carriage is from $2 to $3 per ton, and even that is being diminished.

The success which attended the opening of the Erie Canal led to the construction of that to Lake Champlain, and of branches from the former to points on Lake Ontario. . . .

Satisfactory as were those results, the New York people expected they could improve on them by other enterprises, and by the construction of railways to connect their harbour still farther with the north and west. The traffic on the canals was enormous in quantity, the time occupied in transmitting produce was considerable, much of the merchandise going westward could be sent conveniently by railway, and from the severity of an American winter, the navigation of the canal was obstructed at the very time when farmers and others could most conveniently send their produce to market, and when it was most wanted for consumption. Influenced by these and other considerations, stupendous lines of railways have been constructed or are in progress, to join New York to Lakes Erie and Ontario, and the regions bordering on those lakes in the north and west. One of these lines, the Erie railway, spreads out into a number of lines at each end, forming at each terminus a sort of delta, to accommodate its large business. At the city end it has three outlets, and I believe it touches the western lakes at seven separate points.

From those points on the lakes, bordering on the state of New York, communications are carried on westward to all the other lakes, and thence by rivers, and by canals and railways in course of construction, to various points of the interior. By those channels, the foreign imports into the harbour of New York, and the manufactures of the eastern states reach the consumers of the west; and in return, the latter send by the same routes to the east coast their agricultural and forest productions.

By some of those new enterprises, the valleys of the Mississippi and the Ohio have been approached from New York; and produce, which a very few years ago found its natural outlet to the sea, by the

Gulf of Mexico, is now diverted to the east coast by this newly-opened inland navigation. In this way, the Indian corn of the state of Missouri above St. Louis, reaches Chicago, by the Illinois river and Chicago canal, and thence by lake and canal finds its way to New York; and by the Ohio river and canal, through Cleveland, the provisions from the regions on the Ohio above Louisville, are carried forward to the same destination. It has been even attempted to divert the cotton of Tennessee into this channel, and several cargoes have been brought to the east coast through those new inland routes.

But those advantages, natural and acquired, which New York now enjoys, have secured to it others which will contribute yet further to its prosperity.

It is now the largest—indeed *the* money market of the States; and, therefore, offers facilities to merchants in the transaction of their business, which cannot be afforded by any other city. It is the largest general market in the Union, and therefore commands a preference from buyers and sellers. The extent of its foreign trade ensures a speedy shipment of produce to any part of the world, and average rates of freight; and from its being the point of communication between Europe and America, it affords to merchants at all times, the fullest and latest information upon every subject affecting the commerce of the country.

The future of New York no one can even imagine, far less venture to predict. The position to which it has now attained, seems to have prepared it only for more gigantic strides. Not only is it now in direct communication with many of the most important points in the interior of the country, but it is daily striving to enlarge those communications, and to reduce their cost. The west, as it advances in population and wealth, will almost in the same degree administer to its greatness; for nearly all the surplus produce of those immense regions, will find its natural outlet to the markets of the world, through the ports on the east coast, and through none so readily as New York; and through the same channel will be distributed to the interior, the merchandise which is imported into the Union from all parts of the world. . . .

Undoubtedly most of the trade of the port is carried on by merchants resident there, but as New York offers the best point for shipment of home produce, and for the distribution to the interior of foreign commodities, merchants of the other cities [Boston and Philadelphia] . . . transact much of their business through this city, finding it to afford them the largest, and frequently the most advantageous market.

NEW YORK PANORAMA: 1854

New York City reached an unprecedented peak of prosperity in the middle fifties, and no contemporary travel narrative catches the color and variety of the urban scene more comprehensively or vividly than the work of twenty-three-year-old Isabella Bird, the daughter of an English missionary and in later years the wife of Dr. John Bishop, a medical missionary. The precocious Miss Bird had written an essay on fiscal protection at the age of sixteen. She traveled extensively before her marriage and after her husband's death; and by 1890 she had gained an established reputation as authoress, traveler, and missionary advocate. Her first trip to the United States, undertaken in the interests of her health, resulted in the popular volume, *The Englishwoman in America*. The serious young visitor was in general favorably impressed with the "imposing" New World metropolis. The following excerpts describe the city as she found it upon her arrival by railroad from upstate New York in November 1854.[41]

We had steamed down Tenth Avenue for two or three miles, when we came to a standstill where several streets met. The train was taken to pieces, and to each car four horses or mules were attached, which took us for some distance into the very heart of the town, racing apparently with omnibuses and carriages, till at last we were deposited in Chambers Street, not in a station, or even under cover, be it observed. My baggage, or "plunder" as it is termed, had been previously disposed of, but, while waiting with my head disagreeably near to a horse's nose, I saw people making distracted attempts, and futile ones, as it appeared, to preserve their effects from the clutches of numerous porters, many of them probably thieves. . . .

New York deserves the name applied to Washington, "the city of magnificent distances." I drove in a hack for three miles to my destination, along crowded, handsome streets, but I believe that I only traversed a third part of the city. . . .

Broadway is well paved. . . . Its immense length necessitates an enormous number of conveyances; and in order to obviate the obstruction to traffic which would have been caused by providing omnibus accommodation equal to the demand, the authorities have consented to a most alarming inroad upon several of the principal streets. The stranger sees with surprise that double lines of rails are laid along the roadways; and while driving quietly in a carriage, he hears the sound of a warning bell, and presently a railway-car, holding thirty persons, and drawn by two or four horses, comes thundering down the street. These rail-cars run every few minutes, and the fares are very low. For very sufficient reasons, Broadway is not thus encroached upon; and a journey from one end to the other of this marvellous street is a work of time and difficulty. Pack the traffic of the Strand and Cheapside into Oxford Street, and still you will not have an idea of the crush in Broadway. There are streams of scarlet and yellow omnibuses racing in the more open parts, and locking each other's wheels in the narrower—there are helpless females deposited in the middle of a sea of slippery mud, condemned to run a gauntlet between cart-wheels and horses' hoofs—there are loaded stages hastening to and from the huge hotels—carts and waggons laden with merchandise—and "Young Americans" driving fast-trotting horses, edging in and out among the crowd—wheels are locked, horses tumble down, and persons pressed for time are distracted. Occasionally, the whole traffic of the street comes to a dead-lock, in consequence of some obstruction or crowd, there being no policeman at hand with his incessant command, "Move on!"

The hackney-carriages of New York are very handsome, and, being drawn by two horses, have the appearance of private equipages. . . . The omnibus or stage accommodation is plentiful and excellent. . . . They are sixteen inches wider than our own omnibuses, and carry a number of passengers certainly within their capabilities, and the fares are fixed and very low, 6½ cents for any distance. They have windows to the sides and front, and the spaces between are painted with very tolerably-executed landscapes. . . .

Strangers frequently doubt whether New York possesses a police; the doubt is very justifiable, for these guardians of the public peace are seldom forthcoming when they are wanted. They are accessible to bribes, and will investigate into crime when liberally rewarded; but probably in no city in the civilised world is life so fearfully insecure. The practice of carrying concealed arms, in the shape of stilettoes for attack, and swordsticks for defence, if illegal, is perfectly common; desperate reprobates, called "Rowdies," infest the lower part of the town; and terrible outrages and murderous assaults are matters of such nightly occurrence as to be thought hardly worthy of notice. . . .

The principal stores are situated in Broadway; and although they attempt very little in the way of window display, the interiors are spacious, and arranged with the greatest taste. An American store is generally a very extensive apartment, handsomely decorated, the roof frequently supported on marble pillars. The owner or clerk is seen seated by his goods, absorbed in the morning paper—probably balancing himself on one leg of his chair, with a spittoon by his side. He deigns to answer your inquiries, but, in place of the pertinacious perseverance with which an English shopman displays his wares, it seems a matter of perfect indifference to the American whether you purchase or no. . . .

One of the sights with which the New York people astonish English visitors is Stewart's dry-goods store in Broadway, an immense square building of white marble, six stories high, with a frontage of 300 feet. The business done in it is stated to be above 1,500,000£ per annum. There are 400 people employed at this establishment, which has even a telegraph office on the premises, where a clerk is for ever flashing dollars and cents along the trembling wires. There were lace collars 40 guineas each, and flounces of Valenciennes lace, half a yard deep, at 120 guineas a flounce. The damasks and brocades for curtains and chairs were at almost fabulous prices. Few gentlemen, the clerk observed, give less than 3£ per yard for these articles. The most costly are purchased by the hotels. I saw some brocade embroidered in gold to the thickness of half an inch, some of which had been supplied to the St. Nicholas Hotel at 9£ per yard! There were stockings from a penny to a guinea a pair, and carpetings from 1s.8d. to 22s. a yard! Besides six stories above ground, there were large light rooms under the building and under Broadway itself, echoing with the roll of its 10,000 vehicles.

The hotels are among the sights in New York. The principal are the Astor House (which has a world-wide reputation), the Metropolitan, and the St. Nicholas, all in Broadway. Prescott House and Irving House also afford accommodation on a very large scale. The entrances to these hotels invariably attract the eye of the stranger. Groups of extraordinary-looking human beings are always lounging on the door-steps, smoking, whittling, and reading newspapers. There are southerners sighing for their sunny homes, smoking Havana cigars; western men, with that dashing free-and-easy air which renders them unmistakeable; Englishmen, shrouded in exclusiveness, who look on all their neighbours as so many barbarian intruders on their privacy; and people of all nations, whom business has drawn to the American metropolis. . . .

If there are schools, emigrant hospitals, orphan asylums, and nursing institutions, to mark the good sense and philanthropy of the people of New York, so their love of amusement and recreation is strongly evidenced by the numerous places where both may be procured. There is perhaps as much pleasure-seeking as in Paris; the search after amusement is characterised by the same restless energy which marks the pursuit after wealth; . . . Broadway and its neighbourhood contain more places of amusement than perhaps any district of equal size in the world. These present variety sufficient to embrace the tastes of the very heterogeneous population of New York.

There are three large theatres; an opera house of gigantic proportions, which is annually graced by the highest vocal talent of Europe; Wood's minstrels, and Christy's minstrels, where blacks perform in unexceptionable style to unwearied audiences; and comic operas. There are *al fresco* entertainments, masquerades, concerts, restaurants, and oyster saloons. Besides all these, and many more, New York contained in 1853 the amazing number of 5980 taverns. The number of places where amusement is combined with intellectual improvement is small, when compared with other cities of the same population. There are however some very magnificent reading-rooms and libraries.

The amount of oysters eaten in New York surprised me, although there was an idea at the time of my visit that they produced the cholera, which rather checked any extraordinary excesses in this curious fish. In the business streets of New York the eyes are greeted continually with the words "Oyster Saloon," painted in large letters on the basement story. If the stranger's curiosity is sufficient to induce him to dive down a flight of steps into a subterranean abode, at the first glance rather suggestive of robbery, one favourite amusement of the people may be seen in perfection. There is a counter at one side, where two or three persons, frequently blacks, are busily engaged in opening oysters for their customers, who swallow them with astonishing relish and rapidity. In a room beyond, brightly lighted by gas, family groups are to be seen, seated at round tables, and larger parties of friends enjoying basins of stewed oysters; while from some mysterious recess the process of cookery makes itself distinctly audible. Some of these saloons are highly respectable, while many are just the reverse. But the consumption of oysters is by no means confined to the saloons; in private families an oyster supper is frequently a nightly occurrence; the oysters are dressed in the parlour by an ingenious and not inelegant apparatus. So great is the passion for this luxury, that the consumption of it during the season is estimated at 3500£-a-day.

There are several restaurants in the city, on the model of those in the Palais Royal. The most superb of these, *but not by any means the most respectable,* is Taylor's, in Broadway. It combines Eastern magnificence with Parisian taste, and strangers are always expected to visit it. It is a room about 100 ft. in length, by 22 in height; the roof and cornices richly carved and gilded, the walls ornamented by superb mirrors, separated by white marble. The floor is of marble, and a row of fluted and polished marble pillars runs down each side. It is a perfect blaze of decoration. There is an alcove at one end of the apartment, filled with orange-trees, and the air is kept refreshingly cool by a crystal fountain. Any meal can be obtained here at any hour. On the day on which I visited it, the one hundred marble tables which it contains were nearly all occupied; a double row of equipages lined the street at the door; and two or three hundred people, many of them without bonnets and fantastically dressed, were regaling themselves upon ices and other elegancies. . . . There was a complete maze of fresco, mirrors, carving, gilding, and marble. A dinner can be procured here at any hour of day or night, from one shilling and sixpence up to half-a-guinea, and other meals in like proportion. As we merely went to see the restaurant, we ordered ices which were served from large reservoirs, shining like polished silver. These were paid for at the time, and we received tickets in return, which were taken by the door-keeper on coming out. It might be supposed that Republican simplicity would scorn so much external display; but the places of public entertainment vie in their splendour with the palaces of kings.

It was almost impossible for a stranger to leave New York without visiting the American museum, the property of Phineas Taylor Barnum. . . . His museum is situated in Broadway, near to the City Hall, and is a gaudy building, denoted by huge paintings, multitudes of flags, and a very noisy band. The museum contains many objects of real interest, particularly to the naturalist and geologist, intermingled with a great deal that is spurious and contemptible. . . . There is a collection of horrors or monstrosities attached, which appears to fascinate the vulgar gaze. The principal objects of attraction at this time were a dog with two legs, a cow with four horns, and a calf with six legs—disgusting specimens of deformity, which ought to have been destroyed, rather than preserved to gratify a morbid taste for the horrible and erratic in nature. . . .

The magnificence of the private dwellings of New York must not escape mention. . . . The squares, and many of the numbered streets, contain very superb houses of a most pleasing uniformity of style. . . . These houses are six stories high, and usually contain three reception-rooms; a dining-room, small, and not striking in appearance in any way, as dinner-parties are seldom given in New York; a small, elegantly furnished drawing-room, used as a family sitting-room, and for the reception of morning visitors; and a magnificent reception-room, furnished in the height of taste and elegance, for dancing, music, and evening parties.

In London the bedrooms are generally inconvenient and uncomfortable, being sacrificed to the reception-rooms; in New York this is not the case. The bedrooms are large, lofty, and airy; and are furnished with all the appurtenances which modern luxury has been able to devise. The profusion of marble gives a very handsome and chaste appearance to these apartments. There are bath-rooms generally on three floors, and hot and cold water are laid on in every story. The houses are warmed by air heated from a furnace at the basement; and though in addition open fires are sometimes adopted, they are made of anthracite coal, which emits no smoke. . . .

Having given a brief description of the style of the ordinary dwellings of the affluent, I will just glance at those of the very wealthy, of which there are several in Fifth Avenue, and some of the squares, surpassing anything I had hitherto witnessed in royal or ducal palaces at home. The externals of some of these mansions in Fifth Avenue are like Apsley House, and Stafford House, St. James's; being substantially built of stone. . . .

The best society in New York would not suffer by comparison in any way with the best society in England. It is not in the upper classes of any nation that we must look for national characteristics or peculiarities. Society throughout the civilized world is, to a certain extent, cast in the same mould. . . . Therefore, it is most probable that balls and dinner-parties are in New York exactly the same as in other places, except that the latter are less numerous, and are principally confined to gentlemen. It is not, in fact, convenient to give dinner parties in New York; there are not sufficient domestics to bear the pressure of an emergency, and the pleasure is not considered worth the trouble. . . .

The wharfs . . . are a scene of indescribable bustle from morning to night, with ships arriving and sailing, ships loading and unloading, and emigrants pouring into the town in an almost incessant stream. . . .

A great many of these immigrants were evidently from country districts, and some from Ireland; there were a few Germans among them, and these appeared the least affected by the discomforts of the voyage, and by the novel and rather bewildering position in which they found themselves. They probably would feel more at home on first landing in New York than any of the others, for the lower part of the city is to a great extent inhabited by Germans, and at that time there were about 2000 houses where their favourite beverage, *lager-beer,* could be procured.

The goods and chattels of the Irish appeared to consist principally of numerous red-haired, unruly children, and ragged-looking bundles tied round with rope. The Germans were generally ruddy and stout, and took as much care of their substantial-looking, well-corded, heavy chests as though they contained gold. The English appeared pale and debilitated, and sat helpless and weary-looking on their large blue boxes. Here they found themselves in the chaotic confusion of this million-peopled city, not knowing whither to betake themselves, and bewildered by cries of "Cheap hacks!" "All aboard!" "Come to the cheapest house in all the world!" and invitations of a similar description. There were lodging-touters of every grade of dishonesty, and men with large placards were hurrying among the crowd, offering "palace" steamboats and "lightning express" trains, to whirl them at nominal rates to the Elysian Fields of the Far West. . . .

New York, with its novel, varied, and ever-changing features, is calculated to leave a very marked impression on a stranger's mind. In one part one can suppose it to be a negro town; in another, a German city; while a strange dreamy resemblance to Liverpool pervades the whole. In it there is little repose for the mind, and less for the eye, except on the Sabbath-day, which is very well observed, considering the widely-differing creeds and nationalities of the inhabitants. The streets are alive with business, retail and wholesale, and present an aspect of universal bustle. Flags are to be seen in every direction, the tall masts of ships appear above the houses; large square pieces of calico, with names in scarlet or black letters upon them, hang across the streets, to denote the whereabouts of some popular candidate or "puffing" storekeeper; and hosts of omnibuses, hacks, drays, and railway cars at full speed, ringing bells, terrify unaccustomed foot-passengers. There are stores of the magnitude of bazaars, "daguerrean galleries" by hundreds, crowded groggeries and subterranean oyster-saloons, huge hotels, coffee-houses, and places of amusement; while the pavements present men of every land and colour, red, black, yellow, and white, in every variety of costume and beard, and ladies, beautiful and ugly, richly dressed. Then there are mud huts, and palatial residences, and streets of stately dwelling-houses, shaded by avenues of ilanthus-trees; waggons discharging goods across the pavements; shops above and cellars below; railway whistles and steamboat bells, telegraph-wires, eight and ten to a post, all converging towards Wall Street—the Lombard Street of New York; militia regiments in many-coloured uniforms, marching in and out of the city all day; groups of emigrants bewildered and amazed, emaciated with dysentery and sea-sickness, looking in at the shop-windows; representatives of every nation under heaven, speaking in all earth's Babel languages; and as if to render this ceaseless pageant of business, gaiety, and change, as far removed from monotony as possible, the quick toll of the fire alarm-bells may be daily heard, and the huge engines, with their burnished equipments and well-trained companies, may be seen to dash at full speed along the streets to the scene of some brilliant conflagration. New York is calculated to present as imposing an appearance to an Englishman as its antiquated namesake does to an American, with its age, silence, stateliness, and decay.

"KLEINDEUTSCHLAND" IN THE FIFTIES

The German element was a much more conspicuous ingredient of New York's cosmopolitanism in the 1850's than it was a century later when more recent migrants from southern and eastern Europe had further diversified the city's nationality pattern. Less numerous than the Irish, in the fifties, the German residents were nevertheless more identifiably foreign; and their tendency to dwell among their compatriots, where they could "speak their own language and live according to their own customs," emphasized the differences between them and the native population. By the eve of the Civil War, a majority of the city's some 120,000 German-born residents appear to have been concentrated in the section from Houston to Twelfth Street, eastward from the Bowery. This "Deutschländle," or "Little Germany," was described by Karl Theodor Griesinger, a member of the German liberal generation of the forties. Upon his release from prison, to which he had been sent by the Catholic government of Baden for editing a radical newspaper, he spent the five years from 1852 to 1857 in the United States. He wrote a number of books describing his experiences. The following excerpt is from his *Land und Leute in Amerika: Skizzen aus dem amerikanischen Leben.*[42]

The traveller who passes up Broadway, through Chatham Street, into the Bowery, up Houston Street, and thence right to First Avenue will find himself in a section which has very little in common with the other parts of New York. The arrangement of the streets and the monotony of the brownstone dwellings are similar, but the height and detail of the houses, the inhabitants, and their language and customs differ greatly from those of the rest of New York. This is "Kleindeutschland," or "Deutschländle," as the Germans call this part of the city. . . .

The first floor of the houses along these avenues serves as a grocery or shoemaker's shop, or even an inn; but the upper floors still house from five to 24 families, in some buildings as many as 48. . . . On each floor of such buildings there are eight apartments, four on the street side and four on the back. Naturally the apartments are very small: a living room with two windows and a bedroom with no windows—that is all. The room with the two windows is 10 feet by 10 feet, and such apartments rent for five to six dollars a month. Apartments on the back cost four dollars or less monthly. Apartments in buildings where only ten or twelve families reside rent for eight to nine dollars. These apartments contain a comfortable living room, with three windows, and two bedrooms. According to the standards of the German workingman, one can live like a prince for ten to fourteen dollars a month. Apartments at this price contain two bedrooms, two living rooms, one of which is used for a kitchen, and sufficient room for storing coal and wood.

That's how the Germans live in *Kleindeutschland.* But they are satisfied—happy, contented, and, most significantly, among their own people. . . . *Deutschländle* certainly deserves its name, because 15,000 German families, comprising seventy to seventy-five thousand people live here. New York has about 120,000 German-born inhabitants. Two-thirds of these live in *Kleindeutschland*. They come from every part of Germany, although those from northern Germany are rarer than those from the southern part, and Hessians, people from Baden, Wuertembergers, and Rhenish Bavarians are most numerous.

Naturally the Germans were not forced by the authorities, or by law, to settle in this specific area. It just happened. But the location was favorable because of its proximity to the downtown business district where the Germans are employed. Moreover, the Germans like to live together; this permits them to speak their own language and live according to their own customs. The cheapness of the apartments also prompted their concentration. As the first Germans came into *Kleindeutschland*, the Irish began to move and the Americans followed because they were ashamed to live among immigrants.

Life in *Kleindeutschland* is almost the same as in the Old Country. Bakers, butchers, druggists—all are Germans. There is not a single business which is not run by Germans. Not only the shoemakers, tailors, barbers, physicians, grocers, and innkeepers are German, but the pastors and priests as well. There is even a German lending library where one can get all kinds of German books. The resident of *Kleindeutschland* need not even know English in order to make a living, which is a considerable attraction to the immigrant.

The shabby apartments are the only reminder that one is in America. Tailors or shoemakers use their living rooms as workshops, and there is scarcely space to move about. The smell in the house is not too pleasant, either, because the bedrooms have no windows, and there is a penetrating odor of sauerkraut. But the Germans do not care. They look forward to the time when they can afford a three-room apartment; and they would never willingly leave their beloved *Kleindeutschland*. The Americans who own all these buildings know this. That's why they do not consider improving the housing conditions. They like the Germans as tenants because they pay their rent, punctually, in advance, and keep the buildings neat and clean. The landlords are interested in keeping the German tenants crowded together because such buildings bring more profit than one-story houses. . . .

There are more inns in *Kleindeutschland* than in Germany. Every fourth house is an inn, and there is one for every 200 people. To the stranger, coming for the first time into the section, it would appear that there was nothing but beer saloons. Actually an immense quantity of beer is consumed. Since the German does not care for brandy there is not a single hard liquor saloon in *Kleindeutschland*. Wine is too expensive, so the resident has to be content with beer.

One who has not seen the *Deutschländle* on a Sunday, does not know it at all. What a contrast it presents to the American sections, where the shutters are closed, and the quiet of a cemetery prevails! On Sundays the . . . churches are full, but there is nevertheless general happiness and good cheer. The Protestant Germans do not indulge in much religious observance. They profess to be freethinkers, and do not go to church very often. On the other hand, the Catholic church on Third Street is always overcrowded. It was built from the voluntary contributions of the German workingmen. Saving the money out of their weekly pay, they have built the second largest, and the most beautiful, church in New York City. It has a big tower and three bells, and nearby is a school which the German children attend and where classes are conducted in German. All this has been accomplished through the monthly contributions of the German workingmen, who take great pride in their school and their church.

On Sunday the movement in the streets is like that in a dovecote. People go from the inn to the church and back to the inn again. Everybody wears his Sunday clothes and is in high spirits. In the afternoon, on days when the weather is good, almost everybody leaves town and goes on a picnic. On Sunday night there is still more merriment in *Kleindeutschland*. The inns are crowded, even with women. There is music, in spite of the laws against making noise on Sunday.

The Germans have a *Volkstheater,* although the name theatre can hardly be applied to this long hall where the consumption of beer and cheese is a major activity. At the end of the hall is a small stage; and the performances are not real plays as much as entertainment by comedians whom the proprietor hires to amuse his customers. Their ribald songs receive the enthusiastic applause of the audience. The people enjoy themselves immensely; the entertainment costs only ten cents, and one gets a free beer now and then. Such is the way Sunday is celebrated in *Kleindeutschland*.

THE FIRE LADDIES OF THE FIFTIES

Observers of the fifties were as little impressed with the efficiency of the city's fire-fighting facilities as they were with that of its other municipal services. They nevertheless had to admit that the volunteer "fire laddies" lent color and excitement to the urban scene and enjoyed a prestige far beyond that of similar public servants in European cities. The organization and practices of the fire companies interested Charles Mackay, the British journalist and poet, who undertook an eight-months' lecture tour in the United States and Canada from October 1857 to June 1858. A Scotsman by birth, Mackay was associated in turn with the London *Morning Chronicle,* the Glasgow *Argus,* and the *Illustrated London News,* of which he became editor in 1852. He returned to New York City in 1862 and served as a special correspondent of the London *Times* for the duration of the American Civil War. He was the author of a long list of works of prose and poetry. The following excerpt from his *Life and Liberty in America* describes a parade, or "turn-out," of the city's fire companies in December 1857.[43]

Each company had its favourite engine, of which it is as fond as a captain is of his ship, gaily ornamented with ribbons, flags, streamers, and flowers, and preceded by a band of music. Each engine was dragged along the streets by the firemen in their peculiar costume—dark pantaloons, with leathern belt around the waist, large boots, a thick red shirt, with no coat or vest, and the ordinary fireman's helmet. Each man held the rope of the engine in one hand, and a blazing torch in the other. The sight was peculiarly impressive and picturesque. I counted no less than twenty different companies, twenty engines, and twenty bands of music—the whole procession taking upwards of an hour to pass the point at which I stood. The occasion of the gathering was to receive a fire company on its return from a complimentary visit to another fire company in the adjoining Commonwealth of Rhode Island, a hundred miles off. Such interchanges of civility and courtesy are common among the "boys," who incur very considerable expense in making them, the various companies presenting each other with testimonials of regard and esteem, in the shape of silver claret-jugs, candelabra, tea services, etc. But the peculiarities of the firemen, the constitution of their companies, the life they lead, and their influence in the local politics and government of the great cities of the Union, are quite a feature in

American civic life, totally different from anything we have in England. . . .

The firemen are mostly youths engaged during the day in various handicrafts and mechanical trades, with a sprinkling of clerks and shopmen. In New York, each candidate for admission into the force must be balloted for, like a member of the London clubs. If elected, he has to serve for five years, during which he is exempt from jury and militia duty. The firemen elect their own superintendents and other officers, by ballot, as they were themselves elected; and are divided into engine companies, hook and ladder companies, and hose companies. The engine and accessories are provided by the municipality; but the firemen are seldom contented with them in the useful but unadorned state in which they receive them, but lavish upon them an amount of ornament, in the shape of painted panels, silver plating, and other finery, more than sufficient to prove their liberality, and the pride they take in their business. The service is entirely voluntary and gratuitous, having no advantages to recommend it but those of exemption from the jury and the militia, and leads those who devote themselves to it not only into great hardship and imminent danger, but into an amount of expenditure which is not the least surprising part of the "institution." The men—or "boys," as they are more commonly called—not only buy their own costume and accoutrements, and spend large sums in the ornamentation of their favourite engines, or hydrants, as already mentioned, but in the furnishing of their bunk-rooms and parlours at the fire-stations. The bunk or sleeping rooms, in which the unmarried, and sometimes the married, members pass the night, to be ready for duty on the first alarm of fire, are plainly and comfortably furnished; but the parlours are fitted up with a degree of luxury equal to that of the public rooms of the most celebrated hotels. At one of the central stations, which I visited in company with an editor of a New York journal, the walls were hung with portraits of Washington, Franklin, Jefferson, Mason, and other founders of the Republic; the floor was covered with velvet-pile carpeting, a noble chandelier hung from the centre, the crimson curtains were rich and heavy, while the sideboard was spread with silver claret-jugs and pieces of plate, presented by citizens whose houses and property had been preserved from fire by the exertions of the brigade; or by the fire companies of other cities.

Alexander Marjoribanks, a professional British traveler who visited New York in 1850, described the competitive behavior of the companies at the time of fires. The following comment appears in his *Travels in South and North America,* which was published in 1853.[44]

The fire department in New York . . . is a most wonderful thing. As the point of honor is to be first at a fire, the director of the first engine that arrives, becomes director-general for the evening. He is, as it were, the commander-in-chief of an allied army during a battle. The company attached to each engine amounts to from 20 to 100 men, and it starts from the station-house as soon as three or four have arrived to direct its movements. The people in the streets assist in dragging it with ropes, as no horses are employed. The competition to be first is so ardent, that ambitious young men sleep as if a part of the brain were left awake to watch for the word "fire," or the sound of the . . . alarm-bell. They will sometimes put on their boots and great-coats, carry their clothes in their hands, and dress at the fire. In rushing along the streets, sometimes blowing horns, and ringing the large bells attached to the engines all the time, they often run down and severely injure passengers who are in their way; or if one of themselves fall, the rest drag on the engine, regardless of his fate, and occasionally break his legs or arms with the wheels. When two engines arrive at a fire at the same time, the companies frequently fight for the first place, and then a desperate and bloody battle will rage for a considerable time, while the flames are making an unchecked progress. They are often called out on very trivial alarms, and being once abroad at midnight hours, they adjourn to taverns, and pass the night in nocturnal recreations. . . . On inquiring one day of a bystander, if all this hubbub were necessary, he politely replied, "I guess the youth here need excitement."

7. *NEW YORK IN THE SIXTIES*

COMMENTATORS OF MANY NATIONALITIES described the emerging metropolis in the decade during which it felt the intensifying impact of the Civil War. On the eve of the conflict there were such distinguished visitors as the first official emissaries from Japan; England's Prince of Wales, the future Edward VII; and the party of Prince Napoleon, a cousin of Napoleon III. The war brought a spate of correspondents—William H. Russell of the London *Times,* Edward Dicey of the *Spectator,* George Sala of the *Daily Telegraph,* and John Skinner of the *Daily News,* as well as the French writer and political figure Ernest Duvergier de Hauranne. To portray the city upon the return of peace there was such a varied group, among others, as England's Charles Dickens and Sir Charles Dilke; the Argentinian educator, statesman, and journalist Domingo Sarmiento; Friedrich Gerstäcker, the German travel writer; and America's Mark Twain, viewing the "overgrown" metropolis after an absence of thirteen years. Meanwhile, New Yorkers like George Templeton Strong and Walt Whitman continued their perceptive comment on the changing urban scene.[1]

The "Great White Way" was still a development of the future when New York was host to the members of the initial Japanese mission in May and June of 1860. Nevertheless, it was the illumination of the gaslit city which most impressed the visitors "from Niphon come," as Whitman wrote in describing the pageantry of Manhattan's welcome to the Orientals. "There is a street light in front of each door which when lighted at night makes the street seem as bright as day," one of the Japanese reported. "Some of the buildings have as many as a hundred gas lights over the entrance. The light in the rooms of the houses shining through the glass windows at night is so wonderful and is such a surprise to us that I cannot describe it." The arrival of the Prince of Wales in the following October brought a "week of excitement . . . pervading all classes" which was beyond that of any event which that ubiquitous diarist, Strong, had witnessed in his lifetime. "By ten o'clock, people were stationing themselves along the curbstones of Broadway, . . . one long dense mass of impatient humanity," Strong wrote on October 11. "All the windows on either side were filled. Temporary platforms crowded, at five dollars a seat. . . . What a spectacle-loving people we are!" [2]

Within a year, the pageantry of peace had given way to that of war; and the city's commentators—many of them war correspondents—were reporting New York's reaction to the civil conflict that imperiled the nation (if not the city) between 1861 and 1865. The firing on Fort Sumter brought a burst of enthusiasm for the Union cause which belied earlier attempts of the New York business community to encourage compromise with the seceding Southern states. The city was dazzling in its festival attire, wrote a French clergyman who happened to be in New York during the first two months of the war. "Every window had its one or more flags." Omnibuses and "even the horses of the common carts" were decked out in the national colors.[3]

New York's original coolness toward the crisis had been prompted by its merchants' fear of "offending their Southern friends and connections," wrote the correspondent of the London *Times,* on the basis of observations extending from March to July of 1861. "When, however, [they] . . . saw the South was determined to quit the Union, they resolved to avert the permanent loss of the great profits derived from their connection with the South by some present sacrifices. They rushed to the platforms—the battle-cry was sounded from almost every pulpit—flag raising took place in every square, . . . and the oath was taken to trample Secession under foot, and to quench the fire of the Southern heart forever." [4]

In these early months of the war, mass meetings in Union Square drew hundreds of thousands of shouting, singing spectators. Broadway was thronged with "companies of recruits in citizen's dress parading up and down, cheered and cheering. . . . Every . . . man, woman, and child bearing a flag" appeared to have gone "suddenly wild and crazy." The departure of each regiment was the occasion for a new celebration; and in the opinion of a visiting Frenchman, the Astor House, opposite the recruiting ground in the Park, seemed "to be placed there expressly for the *adieux.*" Champagne "inflated the sails of American eloquence"; and patriotic women presented flags of their own making to the departing regiments.[5]

For Walt Whitman, the war lent an added excitement to the pageant of Manhattan:

. . . Broadway, with the soldiers marching. . . .
(The soldiers in companies or regiments—some starting away, flush'd and reckless,
Some, their time up, returning with thinn'd ranks, young, yet very old, worn, marching, noticing nothing. . . .)
Manhattan streets with their powerful throbs, with beating drums as now,
The endless and noisy chorus, the rustle and clank of muskets. . . .

But many New Yorkers, after the first burst of patriotic ardor, settled down to endure, if not indeed to take advantage of, the civil conflict. In many quarters outright opposition to the war continued. In 1863, a British visitor heard Governor Seymour rallying local Democrats to oppose the "despotic action of the Federal Government" (in Republican hands), an attitude which recalled Mayor Fernando Wood's proposal, early in 1861, that New York disassociate itself from the Union and assume the status of a free city.[6]

By November of 1862, the martial enthusiasm of former months was perceptibly on the wane. Strong confided to his diary that "traitors" were "now beginning cautiously to tamper with the great torrent of national feeling that burst out, April 1861," taking advantage of a prevailing "mass of selfishness, frivolity, invincible prejudice, personal Southern attachment, [and] indifference to national life." At a masquerade at the Belmont mansion, which Strong attended in February 1863, the Marquis of Hartington wore "a showy little secesh flag, conspicuously stuck in his buttonhole." Presumably the young Englishman "had been consorting with W. Duncan and Belmont and naturally thought sympathy with rebellion *the thing* in New York." [7]

Politics also encouraged disaffection from the Union cause. Democratic politicians apparently convinced the city's Irish laborers that the draft was taking a disproportionate share of their number and that emancipation would strengthen the competition of Negroes in the local labor market. This helped to cause the bloody draft riots of mid-July 1863, which took a tragic toll of the city's colored residents. In 1864, Wood and other "Peace Democrats" plotted with Confederate operators in an abortive attempt to foment rebellion in the city during the presidential contest of that year. According to a

British visitor, the "struggle for the election of President" appeared to be attracting more local interest than was the "tremendous struggle going on outside." Partisans even boarded the streetcars to take the votes of the passengers for Lincoln or McClellan; and the "smallest triumph of the kind" the visitor ever saw recorded was "in a communication to the *World,* stating that the vote had been taken on a city car, and that out of twenty-four persons there were eighteen for McClellan, and only six for Lincoln." In view of such behavior, it is not surprising that a French traveler, who visited the city in the summer of 1864, should conclude that New York was "Democratic and pro-Southern. . . . The money interest and the masses, who dominate, desire above everything else, an end of war, relief from taxes, and a cessation of recruitment." [8]

Comments of this kind, however, obscure the very real contribution made by many citizens of the Empire City to the winning of the war. This was true not only in the realm of manpower, but also in the provision of goods, the subscription of funds, and the exertion of political influence in the interest of preserving the Union. Within three weeks after the firing on Fort Sumter, a Union Defense Committee had been organized and a war fund of more than $2,000,000 subscribed. The city's leading merchants were represented on the defense committee, which undertook to organize volunteer regiments, provide local relief, and supply the Army with equipment of all kinds. New York's womanhood also made a signal contribution in the activities of the Woman's Central Association of Relief for the Sick and Wounded of the Army, one of the forerunners of the United States Sanitary Commission. The Metropolitan Fair, held in April 1864, for the benefit of the Commission, netted more than a million dollars.[9]

Such activities, however, were overshadowed by the more conspicuous evidences of the material prosperity which was accruing to New York as a result of the war. As early as 1862, the correspondent of the London *Spectator* reported that, in view of the prevailing prosperity, an "incurious stranger," not given to conversation or reading the newspaper, might almost have inhabited New York for weeks "without discovering that the country was involved in a civil war." "Go into Broadway, and we will show you what is meant by the word 'extravagance,' " counseled the editor of the New York *Independent,* in June of 1864. "Ask Stewart about the demand for camel's hair shawls, and he will say 'monstrous.' Ask Tiffany what

NEW NEW YORKERS

A flood of immigrants from Europe—and especially from its southern and eastern parts—swelled the rapidly expanding population of New York City at the turn of the twentieth century. Contemporaries observed them at the docks, in old-country attire, as in this photograph taken near Battery Park in about 1890. Often they stood bewildered amid boxes and hampers before taking off for sections of the city in which their compatriots lived.

Italian names and swarthy skins identify Mulberry Bend (about 1890, left)—where "Mulberry Street crooks like an elbow"—as the locale of newcomers from Italy's "sunny climes." Jacob Riis found this congested section more like "the market-place in some town of Southern Italy than a street in New York—all but the houses" which were "the same old tenements of the unromantic type."

Yiddish signs and curbstone merchandising characterized the squalid Jewish quarter, centered upon Ludlow, Hester, and Essex streets, on New York's lower East Side. Jacob Riis reported that two small rooms in a six-story tenement on Essex Street held a "family" of "father and mother, twelve children and six boarders."

Picture Credits:
(*top*) Museum of the City of New York
(*center*) Courtesy of *The News*, New York's Picture Newspaper
(*bottom*) Courtesy of *The News*, New York's Picture Newspaper

Courtesy of The New-York Historical Society, New York City

The Jacob A. Riis Collection, Museum of the City of New York

THE HOMES OF THE RICH

Millionaires' Row was an array of palatial residences that by 1900 extended along Fifth Avenue from the Forties to the Seventies. On the left is the Renaissance chateau, designed by Richard Morris Hunt for William K. Vanderbilt, that formerly stood on the northwest corner of Fifth Avenue and Fifty-second Street. Its baronial splendor, borrowed from Europe, contrasts with the adjoining traditional brownstones. Beyond are the spires of St. Thomas's Episcopal Church and the Fifth Avenue Presbyterian Church. In such churches, ministers were said to preach to $250,000,000 every Sunday. On the right is portrayed a fashionable sleighing expedition of about 1900, set against almost the identical background.

Museum of the City of New York

The Jacob A. Riis Collection, Museum of the City of New York

THE HOMES OF THE POOR

Jacob Riis photographed this sweatshop, in a Ludlow Street tenement, in the late 1880's (left). A French observer of the early nineties could hardly "endure the air" of rooms where hollow-faced workers toiled over garments for which they were paid at the rate of a dollar a day.

Malodorous back alleys, like Bandits' Roost on Mulberry Street (at the right), housed many of New York's poor in the 1880's and 1890's. This picture, taken by Jacob Riis, was used to illustrate his *How the Other Half Lives*. The reformer reported that high rates of infant mortality, fiendish abuse, and even murder were the "everyday crop" of this dilapidated section.

The Jacob A. Riis Collection, Museum of the City of New

Museum of the City of New

THE SIDEWALKS OF NEW YORK

Contemporaries deplored the physical sordidness and squalor of many parts of New York City in the 1880's and 1890's. Rubbish and refuse obstructed the streets and sidewalks, as in this photo by Jacob Riis, exposing conditions in Manhattan when municipal graft and corruption governed the provision of urban services. According to Rudyard Kipling, the streets of New York in the 1890's were "kin to the approaches to a Zulu kraal."

Festoons of telephone, telegraph, and electric-light wires, suspended from rough-hewn poles, obscured the New York sky and presented special hazards when they were encumbered with snow, as in the blizzard of 1888 (right). The Legislature had passed a law in 1884 requiring that such wires be placed underground, but this work was still going on at the close of the century.

kind of diamonds and pearls are called for. He will answer 'the prodigious,' 'as near hen's egg size as possible,' 'price no object.'" As for the cause of the prosperity, in addition to war orders, stock speculation, and inflation, the bad grain harvests in Europe, according to one French visitor, had given an impulse to New York's commerce that "nearly compensated for her rupture with the Southern states." [10]

Statistics supported the outward signs of material gains. The value of goods produced in New York County more than doubled during the decade—from less than $160,000,000 in 1860 to nearly $333,000,000, ten years later; bank deposits, during the war years alone, jumped from less than $80,000,000 to nearly $225,000,000; and the value of real and personal property almost doubled, during the decade, to stand at more than a billion dollars by 1870. The Stock Exchange, where securities totaling $3,000,000,000 were handled in 1868, gave Wall Street an attraction to visitors it was not to have again until the 1920's. Two English travelers were fascinated by operations there in 1869: "The vice president stood on the rostrum like an auctioneer, hammer in hand"; and as stocks were sold in rotation, according to a list printed on a blackboard, the dealers "in a wild crowd" proceeded with "a Babel of unearthly yells, which meant bidding." Stock tickers, introduced in 1868, were a novelty characteristic of the times. "Look into any office in Wall Street," wrote the British visitors, "and click, click, goes the machine, spinning out a paper ribbon, upon which is distinctly printed every sale as it is made." [11]

The rising cost of living further reflected the accelerated tempo of the sixties. "The ascendancy of dollars" was written "on every paving stone along Fifth Avenue, down Broadway, and up Wall Street," wrote the English novelist Anthony Trollope, early in the decade. During the war, the demand for houses was unprecedented; "new stores and streets were still building, and notices of 'houses to let'" were very few. Mark Twain, assessing the changes of the war years, after his arrival in 1867, contended that they had "increased the population of New York and its suburbs a quarter of a million souls," covered "her waste places with acres upon acres of costly buildings," "made five thousand men wealthy, and for a good round million of her citizens" made it "a matter of the closest kind of scratching to get along." "Everything is high," he reported. "You pay twelve hundred dollars rental, now, for the dwelling you used to get for five or six hundred. . . . You pay $20 to $25 and $30 a week for the same sort of private board and lodging you got for $8 and $10 when I was here thirteen years ago. . . . I find that with due moderation, a single man can get along after a fashion for forty to fifty dollars a week. God help the married ones!" [12]

Visitor and resident alike lampooned the war-made rich, or "Shoddy aristocracy," which was "tossed to the surface in the convulsion of society caused by the war." In French the invidious label was rendered "Shodés" as Madame Olympe Audouard described the pretentions of the *nouveaux* whom she observed on her visit to the city. According to George Borrett, a fellow of one of the colleges of Cambridge University who was in New York in 1864, Mr. Shoddy had "spent his thousands, and Mrs. Shoddy her tens of thousands, in ornamentation of their respective persons until he and she can see in one another not merely a metaphorical jewel, but a perfect walking museum of gems and gildings." As for the "genuine aristocracy" of the city, they, according to Mark Twain, stood "stunned and helpless under the new order of things." "They find themselves supplanted by upstart princes of Shoddy, vulgar and with unknown grandfathers. Their incomes, which were something for the common herd to gape at and gossip about once, are mere livelihoods now—would not pay Shoddy's house-rent. They move into remote new streets up town, and talk feelingly of the crash which is to come when the props are knocked from under this flimsy edifice of prosperity." [13]

Certainly something of this attitude is reflected in the entries in Strong's diary for 1864 and 1865. "How New York has fallen off during the last forty [could he have meant four?] years!" he lamented in March of 1864. "Its intellect and culture have been diluted and swamped by a great flood-tide of material wealth." He disdained as "hideous," "ugly," and "barbaric" the hundred-thousand-dollar mansions of the newly rich, as well as the social aspirations of men "whose bank accounts are all they can rely on for social position and influence." Even the costliness of the carriages, thronging Fifth Avenue on their way to Central Park, which he described in March 1865, reminded him unpleasantly of the "profits of Shoddy and petroleum." "Not a few of the ladies who were driving in the most sumptuous turn-outs, with liveried servants, looked as if they might have been cooks or chambermaids a very few years ago." [14]

Whether because of the pretentiousness of the war-made wealth, or for some other reason—sympathy for the South, tensions born of diplomatic crises, or even envy of its overweening prosperity—commentators of the sixties were generally more critical of New York City than were those of previous years. What travelers of the fifties thought magnificent was now called "repulsive and vulgar"; Broadway was belittled as a "one-horse boulevard"—without symmetry enough for grandeur nor irregular enough to be picturesque; and even Fifth Avenue, for all the wealth it represented, was criticized for the "dreadful monotony" of its tightly packed brownstone structures and the meretricious elegance of its architecture. French travelers, still looking for palaces and monuments, found them only in the city's quays, its vast stores and hotels, or the dwellings of its merchant princes, like the $2,000,000 residence of A. T. Stewart, rising at the close of the decade at the corner of Thirty-fourth Street and Fifth Avenue. Anthony Trollope found less to admire in the city than had his traditionally more critical mother, a generation earlier. "I know no great man, no celebrated statesman, no philanthropist of peculiar note who has lived on Fifth Avenue," he wrote, following his visit late in 1861. "That gentleman on the right made a million of dollars by inventing a shirt-collar; this one on the left electrified the world by a lotion. . . . Such are the aristocracy of Fifth Avenue." Visitors of the late sixties contended that the race for riches in New York was "perhaps the fastest in the world, and the racers the most unscrupulous." [15]

The most universal subject of criticism was the disgraceful condition of the city's streets: in winter, when horses floundered through "a coating of some three or four feet of snow, indented with holes and furrows . . . of most alarming magnitude"; in summer, when visitors slipped on garbage or had to wade up to the ankles in mud "in front of a marble palace." After a visit in 1867, George Rose, the British monologuist and writer, called New York "one of the worst lighted, worst paved, and worst kept cities in the world"; and even a much more charitable Scottish divine contended that the dirtiest streets of London or Glasgow were "like a drawing-room floor compared with the streets of New York on a slushy day." "The condition of the streets seems to be only a picture of the municipal government generally," he concluded, after visiting New York in 1867 and 1868.[16]

The corruptness of local politics was certainly one of the factors which debased the prestige of New York in the eyes of commentators of the sixties. By the close of the decade the city government was in the grip of the Tweed Ring, which ultimately mulcted the citizens of an estimated $200,000,000. "To be a citizen of New York is a disgrace," Strong stormed in his diary in December 1868. "The New Yorker belongs to a community worse governed by lower and baser blackguard scum than any city in Western Christendom." As did most of the foreign commentators, Strong found an easy explanation for the corruption in the manipulation of the foreign vote, especially that of the Irish. Despite the war, the number of foreign-born increased during the decade. The Irish were still the most numerous, so much so as to make New York an Irish city in the opinion of young Charles Wentworth Dilke, whose tour of the English-speaking world in 1866 and 1867 was ultimately recorded in his *Greater Britain.* Its already broadly cosmopolitan society "denationalized" the huge city, in Dilke's opinion, making it less representative of the America of the past than "the humblest township of New England" or the "most chaotic village of Nebraska." Other commentators, by contrast, declared that the city's very cosmopolitanism made it typical of contemporary American life.[17]

For one branch of the municipal service there was, however, almost universal acclaim. This was the police—"large, fine looking men," whose "blue uniforms, well studded with brass buttons, . . . jack boots, and . . . batons worn like a dagger" gave them, according to Mark Twain, "an imposing military aspect." "New York's finest" impressed visitors of the sixties as they charged through the "tangled vehicles," ordering "this one to go this way, another that," halted the torrent of traffic to conduct timid females through a sea of hurrying conveyances, or gallantly assisted them in boarding an omnibus. "The women like it," Twain reported. "I stood by for two hours and watched one of them cross seven or eight times on various pretences, and always on the same handsome policeman's arm." Charles Dickens, revisiting America in the fall of 1867 to give a series of readings, insisted that "nowhere, at home or abroad," had he "seen so fine a police as the police of New York." Their bearing was "above all praise."[18]

The "torrent of traffic" was no new phenomenon for the "million-footed" city; but observers were now more likely to be exasperated by it than impressed. Visitors complained that the horse-drawn streetcars were always packed. A double row of riders jammed the central aisles; the drivers' platforms were occupied to overflowing;

and passengers even clung, like bees on a bough, to the platform behind. By the mid-sixties there were proposals for an underground railway—"a lower Broadway," along which the city's monotonous business traffic might move "uninterrupted" while "upper and brighter Broadway" remained "the lounge of the flâneur, the Rialto of the merchant, and the promenade of the belle." Although this method of relieving the congested streets was postponed for future development, an experimental elevated line had been inaugurated by the close of the sixties. The incorporation of the Hansom Cab Company in 1869 helped to meet the lack of private conveyances which hitherto had annoyed the city's visitors.[19]

Improvements in ferry service and the first steps in the construction of the Brooklyn Bridge, in the winter of 1866–67, pointed up a flight to the "suburbs" that was dictated by the increasingly high cost of living and the lack of housing on Manhattan. Dickens wrote in 1867 that Brooklyn was "a kind of sleeping-place for New York"; and local commentators were already pointing out that with the removal of middle-class residents, there were but two classes left in the city: the rich and the poor. In the realm of municipal administration, a corollary of this suburban trend was the creation of a number of metropolitan authorities, patterned after the Metropolitan Police District, which had been established in 1857. One of these was the Metropolitan Fire District, which took in both Manhattan and Brooklyn and which was set up for the administration of the paid fire department that was created by the legislature in 1865—"to the great disgust and wrath" of "our ancient, rowdy . . . engine companies," as Strong recorded in his diary. A Metropolitan Sanitary District and other metropolitan agencies followed. Indeed, as early as December 1868, Andrew H. Green proposed bringing the city of New York and its various suburbs under one common government—a forecast of the consolidation that was to be achieved thirty years later.[20]

The congestion of the central city was one of the chief complaints of Mark Twain as he came back to the metropolis from America's "open spaces." In a letter to a San Francisco newspaper, he cited the city inspector's report for 1864 which showed that more than half a million New Yorkers lived in 15,000 tenements—an average of eight families to a house, though "some swarmed with two or three hundred persons." Such was the crowding by the mid-sixties that diarist Strong predicted that by the year 1900 Manhattan's Belgravia would be transferred from Fifth Avenue to King's County, for "Brooklyn has room to expand and New York has not." More precisely prophetic was the appearance, on the crowded island, of a new solution to meet the ever present need for multiple dwellings. The turn of the seventies saw the completion of the city's first modern apartment house, a four-story structure on East Eighteenth Street which contained sixteen suites, each with six rooms and a bath. For the middle-class New Yorker, dwellings of this kind, built on a French model, permitted a compromise between the expensive and almost unavailable single house and hotel or boarding house living.[21]

Contemporary comment on the amusement scene reflects the changes in taste and practice which were dictated by the expanding population, the increasing wealth, and the altered standards of Civil War New York. Theatres multiplied; by the later sixties, close to twenty were offering a broad choice of entertainment nightly—from opera to burlesque; box office receipts totaled $3,000,000 in a good year. The theatre-going public was so numerous that long-run plays were beginning to supplement stock-company repertory. To Dickens' amazement, Niblo's extravaganza, *The Black Crook,* had played "every night for 16 months (!)"; and when the box office opened for the sale of tickets to the author's course of readings, purchasers, including many speculators, were lined up for three quarters of a mile. In Mark Twain's opinion, *The Black Crook*—first of Manhattan's long-run "girl-show" spectacles—exhibited the change in popular taste from the days when *Uncle Tom's Cabin* was all the rage. "The scenery and the legs are everything," he reported. "Girls—nothing but a wilderness of girls—stacked up, pile on pile, away aloft to the dome of the theatre. . . . dressed with a meagreness that would make a parasol blush." Edwin Booth and the legitimate drama still drew "immense houses"; but Twain was of the opinion that the famous tragedian would have to "make a little change and peel some women" if he wished to go along with the popular taste.[22]

Commentators of the sixties noted increasing evidence of "high society"—outdoors in Central Park, where the "carriage parade" and the trotting of fast horses were much in vogue; and indoors, at extravagant banquets and costume balls, at one of which the hostess appeared as "Music," wearing in her hair "a harp contrived in Paris and illuminated by tiny gas jets." The scene of many of the latter occasions was the sumptuous establishment of Lorenzo Delmonico, who opened a new restaurant at Fourteenth Street and Fifth Avenue in April 1862. Here one visitor was introduced to "the best society of New York." "The toilets and the diamonds were resplendent," he wrote in December 1866, "and one figure of the 'German' (cotillion), in which the ladies formed two groups in the centre, facing inwards with their bright trains spread out behind them, was a splendid piece of colour and costume. Prince Doria was there, and most of the magnates of the city looked in." On another level of indoor entertainment was that provided in the "fast houses" and "concert-saloons," a new "feature of the metropolis," according to a French visitor, where "pretty waiter girls" ministered to the desires of the male patrons. It was estimated that there were as many as 12,000 prostitutes in New York City in the late sixties, an aspect of the local scene that came in for full treatment in such lurid accounts as James D. McCabe's *Secrets of the Great City* and Matthew Hale Smith's *Sunshine and Shadow in New York,* both published in 1868.[23]

Wartime wealth made increasingly apparent the extremes of living that separated the rich and poor in the expanding metropolis. London had nothing that could compare for squalor with the "locality in and around the Five Points," according to James D. Burn, a Scotsman who spent three years among American workers during the Civil War. Yet despite the widened gap between the city's "poles of social life," most Europeans were struck with the equalitarianism of many aspects of its society: "ladies and washerwomen, gentlemen and labourers . . . hustled together" in the cars and omnibuses "without the slightest mutual sense of incongruity"—"all clothed in almost the same manner and style: the coachman, the street-porter, the merchant, the artisan, the banker, the lawyer." And there was an individualistic assertiveness in its people, even among the recent immigrants, which not even crowded or squalid living could restrain.[24]

The change-filled sixties speeded the transformation of New York from a bustling city to a metropolis that anticipated the pattern of recent times. The Civil War and its aftermath hastened rather than started the metropolitan trend; but the drastic developments of the decade made observers more conscious of the change. War-created wealth and the commercial, financial, and industrial developments it fostered produced an economy not unlike that of the modern city. At the same time, in the beginnings of apartment houses, the elevated railway, and the Brooklyn Bridge, all occurring at the turn of the seventies, the physical community of the future came into view. Moreover, as is true of the modern metropolis, so in the sixties, for the first time, the population of Manhattan increased at a rate far less rapid than that of Brooklyn and the Bronx, communities that were then on its "suburban" fringe.[25]

Contemporary observers, both native and foreign, caught the import of the changes that were occurring in this significant decade. And not a few deplored the change. George William Curtis, writing in *Harper's Monthly Magazine* for 1862, regretted that New York had lost "much of its old town character" and was becoming "every year more a metropolis." To Mark Twain, the city had grown just "too large"; and George Templeton Strong longed for a residential area that would provide "an open expanse of sky." But the reality of the matter was—as foreign visitors especially were aware—that with its "floating population" and appearance of "mobility," New York had "become a great capital in the European sense of the word." "The entire result of the country's labor seems to seek New York by inevitable channels," wrote Fitz-Hugh Ludlow in 1865, praising the city as a capital of "broad congenialities and infinite resources, . . . widely diffused comfort, luxury, and taste." The Scottish clergyman David Macrae was more inclined to qualify his praise; but he nevertheless could not deny the dynamic drive of the incipient metropolis. This city of "colossal wealth and haggard poverty," this representation of "all that is best and all that is worst in America," he wrote, would soon convert the whole island into "one huge hive of industry," just as already she had "stretched her arms across the river on both sides of her" to build other "great cities for her overflowing population." Such was New York—in contemporary eyes—as the city of continuing commerce and increasing contrasts moved out of the war-invigorated sixties into the metropolitan phase of its urban career.[26]

NEW YORK'S MERCHANTS AND THE CIVIL WAR

The dilemma of New York's merchants at the prospect of a conflict that threatened their Southern market is well reflected in William H. Russell's *My Diary North and South.* One of England's foremost journalists, Russell had already covered the Crimean War and the Sepoy Mutiny when he was sent to the United States to report the sectional crisis for the London *Times.* Upon his arrival in March 1861, he found "the upper world of millionaire merchants, bankers, contractors, and great traders" opposed to the policies of the newly installed Lincoln administration and counseling compromise with the resisting South. When he visited the city again early in July, the atmosphere had greatly changed. With the Confederacy's resort to arms, the city's commercial leaders rallied to preserve the Union. The following excerpt from Russell's diary is dated July 2, 1861.[27]

. . . the first thing which struck me was the changed aspect of the streets. Instead of peaceful citizens, men in military uniforms thronged the pathways, and such multitudes of United States flags floated from the windows and roofs of the houses as to convey the impression that it was a great holiday festival. The appearance of New York when I first saw it was very different. For one day, indeed, after my arrival, there were men in uniform to be seen in the streets, but they disappeared after St. Patrick had been duly honored, and it was very rarely I ever saw a man in soldier's clothes during the rest of my stay. Now, fully a third of the people carried arms, and were dressed in some kind of martial garb.

The walls are covered with placards from military companies offering inducements to recruits. An outburst of military tailors has taken place in the streets; shops are devoted to militia equipments; rifles, pistols, swords, plumes, long boots, saddle, bridle, camp belts, canteens, tents, knapsacks, have usurped the place of the ordinary articles of traffic. Pictures and engravings—bad, and very bad—of the battles of Big Bethel and Vienna, full of furious charges, smoke and dismembered bodies, have driven the French prints out of the windows. Innumerable "General Scotts" glower at you from every turn, making the General look wiser than he or any man ever was. Ellsworths in almost equal proportion, Grebles and Winthrops—the Union martyrs—and Tompkins, the temporary hero of Fairfax court-house. . . .

[Zouaves] are overrunning society, . . . and the dress . . . is singularly unbecoming to the tall and slightly-built American. Songs "On to glory," "Our country," new versions of "Hail Columbia," which certainly cannot be considered by even American complacency a "happy land" when its inhabitants are preparing to cut each other's throats; of the "star-spangled banner," are displayed in booksellers' and music-shop windows, and patriotic sentences emblazoned on flags float from many houses. The ridiculous habit of dressing up children and young people up to ten and twelve years of age as Zouaves and vivandières has been caught up by the old people, and Mars would die with laughter if he saw some of the abdominous, be-spectacled light infantrymen who are hobbling along the pavement. . . .

I was desirous of learning how far the tone of conversation "in the city" had altered, and soon after breakfast I went down Broadway to Pine Street and Wall Street. The street in all its length was almost draped with flags—the warlike character of the shops was intensified. In front of one shop window there was a large crowd gazing with interest at some object which I at last succeeded in feasting my eyes upon. A gray cap with a tinsel badge in front, and the cloth stained with blood was displayed, with the words, "Cap of Secession officer killed in action." On my way I observed another crowd of women, some with children in their arms, standing in front of a large house and gazing up earnestly and angrily at the windows. I found they were wives, mothers, and sisters and daughters of volunteers who had gone off and left them destitute.

The misery thus caused has been so great that the citizens of New York have raised a fund to provide food, clothes, and a little money—a poor relief, in fact, for them, and it was plain that they were much needed, though some of the applicants did not seem to belong to a class accustomed to seek aid from the public. This already! But Wall Street and Pine Street are bent on battle. . . .

[At first,] their sentiments, sympathies, and business bound them with the South; and, indeed, till "the glorious uprising" the South believed New York was with them, as might be credited from the tone of some organs in the press, and I remember hearing it said by Southerners in Washington, that it was very likely New York would go out of the Union! . . .

The change in manner, in tone, in argument, is most remarkable. I met men to-day who last March argued coolly and philosophically about the right of Secession. They are now furious at the idea of such wickedness—furious with England, because she does not deny their own famous doctrine of the sacred right of insurrection. "We must maintain our glorious Union, sir." "We must have a country." "We cannot allow two nations to grow up on this Continent, sir." "We must possess the entire control of the Mississippi." These "musts," and "can'ts," and "won'ts," are the angry utterances of a spirited people who have had their will so long that they at last believe it is omnipotent. Assuredly, they will not have it over the South without a tremendous and long-sustained contest, in which they must put forth every exertion, and use all the resources and superior means they so abundantly possess.

It is absurd to assert, as do the New York people, to give some semblance of reason to their sudden outburst, that it was caused by the insult to the flag at Sumter. Why, the flag had been fired on long before Sumter was attacked by the Charleston batteries! It had been torn down from United States arsenals and forts all over the South; and but for the accident which placed Major Anderson in a position from which he could not retire, there would have been no bombardment of the fort, and it would, when evacuated, have shared the fate of all the other Federal works on the Southern coast. Some of the gentlemen who are now so patriotic and Unionistic, were last March prepared to maintain that if the President attempted to reenforce Sumter or Pickens, he would be responsible for the destruction of the Union. Many journals in New York and out of it held the same doctrine.

One word to these gentlemen. I am pretty well satisfied that if they had always spoken, written, and acted as they do now, the people of Charleston would not have attacked Sumter so readily. The abrupt outburst of the North and the demonstration at New York filled the South, first with astonishment, and then with something like fear, which was rapidly fanned into anger by the press and the politicians, as well as by the pride inherent in slaveholders.

RECRUITING: JULY 1861

The recruiting of volunteers, early in the war, attracted the attention of Lieutenant Colonel Camille Ferri-Pisani who accompanied Prince Napoleon of France on an extensive tour of North America in 1861. The Prince's aide-de-camp was not much impressed with New Yorkers. In his opinion they were as much European as American, as a result of the mixture of Irish, German, Italian, and Dutch blood. Like the correspondent of the London *Times,* he sensed the apprehensions of New York's merchants at the prospective loss of Southern markets as well as the local resistance to the policies of a Republican administration. His account of recruiting operations was written on July 31, 1861, shortly after the defeat of the Federal Army at the Battle of Bull Run. The following excerpt from it is reprinted, by permission of Librairie

Hachette, from Ferri-Pisani's *Lettres sur les États-Unis d'Amérique,* published in 1862.[28]

The recruiting operations which are taking place in New York at this moment, on a huge scale, so excite the populace, and are of such a nature that they almost completely absorb the stranger's attention. . . .

The great Barnum is the model and the master of all the citizens who aspire to avenge the honor of the federal flag, under the title and with the appointment as captain, colonel, general. The genius of advertising, put in the service of the country, is raised to immeasurable heights. The brigade called *Excelsior,* one of the first to be formed, and truly fine, had its center of recruitment established from the outset in a magnificent building, covered with signs and flags. An immense throng pressed in front of the large balcony which was laden with military emblems, and in the midst of which a military band poured torrents of harmony on the crowd. Then at intervals a patriotic speech brought to a peak the enthusiasm which the music and the sight of the flags and trophies had already excited. A movement would spread in the assemblage, and as the extended hand of the orator pointed the way by which one could "follow the crowd," swarms of men entered the rooms and signed the recruitment register.

In general each company being formed in New York has a recruiting office in Broadway, and, besides, a tent where they receive enlistments on the lawn of the City Hall. These tents form a little camp, in the midst of which a grave and curious crowd circulates, for everything is done gravely in the United States, just as everything is done gaily in France. . . .

There is something amusing . . . in the contrast between the imperturbable seriousness of the recruiting officers and the recruits and the style, form, and design of the placards displayed by the former and read avidly by the latter, placards which, transported verbatim to one of the revues of our little theatres, would elicit general hilarity.

These signs, of gigantic size, usually represent a Union soldier exterminating the enemy, but with such exaggerations of attitude, gesture, and expressions that one would think that the crayon of Cham had done them. Below comes a patriotic appeal, adroitly mingled with the enumeration of the titles which the commanding officer and his regiment believe to enlist public confidence. For example: "Attention! young men who wish to avenge their country!

Where will you find a regiment which will improve upon the Lincoln Chasseurs or the New York Zouaves? etc. All the officers are versed in the art of war; the colonel will be a graduate of West Point, etc."

Often the citizen who raises the regiment takes only the position of lieutenant-colonel, leaving the place of the colonel unassigned, in order to attract the public with the hope of seeing it filled by a graduate of West Point. . . .

Then come the details on the advantages assured by the government to the enlistee: sixty francs a month, victuals in abundance, good uniforms, and a tract of land at the expiration of his term of service. The principal parts of the advertisement are almost always drawn to the particular attention of the public by a hand, the finger pointing. . . . It goes without saying that the hand which directs the eye to the sixty francs per month is a gigantic one. I have seen poor famished Irishmen devour these seductive advertisements with their eyes, fascinated as they were by these diabolical hands, at the end of which was found the enticing list of the food of which the rations were composed: bread, wine, meat, vegetables, beer, etc.

Apparently some disloyal practices crept into these half commercial, half military undertakings; for after the announcement of the lucrative conditions of the contract, one often reads a *nota bene* . . . warning the public against the fallacious offers of conscienceless contractors who promised the defenseless citizens advantages not guaranteed by Congress.

For regiments already formed, but which lacked a complement, it was pointed out that only twenty-five men were lacking: "Hurry, there remain only twenty-five enlistments to deliver to the public." As in the sale of coats at an auction, it is always the last coat in the shop that the auctioneer displays to the crowd. Finally, there are demands for enlistment in bloc, for an entire company; for example: "We need a company of men of good morale, commanded by a captain versed in military art. Write to such a street, such a number."

WARTIME NEW YORK, 1862: "A SOBER BUSINESS"

By 1862, New York's initial wartime enthusiasm had waned, and "business as usual" prevailed, albeit with wartime overtones. The fortunes of the federal cause were at their lowest ebb when Edward Dicey, English journalist and magazine writer, arrived early in that year, to report the war for the London *Spectator*. The appearance of the city had less to recommend it than the Londoner had expected, but in spite of some indications of retrenchment, its solid, if somewhat pedestrian, prosperity gave few outward indications of the dislocations of war. The following excerpt is from his two-volume chronicle, *Six Months in the Federal States,* reprinted here by permission of Macmillan and Company, Limited.[29]

The general effect of the "Empire City" is to me disappointing. Simple magnitude is never very striking to anyone accustomed to London; and, except in magnitude, there is not much to impress you. Broadway is, or rather ought to be, a very fine street; and its single stores are as grand as anything can be in the way of shop-front architecture. But a marble-faced palace, of six stories high, has a cast-iron store, with card-paper-looking pillars, on one side, and a two-storied red-brick house on the other. There is no symmetry or harmony about the street, so that it lacks grandeur, without having irregularity enough to be picturesque. The rows of stunted trees on either side give it, in parts, a French look; but still, when I had once heard a candid American describe it as a "one-horse boulevard" I felt he had produced a description which could not be improved upon. Fifth Avenue is symmetrical enough; but its semi-detached stone mansions, handsome as they are, have not sufficient height to justify its American name of the Street of Palaces; while its monotony is dreadful. . . .

There is a popular delusion in England, that New York is a sort of gingerbread-and-gilt city; and that, contrasted with an English town, there is a want of solidity about the whole place, materially as well as morally. On the contrary, I never was in a town where externally, at any rate, show was so much sacrificed to solid comfort. The ferries, the cars, the street railroads, and the houses, are all so arranged as to give one substantial comfort, without external decoration. It is, indeed, indoors that the charm of New York is found. There is not much of luxury, in the French sense of the word—no lavish display of mirrors, and clocks, and pictures—but there is more comfort, more English luxury, about the private dwelling-houses than I ever saw in the same class of houses at home. The rooms are so light and lofty; the passages are so well warmed; the doors slide backwards in their grooves, so easily and yet so tightly; the chairs are so luxurious; the beds are so elastic, and the linen so clean, and, let me add, the living so excellent, that I would never wish for better quarters, or for a more hospitable welcome, than I have found in many private houses of New York. All the domestic arrangements (to use a fine word for gas, hot water, and other comforts) are wonderfully perfect. Everything, even more than in England, seems adapted for a home life. . . .

Undoubtedly, out of doors, you see evidences of a public equality, or rather absence of inequality, among all classes, which cannot fail to strike an inhabitant of the Old World. In the streets, the man in the hat and broadcloth coat and the man in corduroys and fustian jacket never get out of each other's way or expect the other to make way for him. . . . There is a great deal of poverty in New York, and the Five Points quarter—the Seven Dials of the city—is, especially on a bitter winter's day, as miserable a haunt of vice and misery as it was ever my lot to witness in Europe. Still, compared with the size of New York, this quarter is a very small one; and poverty there, bad as it is, is not helpless poverty. The fleeting population of the Five Points is composed of the lowest and most shiftless of the recent foreign emigrants; and in the course of a few years they, or at any rate their children, move to other quarters, and become prosperous and respectable. From these causes, and from the almost universal diffusion of education, there is no class exactly analogous to our English idea of the mob. The fact that well-nigh everybody you meet is comfortably dressed seems to disprove the existence of those dangerous classes which always attract the notice of a foreigner in England. There are few beggars about the town, and of those few, all are children. For an Anglo-Saxon population, there is very little drunkenness visible in the streets; and with regard to other forms of public vice it is not for an Englishman to speak severely. The Broadway saloons, with their so-called "pretty waiter-girls," and the Lager Bier haunts in the low quarters of the town, whose windows are crowded with wretched half-dressed, or undressed women, formed, indeed, about the most shameless exhibition of public vice I have ever come across, even in England or Holland; and I am glad to say that, since I left New York, the State Government, under a republican as opposed to a democratic legislature, has taken means to suppress these social nuisances. But in the streets at night, there are few of the scenes which habitually disgrace our own metropolis.

The great quiet and order of the city are in themselves remarkable. . . . There are no soldiers about, as in a continental capital; and the policemen—nearly as fine a body of men, by the way, as our

London police—appear to devote their energies to preserving Broadway from being utterly jammed up by carts, and to escorting ladies across the most treacherous of thoroughfares. The people seem instinctively to keep themselves in order. How a row would be suppressed if there was one, I cannot say; I only know that, during my stay in New York, I never saw anything approaching to a disturbance in any public place or thoroughfare. . . .

I had left England at the time when the fortunes of the Federal cause seemed the lowest, and when New York was popularly believed to be on the brink of ruin and revolution. It was, I own, a surprise to me to find how little trace there was of either. . . . There were forts being thrown up rapidly along the banks which command the Narrows; but . . . the number of uniforms about the streets was small. . . . A score or so of tents were pitched upon the snow in the City Park, and at the Battery, but rather for show than use. In the Broadway and the Bowery there were a few recruiting offices, in front of which hung huge placards tempting fine young men, by the offer of a hundred dollars' bounty (to be paid not down, but after the war), and the promise of immediate active service, to join the Van Buren light infantry or the New York *mounted* cavalry. It was rare to hear a military band; and in the shop windows I noticed at that time but few pictures of the war, or portraits of the war's heroes. I saw regiments passing through the town on their way to the South, and yet only a few idlers were gathered to see them pass. In fact, the show-time of the war had passed away, and it was become a matter of sober business. . . .

There was no want of interest or feeling about the war. In society it was the one topic of thought and conversation. If you heard two people talking in the street, or in the cars, or at the church doors as you came out of service, you would be sure to find they were talking of the war. The longer I lived in the country, the more I learnt how deep the feeling of the North was; but it was like all English feeling, and came slowly to the surface. . . .

Broadway was daily rendered almost impassable by the never-ending string of carts and omnibuses and carriages, which rolled up and down it for hours. Splendidly-equipped sable-covered sleighs were to be seen at every turning; and, on a fine day, the pavements were thronged with ladies, the expensiveness of whose dresses, if questionable as a matter of taste, was unquestionable as a matter of fact. . . . There was, I have no doubt, much mercantile distress;

and the shopkeepers, who depended on the sale of luxuries to the wealthy classes, were doing a poor trade. But work was plentiful, and the distress, as yet, had not gone down deep. There were few balls or large parties, and the opera was not regularly open, partly because public feeling was averse to much gaiety; partly, and still more, because the wealthy classes had retrenched all superfluous expenditure with a really wonderful unanimity. Residents often expressed their regret to me that I should see their city under so dull an aspect. But I know that, on a bright winter day, when the whole population seemed to be driving out in sleighs to the great skating carnivals at the Central Park, I have seldom seen a brighter or a gayer-looking city than that of New York.

WARTIME NEW YORK, 1864: "A CITY WITHOUT A COUNTRY"

New York in the last years of the Civil War presented a distasteful spectacle to twenty-one-year-old Ernest Duvergier de Hauranne, who arrived in the city in June of 1864 and remained in the United States until February of 1865. The young French traveler was destined to gain some reputation in France as a writer and political figure before his death in 1877. He found New York dominated by "the money interest and the masses," both of which appeared to put their personal welfare above the good of the Union. The following excerpt, representing observations made in June 1864, is from his *Lettres et notes de voyage,* which has been called "the most complete picture of American life written by any French traveller during the period of the Civil War."[30]

The first impression of New York is that it is repulsive and vulgar. The broken pavements, the muddy streets, the squares overrun with grass and underbrush, the disreputable horse cars, and the irregular houses plastered with huge handbills have the careless ugliness of an open-air bazaar. The old cities of Europe all have character; this has nothing but commonplaceness. . . .

Everybody is obsessed with business. Broadway, Wall Street, and all the downtown area are the universal gathering place for ten hours during the day. Thousands of omnibuses traverse the main street, filled every morning with a compact crowd which they bring back in the evening. Neither the boulevards, the Strand, nor the Corso of Rome in carnival time can give an idea of this tumultuous movement. Our Parisian strollers hardly resemble this unpleasant, preoccupied, harried throng which elbows its way among the trucks and carts. . . .

Advertising is the indispensable adjunct of this great village fair. On every hand are floating banners, monstrous signs, flamboyant decoration. Advertising matter extends into the street, onto the edge of the sidewalk between the gutter and the pedestrians' feet. Just now I read "Blood!" written in red letters, but nobody knows its meaning. Last year in the same place an astonished public for six months read the mysterious word, "Sozodont!" and for six months the persevering mystifier kept the word a secret; it was a dental preparation which is now selling profusely. Here is the arresting announcement: "Books at tremendous low prices," and there an impressive row of identical notices: "We need 10,000 volunteers," with detail on the bounties offered and the drinks promised, or then again a large flag on which is displayed in brilliant colors the scene of a fantastic battle. Everything is handled that way, even serious things, even the purchase of blood! . . .

My friends took me to Central Park, vast American "Bois de Boulogne," with its valleys, rocks, cascades, aqueducts, lakes, and cliffs, opening out from the end of Fifth Avenue. The vicinity of the Park, for the length of a league, and the cross streets nearby are the abode of the most fashionable society. . . .

All the researches after luxury are brought together in their handsome dwellings. Each bedroom is supplied with water, gas, and heat, and each has a bathroom. The dimensions of the lots are the established ones: 25 by 100 feet. Each family lives in its own house. There is a great difference between these agreeable dwellings and our crowded ones, with their sombre staircases and narrow courts.

The Park, if one can believe its name, will one day be in the center of the city. Nothing is more American than this ambitious name, given at first sight to wild terrain situated beyond the suburbs. What limits can be assigned to this rapidly expanding city, which already flows into its outskirts and has perhaps doubled in size in the past fifteen years? . . . The Park is recent, hardly finished, yet it already swarms each evening with beaux and carriages, especially those remarkable American vehicles whose slender wheels resemble filigreed jewelry, and which run along like big spiders with long legs. . . .

But what of the darker side of the picture? Between Broadway and the Hudson lies a dirty and ragged section inhabited by Irishmen and colored people. Nothing could be more depressingly miserable than these wooden hovels, these long, muddy streets, and this impoverished population. From time to time, a lumbering horse car, with a cracked bell, rolls along, bearing, to the stranger's amazement, this inscription: "This carriage for colored people." What does this mean? . . . Are there laws against Negroes? Are they outside the common law? No; but public prejudice persecutes them more tyrannically than any law. They are denied the omnibuses, are excluded from the churches. That's how these democrats interpret equality, and these Puritans, Christian charity. . . .

In this America, where national ties are already so fragile, New York is primarily a city without a country. It is the cosmopolitan market, the vast hostelry which America opens to all people. But here sacrifice occurs without devotion. Last year, in connection with conscription, the money of the rich Copperheads fomented a riot among the Irish which even their Archbishop could not quell. This was perpetrated at a moment when the city was stripped of troops and deprived of its militia and so could not resist the insurgents. The riot . . . was a savage one. The mob killed, pillaged, hung Negroes to lampposts, and mutilated and tortured their prisoners. Its cruelty was ungovernable.

WARTIME NEW YORK, 1864: A STROLL DOWN BROADWAY

Surface manifestations of the extravagant living, commercial prosperity, and preoccupation with externals which characterized the New York scene in the last year of the war are mirrored in George T. Borrett's *Letters from Canada and the United States*. A fellow of King's College, Cambridge, Borrett visited New York City late in September of 1864, when the city was in the throes of the presidential campaign of that year.[31]

I was roused, about seven o'clock in the morning, by the attendant of the car, who brought me my boots, and told me that we were in New York. I looked out, and found that our train had become a series of street-cars. It had been split up into segments, two or three cars in a division, to each of which was attached a team of half-a-dozen horses, who rattled us down the centre of the street, through which the rails are carried far into the heart of the city. The time that was occupied in passing to the depôt I spent in a tolerably satisfactory toilet. . . . and though it might seem strange to you to meet a railway-carriage coming down Oxford Street, with a lot of men towelling their faces . . . at one end of it, and a posse of women polishing up their back hair at the other, I can assure you that I took to it all as naturally as if I had been brought up to the system from my vaccination. . . .

But let us saunter down [Broadway] . . . and take a passing glance at its details. My abode on my first visit to New York was at the Fifth Avenue Hotel, and we will start from its wide entrance—across the handsome Square of which it is the chief ornament—pass down a small portion of Broadway into Union Square, still larger—through that, and down another portion of Broadway, consisting chiefly of private residences—by Grace Church, the fashionable church of the "Upper Ten" of New York—and enter upon the straight which will lead us down to Wall Street, and the Battery, two miles distant. . . . On our way we pass the chief theatres, pre-eminent amongst which is Wallack's, and several which go by the name of "Gardens," a title that seems to suit any place of entertainment, in or out of town alike; and before long we are at the St. Nicholas Hotel, a vast white marble edifice looking cool and comfortable . . . by dint of the green Venetian shutters with which its windows, like those of most of the houses, are furnished. Further on is the La Farge Hotel, a similar building, but less aristocratic, and on the other side more hotels, perhaps a step lower in the social scale; and so we come to Tiffany's store. Tiffany is the great jeweller, who has grown so fat on the extravagancies of the Shoddy. . . . Prices are being asked and given for *articles de vertu* which would confound Harry Emanuel himself. But Tiffany is only one of the fatted calves. Ball and Black have gorged themselves as well upon the exorbitant demand for jewellery, and their store is almost opposite. . . . But vast as is the scale on which this business is conducted, it sinks into comparative insignificance by the side of Stewart's stores. Stewart is the great "dry-goods merchant" of New York, whose fame has long reached our shores. He is, I suppose, next to the President, the best known man in America. For "dry-goods" are a surer road to fame than politics and legislation. His white marble stores, one for the wholesale, the other for the retail trade, would dwarf Marshall and Snelgrove's, and Farmer and Rogers' into pigmies. We went over one of them, ascending by the lift which carries up the goods, through the successive tiers of show-rooms and down the magnificent staircases which connect the several flats, in utter amazement at the extent of the area enclosed by the walls, and the business transacted within them. But you must not linger here. A few yards farther on is the City Hall, in a meagre sort of square . . . and . . . rendered still more unsightly by a lot of ill-conditioned recruiting booths, placarded with all sorts of announcements of the inconceivable advantages of serving in the Federal army. . . . Opposite the square is the noted Astor House, one of the chief hotels of the city, with a crowd of idlers upon the steps of its portico, pass it when you will, morning, noon, or night. But over the way is Barnum's museum. . . . "Cultivate externals," has been the motto of his life, and in accordance with this principle he has possessed himself of an enormous block, of which he occupies for his own purposes the mere outside shell. The rest I suppose he lets for warehouses. Consequently, on entering, you find yourself, not in a spacious hall, or even a decent room, but in a dirty narrow strip of gallery, a sort of boarding-school pie, nothing but crust, with a few dusty shelves on the inside, containing a mass of nothing higgledy piggledy, unimaginably mouldy and abominable. . . .

Well, Barnum's is a regular do, and having been there long enough to get properly ashamed of ourselves at being so done, we will pass on down Broadway, which becomes more crowded with foot-passengers on the side-walks, and blocked with carriages in the roadway, as we advance towards the sea, and in a short time we shall be in Wall Street. Wall Street, the New World's "hell," where more fortunes have been made and lost in one year of the last four than in centuries of the lives of other countries. . . .

What I did in New York would fill a volume. . . . There was always, as the Yankees say, "any quantity" to do. . . . And how can I tell you of the endless diversion to be found in the streets themselves? Sometimes it was a procession of the famous fire-brigade, in their Garibaldi shirts and "dress" trousers, with their beautiful steam fire-engines burnished like mirrors, and decorated with flowers and flags innumerable. Sometimes it was a "turn out" of the representatives of some club or union, in procession to the Cooper's Institute to hold a meeting upon the presidential election, or simply airing themselves and their banners. Sometimes it was a string of regiments on their way from or to the front. Sometimes a military funeral, solemn and gorgeous; sometimes an Irish one, grotesque and ludicrous. Then there were the passengers on the sidewalks; goat-faced warriors in brigand hats; blue-cheeked civilians behind enormous cigars; schoolgirls with their bundles of books returning from their studies, to which they had betaken themselves before the rest of the world was astir, though the world of New York is an early bird, and seven o'clock was the ladies' breakfast hour in the boarding-house wherein I spent a week of my visit. There were the omnibuses, too, without conductors, where the driver took your fare or not as you pleased to pay it through a hole in the roof behind him; and the street-cars with their impudent managers, always crammed and uncomfortable.

JOY AND GRIEF: 1865

New York's reactions to the two most stirring events of 1865—the Union victory and the assassination of Abraham Lincoln—are dramatically recorded in the diary of a native Manhattanite, George Templeton Strong. The diarist was born in 1820 of a distinguished New York family. After graduating from Columbia University, he entered the practice of law. He was an ardent supporter of the Union in the conflict that resulted in the Civil War. His four-million-word diary, covering the years from 1835 to 1875, provides a rich chronicle of the New York scene. The following excerpt from it is reprinted, with the permission of The Macmillan Company, from the four-volume edition by Allan Nevins and Milton Halsey Thomas, published in 1952.[32]

April 3. Petersburg and Richmond! *Gloria in excelsis Deo.*

New York has seen no such day in our time nor in the old time before us. The jubilations of the Revolutionary War and the War of 1812 were those of a second-rate seaport town. This has been metropolitan and worthy an event of the first national importance to a continental nation and a cosmopolitan city. . . .

Walking down Wall Street, I saw something on the *Commercial Advertiser* bulletin board. . . . I read the announcement "Petersburg is taken" and went into the office in quest of particulars. The man behind the counter was slowly painting in large letters on a large sheet of brown paper another annunciation for the board outside: "Richmond is"—"What's that about Richmond?" said I. . . . He was too busy for speech, but he went on with a capital C, and a capital A, and so on, till I read the word CAPTURED!!! . . .

An enormous crowd soon blocked . . . part of Wall Street, and speeches began. . . . Never before did I hear cheering that came straight from the heart, that was given because people felt relieved by cheering and hallooing. . . . They sang "Old Hundred," the Doxology, "John Brown," and "The Star-Spangled Banner," repeating the last two lines of Key's song over and over, with a massive roar from the crowd and a unanimous wave of hats at the end of each repetition. I think I shall never lose the impression made by this rude, many-voiced chorale. . . .

I walked about on the outskirts of the crowd, shaking hands with everybody. . . . Men embraced and hugged each other, *kissed* each other, retreated into doorways to dry their eyes and came out again to flourish their hats and hurrah. . . . My only experience of a people stirred up to like intensity of feeling was at the great Union meeting at Union Square in April, 1861. . . .

April 4. . . . Broadway is a river of flags. . . . Guns popping off in every direction tonight. A salute of one hundred guns fired at the foot of Wall Street this morning, and another in front of the Union League Club tonight. . . .

April 10 [following news of the surrender]. . . . It has rained hard all day; too hard for jubilant demonstrations out of doors. We should have made this Monday something like the 3rd of April, 1865, I think, had the sun shone. . . . Guns have been firing all day in spite of foul weather. . . .

April 15. . . . Nine o'clock in the morning. LINCOLN AND SEWARD ASSASSINATED LAST NIGHT!!!!! . . . *Up with the Black Flag now!*

Ten P. M. What a day it has been! Excitement and suspension of business even more general than on the 3rd instant. Tone of feeling very like that of four years ago when the news came of Sumter. . . . People who pitied our misguided brethren yesterday, . . . and hoped there would be a general amnesty, . . . talk approvingly today of vindictive justice and favor the introduction of judges, juries, gaolers, and hangmen among the dramatis personae. . . .

No business was done today. Most shops are closed and draped with black and white muslin. Broadway is clad in "weepers" from Wall Street to Union Square. . . .

April 16. An Easter Sunday unlike any I have ever seen. . . . Nearly every building in Broadway and in all the side streets, as far as one could see, festooned lavishly with black and white muslin. Columns swathed in the same material. Rosettes pinned to window curtains. Flags at half mast and tied up with crape. I hear that even in second and third class quarters, people who could afford to do no more have generally displayed at least a little twenty-five cent flag with a little scrap of crape annexed. Never was a public mourning more spontaneous and general. . . .

April 17. . . . All over the city, people have been at work all day, draping street fronts, so that hardly a building on Wall Street, Broadway, Chambers Street, Bowery, Fourth Avenue is without its symbol of the profound public sorrow. . . .

April 28. . . . Little business has been done in town these ten days. Never, I think, has sorrow for a leader been displayed on so great a scale and so profoundly felt. It is very noteworthy that the number of arrests for drunkenness and disorder during the week that followed Lincoln's murder was less than in any week for very many years! The city is still swathed in crape and black muslin.

THE BOYS COME MARCHING HOME: 1865

Returning veterans were part of the kaleidoscope which New York City presented to visitors and residents in 1865. This aspect of the urban scene was described by John E. Hilary Skinner, British barrister and journalist, in the sketches of postwar America which he published under the title, *After the Storm; or, Jonathan and his neighbours in 1865–66.* As special correspondent for the London *Daily News,* Skinner had covered the activities of the Danish Army in the War of 1864. After his sojourn in the United States, he reported the Austro-Prussian Campaign and the Franco-Prussian War.[33]

The boys were mustered out of service and every train had its quota of discharged veterans, with knapsacks and bronzed faces, loud speech, and strange stories to tell, proceeding to their respective homes. Many who had adopted a civilian costume displayed the metal badge of their corps, and many others who were without such mark could be recognized by their weather-beaten features and easy carriage. . . . In New York the arrival of soldiers was incessant. Some came by sea, but most by the railways to Jersey City, and thence across the ferry to Pier No. 1. They landed near the open space by the Battery and marched up town in full campaigning guise. Pet dogs ran behind many companies, whilst adopted contrabands, acting as water-carriers, trudged in the rear of others. The veterans cared nothing for appearance, but strode forward, beneath the hot summer sun, in wide-awakes or straw hats, as fancy suggested. A few detachments had bands of music, and, where music was wanting, the buglers relieved each other, French fashion, in a lively fanfare. Regiments known in the city were of course more warmly greeted than strangers passing through. The Irish Legion, which returned soon after the Irish Brigade, found itself among enthusiastic friends; so did other bodies of Federal troops. Heavy losses had been sustained by some corps. The New York 52nd regiment, for example, came back less than three hundred strong, having had on its muster rolls, during the war, two thousand six hundred names.

"SCHENCK" AND "SHAUGHNESSY" IN THE SIXTIES

Although by the sixties New Yorkers already represented "almost every nationality upon the face of the earth," visitors agreed that the Irish and the Germans were by far the most numerous among the foreign-born. The Irish ingredient attracted the attention especially of two travelers of the period. One was William H. Russell, correspondent for the London *Times,* who recorded his experiences in *My Diary North and South.* The other was James D. Burn, a Scotsman of humble origins, who came to America in 1862 in a fruitless attempt to better his fortunes, and who published in 1865 an account of his experiences entitled *Three Years Among the Working-Classes in the United States during the War.* The increased affluence of the city's German element was noted by Friedrich Gerstäcker, a German adventurer, travel writer, and novelist who made a second trip to the United States in 1867. The first two of the following excerpts are from Burn and Russell, respectively. The third is from Gerstäcker's *Zwischen Wildnis und Kultur: Reisen und Abenteuer in der neuen Welt,* reprinted with the permission of Deutsche Buchvertriebs- und Verlags-Gesellschaft.[34]

"Schenck" and "Shaughnessy" represent the plodding Teuton and the impulsive Celt, over the portals of lager-beer saloons and whisky stores, in all the leading thoroughfares, from the back slums in the vicinity of the wharves to the pave on the Broadway, where Republican "big bugocracy" sports its jewels, silks and drapery. . . . In New York there is scarcely a situation of honour or distinction, from the chief magistrate down to the police, that is not filled by a descendant of some Irishman who lived in savage hatred of England beyond the pale! The mere labouring Irish, like those of the same class at home, may be seen engaged in all the humbler occupations from shouldering the hod to rag-gathering, but in whatever business they may be employed, they have a decided advantage over their compeers in the old country—as they are sure to be remunerated in such a way as enables them to live comfortably, so far at least as food and clothing are concerned. One of the principal trading branches of business in which Irishmen are generally successful, is that of the liquor store line, a trade which the Irish and Germans may be said to divide between them. As the body is composed of a large number of members, its influence in a political point of view is a matter of no small importance during elections, whether for municipal authorities, state officers, or presidents.

Monday, 18th [March, 1861]—"St. Patrick's day in the morning" being on the 17th, was kept by the Irish to-day. In the early morning the sounds of drumming, fifing, and bugling came with the hot water and my Irish attendant into the room. He told me: "We'll have a pretty nice day for it. The weather's often agin us on St. Patrick's day." At the angle of the square outside I saw a company of volunteers assembling. They wore bear-skin caps, some turned brown, and rusty green coatees, with white facings and cross-belts, a good deal of gold-lace and heavy worsted epaulettes, and were armed with ordinary muskets, some of them with flint-locks. Over their heads floated a green and gold flag with mystic emblems, and a harp and sunbeams. A gentleman, with an imperfect seat on horseback, . . . with much difficulty was getting them into line . . . and the din and clamor in the streets, the strains of music, and the tramp of feet outside announced that similar associations were on their way to the rendezvous. . . .

After breakfast, I struggled with a friend through the crowd which thronged Union Square. Bless them! They were all Irish, judging from speech and gesture and look; for the most part decently dressed, and comfortable, evidently bent on enjoying the day in spite of the cold, and proud of the privilege of interrupting all the trade of the principal streets, in which the Yankees most do congregate, for the day. They were on the door-steps, and on the pavement, men, women, and children, admiring the big policemen—many of them compatriots—and they swarmed at the corners, cheering popular town-councillors or local celebrities. Broadway was equally full. Flags were flying from the windows and steeples—and on the cold breeze came the hammering of drums and the blasts of many wind instruments. [Following an Irish militia regiment came the] long string of Benevolent, Friendly, and Provident Societies, with bands, numbering many thousands, all decently clad, and marching in order, with banners, insignia, badges, and ribbons, and the Irish flag flying alongside the "stars and stripes." . . . The various societies mustered upwards of 10,000 men, some of them uniformed and armed, others dressed in quaint garments, and all as noisy as music and talking could make them. The Americans appeared to regard the whole thing very much as an ancient Roman might have looked on the Saturnalia; but Paddy was in the ascendant, and could not be openly trifled with.

Hoboken is almost exclusively German, while Brooklyn, on the other hand, has maintained its American character. In general, the German element has not only grown in numbers but has won the high esteem of the Americans as well. The German press holds an important position, with such newspapers as the New York *Staatszeitung* and the *Handelszeitung*. In the realm of merchandising many German firms are in competition with the best American ones. Moreover, the German element has succeeded in creating a social life of its own. There are numerous German restaurants, the elegant interiors of which suggest that they are visited by another sort of people than those thirty years ago. It is said that "where Germans are, there is beer, also." There is some truth in this saying, but one can hardly regard beer as the only factor that links the Germans in America.

POST-CIVIL WAR SOCIETY—HIGH AND LOW

Society—both high and low—was affected by the prosperity of the war years and the speculative era that followed. Before the war was half over, dances, card parties, and receptions, somewhat curtailed at the outset of the struggle, became more popular than ever. The world of fashion reached new extremes of extravagance and display. In commercial entertainment there was a variety to suit the most cosmopolitan tastes. The prevalence of commercialized vice impressed a Frenchman, presumably Ferdinand (Frederick?) Longchamp, who wrote an anonymous description of conditions in New York in 1867 and 1868. His account of a tour around New York with an imaginary Asmodeus, "the same that conducted a famous novelist through the labyrinth of human passions," reflects the current increase in amusement facilities. The newly popular "concert-saloons," which he describes, like the brothels on notorious Greene Street and the "parlor houses" in the better quarters of the city, were among the establishments that were giving the emerging metropolis an increasingly lurid reputation for wickedness in the postwar era. The following excerpt is from *Asmodeus in New York,* a translation of his *Asmodée à New-York: revue critique des institutions politiques et civiles de l'Amérique; vie publique et privée, moeurs, coutumes, anecdotes romanesques, etc.*[35]

It was quite dark when we reached the great metropolis of the United States. . . .

Theatres, restaurants, and hundreds of pleasure resorts were crowded with persons. About twenty theatres, including minstrel-halls, are opened to the public every night, and the opera and the drama are there interpreted in divers pleasing ways to suit all tastes. As regards drinking-saloons, their number is beyond calculation.

"A few years ago," said Asmodeus, "the number of restaurants and liquor-saloons was rather limited; eatables and other refreshments could be procured in public hotels only. There were, it is true, a few eating-houses, located in damp basements; but their dirty appearance and offensive smell were not calculated to attract many guests. A great change has taken place; bachelors now live after the Parisian fashion; they rent furnished rooms, and take their meals at some restaurant.

"The number of restaurants or dining-saloons is now larger than that of the French capital; and New York can boast of a few which, for their luxury in every particular, may well challenge comparison."

"What are those places we meet at almost every step, from which issue musical strains?"

"They are concert-saloons—a new feature of the metropolis—I might say, of the country: bar-rooms, where an orchestra delights the frequenters while enjoying some of the one hundred and fifty beverages in vogue in the States. . . . "

By a long flight of steps, we entered one of those concert-saloons, which, according to the sign, promised to be a spacious and shady garden. But, as Asmodeus had said, the walls alone represented the garden in highly inflamed patches of red, green, and yellow paint. Hardly inside, we were almost suffocated with the fumes of liquor and smoke of meerschaums and cigars. To be sure, the place was handsomely fitted up, and crowded with visitors—a number of what they call "pretty waiter girls" flitting about among the customers, and laughing and loudly talking with them. A piano-player, wildly thumping and banging on a cracked and hideously wired instrument, the rattling of glasses, moving of chairs and tables—all contributed to bewilder and madden me with the discordant tumult. . . .

The whole force of female waiters was in attendance—that is, about thirty or forty young women, all busy endeavoring to quench the thirst of several hundred men; and, while executing the multitudinous orders given them, they found sufficient time to distribute their photographs, to talk, and drink with visitors. I noticed that they consumed nearly as much as the men, and wondered how they could stand it.

"The excesses of those poor creatures," said Asmodeus, "are sure to bring their miserable lives to an untimely end. For, as the concert-saloon owners pay them an insufficient salary to live upon, the girls, for the purpose of increasing it, purchase, every morning, a certain number of drinking-tickets . . . with a discount of thirty percent and sometimes more. If you follow their motions, you will perceive that they themselves keep the money received from visitors, and pay the bar-tender with their own tickets, on obtaining from him the ordered refreshments. Now, to dispose of the largest possible number of tickets, the girls have recourse to all conceivable stratagems—the most usual being to ask the visitor to drink a toast to their beauty. Though the latter is generally faded, the visitor accedes for gallantry's sake; and as the Hebe has to keep him company while toasting her charms, he pays for two drinks instead of one. After a few months of such a life, the health of most of those female waiters—I do not speak of their virtue—is utterly ruined. . . . "

The activity of these Hebes was only equaled by that of half a dozen men, protected by a railing, behind which they manipulated the drinks ordered by the crowd.

"It is a business of no small importance," observed Asmodeus, "to be a bar-tender—to thoroughly understand how to properly prepare the almost infinite number of beverages appreciated by the Americans. . . ."

This great metropolis . . . sets examples for other cities, and whether they be good or bad, they are certain to be followed. Dens of corruption, I admit, exist in all large centres of population; but it may be doubted whether vice shows itself elsewhere so impudently

—it recedes from the gaze of the public and dwells in remote streets; while here it displays itself on the most favourite thoroughfare of New York, one which is a sort of Parisian Boulevard for New Yorkers, and at the same time, the pride of commercial men. . . . From what you have seen, you may form an estimate of what is transpiring in saloons removed from the gaze of the police. The least reputable of those resorts are schools for licentiousness; the others, nurseries of crime. In the latter the waiter-girls are prostitutes, connected with professional thieves and assassins; and woe betide the stranger who falls into the snares of those dangerous sirens! More than one has found his grave in the Hudson, dragged there in the darkness of the night, after being drugged by poisonous liquors and robbed of his valuables.

WALT WHITMAN AND MARK TWAIN: OPPOSING VIEWS OF THE METROPOLIS

Americans—and even New Yorkers—of the sixties, like those of later days, had conflicting opinions about the merits of life in the metropolis. The opposing views are well exhibited in the reactions to New York of two American men of letters: Walt Whitman, who extols the fulfillment of urban living, and Mark Twain, who deprecates the frustrations of it.

The city had no more ardent exponent than Walt Whitman, who found emotional sustenance in its vibrant, multitudinous society. Whitman spent most of his early years in Brooklyn and Manhattan. "New York is a great place—a mighty world in itself," he wrote as early as 1842, when he was editing the short-lived New York *Aurora*. His youthful enthusiasm for the city—with its "mighty rush of men, business, carts, carriages, and clang"—had not diminished thirteen years later when he wrote a series of articles for *Life Illustrated,* depicting the human side of "the fullest, fastest, busiest city in the world." Its vibrant humanity found reflection in many of his poems of the fifties and sixties, and on his return to the New York area in 1878, after years of residence in Washington and its vicinity, he continued to regard the great human aggregate as one of the superb manifestations of American democracy. The following excerpt from *Democratic Vistas* expresses his reaction to the city in September 1870.[36]

After an absence, I am now again . . . in New York city and Brooklyn, on a few weeks' vacation. The splendor, picturesqueness, and oceanic amplitude and rush of these great cities, the . . . lofty new buildings, façades of marble and iron, of original grandeur and elegance of design, with the masses of gay color, the preponderance of white and blue, the flags flying, the endless ships, the tumultuous streets, Broadway, the heavy, low, musical roar, hardly ever intermitted, even at night; the jobbers' houses, the rich shops, the wharves, the great Central Park, and the Brooklyn Park of hills, . . . the assemblages of the citizens in their groups, conversations, trades, evening amusements . . . these, I say, and the like of these, completely satisfy my senses of power, fulness, motion, &c., and give me, through such senses . . . a continued exaltation and absolute fulfilment. Always and more and more . . . I realize . . . that not Nature alone is great in her fields of freedom and the open air, in her storms, the shows of night and day, the mountains, forests, seas—but in the artificial, the work of man too is equally great—in this profusion of teeming humanity—in these ingenuities, streets, goods, houses, ships—these hurrying, feverish, electric crowds of men, their complicated business genius, (not least among the geniuses,) and all this mighty, many-threaded wealth and industry concentrated here.

Unlike Whitman, Mark Twain found the magnitude and excitement of the city more nerve-racking than rewarding, its anonymity and variety no substitute for the friendliness of the river town or mining camp. From February to June 1867, he was in New York as correspondent for the San Francisco *Alta California.* His letters to the California newspaper show that he made a conscientious effort to see and understand the city, but he ultimately concluded that he was not at home there: "There has been a sense of something lacking, something wanting, every time," he wrote on June 6, 1867, "and I guess that something was the provincial quietness I am used to. I have had enough of sights and shows, and noise and bustle, and confusion. . . ." The following excerpts are from one of his first letters and one of his last, written from New York. They are reprinted, with the permission of Alfred A. Knopf, Incorporated, from *Mark Twain's Travels with Mr. Brown,* ed. by Franklin Walker and G. Ezra Doane.[37]

February 2, 1867 *The Overgrown Metropolis*

The only trouble about this town is, that it is too large. You cannot accomplish anything in the way of business, you cannot even pay a friendly call, without devoting a whole day to it. . . . The distances are too great. . . . You cannot ride . . . unless you are willing to go in a packed omnibus that labors, and plunges, and struggles along at the rate of three miles in four hours and a half, always getting left behind by fast walkers, and always apparently hopelessly tangled up with vehicles that are trying to get to some place or other and can't. Or, if you can stomach it, you can ride in a horse-car and stand up for three-quarters of an hour, in the midst of a file of men that extends from front to rear (seats all crammed of course,)—or you can take one of the platforms, if you please, but they are so crowded you will have to hang on by your eye-lashes and your toe-nails. . . .

June 5, 1867 *New York*

. . . I have at last, after several months' experience, made up my mind that it [New York] is a splendid desert—a domed and steepled solitude, where a stranger is lonely in the midst of a million of his race. A man walks his tedious miles through the same interminable street every day, elbowing his way through a buzzing multitude of men, yet never seeing a familiar face, and never seeing a strange one the second time. . . . Every man seems to feel that he has got the duties of two lifetimes to accomplish in one, and so he rushes, rushes, rushes, and never has time to be companionable—never has any time at his disposal to fool away on matters which do not involve dollars and duty and business.

All this has a tendency to make the city-bred man impatient of interruption, suspicious of strangers, and fearful of being bored, and his business interfered with. The natural result is . . . the serene indifference of the New Yorker to everybody and everything without the pale of his private and individual circle.

There is something in this ceaseless buzz, and hurry, and bustle, that keeps a stranger in a state of unwholesome excitement all the time, and makes him restless and uneasy . . . a something which impels him to try to do everything, and yet permits him to do nothing. . . . A stranger feels unsatisfied, here, a good part of the time. He starts to a library; changes, and moves toward a theatre; changes again and thinks he will visit a friend; goes within a biscuit-toss of a picture-gallery, a billiard-room, a beer-cellar and a circus, in succession, and finally drifts home and to bed, without having really done anything or gone anywhere.

NEW YORK IN THE NINETIES

Nothing better represented the elegance and glamour of New York in the nineties than the Waldorf-Astoria Hotel (left), which was opened at Thirty-fourth Street and Fifth Avenue in 1897. Contemporaries were of the opinion that with its Peacock Alley, its thousand bedrooms, and its sumptuous service, it exuded the very essence of the metropolis.

The increasing confinement of city living led New Yorkers to seek outdoor recreation. The masses enjoyed themselves at Coney Island's Steeplechase Park (below). Members of "The Four Hundred" took to the bicycle in Central Park (left).

Photos courtesy
Museum of the
City of New York

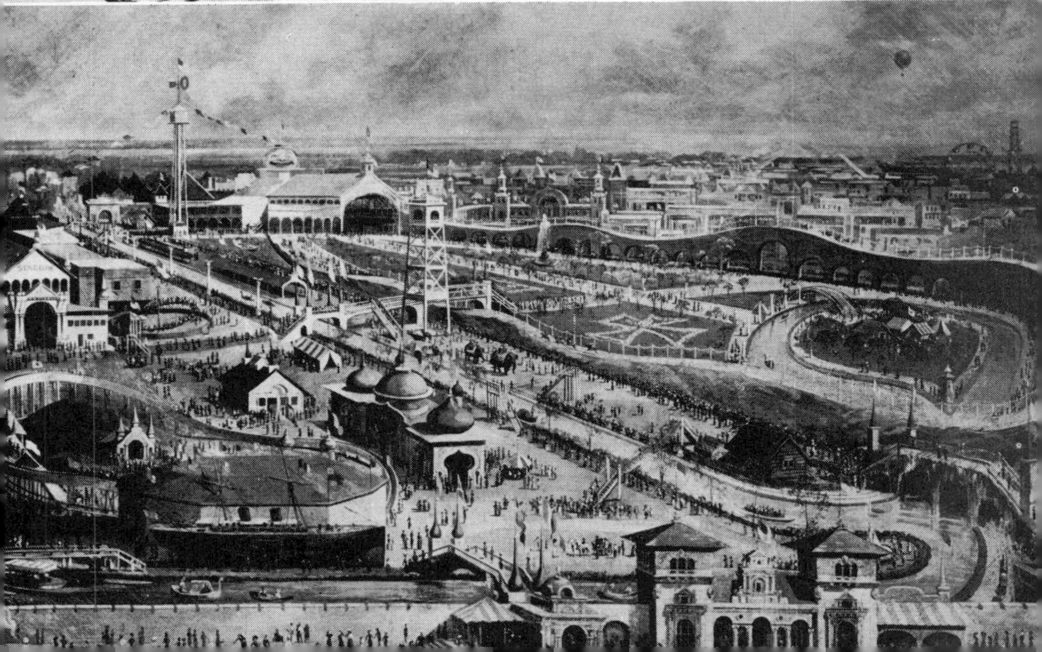

The J. Clarence Davies Collection, Museum of the City of New York

BINDING THE GREATER CITY

Outward signs of the consolidation of Greater New York, which occurred on January 1, 1898, were the mighty span of the Brooklyn Bridge and the elevated lines that facilitated contact as early as the 1880's between the Bronx and Manhattan.

Contemporaries viewed the 6,000-foot bridge, with its 1,595-foot central span, as a sign of the "go-ahead" spirit of New York, proof of the gigantic accomplishment of which the modern metropolis was capable. Designed in 1867 by John A. Roebling, the bridge was completed after his death, through the untiring zeal of his son, Washington A. Roebling. Pedestrians had to pay a toll of one cent after it was opened to the public, with impressive ceremonies, on May 24, 188

The first elevated railroads, steam-powere went into operation at the turn of the sever ties, when construction work on the Brook lyn Bridge was about to begin. By 1900, fou elevated lines reached the remoter parts o the Island. Like the bridge, the "El," appear ing to swing in midair between earth an sky, was one of the "spectacles" of the lat nineteenth-century city.

In the photograph above, taken in 188 the bridge, with its fortress-like piers an tight-strung wires, outmodes the ferry boat whose service it amplified. Below, a treacher ous curve on the elevated before the last o the lines was removed in the 1950's.

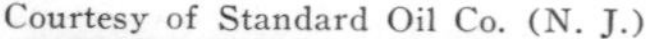

Courtesy of Standard Oil Co. (N. J.)

NEW YORK AND WORLD WAR I

Fifth Avenue was a sea of heads on November 11, 1918, as New Yorkers celebrated Armistice Day, at the close of World War I. The flag-bedecked Avenue, seen here looking northward from Thirty-fourth Street, wore the decorations of war as well as of peace. The appeals of the Red Cross and the United War Work Campaign still spanned the street, and the wall of flags, in which the Union Jack and the French Tricolor mingled with the Stars and Stripes, suggested the spirit in which the war had been waged.

Courtesy of *The News,* New York's Picture Newspaper

BRIGHT LIGHTS OF THE POSTWAR ERA

Speakeasy, 1929, drawn by Joseph Webster Golinkin; reproduced by courtesy of the artist.

The Great White Way: New Year's Eve in Times Square. (January 1, 1939)

Courtesy *The News,*
New York's Picture Newspaper

CHARLES DICKENS REVISITS NEW YORK CITY: 1867–1868

The most distinguished foreign witness to the growth of New York City by the later sixties was Charles Dickens, who returned to New York, a quarter-century after his first visit, to give a course of readings. This enterprise met with spectacular success. At a testimonial dinner, held on the eve of his return to England late in April 1868, the author of the *American Notes* bore testimony to the many changes that had taken place since his first visit, especially the rise of "vast new cities," an increase in the "graces and amenities of life," and "much improvement in the press." The following excerpts from letters written while he was in New York amplify, as well as qualify, his official public reaction.[38]

[December 11, 1867] Amazing success. A very fine audience, far better than at Boston. *Carol* and *Trial* on first night, great: still greater, *Copperfield* and *Bob Sawyer* on second. For the tickets of the four readings of next week there were, at nine o'clock this morning, 3000 people in waiting, and they had begun to assemble in the bitter cold as early as two o'clock in the morning. . . .

[Recalling his visit of 1842] The only portion [of the city] that has even now come back to me is the part of Broadway in which the Carlton Hotel (long since destroyed) used to stand. There is a very fine new park [Central Park] in the outskirts, and the number of grand houses and splendid equipages is quite surprising. There are hotels close here with 500 bedrooms and I don't know how many boarders; but this hotel [the Westminster, on Irving Place] is quite as quiet as, and not much larger than, Mivart's in Brook Street. . . . The waiters are French, and one might be living in Paris. One of the two proprietors is also proprietor of Niblo's Theatre, and the greatest care is taken of me. Niblo's great attraction, the *Black Crook,* has now been played every night for 16 months (!), and is the most preposterous peg to hang ballets on that was ever seen. The people who act in it have not the slightest idea of what it is about, and never had; but, after taxing my intellectual powers to the utmost, I fancy that I have discovered Black Crook to be a malignant hunchback leagued with the Powers of Darkness to separate two lovers; and that the Powers of Lightness coming (in no skirts whatever) to the rescue, he is defeated. I am quite serious in saying that I do not suppose there are two pages of *All the Year*

Round in the whole piece (which acts all night); the whole of the rest of it being ballets of all sorts, perfectly unaccountable processions, and the Donkey out of last year's Covent Garden pantomime! At the other theatres, comic operas, melodramas, and domestic dramas prevail all over the city, and my stories play no inconsiderable part in them. . . . the local politics of the place are in a most depraved condition, if half of what is said to me be true. I prefer not to talk of these things, but at odd intervals I look round for myself. Great social improvements in respect of manners and forbearance have come to pass since I was here before, but in public life I see as yet but little change. . . .

The halls are excellent. Imagine one holding two thousand people, seated with exact equality for every one of them, and every one seated separately. I have nowhere, at home or abroad, seen so fine a police as the police of New York. . . . On the other hand, the laws for regulation of public vehicles, clearing of streets, and removal of obstructions, are wildly outraged by the people for whose benefit they are intended. Yet there is undoubtedly improvement in every direction. . . .

At Brooklyn I am going to read in Mr. [Henry] Ward Beecher's chapel: the only building there available for the purpose. You must understand that Brooklyn is a kind of sleeping-place for New York, and is supposed to be a great place in the money way. We let the seats pew by pew! . . . Each evening an enormous ferry-boat will convey me and my state-carriage (not to mention half a dozen wagons and any number of people and a few score of horses) across the river to Brooklyn, and will bring me back again. The sale of tickets there was an amazing scene. The noble army of speculators are now furnished (this is literally true, and I am quite serious) each man with a straw mattress, a little bag of bread and meat, two blankets, and a bottle of whiskey. With this outfit, *they lie down in line on the pavement* the whole of the night before the tickets are sold: generally taking up their position at about 10. It being severely cold at Brooklyn, they made an immense bonfire in the street. . . .

The Irish element is acquiring such enormous influence in New York city, that when I think of it, and see the large Roman Catholic cathedral rising there, it seems unfair to stigmatise as "American" other monstrous things that one also sees. But the general corruption in respect of the local funds appears to be stupendous.

8. *THE EMERGENCE OF THE MODERN CITY (1870–1900)*

THE GENERATION from 1870 to 1900 saw the advent of present-day New York. Physically the city was still scaled more to the nineteenth than to the twentieth century. Yet contemporary comment depicts a community whose basic features bore a close resemblance to those of the present day. Commentators of the early 1880's began to note the "upward tendency" of its architecture and the innovation of electricity which illumined Broadway, from Union Square to Thirty-fourth Street, with the "radiance of day." Its "Little Italies," its Negro Harlem, and its Hebrew quarter on the lower East Side—all identifiable by the later 1880's—gave it the ethnic pattern of La Guardia's New York; while the squalid congestion of its slums and the exploitation of its industrial workers, which now offended observers' eyes, represented extremes of crowded living and social indifference which succeeding generations were not to see surpassed and which, indeed, the twentieth-century city was in some measure to allay.[1]

The census takers of 1870 listed 942,292 residents in New York City and close to a million and a half in the area which later (in 1898) was consolidated to form Greater New York. By 1900, the population of this wider area had more than doubled, to give the consolidated city a total of 3,437,202. The visitor of 1870 found Manhattan compactly built for more than five miles northward from the Battery point; but although streets were laid out beyond the number 150th, the city still had a "straggling, unfinished look" for some distance south of Central Park. Here and there, "between blocks of imposing houses" were groups of rough wooden huts occupied by Irish squatters with their poultry and pigs. On the east side, buildings straggled irregularly as far as Harlem; on the west, beyond Sixtieth Street, construction, even less continuous, ran, finally, into the "scattered suburban residences of Manhattanville and Washington Heights." By the close of the century, however, virtually all the empty space south of the Park had been occupied; the city had "imparted its peculiar effect to every street"; and population, propelled by the pressure of immigrant newcomers in the lower city, was continuing to spread both northward on Manhattan and across the rivers into the suburbs, some of which, by 1900, had become boroughs of Greater New York.[2]

A "mania for high buildings," noted from the mid-seventies, began the transformation of the horizontal city of 1870 into the skyward-thrusting community of later years. Most visitors were impressed with the eight-, ten-, and eleven-story structures which began to appear in the 1870's, despite the fact that they threatened "to shut out the sky"; but to veteran Manhattanites like George Templeton Strong they were "hideous, top-heavy" nightmares. By 1900, the architectural revolution had been carried to such extremes that, in the opinion of foreign visitors, the Americans had practically "added a new dimension" to space. "They move almost as much on the perpendicular as on the horizontal plane," a British journalist reported in 1899. "When they find themselves a little crowded, they simply tilt a street on end and call it a skyscraper." [3]

The use of elevators—one of the earliest of which was installed in the five-story Equitable Building in 1870—encouraged the vertical trend, permitting hotels and business structures to be built to heights limited only by the capacity of masonry to sustain their weight. The massive walls of the Western Union Telegraph Building, constructed in the early seventies, allowed it to rise 110 feet from the sidewalk. According to one British observer, the Tribune Building, erected in 1874 and 1875, towered "above the surrounding buildings like a sort of brick and mortar giraffe." Its clock tower rose to a height of 285 feet, somewhat higher than the spire of Trinity Church, long the loftiest landmark on the island.[4]

The tall buildings of the 1880's were dwarfed in the succeeding decade as architects substituted a steel skeleton for the mass of masonry that formerly had supplied support. The Tower Building, at 50 Broadway, erected during 1888 and 1889, was the earliest example of the use in New York City of this revolutionary architectural technique, when the first seven of its thirteen stories were supported by a steel frame. By the close of the century, New York could boast of half a dozen structures whose over-all height exceeded 300 feet and of many others almost their equal in altitude. Its tallest skyscraper was then the Park Row Business Building, completed in 1898. The tower above its twenty-nine stories reached an unprecedented height of 392 feet.[5]

As in later years, contemporaries were of mixed minds as to the merits of the towering excrescences, "shooting up with startling abruptness" above the surrounding blocks. The Scottish clergyman David Macrae, returning to the city in 1898 after a lapse of thirty years, found the architectural innovation "startling," "outrageous"; and William Dean Howells condemned the "savage anarchy" that permitted a bare brick wall to rise "six or seven stories above the neighboring buildings." In the opinion of the distinguished British author Frederic Harrison, these nineteenth-century "towers of Babel" hopelessly disfigured the city. If they became general, they would make the streets "dark and windy cañons, and human nature would call out for their suppression," he contended in the impressions of America which he wrote after a visit at the turn of the century. On the other hand, Walt Whitman, writing in 1878, found something heroic in the "cloud touching edifices" of "tall-topt" Manhattan; and to the French novelist Paul Bourget, these human "beehives" with their "thousand offices" connoted the "tireless *forward*," the material achievement, that above all was the essence of New York.[6]

Its almost unalloyed materialism was the quality of the New York scene most universally noted by the commentators of these years. Native and foreigner alike, they agreed that the "besetting sin" of New Yorkers was their "mad race for wealth," their pursuit of the "Almighty Dollar." "The light of Mammon gleams on nearly every face in Broadway and Wall Street," wrote an Englishwoman who sojourned in the city in the early seventies; and in succeeding decades visitors rang the changes on this observation in every tongue. The Polish novelist Sienkiewicz, a traveler of 1876, was repelled by the exclusive preoccupation with the pursuit of wealth; an Italian visitor of 1882 labeled New York *"la Mecca del dollaro"*; and the Cuban revolutionary José Marti was struck in the eighties with the prevailing concern for money. French travelers continued to deplore the lack of taste and refinement in a city whose only monuments were the banks, hotels, and insurance companies dedicated to the "religion" of supplying men with riches. The consensus of observers of the nineties was expressed by George W. Steevens, a British journalist who came to the United States to report the presidential campaign of 1896. The very buildings cried aloud of "struggling, almost savage, unregulated strength," he wrote. "Nothing is given to beauty; everything centres in hard utility. It is the outward expression of the freest, fiercest individualism. The very houses are alive with the instinct of competition, and strain each one to overtop its neighbours." [7]

In the opinion of contemporary observers, this compulsion for material gain was reflected in the frenetic behavior of New Yorkers as well as in the unsightly environment in which they lived. To Sir John Leng, one of Scotland's outstanding journalists, New York and Chicago in 1876 represented "the nervous, spasmodic, excitable phases of commercial activity more than any other American cities." Everything here appeared "to be done at full speed"—as if, to quote a visitor of 1872, the residents seemed "bent on making amends . . . for having come into the world half-an-hour too late." Oscar Wilde, arriving in New York in 1882 to lecture on the English Renaissance, was struck with the fact that everybody seemed "in a hurry to catch a train"; and the British philosopher Herbert Spencer, a visitor of the same year, criticized the restless energy and unceasing ambition of the New Yorkers he had met. "Immense injury is done by this high-pressure life," he asserted. "It is time to preach the gospel of relaxation." But his counsel was little heeded, for Paul Bourget, reflecting upon the "mad haste" of the cable cars a decade later, observed in 1893 that "a fever for getting there" had led New Yorkers even to make "the street walk." [8]

In the unsightliness of the surface scene—even beyond the squalid slums—contemporaries found the most striking proof of what appeared to be the prevailing preoccupation with the race for riches. The city's streets were a continuing disgrace, to which almost no commentator failed to make a scathing reference. Stone paving blocks, "one to two inches higher than their neighbors," the rails used by the horsecars, and the iron girders of the elevated railways were obstructions that made riding "a jolting process," done "at the risk of dislocating your neck." Mud and filth disfigured the thoroughfares, even in front of the most palatial mansions, and, in the opinion of William Dean Howells, gave them an appearance of "arrogant untidiness, . . . immediate neglect and overuse." According to Rudyard Kipling, the streets of this "long, narrow pig-trough"—his term for the New York he visited in 1892—were "first cousins to a Zanzibar foreshore, or kin to the approaches of a Zulu kraal." [9]

Overhead, as well as underfoot, the expanding metropolis had an unkempt and disheveled look. The elevated railroad, perpetually "tearing along" on its stilted, aerial highway, was "an ever-active volcano over the heads of inoffensive citizens," in the opinion of an Australian visitor of 1888. Telephone and telegraph wires, hanging in rakish festoons from "gaunt, untrimmed" timbers, gave the city the appearance of being "covered with gigantic cobwebs." The "acres of wall," produced by the irregular height of the new tall buildings, encouraged a rash of garish advertising that cheapened the physical appearance of the city and further emphasized its commercial tone. The "bills of enormous size" that "papered" the metropolis disfigured New York for the French musician Jacques Offenbach, a traveler of 1875; and twenty years later, the scourge had spread. "There is a product called Castoria—children cry for it, it appears," wrote a British visitor of 1896. ". . . its spirited proprietors have bought up every wall in New York that faces towards the Brooklyn Bridge. As you stand there the red houses seem to be laced with gold letters; the whole city is yelling aloud concerning the virtues of Castoria." [10]

Despite sporadic attempts, this generation saw but little progress in improving the city's physical appearance. Visitors in the fall of 1886 noted that in some places the pavements were being lifted for the purpose of burying the telegraph and telephone wires underground. Begun in this year, pursuant to legislation of June 1884, this improvement was still being carried on in the later nineties. The introduction of asphalt paving brought some relief from "the din of wheels" on rough stone streets; but Howells complained in 1893 that "the sharp clatter of the horses' iron shoes" still tormented the ear; and their pulverized manure, which formed "so great a part of the city's dust," seemed "to blow more freely about on the asphalt than on the old-fashioned pavements." Street cleaning became more systematic and effective after the appointment of Colonel George E. Waring as street-cleaning commissioner in January 1895.[11]

The introduction of electric lighting promised to enhance the appearance of the presently pedestrian gaslit city. Although its use did not become general until the later nineties, electricity illumined a business house on the Bowery as early as 1878 and lighted Broadway, from Fourteenth Street to Twenty-sixth Street, in December of 1880. To commentators of the early eighties, electric lighting was one of the marvels of the metropolis. "The effect of the light in the squares of the Empire City can scarcely be described, so weird and so beautiful is it," wrote a British visitor of 1882. From tall standards, "erected in the centre of each square," light was "thrown down upon the trees in such a way as to give a fairy-like aspect." By the close of the century, the "omnipresence of electricity" already offered a foretaste of the glamor with which it was to suffuse Broadway in the ensuing years. A visitor of 1899 reported that theatres, restaurants, and stores were "outlined in incandescent lamps," as Broadway and many of the cross streets, from Union Square to Herald Square, flashed out at dusk "into the most brilliant illumination." [12]

Lacking, as yet, the spectacular lighting that was to give it its twentieth-century excitement, Broadway, earlier focus of interest, now attracted much less attention than its pretentious neighbor, Fifth Avenue. This very "alderman of streets," where "aristocratic New York" reigned "supreme," epitomized the material accomplishment which gave Victorian Manhattan its most characteristic tone. "Aristocratic dullness" stamped its "monotonous," brownstone vista (*chocolat au lait,* to a French visitor) in the seventies; but the reverse became true of its upper reaches, as the section from Forty-sixth Street to Seventy-second, along Central Park, was embellished, between the early 1880's and 1900, with the residential palaces of the city's millionaires. Here were the homes of the Vanderbilts and the Astors, of Jay Gould, Elbridge T. Gerry, Collis P. Huntington, Charles Crocker, H. O. Havemeyer, Charles T. Yerkes, H. M. Flagler, William Rockefeller, Perry Belmont, William C. Whitney, and other financial titans—an architectural catalog to the owners of much of the nation's wealth.[13]

The architects of these palatial dwellings shunned the monotonous brownstone dignity of the earlier period and turned to Europe for their models. The result was "an architectural pot-pourri," which in the opinion of Frederic Harrison almost rivaled "the Rue des Nations at the Paris Exhibition of 1900." "Facing the Central Park, each millionaire seems to have commissioned his architect to build him a mansion of any ancient style from Byzantine to the last French Empire, provided only it was in contrast to the style of his neighbours," the British publicist wrote, after a sojourn in New York at the turn of the century. "So commissioned, the artist has lavished skilful carving, singular ingenuity, and noble material in stone, marble, and mosaic. Many . . . are interesting . . . and some . . . beautiful, but the general effect of such rampant eclecticism is rather bewildering." [14]

Madison Avenue, which boasted the sumptuous Tiffany residence, had an aura of affluence similar to that of its more famous neighbor.

But the pedestrianism of Sixth Avenue symbolized, by contrast, the ever heightening social diversity in the metropolitan scene. Opposed to the aristocracy, wealth, and elegance of Fifth Avenue were the plebeian sights and sounds of its more menial neighbor to the west—"the carts and vans, the five-cent cars, the workmen's trains, the street-stalls and lager-beer saloons, the odour of fish, and cabbage, and stale tobacco, the bars, the butchers, the democracy of Sixth Avenue." Side by side ran the two contrasting thoroughfares, wrote an English visitor of 1881, "these representatives of the Ten and the Million, patrician velvet and plebeian corduroy." [15]

There were, however, more glaring examples of the contrasts of metropolitan living—the "lights and shadows" which to American commentators of the period were the inevitable accompaniment of urban life. At the opposite extreme from "Millionaire's Row" were the bedraggled slums, which by 1900 housed more than one and a half million of the city's residents. Many European observers, especially visitors of the eighties, contended that these quarters exceeded in misery the worst that London or Paris could offer; and American writers like Jacob Riis and William Dean Howells presented even more graphic evidence of the squalor in which increasing thousands of New Yorkers dwelt.[16]

In his *How the Other Half Lives,* published in 1888, Jacob Riis turned the spotlight of his reporter's pen upon the sordid, downtown back alleys, the malodorous Mulberry Bend, the seven-cent lodging houses, and the teeming tenements of the lower East Side, where human congestion reached an unprecedented figure of as many as 330,000 persons per square mile. An "East-Side Ramble" in the mid-nineties offered Howells a first-hand view of what he called "a typical New York tenement." An alleyway about two feet wide gave access to a court from which the inmates of the dwelling had their "sole chance of sun and air." Two small windows transmitted the "putrid breath of the court, . . . twice fouled by the passage through the living room," into the "black hole in the rear, where the whole family lay on the heap of rags that passed for a bed. . . . All the tenements here were of this size and shape," he reported, "—a room with windows opening upon the court and at the rear the small black bin or pen for the bed." [17]

Multiple dwelling, though of more agreeable character, was also increasingly the lot of middle-class New Yorkers as the pressure of population put an ever greater premium on space. Writers who contrasted New York of the nineties with the city of pre-Civil War days noted the fact that, for many of the residents, the individual home and even, to some extent, the hotel and boarding house life of the earlier period had given way to "housekeeping in flats, or apartments of three or four rooms or more, on the same floor," as was the case in all the countries of Europe, and even England, where flats were beginning to appear. The German geographer Friedrich Ratzel observed this residential trend as early as 1873 and praised it as an improved means of exploiting "the land and capital available for construction." By the turn of the 1880's, apartment houses 90 to 100 feet in height and equipped with the latest labor-saving devices, were among the touted attractions of the metropolis.[18]

Professor Ratzel noted, too, the increasing separation of business and residence, as high rents and the pressure of population forced more and more New Yorkers to "retreat even farther North" for residence purposes or cross "one of the rivers into Long Island or New Jersey." Should one choose the first alternative, according to a British visitor of 1896, he could "either go North of the Harlem River and live in a house, or remain below it and live in a flat"; for by the nineties, land was "too scarce to allow a whole house to any man far short of his million." The other option was to become a "commuter" and live across one of the rivers. The comic papers never tired of representing the commuter "starting out for Lonelyville with a huge bundle of town-bought provisions in his hand," the Britisher reported. The reason for this contempt? "The commuter earns his money in New York, and he spends it in New Jersey; that is his crime." [19]

Observers blamed the bifurcated existence of more and more New Yorkers—as well as the preoccupation with money-getting—for making Manhattan "the worst governed city in the Union." A population "passing nomadically from flat to flat or else settling many miles outside the city" lacked a "steady body of civic opinion." As a result, the municipal government, "with all its vast interests," had been "left to ward politicians of the Tammany class, to their own comfort and that of their friends." In the late seventies and early eighties, Tammany was under the domination of "Honest" John Kelly, and such were the excesses of boss politics that Herbert Spencer asserted, during his visit in 1882, that New York, like the Italian republics of the Middle Ages, was losing the substance, if not the forms, of freedom. A legislative investigation, revealing collusion between the police and criminal elements in the city, brought a momentary reaction against Tammany in the mid-nineties, but it was a short-lived victory for reform.[20]

Meanwhile, a movement to square the structure of the municipal government with the reality of the wider metropolitan area—a "civic three-in-one," according to a Scottish visitor of the early seventies—bore fruit in 1897 in the creation of Greater New York. The Greater New York charter, which went into effect on January 1, 1898, authorized the consolidation of Brooklyn, Queens, and Staten Island with Manhattan and the Bronx. An outward sign of the integration of the wider city's component parts was the completion of the Brooklyn Bridge, which was formally opened on May 24, 1883, in the presence of President Arthur and his cabinet and the governors of the nearby states. In a period when foreign travelers found little in New York to admire, their almost universal praise for this engineering marvel was an agreeable exception. The Reverend John Kirkwood, an English clergyman, spoke for most of the city's visitors when he called the spectacular span "a source of increasing wonder and admiration." To the French novelist Bourget it was another sign of the audacious "go-ahead" spirit of the New World metropolis.[21]

Of the nearly three and a half million persons who made up this Greater New York, at the census of 1900, considerably more than a third were foreign-born; for the flood of immigration continued to leave a numerous residue in the port of entry. Indeed, the immigrants of the eighties and nineties, coming in unprecedented numbers from Italy, Austria, Russia, and the other countries of southern and eastern Europe, were more inclined than those of an earlier period to settle in the metropolis. By 1900, Germans were the most numerous nationality among the city's foreign-born population, and there were some 275,000 natives of Ireland among its extensive Irish stock. Though the city already sheltered representatives of virtually all the nations of the globe, the most spectacular increases were in immigrants from Russia and Italy. By 1900, New Yorkers born in the Russian Empire numbered 155,201, most of them of the Jewish faith; and there were already more than 145,000 natives of Italy.[22]

The daily arrivals of immigrants and their as yet undissolved suspension in the urban scene convinced most foreign observers that New York was too cosmopolitan to be typical of America, if, indeed, they did not predict that the American element in the city would soon be submerged by the foreign flood. "Although in America, it is not American. New York is New York and nothing else," wrote

Thérèse Yelverton, an English travel writer who visited the city in the mid-seventies. To another traveler of her sex, the Finnish feminist Alexandra Gripenberg, New York's cosmopolitanism was the one distinguishing feature of a city which had less individuality and character, in her opinion, than the other large urban centers of the nation. Visitors liked to point out that the Empire City was the second or third largest German city in the world and that it had a larger Irish population than Dublin. One British traveler reported: "An Irishman landing there cries, 'Be dad! it's for all the wurrld loike Corrk!' A German exclaims, 'Ganz wie Berlin'; the Chicagoan bluntly asks, 'What's the next train for the United States?' " The French economist Paul de Rousiers, like other astute observers of the city on the turn of the 1890's, concluded that New York could best be understood as "the connecting link between two very different worlds, American on the one side and European on the other. For Europeans New York is America, but for Americans it is the beginning of Europe." [23]

The sons of Erin were so prevalent when James Macaulay visited the city in 1870 that the Scottish journalist wondered whether he was in "New York or New Cork." He found Irishmen everywhere: servicing the port, driving the omnibuses, keeping stores and saloons, participating in the city council, and dwelling in Fifth Avenue mansions as well as, more numerously, in the slums. The squalid living conditions of the "low Irish" were a continuing subject of comment throughout the generation, although the Irish social reformer Charlotte O'Brien, a visitor of 1881, was impressed with the emotional security and self-respect exhibited by her former countrymen even in their tenement homes. Commentators noted the increasing influence of the Catholic Church upon the Irish element in the population; and local support of such movements as the Fenian agitation—the excuse for a colorful parade when the Irish clergyman Michael Buckley visited New York in 1871—reflected the role of the Irish in fomenting anti-British feeling in this part of the United States. The opinion was widespread, throughout the period, that the solidarity of the Irish vote, "under the bidding of their priests and politicians," was responsible for the excesses of machine politics in New York and the notorious shortcomings of its municipal government.[24]

The Teutonic ingredient of the city, increasing even more rapidly than the Irish in this period, was the subject of comment especially by German visitors. By the late 1860's, the German element had already permeated many parts of the New York area. They made up a considerable portion of the population of Brooklyn, Williamsburg, Jersey City, and especially Hoboken; and German tobacconists, tailors, lithographers, grocers, tavern-keepers and brewers plied their trades in many parts of Manhattan. The center of their society, however, was still the "German town" south of Fourteenth Street on the east side of the city. Here the principal German theatres, beer gardens, and other businesses gave the section the appearance, according to one commentator, of "an immense chain of German sausages, interlinked here and there with material properly American." Visitors of the nineties continued to remark upon the Germanism which stamped whole sections of the city, but they detected a "striking" Anglicization—indicative of the speed with which many New York Germans were taking on American ways.[25]

A significant new nationality element had become the cause of comment by the turn of the 1880's. The vicomte d'Haussonville, a French visitor of 1882, observed among the Irish residents of the fetid Five Points area Italian newcomers, characterized by "more animation and life and less drunkenness" than their Irish neighbors. The decade of the 1870's saw the first major influx of Italians into New York, although they had begun to come in small numbers in the years before the American Civil War. By 1880, there were more than 12,000 natives of Italy in the city. Many of them inhabited the "Little Italy" in the vicinity of Mulberry Street—a miserable world of its own with Italian stores, restaurants, boarding houses, banks, and steamship companies. The Italian was welcomed in the slums as a tenant who made less trouble than "the contentious Irishman or the order-loving German," according to Jacob Riis, who described "The Italian in New York" in the middle 1880's: that is to say, he was "content to live in a pig-sty" and submit to "robbery at the hands of the rent-collector without murmur." [26]

This was the environment in which Giuseppe Giacosa found his former countrymen when he visited New York in the early 1890's. The mud, filth, and disorder of the place were almost beyond the description of Italy's most noted contemporary dramatist and co-author of the librettos for several of Puccini's operas. Overhead, the sky was "spiderwebbed" with faded clothes, hanging from one dilapidated house to another; and in the streets were half-naked children and gaunt and disheveled women, carrying on domestic tasks for which the dark and crowded tenements provided little space. Already, the greater part of the Italian community had been dispersed to the north and west as the newcomers improved their standard of living through employment in the building trades, or as barbers, waiters, or proprietors of fruit shops to which they had "worked up after going around for years with baskets and little carts." Giacosa found their existence still far below the American level, however, a situation to be explained by the fact that many of them sent part of their earnings to their families in the Old World.[27]

Contemporaries—both native and foreign—were equally appalled at living conditions in the Jewish quarter on the lower East Side. Propelled by the proscription of their people in the Czarist Empire after 1880, these newcomers—strange in religion as well as appearance—peopled what Theodore Dreiser called the city's "most radically foreign plexus"—the lower East Side. Here the "amount of poverty, toil, and social degradation" was "positively appalling," in the opinion of Arthur Montefiore, an Englishman of Jewish antecedents who visited this crowded section of the city in 1888. Street after street of six-story tenement houses were "crammed from garret to cellar" with Jewish families, ten to fourteen people of both sexes and of all ages occupying every room. In such quarters, according to Jacob Riis, occurred the bulk of the sweatshop labor in tailoring and garmentmaking by which the residents kept "absolute starvation at bay." Paul Bourget, a visitor of 1893, could hardly "endure the air of these shops, where the odor of ill-cared-for bodies mingled with the odor of spoiled food. . . . For a dozen little children's trousers, over which these hunger-hollowed faces were bent, the contractor pays seventy-five cents," he reported. The worker could make "eighteen in his best days, by not losing half an hour." [28]

The orthodox faith of these newcomers differentiated them from many members of New York's historic older Jewish community. The skullcaps and long-skirted caftans of some of the men attracted the attention of visitors, as did the small parchment scrolls, hanging at the door of almost every tenement, which most of the inhabitants kissed in coming in and going out. Montefiore reported that in this part of the city Saturday was observed as the Sabbath, when the residents *en masse* attended synagogues of their own making—frequently "a scantily furnished room in a rear tenement, with a few wooden stools or benches for the congregation." Describing the city of the later 1880's, Jacob Riis reported that Hebrews had so "crowded out the Gentiles in the Tenth Ward" that, when the great Jewish holidays came round, the public schools had "practically to close up." According to Montefiore, the wealthier Hebrews of New York looked askance upon these newcomers and advocated enforcement of the recently enacted pauper immigration law.[29]

The almost laundered neatness of Chinatown distinguished it from the Hebrew community and the "Little Italy" which flanked it on the east and west; but there was nothing particularly picturesque about the Chinese quarter of this period. To outsiders, it was known chiefly for its "gambling hells" and opium dens, with their little apartments, each "furnished with a rude bed, consisting of a wooden bench upholstered with quilt and blankets," where Montefiore observed "yellow-faced, pig-tailed smokers, endeavoring to court the soothing dreams which first led them to contract the habit." Until the early eighties, New York's Negro citizens were virtually restricted to "Africa," a section which included the vile rookeries of Thompson Street and a narrow strip on the West Side south of Thirty-second. By the later 1880's, however, the encroachment of the Italians in this area was forcing their removal to the upper East Side, from Yorkville to Harlem, where they developed what Jacob Riis described as a "neat and orderly community," far different from the "black and tan slums" in the lower city. The Cuban patriot José Marti, in New York from 1880 to 1895, was impressed with the self-possessed behavior of a community of "well-to-do Negroes" who lived in the vicinity of Sixth Avenue. Their discussion of "the minister's sermons, the happenings at the lodge, the success of their lawyers, or the achievement of some Negro student . . . just graduated from a medical school" suggested the opportunities life in New York was already offering this race.[30]

Save for the communities of Italians and Chinese, the lower city was by now virtually confined to the pursuit of business—a "city" of stores, offices, and banks, which connoted the extensive commercial, financial, and industrial foundations upon which New York's prosperity was now based. By the early seventies, it was apparent to the French economist Claudio Jannet (a nineteenth-century André Siegfried) that the "creation of a powerful money market in New York" was one of the great economic transformations which explained the American economy at the turn of the eighties. "The distribution that New York bankers make of their capital to all points of the Union assures to them an influence which justifies the name of *empire city* given to Manhattan," he wrote in the mid-seventies. By 1890, the value of goods manufactured in the Greater New York area exceeded a billion dollars; and in 1900 the city was still the nation's first industrial center with products valued at $1,371,358,468. Nevertheless, despite the ever increasing financial and industrial prowess of this "empire" city, it was its commercial activities which continued to engage the observer's attention—both as a mart of retail enterprise and as the nerve center of the nation's productive economy. In the opinion of Oscar Wilde, New York in 1882 was "one huge Whiteley's shop." [31]

By this date, as business followed the northward movement of population, the fashionable shopping region was centered at Fourteenth Street, Broadway, and Sixth Avenue. Here the "dry goods stores" of Lord and Taylor and Arnold Constable and Company and the "carpet warehouse" of W. & J. Sloane rose "like giants on either hand." Iza Duffus Hardy, an Englishwoman who reached New York when the city was mourning the death of President Garfield, reported that Fourteenth Street, especially, was "the headquarters of ladies bent on shopping." At certain hours and seasons it was "so thronged" that one could make "but a very slow progress . . . along it." "It is a perfect bazaar," she wrote in her sketches of American travel; "not only is there a brilliant display in the windows of everything good to look at, from exotic flowers to encaustic tiles, and everything one can possibly wear, from Paris imported bonnets to pink-satin boots, but the side-walk is fringed with open-air stalls, heaped high with pretty things, many of them absurdly cheap."

This visitor was intrigued with the new way of giving change in vogue in some of the city's stores. "Instead of the usual yell of 'Cash!' and the small boy or girl pushing breathless through the crowd . . . with our purchases and our money, . . . our five-dollar bill and our account were put into a hollow wooden ball, which the sales-lady (we do not have any shop-girls in New York) deftly tossed into a sort of hanging cradle or network. Quick as a flash, up went cradle, ball, dollars, and bill before our astonished eyes; the ball, jerked into a sort of groove or gallery, rolled with amazing celerity along the ceiling to the far-off end of the establishment, and in a minute or two we saw it flashing back along its groove, leaping down into its cradling net, and thence into the sales-lady's ready hand, its contents being now our correct change and receipted bill." [32]

Near by, on Broadway, A. T. Stewart's dry-goods establishment was still one of the "things to see" in New York of the eighties. With its

2,900 to 3,000 employees, including the sewing girls who were installed with their machines on the top floor, it offered "a sight" perhaps "not to be found in any other shop of the kind in the world." According to Walter G. Marshall, a British visitor of 1879, a great many people dropped in simply "to stare and look about, without intending to make purchases." "Stewart's marble palace"—the wholesale department of his enterprise—was farther downtown in the vicinity of the famous "dry-goods district." Here, in the section from Broome and Grand streets to City Hall Park, throbbed "the pulse of the dry-goods trade of the United States," wrote a British visitor of 1887, "strengthening and weakening as good or poor crops give the agricultural community a surplus to spend for dress." [33]

The northward thrust of residence and the relegation of the lower city to business not only prompted but were made possible by a drastic expansion of transit facilities, as the elevated railroad and, at the close of the century, electric trolleys supplemented and finally superseded the horsecar and the omnibus of Civil War days. In the opinion of the German geographer Friedrich Ratzel, New York's horsecar system gave it transit facilities superior to those of any European city at the time of his visit in 1873. Most contemporaries, however, criticized the vehicles as slow, dirty, and inadequate, especially at rush hours, when, according to a Belgian visitor of 1877, the horse-drawn cars followed one another in a steady stream, "the horse's head of one only a few steps from the car" which preceded it.[34]

An expansion of the elevated railway, which had had "a sickly existence" since the turn of the seventies, marked the first real advance in providing the growing city with more rapid conveyance. In 1878, the addition of a second line, the Sixth Avenue Elevated, supplemented the original unit, which had been built along Greenwich Street on the west side; and by 1900 there were available four main double-track lines, on which cars ran at two- to three-minute intervals. For a decade after its opening, the Sixth Avenue "El," like the Brooklyn Bridge, was one of the city's most spectacular "sights"—in the daytime as the cars sped along at the level of the second-story windows or at night when they seemed "to swing in mid-air between you and the sky," their "green and red fiery eyes staring ahead and plunging into the darkness." [35]

English commentators compared the operation of the aerial railway with the London underground, generally to the latter's disadvantage. They found it an admirable arrangement for traveling New York's long distances speedily and cheaply. With its comfortable and airy cars, it was a "marvellous piece of work," in the opinion of Henry Irving, who traveled the Sixth Avenue line shortly after arriving for his theatrical debut in the fall of 1883. To one of his compatriots, the contrast between the elevated and the underground epitomized the difference between the American and British personalities: the " 'L' road . . . ephemeral, precipitate, hurried," appearing to run "at full speed on nothing through the air" and democratic in the extreme in operation; the British underground less exhilarating, but secure, and adapted to the "privilege of choosing . . . graded classes," according to one's "tastes and means." [36]

At the same time, contemporaries criticized the aerial railway for disfiguring the streets, obstructing traffic, reducing the value of abutting property without the consent of the owners, and intruding upon personal privacy, as it careened "so near to the houses you might shake hands with the inhabitants and see what they had for dinner." Additional disadvantages were the "smoke and flying cinders" issuing from their steam locomotives and the "roar and shriek and hiss" as they passed overhead. To Finland's Alexandra Gripenberg, a Scandinavian visitor in the tradition of Peter Kalm and Fredrika Bremer, the elevated ruined the perspectives of the streets and gave the pedestrian the impression of constantly walking under a bridge. Nevertheless, having an "iron horse . . . above the roofs" connoted, in her opinion, the "new, seething, urgent modernity" of the New World metropolis.[37]

The introduction of cable cars gave young Stephen Crane an opportunity to record a new and somewhat transient urban sound—the cable "whirring" in its underground channel. In the mid-nineties, he described a day in the Broadway cars—"long, yellow monsters" that prowled "intently up and down, up and down," in the daytime, transporting workers, then shoppers, through "a jungle of men and vehicles" and "lofty mountains of iron and cut stone"; in the evening, lighted like brilliant salons, carrying the theatre-going public to the Tenderloin. William Dean Howells found this mode of transportation less romantic. The apparatus for gripping the chain frequently went awry, he reported, and this caused the car to "rush wildly over the track, running amuck through everything in its way, and spreading terror on every hand." Commentators of the nineties noted that New York was "very far behind many American cities of much less importance" in providing electric trolley cars for surface travel.

These had been introduced in Brooklyn and the Bronx in the late eighties, but their use in Manhattan had to await the development of an under-trolley system at the turn of the new century.[38]

As in the sixties, European visitors continued to be struck with the equalitarianism of travel on the public transit facilities, where, according to Giuseppe Giacosa, the gentleman who edged himself into the space beside you on the elevated "might with equal likelihood be the attorney of the richest railroad in the world, a shoe clerk, or a cab driver . . . just finishing his tour of duty." But this was one of the more democratic features of a society in which pretensions to class distinction were increasingly observable. An English traveler of 1874 reported that "our aristocratic circles" was a favorite expression with the newspapers. "Liveried servants are to be seen on Fifth Avenue," she wrote, "and some of the more advanced spirits among the New Yorkers have really succeeded in persuading themselves that they are aristocrats." Lady Duffus Hardy found society in New York City in the later seventies "more exclusive" than in the old country. "Wholesale and retail mix freely in all commercial matters, are 'Hail, fellow! well met!' on the cars or in the streets, but on the threshold of home they part. The merchant, who sells a thousand gallons of oil, will not fraternize at home, or be weighed in the social scale with the vendor of a farthing dip."

This penchant for aristocratic ways may explain the fact that during the seventies and eighties a preference for English styles and manners was in some measure replacing the former imitation of French fashions in the city. Military and official uniforms were still "closely modelled on the French," according to Arthur Montefiore, an English visitor of 1888; but "the *jeunesse doré* of the Fifth Avenue and its environment" were "imitating English fashions and manners with an amusing extravagance. They have indeed out-heroded Herod, and the mashers and aesthetes who have been almost laughed out of England bloom with exotic luxuriance in New York society. No English covert-coats are shorter, or walking-sticks thicker, or trousers baggier than those which are provided for these dudes by their 'custom tailors.' "[39]

It was apparent to observers of the post-Civil War metropolis that Victorian New York boasted a self-conscious "Society," even though visitors came no closer to it than the elaborate setting in which "the 400" moved. In the years from 1872 to 1897, the "Patriarchs," a small group of the city's "untitled aristocracy"—the phrase of a traveler of the mid-1880's—epitomized the exclusiveness of the city's upper social circle. The Patriarchs' famous balls, originally under the management of Ward McAllister, were the most brilliant events of the social season. McAllister, the social arbiter of Gotham in this period, also managed the famous ball for four hundred guests, given by Mrs. William Astor on February 1, 1892, from which the term "the 400" originated.[40]

New York's fashionable hotels and restaurants were the haunts of its high society; and as in earlier generations, the location and character of such establishments mirrored the city's growth and changing ways. In the late seventies, the northward advance of business and residence had put the stately Fifth Avenue Hotel, at Madison Square, in the "center of New York's brilliance." In this area—the city's "Place de la Concorde"—one found the leading "hotels, theatres, [and] clubs," and the "fashionable and celebrated restaurants of Delmonico and Brunswick," as well as the maison Maillard, the famous confectioner. There, during Holy Week, one visitor "thought himself transported to Paris, . . . seeing the fashionable throng (the kings and queens of the dollar-ocracy) come to purchase Easter eggs, exclusive product of the Parisian boulevard." The Clarendon Hotel and the Brevoort, with its portraits of Queen Victoria and the Prince Consort, on lower Fifth Avenue, were somewhat more aristocratic and catered to foreign visitors of note; but the white marble Fifth Avenue Hotel was locally considered the "most desirable and fashionable resort" for hotel living. In the postwar era, to quote an English traveler of 1878, it was "the temporary abode of the 'petroleum' and 'shoddy' aristocracy—rough, illiterate, vulgar creatures for the most part, who claim pre-eminence on the score of their money-bags." [41]

When George Augustus Sala visited New York in 1863, the " 'fashionable' or 'up town' Delmonico restaurant occupied a large building at the corner of East Fourteenth Street and Fifth Avenue." Upon his return in 1879, the English journalist found that Fourteenth Street was "downtown" and that a new "palazzo Delmonico" fronted on Broadway, Fifth Avenue, and Twenty-sixth Street, in the vicinity of the Fifth Avenue Hotel. In the opinion of a French visitor of 1892 its "exaggerated luxury" made it "better and more sumptuous than the finest Parisian restaurant." Sala enjoyed a "baked ice" called an "Alaska" at Delmonico's establishment, but he reported that a "first rate dinner" there was "a very serious affair in the way of dollars." Next in renown to Delmonico's was the restaurant at the Hotel

Brunswick, where prices were also "recherchés." "On the lower rungs of the social ladder," according to Sala, were "the so-called 'fifteen-cent houses,' " where for that small sum you could obtain "a cut from a hot joint with bread, butter, potatoes and pickles." [42]

The opening of the Waldorf-Astoria, at Thirty-fourth Street and Fifth Avenue, in the nineties, symbolized both the relentless advance northward of business and residence and the increasing affluence of the society that patronized its palatial accommodations. The Hotel Waldorf, older half of the hyphenated hostelry, began to operate in 1893. The joint enterprise, with its sixteen stories and 1,000 bedrooms, was opened to an impressed public in November 1897; and it speedily became, for a time at least, a rendezvous for Manhattan's millionaires. The formerly fashionable Fifth Avenue Hotel, ten blocks to the south, was now the gathering place of the Republican politicians; while the once-admired Astor House, "downtown" in the vicinity of City Hall Park, had long since become "purely commercial." By 1900, a trio of fashionable hotels overlooked the Plaza at the Fifth Avenue entrance to Central Park: the stately Plaza, the lofty Netherlands, and the glittering Savoy. A new Delmonico's followed fashion northward and opened in 1897 at Fifth Avenue and Forty-fourth Street.[43]

To commentators of the period, religious observance in the more fashionable sections of the city appeared to reflect the concern for the spectacular and the obsession with wealth which characterized other aspects of the social scene. Choirs of professional musicians supplemented congregational singing and "popular preachers" were regarded as essential in attracting "fashionable congregations." After visiting one of the city's leading Episcopal churches in 1890, the French writer Paul Blouet reported that the church "was literally packed until the sermon began, and then some of the strollers who had come to hear the anthems moved on." The rector had "a big unctuous voice, with the intonations and inflections of a showman at the fair." James F. Muirhead, in America in 1893 collecting information for *Baedeker's Handbook to the United States,* reported that the churches of Fifth Avenue more than hinted at golden offertories. "The visitor is not surprised to be assured (as he infallibly will be) that the pastor of one of them preaches every Sunday to 'two hundred and fifty million dollars!' " [44]

Popular preachers and paid singers represented the attempt of the church to compete with the ever increasing supply of secular entertainment in the late nineteenth-century city. If in its preoccupation with business New York of pre-Civil War years had reminded observers of Liverpool, its facilities for public entertainment, as well as the commercial and industrial expansion which helped to underwrite them, now caused Americans, at least, to claim for it the qualities not only of Liverpool, and even London, but of Paris, as well. And many a foreign traveler agreed. The English actor Henry Irving professed in 1883 to have "seen it all before. It is London and Paris combined." And Robert Louis Stevenson, who visited the Empire City five years later, called it "a mixture of Chelsea, Liverpool, and Paris." [45]

Certainly the city of the later nineteenth century offered pleasure seekers rich and varied entertainment. The number of its theatres, totaling some twenty-four in 1879, had reached forty-five by 1900; and as in the years preceding the Civil War, it was visited by most of the famous actors and singers of the day. Performers of serious drama, like Sarah Bernhardt, Helena Modjeska, Ellen Terry, Henry Irving, and Edwin Booth, vied for public attention with such popular entertainers as the beauteous Lily Langtry and Lillian Russell, glamorous toast of the Casino, which was opened in 1882. Long-run plays, which had become profitable in the sixties, increased in number. *Erminie,* an English operetta, had 1,256 performances, beginning in 1886. The introduction of a new medium, which was in time to make theatrical entertainment available to the ever multiplying urban audience, came in 1896 when Edison's Vitascope was exhibited for the first time at Koster and Bial's Music Hall. Moving figures, projected one-half life-size on a white screen, forecast the development of motion pictures, the most characteristic urban entertainment of the ensuing century.[46]

James Burnley, an English traveler of the late seventies, praised not only the handsome appearance of New York's theatres but also the free programs, not supplied in London houses. The unrestrained practices of the "ticket scalpers" also caused foreign visitors some surprise. Henry Irving was astounded to see his first-night audience "mobbed by a band of ticket speculators," with satchels strapped to their shoulders, announcing in hoarse tones, even under the box office windows, "I have seats in the front row. . . . I have the best seats in the orchestra." [47]

The opening of the Metropolitan Opera House, in October 1883, symbolized the growing affluence of the city's leading citizens as well as the cultural riches which it was within the power of the metropolis to offer. Until the eighties, the Academy of Music on Fourteenth Street was the "really aristocratic theatre of the city," wrote the Italian traveler Carlo Gardini, the only place in which Italian opera was presented to a fashionable audience in which the women wore "elegant gowns" and the men "evening clothes." In time, however, its eighteen boxes were not sufficient for the "so-called aristocracy, . . . the families of those who accumulated their millions in recent times." When the directors of the Academy refused to open the social gates further than to add twenty-six boxes, the new aristocracy determined to erect its own house. The resulting Metropolitan, a yellow brick structure of Italian Renaissance design, which was opened on October 22, 1883, had 122 boxes for the growing ranks of New York's "Society." According to the *Dramatic Mirror,* "The Goulds and the Vanderbilts and people of that ilk perfumed the air with the odor of crisp greenbacks. . . . The tiers of boxes looked like cages in a menagerie of monopolists." [48]

The competition for talent, between the managers of the two opera houses, brought the world's most distinguished artists to the city, among them Adelina Patti, Christine Nilsson, Italo Campanini, and Marcella Sembrich. "That season was really a golden age for the theatre in New York," Gardini reported, in his *Gli Stati Uniti;* "the artists, because of the war between the young and the old aristocracy, pocketed veritable treasures, and the public had the luck to hear in a single winter all the living celebrities of the world, a luxury certainly not afforded by any capital in Europe." The location of the Metropolitan at Thirty-ninth Street and Broadway was indicative of the northward advance of a new theatrical district. By the mid-1880's, Fourteenth Street and its vicinity had been superseded as a theatrical center and a new "Rialto" extended along Broadway from Madison Square to Forty-second Street.[49]

Relief from the ever increasing congestion of the metropolis lent added appeal to the city's meager facilities for outdoor recreation, such as Central Park and, in the summer, the nearby beaches, which one traveler called "the health-breathing lungs of a great city." All levels of society enjoyed the park. In the afternoon its roads were "crowded with fast trotting horses, single and in pairs, in buggies, broughams, and landaus," a Scottish journalist reported, after visiting New York in 1876; and open drays were available for moderate charges "in which parties of work-people and their families can drive round whenever they choose." In the winter months, sleighs by the hundred enlivened the Fifth Avenue highway to the park: "Canadian cutters; 'sulky' sleighs for one selfish bachelor; 'sociables,' with a whole family party; Russian sleighs, with an Oriental, barbaric opulence of bear or tiger skins, with clashing silver bells, and crimson pompons flashing as the horses toss up their proud heads and champ their bits; all speed past making one of the most joyous and brilliant scenes imaginable." [50]

Coney Island, the American Brighton, grew in popularity as the city increased in size and congestion in the seventies. On a hot Sunday, half a million people (making a "carpet of heads") might crowd its wide stretch of sand in a few hours, a traveler of 1887 reported in the London *Times*. "They spread over the four miles of sand strip, with . . . bands of music . . . in full blast; countless vehicles moving; all the miniature theatres, minstrel shows, merry-go-rounds, Punch and Judy enterprises, fat women, big snakes, giant, dwarf, and midget exhibitions, circuses and menageries, swings, flying horses, and fortune telling shops open; and everywhere a dense but good-humoured crowd, sightseeing, drinking beer, and swallowing 'clam chowder.' " Fireworks enlivened the scene at night until time to go home, when "the swelling torrents of humanity," flowing out upon station and pier, emphasized "the vast magnitude of a Coney Island Sunday." While the "masses" frequented Coney Island, the "classes," in this city of increasing contrast, spent a more extended "season" at such resorts for the wealthy as Long Branch, New Jersey, and Newport, Rhode Island.[51]

The city of the later nineteenth century was not without its more intellectual refreshment, such as could be provided at a number of distinguished libraries and museums, although, as an Australian visitor of 1888 complained, "nothing could more strongly emphasize the general devotion of the citizens of New York to the Almighty Dollar than the prevailing indifference to the literary and art treasures in their midst." There was nevertheless a rich fare in the privately endowed collections of the Astor Library, the Lenox Library, and the Tilden Trust, whose holdings were combined to form the New York Public Library in 1895. A German scholar who visited the city on the turn of the 1890's praised the scientific collections at Columbia University, "the most significant temple of education in New York." [52]

The Metropolitan Museum of Art was organized with some difficulty in January 1870. Other collections of paintings included those of the historic National Academy of Design and of an insurgent group of exhibitors known as the Society of American Artists. Unlike the situation in the twentieth-century city, local artists worked against many odds in a period when New Yorkers were more intent upon aping Europe's culture than advancing their own. According to Arthur Montefiore, "the really successful painters of America" were far more readily met in the studios of London and the ateliers of Paris than in New York. Nor was this surprising, he thought, after visiting New York in 1888, since "the millionaires of the New World" appeared to "prefer spending their money in the markets of the Old, thereby depreciating the American school, as a school, and discounting the American artist as a producer." [53]

In the realm of entertainment, New York of the period might have been another Paris, but most foreign observers were of the opinion that for accomplishment in the artistic "professions" this "boss city of the universe" had not yet matched the attainment of London, Paris, Berlin, or Vienna. E. Catherine Bates, an Englishwoman who traveled in the United States in the mid-eighties, expressed the opinion of most of the city's visitors when she wrote, "New York is pre-eminently a city of good food, good theatres, fine horses and pretty women. . . . I believe there is some very good literary and artistic society to be found in the American capital, but you must dig deeper for it here than in Boston, and I think the more superficial social life of ball and opera, bright flowers and charming toilettes, well-groomed horses and jingling sleigh bells is the more characteristic view." [54]

Despite the neglect of the streets, for which most commentators condemned the municipal administration, other services—police, fire, and health—earned the praise of most casual observers. William Hardman, editor of the London *Morning Post,* criticized the police in 1883 for their indifferent attire: "a badly fitting . . . greyish-blue uniform, necktie of the patrolman's choice, and grey felt helmet." But most writers—native and foreign—contended that property was safer in New York than in European capitals, and that the city's crime record compared favorably with that of other American cities. An English visitor of 1885 was impressed with the organizational ingenuity of the city's now professional fire department, whose preparations made it possible, in the short span of two minutes, "for the engine, with horses harnessed, firemen on it, and everything complete, to leave the yard." [55]

To judge from contemporary comment, New York City was physically more unattractive during the decades from 1870 to 1900 than at any other period in its history. In this garish generation, it was too large and mature to be picturesque, too young and unkempt to be imposing. In appearance, it bore the stamp of the new industrialism, but with few of the architectural and mechanical marvels which its material achievement would one day make possible. Socially it presented extremes in both ethnic diversity and standards of living which were sharper than ever before or since. Commentators were no longer surprised at the size of the New World metropolis, nor at its pre-eminent position among American cities; but they were disappointed at its failure to inspire admiration in other respects. [56]

Its size, indeed, and the power it represented were in this generation New York's chief claims to distinction. For all its "uncouth, formless" chaos it nevertheless impressed observers as a "magnificent embodiment of titanic energy and force," one of "the wonderful products of . . . western civilization." And though only an occasional skyscraper as yet escaped its generally earthbound existence, the increase of these "Cyclopean structures," the expanding use of electricity to illumine them, and the introduction of the "horseless carriage" and the subway at the turn of the new century forecast the wonders of the city of the almost immediate future. For the moment, however, late nineteenth-century New York was prevailingly mundane, despite the baronial elegance of its Fifth Avenue mansions and the excitement generated by the "steam-engine proclivities" of its money-getting citizens. It was a city of glaring contrasts, apparent to both resident and outsider alike—Fifth Avenue and Five Points, aspiring architecture and ill-kept streets, a Delmonico dinner and a "fifteen-cent" lunch. The author of *Baedeker's Handbook to the United States* summed up the observers' impressions when he wrote that New York of the nineties was "like a lady in ball costume, with diamonds in her ears, and her toes out at her boots." [57]

NEW YORK IN THE BROWNSTONE AGE

The ostentatiousness and materialistic pretensions of many New Yorkers of the seventies, as exhibited in their desire to live in houses fronted, at least, with "brownstone," were reflected in the observations of Thérèse Yelverton, an Englishwoman who visited New York early in that meretricious decade. The tone of Victorian society in the Empire

City is suggested in her sharp comments on socially ambitious New Yorkers and their aspiring wives. It is reprinted from her two-volume work, *Teresina in America,* which was published in 1875.[58]

In New York . . . most men's ambition is to live in a house with a "brown stone *front.*" It is called brown stone, but is of a reddish chocolate colour, and is one of the handsomest stones I know. No matter what the rest of the house is built of—wood, brick, or plaster and daub—it must have a stone front, and *look* like a stone building. If it cannot be actually veneered with "brown stone," it must at least be plastered to resemble it. Houses are advertised, without any other recommendation than that they have a brown stone front. That is considered the *ne plus ultra* of earthly habitations—the summit of all desires—the crowning effort of the love of make-believe. If his house *looks* like a nobleman's mansion in front—and you could not pay him a greater compliment than to tell him it does—the New Yorker is satisfied. . . .

The "brown stone front" being obtained, the next object seems to be so to furnish the house that it may resemble, as nearly as possible, a royal residence. But every article is painted and varnished to look like what it is not. What is apparently massive oak carving betrays itself as deal; enormous mirrors reflect one foreshortened in a most singular way. The very "Utrecht velvet"—with which even a New York washerwoman, so great and so general is the love of display, will have her chairs seated—is a compound of some trash that Utrecht would scorn to recognize. Most of this ostentatious class go to Europe for no better purpose than to *say* they have been, or to gather ideas for making the grandest display on their return home. Numbers of ladies visit Paris with no desire beyond that of seeing the fashions, and taking home something newer than their neighbours have got. To endeavour to dress like a Frenchwoman is laudable enough, but the first two essentials of *her* dress—appropriateness and unpretentiousness—are always conspicuously absent in the American ladies' toilette. When in Europe they go to state balls and concerts, attend drawing-rooms and aristocratic *réunions;* they see and hear of princesses, duchesses, and other women of fashion, who are clothed in purple and fine linen, ermine, velvets and satins, with diamonds, emeralds, pearls, etc., *ad libitum*—all delicious for a woman to contemplate—and straightway on their returning to their country come down dressed up to this mark, as nearly as circumstances will allow, to the breakfast tables of a common *restaurant,* having partly ruined their husbands to effect their display. American husbands, by-the-way, are models in this respect. They do not complain at extravagance if it only makes a show. On the contrary, the more recklessly money is lavished the more they exult over that fact. "You will find my wife a smart woman," said a husband, glorifying himself and his better half; "quite an elegant lady. These sixteen boxes are her luggage. She spent in Europe thirty thousand dollars on dress." I could have sworn that they lived in a "brown stone front," and that the wife would display her diamonds at the cabin dinner, and so it turned out. Of course, there are Americans—both men and women—of talent and genius who visit European cities for the study of art and of science, and who wish to contemplate the marvellous works of bygone ages, while others seek general improvement or the mere excitement of travel. The greater part, however, visit Europe for the *"say"* of the thing, and because it denotes that they have wealth to squander.

This disposition to ostentation throws an air of flimsiness over all their undertakings. . . . The Fifth Avenue, where are congregated the much-coveted "brown stone fronts," is, *in front*—a very handsome-looking street—the rich colour of the stone being in itself a beauty unrivalled by any building material as yet in use. If New York were built of that stone entirely, as Aberdeen is of granite and Bath of white stone, it would, indeed, be superb. But the houses behind the stone fronts are mere shells; and it is only in Fifth Avenue and Madison Avenue that these stone fronts even predominate. There are, however, some few exceptions to the general want of substantiality. One is a real stone and marble mansion, back, front, sides, and all, which a Scotch capitalist is building for himself. This mansion is called a palace—*faute de mieux*—for ostentation extends even to the naming of the most ordinary things.

TRAVEL AND COMMUNICATION IN THE LATE 1870'S

The effects of the telephone and the elevated railway on the New York scene in the later seventies find matter-of-fact description in the travel account of Walter G. Marshall, an Englishman who visited the United States in 1878 and 1879. By this time, New Yorkers could make telephone calls to a distance of thirty miles; and travel at the level of the second-story windows had supplemented conveyance by horsecar, stagecoach, carriage, or brougham. The following excerpt from Marshall's

Through America; or Nine Months in the United States is reprinted with the permission of Sampson Low, Marston and Company Limited.[59]

In the old or lower part of the city, the streets branching off right and left from the Broadway are the great commercial centres of the metropolis. Glance down any one of these, . . . and . . . above, against the sky, you look upon a perfect maze of telephone and telegraph wires crossing and recrossing each other from the tops of the houses. The sky, indeed, is blackened with them, and it is as if you were looking through the meshes of a net. . . . The sky is really obscured by the countless threads of wire, and the housetops are made free use of to conduct them to their destination. Altogether there are about 5000 miles of telegraph and telephone wires in the Empire City. The telegraph wires are conducted along the streets by means of some 9000 or 10,000 poles.

There were, in February last, 20,000 people in direct telephonic communication in New York. . . . It would take exactly three minutes for the Bell Company at 923, Broadway . . . to connect, say, John Smith, . . . two and a half miles distant, with Richard Roe, of Paterson, New Jersey, seventeen miles distant from the same office. . . . Each subscriber to any one of these companies—the subscription is ten dollars per month—has, of course, a list of all other subscribers to the same company, so that he may know whom he can talk to at any time. At present the furthest places communicated with by telephone in New York are distant thirty miles; but the Bell Company are engaged in getting up lines to Philadelphia, ninety miles distant. . . .

And now how to get about in New York. There is first the elevated railway. Answering to our "underground" in London, in affording rapid conveyance through the city without interfering with the traffic, it is raised high above the streets instead of being tunnelled under them. The effect of the "elevated"—the "L," as New Yorkers generally call it,—is, to my mind, anything but beautiful; but this, perhaps, is only a matter of taste. The tracks are lifted to a height of thirty feet (in some places higher) upon iron pillars, the up line on one side of the street and the down on the other. . . . Beneath the raised lines is the roadway for horses and carriages, and the lines of rail for the tramway cars, with the pavements beyond. As you sit in a car on the "L" and are being whirled along, you can put your head out of [the] window and salute a friend who is walking on the street pavement below. In some places, where the streets are narrow, the railway is built right over the "sidewalks" . . . close up against the walls of the houses. . . .

As might be expected, the elevated railway is immensely patronized. Trains run at frequent intervals on the several lines, from 5.30 in the morning till 12 o'clock at night, and during the crowded hours, namely from 5.30 a.m. to 7.30 a.m., and from 5 p.m. to 7 p.m., they follow each other as fast as can be managed. One company—the Metropolitan, or Sixth Avenue—runs daily 840 trains (420 each way) up and down its lines between 5.30 a.m. and 12 p.m.; seventy trains per hour are run during the crowded hours mornings and evenings. The fare during these busy hours is five cents . . . , at other times, ten cents. Of course it is needless to observe that there are no classes, as in our passenger trains, but all ride together in a long car, or carriage, the seats ranged lengthwise at the sides, with a passage down the middle and a door at each end, four cars being as many as are run at a time on the "elevated." There is, therefore, the same fare for everybody,—no matter how long or short the distance travelled over,—and the three companies working the elevated railways (the Metropolitan, the Manhattan, and New York companies), having carried their lines far into the upper portion of the city, you can, for the sum of five cents, take a ride of some ten or twelve miles, and without changing cars. The trains are run at a good speed, and there is but little delay at the stations; indeed sometimes the train does not pull up at all, and yet people recklessly jump on and off all the same. . . . There are very few cross tracks, so that the chances of collision are reduced to a minimum; but there are sharp curves here and there, which have to be approached slowly and cautiously, else the train would never get round. In rounding these the engine will give a sudden jerk to one side, so much so that you have a full view of the locomotive ahead of you from out of the side-window of your car. . . . Tickets have to be given up almost as soon as bought, before passengers can enter the train. . . . As a financial enterprise the elevated railway has turned out a success beyond even the expectations of its promoters. . . . As a natural consequence of the introduction of the elevated railway, property lying contiguous to the overhead lines has considerably depreciated in value. The nineteen hours and more of incessant rumbling day and night from the passing trains; the blocking out of a sufficiency of light from the rooms of houses, close up to which the lines are built; the full, close view passengers on the cars can have into rooms on the second and third floors; the frequent squirtings of oil from the engines, sometimes even finding its way into the private rooms of a dwelling-house, when the windows are left open—all these are objections that have been reasonably urged by unfortunate occupants of houses whose comfort has been so unjustly molested. . . .

There are other ways of getting about New York besides taking the "elevated." Railways for horse-cars are laid along nearly every avenue (all except Fifth and Lexington avenues, I believe), and many of the cross streets: you are said to travel in this way by "car," but by "stage" if you take another form of conveyance, namely a 'bus. . . . A bobtailed stage or car is one without a conductor or man to collect the fares, there being a box inside with a slit in the top, into which the passenger is trusted to drop the exact amount of the fare. If he wants change out of his money, he can, in a bobtailed horse-car, obtain it from the driver to the amount of two dollars, and no more, and the driver will hand back to the passenger a little sealed packet containing the whole amount returned in the form of small pieces of change, and thus the proper fare, which is generally five cents, can be selected and dropped into the till. In a stage, however, there is no such communication between the passenger and driver, for the former is here left to pay in the exact amount. . . . But the fare-box is so placed that the driver can peep down from his seat and see if everyone inside has paid, and if you don't pay immediately you step in, the driver will "rap away" at you till you do—till he sees you have dropped the proper fare into the box, whereupon he will turn a slide and pass the money out of sight, so that there may be no confusion when the next passenger comes to pay in his fare. Stages are painted red, white, and blue, and have bright-coloured pictures (very dauby-looking) illuminating the sides. They traverse the Broadway, and convey up-town New Yorkers to the ferries for Brooklyn. But it is "fashionable" in the Empire City to travel by horse-car, or else take the "elevated."

Of course there are hackney carriages to be obtained, but these are very few and far between. They consist mostly of big family coaches-and-pairs, with room enough inside to comfortably seat six. . . . There is another form of public conveyance called a "coupé" or small brougham, holding only two people. These coupés are invariably well cushioned, and are as comfortable a class of conveyance as one could well desire. The pity is there is not more of them. But driving about in public carriages in New York comes to be absurdly expensive unless you hire by the hour, when the fare is one dollar. Yet even then there must be an understanding between yourself and the driver before starting, else there may be a "scene."

SUMMER PASTIMES ON THE TURN OF THE EIGHTIES

Aside from the charms of Central Park, the English novelist Mary Duffus Hardy found nothing picturesque or attractive about New York City on the turn of the eighties. In her opinion it was "a wilderness of bricks and mortar" with "streets and houses so closely packed as scarce to leave breathing room for its inhabitants." She nevertheless described it in great detail in reporting upon her trip through the United States in 1879 and 1880. Born Mary Anne MacDowell, Lady Hardy became the wife of Thomas Duffus Hardy, who was knighted in 1869. Her first novel appeared before she was thirty and she continued to write extensively thereafter. She traveled widely, and her trip to the United States resulted in two books: *Through Cities and Prairie Lands* (1881) and *Down South* (1883). In the following excerpt from the former she describes the retreat to parks and beaches and the recourse to soft drinks and "air-conditioned" entertainment by which New Yorkers of the early 1880's countered the discomforts of a hot Manhattan summer.[60]

Our friends, the few who remained in Gotham to battle with the fierce summer sun, regretted that we had come back at the dead season; but they managed to make it lively enough. What with excursions on the water, picnics on land, theatres, and social gatherings at home, the time passed only too quickly. . . .

As the weeks passed on, the temperature became almost unendurable. The coolest place in all New York was the Madison Square Theatre. The thermometer had mounted to 100° when we received a box for an afternoon miscellaneous performance in aid of the Edgar Poe Memorial Statue. Among the many other things selected for the occasion was an abridged version of "The Taming of the Shrew," when Edwin Booth consented to play Petruchio. Nothing less than a desire to see this celebrated actor would have tempted us to stir. The sun, like a ball of burnished copper, filled the skies with a heat-created mist, and poured upon the earth a fiery atmosphere that seemed to burn as it touched you, and the very breeze might have issued from the mouth of a furnace; but we gathered

THE THREADBARE THIRTIES

Crowds mill around the Stock Exchange on Wall Street in late October 1929, after the New York *Times* reports: "Stocks collapse in 16,410,032-Share Day." The ensuing depression hung over the city throughout the early thirties. The magnificent Empire State Building was largely vacant. The Waldorf-Astoria was in the hands of receivers. Apple-sellers beset pedestrians in Times Square; and, for once, there were more beggars in New York than in the large cities of Europe. At the depth of the depression, nearly a million and a half New Yorkers—one in five of the city's population—were on relief. Radical talk resounded in Union Square. Conditions improved by 1936 and 1937, and with the stimulus to employment provided by the outbreak of World War II, recovery was in sight.

Brown Brothers

Bread Line—No One Has Starved, an etching by Reginald Marsh in 1932.
Reproduced by courtesy of Mrs. Marsh;
photograph from Museum of the City of New York.

Courtesy of *The News,* New York's Picture Newspaper

Museum of the City of New York

NEW YORK'S SKYSCRAPERS ARE ITS MONUMENTS

Contemporaries had mixed reactions to the skyscraper, but by the early twentieth century, these towering structures already gave promise of becoming the hallmark of New York City. Most discussed of the early "giants" was the twenty-one story Flatiron Building, completed in 1902 from plans by D. H. Burnham and Company. Its exterior walls and floors were supported at each story by a steel frame—a technique of construction pioneered in Chicago in the mid-1880's which made possible buildings of unprecedented height. The Flatiron Building was built on Broadway and Fifth Avenue at Twenty-third Street.

The sixty-story Woolworth Building, completed in 1913, held the record for nearly twenty years as the world's tallest building. In the photograph above, it dominates the Old Post Office at the edge of City Hall Park and looks down upon the other skyscrapers of the lower city. Its tower rises without a setback from the center of its Broadway front to a height of 792 feet above the curb. Designed by Cass Gilbert, the Woolworth Building, with its gargoyles, terra-cotta ornament, and Gothic spires, typified the "cathedral to commerce," and set an architectural pattern that made the city of later years appear to be "Nineveh and Babylon piled on Imperial Rome."

The 200-foot observation tower is almost out of reach of the camera in a photograph of the Empire State Building (facing page, left) taken in the middle 1930's. Skyscraper construction probably attained its ultimate

The Leonard Hassam Bogart Collection, Museum of the City of New York

Photograph by John Harvey Heffren, reproduced by courtesy of Museum of the City of New York

ıeight in this 102-story, 1,248-foot structure lesigned by Shreve, Lamb, and Harmon and ›uilt at Thirty-fourth Street and Fifth Aveıue between 1929 and 1931. Its silvery shaft ·ises from a five-story base in an unbroken ine, unlike the elaborate façade of the Flatron Building (facing page, left). Statisticians ›ointed out that the Empire State Building :ontained more than 2,150,000 square feet of ·entable floor space, could accommodate 20,›oo workers, and had 6,400 windows and ›even miles of elevator shafts. Another spec:acular skyscraper of the period was the RCA Building in Rockefeller Center, which was :ompleted in 1933 (see frontispiece).

Lever House, executive offices of one of :he world's largest soap companies, represents :he mid-twentieth-century manner in New York's skyscraper style. It was designed by :he firm of Skidmore, Owings, and Merrill and was built on Park Avenue at Fifty-third and Fifty-fourth streets, between 1950 and 1952. More restricted in height than skyscrapers of the 1920's and 1930's, its twenty-four stories of blue-green glass and stainless steel are characteristically mid-century in style. The tower covers only a small portion of the building area. Walls are continuous horizontal glass strips. The ground floor has a glass display room, an open colonnade, and a two-story landscaped court. The third story is "nipped in" to separate tower from base and impart a feeling of lightness to the sleek tower. The structure is fully air-conditioned, and its windows are of heat-resistant glass. Unlike prewar buildings, which used space to the maximum, it follows the modern trend by restricting its floor area, in this instance to six times the lot area.

Courtesy of *The News,* New York's Picture Newspaper

NATIONALITY ON PARADE

"St. Patrick's Day in the after noon." New York celebrates it Irish antecedents as 40,00 marchers pass St. Patrick's Ca thedral at Fifth Avenue and Fiftieth Street, in traditional St Patrick's Day parade, March 17 1936.

A transplanted Italian tradi tion: Feast Day in a Brooklyn parish, 1954. New Yorkers o Italian origin honor the patron saint of the Italian village from which the residents have come

Photo by Irwin Gooen, New York University

ourselves together—all that was left of us, for we were gradually melting away—and, armed with fans, smelling-salts and sundry antidotes to fainting fits, panted our way from Forty-fifth Street to a Sixth Avenue car, which landed us close to the theatre. Immediately on entering, we felt as though we had left the hot world to scorch and dry up outside, while we were enjoying a soft summer breeze within. Where did it come from? The house was crowded—there was not standing-room for a broom-stick; but the air was as cool and refreshing as though it had blown over a bank of spring violets. We learned the reason of this. By some simple contrivance the outer air, circulating through and among tons of ice, is forced to find its way through a thousand frozen cracks and crevices before it enters the auditorium; thus a flow of fresh air is kept in constant circulation, which renders an afternoon in Madison Square Theatre a luxury during the hottest of dog-days.

The death roll is terrible during these hot spells, sometimes amounting from sun-stroke alone to twenty in a single day. The New Yorkers, however, know how to make the best of their semi-tropical summer. The more sensible portion of the masculine population go about in their linen suits and panama hats, though some men cling to their beloved chimney-pot and swelter under a weight of broadcloth; but no man is above carrying an umbrella, white, green, or brown, as the case may be. Rivers of iced lemonade are flowing at the street corners, at two cents per glass. You may see a multitude closing round and pouring in and out of the "drug stores" (chemist's shops). You think there must have been an accident—somebody run over, somebody killed. No such thing; it is only the more aristocratic thirsty multitude, who eschew street corners, crowding in for their iced drinks. The "drug stores" have, every one, a neat white marble fountain, with a dozen shining silver taps, which pour forth streams of fruit-flavored iced drinks—pine, cherry, strawberry, raspberry, and lemon cream soda, the most delicious of all. From early morning till late in the evening these fountains never cease playing; small fortunes pour from their silver mouths into the pockets of their owners.

In the summer evenings the whole indoor population of New York seems to overflow on to the "stoops" of their house. Walking through some of the best streets, you may glance in at the open windows, and see the elegantly furnished vacant rooms, with their luxurious lounges, paintings, mirrors, and gilded magnificence, mellowed in the low-burning gaslight, while the inhabitants are taking the air on their doorsteps. . . . This is an old knickerbocker custom, which still obtains everywhere except on the sacred Fifth Avenue, which confines itself strictly within doors, shrined from the vulgar gaze; perhaps the *nouveau riche* element (being largely represented) is afraid of compromising its dignity by following old-fashioned customs.

As the weeks passed on the weather became more and more trying, and we made daily excursions to the numerous watering-places immediately surrounding New York, leaving home early in the morning and returning the same evening, which is easily done. Coney Island, one of the great resorts for the million, is reached from the foot of Twenty-third Street in about an hour. A few years ago it was a mere wide waste of sand, and was bought by a clever speculator for a mere song; it is now worth millions of dollars, and is covered on all sides with a miscellaneous mass of buildings of all descriptions. Restaurants, shooting galleries, pavilions, and refreshment-rooms to suit all classes, and some monster hotels, of light, airy structure, lift their faces towards the sea. Culver, Brighton, and Manhattan Beaches, the one being a continuation of the other, spread their wide stretch of silver sand along the side of the island and down to the blue Atlantic waves below. There are no pleasant walks or drives, there exists not a tree, there is no shade from the fierce, blinding sun to be found anywhere. No gray rocks or picturesque battlemented cliffs; nothing but the level island, with its wide stretch of silver sand and a world of sea. The hotels are crowded, every nook and corner of the island filled to overflowing during the season; the beach is covered with a lively mass of holiday-makers, all bent on enjoying themselves; gay bunting is flaunting and flying everywhere; musicians are hard at work, beating drums, scraping fiddles, and blowing trumpets, as though their very life depended on the noise they are making. Altogether, it is a gay, stirring scene. Coney Island is not a place where the fashionable or aristocratic multitude most do congregate; it is a rather fast, jolly, rollicking place, and serves its purpose well, as the health-breathing lungs of a great city. . . .

Central Park is the only place where you can enjoy a drive—there driving is a delight, the roads are simply perfect, and scores of splendid equipages and beautiful women are on view daily in the grand drives from three till six o'clock; while the bridle paths, winding through sylvan shades beneath full-foliaged trees, are crowded with fair equestrians and their attendant cavaliers; it is a pleasure to watch them at a trot, a canter, or a gallop, for the American women ride well and gracefully. New York is very proud of Central Park; and well it may be so, for it is one of the finest in the world, there is nothing like it this side of the Atlantic. Twenty years ago it was a mere swampy rocky waste, now it is a triumph of engineering skill and a splendid illustration of the genius of landscape gardening: there are smooth green lawns, shady groves, lakes, beautifully wooded dells and vine-covered arbours; whichever way you turn you come upon delicious bits of picturesque scenery blossoming in unexpected nooks and corners. Here and there huge gray rocks stand in their original rugged majesty, their broken lichen-covered boulders tumbling at their base. From the terrace, which is the highest point, you enjoy a view of the entire park with its numerous lakes, fountains, bridges, and statues, spreading like a beautiful panorama round you. Here, too, you fully realize the cosmopolitan character of the city, for here great men of all nations are immortalized or libelled in stone, and their statues stud the park, side by side with the national heroes. Some idea of the extent of these grounds may be gathered from the fact, that there are ten miles of carriage drives, all as a rule wide enough for six to go abreast, about six miles of bridle paths for riding, and twenty-eight for pedestrian exercise; a wide stretch of lawn is set apart for cricket or croquet playing, and a special quarter for children with merry-go-rounds, swings, etc.; there is also a menagerie containing numerous and varied specimens of animals, the nucleus of what is to be, when completed, a fine zoological collection.

BOSS RULE IN THE EIGHTIES

The sordid state of municipal politics in New York City in the early eighties prompted critical comment from two British visitors. One was the eminent philosopher Herbert Spencer, who traveled incognito in the United States in 1882. The other was Sir Lepel Griffin, distinguished Anglo-Indian administrator, whose writing about the United States in the *Fortnightly Review* made him the prototype of the most hostile critics of this period. At the time of their visits, the Tammany machine had recovered from the setback it had suffered in connection with the exposure of the Tweed Ring in the early seventies. "Honest" John Kelly was now in control of Tammany, and he had made the machine a great vote-getting juggernaut, strengthened through control of the immigrant vote and subsidized by the party's nominees and persons who sought protection or were forced to seek it. Kelly's regime lasted from 1872 to 1886. His successor, Richard Croker, dominated the machine for most of the period from then until 1902 and was a boss of the same stamp.

Spencer eluded the reporters upon his arrival in New York and registered at a hotel as "Mr. Lott's friend." He finally permitted his admirer Professor Youmans to interview him, for publication, and later reluctantly consented to speak at a banquet given in his honor at Delmonico's. Spencer's comments on New York, expressed on these occasions, are reprinted, with the permission of Appleton-Century-Crofts, Incorporated, from his *Essays, Scientific, Political, and Speculative.*[61]

The extent, wealth, and magnificence of your cities, and especially the splendour of New York, have altogether astonished me. . . . If along with your material progress there went equal progress of a higher kind, there would remain nothing to be wished. . . .

After pondering over what I have seen of your vast manufacturing and trading establishments, the rush of traffic in your street-cars and elevated railways, your gigantic hotels and Fifth Avenue palaces, I was suddenly reminded of the Italian Republics of the Middle Ages; and recalled the fact that while there was growing up in them great commercial activity, a development of the arts, which made them the envy of Europe, and a building of princely mansions which continue to be the admiration of travellers, their people were gradually losing their freedom. . . .

You retain the forms of freedom; but, so far as I can gather, there has been a considerable loss of the substance. It is true that those who rule you do not do it by means of retainers armed with swords; but they do it through regiments of men armed with voting papers, who obey the word of command as loyally as did the dependents of the old feudal nobles, and who thus enable their leaders to override the general will, and make the community submit to their exactions as effectually as their prototypes of old. . . . Manifestly, those who framed your Constitution never dreamed that twenty thousand citizens would go to the poll led by a "boss."

Sir Lepel Griffin was not as hesitant to criticize New York as was his philosopher compatriot. Indeed, this successful colonial administrator, who was the author of numerous historical and biographical works on

India, could find nothing good to say of the United States in general. It was "the country of disillusion and disappointment, in politics, literature, culture, and art; in its scenery, its cities, and its people." The following remarks upon the New York political scene, drawn from his sarcastically entitled work, *The Great Republic,* reflect his disapproval of the Empire City in the early eighties. They are reprinted with the consent of Charles Scribner's Sons.[62]

The City of New York has, for many years, been one of the most striking and convenient illustrations of what is known in America as Boss rule, and the many millions that it has cost the people, in waste, peculation, and undisguised and unblushing robbery, form the price which they have had to pay for the pretence of freedom. Matters are now less openly scandalous than of old, but the same system is in full force. Boss Kelly, who sways the destinies of New York, has been able, from his near connection with an Irish cardinal, to defend his position with spiritual as well as temporal weapons, and the whole Irish Catholic population vote solid as he bids them. The result of a generation of this régime has been disastrous. The commercial capital of the United States may now be fairly reckoned, for size and population, the second city in the world, if Brooklyn, New Jersey, and the suburbs be included within its boundaries. Its property is assessed at fifteen hundred million dollars, its foreign commerce is not far from a billion dollars, while its domestic trade reaches many hundred millions. But there is hardly a European city of any importance which is not infinitely its superior in municipal administration, convenience, beauty, and architectural pretensions. With the exception of the Post Office and the unfinished Catholic cathedral, which is neither in size nor design a cathedral at all, there is scarcely a building which repays a visit. The City Hall,* which cost ten or twelve millions of dollars, is certainly worth inspection as an instance of what swindling on a gigantic scale is able to accomplish; as is the Brooklyn Bridge, which cost seventeen millions, or three times the original estimate, and which was further unnecessary, as a subway would have been more convenient and have cost much less. Local taxation is crushingly heavy, and so inequitably assessed that the millionaires pay least and the poor most. The paving of the streets is so rough as to recall Belgrade or Petersburg; the gas is as bad as the pavement; and it is only in Broadway and portions of

* He means County Court House.

Fifth Avenue that an unsystematic use of the electric light creates a brilliancy which but heightens the contrast with the gloom elsewhere. The Central Park, so called from being a magnificent expanse of wilderness in the centre of nothing, is ill-kept and ragged, and at night is unsafe for either sex. The fares of hack-carriages are four to five times as high as in London. The police is inefficient, arbitrary, and corrupt. At its head are four Commissioners, who are politicians in the American sense and nothing more. They are virtually appointed by the aldermen, who have authority to confirm or reject the mayor's nomination of heads of departments. The aldermen are, in many cases, persons to whom the description of Michael Mulhooly might apply—politicians of the drinking-saloons, the tools and slaves of the Boss who made them and whose orders they unhesitatingly obey. When a respectable mayor has chanced to be appointed, he has declared it useless to nominate good men to office, and has lowered his appointments to the level of the confirming aldermen. The Comptroller, who is the financial head of the city, expending between thirty and forty millions of dollars annually, the Commissioners of Excise, Taxes, Charities, Fire, Health, and Public Works, are all controlled, approved, and virtually appointed by the aldermen, who are directed by the Boss. Even the eleven police judges, who should be the independent expounders and enforcers of the criminal law, are appointed by the same agency, so that if their origin be traced to its first cause they are the nominees of the criminal classes they have to try and punish. The result is that it is impossible to procure the adequate punishment of any official, however criminal, since he was appointed as a political partisan. . . .

The carcase over which the New York vultures are now gathered together is the new aqueduct, which is estimated to cost from twenty to thirty millions of dollars, but which, if the precedents of the County Court House and the Brooklyn Bridge be followed, will probably cost sixty millions. Here is a prize worthy of Tammany and a contest—a mine rich in jobbery and corruption for years to come; and there is no doubt that, before the work is completed, many patriotic Irish statesmen of the Mulhooly type, who are now loafing around the saloons on the chance of a free drink, will be clad in purple and fine linen and cheerfully climbing the venal steps which lead to the Capitol.

THE HOMES OF THE RICH: 1887

"Millionaires' Row" on upper Fifth Avenue was the subject of one installment of "A Visit to the United States," which was published serially in the London *Times* during the fall of 1887 and, in 1888, as a book. The articles were unsigned, but they were more complimentary than the accounts of most foreign observers of the period. The following, from the installment entitled "Fifth Avenue and Its Characteristics" in the issue of September 5, 1887, describes the mansions of the city's most famous commercial and industrial tycoons: the Astors, the Vanderbilts, and A. T. Stewart. It is reprinted with the permission of the *Times*.[63]

[Fifth Avenue] presents striking examples of the best residential and church architecture in New York, and the progress of the street northward into the newer portions shows how styles change with the lapse of time. The older houses at the lower end are generally of brick, which gradually develops into brownstone facings and borders, and then into uniform rows of most elaborate brownstone structures with imposing porticoes reached by broad flights of steps. As Central-park is approached the more modern houses are of all designs and varieties of materials, thus breaking the monotony of the rich yet sombre brown. . . .

Mounting gradually up the gentle ascent of Murray-hill, we get to what was a few years ago the centre of the aristocratic neighborhood at Thirty-fourth-street . . . on the opposite corners of which are represented the two greatest fortunes produced in America before the advent of the Vanderbilts. On the west side of Fifth-avenue, occupying the block between Thirty-third and Thirty-fourth streets, are two spacious brick houses with brownstone facings and a large yard between enclosed by a red brick wall. These are the homes of the Astors, John Jacob and William, the grandsons of John Jacob Astor, who amassed the greatest fortune known in America anterior to the Civil War. Near by, in Thirty-third street, lives a great grandson, William Waldorf Astor, who was recently the American Minister at Rome. The Astor estate (valued at £5,000,000 at the death of John Jacob Astor) is typical of the unexampled early growth of New York and of the accumulation of wealth by the advance in the value of land as the city expanded. . . .

On the northwest corner of Fifth-avenue and Thirty-fourth-street is the magnificent white marble palace built by Alexander T. Stewart when at the height of his fame as the leading New York merchant. It was intended to eclipse anything then known on the American continent, and upon the building and its decoration £600,000 were expended. This noted house outshone all other New York dwellings until the Vanderbilt palaces were constructed further out the avenue. The Stewart fortune was an evidence of the enormous possibilities of New York as a place for successful trading, though much of the wealth he amassed was afterwards invested in large buildings in profitable business localities, notably the great hotels on Broadway in the "dry goods district." . . .

The Vanderbilt fortune, the greatest ever amassed in America, represents modern New York's financially expansive facilities, as manipulated by the machinery of corporations and the Stock Exchange, and is the accumulation of two generations, a father and son, within the present century. . . .

On the west side [of Fifth Avenue] at Fifty-first and Fifty-second streets are two elaborate brownstone dwellings with ornamental fronts and having a connecting covered passage, which contains the doorways of both. These are the homes of William H. Vanderbilt's daughters, and are only exceeded in magnificence by his own house, a castellated drab-stone structure, at the upper corner of Fifty-second-street. This is also highly decorated, and is now the home of his eldest son, William K. Vanderbilt, the present president of the New York Central Railway. His second son, Cornelius Vanderbilt, lives in the fourth palace at the corner of Fifty-seventh-street, a brick building with ornamental stone decorations. These palaces were built, decorated, and furnished to outshine any other dwellings in New York, and it is said that £3,000,000 were expended upon them. . . .

All the dwellings in this region are costly, and show that fortunes have been expended in their decoration. . . . Dr. John Hall's Presbyterian Church is at Fifty-fifth-street . . . the largest and wealthiest Presbyterian church in the world. Its pastor is said to preach to £50,000,000 every Sunday.

THE HOMES OF THE POOR: 1881

The contrast between the mansions of the rich and the hovels of the poor appalled resident and visitor alike in the period following the Civil War. The "tenement" came to be the symbol of the airless congestion in which an increasing proportion of the population was forced to dwell. Tenement house statutes passed in 1867, 1879, 1887, and 1895 did little to remedy the situation. Finally, the writings of reformers like Jacob Riis and the publicity attending a housing exhibit in 1900 heightened the demand for action and resulted in the passage of legislation in 1901 which promised real reform. Tenement house living in the early eighties was described at first hand by Charlotte G. O'Brien, an Irish author and social reformer who resolved to witness the experiences of Irish immigrants to America at the time of the augmented migration following the crop disasters of 1879. She made several steerage passages to study conditions of travel and resided for two months in a typical New York tenement. Following is an excerpt from her article, "The Emigrant in New York," which appeared in *The Nineteenth Century,* in October 1884.[64]

New York life among the poor has one central distinguishing feature—namely, the fact that all live in tenements or in houses built on much the same principle. This principle is about as bad as it can possibly be. In the typical tenement house the staircase passes up a well in the centre of the house. It has no light from the open air, no ventilation; it is absolutely dark at midday, except for such light as may find its way in from the open hall door or from the glasses over the doors of the flats, and possibly from a skylight at the top of the house. It is a well for all the noxious gases to accumulate in; it cannot be aired; the rays of the sun never penetrate to it; in the worst houses it is foul with the coming and going of the innumerable denizens of the tenements. On its steps play about the pale, unhealthy children who, even allowing for the enormous death rate, still swarm in these horrible dwellings. Can a more frightfully unwholesome system be imagined? Yet this is not the worst. The tenements, opening in flats off these stairs, may be constituted of more or fewer rooms, but as a rule the bedrooms never have direct access to the open air. They open into the living rooms, and their windows open on to the stairs, so that not alone can the bedrooms never be properly aired, but they are so constructed that they receive all the impure gases that accumulate in the central well.

When I first entered the tenement in which I lodged, in a house occupied by twenty labourers' families, I own to a feeling of something like dismay, finding the room stifling, the family wash going on in the sitting-room, and a red-hot stove. The thermometer at the time was up to 90 degrees in the shade. I found my lodging consisted of a bedroom about 6 feet by 5 feet 6 inches; it was almost dark when the door into the living room was closed, the two tiny trap windows opening one on the dark stairs, the other on the outer room. However, I had come to see the life of the respectable poor, and here I experienced it. The whole tenement consisted of a central room about 10 feet by 14 feet or less; off this opened my bedroom . . . and a second, equally tiny, dark, and unventilated, occupied by my host and his wife. All the work of the day went on in these rooms; at six o'clock the stove was lighted, and from that hour till night it was in constant use. All the washing, cooking, ironing, and housework of every kind went on here. A small recess formed the scullery, where was a small sink with water laid on. For this tenement of three rooms . . . twelve dollars a month was paid. That amounts to nearly 29£ a year. As there were said to be twenty tenements in this house, and the one I occupied appeared about the same as the others, the total rental must have been very considerable, though the house was a poor-looking place in a very poor district. It may be asked, What was to be seen outside in the street? Filth undescribable, naked-limbed children, slatternly women, emigrant boarding houses, saloons, and a population which can be estimated by calculating twenty or thirty families, sometimes many more, to each house. As a sample of the infant mortality resulting from these and other conditions which I shall not describe, I may mention that the dwellers in the tenement adjoining ours, who had lived there twenty-eight years, had had eleven children born to them, of whom two pale boys were the survivors. . . .

I found wages to be in New York as high as in any of the large towns I afterwards visited—that is, two dollars a day seemed the standard wages of those who call themselves "private working men," what we should call day labourers. "Long-shore men"—men working in bakeries, stores, &c.—received this wage, very high pay apparently; but when it is remembered that a tenement such as I have described costs nearly 30£ a year, and that everything in the way of clothes is more than double the price in England, the difference is not so remarkable.

LOWER NEW YORK IN THE LATER EIGHTIES

Immigration from southern and eastern Europe, becoming increasingly noticeable by the mid-1880's, not only aggravated the problem of housing the city's poor but augmented the ethnic variety of the already cosmopolitan city. Both of these aspects of the metropolitan scene were described by Jacob A. Riis, an urban crusader who had viewed New York through the eyes of an immigrant before he undertook to acquaint New Yorkers with how "the other half" lived. A native of Denmark, Riis migrated to America in 1870. As a police reporter for the New York *Tribune* (1877–88) and the *Evening Sun* (1888–99), he gained a first-hand impression of the festering environment of the lower city in which most of the newcomers lived. The following observations on the ethnic pattern of the city in the eighties are drawn from his *How the Other Half Lives* (1890), the best known of the writings by which he advanced his lifelong crusade to improve living conditions for the underprivileged citizens of New York. The excerpt is reprinted with the consent of Charles Scribner's Sons.[65]

When once I asked the agent of a notorious Fourth Ward alley how many people might be living in it I was told: one hundred and forty families, one hundred Irish, thirty-eight Italian, and two that spoke the German tongue. Barring the agent herself, there was not a native-born individual in the court. The answer was characteristic of the cosmopolitan character of lower New York, very nearly so of the whole of it, wherever it runs to alleys and courts. One may find for the asking an Italian, a German, a French, African, Spanish, Bohemian, Russian, Scandinavian, Jewish, and Chinese colony. Even the Arab, who peddles "holy earth" from the Battery as a direct importation from Jerusalem, has his exclusive preserves at the lower end of Washington Street. The one thing you shall vainly ask for in the chief city of America is a distinctively American community. There is none; certainly not among the tenements. . . .

The Irishman is the true cosmopolitan immigrant. All-pervading, he shares his lodging with perfect impartiality with the Italian, the Greek, and the "Dutchman," yielding only to sheer force of numbers, and objects equally to them all. A map of the city, colored to designate nationalities, would show more stripes than on the skin of a zebra, and more colors than any rainbow. The city on such a map would fall into two great halves, green for the Irish prevailing in the West Side tenement districts, and blue for the Germans on the East Side. But intermingled with these ground colors would be an odd variety of tints that would give the whole the appearance of an extraordinary crazy-quilt. From down in the Sixth Ward, upon the site of the old Collect Pond . . . the red of the Italian would be seen forcing its way northward along the line of Mulberry Street to the quarter of the French purple on Bleecker Street and South Fifth Avenue, to lose itself and reappear, after a lapse of miles, in the "Little Italy" of Harlem, east of Second Avenue. Dashes of red, sharply defined, would be seen strung through the Annexed District, northward to the city line. On the West Side the red would be seen overrunning the old Africa of Thompson Street, pushing the black of the negro rapidly uptown, against querulous but unavailing protests, occupying his home, his church, his trade and all, with merciless impartiality. There is a church in Mulberry Street that has stood for two generations as a sort of milestone of these migrations. Built originally for the worship of staid New Yorkers of the "old stock," it was engulfed by the colored tide, when the draft-riots drove the negroes out of reach of Cherry Street and the Five Points. Within the past decade, the advance wave of the Italian onset reached it, and to-day the arms of United Italy adorn its front. The negroes have made a stand at several points along Seventh and Eighth Avenues; but their main body, still pursued by the Italian foe, is on the march yet, and the black mark will be found overshadowing to-day many blocks on the East Side, with One Hundredth Street as the centre, where colonies of them have settled recently.

Hardly less aggressive than the Italian, the Russian and Polish Jew, having overrun the district between Rivington and Division Streets, east of the Bowery, to the point of suffocation, is filling the tenements of the old Seventh Ward to the river front, and disputing with the Italian every foot of available space in the back alleys of Mulberry Street. The two races, differing hopelessly in much, have this in common: they carry their slums with them wherever they go, if allowed to do it. Little Italy already rivals its parent, the "Bend," in foulness. . . . Between the dull gray of the Jew, his favorite color, and the Italian red, would be seen squeezed in on the map a sharp streak of yellow, marking the narrow boundaries of Chinatown. Dovetailed in with the German population, the poor but thrifty Bohemian might be picked out by the sombre hue of his life as of his philosophy. . . .

Down near the Battery the West Side emerald would be soiled by a dirty stain, spreading rapidly like a splash of ink on a sheet of blotting paper, headquarters of the Arab tribe, that in a single year has swelled from the original dozen to twelve hundred, intent, every mother's son, on trade and barter. Dots and dashes of color here and there would show where the Finnish sailors worship their djumala (God), the Greek pedlars the ancient name of their race, and the Swiss the goddess of thrift. And so on to the end of the long register, all toiling together in the galling fetters of the tenement.

"LITTLE ITALY" IN THE EARLY NINETIES

The accelerating stream of migrants from Italy, which began to be apparent in the 1880's, typified the new sources from which New York's swelling population was recruited in the later nineteenth century. Throughout this decade, Italians crowded into the Five Points area and the old Irish neighborhoods south of Washington Square, while Russian and Polish Jews were displacing the German residents on the lower East Side. The squalid living conditions of the poorest Italian newcomers were observed by Giuseppe Giacosa, noted Italian dramatist, who came to New York in October 1891 to direct Sarah Bernhardt in a performance of his *La Dame de Challant.* The following excerpt, reprinted by permission of the publisher, is from his article "Gli Italiani a New York ed a Chicago," which appeared in August 1892, in the Italian periodical, *Nuova Antologia di Scienze, Lettere, ed Arti.* It was later incorporated in his *Impressioni d'America,* published in 1898.[66]

Let us look briefly at the Italian quarter of New York. . . .

Here the mud, dirt, and filth, the stinking humidity, the incumbrances, the disorder of the streets are beyond description. . . .

Men in tattered, filthy attire move from one shop to another or form small groups at the entrances of those beer taverns where they are served the bitter dregs of the barrels from which beer is sold in healthy quarters to healthy people. In the doorways, on the steps of the staircases, on little wooden and straw stools almost in the middle of the street, women carry on all the pursuits of their pathetic domestic life. They nurse their young, sew, clean the withered greens which are the only ingredient of their soup, wash their clothes in grimy tubs, untangle and arrange one another's hair. They chatter, but not in the happy and playful mood of Naples, but in a certain angry importuning way that stings the heart.

Now and then a confusion of carts—in those streets carriages never pass—forces them to move and hurriedly collect their belongings. Then follow shouting and swearing from the wagoners and cries and improprieties from the whole swarm of females. Some old, disfigured women pass by, laboriously carrying a foul burden in large baskets. Vain toil: for should not everything here be thrown on the dung heap—the clothes the people wear, the displayed merchandise, the fruit, the herbs, the old yellowed meat which hangs in the butcher shops, the furniture which one glimpses in the open stalls, the sordid Italian and American bank notes in the windows of the frequent banks, even the huge pictures of King Victor, of Garibaldi, and of Umberto and the tri-color flags that hang and flutter from nearly all of the windows and frame the entrances to the small shops? Those flags give you a sense both of tenderness and of national shame. These poor folk, so sorely tried, so far removed from their native land, and in the midst of so many urgent and sorrowful realities, apparently still find solace in the image of the homeland which these symbols evoke.

Such miserable spectacles are found only in those few streets where the dregs of the Italian emigration accumulate. Yet these are still a hundred times preferable to the dregs of the Irish, whose degradation stems from bad habits, rather than, as in our people, from economic prejudice and ignorance. Nor should one think that all Italians live there; not by far. There are many Italians in New York and Brooklyn, supplying a large part of the stonemasons, sculptors, stucco workers, painters, many many barbers, waiters, nearly all the fruit merchants, from the many who are established in fine stores to those who go around with baskets and carts, and, until a few years ago, all the bootblacks. These, for the most part, live in dispersed parts of the city as their work requires, and aside from assuming the bourgeois attitudes of the majority which they do not know how or want to accept, they live more or less like Americans. They still exhibit a certain minute concern over savings, a frugality which borders on privation, a meticulous debating of pennies, shabby clothes, crowded living in cramped quarters, in short a thousand parsimonious practices that twenty years ago every one called exercises in virtue and which many do, even today. These practices cause Americans to associate even those whose condition is improved with those of their compatriots who infest Baxter and Mulberry streets, thinking the latter characteristic of all Italians.

Men commonly think of the characteristics of each race only in terms of its extremes; those essentially are the only ones that are differentiated, and those alone form the conception that gets fixed in the popular mind. Subtle ethnic differences cannot be detected by a people born of and springing from the fusion of so many different elements, especially elements which are the most indomitable, the most ambitious, the most audacious, and the most eager for the good things in life of any people in the world.

But do Americans realize the condition of these people, divorced from the wives and children who expect them to send back a few pennies to pay the rent, who are pressed with the need of accumulating the sum needed to redeem their mortgaged lands? Americans are not aware of the urgent pressures which make heroic the resignation of these wretched folk. . . .

But we who know the real condition of these fellow countrymen of ours, the cruel necessities which drove them to America, and the affections which incline them to their native land and cause them to make such sacrifices—we must make a very different judgment of them [than do the Americans]. If the concept of the standard of living in America is more elevated, it is not their fault. One cannot deny that part of their wretchedness is the fruit of ignorance. If they were better educated they would not fall into the traps which injure many of the best of them, but surely the greater part of their suffering follows from behavior that is virtuous in intent.

RUDYARD KIPLING DEFAMES NEW YORK: 1892

The physical squalor of the city in the early nineties and the relationship of municipal corruption to this unpleasant situation prompted some brutally critical comment from the English novelist Rudyard Kipling. Kipling made no reference to New York in his *American Notes,* which he wrote after visiting the country en route from India in 1889. The present strictures upon the metropolis were written in 1892 when Kipling and his American bride stopped in New York on a projected journey around the world. The failure of a bank in Yokohama prevented the completion of the trip, so the young couple returned by way of Canada to Mrs. Kipling's home in Brattleboro, Vermont. Here they lived for four years, until an altercation with their neighbors prompted a somewhat precipitate return to England. The following is an excerpt from Kipling's *Letters of Travel (1892–1913)*. It is published with the permission of Mrs. George Bambridge, owner of the copyright, Doubleday and Company, Incorporated, and the Macmillan Company of Canada.[67]

It is not easy to escape from a big city. An entire continent was waiting to be traversed, and, for that reason, we lingered in New

York till the city felt so homelike that it seemed wrong to leave it. And further, the more one studied it, the more grotesquely bad it grew—bad in its paving, bad in its streets, bad in its street-police, and but for the kindness of the tides would be worse than bad in its sanitary arrangements. No one as yet has approached the management of New York in a proper spirit; that is to say, regarding it as the shiftless outcome of squalid barbarism and reckless extravagance. No one is likely to do so, because reflections on the long, narrow pig-trough are construed as malevolent attacks against the spirit and majesty of the great American people, and lead to angry comparisons. Yet, if all the streets of London were permanently up and all the lamps permanently down, this would not prevent the New York streets taken in a lump from being first cousins to a Zanzibar foreshore, or kin to the approaches of a Zulu kraal. Gullies, holes, ruts, cobblestones awry, kerbstones rising from two to six inches above the level of the slatternly pavement; tram-lines from two to three inches above street level; building materials scattered half across the street; lime, boards, cut stone, and ash-barrels generally and generously everywhere; wheeled traffic taking its chances, dray *versus* brougham, at cross roads; swaybacked poles whittled and unpainted; drunken lamp-posts with twisted irons; and, lastly, a generous scatter of filth and more mixed stinks than the winter wind can carry away, are matters which can be considered quite apart from the "Spirit of Democracy" or "the future of this great and growing country." In any other land they would be held to represent slovenliness, sordidness, and want of capacity. Here it is explained, not once but many times, that they show the speed at which the city has grown and the enviable indifference of her citizens to matters of detail. One of these days, you are told, everything will be taken in hand and put straight. The unvirtuous rulers of the city will be swept away by a cyclone, or a tornado, or something big and booming, of popular indignation; everybody will unanimously elect the right men, who will justly earn the enormous salaries that are at present being paid to inadequate aliens for road sweepings, and all will be well. At the same time the lawlessness ingrained by governors among the governed during the last thirty, forty, or it may be fifty years; the brutal levity of the public conscience in regard to public duty; the toughening and suppling of public morals, and the reckless disregard for human life, bred by impotent laws and fostered by familiarity with needless accidents and criminal neglect, will miraculously disappear. . . .

In a heathen land the three things that are supposed to be the pillars of moderately decent government are regard for human life, justice, criminal and civil, as far as it lies in man to do justice, and good roads. In this Christian city, they think lightly of the first—their own papers, their own speech, and their own actions prove it; buy and sell the second at a price openly and without shame; and are, apparently, content to do without the third. One would almost expect racial sense of humour would stay them from expecting only praise—slab, lavish, and slavish—from the stranger within their gates. But they do not. If he holds his peace, they forge tributes to their own excellence which they put into his mouth. . . . If he speaks—but you shall see for yourself what happens. . . .

The blame of their city evils is not altogether with the gentlemen, chiefly of foreign extraction, who control the city. These find a people made to their hand—a lawless breed ready to wink at one evasion of the law if they themselves may profit by another, and in their rare leisure hours content to smile over the details of a clever fraud. Then, says the cultured American, "Give us time. Give us time, and we shall arrive." The otherwise American, who is aggressive, straightway proceeds to thrust a piece of half-hanged municipal botchwork under the nose of the alien as a sample of perfected effort. . . . It is neither seemly nor safe to hint that the government of the largest city in the States is a despotism of the alien by the alien for the alien, tempered with occasional insurrections of the decent folk. Only the Chinaman washes the dirty linen of other lands.

THE MATURING METROPOLIS: 1893

The reactions of the Frenchman Paul Bourget were much more favorable to the city of the early nineties than were those of his fellow novelist Rudyard Kipling. Already New York was "an achievement and not a beginning," in the opinion of the distinguished French novelist, dramatist, and critic, who arrived in New York for a year's visit to the United States in August 1893. Articles on America which he wrote for the New York *Herald* became the subject of controversy, and he was lampooned by Mark Twain in the *North American Review* for his observations upon life in the United States. Bourget's flair for psychological interpretation is seen in his concern with the tone of the city, as reflected in the dynamic magnitude of the Equitable Building and the Brooklyn Bridge. Following is an excerpt from his *Outre-Mer:*

Impressions of America, published in 1895 and reprinted with the consent of Charles Scribner's Sons.[68]

. . . you have only to come in contact with things as a whole [in New York] to receive again that impression of a Babel with a splendor all its own, an impression which—shall I avow it?—I have felt most strongly in connection with a building devoted entirely to business offices, and a bridge over which runs a railway!

The building is called the Equitable, from the name of the insurance company that built it. It is a gigantic palace with a marble façade, rising up almost at the end of Wall Street. . . .

The hum of life in the enormous building, the swarms of comers and goers, the endless ramifications of the corridors, reduce your mind almost to a stupor of admiration, such as you also feel when looking from above upon this great city.

Far as the eye can reach it stretches away . . . broad, longitudinal avenues cut at right angles by streets, thus distributing the blocks of houses in equal masses. . . . This is not even a city in the sense in which we understand the word, we who have grown up amid the charm of irregular cities which grew as the trees do, slowly, with the variety, the picturesque character of natural things. This is a table of contents of unique character, arranged for convenient handling. Seen from here it is so colossal, it encloses so formidable an accumulation of human efforts, as to overpass the bounds of imagination. You think you must be dreaming when you see beyond the rivers two other cities—Jersey City and Brooklyn—spread out along their shores. The latter is only a suburb, and it has nine hundred thousand inhabitants.

A bridge connects New York with Brooklyn, overhanging an arm of the sea. Seen even from afar, this bridge astounds you like one of those architectural nightmares given by Piranesi in his weird etchings. You see great ships passing beneath it, and this indisputable evidence of its height confuses the mind. But walk over it, feel the quivering of the monstrous trellis of iron and steel interwoven for a length of sixteen hundred feet at a height of one hundred and thirty-five feet above the water; see the trains that pass over it in both directions, and the steamboats passing beneath your very body, while carriages come and go, and foot passengers hasten along, an eager crowd, and you will feel that the engineer is the great artist of our epoch, and you will own that these people have a right to plume themselves on their audacity, on the *go-ahead* which has never flinched.

At the same time you ask yourself what right they have to call themselves, as a people, young. They are recent, their advent is so astonishingly new that one can hardly believe in dates in the face of these prodigies of activity. But recent as is this civilization, it is evidently *mature,* at least here. The impression upon me this evening is that I have been exploring a city which is an achievement and not a beginning. Its life is not an experiment; it is a mode of existence, with its inconveniences as well as its splendors.

MONEY AND POLITICS—THE ELECTION OF 1896

A political manifestation of the materialistic spirit of New York City in the nineties was observed by a young English journalist, George W. Steevens, who witnessed the behavior of New Yorkers during the heated presidential campaign of 1896. Visiting the United States under the auspices of the London *Daily Mail,* Steevens sensed the intensity of the contest as Bryan and the Democrats argued for "free silver" and the Republicans attempted to counter this threat of inflation. Pressure and propaganda in the interest of sound money were so effective in New York City as to give the Republican Party its first victory in a presidential contest in this traditionally Democratic stronghold. In his letters from America Steevens described the famous "gold parade" held in New York on the eve of the election and the reactions of the residents on election day. He concluded that concern for the dollar, so apparent in the campaign, set the prevailing tone of the urban society at the time. His letters were collected in a book which he called *The Land of the Dollar.* The following excerpt from this work is reprinted with the permission of Dodd, Mead and Company.[69]

I landed myself in New York just in time for the biggest political demonstration in the world's history. Exactly how many men turned out on Saturday to parade for McKinley and Gold it is hard to estimate. The Silver partisans admit that more than eighty thousand men marched in the great procession, while enthusiastic goldbugs put the figure at nearly double. Probably a hundred to a hundred and ten thousand would about hit it. Anyhow, there were so many that it hardly matters to an odd ten thousand how many there were. It was the greatest assembly of organised men this country has seen since the muster of Union veterans in Washington to disband after the close of the Civil War. It is estimated that there were more men tramping the streets of New York in Saturday's parade than there are voters in the States of Colorado, Idaho, and Nevada put together. There was every manner of man in the procession: millionaires in shining silk hats, and working men in corduroy trousers. The men in one line alone were appraised by expert valuers at thirty million dollars. The head of the procession reached the reviewing stand in Madison Square at a quarter to eleven in the morning; the tail did not arrive until half-past six in the evening. Looking from the window of the "Daily Mail" office, Fifth Avenue was dark for miles with the steadily rolling lines of paraders. Nobody ever saw so many American flags in one day. Every man shouldered this weapon, and the blending of the red, white, and blue made a violet embroidery over the black masses. . . .

At dead of night, when rival Bryan and McKinley meetings were held in Madison Square, the opposing crowds exchanged first arguments, then fierce volleys of cheers; presently the cheers became insults, and then the insults became assaults. The first faction-fight of the campaign in New York was promisingly under way when the police arrived. . . . It must have been nearly daylight before the police finally swept up the scraps, and then New York enjoyed such quiet as it ever gets.

Yet even on Saturday night hundreds gathered quietly in the hotels of the city, not discussing, not drinking,—doing nothing but simply waiting the result. New York is holding its breath ready to break out in huzzas or lamentations, according as the dice may fall. Never was so huge a mass of people so completely centered in one thing. In Wall Street there is no panic, but utter stagnation. . . .

The belated demonstrators were hardly silent when the day of destiny dawned. And almost before it had actually dawned the day's work had begun. The polls open at six o'clock in New York, and even by that hour millionaire and beggar had lined up in front of the polling-booths as if they were the pit-door of a theatre. The strain of the last few days had become no longer bearable. . . .

It must be explained that Americans do not vote, like us, in a public building. During the last few days, broad, dark-green wooden sheds have squatted on the streets all over the city. In these tabernacles they take the sacrament of citizenship. In the poorer quarters, where the streets are narrower, shops are consecrated to the solemn rite. Usually cigar-stores are chosen—sometimes, with genial irony for the defeated candidate, an undertaker's.

By the time the city ordinarily wakes up nearly half the votes had been cast. Already New York, its duty done, had settled itself down to enjoy a holiday under the clear sunlight of an Indian summer's day. The polling-places were soon deserted, but for a little knot of party watchers, tallymen all decked out with ribbons like prize short-horns, and the police. . . . Wall Street and the other business quarters were ablaze with the national colours, but there were no business-men. The Broadway shops and restaurants were all decked out in bunting, but all were closed. Fifth Avenue was as depopulated as in the middle of August. . . . Meanwhile crowds of people were streaming to the ferries and the railway stations, seeking the country. The streets gradually filled with citizens' wives and children, all in their Sunday clothes. It was a Sabbath without any Sabbatarianism. You would say the city was quietly enjoying victory instead of being in the midst of battle. . . .

Hours before any news was possible great crowds had massed in the City Hall Park and in Printing House Square. . . .

The anxious crowd outside surged denser and more terrible in its ungovernable weight. . . .

From the first moment of the arrival of returns, the direction of the stream was clearly apparent. New York City, where never before had a majority been given for a Republican President, was going steadily and surely for Mr. McKinley. One hundred districts, two hundred districts, three hundred districts, were heard from, and Mr. McKinley forged steadily ahead, till his majority in the city was certain to be at least 20,000. Then the serried masses began to open their lungs, and fierce yells and whoops and cheers crashed from side to side of the great square.

Thence I went up deserted Broadway to Madison Square. Here a dense crowd was packed across the thoroughfare before the bulletin-boards of the uptown newspaper offices. . . . At each new triumph of Republicanism the ear-splitting bray of . . . tin trumpets boomed out. This was the form which the voice of the people chose to manifest its exultation. White men and black men, sober men and hilarious men, young men, staid middle-age and grey-beards, matrons and maidens, all were gravely tootling these babies' tin trumpets. Everybody was too exultant to care whether he behaved like an infant or not. There was no escape from the infernal din. . . .

Passing on to the University Club, I found every member present exulting and dancing like schoolboys, as a waiter read item after item of the colossal pile of victories. These fine gentlemen of New York cried for cheers for McKinley, hurled stentorian congratulations at entering friends, clasped each other round the waist by threes and fours, and waltzed round the room under the approving smiles of the head-waiters.

My next task was to fight my way up to Herald Square. . . . The wide square was one riot of delirium. The crowd spread itself over the tram rails, and almost sought to push back the crawling cable-cars which attempted to jostle them from an immediate view of the next undreamed-of success posted on the bulletins. Now rockets and Roman candles were blazing on every side. Gunpowder flared, bands crashed, bugles rang; overhead the late trains puffed and clattered, and above all rang volleys of cheers and the interminable discordant blare of tin trumpets, all blended in a furious jangle of jubilation. The whole place was mad, demoniac, inspired with a divine frenzy.

9. *THE GOLDEN GENERATION* (*1900–1930*)

THE TWENTIETH CENTURY brought a new New York and an acclaim from commentators such as the city had not known since the ebullient decade before the Civil War when the bustling vigor of its streets and wharves had led to predictions that it would one day outclass every other city on the globe. By the turn of the twentieth century, New York, with its "thousand and one mechanical conveniences," was already displaying a standard of living which Old World capitals could not match; its contribution during World War I predisposed many Europeans at least temporarily in its favor; and in the golden decade which preceded 1929 its ever increasing height, wealth, and physical magnitude lent it a titanic quality with which even basically critical observers were impressed. "New York gives the sensation of a city of giants, more than any other city, even London," wrote a French engineer, as early as 1905; and in the succeeding quarter-century the stunning size of the city and the magnificence at least of some parts of it won it general, if sometimes grudging, praise.[1]

It was its skyscraper architecture which more than anything else induced this reaction to New York. At the opening of the century, the new "steel-cage" structures stood out in contrasting isolation above the generally horizontal mass of the metropolis—as Henry James wrote, like "extravagant pins in a cushion already overplanted." But by the late twenties the whole city was "being lifted up" to match the "Himalayan" pinnacles of 1898. The skyscrapers had not only swept uptown, but in height were achieving elevations at which, according to one French traveler, "Europeans seek only the stars." "Skyscrapers are the first thing which a foreigner sees when he comes to America," wrote the editor of the *Frankfurter Zeitung,* after visiting New York in the mid-twenties. "The dizzy loftiness of the Manhattan skyline" looms "like a citadel raised on high by the cyclops." Even when, in some quarters, wartime affinities had given way to "surly admiration," as a French journalist wrote of his compatriots' reaction to America at the turn of the thirties, European visitors admitted that the "forests of skyscrapers" lent an "intense beauty," an undeniable "excitement," novelty, and suggestion of power to the New World metropolis. *"Stelle?"* asks the Italian novelist Arnaldo Fraccaroli, on first viewing the city. *"No. Finestre. Finestre ancóra. Un altra città, aerea."* [2]

By the close of this generation, the elevation of New York's skyscrapers had been pushed to what is probably an all-time high. In whatever language they were described—as *égratineurs de ciel, Himmelskrätzer, grattacieli,* or *rascacielos*—the towering structures rose into new realms of altitude and literally touched the clouds and scratched the sky. The 47-story Singer Building (1908) and the 60-story Woolworth tower (1913), in the lower city, far outclassed the Flatiron Building, whose twenty-one stories had made it a show place early in the century. By the later twenties, builders in the midtown area had followed suit with such soaring structures as the 56-story Chanin Building (1929) and the 77-story Chrysler shaft (1929), with its almost evanescent, needlelike spire. The turn of the thirties saw the completion of the lofty Empire State Building, whose 102 stories truly penetrated the clouds; and the traditions of the Waldorf-Astoria, which it replaced, were continued in a twin-towered, 47-story hotel opened on Park Avenue in 1931. Still farther north, other skyscraper hostelries, like the Sherry-Netherland (1927), the Savoy-Plaza (1928), and the Pierre (1930), were matched by towering apartment houses on the south and west sides of Central Park. "You find them all over town, these landmarks of the new builders," wrote a British journalist, who visited the city in 1920. "Height is the new destination of American architecture. Even in the distant suburbs of Manhattan . . . the twelve-floor building is there and the cottage is not." [3]

Contemporaries differed in their reactions to this "cyclopean pell-mell of towers," especially during the first dozen years of the new century. The English artist Sir Philip Burne-Jones, a visitor of 1902, called the Flatiron Building a "vast horror," and to H. G. Wells, who was in New York four years later, the new structures had an effect of "immense incompleteness," unlike "St. Peter's great blue dome" or the "dark grace" of St. Paul's. The French novelist Pierre Loti, a visitor of 1912, found it hard to get used to these "gaunt giants" as they "stretched their necks inordinately to see better," rising "higher and higher, terrifying and unbelievable." Some criticized the "giraffe-like" shafts for dwarfing the men who inhabited them or, in the opinion of the Danish journalist Johannes V. Jensen, for casting the neighboring churches into their shade. Most outspokenly uncomplimentary was the Russian novelist Maxim Gorky, who came to New York in 1906 to raise funds for the Revolution. In Marxian eyes, the "monstrous height" of these "dull, heavy piles" imparted an air of "cold and haughty presumption" and gave the city the look of "a huge jaw with black, uneven teeth," belching forth clouds of smoke and sniffing "like a glutton suffering from over-corpulency." [4]

Even in these earliest years of the century, however, some observers thought the gargantuan structures worthy of praise. To the American journalist and critic John Corbin, there was the promise of new urban vistas in the dynamic thrust of the Flatiron Building as it dominated Madison Square like "an ocean steamer with all Broadway in tow." The French illustrator and travel writer Charles Huard found its "limitless silhouette" equally exciting, as did his compatriot Camille Saint-Saëns, a visitor of 1906, for whom New York's strange towers with their fabulous dimensions made a "fantastic and marvelous spectacle." The German dramatist Ludwig Fulda, in New York in 1906 and again in 1913, was at a loss to understand "the awed distaste" with which the European traditionally viewed the skyscrapers. The "newest and mightiest example," the Woolworth Building (in which the architects had at last found an effective tower form), was in his opinion "not only colossal but beautiful." [5]

Indeed, from 1913 forward, with this imposing structure to represent the new architectural style and with the developments of World War I to encourage more generous attitudes toward Europe's new ally, observers of whatever nationality rarely failed to find New York's "sky-climbing buildings" a source of wonder and admiration. To Rupert Brooke, in New York in 1913, "their strength . . . of line and the lightness of their colour gave a kind of classical feeling, classical, and yet not of Europe. . . . that characteristic of the great buildings of the world, an existence and meaning of their own." His compatriot Rebecca West placed them among the wonders of the world, detecting an emotional, religious quality in New York's skyscrapers that was not apparent elsewhere in the country. To Blasco-Ibáñez, touring the globe in 1923, the "soaring edifices" of Manhattan had the "beauty of a Colossus"—a "massive beauty," in the opinion of André Maurois, that in its way equaled the beauty of Florence or Egypt. An English journalist expressed the consensus of observers of the twenties when he wrote in 1929 that Manhattan's skyline was "startling, supreme, superb." [6]

Next to the skyline, the marvel of New York for which outsiders of this period were most unprepared was a product of electricity: the "Great White Way." Broadway had again come into its own as a feature attraction. Eclipsed for a time by the aristocratic splendor of Fifth Avenue, it now made a supreme bid for attention with the electric display advertising that then, as now, transformed its garish commercialism into a wonderland after dark. Its "multicolored bouquets of luminous advertising" impressed a French visitor as early as 1903; and by 1910, Broadway at night, with its "immense blaze of legends and pictures, most of them in motion," was reported to be "the finest free show on earth." "Fabulous glow-worms crawl up and down," wrote a British visitor in 1917. "Zig-zag lightnings strike an acre of signboard—and reveal a panacea for over-eating! A four-storey Highlander dances a whisky-fling; another pours out a high-ball, with a hundred feet between his bottle and the glass. Household words race with invisible pen across a whole city block. An electric kitten plays with a mighty spool of Somebody's silk, then jumps with a bound to the top of a skyscraper." Travelers of the twenties were convinced that no European city "illuminated for a Coronation or a Jubilee could come near Broadway on a normal evening." Then it was "a hundred Eiffel towers, a thousand Rue Pigalle, . . . luminous epilepsy, incandescent hypnotism," wrote Philippe de Rothschild, a French visitor of 1930. "Pity the sky with nothing but stars." [7]

These developments gave the connotation of amusement center to what had once been Manhattan's main residential and business street. At the same time, a newer Fifth Avenue, which by 1909 had "risen in marble and Indiana limestone from the brownstone and brick of a former age," bore increasing testimony to the wealth and commercial specialization of the metropolis. H. G. Wells marveled at the "great torrent of spending and glittering prosperity in carriage and motor car" which poured along its well-groomed expanse in 1906; and five years later Arnold Bennett fairly rhapsodized over the proud and lavish grandeur of this "principal shopping street of the richest community of the world." By the late twenties the baronial residences of "Millionaire Row," on Fifth Avenue in the vicinity of Central Park, were giving way to "soaring masterpieces of stone and steel," surpassing "in audacity anything that the Gothic masters dreamed of," but which were "hotels, not cathedrals!" as a traveler of 1928 reported with some degree of irony.[8]

What many regarded as the ultimate in New York's street architecture was now to be found in newly built Park Avenue—symbol of the pullulating prosperity of the twenties. The development of this fashionable thoroughfare, once the railroad backyard of the middle city, lagged behind that of Fifth and Madison, its more affluent neighbors. It was not until the twenties that postwar prosperity transformed the monotony of its eight- and nine-story elevator apartments into "a place of gold unalloyed." "For sheer magnificence there is nothing in the world like the new Park Avenue," wrote the Liberal journalist J. A. Spender, a traveler of 1928, who saw in the dignified elegance of its apartment buildings the latest and most splendid examples of New York's multiple residential dwellings. Here were duplex and even triplex flats, with "whole floors removed, and no doubt baronial halls built into them." Outside, ornament had been minimized above the third floor, thus "bringing the great twenty-storied masses into a uniform relation with each other." [9]

Other visitors agreed that Park Avenue's "communal palaces," unlike the ornate mansions on Riverside Drive, were "masterpieces of restraint and good taste." Their tenants made the section from Forty-sixth to Ninetieth Street the wealthiest residential highway in the world. The French novelist Paul Morand, who described the avenue in 1929, asserted that of its 5,000 families, 2,000 were millionaires, each of whom was reported to spend $150,000 a year. Apartment rentals of $40,000 were not uncommon, and Riesner cabinets and genuine Rembrandts decorated the rooms of the most expensive hotels. The 42-story Ritz Tower, erected at Park Avenue and Fifty-seventh Street in 1925, epitomized the avenue's expensive grace. Like the phrase "Park Avenue" the name "Ritz," too, came to stand colloquially for the highest fashion of the time. And it was not inconsistent with past experience, that in the now traditional northward migration of the city's fashionable hostelries, the Waldorf-Astoria should have sought a Park Avenue setting at the turn of the thirties.[10]

Three already traditional qualities of New York—unceasing noise, constant movement, and perpetual change—struck contemporaries more forcibly than ever in this generation. The "heavy, low, musical roar, hardly ever intermitted," which to Walt Whitman had connoted the city of the sixties, was increased to pandemonium, fifty years later, in the opinion of commentators assaulted by the "nerve-shattering din" of the elevated railway and the "never-ending" and "infernal" uproar of traffic mounting from the streets. The compulsion to haste had aggregated Whitman's "hurrying . . . electric crowds" into "shoving and elbowing masses, making them stand clinging to straps, jerking them up elevator shafts, and pouring them into ferry boats." Subway excavation and skyscraper construction perpetuated the impression that New York was in a "chronic state of pulling down and rebuilding." "The note of New York is impermanence," wrote William George Fitzgerald, a British author who visited the United States in 1917. "Great pits yawn here and there—perhaps for the leg-rests of yet another skyscraper. Or the hole may be part of the city tube." The residents' reaction had already been expressed by William Dean Howells. New Yorkers were never surprised, he remarked in 1913, to return from a vacation and find that an "architectural geyser" had shot up where formerly "a meek little ten-story edifice cowered." [11]

Disturbing as were these features of the New York scene, most contemporaries regarded them as concomitants of the dynamic drive of the metropolis. The relentless noise and human hurry reflected the "blindly furious energy of growth," just as the skyscraper—"conceived in constriction" and "sired by aspiration" as Ernest Gruening wrote in the early twenties—represented not only an adaptation to the environment but also the vertical thrust of the city's aggressive economy. By 1930, there was no denying New York's physical magnitude—nor its economic power in the nation and the world. Its population, which had outdistanced London's by 1910, more than doubled between 1900 and 1930 to reach a total of nearly seven million within a wider metropolitan area that included nearly four million more. Channeling as it did so much of the nation's productive energies, by the close of World War I it superseded the British capital as the financial center of the globe. The French scholar André Chevrillon, comparing the changes of thirty years, concluded in 1922 that New York, with its grandeur and its activity, was now truly "the first capital of the world." [12]

In this, as in preceding generations, the economy of the city rested on commerce, industry, and finance. "The wholesale merchants, the banker potentates, and the corporation attorneys set the pace . . . and dominate all the activities of the metropolis," was the opinion in 1904 of Hugo Munsterberg, German-born professor of psychology, whose residence at Harvard University did not prevent him from viewing American society through the eyes of an outsider. The dominance of office buildings—"cathedrals to commerce"—on the horizon furthered the prevailing impression that "commerce, trade, traffic—what is commonly called 'business,' " as John C. Van Dyke wrote in 1908, provided the basic energy for the city's economic advance.

Actually, as early as 1900, New York's shippers were handling, in terms of value, well beyond a third of the nation's exports and as much as two thirds of its imports. A threefold increase in exports occurred during World War I; and thanks to improvements instituted by the Port of New York Authority, created in 1921, New York was able to retain, as late as 1929, its prewar share of the export trade and almost 50 per cent, in dollar value, of the nation's imports. In that year the value of its wholesale trade was nearly 23 per cent of the national total. Its unquestioned pre-eminence in retail merchandising was symbolized in its fashionable shopping center, which had moved northward to Thirty-fourth Street, on Fifth Avenue, by the eve of World War I, and to the vicinity of the Fifties and Madison Avenue in the expansive era that followed it.[13]

The outbreak of war in Europe momentarily unsettled business in New York, but war money soon stimulated all phases of the economy. With Paris no longer accessible, visitors from Latin America "piled in"; and the city appeared to be overrun by brokers and speculators celebrating with "any-price" dinners, and by farmers, contractors, and manufacturers from America's Middle West, intent upon circulating some of the money which "deluged" the country as a result of wartime demands. It was impossible to exaggerate the "nightly riot" or the prices asked for "food and wine, amusements, and souvenirs," a British commentator reported, describing conditions in the fall and winter of 1916–1917.[14]

Once the United States had entered the conflict, New York, like most of America, took its patriotism seriously and participated with a "high heart." "The war was everywhere," wrote commentators from France and England, several of whom were in America on missions to advance the war effort. They found the Harbor girded for war, as battleships rode at anchor and aircraft hovered overhead. On Fifth Avenue, afloat with flags, the Union Jack, the French tricolor, and the blue-starred service emblem mingled with the Stars and Stripes. Miniature flags waved from the hoods of most of the motor cars and hung in the windows behind. "Give Till It Hurts" was the message of banners, strung high across the streets. Impassioned speeches, delivered on street corners and from theatre stages, carried bond drives "over the top." "Hooverish" hostesses served rice and potato bread and spent long hours in organized war work. Yet for all the vigor of such patriotic responses, the gaiety of the hotel amusements, the dazzling brilliance of the streets, and the manifest evidence of prosperity in the wartime city impressed European observers with the contrast between the sacrifices of New Yorkers and those of their overseas allies.[15]

The prosperity that had prevailed on the eve of the war was only a pale preview of the spending spree that followed it. To a native New Yorker, "overflowing wealth" was one of the city's chief characteristics, at the turn of the twenties; and to postwar visitors from Europe—like the British journalist Harold Spender—its affluence and luxury, as exhibited in "gigantic shops . . . , lavish display of furs and jewellery, . . . and teeming motorcars," were positively mythical. "Magnificence is the first thing that strikes one in New York," wrote another visitor of 1920; in the opinion of a not uncomplimentary French scholar, who was in the city two years later, postwar New York was "under the sign of gold." [16]

By the later 1920's, the reactions of some foreign observers to the opulence and extravagance of life in New York—by contrast with Europe's distresses—reflected a growing antagonism toward the United States on the part of its former allies. French commentators like Bernard Faÿ, Georges Duhamel, and Paul Achard found less praise for New York at the close of the twenties than had their compatriots some years earlier. In the opinion of C. H. Bretherton, a British visitor of 1925, New York was "a vast cash register" that "toils night and day to amuse—and charges accordingly." It was a "terrifying city" to Oxford-trained Vera Brittain and her scholar husband, during this "crazy period of indiscriminate money-getting," as they tried to subsist there in 1926 on a research worker's pay. Even the sophisticate Ford Madox Ford, who found the temper of the city distinctly to his liking, sensed "its gaiety, its tolerance, its carelessness" to be "that of a storming-party hurrying towards an unknown goal." "It is the city of the Good Time," he wrote, "and the Good Time is there so sacred that you may be excused anything you do in searching for it." [17]

New York's prosperity in these golden years was nurtured by the city's leadership in the realm of finance. From 1890 to 1930, New

York held the reins of the nation's finances more tightly than ever before or since, for after 1930 came wider decentralization and greater direction from Washington, D. C. In the period preceding World War I, the city's predominance in the money market was in part the consequence of the activities of a triumvirate of financial titans, J. P. Morgan, Sr., James Stillman, head of the National City Bank of New York, and George F. Baker, president of the First National Bank of New York. It was furthered by the presence in the city, by the turn of the century, of the chief offices of more than a third of the largest industrial combinations of the nation and of the country's four largest life insurance companies, with their fast-accumulating assets.[18]

In the wake of the demands of World War I, money flowed toward America, according to one British observer, "as water down hill." "Only by the most careful and constant extravagance can we keep it from bursting the banks!" he reported a local humorist as explaining in 1917. With the generally pervasive prosperity of the middle twenties a torrent of money poured into New York City for investment in stocks and bonds. The big banks of the city organized security-selling affiliates and established branches in foreign countries, helping to set the stage for the runaway stock market that was to bring this extravagant era to a close.[19]

Visitors to the city in the period of postwar speculation were eager to observe the operations of New York's two large securities markets. The famous British war correspondent Sir Philip Gibbs visited the Curb Exchange in 1919 when its activities actually took place outside on the curb, a practice which was abandoned two years later. Sir Philip was reminded of a madhouse as he observed the raucous bidding of the brokers in front of one narrow building. From its windows "poked two rows of faces, one above the other," some with telephone receivers at their ears. "Hideous grimaces" on each of the faces were "accompanied by strange, incomprehensible gestures of the man's fingers," signals to the curb brokers "who wore caps of different colors in order to be distinguished from their fellows." "Up and down the street, and from the topmost as well as the lower stories of the buildings, I saw the grimaces and the gestures of the window-men," Gibbs reported. "It was a lively day in Wall Street, and I thanked God that my fate had not led me into such a life. It seemed worse than war." [20]

A French traveler witnessed the activity at the Stock Exchange in the peak year of 1929 when seats were selling there for as much as $625,000. After visiting the offices of the only French brokerage firm on the exchange he found himself in what appeared to be an army headquarters in the midst of battle. "A panting, sweating, shirt-sleeved personnel" was "plunged in its task, helmeted men connected with the ceiling by wires that enter their ears, and clamped to the floor by curving tubes that enter their mouths, one hand on the telegraph, the other entering o's and staff and serpent dollar signs in huge ledgers." Normal operations could not keep pace with "the great increase in speculation." "Sunday shifts" and "night shifts" reflected the accelerated activity; and the "downtown section, which before the war was plunged in darkness after seven in the evening," was "now lighted all night long." Elsewhere in the building a similar tumult prevailed: "a flood of excited secretaries, a storm of messengers, a cyclone of page-boys, a hurricane of middle-men dashing bare-headed, in black coats and striped trousers, as in London," among them "a few specimens of the old white-spatted business men with carnations in their buttonholes." Finally, the closing gong "booms out. The turmoil settles. The great generals instantly leave the battlefield, leap into the still empty subway, in the trains of which, a couple of hours later, the man-in-the-street will be avidly reading the price columns." [21]

While trade and finance appeared, to the casual observer, to set the tone of the city's economy, the largest proportion of its working population in these years was engaged in manufacturing and mechanical pursuits. Nearly half the total working population was so occupied in 1900, and fully a third, thirty years later. "Those who are accustomed to think of cities in terms of manufacturing do not ordinarily count New York City among the great industrial centers of the United States, but this is an error of the first order," wrote Charles A. Beard, in 1924, speaking not as a historian but as a contemporary observer. To be sure, the myriad store windows of Manhattan, as well as the office-type buildings used in industries such as the garment trades, furthered the impression that New York was "not so much an industrial city as a city of commerce, a city of financiers." Nevertheless, the smokestacks in the boroughs and suburbs that flanked Manhattan Island were symbols of industrial activity that kept New York City the "number-one" manufacturing center of the nation. Production within the city limits was valued at one and a third billion dollars at the turn of the century and nearly six billion dollars three decades later. Manhattan may have given visitors the impression of being essentially a "shop," selling, consuming, and

Collection, The Museum of Modern Art, New York. Mrs. Simon Guggenheim Fund

THE MID-CENTURY CULTURAL SCENE: A WEALTH OF RESOURCES

Commentators of the 1930's and 1940's were impressed with New York's "unimaginable riches" in the fields of music and art and with the variety and resources of its libraries and museums. The Metropolitan Museum of Art was a storehouse of masterpieces; and the finest of contemporary work could be seen at the Museum of Modern Art, as in the display of sculpture and painting by Modigliani, Picasso, and Maillol, in one of its exhibits, shown above. Among the many treasures of the New York Public Library was its Gutenberg Bible (right), a rare copy of the first printed book. "In winter there is almost too much good music," wrote one visitor in 1947. At the Metropolitan Opera, the opening-night audience on December 21, 1936, photographed at intermission, below, heard a performance of *Die Walküre,* with a cast that included such world-famous Wagnerian singers as Flagstad, Rethberg, Thorborg, Melchior, List, and Schorr.

Courtesy of the New York Public Library

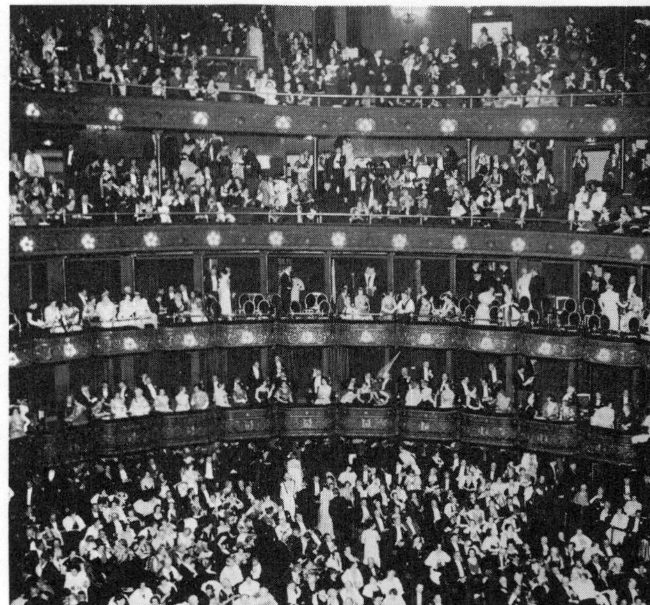

Courtesy of *The News,* New York's Picture Newspaper

Pictures on this page courtesy Standard Oil Co. (N. J.); opposite, courtesy *The News,* New York's Picture Newspape

NEW YORK AT NIGHT

As early as the 1880's, visitors began to note the "weird" and "beautiful" effect of electric lights upon some of the city's squares. Fifty years later, the "sky-soaring citadel" blazed, as Thomas Wolfe wrote, "like a magnificent jewel in its fit setting of sea, and earth, and stars."

Above, the skyline of midtown Manhattan flashes out in the early evening from Radio City southward to the glowing eminence of the Empire State Building. Left, the gleaming ribbon of Fifth Avenue borders Central Park and the residential Upper East Side.

New York City takes wartime precautions during World War II. Above, right, lights flare below (and some even above) the fifteen-story dimout limit, looking west on Forty-second Street from the *Daily News* Building in June of 1942. Below, the pall of a complete blackout settles over midtown Manhattan.

THE TWENTIETH-CENTURY BUSINESS SCENE

Business and finance combined with trade and industry to underwrite New York's economy in the twentieth century. By the 1930's the dwellings of Millionaires' Row, on Fifth Avenue south of Central Park, had been replaced by fashionable department and specialty stores. In the picture at top, autos and motorbuses (the double-deckers were retired in 1953) move in a continuous stream along the Avenue in the vicinity of Radio City; and to the north, the "wedding-cake modern" lines of the First National City Bank typify the structures that were changing the façade of the street at the mid-century. Visitors constituted one of New York's biggest businesses; and the city's facilities for conventions and exhibits were expanded in 1956 with the opening of the $35,000,000 Coliseum, the world's largest exhibition building (center). Pictured below is the financial nerve-center of the city's (and the nation's) economy—the floor of the New York Stock Exchange, on Wall Street. Here members of the exchange crowd around horseshoe-shaped trading posts at which listed stocks are bought and sold.

Picture credits:
(*top*) Underwood and Underwood
(*center*) Courtesy, Coliseum Exhibition Corporation
(*below*) Courtesy, New York Stock Exchange

using things, "all with a great show"; but, as one visitor observed, "behind all this," the Bronx was "clothing her, Brooklyn feeding her, and Jersey City . . . making the steel of her houses." [22]

Although most contemporary commentators concerned themselves less with industrial pursuits in New York than with other features of the economy, one of them—Egon Kisch, a Czech visitor of the late twenties—turned his attention to this aspect of the New York scene and specifically to the garment trades, the city's largest industry in terms of value of product and persons employed. The operatives were principally "fugitives from the Russo-Polish pogroms and their sons," Kisch reported. He found that the establishments where they worked, in the tall buildings of the needle district, were practically identical, whether they turned out dresses, cloaks, or men's suits. Ten to fifteen workers were the complement of employees. Along the windows stretched the cutters' tables, crowded with rolls of fabric. In the smaller places, the cutting was done by hand, in the larger, by electric shears which, "under the guidance of a master cutter," would "trim thirty different cloths to an exact pattern." Beyond these tables were more men and women, "bent over sewing machines, sewing buttonholes by hand, or moving mechanically with the motions of their pressing irons." [23]

Observers, early in the century, were convinced that the living conditions of New York's humblest workers—"packed together like herrings in a barrel"—were far worse than those in the East End of London. New York's East Side "seemed to sweat humanity at every window and door," when Arnold Bennett visited it in 1911. "The thought of the hidden interiors was terrifying . . . would not bear thinking about." To the British literary critic Stephen Graham, a visitor of 1913, Manhattan's slums were "slums at their intensest"; and even in the postwar twenties the "broken windows, leaky roofs" and "stairs thick with dirt and vermin" in this "clearing station of the New World" contrasted sharply with the comfort and luxury in other parts of the metropolis. Unionization, after 1910, brought some diminution in the hardships of sweatshop labor; and compliance with tenement house legislation of 1901 reduced the congestion in the most crowded quarters from 1,000 persons per acre in 1900 to 500 per acre in 1925. However, despite such improvements, the living conditions of New York's poor, as late as the turn of the 1930's, were still the subject of fully deserved criticism by contemporary observers.[24]

The "middle classes," whom both the rich and the poor continued to crowd out of the central city, were now pouring into the Bronx or spilling over into remoter suburbs. Arnold Bennett visited the Bronx in 1911 on the conviction that "a place with a name so remarkable must itself be remarkable." Here he found four-room flats renting for $26, equipped with central heating, gas, and electricity and supplied with a refrigerator, a kitchen range, a bookcase, and a sideboard—"amenities for the people" which did "not even exist for the wealthy in Europe." For residents higher in the "social-financial scale" there were apartment buildings with doormen, the "plutocratic luxury" of a mail chute, and fittings which, though "artistically vulgar," resulted in a "harmonious effect of innocent prosperity." In the Grand Central or Pennsylvania stations, travelers of the twenties mingled with increasingly numerous "daytime" New Yorkers—"commuters" who, after business hours, hurried away to "suburbs . . . beyond the turmoil of the city . . . with bustling little high streets of their own," good shops, and "neat little houses of wooden framework." [25]

Individual houses within the city were, indeed, increasingly the exception as the rapid growth of population augmented New York's traditional tendency to resort to multiple dwelling. The "kitchenette-apartment"—a New York colloquialism, according to a contemporary commentator—generally replaced the boarding house of an earlier period, except among European newcomers; and sumptuous suites in the apartment houses on Park Avenue or Central Park were twentieth-century substitutes for the spacious individual town houses of the mid-nineteenth century. To foreign observers of the 1920's, apartment living imposed an unfortunate "temporariness" upon existence in the city; in their opinion, as in that of visitors of pre-Civil War days, it was the scarcity and expense of domestic servants that induced this inadequate way of life. Cooks demanded $80 a month, their room and board, and freedom from heavy work, a German visitor of 1927 reported, commenting that "servile spirits" were "rare in the United States and must, therefore, be handled with kid gloves." Britishers were surprised to see the wives of men worth as much as ten thousand dollars a year doing their own work with the aid of a charwoman who earned three to four dollars a day. The "total absence of servants," they predicted, would give rise to a new and more transient kind of home—"one room and a concealed bed" and flats or apartments of an advanced type with "the latest heating, air cleaning, dust removing appliances and restaurants in which or from which all meals" would "be served." [26]

Feminine New Yorkers of the period may have suffered from a scarcity of domestic help, but in the opinion of commentators from abroad they were the best-dressed women in the world. "One of the first things that strikes the stranger in New York is the extreme smartness of the women," wrote the artist Burne-Jones, after visiting America in 1902 and 1903. "One rarely comes across a really badly dressed woman in any rank of life. . . . Her Parisian sister, to whom I suppose she would herself admit that she was occasionally indebted for ideas, is not her superior in this respect." A traveler of 1917 was impressed with the "trimness, the taste, the polish" of the thousands of girls who were engaged in office work in the city during World War I. And by the late twenties, when it appeared that "all the furred fauna of creation" had been butchered to clothe the fair New Yorker—with her "plucked and painted eyebrow, lips freshly penciled and reddened, tight-fitting hats" and "admirable leg except for the small rubber galoshes that make her feather-footed"—even French travelers admitted that New York contained "the most beautiful women in the world." [27]

The smartness and vivacity of New York's business girls, according to a visitor in 1913, sprang from the fact that they were "the children of foreigners" and had "peasant blood in them and immigrant hope." As earlier, the cosmopolitanism of New York was its most conspicuous human feature; but the novelty of this generation was the increasing evidence of the recent immigration from southern and eastern Europe. Visitors who compared the city of the 1920's with that of the late 1890's were struck with the change in its ethnic composition. The French scholar André Chevrillon, on a return visit to New York in 1922, found that Poles, Hungarians, Russians, and Armenians had "begun to change the color and even the substance" of the basically Anglo-Saxon community he had visited in 1898. The editor of the London *Spectator* expressed surprise at the comparative absence of Nordic faces in the New York of 1928, upon visiting it after an absence of thirty years. Migrants from southern and eastern Europe had been outnumbering those from the older source since the middle 1890's; but it was not until the first decades of the new century that the human fabric of the community began to show the results. By 1930, Russians and Italians had replaced Irishmen and Germans as the most numerous of the city's always abundant foreign-born; and commentators, who formerly had spoken of New York as another Dublin or Berlin, now equated its population with that of Naples, Rome, or "Jerusalem in its palmiest days." [28]

They described the newcomers at the docks, where in 1905 the French illustrator Charles Huard witnessed the torrent of arrivals from "the sunny climes"—clothed in the costumes of the old country—standing bewildered among broken boxes and loosely covered hampers that revealed "tools, kitchen utensils, [and] bottles of all kinds." They observed them "come from all quarters of the globe" in the slums around First Avenue and under the Brooklyn Bridge, or in the increasingly compact colonies of their own nationalities. They heard them speaking in unfamiliar tongues, at breaks in the working day, on the tramcars or in the streets. Rupert Brooke traveling on a streetcar at sundown, in 1913, was engulfed in "Yiddish, Italian, and Greek, broken by Polish, or Russian, or German"; and his compatriot, the British journalist J. A. Spender, was similarly conscious of the "babel of tongues" as he walked down a long stretch of Sixth Avenue during a lunch hour in 1928. By that date, the new migration had put the stamp of its personality on whole sections of the city. "Many Italians hardly know they are outside their native land," wrote the Italian novelist Arnaldo Fraccaroli, after visiting the city in 1928, "because here they have everything Italian: friends, churches, schools, theater, banks, businesses, daily papers, societies, meeting places. And they can travel for many kilometers without hearing spoken any language except the Italian, or Italian dialect."

To judge from the accounts of their visiting compatriots, by the later twenties the Italians of New York were much better off than when Giuseppe Giacosa had described their squalid state some forty years earlier. The travel writer Luigi Barzini, a visitor at the turn of the thirties, saw little evidence of an evil which until recently had made life difficult for these newcomers—their exploitation by bosses to whom they owed their passage money. On the other hand, Barzini saw many signs of the increasing prestige of the Italian community. This he laid to several causes: the growing recognition of Italy under the Mussolini regime; the gradual improvement in the economic position of the earlier Italian immigrants to New York; and the more professional character of the recent arrivals, among whom were technicians, engineers, and specialists easily adapted to American life. Barzini detected at least seven Italian quarters—the oldest in the lower city and others in Brooklyn, the Bronx, Harlem, and Queens.

Here one heard an "outright Italo-American language—half English and half Italian or some dialect of it, but equally incomprehensible to either the Italian or American." The advances of the second generation, in Barzini's opinion, promised to erase, as in the case of the Irish, the prejudices to which the condition of the earliest Italian migrants had given rise. He nevertheless perpetuated the often repeated cliché that New York was "built by the Italians, run by the Irish, and owned by the Jews." [29]

It was perhaps a sign of the still increasing intensity of New York's cosmopolitanism that many observers saw less evidence of assimilation of the more recent immigrant stocks than had been the case with the earlier immigration. There was considerable glib talk of the city as a "magic cauldron" or "giant crucible" in which the residents of diverse nationality were recast to a new and common mold; early in the century, Henry James asserted perversely that the newcomers were remaking New York more than it was remaking them. But a more common view was that of André Siegfried, who concluded, following a visit in 1914, that, despite a common bearing, the population seemed less assimilated than it had appeared to be ten years earlier. Returning again in 1925, preparatory to writing his prize-winning *America Comes of Age,* he was struck with the increasing evidences of a "fantastic cosmopolitanism" which had submerged the original Protestant Anglo-Saxon stock.[30]

These reactions were undoubtedly colored by local expressions of hostility toward this newer immigration. The Americans found it "appalling," wrote a correspondent of the London *Daily Telegraph* in December 1920, reporting an attitude which was to result in the enactment of the first quota law in the following year. "The worst of this immigration is that it is apt to remain in New York, insufferably crowding that already crowded city, swelling the immense foreign and undigested populations and creating a problem of non-assimilation which is growing more alarming every year." As late as 1930, the German scholar M. J. Bonn described New York as "the sieve through which the muddy stream of immigration poured into the Promised Land." Caught in its fine meshes the newcomers had "spread in a thickish layer over the peninsula of Manhattan and the islands and shores in its vicinity." Over its "thousand ghettoes, both Christian and Jewish," only a diaphanous veil of Americanism was spread, he asserted, one that was "easy to tear asunder" and was "frequently torn." [31]

To judge from contemporary comment, the most conspicuously novel aspect of the recent immigration was the magnitude of its Jewish ingredient. In 1903, when the number of New Yorkers of that faith totaled 600,000 (a tenfold increase since 1880), a French visitor marveled that this was "seven times as many as in all France." "Hebrews are everywhere," wrote Walter R. Hadwen, a distinguished British physician who visited New York in 1921, listing this group first in a catalog of the constituents of New York's cosmopolitanism. "Practically all the Jews of America concentrate in New York, and some of the trades, such as those of tailors and jewellers, are almost entirely in their hands. They own most of the cinemas and theatres, and that they have much to do with finance goes without saying." By the late twenties, there were nearly two million Jews in New York and the Jewish population of "the largest Jewish city in the world" was then as heterogeneous in character as the Empire City's population as a whole. "There are German Jews, Spanish and Portuguese Jews, Levantine Jews, Jews from Holland, Galicia, Hungary, Rumania, the Ukraine," wrote Paul Morand after visits extending from 1925 to 1929; "there are the multi-millionaire Jews of Riverside Drive, the poor Jews of Harlem and the Bronx and Brooklyn." [32]

Popular reactions to the poverty and congestion of the Jewish quarter on the East Side, as well as to the strangeness of the Hebraic customs practiced there, were reminiscent of attitudes toward the Irish in the mid-nineteenth century and toward the Italians a half-century later. As early as 1903 a French traveler reported that the local merchants viewed the growing power of Jews in the commercial world with considerable alarm. On the other hand, travelers of the late twenties pointed out the contribution of New Yorkers of the Jewish faith who had created huge businesses, founded great institutions, or become philanthropic millionaires. An Englishman who visited the city in 1910 and 1911 found the Jews, along with the other non-British stock, the chief audience for the city's offerings of concert and opera; and in the opinion of the British novelist Ford Madox Ford, a visitor of 1926, the "Israelite support of the arts" made the "difference between hardly supportable indigence and just bearable comfort" for the creative talents residing in the city.[33]

As for the perennial question, "Was New York really America?" some foreign visitors still continued to regard the city as alien to the American norm. To some it was still only the dockyard, threshold, or gateway to the real United States. Count Keyserling, on the other hand, gave the customary interpretation a different turn. He described the city as "America's window opening onto Europe," the guarantor because of its "world-wide interest," by contrast with some other parts of the nation, that "George Babbitt and what he stands for" would not control the foreign policy of the now powerful postwar United States.

Increasingly, however, observers were convinced that in its very cosmopolitanism New York epitomized the variety of American society; and in a generation of greatly speeded and expanded communication the city was seen, more than ever before, to be setting the fashion, not only in dress but in attitude, for the nation at large. "Its magazines go everywhere, standardising ideas," wrote a British journalist in 1928, echoing a point of view that some American observers had expressed earlier in the century; "its slang invades the remotest recesses, standardising speech; its melodies are in every home, standardising entertainment; the very thought of Broadway, the Main Street of all America, thrills millions who are scattered far and wide." "New York is not America," a French visitor of the succeeding year asserted, "but it is plain to all beholders that all America would like to be New York." In the opinion of an English scholar, the city, in its collective life and character, was "the most American thing . . . on the American continent," a sort of "Americaniser" for the nation as a whole.[34]

Even in the pursuit of art and letters, so long subordinated in the prevailing preoccupation with business, New York began to exert an unprecedented influence by the turn of the 1920's. In the early years of the century, its intellectual life still reflected the "undisguised triumph of mechanics over aesthetics," in the opinion of foreign visitors; and to residents like William Dean Howells the average New Yorker seemed to care far less for books than for horses or for stocks. Observers of the twenties, however—when the flow of money was such as to offer "a tranquil perch for art"—testify to the transformation that was taking place. New York could then boast a keener intellectual life than London, in the judgment of visiting British authors—one in which the literati of other capitals "could feel perfectly at home." Its already distinguished musical offering, especially in opera, which had impressed Camille Saint-Saëns in 1906, became increasingly abundant, as did its dramatic fare, as well. "There were more orchestral concerts in New York last winter than there were in Berlin," H. L. Mencken had to admit in 1927, despite a genuine distaste for the metropolis. "The town has more theaters, and far better ones, than a dozen Londons. It is . . . loaded with art to the gunwales and steadily piling more on deck." A French traveler of 1929 contended that New York had become what "Rome was for Corot or Poussin," and that in view of the copiousness of its libraries and museums it was the refuge of Western culture, alone possessed of the profusion that is "mother of the arts." [35]

The major innovations in the realm of popular entertainment were the cinema "palace" and the neighborhood movie theatre, which catered to the mass demand of the metropolis for dramatic fare. Vaudeville houses began to exhibit one-reel pictures in 1899; by 1927 when sound film was introduced, the movie theatres outshone the legitimate playhouses in architectural glamor. The Roxy, built at a cost of $15,000,000 in 1926, was one of the spectacles of New York to visitors of the later twenties. Its wide, thickly carpeted corridors and elaborate lighting and decoration reminded Count von Luckner of one of the palaces of Louis XIV. "As we entered, an orchestra of 110 men were playing a selection from one of the Beethoven symphonies," wrote the famous Sea Devil of World War I, after his visit to the United States on a lecture tour in 1926 and 1927. "Then the whole orchestra, the 110 men and their instruments, conductor and all, slowly and quietly sank into some underworld. To take its place, three great organs rose out of the depths," their mighty tones filling the theatre. Variety acts supplemented the "feature presentation"—a showing of the film *What Price Glory?* [36]

Its hotels and restaurants, too, reflected the affluence and increasing sophistication of the metropolis. The pre-eminence of individual hotels was hardly less fleeting than any other aspect of the New York scene; but none better symbolized the spirit of its time than the original Waldorf-Astoria on Fifth Avenue, at Thirty-fourth Street, which, from the late nineties to the outbreak of World War I, bespoke the increasing magnificence of the new New York. Travelers agreed that in its monied magnitude, its splendor, its cosmopolitanism, it was New York personified. Here, "condensed and accumulated," as Henry James asserted after a visit in 1904 and 1905, was the *"characteristic"* of the metropolis as one elsewhere could rarely find it. Its daily average of 1,400 guests, its staff of well beyond that number, and the floating throng that patronized its lavish dining rooms or lingered curiously in its ground floor "Peacock Row" made it seem less a hotel than some fabulous, exciting urban spectacle. On the eve of World

War I, the more northerly Plaza, opened in 1907, and the St. Regis, with its suggestions of Versailles and the Petit Trianon, outclassed the Waldorf in studied luxury; and in the years following the war, hotels like the Commodore and the Pennsylvania (a city in itself, according to Vera Brittain) better represented the impersonal vastness and the unlimited resourcefulness of the New York hotel of the speculative era.[37]

Even the churches took their cue from the impressiveness which pervaded the fashionable streets of the metropolis. As they had begun to do in the later nineteenth century, those on Fifth Avenue offered the eloquence of preachers imported from Britain and the music of expensive choirs. An English visitor of 1910 heard these houses of worship called "Sunday Music-Halls" and "Sunday Opera-Houses." One of the attractions of the Fifth Avenue Baptist Church was the chance of glimpsing John D. Rockefeller or his son. "The crowds that fill all these churches on a Sunday morning are attracted by the razzle-dazzle 'tone' given to these meeting places by the millionaires and their fashionable wives and daughters," wrote the author of *An Englishman in New York*. "The preacher comes into the show as a sort of master of religious ceremonies, and his sermon figures as a sort of light dessert after a feast of music. He is paid to make himself visible at the proper time, just like the organist and the singers." In the twenties, the activities of the churches (with their "air of children whom the buildings hold by the hand") appear to have been overshadowed, to contemporary observers, by the more spectacular character of the secular scene.[38]

Jazz, cabaret clubs, bootleggers, and speak-easies were part of the New York that commentators of all nationalities described in the postwar Prohibition era. Aldous Huxley sensed a "general atmosphere of hilarious inebriation" in its night life in the mid-twenties; and the German radical Ernst Toller, arriving in 1929 to lecture to German workers, gained the impression that the patronage of speak-easies, as well as a general disregard for the law, was standard practice in the metropolis. Many observers contended, however, that the city did not "flame" as much as the movies and the magazines had led them to expect. England's Philip Guedalla professed to have searched in vain for the "ruthless, devouring" city of legend. The lurid was there, but its manifestations were often lost sight of in the overwhelming magnitude of the city.[39]

The automobile and the subway were also features of the new New

York that distinguished it from the nineteenth-century city. The horseless carriage, a novelty in the nineties, had become common enough by 1908 and 1909 to obsess William Dean Howells with the hazards it presented to the urban pedestrian. "The motorist whirs through the intersecting streets and round the corners, bent on suicide or homicide," he wrote from the relative safety of the "Editor's Easy Chair" in *Harper's Monthly Magazine;* "the kind old trolleys and hansoms that once seemed so threatening have almost become so many arks of safety from the furious machines replacing them. But a few short years ago the passer on the Avenue could pride himself on a count of twenty automobiles in his walk from Murray Hill to the Plaza; now he can easily number hundreds." By the extravagant twenties, the number of automobiles was such as to amaze the European visitor. Broadway, according to an English traveler of 1920, was so packed with motor cars that "you could almost jump from roof to roof across the road." Germany's Count von Luckner, after a sojourn in 1927, reported that there were more automobiles in New York alone than in all of Europe, that every fourth person owned a car. An Italian commentator devoted a chapter to "*Automobili per tutti*" in a description of New York he published in 1931.[40]

The subway system was another of the gargantuan developments which, in the view of contemporaries, revealed the accomplishments of which twentieth-century New York was capable. The first subterranean line was begun in 1900 and opened for travel in 1904. In the opinion of the German dramatist Ludwig Fulda, the city's transportation system, like its towering buildings, appeared to have been built "by the hand of giants." The elevated trains, electrically propelled after 1901, continued their screeching way overhead, as did the speeding, open-sided tramcars, on the surface. The tunnel of the Hudson and Manhattan Railroad Company, completed in 1908, connected the populous New Jersey shore with Manhattan Island, and the Holland Tunnel did so by the late twenties. Motor buses, employed on Fifth Avenue, since the early years of the new century, competed with the ancient horse-drawn omnibuses until the latter were finally retired from service in 1907. By the eve of World War I, mechanical devices, with their inhibiting signals, were replacing the human traffic control which the police department had inaugurated in 1904.[41]

Observers noted that motorization and mechanization were applied, as well, to other aspects of the urban service: the policemen's motorcycles and their streetside telephones, as well as the increasingly elaborate fire-fighting equipment, which, as in earlier times, rarely failed to catch the traveler's eye. "Nowhere do firemen rush to and fro so much as here," wrote a French visitor of the later twenties. ". . . every few yards there is a fire-alarm or a fire hydrant as big as a siege-gun. The firemen arrive on the scene of the outbreak forty seconds after the alarm. Everything stops at the first piercing wail of their sirens and the accompanying clang of the bells, and the engines, beautiful as fire itself, go past with the swiftness of flames." Such mechanization led some commentators to regard New York as the heartless product of the Machine Age—the "steel-souled machine room" that Henry James described in 1904, or the "automatic city" (*la ciudad automática*) which the Spanish satirist Julio Camba called it in 1932. Viewing the lower city in 1906, H. G. Wells concluded that here "individuals count for nothing. . . . the distinctive effect is the mass, . . . the unprecedented multitudinousness of the thing." [42]

Few of the city's visitors commented upon the services that might reflect a municipal conscience, if not a soul, but those who did reported the current interest in building codes, sanitation, and public recreation which were inspired by the municipal progressivism of the early twentieth century. Annette Meakin, a British visitor of 1907, saw "places being cleared in the busiest parts of the city for 'playgrounds,' not . . . simply for open spaces where poor children could play between their school hours, but for regular club-houses, standing in their own grounds, with gymnasia and bathing-pools," such as were also being developed at the moment in Chicago. The decade of the thirties was to see much more spectacular developments along these lines.[43]

In the early years of the new century, the city's chroniclers still identified a "social hierarchy" which prided itself on being "the élite of the first city of America." But as the generation advanced, the torrent of population and prosperity submerged even the once much publicized social leaders of the gilded age. "There appear to be no great social names in New York nowadays in the sense that twenty years ago there were the Astor and Vanderbilt families and their rather tyrannous two or three hundred of supporters," wrote Ford Madox Ford after a visit in the mid-twenties. "There is a very gay, insouciant, and enormously expensive social life in New York, but relatively few names swim to the surface of its whirlpool and those that do are forever changing." In the increasing anonymity of the metropolis, Park Avenue apartments swallowed up the individual as surely as the teeming tenements of the lower East Side.[44]

New York was riding higher by the late twenties than ever before or since. Like the United States as a whole, her economic self-confidence was not as yet shaken by the crash of 1929 nor her sense of security unsettled by the sobering atomic aspects of World War II. In a generation which put a premium on bigness, her physical magnitude expressed the ultimate to observers for whom her soaring skyscrapers still came as a surprise; and her seemingly unlimited wealth bolstered an influence in the nation and the world that appeared to preclude a challenge. From the opening of the century, New York, more than any other city, seemed to be scaled to the potential of the New World and modern times; and the "exultant sense of power," noted early in the century, mounted, like her skyscrapers, to become an overwhelming confidence in titanic achievement as this dynamic generation closed. Even Mencken, for all his scorn for its distractions, its materialism, and its "frauds and scoundrels," admitted that New York was the place "where all the aspirations of the Western World" met to form "one vast master aspiration, as powerful as the suction of a steam dredge."

Some contemporaries were frightened, or even repelled, by the limitless "bigness" of this urban monster, but most of them were impressed in spite of themselves. They recognized in this "New Cosmopolis" the "colossal flower" of "America's colossal agricultural and industrial civilization," the symbol of "some new attitude of enterprise and audacity" that refused to be confined by the conventions of former times and an older world. Merciless, maybe, but vital and fascinating, it was "the magnum opus of modern material civilization," "the great image of towndom," "microcosm of the United States,"—"Metropolis, city of Giants."[45]

SYMBOL OF MATERIAL PROGRESS: NEW YORK, 1906

H. G. Wells saw in New York of the early twentieth century a foretaste of that world of a fantastic future about which he frequently wrote. The prolific British novelist was forty years old when he made the journey to the United States which resulted in the volume *The Future in America.* To the future author of *The Outline of History,* as to most visitors of the early twentieth century, New York was a somewhat frightening monument to material progress. He saw in it the still unfinished product of some mechanical, inhuman force which was driving society toward a more ideal world. Wells visited New York in the spring of 1906, and the resultant *The Future in America* was published late in that year. The following excerpt from it is reprinted with permission of Harper and Brothers (copyright, 1906, by Harper and Brothers; 1934, by Herbert George Wells).[46]

My first impressions of New York are enormously to enhance the effect of . . . material progress . . . as something inevitable and inhuman, as a blindly furious energy of growth that must go on. Against the broad and level gray contours of Liverpool one found the ocean liner portentously tall, but here one steams into the middle of a town that dwarfs the ocean liner. The sky-scrapers that are the New-Yorker's perpetual boast and pride rise up to greet one as one comes through the Narrows into the Upper Bay, stand out, in a clustering group of tall irregular crenellations, the strangest crown that ever a city wore. They have an effect of immense incompleteness; each one seems to await some needed terminal,—to be, by virtue of its woolly jets of steam, still as it were in process of eruption. . . . New York's achievement is a threatening promise, growth going on under a pressure that increases, and amidst a hungry uproar of effort. . . .

Noise and human hurry and a vastness of means and collective result, rather than any vastness of achievement, is the pervading quality of New York. The great thing is the mechanical thing, the unintentional thing which is speeding up all these people, driving them in headlong hurry this way and that. . . . Much more impressive than the sky-scrapers to my mind is the large Brooklyn suspension-bridge. . . . One sees parts of Cyclopean stone arches, one gets suggestive glimpses through the jungle growth of business now of the back, now of the flanks, of the monster; then, as one comes out on the river, one discovers far up in one's sky the long sweep of the bridge itself, foreshortened and with a maximum of perspective effect; the streams of pedestrians and the long line of carts and vans, quaintly microscopic against the blue, the creeping progress of the little cars on the lower edge of the long chain of netting; all these things dwindling indistinguishably before Brooklyn is reached. Thence, if it is late afternoon, one may walk back to City Hall Park and encounter and experience the convergent stream of clerks and workers making for the bridge, mark it grow denser and denser, until at last they come near choking even the broad approaches of the giant duct, until the congested multitudes jostle and fight for a way. They arrive marching afoot by every street in endless procession; crammed trolley-cars disgorge them; the Subway pours them out. . . . The individuals count for nothing, they are clerks and stenographers, shopmen, shop-girls, workers of innumerable types, black-coated men, hat-and-blouse girls, shabby and cheaply clad persons, such as one sees in London, in Berlin, anywhere. Perhaps they hurry more, perhaps they seem more eager. But the distinctive effect is the mass, the black torrent, rippled with unmeaning faces, the great, the unprecedented multitudinousness of the thing, the inhuman force of it all. . . .

I corrected that first crowded impression of New York with a clearer, brighter vision of expansiveness when next day I began to realize the social quality of New York's central backbone, between Fourth Avenue and Sixth. The effect remained still that of an immeasurably powerful forward movement of rapid eager advance, a process of enlargement and increment in every material sense, but it may be because I was no longer fatigued, was now a little initiated, the human being seemed less of a fly upon the wheels. . . . I became aware of effects that were not only vast and opulent but fine. It grew upon me that the Twentieth Century, which found New York brownstone of the color of desiccated chocolate, meant to leave it a city of white and colored marble. I found myself agape, admiring a skyscraper—the prow of the Flatiron Building, to be particular, ploughing up through the traffic of Broadway and Fifth Avenue in the afternoon light. . . . New York is lavish of light, it is lavish of everything, it is full of the sense of spending from an inexhaustible supply. For a time one is drawn irresistibly into the universal belief in that inexhaustible supply. . . .

One assumes . . . that all America is in this vein, and that this is the way the future must inevitably go. One has a vision of bright electrical subways, replacing the filth-diffusing railways of to-day, of clean, clear pavements free altogether from the fly-prolific filth of horses coming almost, as it were, of their own accord beneath the feet of a population that no longer expectorates at all; of grimy stone and peeling paint giving way everywhere to white marble and spotless surfaces, and a shining order, of everything wider, taller, cleaner, better. . . .

So that, in the meanwhile, a certain amount of jostling and hurry and untidiness, and even—to put it mildly—forcefulness may be forgiven.

WHAT IS A NEW YORKER? 1907

The bearing of immigration upon the personality of the New Yorker and of New York upon the personality of the newcomers, now arriving in unprecedented numbers, was a subject of interest to commentators in the first decade of the new century. In the opinion of Charles Whibley, English literary critic and journalist, New York was a "magic cauldron." Its effect upon the immigrant was to make a new type, not immediately devoid of old accents and habits but with a self-assurance and an air of patronizing familiarity which distinguished him from similar residents of the Old World. Whibley was a professional writer, a contributor to the *Pall Mall Gazette, Blackwood's Magazine,* and the *Daily Mail,* as well as the author of numerous books. He visited the United States in 1907, at a moment when immigration was reaching peak proportions. The following excerpt from his *American Sketches,* published in 1908, is reprinted by permission of William Blackwood and Sons, Limited.[47]

As America is less a country than a collection of countries, so New York is not a city—it is a collection of cities. Here, on the narrow rock which sustains the real metropolis of the United States, is room [f]or men and women of every faith and every race. The advertisements which glitter in the windows or are plastered upon the hoardings suggest that all nationalities meet with an equal and a flattering acceptance. The German regrets his fatherland the less when he finds a brilliant Bier-Halle waiting for his delight. The Scot no doubt finds the "domestic" cigar sweeter to his taste if a portrait of Robert Burns adorns the box from which he takes it. The Jew may be supposed to lose the sense of homesickness when he can read the news of every day in his familiar Yiddish. . . .

What, indeed, is a New Yorker? Is he Jew or Irish? Is he English or German? Is he Russian or Polish? He may be something of all these, and yet he is wholly none of them. Something has been added to him which he had not before. He is endowed with a briskness and an invention often alien to his blood. He is quicker in his movement, less trammelled in his judgment. Though he may lose wisdom in sharpening his wit, the change he undergoes is unmistakable. New York, indeed, resembles a magic cauldron. Those who are cast into it are born again. For a generation some vague trace of accent or habit must remain. The old characteristics must needs hang about the newly-arrived immigrant. But in a generation these characteristics are softened or disappear, and there is produced a type which seems remote from all its origins. As yet the process of amalgamation is incomplete, and it is impossible to say in what this hubble-shubble of mixed races will result. . . .

And by what traits do we recognise the citizen of New York? Of course there is no question here of the cultivated gentleman . . . but of the simpler class which confronts the traveller in street and train, in hotel and restaurant. The railway guard, the waiter, the cab-driver—these are the men upon whose care the comfort of the stranger depends in every land, and whose tact and temper are no bad index of the national character. In New York, then, you are met everywhere by a sort of urbane familiarity. The man who does you a service, for which you pay him, is neither civil nor uncivil. He contrives, in a way which is by no means unpleasant, to put himself on an equality with you. . . .

And familiarity is not the only trait which separates the plain man of New York from the plain man of London. The New Yorker looks upon the foreigner with the eye of patronage. To his superior intelligence the wandering stranger is a kind of natural, who should not be allowed to roam alone and at large. Before you have been long in the land you find yourself shepherded, and driven with an affability, not unmixed with contempt, into the right path. Again, you do not resent it, and yet are surprised at your own forbearance. A little thought, however, explains the assumed superiority. The citizen of New York has an ingenuous pride and pleasure in his own city and in his own prowess, which nothing can daunt. He is convinced, especially if he has never travelled beyond his own borders, that he engrosses the virtue and intelligence of the world. . . .

Thus you carry away from New York a memory of a lively air, gigantic buildings, incessant movement, sporadic elegance, and ingenuous patronage. And when you have separated your impressions, the most vivid and constant impression that remains is of a city where the means of life conquer life itself, whose citizens die hourly of the rage to live.

FIFTH AVENUE: 1911

In its proud elegance, Fifth Avenue connoted the growing magnificence of early twentieth-century New York. It fairly intoxicated Arnold Bennett with its vista of impressive cornices and other architectural reminders of Florence and the Italian Renaissance. By 1911, when

Bennett visited America, the publication of his *The Old Wives' Tale* and *Clayhanger* had already placed him in the top rank of contemporary British novelists. He was accorded a welcome in the United States unequaled by that given any English author since Dickens. The following excerpt is from *Your United States: Impressions of a First Visit,* the book that inevitably resulted from his trip. It is reprinted with the permission of "The Owners of the Copyright," of Doubleday and Company, and of A. P. Watt and Son.[48]

When I first looked at Fifth Avenue . . . I thought it was the proudest thoroughfare I had ever seen anywhere. The revisitation of certain European capitals has forced me to modify this judgment; but I still think that Fifth Avenue, if not unequaled, is unsurpassed. . . .

A lot of utterly mediocre architecture there is, of course—the same applies inevitably to every long street in every capital—but the general effect is homogeneous and fine, and, above all, grandly generous. . . .

And the glory of the thoroughfare inspires even those who only walk up and down it. It inspires particularly the mounted policeman as he reigns over a turbulent crossing. It inspires the women, and particularly the young women, as they pass in front of the windows, owning their contents in thought. . . . I have driven rapidly in a fast car, clinging to my hat and my hair against the New York wind, from one end of Fifth Avenue to the other, and what with the sunshine, and the flags wildly waving in the sunshine, and the blue sky and the cornices jutting into it and the roofs scraping it, and the large whiteness of the stores, and the invitation of the signs, and the display of the windows, and the swift sinuousness of the other cars, and the proud opposing processions of American subjects . . . I have been positively intoxicated!

And yet possibly the greatest moment in the life of Fifth Avenue is at dusk, when dusk falls at tea-time. The street lamps flicker into a steady, steely blue, and the windows of the hotels and restaurants throw a yellow radiance; all the shops—especially the jewelers' shops—become enchanted treasure-houses, whose interiors recede away behind their façades into infinity; and the endless files of innumerable vehicles, interlacing and swerving, put forth each a pair of glittering eyes. . . .

It is not easy for a visiting stranger in New York to get away from Fifth Avenue. The street seems to hold him fast. There might almost as well be no other avenues; and certainly the word "Fifth" has lost all its numerical significance in current usage. A youthful musical student, upon being asked how many symphonies Beethoven had composed, replied four, and obstinately stuck to it that Beethoven had only composed four. Called upon to enumerate the four, he answered thus, the C. minor, the Eroica, the Pastoral, and the Ninth. "Ninth" had lost its numerical significance for that student. A similar phenomenon of psychology has happened with the streets and avenues of New York. Europeans are apt to assume that to tack numbers instead of names on to the thoroughfares of a city is to impair their identities and individualities. Not a bit! The numbers grow into names. That is all. Such is the mysterious poetic force of the human mind. That curt word "Fifth" signifies as much to the New-Yorker as "Boulevard des Italiens" to the Parisian.

TRANSPORTATION AND TRAFFIC: 1913

The expanded facilities for getting about in the city, as well as the problem of traffic control, interested a German visitor who described New York after a visit in 1913. He was Ludwig Fulda, one of the trio of modern German dramatists which included Hauptmann and Sudermann. Fulda made two trips to the United States—one in 1913 and one, earlier, in 1906, when he came for a series of readings from his own works and to superintend rehearsals for his play *Masquerade*. He was much impressed with New York, which he regarded as "a symbol of the titanic strength and energy of Americanism." The following excerpt is from the 1914 edition of his impressions, his *Amerikanische eindrücke*. It is published with the permission of J. G. Cotta'sche Buchhandlung Nachfolger, Stuttgart.[49]

One could believe that giants had built this city for giants, and if you walk in lower Broadway among these monsters, you get the illusion of being in a deep mountain canyon. In this instance, however, the cliffs, which rise to such dizzy heights, have windows and doors, and in their interiors they have elevators which lift you as quick as lightning to the top. Sometimes more than a dozen of these elevators are in operation so that one might compare them with a vertical railroad system. There are "slow trains" which stop at every floor, and "express trains" which always skip some stations, and other fast trains which fly in a quarter of a minute from the basement to the roof. . . .

Among the praiseworthy marvels of New York, one must not overlook its transportation system. In its layout, this too appears to have been built by the hand of giants, and it surpasses that of all European cities. The subway, the electric underground which was opened hardly ten years ago, goes in four lanes from the southern to the northernmost part of the city. It travels beneath the two rivers which separate Manhattan from the mainland and from Long Island, and within a short time it will be continued up to the ocean's edge, without a rise in fare, although the distance is twice as long as that from Berlin to Potsdam. Two lanes serve the local and two the express trains. . . .

The tracks of the Pennsylvania Railroad go under the river, and the tracks of the New York Central under the streets. In spite of this, there is little noise and no smoke because the steam locomotion is replaced by electric power within the city limits. This is a better solution of the transportation problem than that of Berlin, where the city is cut up by the broad tracks of the Anhalter and Potsdam stations. New York has a much larger transportation system than Berlin, yet only these two beautiful stations suffice. Both have become a proud ornament of the city—marvelous, monumental buildings which do not suggest their function. They are proof of the awakened interest in combining beauty of form with utility of function; they are proof of the inevitable triumph of American architecture. This becomes evident in everything that has been built in recent years, the garden homes, simple as well as elaborate; the apartment houses, which are more and more in the majority in the residential sections; the numerous imposing hotels; and particularly the luxuriously ornamented public buildings, among which the new post office and particularly the library seem outstanding. Both use classic styles, yet they show an independent development toward modernistic art; both are impressive in their dimensions and in the quality of the material used.

On my second visit the better pavement and greater cleanliness of the streets were particularly striking and the improved traffic control in certain areas and at certain times. Now one who wishes to cross the street need not make his last will and testament because, as a result of a practice patterned after London and Berlin, a policeman directs the flow of traffic. This direction of the flow of pedestrians is made necessary because the automobile has won out over the horse and carriage and appears in numbers unbelievable to the European, even in his dreams.

NEW YORK DURING WORLD WAR I: NEUTRAL PHASE

The accounts of several British travelers mirror the impact of World War I upon the Empire City during the period of interested neutrality, the months of zealous participation, and the buoyant aftermath. A witness for the neutral period is William George Fitzgerald who from 1916 to 1938 was a prolific contributor to serious English periodicals, writing under the pen name of Ignatius Phayre. In the United States during 1916 and 1917, Fitzgerald found New York more sensitive to the drift of European affairs than other American cities. "Dramatic events of the war were calmly received elsewhere," he reported; "only New York was really excited in the early days, and crowded to the bulletin boards debating belligerent chances the whole night long." The following excerpts from his chronicle of the period, *America's Day,* suggest the economic reaction to the outbreak of war, the tensions resulting from the city's ethnic variety, and some of the relief activities of New Yorkers in the "Neutral Day." They are reprinted by permission of Dodd, Mead and Company.[50]

The outbreak of a world-war threw the United States into profound distress and gloom; it is curious to recall this fact in view of the roaring times that followed. The South was in despair, unable to sell its cotton. New York, for all its wealth and careless pride, was afraid it could not pay its debts, and therefore closed her Stock Exchange for four months. "In all previous panics," says the official chronicle of that institution, "the markets abroad were counted upon to come to the rescue and break the fall. Imports of gold, foreign loans and foreign buying were safeguards which prevented complete disaster. But now our market stood unaided. An unthinkable convulsion had seized the world. Our boasted bonds of civilization burst overnight and plunged us all into barbarism."

The savings banks fell back on a panic law, and would only pay deposits upon sixty days' notice. . . . How the scene changed in 1915 as [is] an industrial drama of historic interest! For three months the export of food-stuffs rose; and by April the first big order was placed for $83,000,000 worth of munitions of war. Thereafter the clouds lifted with dream-like swiftness until America had paid off a mortgage of five thousand million dollars, thanks to Europe's ravening needs. The export trade of 1916 was nearly $2,000,000,000 beyond that of 1915; the excess of exports over imports was ten times greater than in 1914. There are no records comparable with these in the whole story of American commerce. . . .

Money appeared to have lost its value. There were yellow-back tips (of $100) for the bowing *mâitre d'hôtel,* five dollars for the boy that "boosted" an overcoat and handed out a hat from the cloak-room. Two dollars was paid to enter a noisy cabaret; here one sat down exhausted to a supper-dish of eggs at one dollar a plate. Champagne poured freely as ice-water on a sultry night. The men who speculate in theatre tickets got fifty dollars for a stall. . . .

Quaint tales are told of spendthrift "stunts" that vied with one another, until folly fell exhausted for a space of new germination. There was the hostess who bought boxes for three plays, that her guests might choose according to their after-dinner mood. There was Mrs. So-and-So's ball with costly jewels for cotillion favours; the banquet with dancers on the table, and stocks and bonds folded in the serviettes as little gifts. There were ballets on the Long Island lawns brought *en masse* from the Metropolitan Opera, with Caruso himself to sing "Hail Columbia" at the close. . . . Today [late 1917] this riot is voted bad form. It is a crudity of jaded senses which the best people leave to the unsophisticated newly-rich who block Broadway at night with a tangle of sumptuous cars. . . .

The Clan-na-Gael orators cried "Death to England!" from a soap-box at the street corner. The Irish-American press preached open sedition; at a hyphenate meeting in New York, an officer of the Irish Volunteers struck a reporter with his sword because the man refused to rise when "Die Wacht am Rhein" was played by the orchestra.

All this faction was condemned; American common sense would have none of it. . . .

Mayor Mitchel of New York, himself the grandson of an outlawed Irish patriot—forbade anti-Ally speeches, and refused police protection to Jeremiah O'Leary and other firebrands of the Clan-na-Gael. Of course, mob fights ensued. An Irish captain of police gave an order to his Irish squad—and the New York streets beheld civil war of a new kind, with citizen "Vigilantes" aiding the forces of order against the Clan-na-Gael mob. . . .

War relief work in the neutral Day covered Europe from Brussels to Belgrade, and thence to Beirut and starving Palestine. Through the Federal Council of Churches the city appealed to 35,000,000

Americans, and through Cardinal Gibbons to America's 16,000,000 Catholics. It was New York, in short, that mobilized the impulsive generosity of the continent. There were In-aid-ofs of inexhaustible ingenuity; "chain-letters" crossed over to the Pacific, gathering millions of dollars as they went. You were bidden buy eyes for the blinded soldier, milk for the Armenian babe, clothing for Serbian refugees, an ambulance for the Somme; a soup-kitchen for Berlin, or Warsaw, or Paris.

At emotional meetings women gave the jewels from their necks and wrists. The illiterate immigrant threw twenty cents on the platform. Jacob Schiff handed up $100,000; the Rockefeller Foundation voted $1,000,000 for relief in Poland and the Balkans.

The Clearing House Wharf at the foot of Charlton Street showed how great was New York's anxiety to alleviate some of Europe's woe with some of her own prosperity. But the metropolis, like the rest of America, longed for peace, and the ceasing of a havoc too strange for transatlantic minds to grasp. "Yes," said the typical New Yorker at a naval review, "the *Pennsylvania's* a wonderful gun-platform; so is her sister, the *Arizona*. The new *Mississippi* will be greater still, I guess. But we'd rather have the *Mauretania* racing in once more for our Christmas mails. Can't you *see* her, man, sighted from Nantucket in the tail-end of a December blizzard? What a vision of power and utility in grey-white tones, shining with frozen spray! Her towering bows awash, cascades of water streaming from her scuppers, and four enormous funnels belching flame and smoke. A regular Pittsburg tumbling through our wintry bay. . . . Watch her back up the Ambrose Channel, her course lit with blazing buoys, her upper works higher than the roofs on the wharfs! Ah, my friend, that's the old-time social link—the giant shuttle of brotherhood between the Old World and the New! You may keep your destroyers, your *Revenges* and *Warspites* and *Iron Dukes*. Only send us the *Mauretania* again, and by God! we'll give her skipper such a welcome as Columbus never knew!"

NEW YORK DURING WORLD WAR I: PARTICIPATION

The crusading spirit in which New York, like most of America, entered World War I was observed by Frank Dilnot, prominent British foreign correspondent, who was in the United States during most of the period of America's participation. Dilnot arrived in January 1917, when brightly lighted Broadway contrasted sharply with bedimmed London, then threatened by German aircraft. By April, the New World had gone to the rescue of the Old, and New York was vibrant with wartime activity. The following excerpts from Dilnot's *The New America* depict the urban scene in the fall and winter of 1917–1918.[51]

. . . the American flag was mingled with the colours of Britain; the Union Jack on the one side and the Tricolour of France on the other were to be found in quarters where for generations the Union Jack was unknown—and if known was disliked. . . . It was hard to realize this in the autumn of 1917 as one surveyed Fifth Avenue a blaze of colour in which the Union Jack was prominent. The American temperament never displays its difference from the English more strikingly than in its fearlessness of its own feelings. There has been comparatively little bunting shown in Britain during the war. In America not only was the national flag freely displayed on every possible occasion and in many cases hung out continuously on buildings public and private, but a further display followed as the men began to be drafted. There was devised a white flag with a red border and on the white ground were placed blue stars indicating the number of men who had gone to service from the particular place which showed the flag. Private houses, shops, public institutions, clubs, all had these flags and a brave show they made. A variation and extension was in the enameled brooches and lapel pins indicating by their stars the number of those in service from the wearer's family. America went into the war sternly but with high heart, and with something of that chivalrous display which marked a cause in ancient days of knightly service.

War songs began to appear. They were direct and not oblique as in Britain where the soldiers adopted a music hall ditty like "Tipperary" which had no possible relevance to battle efforts. Nor did the people in America take readily to plaintive melodies like "Keep the Home Fires Burning," which replaced "Tipperary" as the favourite among British soldiers. The ardent nervous temperament required something direct, something with a lilt and a march and a ring about it. And thus the popular places of amusement rattled with such choruses as,

Over there, over there, send the word, send the word, over there,
That the Yanks are coming, the Yanks are coming,

The drums rum-tumming everywhere, . . .
We'll be over, we're coming over, and we won't come back till it's over over there.*

At the various times when a week or a fortnight was set aside for subscriptions either to Liberty Loan issues or the Red Cross Fund the great cities were in a ferment. . . . In New York at the start of one of the Liberty Loan campaigns cardboard representations of a bell—the Liberty Bell—were made by the million, and in the early hours of the first morning they were hung on door knobs not only of houses and shops and offices but on the doors of flats and apartments in hundreds of thousands of homes; crowds of enthusiastic boys were enlisted for the work. There were bands and banners at street corners from early morning till early the next morning. Impassioned speeches were made from the stage of every theatre, moving picture palace and every vaudeville show, and clever orators both men and women extracted competitive announcements from individuals in the audiences, pitting city against city, country against country, in the amount of subscriptions. Every office in New York, large or small, was invaded once, twice, or thrice in a week by a collector who might be a nurse in uniform, a boy scout, a sailor or a bank official; there was no escape for the stingy. At various busy points in the city a large coffin on trestles on the sidewalk, with nails resting on the lid, was forced on the attention of passing crowds by collectors, hammers in hand, who invited men and women to drive nails into "the Kaiser's coffin" at the price of a dollar. Sums amounting to millions of dollars for the Red Cross, and billions of dollars for the war loan were readily obtained. It was a wonder where the money came from.

When the Government put restrictions on the use of fuel and light during an exceptionally cold winter there was but little grumbling. And when the country was appealed to for voluntary food rationing so that the necessary supplies might be sent to the Allies there was a response which practically did away with the use of white bread, and put a sweet-loving nation to the test of the smallest lump of sugar in a cup of coffee.

In the streets . . . could be seen each evening couples and groups of British and French soldiers and sailors (principally sailors) enjoying themselves amid strange scenes and with hospitable hosts. I was

* Quotation from "Over There" by George M. Cohan—copyright, 1917; copyright renewal, 1945, Leo Feist Inc. Used by special permission of the Copyright Proprietor.

in one of the table-d'hôte restaurants in 49th Street crowded with diners when a couple of French blue-jackets, attracted by the French name on the sign outside, came in looking rather at a loss and perhaps a little shy. Directly the man at the piano and his companion with the violin saw them they struck up the Marseillaise. The whole of the crowded gathering rose to its feet and sang the chorus, while the French soldiers, staggered at this blast of welcome, were conducted to a table by the proprietor, and had set before them the best the establishment could provide at no cost to themselves. . . .

A spectacle never to be obliterated was the first parade down Fifth Avenue of thousands of soldiers on their way to the camps preparatory for France.

NEW YORK AND WORLD WAR I: SEQUEL

In the months following the Armistice, New Yorkers expressed the highhearted assurance that came with victory. To British visitors, predisposed to admire their new-found ally, the "colossal scale" of New York City and the magnitude of its "height, spirit, and emotion" typified the now recognized power and material prosperity of the United States. The writings of two British journalists, Sir Philip Gibbs and W. L. George, are characteristic of the Briton's admiration for America from the close of the war through the early twenties. Gibbs had distinguished himself as a war correspondent; he was to become a prolific novelist and commentator on the European scene. The following excerpt describing New York City in the era of homecoming is taken from his *People of Destiny,* a work that resulted from his lecture tour through the United States in 1919. It is reprinted by permission of the author and of Harper and Brothers.[52]

I had the luck to go to New York for the first time when the ordinary life of that City of Adventure . . . was intensified by the emotion of historic days. The war was over, and the warriors were coming home with the triumph of victory as the reward of courage. . . . The emotion of New York life was visible in its streets. The city itself, monstrous, yet dreamlike and mystical as one sees it first rising to fantastic shapes through the haze of dawn above the waters of the Hudson, seemed to be excited by its own historical significance. There was a vibration about it as sunlight splashed its gold upon the topmost stories of the skyscrapers . . . and flung back bars of shadow across the lower blocks. Banners were flying everywhere in the streets that go straight and long between those perpendicular cliffs of masonry, and the wind that comes blowing up the two rivers ruffled them. . . . In those decorations of New York I saw the imagination of a people conscious of their own power, and with a dramatic instinct able to impress the multitudes with the glory and splendor of their achievement. . . . When the men of the Twenty-seventh Division of New York came marching home down Fifth Avenue they passed through triumphal arches of white plaster that seemed solid enough to last for centuries, though they had grown high, like Jack's beanstalk, in a single night. . . .

The adventure of life in New York, always startling and exciting . . . was more stirring . . . because of this eddying influence of war's back-wash. The city was overcrowded with visitors from all parts of the United States who had come in to meet their home-coming soldiers. . . . This floating population of New York flowed into all the hotels and restaurants and theaters. Two new hotels—the Commodore and the Pennsylvania—were opened just before I came, and, with two thousand bedrooms each, had no room to spare, and did not reduce the population of the Plaza, Vanderbilt, Manhattan, Biltmore, or Ritz-Carlton.

Equally enthusiastic about the postwar city was W. L. George, an English journalist and novelist of some reputation who spent six months in the United States in 1920. George was prepared to like America before he arrived in the country, and he was not disappointed. He found "magnificence" to be the prevailing quality of the city and saw in New York "the microcosm of the new civilization of America." The following excerpt from his *Hail Columbia* is typical of the reaction of observers of the period who viewed the city as the startling product of "a land of Titans." It is reprinted through the kindness of the author's widow and of Coutts and Company, the Trustee of his estate.[53]

The colossal scale of New York naturally makes upon the stranger his first important impression. The American does not realize what a shock New York can be to a European who has never before seen a building higher than ten floors; the effect is bewildering. The monster hotel where the stranger makes his first acquaintance with America is itself a shock. I began in a hotel which seems to have two thousand bedrooms and to carry a rent roll of $20,000 a day. In other words, this is Brobdingnag, the land of the giants. Gigantic chaos, that is the first feeling I had in New York. Differences forced themselves upon me. I missed the public houses of England and the cafés of the Continent. (The soda cafés, where so few people sit down, did not seem to correspond.) Fifth Avenue, people so many, traffic so thick that one has to take one's turn at a crossing, that police control has become mechanical, beyond the power of man. Then one goes into a store; one wanders through endless departments, on endless floors, one goes through tunnels and never comes out by the same block as one went in. There is so much in the streets; everything hurries—motor cars, street cars, railway cars. In the restaurants endless vistas of napery and crystal extend away. One goes up Broadway at night to see the crowded colored signs of the movie shows and the theaters twinkle and eddy, inviting, clamorous, Babylonian! You see, all the great cities of the present and the past come into my mind and make my judgment fantastic. For New York is all the cities. It is the giant city grouped about its colossal forest of parallelepipeds of concrete and steel. One can't find one's way. The plan of the city is simple, but it is so large and hangs so heavily over you that you become dazed. . . . It is only little by little, as you grow used to this enormity, that you reach comfort in New York, that you look casually at the Equitable Building, and contemptuously at the little apartment houses of eight floors.

NEW YORK, CULTURAL CAPITAL: MID-TWENTIES

The increasing stature of New York as an intellectual center was recognized by writers who visited the city in the later twenties. In their opinion, the manner of its intellectuals suggested Paris rather than London, without the exclusiveness of artistic circles in the French capital. "New York confronts the incoming tides of art with a broad gesture of acceptance," wrote the English historian and essayist, Philip Guedalla, after visiting the city in 1927. "Symbolists from Prague, Ukrainian wood-sculptors, performers on unheard-of instruments from recently discovered countries, practitioners of every known and unknown variety of art, even historians from England—each and all are assured of welcome." Since about 1910, historic Greenwich Village had attracted a distinguishable colony of writers and artists, making it reminiscent of London's Chelsea or Paris's Montmartre; but travelers of the later twenties found that intellectual interest and activity in the city were by no means so narrowly localized. This aspect of the New York scene elicited comment from the sophisticate Ford Madox

Ford, prolific English author, who found New York in 1926 the only place outside Provence where everybody was "rich and gay." The following excerpt from his book *New York Is Not America* is reprinted with the kind permission of his widow, Mrs. Janice Biala Brustlein.[54]

New York differs from London in having a keener intellectual life; it differs from Paris in that intellectual circles are smaller. Perhaps the products of the intellect are less valued here by the bulk of the people than is the case in other cities—but New York is becoming more and more of an intellectual center as the days go on—and that adds enormously to the world. . . .

Any one accustomed to the artistic and thinking lives of other capitals can here feel himself perfectly at home—and perfectly normal. About the same views of the arts are held in Greenwich Village and in Chelsea and in drawing-rooms on Park Avenue as will be found in the corresponding districts in Paris. Probably on Riverside Drive—postulating for convenience that Riverside Drive is the rich-Jewish quarter—you will find more "advanced" views held than are held in average Parisian drawing-rooms—and you will find artistic or intellectual conversation anywhere in New York to be infinitely more advanced than in the most advanced attic-studios of London.

This intellectual vividness New York owes partly to the presence of an immense Jewish population, partly to the absence of a Governing Middle Class. . . . At any rate the only people I have found in New York—and I have not found them anywhere else at all—who really loved books with a real, passionate, yearning love that transcended their attention to all other terrestrial manifestations were Jews—and the only people who subsidized young writers during their early non-lucrative years. . . .

For a city to be an artistic—or any other—center there must be a social life for the artists or others and that social life must be of a kind to attract outsiders. Thus in New York you will find great numbers not only of resident practitioners of one or other of the arts but you will find attracted to her increasingly considerable numbers of foreigners like myself and in addition all the practitioners of the arts of other American cities which might legitimately expect to retain their artists for themselves. This is very marked indeed in the case of the art of letters.

It is strikingly the case with artistic as opposed to social life. . . . Of course in these matters I do not want to give myself the airs of one who dogmatizes or of a specialist. But I think that it may be accepted as a fairly safe generalization—as two fairly safe generalizations—that, firstly, New York is not the exclusive social capital of America that London is for England, Rome for Italy—or even Chicago for the Middle West. And then that New York *is* the artistic center of the Western Hemisphere. . . .

In any case the artistic life of New York is assimilating itself more and more to that of Paris—and I do not know that it does not carry the process of international fusion further than Paris allows it to be carried. The distinguished French that one begins to meet profusely on Fifth, or Park Avenues mingle with the natives, are welcomed and overwhelmed by the natives, in a way that never happens in the capital of France. There foreigners are kept rather severely at a distance—and the Middle-Westerner-become-New-Yorker goes to Paris rather to meet other Middle-Westerners-become-New-Yorkers than with any hope of meeting members of the Académie Française. . . .

New York will achieve its position—it has achieved the position it has—rather by in- than by exclusiveness, and it is good that there should be a place where all sorts of foreignesses—*all* sorts—should be united as it were in a common frame.

THE ROARING TWENTIES: NEW YORK, 1925–1929

The excitement—violence, even—of New York in the roaring twenties is sharply etched in a book-length account written by Paul Morand, French author and diplomat, who made four visits to the city between 1925 and 1929. Morand's diplomatic career took him successively to London, Rome, and Madrid; and he had his first view of New York City when he was en route to the Bangkok legation in 1925. He engaged in writing and lecturing at the close of the decade; but in 1932 he returned to the Ministry of Foreign Affairs where he was assigned to the official Tourist Bureau. His volume entitled *New York* gives a colorful yet penetrating picture of the urban scene in the later twenties. It reflects, as well, some of the more sensational sides of the city in this carefree era, as the following excerpt reveals. It is reprinted from the translation of Hamish Miles with the permission of William Heinemann, Limited.[55]

Open a book or newspaper of a few years ago and you will seek the term "speakeasy" in vain. It was born of Prohibition. The speakeasy (the name suggests a whispered password) is a clandestine refreshment-bar selling spirits or wine. They must be visited to understand present-day New York. . . . There are a few in the downtown streets, but they are mainly set up between Fortieth Street and Sixtieth Street; they are usually situated downstairs and are identifiable by the large number of empty cars standing at their doors. The door is closed, and is only opened after you have been scrutinized through a door-catch or a barred opening. At night an electric torch suddenly gleams through a pink silk curtain. There is a truly New York atmosphere of humbug in the whole thing. The interior is that of a criminal house; shutters are closed in full daylight, and one is caught in the smell of a cremation furnace, for the ventilation is defective and grills are prepared under the mantelpiece of the fireplace. Italians with a too familiar manner, or plump, blue pseudo-bullfighters, carrying bunches of monastic keys, guide you through the deserted rooms of the abandoned house. Facetious inscriptions grimace from the walls. There are a few very flushed diners. At one table some habitués are asleep, their heads sunk on their arms; behind a screen somebody is trying to restore a young woman who has had an attack of hysteria. . . . The food is almost always poor, the service deplorable; the staff regard you with the eyes of confederates and care not two pins about you. The Sauterne is a sort of glycerine; it has to go with a partridge brought from the refrigerator of a French vessel; the champagne would not be touched at a Vincennes wedding-party.

Yet the speakeasy pervades Manhattan with a fascinating atmosphere of mystery. If only one could drink water there! Some speakeasies are disguised behind florists' shops, or behind undertakers' coffins. I know one, right in Broadway, which is entered through an imitation telephone-box; it has excellent beer; appetizing sausages and Welsh rabbits are sizzling in chafing-dishes and are given to customers without extra charge; drunks are expelled through a side-door which seems to open out into the nether world, as in *Chicago Nights*. In the poorer quarters many former saloons for the ordinary people have secretly reopened. All these secret shrines are readily accessible, for there are, it is said, 20,000 speakeasies in New York, and it is unlikely that the police do not know them; I think myself that they are only forced to close down when they refuse to make themselves pleasant to persons in authority, or when they sell too much poison. . . . The speakeasy is very popular in all classes of society; women go there gladly, even a few young girls. . . .

An intelligent lady remarked to me once that Prohibition was very pleasant. "Before it," she said, "no decent woman could go into a bar, but now nobody is surprised at our being there." . . .

A town of contrasts, puritan and libertine; the two-sided picture of a well-policed America and a savage continent, of East and West; a few yards from the luxury of Fifth Avenue and one is in battered and dirty Eighth Avenue. New York is the symbol of America, and half of its population is foreign; it is a center of Anglo-Saxon culture, speaking Yiddish; . . . after making you rich in a week, it ruins you in one morning. . . .

New York's supreme beauty, its truly unique quality, is its violence. Violence gives it nobility, excuses it, makes its vulgarity forgettable. For New York is vulgar; it is stronger, richer, newer than anything you like, but it is common. . . .

People are always moving. . . . The only permanent addresses are those of banks. People change jobs as they change houses. The town is no less changing. One builds for thirty years; those buildings have no past and no future either. Some districts alter their appearance in one season. . . .

Night is abolished. . . . We have seen restaurants full at dawn—with people who will be at work four hours later. New York is a town that never halts, never slacks off. Subways and street-cars run up and down all night long, twenty-four hours a day. . . .

Everything goes fast. . . .

New York is a perpetual thunderstorm.

NEW YORK—"MODERNOPOLIS": LATE TWENTIES

To the French historian Bernard Faÿ, New York of the late 1920's, more than any other city, was scaled to modern times. Faÿ was a frequent visitor to the United States, where he is best known for his studies of Benjamin Franklin and his age. In *The American Experiment,* he turned his scholarly eye upon contemporary America at a time when the United States was the object of growing hostility in many parts of Europe and attempted to explain the phenomenon of New York City by placing it in the context of developments in the United States in recent times. The following excerpt is from *The American Experiment* by Bernard Faÿ in collaboration with Avery

Claflin, copyright, 1929, by Harcourt, Brace and Company, Incorporated. It is reprinted by permission of the publishers.[56]

New York dominates. Thanks to it I have been able to understand Rome, which previously seemed a vain illusion of archaeological dreamers, and whose ruins appeared like shabby traitors to its past. New York, like every great metropolis, overwhelms us with its incongruous magnificence, its power and voluptuousness. Buildings fifty stories high, covered with marble. . . . Straight lines everywhere, horizontal and vertical, which affirm the will to . . . act directly, to make room for millions of people. . . . New York is . . . a city of rectangles, harsh and brilliant, the center of an intense life which it sends out in all directions. Buildings lift it towards the sky and radios broadcast it; monumental railway stations launch it forth along their trunk lines into the interior; docks and wharves direct it towards distant regions to which the great ships anchored in the Hudson will carry it. New York is wretched and opulent, with its countless tiny brick houses squatting beneath the marble palaces which house banks and industrial offices. But New York is the only city in the world rich enough in money, vitality, and men to build itself anew in the last twenty years, the only city sufficiently wealthy to be modern. . . . One is stunned at the sight of these upright masses. . . . Some say that . . . these buildings . . . are out of proportion. By European standards this may appear exact, but not when measured by America. New York is constructed to the scale of the United States, as Athens was built for the Greek Republic, and Paris for the Kingdom of France. The very thing which I admire most in New York is its adaptation to the continent. In this sense, its architecture is intellectually reasonable, logical, and beautiful. Skyscrapers are the dwellings of the supertrusts; they are Eiffel Tower cathedrals which shelter Mr. Rockefeller, the Emperor of Petroleum, or Mr. Morgan, the Czar of Gold. . . .

Some say that New York crushes them—and not without reason; the individual is overwhelmed by these great buildings. This is not an architecture for men, like the Parthenon or the châteaux of the Loire and Versailles. It is an architecture for human masses. Such buildings do not shelter or isolate men as do those of Europe. They gather and shuffle them. Often more than five thousand persons are united under one roof. The Woolworth Building, over one-eighth of a mile high, and the Equitable, whose estimated value is over $30,-

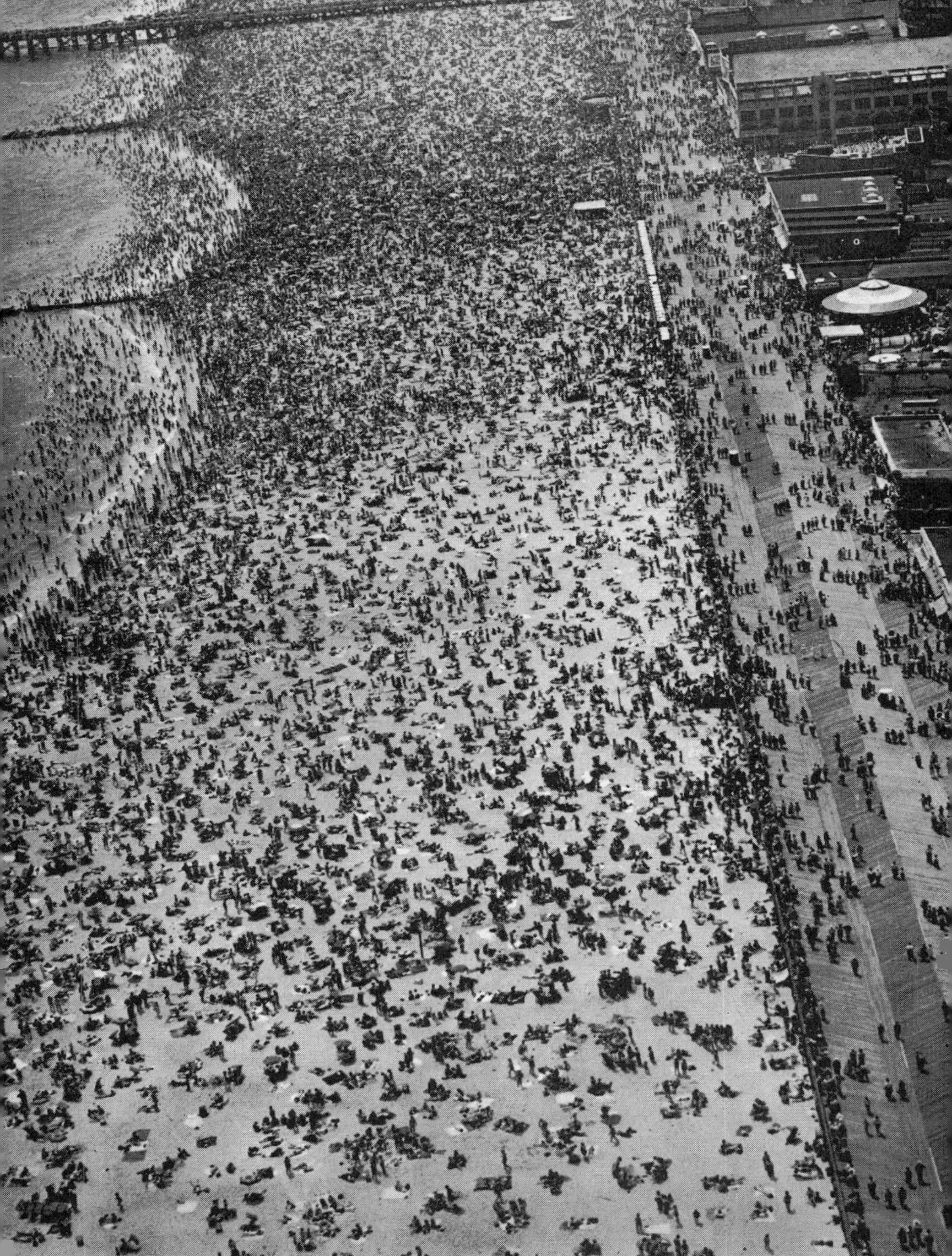

Courtesy of *The News,* New York's Picture Newspaper

CONEY ISLAND: MID-TWENTIETH CENTURY

"The world's largest playground" for "the world's largest city." Serving as the "lungs" of New York since the 1830's, Coney Island's recreational facilities expanded with the city. Now nearly a million pleasure seekers throng its six miles of beach and boardwalk and enjoy its hot dogs, roller coasters, and shooting galleries on a summer Sunday.

Fairchild Aerial Surveys, Inc.

THE HEART OF THE METROPOLIS

This aerial photo reveals the architectural topography of Manhattan—the heart of the twentieth-century metropolis. At the southern tip of the island, canyons of skyscrapers dedicated to big business and high finance monopolize the site of the original village. The spires of the midtown area just south of the open rectangle of Central Park identify the point to which the fashionable shopping, entertainment, and residential section had advanced by the mid-twentieth century. The fringe of piers jutting into the Hudson River on the left are the American berths of the world's largest ocean liners; and on the eastern rim of the island may be seen clusters of modern housing developments, replacing former slum areas along the East River front. The Jersey shore, at the upper left, connected with Manhattan by the George Washington Bridge, represents part of the wider New York–northeastern New Jersey metropolitan area, which at the mid-century numbered nearly 13,000,000 people. Across the Harlem River to the north is the Bronx and to the right are portions of Queens and Brooklyn, tied to Manhattan, as one looks southward, by the Triborough, Queensborough, Williamsburg, Manhattan, and Brooklyn bridges. By 1954, the population of the five boroughs of New York City (Manhattan, the Bronx, Brooklyn, Queens, and Richmond, on Staten Island) totaled 8,000,000 people.

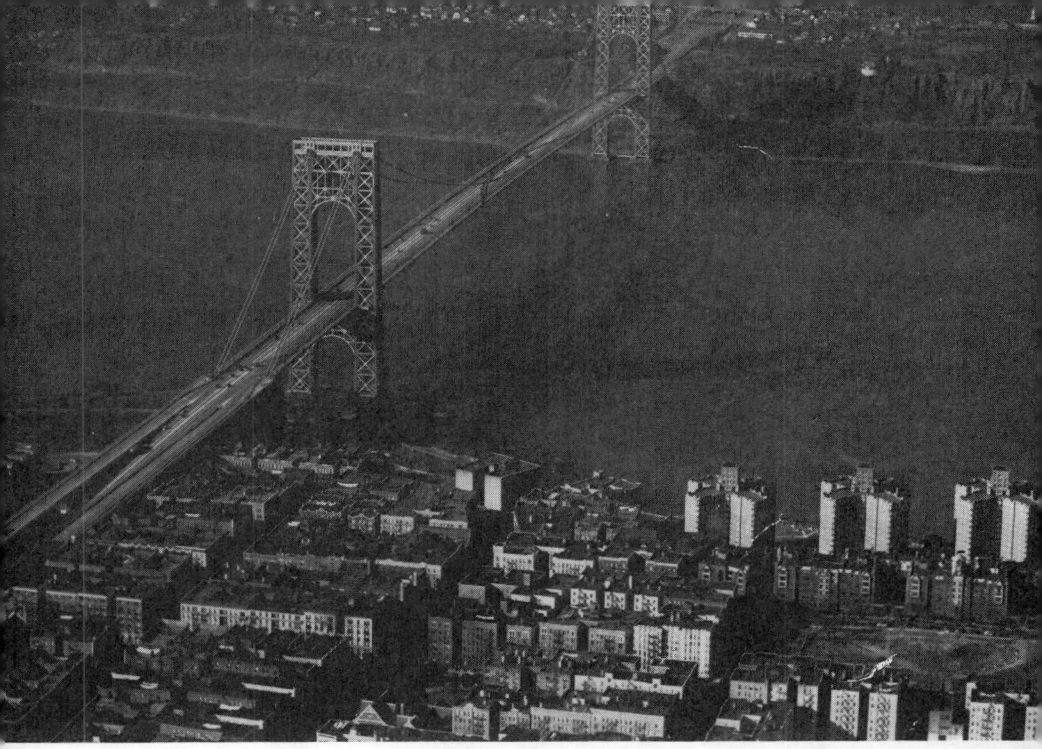

THE PULL OF SUBURBIA

Improved roads and bridges, a shortened working day and week, the dispersion of entertainment facilities by way of movies, radio, and television, and the existence of higher income levels—all combined to strengthen the appeal of suburban living for "daytime" New Yorkers in the middle years of the twentieth century. The flight to the suburbs, and especially to northeastern New Jersey, was encouraged by the completion of the George Washington Bridge, in October of 1931. It was built under the auspices of the Port of New York Authority. The engineer was O. H. Ammann; the architect, Cass Gilbert, who designed the Woolworth Building. Above, the swooping cables and tapering verticals of its 3,500-foot main span cast their shadow on the surface of the Hudson River between 178th Street in Manhattan and Fort Lee, New Jersey. The naked steel grillwork of its towers proved to be so striking in appearance that their intended masonry covering was omitted. Below is a view of heavy traffic on the Jersey side of the bridge—some of the 200,811,678 vehicles that used its eight traffic lanes in the first twenty years of its operation.

Both pictures courtesy of Standard Oil Co. (N. J.)

URBAN SERVICES: TWENTIETH-CENTURY STYLE

Two of "New York's finest" about to take off in a police helicopter—a service introduced in 1949 for aerial patrol at points inaccessible to radio cars. New York's police force numbered more than 19,000 in 1950.

Mayor Fiorello La Guardia on the job with Fire Commissioner McElligott. New York's ubiquitous fire fighters numbered more than 10,000 by 1950. Unlike the unpaid volunteers of a century earlier, a fireman first grade in 1950 received $4,150 annual pay.

Below, the Navy in a rural retreat. The Bronx Zoo and gardens typify the many recreational facilities at least partially subsidized by the municipal government in the twentieth century.

Picture Credits:
(*top*) Courtesy of *The News*, New York's Picture Newspaper
(*center*) Courtesy of *The News*, New York's Picture Newspaper
(*bottom*) Courtesy of Standard Oil Co. (N. J.)

000,000, are worthy of the land where senators are elected by 500,000 voters, a governor by several millions, and where the president can unite 16,000,000 citizens on election day. The New York skyscrapers are the most striking manifestation of the triumph of numbers. One cannot understand or like them without first having tasted and enjoyed the thrill of counting or adding up enormous totals and of living in a gigantic, compact, and brilliant world.

10. *THE MATURING METROPOLIS: WORLD CAPITAL*

THERE IS AN ELEMENT of anticlimax in contemporary descriptions of New York City in the sober and unsettling years between 1930 and 1950. The effects of depression and war reduced both the physical glamor and the prestige and self-confidence of the glittering giant of the twenties. Only at the mid-century, when an economic upswing prompted large-scale new construction, and the location of the United Nations in the metropolis underlined New York's position as a world capital, did the city's dynamism exert again its customary spell.[1]

The impact of the depression engrossed the attention of commentators of the thirties, especially between 1931 and 1935. Queues of unemployed; men, obviously of good background, selling apples at the street corners; the destitute sleeping in Central Park—sights such as these convinced European visitors that reputedly invincible New York had been harder hit by the crisis than many parts of Europe. They noted the seeming paralysis at the wharves, the stores for rent and sales at broad reductions, the half-empty skyscrapers—"tombstones of capitalism . . . with windows," as one observer wrote, referring to the R.C.A. Building which was rising skyward in the thirties. On a Saturday night in 1931, a French visitor counted less than 300 spectators at the Roxy theatre, where "a year ago . . . it was necessary to stand in line an hour" for one of its 3,000 seats.[2]

New York's reaction to the depression, as observed by contemporaries, revealed the city, as always, to be a "sounding board for extremes." In some quarters optimism died hard; for many New Yorkers could not believe that "the age of gold" was past. On the other hand, numerous young intellectuals were "going over to Communism," responsible English observers reported. Books on radical subjects were prominently displayed, "even on Fifth Avenue"; and visitors listened to talk of proletarian revolution at Union Square. In Ivan Kashkin's *New York,* an anthology of vignettes depicting the sordid side of Manhattan published in Moscow in 1933, the

Empire City was called "the stronghold of both capitalism and Communism in America. . . . the center from which the American workers are being rallied to defend their proletarian fatherland." At the other extreme, Wall Street brokers—in an "unhappy and unchastened mood"—were heard contending that the New Deal was a dangerous experiment for which they would have to pay the bill. In the opinion of M. Philips Price, veteran British correspondent and member of Parliament, Franklin D. Roosevelt's program was unpopular with both the "revolutionaries" and the "reactionaries" in the city; but the average New Yorker was "prepared to give the President a chance for the next year or two." [3]

Conditions had improved by the mid-thirties, to judge from the comment of J. B. Priestley, who came to the city in September 1935 to supervise the production of a play. The bread lines and apple-sellers had disappeared, famous dance bands had returned to the supper clubs, and new shows were opening. Vera Brittain, revisiting New York late in 1937, missed "the atmosphere of stringency and strain" which had overwhelmed the visitor in 1934. In its place was "a consciousness of sufficiency without ostentation," which she considered closer to "sane normality" than the "boastful affluence" of the middle twenties. The demands of World War II, which began to be felt by the close of the thirties, erased most of the unemployment that had plagued New York in the depression decade.[4]

The city had fewer advocates in the depressed thirties than at any other time in its often criticized career. As if emboldened by its momentary defenselessness, English visitors called it hard, ugly, vulgar, and blatant—an "iridescent harlot of the nations," as the critic John Cowper Powys put it, with her "dazzling tiara" and "trailing, unwashed skirts." For J. B. Priestley, all the frustrations of life were magnified amid "so much steel and concrete and gasoline vapour." A New Zealand visitor of 1938 found New Yorkers, in the mass, "only a shade less impersonal than the automatic traffic lights"; and to L. P. Jacks, Oxford professor and Unitarian clergyman, this characteristic of the city made everybody "a nonentity to everybody else" and brought "all men down to the zero level of value." The French writer, Odette Keun, was repelled by the griminess of the elevateds, the filth of the subways, and the cheap commercialism of Broadway. New York was an "excruciating city" to two Soviet visitors in 1935, with its "bad food," "smelly streets," and "hellish, screeching" traffic. In the opinion of the expatriate writer Henry Miller, even the "progressive" features of this "most horrible place on God's earth" helped to make life in America a loathsome "air-conditioned nightmare." So common was criticism of the city that Sinclair Lewis concluded in 1938 that "it would be as iconoclastic to praise New York as to damn the Y.M.C.A." [5]

With the outbreak of World War II, commentators found additional grounds for taking the Empire City to task. Correspondents and propagandists from the democracies were struck by the contrast between the blacked-out cities of Europe and the "luminous . . . gaiety" of New York. "No shadow of war was here," wrote the British author and playwright Cecil Roberts, who came to the United States as a "self-appointed propaganda agent" in October of 1939. "Here in this bright new world the darkness of the old world seemed the symptom of a disease that could not attack so young and healthy a continent as America. I sensed an impatience with the bellicosity of Europe." In the opinion of the Polish novelist Maurice Dekobra, correspondent for a Paris newspaper, the war, to New Yorkers, was "a drama played by other people, a far-off film whose sounds do not even reach their ears." Only the foreign refugees, now flocking to New York by every subterfuge, appeared to sense the danger. "You see the first stages of the German conquest before your eyes," Dekobra reported a Viennese migrant of 1935 as saying. "First, we Austrians, victims of the *Anschluss*. Then this Czech girl, second victim. Then this Pole, third victim. Whose turn next?" [6]

The exceeding variety of New York's cosmopolitanism complicated its reaction to events in Europe, even though visitors found the United States and especially its largest city "not . . . as truly neutral" in 1939 as when war broke out in 1914. André Maurois, revisiting New York in April 1939, heard its older society debating the merits of "isolationism" versus "interventionism." Its newer residents exhibited more subtle shades of opinion, according to his compatriot Pierre de Lanux, former director of the Paris office of the League of Nations, who arrived in New York in February 1940 to lecture on behalf of the democratic cause. At the extreme of isolationism, there were Nazis, "numerous in Yorkville"; fascists, "distributed in various organizations more or less camouflaged under patriotic titles"; business interests tied to Germany; many Irishmen, unwilling to support Great Britain; and, finally, the Communists, under orders to oppose participation in wars of the "imperialist nations." More numerous were the many New Yorkers of neutral sentiment, though potentially favorable to the nation's former allies, who feared that aid to the democracies would again take the United States down the road to war. Most militantly interventionist were "the majority of Jews, the Czechs, the Spanish Republicans, and the other actual victims of Nazism." In addition, many artists, writers, professors, and actors were observed to be supporting the interventionist point of view.[7]

The primary concern of the agents of the democracies was to recruit "partisans" who would press Congress for action favorable to the antifascist cause. They were aided, according to de Lanux, by the columnists in such papers as the New York *Times*, the *Herald Tribune*, and the *Post*, who succeeded in awakening many New Yorkers to the urgency of the crisis, despite the counteracting influence of "the Hearst press, always anti-British because of its Irish and German clientele," and certain tabloids "more or less demagogical in tone." They counted on the hope that once New York was awakened, the nation would follow suit, for in their opinion the Empire City, through its radio commentators and syndicated columnists, was in the habit of "enlightening" the country, "stimulating it, and pushing it along." With the assault on Pearl Harbor, most of the "propagandist visitors" appeared to realize that their work was done. "Isolationism, the sense of hemispherical security," had "been blown out of America in a few hours," wrote W. G. Brown, who as General Secretary of the Civil Service Clerical Association had come to America to acquaint American civil servants with the British war effort. New York's reaction to the events of December 7, 1941, reminded him of Britain's earlier response. He saw "no excitement, no jubilation, no flag-waving, no cheers—only the same sort of grim acceptance of inevitability as one saw in England in 1939 when the war came to us." [8]

Wartime New York City, was, however, to be a far more carefree place than London or Paris, as commentators from areas closer to the war effort neglected no opportunity to show. To be sure, there was for a time a dim-out, ordered not so much through fear of bombs as because the glow of the city's lights silhouetted shipping for enemy U-boats lurking out at sea. In this halfway measure, the streets were still lighted, a British visitor of 1942 reported; but the "glaring advertisements" which formerly kept Broadway "in perpetual light" were now extinguished, and "all windows above the 10th floor . . . screened." New Yorkers gained some sense of participation in the struggle as air-raid precautions, inaugurated six months before Pearl Harbor, were "practiced and more or less perfected," sirens were tested, and wardens and plane spotters began to stand watch on tall buildings and rural hilltops. Women took over tasks formerly performed by men—driving cabs, operating elevators, and serving as telegraph messengers—when Selective Service pulled nearly 900,000 New Yorkers into uniform. The rationing of food and gasoline prompted the most obvious sacrifices, at least for those to whom the black market was not available. But for New Yorkers without close friends or relatives overseas, the sight of servicemen on leave and of the cargo vessels and tankers, "lined up on the Hudson and East River, with their camouflage and artillery, awaiting the formation of convoys," constituted the closest contact with the shooting war.[9]

To the casual observer, New York seemed hardly touched by the conflict. The British novelist James L. Hodson saw no sign of a dim-out in the winter and spring of 1943–1944; and the naïveté of the air-raid instructions he found in his hotel bedroom showed him "how far" New York really was "from the war." At Christmas time the city was gay with holiday decorations. Cocktail parties preceded dinners boasting menus "astounding to British eyes." The season was described as "the craziest Christmas for spending" ever known. "There is no war here," Carlos Romulo contended, in amazement, when he reached New York shortly after the fall of the Philippines. He was horrified at what appeared to be the "holiday air of the people," rushing madly about—in a "Coney-Island" dim-out—"spending fabulous sums as if they were in the midst of a carnival." [10]

Only after he had observed the city more closely did the Philippine statesman realize that New York, too, was fighting the war—giving blood, buying bonds, and, above all, moving men and goods in a degree that contributed significantly to victory. The city's surface frivolity, he ultimately concluded, was in part, at least, a reflection of the way that New York showed its fighting spirit. It was a consequence, too, as other commentators were aware, of the very nature of New York's most important wartime contribution—the production and movement of goods essential to the war effort. As production expanded and shipping throve, wages increased, and New Yorkers had more to spend than ever before. At the same time, fewer necessities were available for purchase as a result of wartime restrictions. Hence an unprecedented portion of the worker's income was at hand for spending at theatres, movie houses, race tracks, restaurants, and bars. It was this, in the opinion of Pierre de Lanux, which caused the erroneous impression that "what was happening overseas had no repercussion on life in the United States" and gave service personnel returning from combat the generally unjustified feeling that New Yorkers were blind to the realities of the conflict.[11]

De Lanux is the authority, too, for New York's reaction to the victory when it came in 1945. Despite the scarcity of paper, ticker tape rained on Broadway following news of the German armistice in May; and with the defeat of Japan, in August, the sobering implications of Hiroshima did not prevent New Yorkers from staging a real celebration. "From the dignified flag-bedecked residences, uptown, to the gaudily decorated tenements of the East Side and 'Little Italy,' the national colors floated amid clouds of confetti, cheering cries, the honking of horns, and the wail of sirens," the French chronicler reported. The churches were filled in the morning; then a general rejoicing took possession of the entire city, which reached a climax by evening. At Times Square, the crowds were so dense that the police had difficulty intervening when soldiers and sailors, sharing their joy with the civilians, "embraced and mussed up some of them" in the bargain. "Statisticians will never say exactly how much alcoholic beverage passed from production to consumption that night," de Lanux asserted, "but the figure would certainly be expressed in tons rather than liters." [12]

Like the commentators of earlier days, those of the thirties and forties recognized the role of the port in the city's economy, especially in connection with the nation's colossal war operation; but increasingly their attention turned to the magnitude of the city's industrial output, as well. Referring to New York of the mid-forties as "the greatest manufacturing town on earth," John Gunther pointed out, in his *Inside U. S. A.,* that Manhattan alone employed "more wage earners than Detroit and Cleveland put together," Brooklyn more than Boston and Baltimore, and Queens more than Washington and Pittsburgh, combined. More persons were engaged in New York's garment trades than made automobiles in Detroit or steel in Pittsburgh, according to a similar comment in the New York *Times.*[13]

Yet for all their recognition of New York's industrial might, in this as in other aspects of the urban scene the commentators of the generation found cause for reservations. In the opinion of the American journalist Richard Rovere, the war, like the depression, was hastening New York's "relative (if not absolute) decline." War orders were stimulating the growth of manufacturing in cities better suited to heavy industry, he wrote in 1944. The development of new trade routes was threatening the city's pre-eminence in shipping, and the competition of the federal government and of local banks in other parts of the country was challenging its financial supremacy. In the context of these apprehensions, the French philosopher Jean-Paul Sartre, writing of Manhattan in 1945, viewed New York's skyscrapers as the "ruins" of an era now gone—when optimism suffused the American mind. Even at the mid-century, when the value of the commercial and industrial activity in the area equaled, if not exceeded, that of 1929, the insecurities of an atomic age still prompted an unprecedented concern as to the economic future of New York City. To the American essayist E. B. White, the subtlest change in New York of the late forties was "something people don't speak much about, but that is in everyone's mind. The city, for the first time in its long history, is destructible." [14]

Population figures tended to support the idea that the Empire City was on the decline. During the thirties, the central city added little more than half a million people, by contrast with the increase of one and a third million during the flourishing twenties. During the forties the increase dropped to less than 437,000. To be sure, the metropolitan district of which New York was the core swelled from less than eleven to nearly thirteen million people in the years from 1930 to 1950; but the flight to the suburbs appeared in a sense to be a repudiation of life in the older city. Nor were there as many newcomers from overseas, as formerly, to take the place of those who were moving to the suburban fringe. Federal restrictions on immigration, in effect by the thirties, helped to reduce the number of foreign-born in the population—from two and a quarter million in 1930 to hardly a million and three quarters, twenty years later.

The curtailment of foreign immigration did not prevent New York from remaining what, in the opinion of contemporary observers, the migrants of the preceding generation had helped to make it—"the first Jewish city in the world, the second Italian, the third German," as well as "the capital of Ireland." As Douglas Reed, subeditor of the London *Times,* described it, after a visit in 1949, it was "New Minsk, New Pinsk, or even New Naples," but "distinctly not New *York* or New *Amsterdam.*" To his compatriot Priestley, the city in the later forties appeared to be more "foreign" than it had before World War II, an impression which undoubtedly was fostered by the marked increase in the city's Negro population, the relatively recent influx of Puerto Ricans, and the presence of war refugees and persons associated with the United Nations.[15]

The Negro ingredient of the city's population attracted more attention from commentators in the second quarter of the century than at any time since the 1830's. This was in part a consequence of the spectacular increase in Negro residents—from hardly more than 150,000 in 1920 to almost 750,000 by 1950. At this date, more than a million Negroes dwelt in the New York-Northeastern New Jersey metropolitan area. Observers found Harlem, the best-known of the Negro sections, to be "a city within a city," with its professional men, small shopkeepers, and café society, as well as an often squalid dormitory for the large number of Negroes who worked elsewhere in the city. Harlem's night clubs, shabbier than some visitors of the 1940's had expected, no longer appealed to New York's socialites as much as they had in the sensation-seeking twenties; but visitors still found the Savoy Ballroom—palace of "swing"—one of the few places on the continent where dancing appeared to be "the expression of primitive joy." Though still localized, generally, in their residence throughout the city, Negroes were by the thirties and forties a pervasive element in the New York scene; and contemporary comment reflects the very considerable degree of opportunity for Negroes as well as harmony among the races that prevailed in the mid-century metropolis.[16]

The observers of these years testify indirectly to the existence of a readier adjustment and more harmony and mutual respect among the city's ethnic and racial groups, generally, than had been the case earlier in the century. Some refer to nationality tensions generated in Europe; but their writings, especially in the forties, rarely reflect the distrust of and antagonism toward the foreign-born which made the comments of visitors at the turn of the century an echo of local antipathy toward the "new" immigration. Paul Crowell and A. H. Raskin, staff writers on the New York *Times,* asserted in the late forties that racial tension was more readily resolved in New York than in most American cities. They cited Mayor La Guardia's contention that "here, as nowhere else in the world, . . . the people of all races, religions, creeds, and color can live as neighbors and contribute the finest in their cultures to the composite culture of the city." European visitors marveled at the multiplicity of foreign-language newspapers and of mosques, synagogues, and churches, as well as at other signs of the ethnic diversity of the community. Here, as J. B. Priestley wrote in 1949, one could "dine, drink, and amuse oneself on three continents." Yet in these, as in the parades they witnessed on Fifth Avenue, they sensed a pride in nationality origins that in no way suggested disloyalty to the adopted land.[17]

"As each nationality tries to preserve the customs of its fatherland, some kind of parade or procession occurs nearly every day," wrote Chiang Yee, Chinese artist and author, after revisiting New York in 1946. Three such events especially impressed the Oriental visitor—the Holy Name Parade, "led by dark-faced gentlemen in shining silk toppers," a procession of 300 Chinese-Americans, in military uniform, celebrating the formation of the first Chinese post of the American Legion in the East, and the traditional St. Patrick's Day Parade, which, in his opinion, "surpassed all the others." Early in the century, it was claimed that the recent migrants remained aloof in their nationality ghettos; but by the late thirties, in Cecil Beaton's opinion, at least, the "intrinsic personality" of New York was such that even in sections where foreign tongues alone were spoken the residents had become "impregnated by the national character" and way of life. The city fascinated Johannes V. Jensen as an "anthropological laboratory," in which, according to the Danish travel writer, there was already being developed a "new human type." Every language was spoken, he wrote in the later thirties, "but over them all, the American."[18]

Few observers of the period commented upon the one relatively new nationality group that was added in considerable numbers to the New York community in the decade of the forties. These were the Puerto Ricans, of whom there were probably as many as 325,000 in the city by 1950. The demand for workers during World War II, together with marked reductions in the time and cost of air travel, accelerated the movement of these American territorials to New York. Commentators who did take account of this migration were appalled at the squalor in which the newcomers lived—conditions that recalled the lot of the Irish migrants in the period preceding the Civil War and of those from southern and eastern Europe at the turn of the twentieth century.[19]

New York's soaring skyline—"chiseled out of the megalith," to quote an awe-struck New Zealander—continued to impress commentators of the thirties and forties as it had those of the pre-depression era. Rearing up out of the lonely Atlantic, the clumps of lofty structures reminded China's admiring "Silent Traveller" of the mountain peaks in a Chinese painting; and at night, suffused with a "weird, bluish" glow, they became, for a Japanese visitor, "a million matchbox-like cubes of phosphorescent light." Travelers of the thirties noted that the Woolworth Building was already the "symbol of a past age" as more chaste structures like the R.C.A. Building thrust their "mystical purity" into the clouds. The "vertical city" was "under the sign of the new times," in the opinion of the architect Le Corbusier, who ultimately was to influence the design of the United Nations buildings in New York. The combination of stone, steel, and glass, rising a thousand feet into a magnificently blue sky, impressed the distinguished Franco-Swiss visitor as "a new event in human history which up to now had only a legend on that theme: that of the Tower of Babel." [20]

In the appearance of the "vertical city" commentators nevertheless found much to criticize, as was their custom in these uncertain years. Most of the skyscrapers were a "catastrophe" to Le Corbusier because they lacked surrounding open space. Their ornate decoration frequently prompted disparaging references to "Bagdad-on-the-Subway," or to "Nineveh and Babylon piled on Imperial Rome." Some commentators found a quality "definitely hostile" in architecture that "strait-jacketed" human beings in airless chasms and forced them to work and live, "one batch over another, like birds on the rung of a ladder." Odette Keun confessed that her first impulse was to "punch a hole in every damned high building in every damned narrow street" to "let in the space, light and sky." [21]

The tawdriness of Broadway by day now came in for as much attention as its neon-lit scintillation by night. "Broadway is a lady of the evening," wrote C. V. R. Thompson, who arrived in the city in 1933 as the American representative of the London *Daily Express*. "In the sunlight she looks like a suddenly awakened chorus girl who went to bed with her make-up on. Her buildings, covered with the unlighted framework of a thousand electric signs, look like a set-piece of fireworks after the fireworks have gone off. Her shops are tawdry. . . . There is cheapness and vulgarity everywhere, all masquerading under Broadway's favorite word, showmanship." Jules Romains—an exception to the rule—found the boisterous, joyful, noctambulant society of the Times Square area the epitome of the "laughing and democratic" city. But Priestley spoke for the majority when he insisted that New Yorkers, even, had "no illusions about Broadway." In his own opinion it was "an angry carbuncle" on the face of the metropolis.[22]

Conditions during the depression heightened the contrast between the affluent appearance of Manhattan's central section and the squalor of its slum-bedraggled shell. You step for one moment off the great thoroughfares, wrote a British visitor at the turn of the thirties, referring to the core of the city between Lexington and Sixth avenues, "and the slums are yelling about you." But even in Fifth Avenue and its impressive neighbors they saw the corrosive effects of the depression of the thirties and of the shortages during World War II. Cecil Beaton, revisiting America in 1947, found that in a superficial sense the edge had been "taken off the glamour that once was New York." Its "glitter" was somewhat tarnished, the English artist reported; buildings needed cleaning and houses repainting; almost everywhere there were signs of "change and decay." New Yorkers themselves admitted—to quote Priestley again—that "Fifth Avenue and its superb neighbors" had "come down a few pegs" since the war. A subjective reaction to the change is reflected in the contrasting comment of two American novelists who characterized New York in these years. To Thomas Wolfe, writing with an enthusiasm for the city of the thirties that is reminiscent of Walt Whitman's kinship with the "million-footed" metropolis, the "sky-soaring citadel" blazed "like a magnificent jewel in its fit setting of sea, and earth, and stars." To Truman Capote, a decade later, New York was "a diamond iceberg," floating in river water.[23]

Surprisingly enough, the "lengthwise" character of the "citadel" inspired almost as much comment in these years as did its already well-advertised vertical lift. Perhaps it was the more conspicuous social contrasts of the thirties that fostered this reaction, or the attentuated "licourice ribbons" of automobiles, the traffic lights alternating into the distance, and the new vistas created by the removal of trolleys, overhead wires, and elevated tracks; but from the late thirties forward many observers were struck with the fact that New York was a city of parallel strips. According to Jules Romains, Manhattan was made up of strips, "totally unlike one another," each pursuing "its growth by itself, always from north to south, preserving its own character." One could pass "from the sumptuous to the sordid within a good deal less than five hundred yards," he wrote in 1941.

"There are certainly numberless women of fashion who consider it perfectly natural to go miles down Fifth Avenue, or Madison Avenue, yet for whom a voyage of a half a dozen blocks to east or west would be an adventure, almost a dangerous impairment of good breeding." To his philosophical compatriot Jean-Paul Sartre, New York of 1945 was a complex of "longitudinal worlds," a city "striped with parallel, uncommunicable meanings." [24]

The removal of all but one of the elevated railway lines, the replacement of trolleys with buses, and the city's assumption of management of the unified subway system, in 1940, were the major developments of the generation in the ever vital field of urban transit. In 1945, the city's transit facilities were said to comprise 554 miles of route and 1,237 miles of track, not to mention the almost countless taxicabs which, to the amazement of the average European, were so readily available that you had only to "raise your hand" and one pulled up by your side. The operation of the motor buses interested an English visitor of 1945 who was surprised to observe that the drivers served as conductors, as well. "You enter the bus by the driver's seat, and slip your fare into a slot," he reported; "the driver will give you change if necessary. As he drives along, a machine sorts out the coins, and he places them in the appropriate slots. All the time he is dashing from block to block, dodging a swarm of indignant taxis." [25]

The subway, which by 1945 was the largest passenger railway in the world, served nearly 7,750,000 persons per day at the peak of its activity in that year. It was more than "the vehicle of the poor," as Odette Keun called it; and its patrons provided foreign visitors with striking evidence of the ethnic variety in the New York community. The Orientals who have left accounts of visits to New York seemed to be especially interested in suffering the ordeal of subway travel. Sampling the five o'clock rush hour in the subway station at Times Square, the Chinese traveler Chiang Yee made three attempts to enter the cars before he was carried in with the human tide, his feet suspended a few inches above the ground. For a Japanese woman visitor subway travel presented similar complications. Once inside the train, she found her sight "blocked by a wall of buttoned waistcoats," and the passengers pressed together "like dried figs done up in cellophane." They filled the car "like plaster poured into a mould," she reported, "and when at junctions some of them got in and out of the train, their limbs were entangled with one another, and it was a mercy for them that they were not octopuses." [26]

For all the eyesores and frustrations of which they took almost overeager note, observers of the thirties and forties saw developments that promised to bring the surface of the city—however sociologically striped—into closer physical harmony with the increasingly sleek trimness of its vertical lines. Streets were improved and cleared of obstructions. Large-scale neighborhood renovation, with aid from the W.P.A., made way for modern housing projects at both public and private expense. Constructed in superblocks along modern lines, these were the latest response to New York's perennial need for multiple dwelling. Newly built parks and playgrounds ventilated congested areas; and new bridges and express highways helped to relieve the traffic problem. Upon revisiting the city in 1936, Jules Romains reported that New York's streets were cleaner and better paved and lighted than they had been a dozen years earlier; and his compatriot Odette Keun, for all her criticism of the city's housing arrangements, conceded that the improvements of the thirties had made "the unspeakable conditions . . . of . . . Dreiser's period . . . the exception rather than the rule." [27]

Visitors noted, too, the expanded activity of the municipal government in other fields. Victor Vinde, a wartime visitor from Sweden, praised the current multiplication of hospitals and day nurseries, the improvements in fire and police administration, and the cultural and recreational outlets provided for the citizenry. With its city colleges and museums, park concerts, municipal broadcasting system, and subsidized opera, ballet, and theatre, as well as its beaches, baseball fields, and recreation centers, La Guardia's New York gave promise of becoming, as the Swedish journalist predicted, "a model city even from the social point of view." "The city works pretty hard on organizing the citizen's play," Alistair Cooke reported in his broadcasts to Britain in the forties; "in summer there are handball . . . , city band concerts, city outdoor opera, city fish . . . fed into the surrounding streams, and swimming for thousands who leap the trains for the vast city-sponsored lay-out of Jones Beach." [28]

In increasing the accessibility of music, art, and drama, the city was amplifying the facilities of a community where almost the ultimate in these fields was now recognized to be already professionally available. European visitors, like the Norwegian journalist Theodor Findahl, were impressed with New York's "unimaginable riches" in music and art; and even native authors, though frustrated by its tempo and its tawdriness, were willing to admit that New York was "the cultural center of the world"—not, as Clifford Odets wrote, "because of anything we've consciously done, but because of the ceaseless flow here of talent from everywhere." [29]

In the opinion of Cecil Beaton, "intensification" rather than "innovation," as in the twenties and early thirties, was now the prevailing trend. "In New York today we can see the finest contemporary art," he wrote, upon surveying the cultural life of the city in 1947. "In winter there is almost too much good music. . . . Foreign pianists, conductors, and singers are continually arriving and departing. The symphony concerts are of the highest quality in the world and Toscanini has as much fame as a cinema star and more power than most politicians. New York audiences are the most enthusiastic and critical in the world." Beaton's compatriot, the English author and journalist Cyril Connolly, asserted in the later forties that New York had very nearly achieved "the ideal of a humanist society, where the best of which an artist is capable is desired by the greatest number." [30]

It was perhaps a reflection of the local mood that commentators of these years concerned themselves with this more temperate side of the community rather than with the night life which had attracted so much attention from their predecessors in the twenties. Indeed, the visitors of this period showed as much interest in the New Yorkers' habits of "eating at automats, cafeterias, or perched on stools at drug stores, milk bars, and coffee shops" as had their predecessors in their patronage of night clubs and speak-easies. To Europeans of this generation, the "multifarious profusion" of New York's drugstores was one of the marvels of the metropolis. The French writer Jean Joseph-Renaud was astonished to find them "bazaars and restaurants" as well as pharmacies. "You can buy an alarm clock, a doll, a novel, cigars, knives, ornaments, rugs; eat a light lunch, telephone, even get drugs there!" he wrote after a visit in the early thirties. "It is the classic place for an ice cream soda—the 'bock beer' of New York." [31]

A new emphasis on the city as a collection of self-contained neighborhoods also reflected the contemporary recognition of a more personal, less pretentious side to life in the metropolis—a development encouraged by the fact that with the housing shortage that attended World War II, New Yorkers changed their residence less than had been their May or October habit in earlier years. Alistair Cooke, an adopted New Yorker, confessed to feeling like a "displaced person" when he moved out of the three-block-long neighborhood which had ministered to almost all his material needs for a period of six years. "This great, plunging, dramatic, ferocious, swift, and terrible big city is the most folksy and provincial place I have lived in," he explained in one of his broadcasts to Britain in the late forties. "New York is the biggest collection of villages in the world." As John Steinbeck put it: his neighborhood in the East Seventies had "every quality of a village except nosiness." [32]

It was this more sober and more humane quality in the city which impressed the American journalist Clair Price, returning in 1940 after a sojourn of twenty years on the European Continent. "Some new impulse has been acting on the town," wrote the expatriate author, in noting the signs of an unexpected humanity, a quality upon which observers had been commenting since the early thirties. "Some sense of community design and purpose has tempered the obsession with buying and selling. . . . There is a new maturity, a new tranquillity on the face of the Seven Million." In the opinion of Price and several others, it was the depression that had brought the change; but recognized also was the influence of Fiorello La Guardia, with his avowed ambition to create "a new kind of city—more beautiful, healthful, and convenient; a more comfortable place in which to live, work, and play." To the French novelist Simone de Beauvoir, a visitor of the later forties, the city's humanity was so obvious as to belie its reputation for being hard and cold.[33]

Commentators of the thirties and forties, no less than those of the preceding generation, still found cause to debate the question as to whether New York was representative of America, or whether, ethnically and temperamentally, it was apart from it. The Swedish novelist Vilhelm Moberg, a none too enthusiastic visitor of the later 1940's, found American traits elusive in New York. In his private opinion, he confessed, the city was "chiefly Europe." Some observers were inclined to regard the Empire City as "a world in itself," as a French journalist asserted in 1931, "a planet which doesn't have the same manners and atmosphere as other cities," where the residents give the impression of being "more New York than American." To others, in this as in earlier generations, New York was the nation in microcosm. But whatever their opinions on this controverted subject, no one denied the still increasing magnitude of the city's influence upon life in the United States and the world.[34]

"You can hear New York anywhere," wrote a correspondent of the London *News Chronicle,* in the later 1930's, referring to the way the metropolis was imposing its standards upon the nation by means of radio, national advertising, and the syndicated features of the daily press, most of which emanated from Manhattan. Even politically its influence was pre-eminent, in the opinion of William Allen White, despite the centralizing tendencies of the New Deal. "America rules through New York, if no longer by way of Wall Street," the Kansas editor-philosopher contended in 1937—strange as was the admission, coming out of America's Middle West. "New York is the real symbol of our national life—not Washington." Carlos Romulo characterized the Empire City's influence upon the nation in more popular terms. "It has been said that New York is not part of America," he wrote in the mid-forties. "That may be true. . . . But it is the fire under the boiling pot, and, as Jimmy Durante might paraphrase, I doubt if America could get along without New York." [35]

More novel was the now recognized role of the twentieth-century city in an international sense. Even before late 1946 when the United Nations settled upon Manhattan as a permanent abode, New York gave observers the impression that it had an influence in the world and was of the world to an extent not true of other American cities. New York is "a world capital and has no frontier," Le Corbusier asserted, as early as 1936. "I myself have the right to become a *New Yorker,* if I am strong enough to cut a furrow in New York. I should not thereby become an American." To Cecil Beaton, prewar New York was already the one great "world city"—with "the greatest banks, railways, stores, shipping lines, and entertainment," a center to which "artists, writers, and musicians necessarily migrate." The developments attending World War II advanced its position in this respect and increasingly brought it into focus as the cultural and even the political center of the Western world. "The New York that O. Henry described forty years ago was an American city," wrote J. B. Priestley late in 1947; "but today's glittering cosmopolis belongs to the world, if the world does not belong to it." [36]

The New York that presented itself to observers at the mid-century was, in its ever changing way, retrieving the glamor and prestige of which the depression and World War II had threatened to deprive it. As the seat of the United Nations its already recognized position as an international capital was inevitably enhanced; its physical appeal was newly heightened by a resumption of skyscraper construction that added exciting shafts of glass and aluminum to its already impressive towers. By now its eminence among cities was so generally accepted, so taken for granted, that commentators rarely marveled, as so often they had earlier, at the miracle of its progress from wilderness outpost to teeming metropolis.

At the same time, contemporaries voiced more serious reservations regarding its merits than was true at earlier periods in its phenomenal career. In some, especially from Europe, there was an unprecedented bitterness, an attitude suggesting, if not the influence of the Communist line, resentments born of the contrast between New York and cities physically and spiritually more affected by World War II. To the Norwegian war correspondent Theodor Findahl, who revisited New York in 1946, the return to America after twenty years was like "taking a step backward in time." New York's "stimulating cocktail of movie sensations" was there as before. Its "orchestra" played stronger than earlier. But "the war orchestra in Europe" had "left deeper marks on one's mind." To J. B. Priestley, viewing New York through eyes opened by "a half ruined Europe," there was something offensive in finding "all the rich loot of civilization" in the shop windows of a city that had become "Nineveh and Babylon piled on Imperial Rome." [37]

To such critics of the city, even its alleged advantages were more apparent than real. New York was a myth, they said, a fantasy, compounded of its conspicuous material and cultural abundance and of its almost unearthly architectural splendor—a myth which often obscured the ugly realities of urban living as clouds at times obscured its fantastic architectural peaks. Yet to many observers, the city's inexhaustible resources, its endless variety, its unfailing excitement, and its challenge to achievement were sufficiently real to outweigh the frustrations that living in it entailed. As one commentator conceded, New Yorkers "do not expect happiness . . . they gave it up for the privilege of living in New York." Certainly its residents were quick to admit the ugliness of many aspects of its society: the dirt, the traffic, the crowds, the politics, and the pressure of competition. Yet, as John Steinbeck wrote at the mid-century, "once you have lived in New York and it has become your home, no place else is good enough." John Gunther expressed the mixed reactions of the average commentator of the postwar period when he called New York "the supreme expression of both the miseries and splendors of contemporary civilization." [38]

Though they were of mixed minds as to the merits of life in New York, commentators at the mid-century were universally moved by the dynamism and splendor of the many-sided metropolis. However much they feared it, resented it, admired it, or were frustrated by it, they could not be indifferent to it. It excited as it frustrated, this mixture of fantasy and realism, of emerging maturity and still youthful energy and drive. Less touched than European cities by the war, it reflected more than they a continued faith in the individualistic way of life. More cosmopolitan than Europe's cities had ever been in modern times, it presented an example of ethnic harmony to still contentious national powers. And for all its provincial self-centeredness with international overtones, contemporaries saw in this "capital of everything" a vital manifestation of American life—at once the supreme expression of the nation's material accomplishment, the symbol of its cultural variety, the originator of many of its standards, and the promise and guarantor of its augmented participation in world affairs.[39]

"New York is a great world capital," wrote Victor Vinde, a Swedish journalist who arrived in the city by airborne transatlantic clipper in 1942. "It is varied, capricious, brutal and hard. It is alarmingly crowded and indescribably beautiful. . . . New York is not America, but it is part of America, something of that which is in process of being shaped and developed throughout the vast continent. New York still lives in a Babylonian confusion of tongues. . . . New York is both in the van of America and by the side of America. . . . But from New York comes standardization, the cheap but excellent goods which make life more bearable, easier and perhaps more beautiful. . . . New York is the great, open window to the world: the window through which novelty comes, the window through which the U.S.A. looks out over world events and Europe.

"New York is New York." [40]

THE THREADBARE THIRTIES: NEW YORK, 1931, 1932

New York's distress, in the days of the depression, was described by Mary Agnes Hamilton, a distinguished English visitor who came to the United States on a lecturing tour, in late December 1931. Active as a member of the Labor Party, Miss Hamilton served in Parliament from 1929 to 1931. She was twice a member of the British delegation to the Assembly of the League of Nations and from 1933 to 1937 a governor of the British Broadcasting Corporation. In the following excerpt from her volume *In America Today,* published in 1932, she views the New York scene against the background of impressions gained from visits in more prosperous times. The passage is reprinted with permission of Hamish Hamilton, Limited.[41]

I landed in New York on December 24th, 1931. . . . Friends met me at the dock. "I'm afraid you won't have much of a trip," said the first. . . . "These bank failures. . . . The clubs are all going bust."

"Things are just appalling," said the other. "A million and a half unemployed in the city alone."

I looked about me, as we moved out. Yes: those grey-faced, shambling men, standing about in serried rows and groups, had never been there, looking like that, before. More of them: masses, indeed, as we drove along and across the high-numbered avenues: listlessly parked against the walls, blocking the sidewalks. . . .

I am not denying that "things are bad," as they put it, in the United States. Every day, one sees the degrading misery of bread lines. Every day one is told that this great industry and that, from railroads to publishing, is collapsing. The building slump spreads. In New York, for example, the most salient new structure, the magnificent Empire State, stands unlet and can only pay its taxes by collecting dollars from the sightseers who ascend to its eyrie for the stupendous view to be got thence, while another, even newer, the New Waldorf, is in the hands of the receivers. Stories of failing banks, turned-in motor-cars, despairing suicides, are dinned into one's ears. . . .

One has only to pass outside the central island bounded by Lexington and Sixth Avenues, to see hardship, misery and degradation, accentuated by the shoddy grimness of the shabby houses and broken pavements. Look down from the Elevated, and there are long queues of dreary-looking men and women standing in "bread-lines" outside the Relief offices and the various church and other charitable institutions. Times Square, at any hour of the day and late into the evening, offers an exhibit for the edification of the theatre-goer, for it is packed with shabby, utterly dumb and apathetic-looking men, who stand there, waiting for the advent of the coffee waggon run by

Mr. W. R. Hearst of the *New York American.* . . . At every street corner, and wherever taxi or car has to pause, men try to sell one apples, oranges or picture papers. . . . On a fine day, men will press on one gardenias at fifteen cents apiece; on any day, rows of them line every relatively open space, eager to shine one's shoes. It is perhaps because so many people are doing without this "shine," or attempting with unfamiliar hands . . . to shine their own, that the streets look shabby and the persons on them so much less well-groomed than of yore. The well-shod feet of the States struck me, forcibly, on my first visit; the ill-cleaned feet of New York struck me as forcibly in January and April, 1932. In 1930 an English friend, long domesticated in New England, told me that she hesitated to bring her children to London, since the sight of beggars would make so painful an impression on them; in 1932 there are more beggars to be met with in New York than in London. Yes; distress is there; the idle are there. How many, no one really knows. Ten million or more in the country: a million and a half in New York are reported. They are there; as is, admittedly, a dark undergrowth of horrid suffering that is certainly more degraded and degrading than anything Britain or Germany knows.

MEALS FOR THE MASSES: 1935

Restaurants for the "average man" attracted the interest of two Soviet travelers who visited New York in the middle thirties. They were Ilya Ilf and Eugene Petrov, Russian journalists whose *Diamonds to Sit On* and *The Little Golden Calf* had satirized Soviet enterprise. In the volume *Little Golden America,* which resulted from a trip that took place in the fall and winter of 1935–1936, they nevertheless view American institutions through orthodox Soviet eyes and find in the "economic system" the reason why American foods, "so appetizing in appearance," do not suit their taste. The following excerpt is reprinted from *Little Golden America,* copyright, 1946, by Ilya Ilf and Eugene Petrov, with the permission of Rinehart & Company, Incorporated, New York, Publishers, and of Routledge & Kegan Paul, Limited, London.[42]

Over the large show window of a corner store, despite the sunny morning, gleamed the blue letters "Cafeteria" in electric lights. The cafeteria was large, bright, and clean. Along the walls were glass cases filled with beautiful, appetizing edibles. To the left of the entrance was the cashier's booth. On the right was a metal stand with a small slot athwart as in a coin bank. From the opening emerged the end of a blue pasteboard stub. Those who entered tugged at this end. We also tugged. The melodic clang of a bell resounded. One stub was in our hand, and through the slot of the coin bank another blue stub popped out. Then we did what all New Yorkers do when they dash into a cafeteria for a hurried bite. From a special table we each took a light brown tray, placed on it forks, spoons, knives, and paper napkins; and, feeling extremely awkward in our heavy overcoats and hats, went to the right end of a glass-enclosed counter. Down the entire length of this counter ran three rows of nickelled pipes on which we conveniently placed our trays and slid them along after placing each dish upon them. The counter itself was a tremendous camouflaged electric plate. Soups, chunks of roast, sausages of various lengths and thicknesses, legs of pork and lamb, meat loaves and roulades, mashed, fried, baked, and boiled potatoes and potatoes curiously shaped in pellets, globules of Brussels sprouts, spinach, carrots, and numerous other side dishes were kept warm here. White chefs in starched nightcaps, aided by neat but heavily rouged and marcelled girls in pink headdresses, were busy placing on the glass cover of the counter plates of food and punching that figure on the stub which indicated the cost of each dish. Then came salads and vinaigrettes, various hors d'oeuvres, fish in cream sauces and fish in jellied sauces. Then came bread, rolls, and traditional round pies with apple, strawberry, and pineapple fillings. Here coffee and milk were issued. We moved down the counter, pushing our trays. On the thick layer of chipped ice were plates of compotes and ice-cream, oranges and grapefruit cut in half, large and small glasses with various juices. Persistent advertising has taught Americans to drink juices before breakfast and lunch. . . .

In the middle of the cafeteria stood polished wooden tables without tablecloths, and beside them coat-racks. Those who wished could put their hats under their chairs, where there was a special shelf for that purpose. On the tables were stands with bottles of oil, vinegar, catsup, and various other condiments. There was also granulated sugar in a glass flagon wrought in the manner of a pepper-shaker with holes in its metal stopper.

The settling of accounts with the customers was simple. No one could leave the cafeteria without sooner or later passing the cashier's booth and presenting the stub with the total punched in it. Here also cigarettes were sold and one was free to take a toothpick.

The process of eating was just as superbly rationalized as the production of automobiles or of typewriters.

The automats have progressed farther along this road than the cafeterias. Although they have approximately the same outward appearance as the cafeterias, they differ from the latter in that they have carried the process of pushing food into American stomachs to the point of virtuosity. The walls of the automats are occupied throughout with little glass closets. Near each one of them is a slit for dropping a "nickel" (a five-cent coin). Behind the glass stands a dour sandwich or a glass of juice or a piece of pie. Despite the shining glass and metal, the sausages and cutlets deprived of liberty somehow produce a strange impression. One pities them, like cats at a show. A man drops a nickel, acquires the right to open the little door, takes out his sandwich, carries it to his table and there eats it, again putting his hat under his chair on the special shelf. Then the man goes up to a tap, drops his "nickel," and out of the tap into the glass drips exactly as much coffee and milk as is supposed to drip. One feels something humiliating, something insulting to man in that. One begins to suspect that the owner of the automat has outfitted his establishment, not in order to present society with a pleasant surprise, but in order to discharge from service poor marcelled girls with pink headdresses and thereby earn a few more dollars.

But automats are not over popular in America. Evidently the bosses themselves feel that there must be some limit to rationalization. Hence, the normal little restaurants, for people of modest means, belonging to mighty trusts, are always full. The most popular of these—Childs—has become in America a standard for inexpensive food of good quality. "He dines at Childs": that means that the man earns $30 a week. In any part of New York one can say: "Let's have dinner at Childs," and it would not take him more than ten minutes to reach Childs. At Childs one receives the same clean handsome food as in a cafeteria or at an automat. Only there one is not deprived of the small satisfaction of looking at a menu, saying "H'm," asking the waitress whether the veal is good, and receiving the answer: "Yes, sir!" . . .

Model cleanliness, good quality of produce, an extensive choice of dishes, a minimum of time lost in dining. All that is so. But here is the trouble. All this beautifully prepared food is quite tasteless—

colourless in taste. It is not injurious to the stomach. It is most likely even of benefit to it. But it does not present man with any delights, any gustatory satisfaction. . . .

For a long time we could not understand why American dishes, so appetizing in appearance, are so unappealing in taste. At first we thought the Americans simply do not know how to cook. But then we learned that that alone is not the point: the crux of the matter is in the organization itself, in the very essence of the American economic system. . . . Sitting in a cafeteria, we read Mikoyan's speech, which said that food in a socialist country must be palatable—that it must bring joy to people—and it sounded like poetry to us.

BROADWAY: TWENTIETH-CENTURY STYLE

Broadway, in the mid-twentieth century, connoted a tawdry gaiety that would have surprised contemporaries a century earlier. This quality of the once commercially resplendent thoroughfare was described by Odette Keun, a Frenchwoman who visited the United States in 1936 and again late in 1938. Madame Keun warmed only slowly to an appreciation of New York City, and much of her comment upon it was devastatingly critical. Her first visit to America resulted in a volume entitled *A Foreigner Looks at the T.V.A.* (1937); the second led to the publication in 1939 of *I Think Aloud in America,* which deals extensively with New York City, and from which the following excerpt is drawn. It is reprinted from *I Think Aloud in America;* Longmans, Green and Company; copyright, 1939, by Odette Keun.[43]

Broadway . . . must have a description to itself. A very independent thoroughfare, it wanders and rambles unprofessionally and quite contrary to the city plan. . . . It also changes its aspect according to the part of town in which it happens to have strayed: sometimes it is pure slum, sometimes millions-worth, ponderous, ornate, financial skyscrapers. But its fame comes from its central portion, the "Roaring Forties," chockful of theatres, cinemas, music halls, cabarets and eating-houses.

In the daytime Broadway reveals itself to be the most incongruous street in the city, grey, askew, undignified, with a skyscraper here and a wooden shack there. A Greek temple complete with pediment, columns and capitals is surmounted by an enormous jackboot and rubs shoulders with a sweetshop decorated with coconuts and fetishes in the West African style; a modern theatre lies side by side with a village fair-booth or a soft-drinks stall representing a corner of Tahiti, where bananas smother you and pseudo American sailors serve out spurious fruit juices in tall glasses. The Times Building rears up like the prow of a dreadnought; everywhere cluster Chinese restaurants, Negro shows, Italian movies, Sports Palaces in which you lose your money at the most ingeniously silly games, and hundreds of small, flashy, amazingly low-priced shops overflowing with hats, lingerie, dresses, and false jewellery, which remain open so far into the night that you can't help wondering what their real business is. Impossible to imagine a more shoddy, incompatible, fantastic medley.

But as soon as dusk falls, Broadway bursts into a scintillation which has no equal in America or anywhere else in the world. In an illumination more blinding than a tropical day at its zenith, amid the thump and clatter and purr of trams and cars, among a multitude of kiosks, roasters, shoeblacks, itinerant vendors of newspapers, fruit, flowers, toys, under a gigantic clock apparently suspended in the sky, eddy and mill and bustle the common, garish, variegated crowds. All around you is the apotheosis of electricity. It makes your head reel, for that blaze and riot of light isn't static; it flares, flows, writhes, rolls, blinks, winks, flickers, changes color, vanishes and sparkles again before you can open your mouth to gape.

The whole street is encircled with swirling, whirling, pouring, dazzling hues. Red, white, green, yellow, blue, orange, purple, they urge, solicit, press, command you to go somewhere or buy something. Bottles of beer appear on the firmament and transform themselves into dwarfs drinking; showers of gold peanuts fall from the skies; dragons breathing smoke become a film title; cigarettes are ignited; automobiles materialize. Mountains, towns, lamaseries, men with top hats, nude women with teeth, spring into existence on the façades and are wiped off into oblivion. The latest items of news gallop high up through the black air; telegrams of fire ring unseen buildings. . . .

You cannot realize, on Broadway, that you are in America. This is the rendezvous of an international *populo,* especially on a Saturday evening. . . . At every moment I meet nose to nose a racial type that comes from my own Continent, or Africa, or Asia. The language you overhear isn't English either: Irish, German, Russian, Italian, Greek, Scandinavian, Jewish, all the accents, rolling, slurring, gargling, high-pitched, guttural, clipped, mangle and murder the Anglo-Saxon idiom. . . .

Broadway and its adjoining streets are riddled with dens, dives, places of assignation, the haunts of racketeers and unlawful activities. . . . But . . . it impressed me, an innocent stranger, only as a fabulous playground. Its boast, literally true, is that it never stops and never goes to sleep. It is entirely bent on trivialities, a perpetual fair of cheap amusements for juveniles, it displays a vivid and incoherent vulgarity, and with a noisy zest everybody in it strives to live up to that ideal. . . . Anyhow, though I'd hate to think Broadway is the apex of twentieth-century democratic civilization, that jingling tawdry bit of brilliant tinsel certainly has a lunatic, quite irresistible charm.

NATIONALITIES ON PARADE: 1937–1939

Despite the curtailment of immigration in the middle 1920's, New York's broad cosmopolitanism continued to affect the tone and color of the urban scene. Indeed, with the increasing assimilation and resultant self-assurance of the foreign stocks came more assertive efforts to preserve the traditions of the native country within a broader loyalty to the adopted land. This development was fostered by the activities of fraternal societies and religious organizations catering to special nationality groups, as well as by the existence of a vigorous and prolific foreign-language press. Parades and festivals in honor of Old World saints and heroes symbolized this trend. This aspect of life in New York on the eve of World War II attracted the attention of Robert Waithman, who came to the United States in November 1937 to succeed Raymond Gram Swing as the New York correspondent of the London *News Chronicle.* The following excerpt from his *Report on America,* published in 1940, is reprinted with the permission of Frederick Muller, Limited.[44]

New York is the American city with the most foreign white stock. The New York figures are astonishing. Out of about 7,000,000 people there are 5,000,000 who were either born in a foreign country or are the children of foreign-born fathers or mothers. The population of New York contains: 1,070,000 Italians, 945,000 Russians, 600,000 Germans, 535,000 Irish (and 79,000 Northern Irish), 458,000 Poles, 288,000 Austrians, 178,000 English (and 71,000 Scots and 5,000 Welsh), 115,000 Hungarians, 93,000 Rumanians, 72,000 Czechs, 66,000 Swedes, 62,000 Norwegians, 47,000 French, 43,000 Greeks, 31,000 Lithuanians, 22,000 Spaniards, 20,000 Danes, 19,000 Swiss, 11,000 Dutch.

With them are 30,000 Syrians, 22,000 Armenians, 18,000 Chinese, 2,000 Japanese. There are 77,000 Canadians and French-Canadians,

19,000 men and women from the West Indies, 18,000 from Central and South America.

In New York on St. Patrick's Day every year 50,000 Irish swing down Fifth Avenue to the tune of fife bands. On Pulaski Day 50,000 Poles parade. The orthodox Russians hold their Christmas in January close to the time when the Chinese are celebrating their New Year's Day. The British go to church on St. George's Day, there is a message from the King and Queen, and the British Consul reads the lesson. The Italians parade often; the San Vincent Society, the San Rocco, the San Genaro and all the lesser Societies have their Saints' Days. The Spaniards march on the *Dia de la Raza,* the Day of the Spanish Race, on October 12. The Rumanians celebrate the day of deliverance from Turkish rule on May 10. The Turks celebrate the founding of their Republic on October 27. The Yugoslavs hail December 1, the day when one flag flew over the kingdom of the Serbs, Croats, and Slovenes. The Armenians' Independence Day is May 20, the Syrians' September 1, the Greeks' March 25. The Hungarians salute their national hero, Kossuth, on May 15; the Scandinavians theirs, Erikson, on October 9 (while the Danes have June 5, and the Swedes have November 6 as other days of national celebration).

Banners are raised and music plays, unfathomable thoughts and emotions are seizing the transplanted men and women who march or watch the parades and celebrations. The parades are helping to keep alight flames of patriotism that might have flickered and died more quickly if they had not been tended.

Scores of foreign churches are influencing their congregations; and it may be that the foreign-language newspapers and magazines are exciting the more powerful influence. What these newspapers are telling their people, what opinions they are encouraging, no one man in New York is likely to know. But there are occasional revelations that not all the national groups are thinking as they were supposed to think.

It is understood that the Italians in New York hate Mussolini: but one day in 1938 an Italian audience cheered the name of Mussolini and booed the name of Mayor La Guardia (himself the New York born son of an Italian father and mother) because La Guardia had denounced Fascism. It is frequently said that Hitler has no more bitter enemies than the Germans in New York: but on the night of February 20, 1939, a crowd of 20,000 in Madison Square Garden, marshalled by 3,000 uniformed members of the German-American Bund, hailed enthusiastically a series of pro-Nazi and anti-semitic speeches.

No easy generalization about the Germans or the Italians or about any other division of New York's foreign stock can be true. A man renounces his country and swears allegiance to another, but nobody can say how deep the old patriotism went, how long it will persist, how it will affect his life, and the life of his children.

It is possible to live in New York for a long time without sensing this undercurrent. Then a Greek running a delicatessen store, or a Pole working on a road gang, or an Italian taxi-driver or a German salesman may reveal a glimpse of it. It will suddenly become clear that he is not listening to your talk. He will be looking into the distance, thinking about the country he used to belong to, the country his father came from.

NEW YORK IN WORLD WAR II: 1942–1945

The surface frivolity as well as the underlying resolution of New Yorkers during World War II is well reflected in Carlos P. Romulo's *My Brother Americans.* The Filipino statesman, journalist, and educator arrived in New York not long after the fall of his native country to the Japanese, an experience which he reported in his *I Saw the Fall of the Philippines* (1942). The son of a Filipino guerrilla fighter, Romulo was educated at the University of the Philippines and at Columbia University. After a peacetime career as a professor of English at the University of the Philippines, as member of the Independence Mission to the United States, and as editor and publisher of the *Philippine Herald,* he became press aide to General Douglas MacArthur on December 10, 1941. He escaped from Bataan on the night of April 8, 1942. Reaching the United States shortly thereafter, he engaged during the war years in speaking activities which brought him frequently to New York. The following excerpts mirror his changing reactions to life in the wartime city from 1942 to 1945. They are from *My Brother Americans,* by Carlos P. Romulo. Copyright 1945 by Carlos P. Romulo, reprinted by permission of Doubleday & Company, Incorporated.[45]

What was New York really like, and what were its thoughts in wartime?

I can admit now how thoroughly the greatest of America's cities horrified me upon my return from the Philippines. Then I was filled with a righteous anger and terrible fears, and I carried these into a city living apparently in a state of fiesta. I came from the battlefield into the Starlight Room of the Waldorf where men and women in evening clothes were dancing to Cugat's music. That first night in New York I sat at a table by the orchestra in bewilderment, staring at couple after couple in the soft whirling lights.

I kept repeating: "But there is no war here! No war. . . ."

Not only in the gayer night places was there this dearth of anxiety and fear. Broadway was no longer the Great White Way. It was Coney Island in dim-out. Everyone was out hunting fun, and only the paper hats and horns were lacking to make every night a perpetual New Year's Eve from Forty-second Street to Fifty-second. Apparently all the civilians were having a wonderful time.

But the lone gob or marine or soldier wandering in the streets did not seem to be having such a happy time of it, and his kind became legion as the months went by and the war went on. . . .

And try as I might, I could see few signs of war preparation in Manhattan in the first months of the war.

Nor, to be truthful, would they be apparent even after two and a half years.

Sometimes a line of uniformed men created a long ripple in a crowded street. Sometimes the war bond drive shows caused congestions on the streets. These were small disturbances in a swarming, shouting, always-moving surface of humanity that is New York.

It took me a long time to discover that the mighty war effort in New York worked unseen. It was not on the surface, as in smaller cities. And in a great many individual cases, of course, it was not there at all.

In the small towns each citizen had to do his part or endure the pitiless glare of public disapproval. The New Yorker has no such condemnation to move him. No one could note whether he donated to the blood bank, or bought bonds, or, on the other hand, griped at every small necessary sacrifice and bought black market steaks and nylons for his wife. The average New Yorker is without neighbors. Which is to say he is, socially speaking, on his own.

This may account for the seemingly heartless indifference of New York toward the war situation, as I felt it after my arrival from the Philippines. . . .

New York newspapers gave the war on all fronts remarkable coverage, interpretation, and emphasis, so that no other city on earth was quite so well informed. But the average civilian seemed unaware of the fact that the United States was locked in combat on either side of the world with bitter, powerful, and determined foes. One read of rationing and shortages, but one also seemed able to buy pretty much anything one desired, if the price were in his pocket. And most New Yorkers seemed to have the price. . . .

It was because the apparent lack of concern of New York as a city for the war effort seemed at first glimpse an affront to Americanism itself that I was, in the beginning, alarmed and infuriated.

Then, out of that indignation, came an understanding. As the months brought me back again and again to the big city I came to glimpse something below that bubbling and indifferent surface. Out of this came a great and awed respect. . . .

Without its gay and absurd, seeming heartless, bravery New York could not have accomplished all it has in this present war. Without its general loosening of pockets it could not have poured out its fabulous largess into bonds. It could not have sent so many of its sons into the fighting channels of the earth. Without this courage it could not have given of its blood—enough mixed blood of many nationalities to have run Broadway red—and rushed straight back to work or play again.

New Yorkers did all these things and kept on going, "on the double," because there is so much to be seen and done in New York, and they didn't have time to stop and talk about what they had done. Their sons were fighting on Saipan, their daughters dropped in at the blood bank on their way home from work and gave another blood donation, men of seventy went out in the bitter cold to stand watch as observers or wardens, and every spare penny and minute they had was spent on having a good time.

Had I resented not finding a country steeped in gloom as it readied for war? I might have known better! Two and a half years later, ready for D-day in France, and A-day in the Pacific, found America still unsuppressed. New York was still making wisecracks, dancing in the night clubs, prowling Broadway by night, paying too much for the small fragments of pleasure snatched from impending danger. Those who were back out of the blood and mud of the lines were out hunting amusement, too, and finding new courage in such pleasures.

New York, I found, had a fighting spirit of its own, developed in its own peculiar and insulated fashion while America was deep in war. If it showed less than in smaller places, that may be because more courage is required of those who live in New York. It is not easy for the individual to make his way. It takes a tough mind to fight its way through to the top of this tough and fascinating city.

NEW YORK UNDER LA GUARDIA

The social and physical transformation of the city initiated in the La Guardia administration was reported by a visitor who approached Manhattan in twentieth-century fashion—"out of the clouds." He was Victor Vinde, a prominent Swedish journalist, who came to the United States by clipper in the summer of 1942 at the invitation of the United Press Club. He spent six months visiting the nation's farms, factories, mines, and shipyards for the purpose of describing the nation's war effort. In the following excerpt from his *America at War* he describes the expansion of urban services and municipal amenities in New York City which resulted in large measure from the impulse generated by Mayor Fiorello La Guardia and such aides as Commissioner Robert Moses in the years following La Guardia's accession as mayor in 1934. It is reprinted with the permission of Hutchinson and Company, Limited.[46]

New York, like all great cities, is a city of contrasts. Perhaps it has more contrasts than any other city in the world. It is difficult to imagine more glaring contrasts than between Park Avenue and some back street in Harlem. But a large section of the population works in the very heart of Manhattan and participates in its luxury. They share the tip of Fifth Avenue, which does not consist only of luxury shops, and they go in the afternoon across Park Avenue or Madison Avenue down to the Grand Central to take a train home; they stand about and hang over the barrier at Rockefeller Plaza and inhale the undefinable air of light and beauty which lies around the modern Manhattan.

In the last ten years an inexorable war has been waged against disease and slums, against misery and crime in New York. . . .

Here, as in so many other parts of America, the new spirit which came with Franklin Roosevelt has worked wonders—New York's mayor, La Guardia, with the odoriferous Christian name Fiorello, is a little stubbly Italian with blazing eyes and small plump fists which resound when he strikes a table. He is one of the men who have transformed the giant city, who has taken up the fight against slums. He has no political abode: he has been Socialist, Republican and Democrat. Now he is just La Guardia, without any label. The name is a programme in itself.

In recent years enormous slum areas have been pulled down, nearly 40,000 new dwellings have been erected—a drop in the ocean—and open spaces, broad avenues and parks now stand where formerly there were dilapidated slums. And yet an immeasurable slum still remains. However, a beginning has been made and there is hope that one day New York will become a model city even from the social point of view. Hospitals and crêches have multiplied. Fire and police administrations have been improved and extended. And La Guardia, who is at heart a dreamer, has in the last two years organized public concerts for hundreds of thousands of listeners. Symphony orchestras play Beethoven. It is not true that people like bad music, says the music-lover La Guardia. He is a man of temperament and he has probably as many enemies as friends. . . . And he has the broad masses behind him.

New York's 7,000,000 inhabitants have long been imprisoned in a stony desert. The ring around them has now been broken. In half a decade enormous work has, under the direction of the New York State Commissioner, Moses, been practically completed. Around the city there has been created an enormous belt of air and greenery. New York has acquired real lungs. From the city there now emerge hundreds of new and broad motor roads out to Long Island and Connecticut, leading to golf-courses and camping-grounds, to lakes and bathing beaches. . . . On a summer day even in war-time there is a teeming life on the bathing-beaches. From the Atlantic there blow fresh strong winds, the sand shines gleaming white and the New Yorkers are burned as brown as if they were on an African coast. The masses of stone of the city are far away and the sun is within reach of the multitude also.

FRUSTRATION ON THE SUBWAY: URBAN TRANSIT IN THE TWENTIETH CENTURY

The hazards of subway travel for strangers unacquainted with the system were amusingly related by Anthony Armstrong Willis, British author and playwright, who contributed to *Punch* from 1925 to 1933. The following account of his experience with the New York "underground" appeared in a volume entitled *Britisher on Broadway*. It is

Courtesy of Standard Oil Co. (N. J.)

NEW YORK IS A PORT

New York is "above all, a harbour and a port," wrote the English historian D. W. Brogan in 1939. The huge land-locked area, easily accessible to both the sea and the interior, consists of eight large bays, four straits, and four rivers. In 1950, workers at the port unloaded and dispatched nearly a third of all the foreign cargo that reached the shores of the United States. Above, in the Hudson, as viewed from Weehawken, New Jersey, lie some of the 150 to 175 deepwater vessels which daily use the port's 520 miles of frontage. Below, the Statue of Liberty stands watch over this great port at night.

Courtesy of Standard Oil Co. (N. J.)

Courtesy of United Nations

THE WORLD'S CAPITAL CITY

The selection of New York as the site for the headquarters of the United Nations deepened the already international tone of the metropolis, even though the seventeen-acre East River plot, on which the buildings stand, is not New York but rather United Nations territory. Here the buildings, as constructed between 1949 and 1954, are seen against the mid-Manhattan skyline. The rectangular glass shaft houses the offices of the Secretariat; council chambers and conference rooms are located at the river's edge; and the General Assembly meets in the domed building at the right.

reprinted by permission of the author and of A. M. Heath and Company, Limited.[47]

For a long while after my first experience with the New York subway I avoided the thing like Prohibition, and would sheer off nervously from any corner where I saw a subterranean entrance leering at me. Then I got on my mettle about it. Why should I be laughed at by a cheap New York subway, a mere five-cent automatic subway—I, who could take an eightpenny ticket in a London tube without turning a single stile? I must get to grips with the damn thing—and at once.

So I determined I would use it to visit a friend who lived up on 24th Street at the corner of Fourth Avenue. I chose him because I was then down on the extreme south point of Manhattan Island, and so felt that at least I couldn't help *starting* in the right direction. Moreover, I was only twenty yards from a subway station called South Ferry, which seemed a good starting-point.

So using South Ferry as a base, I decided after intense business with a map outside, that I must somehow get on a line that ran up north underneath Fourth Avenue, and thus come to the 23rd Street station. Possessing, as I do, a good bump of locality, I had a shrewd idea I would then be quite close to 24th Street.

So I went down, a lone British dare-devil, into the New York subway system and the irrevocable turnstiles closed behind me.

There are three things about the New York subway which discourage the stranger. First, there are no officials from whom to ask your way (except a harassed subway guard who, though pressed for time, can yet pause to be as rude as the next man). Secondly, there are no maps on the platforms and only a few incomplete ones in the trains themselves, so that you can't tell whether you are going wrong till you have done it. Thirdly, there is an express train service, which plays old Harry with your preconceived ideas of where you are going to get out. Otherwise it's easy.

I got into a train. It was not crowded. Only two flappers, a negro, and an Italian woman got in too. Then we went off. The next station was called Bowling Green. Two Jews got in; the Italian woman and the negro and the two flappers got out. Then the flappers looked at me sitting there, giggled, and got in again. I blushed and tried to appear high-minded. The train moved off.

At the next station the two Jews got out, but the flappers remained.

They were still giggling at me. The name of the station was South Ferry. For a moment I thought it was the same one, till I remembered that in New York very often two subway stations had the same name.

We moved off again. The next station was Bowling Green, and, by now a little distrait, I had to admit that the name seemed familiar. The flappers, however, who must have been going somewhere, did not get out, so I stayed tight. The train moved off.

The next station was South Ferry. I crossed myself secretly, and looked round for a map. At this one of the flappers asked me if I wanted to get anywhere. I said a trifle haughtily that I was going to 23rd Street, and they retorted that I'd never make it at that rate, as I was merely on a shuttle railway between Bowling Green and South Ferry. I ventured to point out that I'd have realized that sooner if I hadn't seen them staying in it. They replied they had just been waiting to see what in hell I thought I was doing anyway. We then all got out at Bowling Green and the party broke up.

After an interval of wandering in passages I got pushed into a train which, under the title of "Lexington Avenue Express," volunteered to take me up Fourth Avenue, but for some while it only looked in at places like Wall Street, where I happen to own some shares that used to go up and down, and now just go down. Then to my joy we suddenly stopped at 14th Street.

"Getting near 23rd," I murmured encouragingly to myself, adding: "A nine point rise will do it," for my thoughts were still on Wall Street.

The next station, however, called itself by the imposing name of Grand Central, and before I could remember what number street it was on, we were off again.

The next stop staggered me. It was 86th Street. And I thought we hadn't reached twenty. I leapt out like a bear operator caught short, as the express whizzed off, *en route* for a new high. If I hadn't I don't doubt I'd have been well beyond par by the next stop.

Feeling that I'd better travel on a falling market this time, I got in a return train. This one, calling itself a local, dropped my street stock carefully from 86 to 77 to 68 to 59 to 51, and then I was at Grand Central again. At this I shuddered and got out, although I hadn't intended to close the deal till 23. But I had learnt already that Grand Central had a queer effect on trains. They seem to get all funny after looking in at Grand Central. If I'd stayed in that train I'm certain that before I knew where I was I'd have found myself at 1st Street with the bottom out of the market.

So, resolved now to speculate with caution, I began to explore Grand Central. And I just got lost.

Grand Central is a fine place to get lost in, for, in addition to being an indefatigably conscientious subway station, it is a proper railway station and a shopping centre and hotel into the bargain, and as it is one of the only two real railway stations in Manhattan it is a big one. In fact, it is bigger than that. I wandered about till I was tired, getting into subway trains here and there to look at the maps in the carriages and getting out and into others, and I could not get away from Grand Central. At last I found myself in Times Square subway station. I don't know how I got there, but personally I think it is also a part of Grand Central.

Here I clambered, tired but joyful, into a train that had Fourth Avenue on it, and wonderful as it may seem, the next stop was at 34th Street. I scarcely dared breathe in case the next might take it into its head to be 3rd or 180th.

To my annoyance it was called Union Square, which put me right out. I am pretty safe on numbers, but I cannot follow these names. The next was Canal Street, which had a familiar ring, but when I came after a ten-minute run to a station named deKalb Avenue I felt I had had just about enough. I climbed out and found our first porter.

"I want 23rd Street," I said. He told me I meant 25th, five stations away. I didn't argue about it. On most of the subway maps I had been able to glance at, a number might be anything—and probably is.

I was at 25th Street station in six minutes. It was still daylight I remember when I came above ground. But I could not locate our friends in 24th Street. . . .

I had quite a crowd round me before I was made to realize the truth of the saying, "New York is not America," and that I had got to 24th Street, *Brooklyn.* I took a taxi back over the East River to Manhattan and went to bed. I have promised myself never to touch another subway as long as I live.

NEW YORK: VERTICAL CITY

Qualified praise for the skyscraper city of the twentieth century resulted from the visits of the Franco-Swiss architect and artist Charles-Édouard

Jeanneret, better known as Le Corbusier. A specialist in city planning as well as one of the world's most distinguished architects, Le Corbusier was in New York in 1935 and 1936 and again in January 1946, this time in connection with his duties as a member of a commission to find a permanent site for the United Nations in the neighborhood of New York. He was impressed more with the principle of a towering city than with the performance of the city's builders in this respect. Only the planning of Rockefeller Center, under construction in the thirties, conformed to his idea that tall buildings should not be built flush with the street but grouped in superblocks so as to provide more "sun, space, and silence." His comments on the dynamism and flexibility of the urban society echoed those of other travelers of this and earlier generations who called change the most constant characteristic of the New York scene. Following are excerpts from *When the Cathedrals Were White* by Le Corbusier; copyright, 1947, by Reynal and Hitchcock; reprinted by permission of Harcourt, Brace and Company, Incorporated.[48]

New York is a vertical city, under the sign of the new times. It is a catastrophe with which a too hasty destiny has overwhelmed courageous and confident people, though a beautiful and worthy catastrophe. Nothing is lost. Faced with difficulties, New York falters. Still streaming with sweat from its exertions, . . . it sees what it has done and suddenly realizes: "Well, we didn't get it done properly. Let's start over again!" New York has such courage and enthusiasm that everything can be begun again, sent back to the building yard and made into something still greater, something mastered! . . . In reality, the city is hardly more than twenty years old, that is the city . . . which is vertical and on the scale of the new times. . . .

My heart . . . had been torn every day for two months by hate and love of this new world which must be seen to be really known as it is. . . . Hours of despair in the violence of the city (New York or Chicago); hours of enthusiasm, confidence, optimism, in the fairy splendor of the city.

I am not able to bear the thought of millions of people undergoing the diminution of life imposed by devouring distances, the subways filled with uproar, the wastelands on the edges of the city, in the blackened brick streets, hard, implacably soulless streets—tenement streets, streets of hovels that make up the cities of the century of money—the slums of New York or Chicago.

I am offended by this blow at legitimate human hopes. Nevertheless, if I am observant, I discover that my despair is not always shared by the victims themselves. In New York, the people who have come in order to "make money" shake off black thoughts and, looking at the sparkle of the great avenues, the entrances of apartment houses and fine homes, think: "O.K., it will be my turn tomorrow!" . . .

New York is not a completed city. . . . It is a city in the process of becoming. Today it belongs to the world. Without anyone expecting it, it has become the jewel in the crown of universal cities. . . . Crown of noble cities, soft pearls, or glittering topazes, or radiant lapis, or melancholy amethysts! New York is a great diamond, hard and dry, sparkling, triumphant. . . .

New York is not a finished or completed city. It gushes up. On my next trip it will be different. Those of us who have visited it are asked this question: "When you were there in 1939, or in 1928, or in 1926, or in 1920, was such and such already there? Oh, really, you don't know then what an effect that makes!" Such is the rhythm of the city. . . .

A thousand feet of height is the rule in this frightening type of football. . . . A thousand feet of height, in stone, steel and glass, standing up in the magnificently blue sky of New York, is a new event in human history which up to now had only a legend on that theme: that of the Tower of Babel. . . .

At present, it is like a house-moving, all the furniture in confusion, scattered about, unkempt. But order will come. . . .

The skyscrapers of New York are too small and there are too many of them. They are proof of the new dimensions and the new tools; the proof that henceforth everything can be carried out on a new general plan, a symphonic plan—extent and height. . . .

Consider the most recent skyscraper, Rockefeller Center. It is rational, logically conceived, biologically normal, harmonious in its four functional elements: halls for the entrance and division of crowds, grouped shafts for vertical circulation (elevators), corridors (internal streets), regular offices.

. . . imagine the disaster caused by the overnumerous small skyscrapers. The blocks between streets and avenues, that is the building sites, are tiny parcels of land. In accordance with universal practice skyscrapers, like other buildings, are placed on the edge of the sidewalk, and shoot up straight from the street. To say skyscrapers is to say offices, that is, businessmen and automobiles. Can hundreds of cars park at the foot of skyscrapers? The necessary space is lacking, there as elsewhere. . . . New York has hardening of the arteries. A skyscraper should not be a coquettish plume rising straight up from the street. It is a wonderful instrument of concentration, to be placed in the midst of vast open spaces. The density in the skyscraper and the free area at the foot of the skyscraper constitute an indissoluble function. The one without the other is a catastrophe. That is what New York has arrived at!

"HARLEM": MID-FORTIES

At the census of 1950, more than a million Negroes dwelt in the New York-Northeastern New Jersey metropolitan area. From colonial days, New York's Negro community has been sufficiently numerous and individual to attract the attention of visitors and commentators, partly because of the novelty of color to European travelers and partly because of the types of entertainment for which the Negro quarters, and especially Harlem, became famous. By the twentieth century, "Harlem," though by no means the only locale of Negro residence, nor confined to Negroes alone, had become the symbol of the populous Negro ingredient in New York's traditionally heterogeneous society. It was well characterized, in brief compass, by the inveterate American traveler and commentator John Gunther. After serving for a dozen years, beginning in 1924, as foreign correspondent for the Chicago *Daily News,* Gunther turned to a coverage in book form of the contemporary scene "inside" Europe, Asia, Latin America, and the United States. Having resided in New York for periods of time since the middle twenties, he was better equipped than was the average commentator to comprehend the complexity of the Harlem scene. Following is an excerpt from his *Inside U. S. A.,* which appeared in 1947, and which is reprinted by permission of Harper and Brothers (copyright, 1947, by John Gunther).[49]

Though not necessarily the biggest, Harlem is by all odds the most important concentration of Negroes in America. Roughly from 110th Street to 155th on the east side, and from Madison Avenue to St. Nicholas, live some 310,000 Negroes. This is more than the population of whole cities like Atlanta, Dallas, or Portland, Oregon. Yet Harlem holds only about half the total number of Negroes (600,000) in New York City as a whole; there are approximately 150,000 in Brooklyn, about 30,000 in the Bronx, and about 30,000 in Queens. Years ago, New York Negroes lived in a few scattered and isolated enclaves: Minetta Lane in Greenwich Village, "San Juan Hill" on West 63rd Street near the river, and some areas in German Yorkville (especially on East 88th near Third). Now, as everybody knows, they have spread all over the city. Harlem itself is expanding all the time. It has no fixed frontiers.

Since "Harlem" has become a kind of abstraction (like "Hollywood"), it is extremely difficult to describe. The easiest thing to say is that it is a profoundly complex cross section of the whole of New York in black miniature. People are tempted to think of Harlem as exclusively a slum; it is also talked about as if it were a cave full of night clubs. Many Harlemites have of course never seen a night club. Some parts of it are indeed slums, and one block, near Lenox and 143rd Street, is commonly said to be the most crowded in the world. A recent commissioner of housing and building visited a sixty-four-year-old tenement in the neighborhood of Fifth and 117th not long ago, and found it "infested, scaly, shabby," a menace to health, a disgrace otherwise, and a fire trap. . . .

But Harlem as a whole is by no means a slum. . . . A good many apartment blocks, built long before the district became Negro, are still in good shape; the trouble is that they are viciously overcrowded and badly maintained. For instance there will be only one superintendent for six buildings, jammed with sublet flats, and containing literally hundreds of families. Also Harlem has several handsome, modern, and well-maintained apartment buildings. One, at 409 Edgecombe, is in the area known locally as "Sugar Hill"; here lives, as I heard it put, "the glamor set of Black America." But this description makes Sugar Hill sound frivolous, which it is not. A great number of eminent Negroes live there. . . .

[Harlem] is a community constantly in motion. Like New Rochelle, it is a kind of bedroom for the rest of New York; people live here, and work downtown. It has several Negro newspapers, including the conservative *Amsterdam News* and the radical *People's Voice*. There is no Negro department store; most of the shopkeepers on the main street (125th) are Jews. Almost all real estate is white absentee owned, though one Negro businessman, A. A. Austin, is a substantial owner; there is no Negro bank (but local branches of the great white banks employ Negro personnel); about seventy-five saloons and one movie house are Negro owned, but no more; the chief hotel is a remarkable establishment called the Theresa, almost exclusively Negro, but it is white owned, and several whites live in it. The chief Negro business in Harlem on a broad level is insurance (unless you want to count religion as a business), and on a narrower level hairdressing.

The whole community is, of course, strongly labor conscious. . . . Probably some single streets in Harlem have more Negro trade unionists than the entire state of Georgia. In New York as a whole there is probably less discrimination against Negroes, in employment and otherwise, than in any other city in America. In fact many familiar forms of anti-Negro discrimination are illegal in New York. Of course some discriminations, illegal or not, do continue to exist. . . .

To sum up: the chief characteristic of Harlem is that, by and large, its Negroes (and others in New York) have greater opportunities in more fields than in any comparable city; they have better chances in education, jobs, social evolution, and civil service; they are the nearest to full citizenship of any in the nation.

MID-CENTURY METROPOLIS: WORLD CAPITAL

Even before the United Nations occupied its permanent headquarters in the heart of Manhattan, travelers were aware, more than the city's residents, that New York was an international capital, that in appearance and spirit it was as much of the world at large as of the nation that claimed it. This resulted in part from the strength of the United States following World War II. It was a natural culmination of New York's long-time attraction for peoples of all nationalities and creeds, and, in recent years, for refugees from war and prejudice. It was fostered by the structural magnificence, the show of wealth, and the extensive cultural offering that its commercial and industrial pre-eminence made possible. As Cecil Beaton wrote, upon intimate acquaintance with the city, New York of the thirties and forties was "the one great world city." Equally sensitive to the international character of postwar New York City was Beverley Nichols, English essayist, novelist, and travel writer, who, like Beaton, had a wide acquaintance with the city. Educated at Oxford, he made his first trip to America during World War I as a member of the Universities Mission. During 1928 and 1929 he was again in New York, this time as editor of the *American Sketch*. In the following selection, resulting from a visit in the late forties, he catches both the pull of the city for the foreign traveler and the international flavor of the metropolis at the mid-century. It is an excerpt from his *Uncle Samson,* a description of life in postwar America, which was published in 1950. It is reprinted by permission of the author.[50]

The Englishman who crosses the Atlantic today is no longer crossing from the Old World to the New; he is crossing from the New World to the Old.

It is only when one goes to America that one realizes how very far, in Britain, we have gone along the road to the complete socialization, not only of our economy, but of our habits of thought. . . .

Just as Park Avenue is now, in spirit, a million miles from Park Lane, so is Wall Street a million miles from Lombard Street. If you were to venture towards the maelstrom of Wall Street at the hour of luncheon, if you were to plunge into the scurrying rapids of humanity that swirl beneath its jagged cliffs, and if, on some temporary raft of refuge, you were to get into conversation with some young man—in the shelter of a doorway or in the comparative seclusion of an elevator—and if, having made your contact, you were to ask your young man whether he wanted to be a millionaire, what would happen? He might stare at you with some astonishment, suspect that you were a religious maniac, and, quite possibly, turn his back. If, however, he decided that your question was seriously meant, he would reply, with some force, that of course he wanted to be a millionaire, and not only did he want to be a millionaire, but that he had every intention of becoming one, without too much darned delay, either. And before you had detached yourself from him he might well have sold you a packet of life insurance. . . .

I stood on the pavement in Park Avenue as dusk was falling, and sniffed. Yes, the smell of New York was just the same. Ten years had passed since I had last stood in this spot, and in that period one's nostrils had been affronted by many warring odours on land and sea; but here the atmosphere was unchanged. It was the same dry, astringent odour of ozone and gasoline, the scent of open spaces caught up in the scent of the towering metropolis, blended in a unique and heady essence. And I knew that wherever I turned in the great city this essence would envelop me; it would be impossible to escape it. Of course, there would be minor variations. In Central Park there would be a faint tang of autumn leaves, and down Lexington Avenue the whiff of hamburgers; outside the Ritz, as the great doors revolved, there would be little spicy gusts that came from the hot mass of scented womanhood, and up at Harlem, the salt-sweet atmosphere—for it is an atmosphere rather than an aroma—that seems for some of us to tinge the air around the dwellings of the coloured races. But the main formula was fixed; gasoline and ozone, ozone and gasoline; that was New York. . . .

Where should I go, on this, my first evening? . . . a first night in New York is as a first night in no other city. In Paris one can lie in a chaise-longue and watch the street-lamps glowing through the chestnut trees; in Venice one can sit at a window and listen to the water lapping against the walls; in London one not only can but *must* go straight to bed, as there is nothing else to do. . . . Not so in New York. Here the city orders you to come out and greet it, in a thousand strident voices, with a million golden, beckoning fingers. . . .

I decided to drift at random; . . . at every twist and turn there were marvels. . . . black torrents of sleek cars . . . charging throngs of women who all appeared to be wearing a compulsory uniform of mink. But it is the beauty rather than the opulence of New York that catches the traveller by the throat as he turns from 60th Street into Fifth Avenue. For now the dusk was trembling into night; it was the city's *heure exquise,* and ahead stretched the bewildering façade of the buildings that run west of the Park. The geometrical masses of the Plaza Hotel had been transformed into a frail filagree of light and shade, linked by chains of diamonds to distant towers and temples, as tall flowers might be linked by spiders' webs in a garden after rain.

I turned down the Avenue. . . . More than ever before, as the shop windows filed past in a glittering parade, there was the sense of New York as a great international city to which all the ends of the world had come. London used to be like that, but somehow one had forgotten it, so long had it been since the Hispanos and the Isottas had glided down Piccadilly, so many aeons since the tropical fruits had glowed in the Bond Street windows. Coming from that sort of London to America, in the old days, New York had seemed just—American; not typical of the continent maybe, but American first and foremost. Now it was the centre of the world.

NOTES

CHAPTER 1

1. Giovanni da Verrazano, *Cèllere Codex,* as quoted in Jacques Habert, *When New York Was Called Angoulême* (New York, 1949), pp. 43–44. See Edward Channing, *History of the United States* (6 vols., New York, 1905–1930), I, 91–92.

2. Robert Juet, "The Third Voyage of Master Henry Hudson," as excerpted in J. Franklin Jameson, ed., *Narratives of New Netherland* (New York, 1909), pp. 20–21. See John Bakeless, *Eyes of Discovery* (Philadelphia, 1950), pp. 237–39; Channing, I, 439–41.

3. Victor H. Paltsits, "The Founding of New Amsterdam in 1626," *Proceedings of the American Antiquarian Society,* n.s. XXXIV (April 1924), pp. 41, 53, 58–59, 62.

4. Nicolaes Janzoon van Wassenaer, *Historisch Verhael,* pt. XII, November 1626, as excerpted in Jameson, ed., *Narratives of New Netherland,* pp. 82–83.

5. *Ibid.,* p. 83; Isaack de Rasière to the Amsterdam Chamber of the West India Company, September 23, 1626, in A. J. F. van Laer, tr. and ed., *Documents Relating to New Netherland 1624–1626 in the Henry E. Huntington Library* (San Marino, Cal., 1924), pp. 207–8, 223–24, 227–28, 231–32, 235–36.

6. Rev. Jonas Michaëlius to Adrianus Smoutius, 1628, in Jameson, ed., *Narratives of New Netherland,* pp. 122–33.

7. Father Isaac Jogues, "Novum Belgium, 1646," in Jameson, ed., *Narratives of New Netherland,* pp. 259–60; Ellis L. Raesly, *Portrait of New Netherland* (New York, 1945), p. 39; David P. De Vries, *Short Historical and Journal-Notes of various Voyages . . .* (Alkmaar, 1655), in Jameson, ed., *Narratives of New Netherland,* p. 212.

8. Jogues, in Jameson, ed., *Narratives of New Netherland,* pp. 259–60.

9. [Anon.], "Concerning New Netherland, or Manhattan," in "The Clarendon Papers," in New-York Historical Society, *Collections,* II (1869), 1; William R. Shepherd, *The Story of New Amsterdam* (New York, 1926), pp. 64–75.

10. See reproduction of so-called Prototype View ("New Amsterdam Now New York on the Island of Manhattan"), in I. N. Phelps Stokes, *New York Past and Present* (New York, 1939), p. 4; [Anon.], "Description of the Towne of Mannadens, 1661," in Jameson, ed., *Narratives of New Netherland,* p. 421; Charles M. Andrews, *The Colonial Period of American History* (4 vols., New Haven, 1934–1938), III, 78.

11. Shepherd, pp. 94–132.

12. *Ibid.,* pp. 155–65; "Description of the Towne of Mannadens, 1661," in Jameson, ed., *Narratives of New Netherland,* p. 421.

13. Jogues, in Jameson, ed., *Narratives of New Netherland,* pp. 259–60; Carl Bridenbaugh, *Cities in the Wilderness* (New York, 1938), p. 95.

14. "Description of the Towne of Mannadens, 1661," in Jameson, ed., *Narratives of New Netherland,* pp. 423–24.

15. Nicasius de Sille to Maximiliaen van Beeckerke, May 23, 1654, in New York State Historical Association, *Quarterly Journal,* I (1920), 100–3; Raesly, p. 287.

16. Andrews, III, 50, 52–60.

17. Shepherd, pp. 176–87.

18. van Wassenaer, *Historisch Verhael,* in Jameson, ed., *Narratives of New Netherland,* pp. 83–84, 86, 88.

19. "Description of the Towne of Mannadens, 1661," in Jameson, ed., *Narratives of New Netherland,* pp. 421–23; Andrews, III, 61.

CHAPTER 2

1. For the physical growth of the community during the eighteenth century, see Thomas A. Janvier, *In Old New York* (New York, 1894), pp. 36–44.

2. Daniel Denton, *A Brief Description of New-York: Formerly Called New-Netherlands. With the Places thereunto Adjoyning* (London, 1670), p. 3 (Facsimile Text Society edition, ed. by Victor H. Paltsits); Benjamin Bullivant, "A Journall with observations on my travail from Boston in N. E. to N. Y. New-Jersies & Philadelphia in Pensilvania. A. D. 1697," edited as "A Glance at New York in 1697: The Travel Diary of Dr. Benjamin Bullivant," by Wayne Andrews, in *The New-York Historical Society Quarterly,* XL (January 1956), 65; Madam Sarah Kemble Knight, *The Private Journal of a Journey from Boston to New York in the Year 1704* (Albany, 1865), pp. 66–67.

3. Bullivant, pp. 62, 63; Thomas Pownall, *A Topographical Description of the Dominions of the United States of America,* ed. by Lois Mulkearn (Pittsburgh, 1949), p. 43; [Anon.], "Journal of a French Traveller in the Colonies, 1765," in *American Historical Review,* XXVII (October 1921), 82; Michel Guillaume Jean de Crèvecoeur, *Lettres d'un Cultivateur Américain, écrites à W. S., écuyer, depuis l'Année 1770, jusqu'à 1781* (2 vols., 1784), as published in *Magazine of American History,* II (1878), 749.

4. *Journal of Jasper Danckaerts, 1679–1680,* ed. by Bartlett B. James and J. Franklin Jameson (New York, 1913), p. 44; Peter Kalm, *Travels into North America,* tr. by John R. Forster (2 vols., London, 1772), I, 193–94.

5. "Journal of a French Traveller in the Colonies, 1765," p. 82; [Lord Adam Gordon], "Journal of an Officer Who Travelled in America and the West Indies in 1764 and 1765," in Newton D. Mereness, ed., *Travels in the American Colonies, 1690–1783* (New York, 1916), p. 414; Crèvecoeur, p. 749; Rev. Andrew Burnaby, *Travels Through the Middle Settlements in North America in the Years 1759 and 1760* (London, 1798), ed. by Rufus R. Wilson (New York, 1904), p. 111; Bridenbaugh, *Cities in the Wilderness,* pp. 321–22; Ernest S. Griffith, *History of American City Government: The Colonial Period* (New York, 1938), p. 270.

6. Pownall, pp. 43–44; Bullivant, p. 65.

7. [John Fontaine], "Journal of John Fontaine," in Ann Maury, *Memoirs of a Huguenot Family* (New York, 1853), p. 297; Crèvecoeur, p. 748; Bullivant, p. 65.

8. "Answers of Gov. Andros to Enquiries about New York; 1678," in *The Documentary History of the State of New York,* ed. by E. B. O'Callaghan (4 vols., Albany, 1850–1851), I, 60; *Journal of Jasper Danckaerts, 1679–1680,* pp. 45–46; Bullivant, pp. 61–62; "Gov. Dongan's Report to the Committee of Trade on the Province of New-York, dated 22d February, 1687," in *Documentary History . . . New York,* I, 96; Fontaine, p. 296; Kalm, I, 196; Gordon, p. 415; "Journal of a French Traveller in the Colonies, 1765," p. 82.

9. "Gov. Dongan's Report . . . 1687," in *Documentary History . . . New York,* I, 102.

10. Charles Lodwick to Francis Lodwick, May 20, 1692, quoted in I. N. Phelps Stokes, ed., *The Iconography of Manhattan Island . . .* (6 vols., New York, 1915–1928), IV, 375.

11. [Anon.], "New York in America," in *Documentary History . . . New York,* I, 494–95. See also "Cadwallader Colden on the Trade of New York; 1723," *ibid.,* I, 487–91.

12. Kalm, I, 197–200; George W. Edwards, *New York as an Eighteenth Century Municipality, 1731–1776* (New York, 1917), p. 62; "Journal of a French Traveller in the Colonies, 1765," p. 82.

13. Knight, pp. 69–70; Bridenbaugh, *Cities in the Wilderness,* pp. 192, 343.

14. Kalm, I, 201; "Gov. Hunter to the Board of Trade, 12 Novr 1715," in *Documentary History . . . New York,* I, 486; Burnaby, p. 115.

15. "Gov. Moore to the Lords of Trade," January 12, 1767, in *Documentary History . . . New York,* I, 498–99.

16. Patrick M'Robert, *A Tour through Part of the North Provinces of America: Being A Series of Letters wrote on the Spot, in the Years 1774 & 1775* (Edinburgh, 1776), p. 5. This may be found, edited by Carl Bridenbaugh, in *The*

Pennsylvania Magazine of History and Biography, LIX (April 1935), 134–75.

17. William Byrd I to "Bro. Dan'l" [Horsmanden], March 8, 1685/86, in "Capt. Byrd's Letters," in *The Virginia Historical Register, and Literary Advertiser,* II (1849), 208; "Gov. Dongan's Report . . . 1687," in *Documentary History . . . New York,* I, 103; Charles Lodwick, quoted in Stokes, *Iconography,* IV, 375; Antoine de la Mothe Cadillac, "Memoir," quoted, *ibid.,* IV, 373; Fontaine, p. 298; M'Robert, p. 5; Evarts B. Greene and Virginia D. Harrington, *American Population before the Federal Census of 1790* (New York, 1932), p. 102; "Peter Kalm, Scientist from Sweden," in Oscar Handlin, *This Was America* (Cambridge, 1949), p. 32; "Journal of a French Traveller in the Colonies, 1765," p. 82.

18. [Dr. Alexander Hamilton], *Gentleman's Progress: the Itinerarium of Dr. Alexander Hamilton, 1744,* ed. by Carl Bridenbaugh (Chapel Hill, 1948), pp. 88–89; Kalm, I, 211; James Birket, *Some Cursory Remarks Made by James Birket in his Voyage to North America, 1750–1751* (New Haven, 1916), p. 45.

19. "Gov. Dongan's Report . . . 1687," in *Documentary History . . . New York,* I, 116; Byrd to Horsmanden, *op. cit.,* p. 208; Bullivant, p. 62.

20. *Journal of Jasper Danckaerts, 1679–1680,* pp. 75–76; Charles Wolley, *A Two Years' Journal in New York,* ed. by Edward G. Bourne (Cleveland, 1902), pp. 66–67.

21. Kalm, I, 196; M'Robert, pp. 3–4. See also Robert Rogers, *A Concise Account of North America* (Dublin, 1770), p. 79.

22. Kalm, I, 192–93. See also Dr. Alexander Hamilton, p. 178.

23. Rev. John Miller, *A Description of the Province and City of New York; with Plans of the City and Several Forts as they existed in the year 1695* (London, 1843), pp. 12–15.

24. Knight, p. 69; Dr. Alexander Hamilton, p. 88; Crèvecoeur, p. 749; M'Robert, p. 5; Bullivant, p. 66.

25. Knight, p. 69; Dr. Alexander Hamilton, pp. 44, 89; Bridenbaugh, *Cities in the Wilderness,* pp. 414–16; Rogers, p. 73; "Journal of a French Traveller in the Colonies, 1765," p. 82.

26. "Diary of Ezra Stiles," in Massachusetts Historical Society, *Proceedings,* 2d series, VII (1891–1892), 339.

27. Burnaby, pp. 117–18, 260; Dr. Alexander Hamilton, p. 89; Bullivant, p. 64.

28. Fontaine, p. 299; Dr. Alexander Hamilton, pp. 88–89, 177.

29. *Ibid.,* p. 48; "Diary of Ezra Stiles," p. 339; Thomas J. Wertenbaker, *The Golden Age of Colonial Culture* (New York, 1949), p. 55; Bridenbaugh, *Cities in the Wilderness,* p. 462; "Journal of Josiah Quincy, Junior, 1773," in Massachusetts Historical Society, *Proceedings,* XLIX (1915–1916), 479.

30. *Ibid.,* pp. 478–79; Wertenbaker, *Golden Age,* pp. 52–55.

31. *The Works of John Adams,* ed. by Charles F. Adams (10 vols., Boston, 1850–1856), II, 353.

32. Burnaby, pp. 112, 117; Stokes, *Iconography,* IV, 677; Crèvecoeur, p. 749; *The Works of John Adams,* II, 353.

33. *Ibid.,* II, 352; Bullivant, p. 64.

34. Kalm, I, 196–97; Dr. Alexander Hamilton, p. 88; Birket, p. 44; Burnaby, p. 112.

35. Crèvecoeur, p. 750; Edwards, pp. 132, 135–36, 139–41.

36. *Ibid.,* pp. 119–26; Capt. William Owen, R. N., "Narrative of American Voyages and Travels . . . ," ed. by Victor H. Paltsits, in *Bulletin of the New York Public Library,* XXXV (March 1931), p. 151.

37. "Journal of Josiah Quincy, Junior," p. 480; Crèvecoeur, p. 749. A similar impression of the comforts and abundance of life in New York is reflected in a report by Joseph H. Mandrillon, a Frenchman who presumably visited the city on the eve of the Revolution. Comfort was so universal, he asserted, as to produce a softness and laziness in the people. His comments, entitled *Précis sur l'Amérique Septentrionale & la République des Treize-États-Unis,* appear as an appendix to [Alexander Cluny], *Le voyageur américain* (Amsterdam, 1782). See pages 99–101.

38. Bullivant, pp. 61, 62, 64, 66.

39. Kalm, I, 198–200. See Handlin, *This Was America,* p. 14.

40. M'Robert, pp. 3–5, 9, 10.

CHAPTER 3

1. Oscar T. Barck, Jr., *New York City during the War for Independence* (New York, 1931), pp. 74–79.

2. Gordon, p. 415; "Journal of a French Traveller in the Colonies, 1765," p. 85.

3. Excerpt from William Smith, "Diary," quoted in Stokes, *Iconography,* IV, 840; Lieut. Gov. Colden to Lord Dartmouth, July 6, 1774, *ibid.,* IV, 859.

4. *The Works of John Adams,* II, 350.

5. *Colonial Panorama, 1775: Dr. Robert Honyman's Journal for March and April,* ed. by Philip Padelford (San Marino, Cal., 1939), pp. 29, 31, 68, 70.

6. Barck, pp. 40–41; Ewald G. Schaukirk, "Diary," published as *Occupation of New York City by the British,* a reprint from *Pennsylvania Magazine of History and Biography,* I (January 1877), pp. 1–2; William Smith, "Diary," quoted in Stokes, *Iconography,* IV, 883.

7. New York *Packet,* February 15, 1776, *ibid.,* IV, 914. See also extracts from the diary of the Moravian Congregation, in "Occupation of New York City by the British, 1776," in *Pennsylvania Magazine of History and Biography,* I (1877), 134–37.

8. Extract of a letter from New York, April 12, 1776, in *Historical Magazine,* 1st series, X, pt. 2, p. 111; Frederick Rhinelander to Peter Van Schaack, February 23, 1776, in Henry C. Van Schaack, *The Life of Peter Van Schaack* (New York, 1842), pp. 53–54; "Extracts from the Diary of Dr. James Clitherall, 1776," in *Pennsylvania Magazine,* XX (1898), 472–74.

9. *Journal of Lieutenant Isaac Bangs, April 1 to July 29, 1776,* ed. by Edward Bangs (Cambridge, Mass., 1890), pp. 24–26, 29–31, 59.

10. Extract of a letter from New York, April 12, 1776, *op. cit.; The Journal of Nicholas Cresswell, 1774–1777* (New York, 1924), pp. 158–59.

11. Barck, pp. 46–48; *The American Journal of Ambrose Serle,* ed. by Edward H. Tatum, Jr. (San Marino, Cal., 1940), xii, xiv, 103–11, 134; *Archibald Robertson, His Diaries and Sketches in America,* ed. by Harry M. Lydenberg (New York, 1930), p. 98.

12. William Eddis, *Letters from America, Historical and Descriptive, comprising Occurrences from 1769, to 1777, Inclusive* (London, 1792), p. 421; Loyalist letter, September 23, 1776, printed in *St. James's Chronicle,* November 7–9, 1776, quoted in Stokes, *Iconography,* V, 1020.

13. "Letter from an Officer at New-York to a Friend in London" (London, 1777), *ibid.,* V, 1041-42; [Anon.], "Journal of an Irishman in New York at the Close of the American Revolution," ed. by Victor H. Paltsits, in *Bulletin of the New York Public Library,* XXVII (November 1923), 892–93.

14. Eddis, p. 426; Schaukirk, pp. 8, 23; Frederika Riedesel, *Letters and Journals Relating to the War of the American Revolution, and the Capture of the German Troops at Saratoga,* tr. by William L. Stone (Albany, 1867), p. 173; Thomas J. Wertenbaker, *Father Knickerbocker Rebels* (New York, 1948), pp. 216–17; *The American Journal of Ambrose Serle,* p. 168. See "Journal" of Lieut. John Charles Philip von Krafft, 1776–84, in New-York Historical Society, *Collections,* XV (1882), 82.

15. Barck, p. 143; *Letters from America, 1776–1779,* tr. by Ray W. Pettengill (Cambridge, Mass., 1924), pp. 166, 232–33.

16. Schaukirk, p. 10; Riedesel, p. 173; [Thomas Anburey], *Travels through the Interior Parts of America. In a Series of Letters. By an Officer* (2 vols., London, 1789), II, 541. Anburey appears to have lifted most of his observations from the accounts of earlier travelers, although he apparently visited New York late in 1781, en route to England. See Whitfield L. Bell, "Thomas Anburey's 'Travels through America': a note on eighteenth-century plagiarism," in Bibliographical Society of America, *Papers,* XXXVII (1943), 23–36. One of Anburey's sources was the work of J. F. D. Smyth, an English visitor who arrived in New York in August, 1784, and who described the city briefly in his *A Tour in the United States of America* (2 vols., London, 1784).

17. Sidney I. Pomerantz, *New York an American City, 1783–1803* (New York, 1938), p. 21; [Robert Hunter, Jr.], *Quebec to Carolina in 1785–1786, Being the Travel Diary and Observations of Robert Hunter, Jr., a Young Merchant of Lon-*

don, ed. by Louis B. Wright and Marian Tinling (San Marino, Cal., 1943), pp. 11, 132–33, 282; Barck, 73, 221.

18. "Citizen" to editor, *Loudon's New-York Packet,* December 16, 1784; *Life, Journals and Correspondence of Rev. Manasseh Cutler, LL.D.,* ed. by William P. and Julia P. Cutler (2 vols., Cincinnati, 1888), I, 306, 309.

19. Luigi Castiglioni, *Viaggio negli Stati Uniti dell' America Settentrionale, fatto negli anni 1785, 1786 e 1787* (2 vols., Milan, 1790), I, 177–81. See also Howard R. Marraro, "Count Luigi Castiglioni, an early traveller to Virginia," in *Virginia Magazine of History and Biography,* LVIII (1950), 473–91. J. P. Brissot de Warville, *New Travels in the United States of America, Performed in 1788* (2 vols., London, 1792), I, 75, 155, 157; Handlin, pp. 67–68.

20. *Life, Journals and Correspondence of Rev. Manasseh Cutler,* I, 307, 309; [Anon.], "General Description of the City of New York," in *The American Magazine* (March 1788), 226.

21. Barck, p. 229; Pomerantz, p. 155; Brissot de Warville, I, 160–61.

22. Bangs, pp. 3–6, 24–25, 39, 43–44, 56–57, 59, 60, 64.

23. Schaukirk, pp. 1–4, 8, 10, 16–17, 23, 28.

24. *Letters from America, 1776–1779,* pp. 165–66, 232–33.

CHAPTER 4

1. François Alexandre Frédéric, duc de La Rochefoucauld-Liancourt, *Travels through the United States of North America, the Country of the Iroquois, and Upper Canada in the Years 1795, 1796, and 1797; with an Authentic Account of Lower Canada* (2 vols., London, 1799), II, 456; [Barthélemi Sernin du Moulin de la Barthelle, baron de Montlezun], *Souvenirs des Antilles: voyage en 1815 et 1816, aux États-Unis, et dans l'archipel Caraïbe; aperçu de Philadelphie et New-Yorck . . . Par M. . . .* (2 vols., Paris, 1818), I, 97, 152. Robert Hunter wrote after a trip in 1785–86: "Philadelphia is the only decent city I have seen. Boston, New York, and Baltimore are the three next." *Quebec to Carolina in 1785–86,* Wright and Tinling, eds., p. 282.

2. In 1810, Philadelphia City, plus the thickly built parts of Southwark, Passyunk, and Moyamensing, adjoining the southern quarter of the city, totaled 96,664. At this date, New York's population was officially listed as 96,363. By 1820, Philadelphia City plus the contiguous settlements totaled 108,709 to New York's 123,706. A petition of Thomas Stagg to the New York Assembly in February 1811 referred to New York as the most populous city in the United States. James Mease, *The Picture of Philadelphia* (Philadelphia, 1811), pp. 35, 37; *U.S. Census of 1810,* p. 33; *U.S. Census of 1820,* pp. 15, 19; Stokes, *Iconography,* III, 494. A count of the population, authorized by the Common Council, gave New York a population of 100,619 in 1816. See [Edmund M. Blunt], *The Picture of New-York and Stranger's Guide to the Commercial Metropolis of the United States* (New York, 1828), p. 171. Adam Heinrich Dietrich von Bülow, *Der Freistaat von Nordamerika in seinem neuesten Zustand* (2 vols., Berlin, 1797), II, 83–84.

3. [Charles Maurice de Talleyrand-Périgord], *Talleyrand in America as a Financial Promoter, 1794–1796,* unpublished letters and memoirs, tr. and ed. by Hans Huth and Wilma J. Pugh, in American Historical Association, *Annual Report, 1941,* vol. II, 94–95; Montlezun, I, 142; John Bernard, *Retrospections of America, 1797–1811,* ed. by Mrs. Bayle Bernard (New York, 1887), p. 51. See also Timothy Dwight, *Travels; in New-England and New-York* (4 vols., New Haven, 1821), III, 467; John W. Devereux, "My Journal of one of my trips to New York," in *Georgia Historical Quarterly,* XV (1931), 46–80.

4. [François Marie] Perrin du Lac, *Voyage dans les deux Louisianes et chez les nations sauvages du Missouri, par les États-Unis, l'Ohio et les provinces qui le bordent, en 1801, 1802, et 1803* (Lyon, 1805), pp. 20–22. See also La Rochefoucauld-Liancourt, II, 456; William Priest, *Travels in the United States of America; commencing in the Year 1793 and Ending in 1797* (London, 1802), p. 151; *Jeffersonian America: Notes on the United States of America Collected in the Years 1805–6–7 and 11–12 by Sir Augustus John*

Foster, Bart., ed. by Richard B. Davis (San Marino, Cal., 1954), p. 294.

5. "Diary of the Honorable Jonathan Mason," in Massachusetts Historical Society, *Proceedings*, 2d series, II (1885–1886), 8, 11; "A Young Man's Journal of 1800–1813 [William Johnson of Newton, N. J.]," in New Jersey Historical Society, *Proceedings*, n.s., VIII (1923), 151; *Writings of John Quincy Adams*, ed. by Worthington C. Ford (7 vols., New York, 1917), III, 142.

6. John Lambert, *Travels through Canada, and the United States of North America, in the Years 1806, 1807, & 1808* (2 vols., London, 1814), II, 49, 64–65, 295; Timothy Dwight, III, 470; Charles W. Janson, *The Stranger in America, 1793–1806*, reprinted from the London edition of 1807 with introduction and notes by Carl S. Driver (New York, 1935), p. 92; Samuel S. Bridge, "Diary," printed in "New York A Hundred Years Ago," in *Munsey's Magazine*, XL (November 1908), 205.

7. François Auguste, Viscount de Chateaubriand, *Travels in America and Italy* (2 vols., London, 1828), I, 97–98; *Life, Journals and Correspondence of Rev. Manasseh Cutler*, I, 305; John Drayton, *Letters Written During a Tour through the Northern and Eastern States of America* (Charleston, S. C., 1794), pp. 9–10; Thomas Cooper, *Some Information Respecting America collected by Thomas Cooper, late of Manchester* (London, 1795), p. 48; *Jeffersonian America* (Foster), p. 290.

8. Timothy Dwight, III, 451; Lambert, II, 55–57, 59. See also Isaac Weld, Jr., *Travels through the States of North America and Provinces of Upper and Lower Canada during the Years 1795, 1796, and 1797* (London, 1800), p. 192; John Melish, *Travels through the United States of America, in the years 1806 & 1807, and 1809, 1810, & 1811 . . .* (London, 1818), p. 57; Félix de Beaujour, *Sketch of the United States of North America at the Commencement of the Nineteenth Century, from 1800 to 1810*, tr. by William Walton (London, 1814), pp. 75–76; "Diary of . . . Mason," p. 8.

9. Lambert, II, 56–57; Hunter, pp. 129–30; [Francisco de Miranda], *The Diary of Francisco de Miranda: Tour of the United States, 1783–1784*, the Spanish text, ed. by William S. Robertson (New York, 1928), p. 51; Meryle R. Evans, "Knickerbocker Hotels and Restaurants, 1800–1850," in *The New-York Historical Society Quarterly*, XXXVI (October 1952), 382–85; Montlezun, I, 137; Timothy Bigelow, *Diary of a Visit to Newport, New York, and Philadelphia, during the Summer of 1815*, ed. by Abbott Lawrence (Boston, 1880), pp. 12, 13, 21.

10. Perrin du Lac, p. 9; Drayton, p. 19; J. E. Bonnet, *États-Unis de l'Amérique à la fin du XVIIIe siècle* (2 vols., Paris, [1802?]), II, 367, 369; Beaujour, p. 76; Weld, p. 191; [Médéric-Louis-Élie Moreau de St. Méry], *Moreau de St. Méry's American Journey [1793–1798]*, tr. and ed. by Kenneth Roberts and Anna M. Roberts (New York, 1947), p. 146; Constantin F. Chasseboeuf, Count de Volney, *View of the Climate and Soil of the United States of America* (London, 1804), p. 322. See also Lieut. John Harriott, *Struggles through Life, Exemplified in the Various Travels and Adventures in Europe, Asia, Africa, and America of Lieut. John Harriott* (2d ed., London, 1808), quoted in Stokes, *Iconography*, V, 1295. The Baron de Montlezun wrote in 1815: "New York is lighted with reflector-type lamps; the convenience is all the greater since the sidewalks are neglected and the holes make traps." I, 143.

11. Brissot de Warville, I, 155; Timothy Dwight, III, 469; Henry Wansey, *An Excursion to the United States of North America in the Summer of 1794* (Salisbury, 1798), p. 59; Frances S. Childs, *French Refugee Life in the United States* (Baltimore, 1940), pp. 9–10; Pomerantz, pp. 204–5; Édouard Charles Victurnien Colbert, Le Comte de Maulevrier, *Voyage dans l'intérieur des États-Unis et au Canada*, ed. by Gilbert Chinard (Baltimore, 1935), p. 72. A visitor in 1798, Colbert found the New Yorkers more hospitable than the residents of Philadelphia.

12. Alexandre Maurice Blanc de la Naulte, Comte d'Hauterive, "Journal" (manuscript in New-York Historical Society), entry for October 23, 1793; Ferdinand-M. Bayard, *Voyage dans l'intérieur des États-Unis . . . pendant l'été de 1791* (Paris, 1798), pp. 243, 257, 260, 264.

13. Moreau de St. Méry, p. 125.

14. "The Travels of Louis Ange Pitou in the United States, 1801," tr. by Sylvia H. Monaghan, in *Légion d'Honneur*, IV

(April 1934), 247–48. For the reactions of a French Canadian in 1810, see Gabriel Franchère, *Narrative of a Voyage to the Northwest Coast of America in the Years 1811, 1812, 1813, and 1814 . . .*, tr. by J. V. Huntington, in *Early Western Travels,* ed. by Reuben G. Thwaites (Cleveland, 1904), VI, 190–92. See also Henriette Lucie, Marquise de la Tour du Pin de Gouvernet, *Journal d'une Femme de Cinquante Ans, 1778–1815* (2 vols., Paris, 1924), II, 81–84.

15. Lambert, II, 58, 90–91.

16. "Diary of . . . Mason," pp. 9–10; Timothy Dwight, III, 473.

17. Pomerantz, pp. 373, 475, 479; Francis Baily, *Journal of a Tour in Unsettled Parts of North America in 1796 and 1797* (London, 1856), pp. 121–22; Samuel Davis, "Journal of a Tour to Connecticut—Autumn of 1789," in Massachusetts Historical Society, *Proceedings,* XI (1869–1870), 22, 23; Lambert, II, 95, 101–2; Weld, p. 193; Montlezun, I, 143. See also Perrin du Lac, pp. 24–25; John Mair, "Journal of John Mair, 1791," in *American Historical Review,* XII (1906), 83.

18. Samuel Davis, p. 22; *Diary of William Dunlap, 1766–1839* (3 vols., New York, 1930), I, 13–14; Elias Boudinot to his wife, April 24, 1789, quoted in Stokes, *Iconography,* V, 1240.

19. Samuel Davis, p. 22; *The Journal of William Maclay* (New York, 1927), pp. 66, 98; "Diary of Dr. Alexander Anderson," in *Old New York,* I (1890), 97, II (1890–1891), 435; "Diary of . . . Mason," p. 10.

20. Lambert, II, 79–80, 95; Timothy Dwight, III, 473; Perrin du Lac, pp. 26–27; "Diary of . . . Mason," p. 8; Montlezun, I, 143; Pomerantz, 488–90. Perrin du Lac contended that music, painting, and the dance would still be ignored if several Frenchmen had not brought the taste for them some years before. *Op. cit.,* p. 27. For references to a lack of "literary society" in New York, see a rather supercilious tutor's account: *Travels of John Davis in the United States of America, 1798–1802,* ed. by John V. Cheney (2 vols., Boston, 1910[?]). Data on the literary, commercial, and recreational institutions of New York City are to be found in two guidebooks, among the earliest to be written describing New York City, the first of them patterned after the *Picture of London,* the *Oxford Guide,* and the *Tableau de Paris:* [Samuel Latham Mitchill], *The Picture of New-York; or the Traveller's Guide, through the Commercial Metropolis of the United States. By a Gentleman residing in this City* (New York, 1807); [Edmund M. Blunt], *The Picture of New-York and Stranger's Guide to the Commercial Metropolis of the United States* (New York, 1828).

21. Alexander Flick, ed., *History of the State of New York* (10 vols., New York, 1933–1937), V, 243–47; R. S. Guernsey, *New York City and Vicinity during the War of 1812–1815* (2 vols., New York, 1895), II, 39, 219, 304–8, 459.

22. Cooper, pp. 48–50; *Dictionary of National Biography,* XII, 151; *Dictionary of American Biography,* IV, 414.

23. Wansey, pp. 57–59, 65–66, 221, 226; Allan Nevins, *America Through British Eyes* (New York, 1948), pp. 35–36.

24. La Rochefoucauld-Liancourt, II, 456–58; Childs, pp. 30–31.

25. Bernard, pp. 51–52; Nevins, *America Through British Eyes,* p. 24.

26. Lambert, II, 49, 55–61, 62–65, 75–80, 95, 98–100, 104, 106–7, 295.

27. Guernsey, II, 39.

28. *Ibid.,* II, 232.

29. New York *Evening Post,* August 20, 1814, quoted in Stokes, *Iconography,* V, 1574.

30. Guernsey, II, 456–57.

CHAPTER 5

1. [Baron Axel Klinkowström], *Baron Klinkowström's America,* ed. by Franklin D. Scott (Evanston, Ill., 1952), p. 6. This is a translation of Baron Axel Klinkowström, *Bref om de Förenta Staterna, författade under en resa till Amerika, åren 1818, 1819, 1820* [Letters concerning the United States, written during a journey to America in 1818, 1819, 1820] (Stockholm, 1824). See also Friedrich L. G. von Raumer, *America and the Americans* (New York, 1846), p. 468. This is a translation by William Turner of *Die Vereinigten Staaten von Nordamerika* (2 vols., Leipzig, 1845). See also *Walt Whitman of the New York "Aurora,"* ed. by

Joseph J. Rubin and Charles H. Brown (State College, Pa., 1950), p. 19; [Edward Ruggles], *A Picture of New-York in 1846; with a Short Account of Places in Its Vicinity designed as a Guide to Citizens and Strangers* (New York, 1846), p. 107.

2. Lieut. Francis Hall, *Travels in Canada and the United States in 1816 and 1817* (2d ed., London, 1819), p. 8; Sarah M. Maury, *An Englishwoman in America* (London, 1848), p. 164; *The Diary of George Templeton Strong,* ed. by Allan Nevins and Milton Halsey Thomas (4 vols., New York, 1952), I, 302.

3. [John Pintard], *Letters from John Pintard to his Daughter Eliza Noel Pintard Davidson, 1816–1833,* ed. by Dorothy C. Barck, in New-York Historical Society, *Collections,* LXX-LXXIII (1937–1940), LXX (1937), 7, 129; LXXI (1938), 220, 222, 350; LXXIII (1940), 106, 180; *The Diary of Philip Hone,* ed. by Allan Nevins (2 vols., New York, 1927), I, 202; *The Diary of George T. Strong,* I, 262.

4. James Hardie, *The Description of the City of New-York; containing its population, institutions, commerce, manufactures, public buildings, courts of justice, places of amusement, etc.* (New York, 1827), p. 309; Pintard, in New-York Historical Society, *Collections,* LXXI (1938), 58, 265; James Fenimore Cooper, *America and the Americans* (2d ed., 2 vols., London, 1836), I, 166, II, 109; [Mrs. Anne Royall], *Sketches of History, Life, and Manners in the United States, By a Traveller* (New Haven, 1826), p. 243; Theodore Dwight, *Things As They Are; or, Notes of a Traveller through Some of the Middle and Northern States* (New York, 1834), pp. 63–64.

5. Michel Chevalier, *Lettres sur l'Amérique du Nord* (2 vols., Brussels, 1837), II, 36; Frances Trollope, *Domestic Manners of the Americans,* ed. by Michael Sadleir (reprinted from 5th ed., New York, 1927), p. 357; Charles Dickens, *American Notes for General Circulation* (London, 1892), p. 138. See also Thomas Colley Grattan, *Civilized America* (2 vols., London, 1859), II, 184.

6. Henry B. Fearon, *Sketches of America* (London, 1819), pp. 10–11; John M. Duncan, *Travels Through Part of the United States and Canada* (2 vols., Glasgow, 1823), I, 27, 29–31; *The Diary of Philip Hone,* I, 394–95, II, 730; Isaac Candler, *A Summary View of America: comprising a description of the face of the country, and of several of the principal cities; and remarks on the social, moral, and political character of the people* (London, 1824), p. 24; William Dalton, *Travels in the United States of America and Parts of Upper Canada* (Appleby, 1821), p. 5; William N. Blane, *An Excursion through the United States and Canada during the Years 1822–23* (London, 1824), pp. 11–12; comment of Mr. Hedderwick, in Glasgow *Chronicle,* May 24, 1823, quoted in Stokes, *Iconography,* V, 1630; "Diary of Nicholas Garry," ed. by F. N. A. Garry, in Royal Society of Canada, *Proceedings and Transactions,* 2d series, VI (1900), section II, 83–84.

7. Lieut. Frederick Fitzgerald De Roos, *Personal Narrative of Travels in the United States and Canada* (London, 1827), p. 6; Carl August Gosselman, *Resa i Norra Amerika* (2 vols., Nyköping, Sweden, 1835), I, 10, 322; James Stuart, *Three Years in America* (2 vols., Edinburgh, 1833), I, 23; George Combe, *Notes on the United States of North America, during a Phrenological Visit in 1838–9–40* (3 vols., Edinburgh, 1841), I, 28; Thomas Hamilton, *Men and Manners in America* (2 vols., London, 1833), I, 31–32; Charles G. B. Daubeny, *Journal of a Tour through the United States and in Canada, made during the years 1837–38* (Oxford, 1843), pp. 13–14; Frances Trollope, pp. 297–98; Maximilian, Prince of Wied, *Travels in the Interior of North America,* tr. by Hannibal E. Lloyd, in *Early Western Travels,* ed. by R. G. Thwaites (Cleveland, 1906), XXII, 57; Capt. Frederick Marryat, *Diary in America, with remarks on its institutions* (New York, 1839), p. 21.

8. Grattan, I, 17; Evans, p. 388; James S. Buckingham, *America, Historical, Statistic, and Descriptive* (3 vols., London, 1841), I, 47, 49–50; William Brown, *America: a Four Years' Residence in the United States and Canada* (Leeds, 1849), pp. 5–6; Marryat, p. 21; Maury, p. 164.

9. Charles J. Latrobe, *The Rambler in North America* (2 vols., New York, 1835), I, 31; Gustaf E. M. Unonius, *A Pioneer in Northwest America* (Minneapolis, 1950), being a translation by Jonas Oscar Backlund of Unonius, *Minnen från en sjuttonårig vistelse i nordvestra Amerika*

(Upsala, 1861–1862), I, 30–31; "Diary of John Gage," in *Vineland Historical Magzine,* IX (1924), 189.

10. Andrew Bell [pseud., A. Thomason], *Men and Things in America* (London, 1838), p. 26; von Raumer, p. 468; *Walt Whitman of the New York "Aurora,"* p. 125. Salvatore Abbate e Migliore, an Italian traveler, characterized American cities in 1845, as follows: "New York is noisier, Philadelphia more retiring, Baltimore more visually attractive, Washington prouder; but the capital of New England is without doubt the center of all that is refined, noble, and generous in the American character." A. J. Torrielli, *Italian Opinion on America As Revealed by Italian Travelers, 1850–1900* (Cambridge, Mass., 1941), p. 209. See also Herbert Adams, *The Life and Writings of Jared Sparks* (2 vols., Boston, 1893), I, 517.

11. Godfrey T. Vigne, *Six Months in America* (Philadelphia, 1833), p. 7; Dickens, *American Notes,* p. 117; Klinkowström, pp. 6–7; [Barthélemi Sernin du Moulin de la Barthelle, Baron de Montlezun], *Voyage fait dans les années 1816 et 1817, de New-Yorck à la Nouvelle-Orléans . . . par l'auteur des souvenirs des Antilles* (2 vols., Paris, 1818), I, 174; Royall, *Sketches,* p. 244; James Flint, *Letters from America* (Edinburgh, 1822), in *Early Western Travels,* ed. by R. G. Thwaites (Cleveland, 1904), IX, 29; Isaac Holmes, *An Account of the United States of America derived from actual observation, during a residence of four years in that republic* (London, 1823), pp. 264–68; Karl Bernhard, Duke of Saxe-Weimar-Eisenach, *Travels through North America, during the years 1825 and 1826* (2 vols., Philadelphia, 1828), I, 118; Pintard, in New-York Historical Society, *Collections,* LXX (1937), 61; LXXI (1938), 78, 84, 87, 127, 165; Peter Neilson, *Recollections of a Six Years' Residence in the United States of America* (Glasgow, 1833), p. 37; Robert G. Albion, *The Rise of the New York Port [1815–1860]* (New York, 1939), chaps. III through VI; Francis Lieber, *The Stranger in America* (Philadelphia, 1835), p. 54; Michel Chevalier, *Society, Manners, and Politics in the United States* (Boston, 1839), pp. 231–32; Unonius, I, 30; Gosselman, I, 325. Traugott Bromme, in his three-volume account of a trip through the United States, stressed the commercial pre-eminence of New York: *Reisen durch die Vereinigten Staaten und Ober-Canada* (2 vols., Baltimore, 1834), I, 153, 162.

12. Hardie, p. 329; Chevalier, *Society,* pp. 39, 78, 305.

13. Thomas Hamilton, I, 14; Adolphe Fourier de Bacourt, *Souvenirs of a Diplomat* (New York, 1885), p. 32; De Roos, p. 55; Jacques Benj. Maximilien Bins, Comte de Saint-Victor, *Lettres sur les États-Unis d'Amérique, écrites en 1832 et 1833* (2 vols., Paris, 1835), I, 6, 26.

14. Flint, pp. 30–31; Frances Wright [Mrs. Darusmont], *Views of Society and Manners in America; in a series of letters from that country to a friend in England, during the years 1818, 1819, & 1820, By an Englishwoman* (London, 1821), p. 22; Klinkowström, p. 112; Harriet Martineau, *Retrospect of Western Travel* (3 vols., London, 1838), I, 46; James Boardman, *America and the Americans* (London, 1833), pp. 11–12; Francis J. Grund, *The Americans in Their Moral, Social, and Political Relations* (2 vols., London, 1837), I, 48.

15. Unonius, I, 38–40. The Hauswolff work was entitled *Teckningar utur sällskapslifvet i Nordamerikas förenta stater* (Norrköping, 1835).

16. S. A. Ferrall, *A Ramble of Six Thousand Miles through the United States of America* (London, 1832), pp. 326–29; Thomas Hamilton, pp. 299–303; E. S. Abdy, *Journal of a Residence and Tour in the United States of North America, from April, 1833, to October, 1834* (3 vols., London, 1835), I, 30–32; Buckingham, I, 59; Boardman, pp. 11–12; Chevalier, *Society,* p. 107, 342–43; Unonius, I, 38.

17. Buckingham, I, 59, 63; *The Diary of Philip Hone,* I, 201–2; Chevalier, *Society,* pp. 305–6. See *Diary of John Quincy Adams, 1794–1845,* ed. by Allan Nevins (New York, 1951), p. 460.

18. *The Diary of George T. Strong,* I, 63–65; *The Diary of Philip Hone,* I, 253, 262–63; Marryat, pp. 16–20; Bacourt, p. 117; John R. Godley, *Letters from America* (2 vols., London, 1844), I, 27–28. See also Combe, III, 107–10; Clara von Gerstner, *Beschreibung einer Reise durch die Vereinigten Staaten von Nordamerica in den Jahren 1838 bis 1840* (Leipzig, 1842), p. 39.

19. Charles H. Wilson, *The Wanderer in America, or Truth at Home* (2d ed., Thirsk, 1822), p. 16; *The American Diaries of Richard Cobden*, ed. by Elizabeth H. Cawley (Princeton, 1952), p. 121; Lieut. Francis Hall, p. 9; Henry Cooke, "Notes of a Loiterer in New York," in *Bentley's Miscellany*, XVI (1844), 601; Robert Heywood, *A Journey to America in 1834* (Cambridge, Eng., 1919), p. 25.

20. Dalton, p. 4; Candler, pp. 488–90; Wilson, pp. 27–30; Robert H. Collyer, *Lights and Shadows of American Life* (Boston, [1844?]), pp. 2–3.

21. Fearon, p. 86; Ramon de la Sagra, *Cinq Mois aux États-Unis de l'Amérique du Nord . . .*, tr. de l'espagnol par M. René Baïssas (Brussels, 1837), p. 63; Patrick Shirreff, *A Tour through North America; together with a Comprehensive View of the Canadas and the United States as adapted for agricultural emigration* (Edinburgh, 1835), p. 9; Cooke, pp. 599–600.

22. Frances Wright, pp. 26–27; Boardman, p. 12; Grattan, I, 17; Frances Kemble [Mrs. Butler], *Journal* (2 vols., Philadelphia, 1835), I, 103–4; Fearon, p. 12; Alexis de Tocqueville, *Democracy in America*, ed. by Phillips Bradley (2 vols., New York, 1945), I, 289–90.

23. George W. Pierson, *Tocqueville and Beaumont in America* (New York, 1938), pp. 67–73, 77; Madame La Comtesse Merlin, *La Havane* (3 vols., Paris, 1844), I, 63; Théodore Pavie, *Souvenirs Atlantiques . . .* (2 vols., Paris, 1833), I, 27–35.

24. Henry Tudor, *Narrative of a Tour in North America . . .* (2 vols., London, 1834), I, 32; Boardman, p. 13; Bell, p. 40; Stuart, I, 25; Frances Wright, p. 37; Mrs. Felton, *Life in America: A Narrative of two years city and country residence in the United States* (Hull, 1838), p. 81; *The American Diaries of Richard Cobden*, pp. 88–89; Collyer, p. 2; "Journal" of Lieut. George Kirwan Carr, ed. by Deoch Fulton as *A Short Tour Through the United States & Canadas, October 10th to December 31st, 1832* (New York, 1937), p. 25; Buckingham, I, 54; Kemble, I, 55; [Mrs. Basil Hall], *The Aristocratic Journey, Being the Outspoken Letters of Mrs. Basil Hall. Written during a Fourteen Months' Sojourn in America 1827–1828*, ed. by Una Pope-Hennessy (New York, 1931), p. 20; Klinkowström, pp. 117–18; Royall, *Sketches*, pp. 243, 260–61; Grattan, I, 102.

25. Neilson, pp. 22–23; Buckingham, I, 55; Bell, p. 40; *The American Diaries of Richard Cobden*, p. 89; Thomas Horton James [Rubio], *Rambles in the United States and Canada during the year 1845* (London, 1846), p. 22; Cooke, p. 599; John Bill, "Extracts from the Journal of Philo-Jocundus," manuscript in New-York Historical Society, pp. 273–74; Thomas Hamilton, I, 276; Frances Wright, p. 38; Sagra, p. 75.

26. Pintard, in New-York Historical Society, *Collections*, LXX (1937), 216, 217; LXXIII (1940), 44; J. F. Cooper, I, 165, 410; Auguste Levasseur, *Lafayette in America in 1824 and 1825; or Journal of a Voyage to the United States*, tr. by John D. Godman (2 vols., Philadelphia, 1829), I, 125; [Anon.], "A Few Weeks in New York, by a Returned Emigrant," in *The New Monthly Magazine and Humorist*, XLVIII, pt. 3 (1836), 358; Theodore Dwight, p. 55; Francis Lieber, *The Stranger in America* (2 vols., London, 1835), I, 57, 58, 207; Felton, pp. 51–52; Ezekiel Porter Belden, *New York: Past, Present, and Future* (New York, 1851), pp. 44–45; Robert Ernst, *Immigrant Life in New York City, 1825–1863* (New York, 1949), p. 184; Nathaniel P. Willis, *The Complete Works* (New York, 1846), p. 584. Mrs. Anne Royall professed to have been victimized by Irish hack drivers. See *The Black Book; or, a Continuation of Travels in the United States* (vols. I and II, Washington, 1828; vol. III, Washington, 1829), II, 90–91.

27. [Anon.], Letter to *Cymro America*, June 1, 1832, ed. by R. T. Berthoff, in *New York History*, XXXVII (January 1956), 80–84.

28. Tyrone Power, *Impressions of America, during the Years 1833, 1834, and 1835* (2 vols., London, 1836), I, 48; Capt. Basil Hall, *Travels in North America in the Years 1827 and 1828* (3 vols., Edinburgh, 1829), I, 6; John Palmer, *Journal of Travels in the United States of North America and in Lower Canada, Performed in 1817* (London, 1818), quoted in Stokes, *Iconography*, V, 1592; U.S. Bureau of the Census, *Negro Population 1790–1915* (Washington, 1918), p. 55; *Sixth Census of the United States* (Washington, 1841), p. 114; I. Finch, *Travels in*

the United States of America and Canada (London, 1833), p. 35; Flint, p. 47; Dickens, *American Notes,* pp. 129–30; D. Lorenzo de Zavala, *Viage a los Estados-Unidos del Norte de América* (Paris, 1834), p. 165.

29. Klinkowström, p. 78; C. F. Arfwedson, *The United States and Canada, in 1832, 1833, and 1834* (2 vols., London, 1834), I, 27 [published in Stockholm, 1835, under title *Förenta Staterna och Canada, ären 1832, 1833, och 1834*]; Frances Trollope, pp. 309–10; Maury, pp. 178–79; Lieber, pp. 103–4.

30. Fearon, p. 7; Klinkowström, pp. 66–67; Buckingham, I, 47; descriptions of Astor House from contemporary press, quoted in Stokes, *Iconography,* V, 1741; Theodore Dwight, pp. 175–76.

31. Tudor, I, 36–39; Lieut. Francis Hall, p. 10; Grattan, I, 17, 112–13; Boardman, pp. 24–27; Levasseur, p. 128; Bell, p. 49; Neilson, pp. 16–17. Lieutenant De Roos gave the City Hotel a very bad reference after 1826, and denied that meals were served in the guests' rooms. *Op. cit.,* pp. 5–6.

32. Klinkowström, p. 67. See also Buckingham, I, 232–35; Royall, *Sketches,* pp. 241–42; Pintard, in New-York Historical Society, *Collections,* LXXI (1938), 341. For full description of a boarding house in 1841, see Unonius, I, 31–33.

33. Rev. Isaac Fidler, *Observations on Professions, Literature, Manners, and Emigration, in the United States and Canada, Made During a Residence There in 1832* (New York, 1833), pp. 107–8; Boardman, p. 27; *The New Monthly Magazine and Humorist,* XLVIII, pt. 3 (1836), 352; von Gerstner, pp. 33–35; Harriet Martineau, I, 46; Felton, pp. 76–79; *Walt Whitman of the New York "Aurora,"* pp. 22–23.

34. Felton, pp. 75–76; Salvatore Abbate e Migliore, *Viaggio nella America Settentrionale* (Palermo, 1853), pp. 201–3.

35. Karl Bernhard, Duke of Saxe-Weimar-Eisenach, p. 126; Frances Trollope, pp. 298, 309; Felton, pp. 58–59; Boardman, pp. 332, 334; J. F. Cooper, I, 201–2; *The Diary of George T. Strong,* I, 272; *The Diary of Philip Hone,* II, 262. Senator Maclay noted the existence of a May 1st moving day as early as 1790. *Diary,* p. 245.

36. Achille Murat, *America and the Americans* (New York, 1849), p. 244; Ernst, pp. 15–16; Thomas Hamilton, pp. 389–90; George William Frederick Howard, seventh earl of Carlisle, *Travels in America* (New York, 1851), p. 28; J. F. Cooper, I, 219–21.

37. Willis, p. 583; Dickens, *American Notes,* p. 138.

38. Finch, pp. 16, 32–33; Combe, pp. 28–29; "The Diary of Robert Gilmor, 1774–1848," in *Maryland Historical Magazine,* XVII (1922), 324–25.

39. George C. D. Odell, *Annals of the New York Stage* (14 vols., New York, 1927–1945), II, 446; Phyllis Hartnoll, ed., *The Oxford Companion to the Theatre* (New York, 1951), pp. 97–98; E. T. Coke, *A Subaltern's Furlough: descriptive of scenes in various parts of the United States . . . during the summer and autumn of 1832* (New York, 1833), pp. 133–34; Buckingham, I, 47; Kemble, I, 52–53; Power, I, 62; Frances Trollope, p. 300.

40. *The Diary of Philip Hone,* II, 573; *The Diary of George T. Strong,* I, 195.

41. *Ibid.,* I, 215, 219, 287–88; Gosselman, I, 300–1; Donald J. Grout, *A Short History of Opera* (New York, 1947), p. 500; Stokes, *New York Past and Present,* p. 77; Bernhard, Duke of Saxe-Weimar-Eisenach, II, 196–97; Power, I, 164–65; *Musical U.S.A.,* ed. by Quaintance Eaton (New York, 1949), pp. 19–20; Esther Singleton, "History of the Opera in New York from 1750 to 1898," in *Musical Courier,* December 8, 1898, unpaged.

42. Pierson, p. 73; Lieut. Francis Hall, pp. 11–13; *King's Handbook of New York City,* ed. by Moses King (2d ed., Buffalo, N. Y., 1893), pp. 34, 308; Maury, pp. 182, 187, 189–90; "Extracts from the Diary of James B. Longacre," in *Pennsylvania Magazine of History and Biography,* XXIX (1905), 134–36.

43. Pintard, in New-York Historical Society, *Collections,* LXXII (1939), 240; Theodore Dwight, p. 34; *The Diary of Philip Hone,* I, 19, 92, 344–45.

44. Klinkowström, pp. 114–17; *The American Diaries of Richard Cobden,* pp. 90–91, 126; Heywood, p. 77; Zerah Hawley, *A Journal of a Tour through Connecticut, Massachusetts, New-York, the North Part of Pennsylvania and Ohio . . .* (New Haven, 1822), 143; Willis, p. 708.

45. Levasseur, I, 26–27; Édouard de Montulé, *Travels in America,* tr. by Edward D. Seeber (Indiana University Publications, Social Science Series, no. 9, 1950), pp. 21–22; Neilson, p. 56; Capt. Basil Hall, I, 19–24; Godley, II, 221–22; Karl Bernhard, Duke of Saxe-Weimar-Eisenach, II, 196; Combe, II, 278; J. F. Cooper, II, 407–10; *The Diary of Philip Hone,* I, 15, 190, 434; Unonius, I, 49; *The Diary of George T. Strong,* I, 10.

46. James Lumsden, *American Memoranda, by a Mercantile Man, during a short tour in the summer of 1843* (Glasgow, 1844), pp. 7–8; Klinkowström, pp. 68–69; Levasseur, I, 123; *The Diary of Philip Hone,* I, 65, 71, 74.

47. Nelson M. Blake, *Water for the Cities* (Syracuse, N. Y., 1956), pp. 142, 165, 167.

48. William Faux, *Memorable Days in America: Being a Journal of a Tour to the United States* (London, 1823), I, 159; Blane, pp. 9–13; Neilson, pp. 4–7; Coke, pp. 130, 143–47; Brown, pp. 5–6; Dickens, *American Notes,* p. 123; Buckingham, I, 221–22; Karl Bernhard, Duke of Saxe-Weimar-Eisenach, I, 121; Collyer, pp. 6–8; Grund, I, 49; Combe, I, 280.

49. Theodore Dwight, p. 31.

50. [Asa Greene], *A Glance at New York* (New York, 1837), pp. 263–64; Kemble, I, 143.

51. Fearon, pp. 5–7, 9–12, 28–29, 85–87; Nevins, *America Through British Eyes,* pp. 53–54.

52. Neilson, pp. 5–7; Robert Sutcliff, *Travels in Some Parts of North America in the Years 1804, 1805, & 1806* (Philadelphia, 1812), pp. 113–15; Klinkowström, pp. 63–65; *Dictionary of National Biography,* XL, 184; Coke, pp. 143–44, 147.

53. Cooper, *America and the Americans,* I, 173–75, 181, 219–21.

54. Hall, *Travels in North America,* I, 6, 19–24, 31–34, II, 208–10; Nevins, *America Through British Eyes,* pp. 103–104.

55. Karl Bernhard, Duke of Saxe-Weimar-Eisenach, I, 121, 126, 133; Handlin, *This Was America,* p. 155.

56. Boardman, pp. viii, 11–12, 27, 87–88, 306–7, 309, 333–35. See also Pintard, in New-York Historical Society, *Collections,* LXXIII (1940), 44.

57. *Ibid.,* p. 130.

58. Hamilton, *Men and Manners in America,* I, 299–303; *Dictionary of National Biography,* XXIV, 213.

59. Trollope, *Domestic Manners of the Americans,* 297–99, 310–12, 357; *Dictionary of American Biography,* XX, 549.

60. Sagra, pp. 27–29.

61. Marryat, pp. 16–19; Nevins, *America Through British Eyes,* pp. 171–72.

62. Dickens, *American Notes for General Circulation,* pp. 114, 117–18, 123–31, 137; John Forster, *The Life of Charles Dickens* (2 vols., New York, 1907), I, 223–24, 239.

CHAPTER 6

1. *The Diary of George T. Strong,* II, 24; Archibald Prentice, *A Tour in the United States* (7th ed., London, 1850), p. 10; Sir Charles Lyell, *A Second Visit to the United States of North America* (2 vols., New York, 1849), I, 180; James Grant Wilson, *Thackeray in the United States, 1852–53, 1855–56* (2 vols., New York, 1904), I, 85; Isabella Lucy Bird Bishop, *The Englishwoman in America* (2d ed., London, 1856), p. 386; Fredrika Bremer, *The Homes of the New World; Impressions of America,* tr. by Mary Howitt (2 vols., New York, 1853), I, 12; Lady Emmeline Stuart-Wortley, *Travels in the United States, etc. during 1849 and 1850* (3 vols., London, 1851), I, 306; Henri Herz, *Mes Voyages en Amérique* (Paris, 1866), p. 60.

2. *The Diary of George T. Strong,* I, 302, 335; [Anon.], "London, Paris, and New-York," reprinted from the American edition of *Bentley's Miscellany* for July 1851, in *The International Monthly Magazine of Literature, Science, and Art,* IV (August–December 1851), 101; Walt Whitman, *New York Dissected* (New York, 1936), p. 199; Bishop, pp. 334, 337–38; J. J. A. Ampère, *Promenade en Amérique* (2 vols., Paris, 1855), I, 291; Thackeray, in Wilson, I, 85; Stuart-Wortley, I, 2, 5, 279; Bremer, I, 11; Capt. John W. Oldmixon, *Transatlantic Wanderings* (London, 1855), pp. 23–24; Alexander Marjoribanks, *Travels in South and North America* (London, 1853), pp. 306–7; Leon Beauvallet, *Rachel and the New World: a Trip to the United States and Canada* (New York, 1856), pp.

106–8; Charles Mackay, *Life and Liberty in America: or Sketches of a Tour in the United States and Canada, in 1857–8* (2 vols., London, 1859), I, 13, 17–18; James F. W. Johnston, *Notes on North America, Agricultural, Economical, and Social* (2 vols., Boston, 1850), II, 376; William Chambers, *Things as They Are in America* (London and Edinburgh, 1857), p. 192; Ida Pfeiffer, *A Lady's Second Journey Round the World* (2 vols., London, 1855), II, 359; William Edward Baxter, *America and the Americans* (London, 1855), pp. 24–25; Rev. Georges Fisch, *Nine Months in the United States during the Crisis* (London, 1863), p. 3.

3. Walt Whitman, "Mannahatta," in *Complete Poetry and Prose*, ed. by Malcolm Cowley (2 vols., New York, 1948), I, 409; Chambers, pp. 176–77; James Robertson, *A Few Months in America: containing remarks on some of its Industrial and Commercial Interests* (London, n.d.), p. 152; "Lord Acton's American Diaries," pt. I, in *Fortnightly Review*, n.s., CX (1921), 734; *The Diary of Philip Hone*, II, 896–97.

4. C. S. Francis and Co., *The Stranger's Hand-Book for the City of New York; or, What to See, and How to See It* (New York, 1853), quoted in Stokes, *Iconography*, V, 1845; [William N. Bobo], *Glimpses of New York by a South Carolinian (who had nothing else to do)* (Charleston, 1852), p. 51; "Lord Acton's American Diaries," p. 735; Chambers, pp. 178–79; Charles Mackay, I, 18; William Ferguson, *America by River and Rail; or, Notes by the Way on the New World and its People* (London, 1856), p. 72; Baxter, p. 28; Rev. A. P. Moor, *Letters from North America written during the Summer of 1853* (Canterbury, 1855), p. 24.

5. Bishop, pp. 334–35; Moor, p. 24; *Miller's New York As It Is* (New York, 1859), quoted in Stokes, *Iconography*, V, 1878–79; New York *Herald*, August 25, 1859, *ibid.*, V, 1881; J. and A. C——, *The United States and Canada, as Seen by Two Brothers in 1858 and 1861* (London, 1862), p. 17; Charles Mackay, I, 17.

6. Henry Philip Tappan, *The Growth of Cities: a Discourse delivered before the New York Geographical Society, on the evening of March 15th, 1855* (New York, 1855), pp. 31–32.

7. von Raumer, *America and the Americans*, p. 467; Charles Mackay, I, 11; Bishop, pp. 334–35; Chambers, p. 174; Marjoribanks, p. 306; Willis, p. 631; *The Diary of George T. Strong*, II, 61.

8. Walt Whitman, "Crossing Brooklyn Ferry," in *Complete Poetry and Prose*, Cowley ed., I, 171; "A Broadway Pageant," *ibid.*, I, 234; "Mannahatta," *ibid.*, I, 410; *The Stranger's Hand-Book*, quoted in Stokes, *Iconography*, V, 1845–46.

9. Albion, p. 418; Ivan Golovin, *Stars and Stripes, or American Impressions* (London, New York, 1856), p. 25 [a reference to the growth of Brooklyn]; George William Curtis, "Editor's Easy Chair," in *Harper's New Monthly Magazine*, XXIV (February 1862), 409; Chambers, p. 175. "As the Atlantic port of a growing interior country of boundless extent, New York has certainly attracted many native-born Americans from the interior of the State and from New England to settle within its bounds for the purposes of traffic, but it has drawn its main increase from this side of the Atlantic. Every manufacturing district in Europe, and every large commercial port, has sent its agencies and branch establishments with similar trading objects, so that, during these sixty years, New York may be said to have been built up by Europe rather than by the exertions of America herself." Johnston, II, 377.

10. [Domingo F. Sarmiento], *A Sarmiento Anthology*, tr. from the Spanish by Stuart E. Grummon (Princeton, 1948), p. 229; Bishop, p. 381; Charles Mackay, I, 22–23; Ampère, I, 388; Albion, p. 418; U.S. Census, 1860, *Population* (Washington, 1864), p. xxxii; J. Benwell, *An Englishman's Travels in America* (London, 1853), p. 16; Johnston, II, 377–79; Ezekiel P. Belden, *New York: Past, Present, and Future* (New York, 1849), p. 44.

11. David W. Mitchell, *Ten Years in the United States: Being an Englishman's Views of Men and Things in the North and South* (London, 1862), p. 145; Ernst, p. 41.

12. Franz von Löher, *Geschichte und Zustände der Deutschen in Amerika*, quoted, *ibid.*, p. 42; Christoph Vetter, *Zwei Jahre in New-York: Schilderung einer Seereise von Havre nach New-York und Charakteristik des New-Yorker politischen und socialen Lebens* (Hof, 1849), pp. 99–114; Karl Theodor Griesinger,

Land und Leute in Amerika: Skizzen aus dem amerikanischen Leben (2d ed., 2 vols., Stuttgart, 1863), II, 548, 555–56, 564, 569–70, 572; Mitchell, p. 158; Georg Techla, *Drei Jahre in New-York: eine Skizze, für das Volk nach der Natur gezeichnet* (Zwickau, 1862), pp. 95–112.

13. Ernst, pp. 38–40.

14. Mitchell, pp. 144, 149; J. and A. C——, p. 21; Johnston, II, 379; Florence E. Gibson, *The Attitudes of the New York Irish Toward State and National Affairs, 1848–1892* (New York, 1951), pp. 16–18; Lyell, I, 189; *The American Diaries of Richard Cobden,* p. 73; [Anon.], "London, Paris, and New-York," p. 102.

15. [Ole Munch Raeder], *America in the Forties: the Letters of Ole Munch Raeder,* tr. and ed. by Gunnar J. Malmin (Minneapolis, 1929), pp. 164–65; Marjoribanks, pp. 433–36; Mitchell, pp. 158–59; N. Reiss, *Excursion à New York* (Brussels, 1851), p. 43.

16. Herman Melville, *Moby-Dick or the Whale* (New York, 1950, Everyman's Library ed.), p. 3; Prentice, p. 14; Ferguson, p. 61. See also Adam G. De Gurowski, *America and Europe* (New York, 1857), pp. 397–98.

17. The value of exports increased from $32,000,000 in 1844 to $145,000,000 in 1860; the value of imports from $65,000,000 in 1844 to $248,000,000 in 1860. There was a serious setback in 1858. Albion, pp. 386, 390–91, 417; Robertson, p. 14.

18. Chambers, p. 177; Edward W. Watkin, *A Trip to the United States and Canada: in a series of letters* (London, 1852), p. 11. In 1862, A. T. Stewart built a new store on Broadway near Astor Place. It had a cast-iron front. *New York City Guide* (New York, 1939), pp. 136–37.

19. Robertson, p. 15; U.S. Census, 1860, *Statistics of the United States . . . in 1860* (Washington, 1866), xviii; Ernst, p. 18.

20. Alexander Mackay, *The Western World* (3 vols., London, 1850), I, 205–6; [Anon.], "London, Paris, and New-York," p. 108.

21. Bobo, pp. 137–38, 145; De Gurowski, pp. 371–72; Whitman, *New York Dissected,* p. 92.

22. Francis and Theresa Pulszky, *White, Red, Black: Sketches of American Society in the United States* (2 vols., New York, 1853), I, 60, 66; Thackeray, in Wilson, I, 146, 149; Bishop, pp. 361–62; Charles Mackay, I, 14, 21–22.

23. *Ibid.,* I, 40–44; Baxter, pp. 90–91; Robertson, pp. 155–57; Whitman, *New York Dissected,* p. 96.

24. Marie Fontenay [Mme. Manoel] de Grandfort, *The New World,* tr. by Edward C. Wharton (New Orleans, 1855), p. 18; Ferguson, pp. 48, 91; Baxter, p. 24; Maj. H. Byng Hall, "New York As It Is," in *St. James's Magazine,* VIII (August–November 1853), 64.

25. Ampère, I, 296, 386; Johnston, II, 390; Chambers, p. 198; Mitchell, p. 144; Pfeiffer, II, 381; Bremer, II, 601–2; Beauvallet, p. 108; Golovin, pp. 23, 191; Bishop, p. 339; Pulszky, II, 239; Whitman, *New York Dissected,* p. 200. Ole Raeder contended in 1848 that New York was "the Gomorrah of the New World," to be "compared with Paris when it comes to opportunities for the destruction of both body and soul." Raeder, p. 230.

26. *The Diary of Philip Hone,* II, 785; *The Diary of George T. Strong,* II, 56–57, 99, 320.

27. [George G. Foster], *New York in Slices by an experienced carver: being the original slices published in the New York Tribune* (New York, 1849), *passim;* George G. Foster, *New York by Gas-light: with here and there a streak of sunshine* (New York, 1850), *passim.*

28. Johnston, II, 389–90; Chambers, pp. 197–98; Ferguson, pp. 73–77; Prentice, p. 15; Fisch, pp. 52–56.

29. Samuel Rezneck, "The Influence of Depression upon American Opinion, 1857–1859," in *Journal of Economic History,* II (May 1942), 18; *The Diary of George T. Strong,* II, 354–70.

30. James, p. 43; Ampère, I, 295; "Lord Acton's American Diaries," p. 736; Bishop, p. 338; Chambers, quoting New York *Herald,* November 28, 1853, pp. 193–94; Arthur C. Cole, *The Irrepressible Conflict, 1850–1865* (New York, 1934), p. 157; Robertson, pp. 5–7; Alfred Pairpont, *Uncle Sam and His Country, or, Sketches of America, in 1854–55–56* (London, 1857), pp. 24, 28–29; Pfeiffer, II, 359; Chambers, pp. 192–93; James, pp. 31–33; Stuart-Wortley, I, 286; Marjoribanks, pp. 432–33; Charles Mackay, I, 29–30, 48–51; J. and A. C——, p. 16. "Foreigners complain, 'Will the city never be finished?' Not very soon, we think. It is difficult to do in fifty years the work of five hundred, without a good deal of bustle and inconvenience. Rapid

growth in population and wealth necessitates continual improvement in accommodation. We may, indeed, be allowed to fret a little, when the street is for weeks or months encumbered by the building materials of a merchant who sees fit to pull down a very good house in order to erect one that shall cost a quarter of a million, merely because his neighbor has contrived to outshine him in that particular. But when sewers and gas, and Croton water, are in question, we must not grumble. The great public blessings are spreading into every quarter, carrying health and decency with them. The great sewers are arched canals of hard brick, from three to nine feet in diameter, and laid in mortar in the most durable manner. Above them are the gas-pipes, an immense net-work; and nearly on a level with these last are the huge veins and arteries, by means of which the Croton supplies life and health to the inhabitants." [Anon.], "London, Paris, and New-York," p. 105.

31. Lyell, II, 249; Marjoribanks, pp. 306–8; Beauvallet, p. 106; Stuart-Wortley, I, 280; Chambers, p. 192; Oldmixon, p. 23; Bishop, p. 337; Charles Mackay, I, 19–20.

32. Alexander Mackay, I, 71, 92; Bishop, pp. 351, 353; Pfeiffer, II, 365; Stokes, *Iconography,* V, 1770; Robertson, p. 18; J. and A. C——, pp. 18–19; *Schliemann's First Visit to America, 1850–1851,* ed. by Shirley H. Weber (Cambridge, Mass., 1942), pp. 23–24; Whitman, *New York Dissected* ("A Visit to the Opera"), pp. 18–19; *The Diary of George T. Strong,* II, 17–19; "Letters from New York," in *Southern Literary Messenger,* XVI (1850), 755; Maj. H. Byng Hall, p. 66.

33. Charles Mackay, I, 25, 45–46; Bishop, pp. 353–54; Ferguson, pp. 49–52.

34. Tappan, p. 33; Chambers, pp. 178, 203; "Lord Acton's American Diaries," p. 733; Pulszky, II, 240; Stokes, *Iconography,* V, 1701; "Letters from New York," in *Southern Literary Messenger,* XVI (1850), 670–71.

35. Pairpont, pp. 124–25; Alexander Mackay, I, 74; Johnston, II, 389–90; Mitchell, pp. 173–74; Tappan, p. 35.

36. Walt Whitman, "Mannahatta," I, 409–11, "Song of Myself," I, 68–69, in *Complete Poetry and Prose,* Cowley, ed.; *The Diary of George T. Strong,* II, 28; Marjoribanks, p. 305; Chambers, p. 178; Robertson, p. 17; Beauvallet, p. 107; De Gurowski, p. 397; Mitchell, p. 142; J. and A. C——, p. 21; [Anon.], "London, Paris, and New-York," p. 109; Bobo, p. 139.

37. Lyell, I, 180, 184, II, 248–49; Nevins, *America Through British Eyes,* p. 233.

38. Stuart-Wortley, I, 279–83, 286–88, 298–302; Max Berger, *The British Traveller in America, 1836–1860* (New York, 1943), p. 215.

39. Chambers, pp. 173–78, 191–93, 195–96, 203–4; *Dictionary of National Biography,* X, 27–29.

40. Robertson, pp. 8–15; Berger, p. 212.

41. Bishop, pp. 332–33, 336–42, 351–56, 358, 369, 380–82, 386–88; *Dictionary of National Biography,* Second Supplement, I, 166–68.

42. Griesinger, II, 547, 551–52, 554–59, 564–65, 569–72; *Meyers Konversations-Lexikon,* VII, 978; Handlin, p. 252.

43. Mackay, *Life and Liberty in America,* I, 29–30, 49–51; *Dictionary of National Biography,* XXXV, 120–21.

44. Marjoribanks, pp. 432–33.

CHAPTER 7

1. [Yanagawa Masakiyo], *The First Japanese Mission to America (1860), Being a Diary Kept by a Member of the Embassy,* tr. by Junichi Fukuyama and Roderick H. Jackson and ed. by M. G. Mori (Kobe, Japan, 1937), pp. i, ii, 73; Stokes, *Iconography,* V, 1888, 1899, 1924. "Inasmuch as that New York is the general focus to which capital tends for employment, as well as for persons of leisure and those seeking business, there is an affluence of money persons at the metropolis this season. The attractions at this time are the visit of the Great Eastern, the popular 'progress' of the Japanese, and the 'royal progress' of the Prince of Wales. These, in connection with the fame of the great Central Park, swell the number of those visitors who seek the city in such increasing numbers, coming and going from Europe. . . . These crowds of persons swell the hotel business, both going and coming, and should be doubled to indicate the number of visitors. This would be 260,000 in the last five years, or 52,000 per annum—

say, 1,000 per week." *Merchants' Magazine and Commercial Review,* XLIII (July 1860), 71–72.

2. Yanagawa Masakiyo, p. 73. See Walt Whitman, "A Broadway Pageant," in *Complete Poetry and Prose,* Cowley ed., I, 234; *The Diary of George T. Strong,* III, 45.

3. Fisch, pp. 159–62; *The Diary of George T. Strong,* III, 57, 60, 64, 89, 120, 124.

4. Philip S. Foner, *Business and Slavery: The New York Merchants and the Irrepressible Conflict* (Chapel Hill, 1941), *passim;* William H. Russell, *My Diary North and South* (Boston, New York, 1863), p. 370.

5. *The Diary of George T. Strong,* III, 125–35; Lieutenant Colonel Camille Ferri-Pisani, *Lettres sur les États-Unis d'Amérique* (Paris, 1862), p. 28; Édouard Polydore Vanéechout [pseud., L. Du Hailly], *Campagnes et Stations sur les côtes de l'Amérique du Nord* (Paris, 1864), p. 8; Charles W. Dilke, *Greater Britain: a record of travel in English-speaking countries during 1866 and 1867* (2 vols., London, 1868), I, 40; Count Agénor de Gasparin, *The Uprising of a Great People. The United States in 1861,* tr. from the French by Mary Booth (New York, 1861), p. 31.

6. Walt Whitman, "Give Me the Splendid Silent Sun," in *Complete Poetry and Prose,* Cowley ed., I, 288; James W. Massie, *America: the Origin of her present conflict, her prospect for the slave, and her claim for anti-slavery sympathy; illustrated by incidents of travel, during a tour in the summer of 1863, throughout the United States, from the eastern boundaries of Maine to the Mississippi* (London, 1864), p. 130; Foner, pp. 285–88.

7. *The Diary of George T. Strong,* III, 270, 296, 301.

8. Gibson, pp. 141–59, 170–71; Samuel A. Pleasants, *Fernando Wood of New York* (New York, 1948), pp. 139, 143; Robert Ferguson, *America during and after the War* (London, 1866), pp. 13–14; Ernest Duvergier de Hauranne, *Lettres et Notes de Voyage 1864–1865* (2 vols., Paris, 1866), I, 25.

9. Foner, pp. 306–17, 322; James G. Wilson, ed., *The Memorial History of the City of New York* (4 vols., New York, 1892–1893), III, 487, 489, 494, 495, 508–10.

10. Edward Dicey, *Six Months in the Federal States* (2 vols., London and Cambridge, 1863), I, 23–25; New York *Independent,* June 25, 1864, quoted in E. D. Fite, *Social and Industrial Conditions in the North During the Civil War* (New York, 1910), pp. 259–60; Vanéechout, pp. 7, 24–26; Ludwig Haecker, *Amerikanische Reise-Skizzen aus dem Gebiete der Technik, Landwirthschaft und des socialen Lebens* (Braunschweig, 1867), p. 7; J[ohn] Walter, *First Impressions of America* (London, 1867), p. 24. According to the New York *Evening Post,* "extravagance, luxury, these are the signs of the times." Quoted from *Scientific American,* May 21, 1864, Fite, p. 274. See also James D. McCabe [pseud., Edward W. Martin], *The Secrets of the Great City* (Philadelphia, 1868), pp. 79–82; Haecker, p. 7.

11. U.S. Census, 1860, *Population and Manufactures,* p. xviii; U.S. Census, 1870, III, *Statistics of the Wealth and Industry of the United States,* pp. 702–3; Fite, p. 123; Stokes, *Iconography,* V, 1936; George Rose [pseud., Arthur Sketchley], *The Great Country; or, Impressions of America* (London, 1868), p. 7; William Robertson and W. F. Robertson, *Our American Tour* (Edinburgh, 1871), pp. 132–33; Allan Nevins, *The Emergence of Modern America* (New York, 1927), p. 297.

12. Anthony Trollope, *North America* (2 vols., London, 1862), I, 284–85; New York *Times,* October 9, 1863, quoted in Stokes, *Iconography,* V, 1910; Dicey, I, 25; *Mark Twain's Travels with Mr. Brown, . . . sketches written by Mark Twain for the San Francisco "Alta California" in 1866 & 1867, . . . ,* collected and edited with an introduction by Franklin Walker and G. Ezra Dane (New York, 1940), pp. 106–9; David Macrae, *The Americans at Home: Pen and Ink Sketches of American Men, Manners, and Institutions* (2 vols., Edinburgh, 1870), I, 69–71; Joseph von Koeller, *Nordamerikanische Schilderungen (1855–65)* (Hilpoltstein, 1880), pp. 10–11; Walter, p. 24; *Sarmiento Anthology,* p. 269.

13. Mme. Olympe Audouard, *À travers l'Amérique . . .* (Paris, 1907), pp. 136–37; George T. Borrett, *Letters from Canada and the United States* (London, 1865), p. 277; George Augustus Sala, *My Diary in America in the Midst of War* (2 vols., London, 1865), I, 64; *Mark Twain's Travels with Mr. Brown,* p. 107. Two English travelers on the turn of the seventies as-

serted that "the characteristics of the people of the three principal eastern cities" came out in the questions they asked of strangers who sought admission to their society. In Boston it was asked of a young lady if she were clever, in Philadelphia, if she were pretty, in New York, if she were rich. Two Englishmen [—— Rivington and —— Harris], *Reminiscences of America in 1869* (London, 1870), pp. 44–45. According to an Italian visitor of 1867, "There is a current saying: 'Boston, the city of science; New York, the city of business; Philadelphia, the city of aristocracy; Baltimore, the city of beauty; Washington, the city of nothing.' " Luigi Adamoli, "Letters from America, I," in *The Living Age,* CCCXII (March 1922), 588.

14. *The Diary of George T. Strong,* III, 411, 416, 422, 430, 566–67.

15. De Hauranne, I, 13–14; Vanéechout, p. 33; Dicey, I, 9–12; Henry Latham, *Black and White, a Journal of a Three Months' Tour in the United States* (London, 1867), p. 7; Russell, pp. 11–12, 24–25; Walter, p. 12; Anthony Trollope, I, 319; Robertson and Robertson, p. 142. In an article in *Leslie's Weekly,* it was estimated that $20,000 was the minimum price for most of the dwellings on Fifth Avenue. Stokes, *Iconography,* V, 1919.

16. Rose, p. ix; Walter, p. 13; Dicey, I, 20; Friedrich Gerstäcker, *Zwischen Wildnis und Kultur: Reisen und Abenteuer in der neuen Welt* (Berlin, 1943), a reprint of the author's *Neue Reisen durch die Vereinigten Staaten, Mexiko, Equador, Westindien und Venezuela* (1868), p. 7; Sala, *My Diary in America,* I, 403; Macrae, *The Americans at Home,* I, 68–69.

17. *The Diary of George T. Strong,* IV, 236; Forster, *The Life of Charles Dickens,* II, 402, 413; Russell, p. 21; Dilke, pp. 40–49; Two Englishmen, p. 17; Dicey, I, 13–14; Macrae, *The Americans at Home,* I, 66–67; *A Compendium of the Ninth Census* (June 1, 1870) (Washington, 1872), pp. 448–49; Ferri-Pisani, p. 54; Rose, p. 1; Vanéechout, p. 31; McCabe, *The Secrets of the Great City,* pp. 36, 50–51. Matthew H. Smith asserted that the foreign-born were changing the character of the New York Sunday: "The Sabbath of the Continent is becoming common in the city. The observance of the day grows less and less. Pleasure-seekers are more open, and their number is increased by the fashionable and influential. Every wave of foreign emigration lessens the dry land of religious observance." Smith, *Sunshine and Shadow in New York,* p. 145. See also Marc-Gabriel Hurt-Binet, *Neuf Mois aux États-Unis d'Amérique* (Geneva, 1862), p. 63. It is interesting to note that while some Englishmen saw danger in the large number of Irishmen in the city, a French visitor viewed with similar apprehension the large number of Germans. "They already call New York the third capital of Germany," wrote Henri Kowalski, *À travers l'Amérique: Impressions d'un musicien* (Paris, 1872), p. 103. For a description of the German element, see Charles Dawson Shanly, "Germany in New York," in *The Atlantic Monthly,* XIX (1867), 555–64.

18. *Mark Twain's Travels with Mr. Brown,* pp. 90–91; Cleveland Rodgers and Rebecca B. Rankin, *New York: The World's Capital City* (New York, 1948), p. 72; Émile Malézieux, *Souvenirs d'une Mission aux États-Unis d'Amérique* (Paris, 1874), p. 12; Ferri-Pisani, pp. 60–61; Dicey, I, 18; Borrett, pp. 284–85; Latham, p. 257; Vanéechout, p. 55; Forster, *The Life of Charles Dickens,* II, 403; Sala, *My Diary in America,* II, 208–11; McCabe, *The Secrets of the Great City,* p. 69; Smith, *Sunshine and Shadow in New York,* pp. 26–27.

19. Dicey, I, 19; Anthony Trollope, I, 294; Borrett, p. 289; Stokes, *Iconography,* V, 1912, 1916, 1932, 1935; Nevins, *Emergence of Modern America,* p. 80; Fisch, p. 3; *Mark Twain's Travels with Mr. Brown,* pp. 226–28; [Anon.], "The Future of New York," in *Galaxy,* IX (1870), 549, 553.

20. Anthony Trollope, I, 320; Gerstäcker, pp. 6–7; Forster, *The Life of Charles Dickens,* II, 412; Macrae, *The Americans at Home,* I, 66; *The Diary of George T. Strong,* III, 572. "Living in New York is so expensive that persons of moderate means reside in the suburbs, some of them as far as forty miles in the country. They come into the city, to their business, in crowds, between the hours of seven and nine in the morning, and literally pour out of it between four and seven in the evening." McCabe, *Secrets of the Great City,* pp. 38–40.

21. Stokes, *Iconography,* V, 1915, 1921, 1933; *Mark Twain's Travels with Mr. Brown,* p. 235; Nevins, *Emergence of Modern America,* p. 208.

22. [Ferdinand (Frederick?) Longchamp], *Asmodeus in New York* (New York, 1868), p. 239; Lloyd Morris, *Incredible New York* (New York, 1951), pp. 64–66; Forster, *The Life of Charles Dickens,* II, 399, 401; Stokes, *Iconography,* V, 1899; *Mark Twain's Travels with Mr. Brown,* pp. 84–87. See also Rose, p. 13. The location of the two most modern theatres of the period, Wallack's, opened at Broadway and Thirteenth Street in 1861, and Booth's, at Twenty-third Street and Sixth Avenue, in 1869, reflected the city's inevitable northward march.

23. Two Englishmen, p. 23; Latham, pp. 13–14; Adamoli, in *The Living Age* (March 11, 1922), 587; Borrett, pp. 286–87; Walter, p. 20; Morris, p. 29; Vanéechout, pp. 63–65; Stokes, *Iconography,* V, 1893; Rose, p. 24; Longchamp, p. 239; Nevins, *Emergence of Modern America,* pp. 325–26; Dilke, pp. 46–47. "Though this city is not so large as London, life here is more intense; crime is more vivid and daring; the votaries of fashion and pleasure are more passionate and open." Smith, *Sunshine and Shadow in New York,* pp. 706, 371–72.

24. James D. Burn, *Three Years Among the Working-Classes in the United States during the War* (London, 1865), pp. 14, 120; John E. Hilary Skinner, *After the Storm; or, Jonathan and his neighbours in 1865–66* (2 vols., London, 1866), I, 14; Dicey, I, 16, 18–19; Ferri-Pisani, p. 56; John Burroughs, "From London to New York," in *Galaxy,* XV (January–June 1873), 198 ("native nonchalance and independence"). See also Edward Crapsey, "The Nether Side of New York," in *Galaxy,* XI (January–July 1871), 188–97, 401–9, 559–67, 652–60, 827–35; XII (July–December 1871), 57–65, 170–78, 355–63; XIII (1872), 314–23, 489–97. "This is a city of princes and paupers. Great wealth and extreme poverty are found elbow to elbow almost everywhere from the Battery to Spuyten Duyvel." *Op. cit.*, XIII, 314.

25. Édouard Vanéechout wrote in 1861 that the war assured New York of new rights to the title of metropolis: "it is in its breast that henceforth the heart of the Union will beat." *Op. cit.*, p. 67.

26. George William Curtis, "Editor's Easy Chair," in *Harper's New Monthly Magazine,* XXIV (February 1862), 409; *Mark Twain's Travels with Mr. Brown,* p. 82; *The Diary of George T. Strong,* III, 566; Joseph Alexander, graf von Hübner, *Promenade autour du monde, 1871* (Paris, 1873), in Handlin, pp. 297–98; Fitz-Hugh Ludlow, "The American Metropolis," in *The Atlantic Monthly,* XV (1865), 77, 87. "Fling together Tyre and Sidon, the New Jerusalem, Sodom and Gomorrah, a little of heaven and more of hell, and you have a faint picture of this mighty Babylon of the New World." Macrae, *The Americans at Home,* I, 66.

27. Russell, pp. 368–71; Pierce, p. 171; Russell, p. 21.

28. Ferri-Pisani, pp. 68, 77–81.

29. Dicey, I, 11–12, 15–18, 22–26; Nevins, *America Through British Eyes,* pp. 273–74.

30. Duvergier de Hauranne, I, 13–16, 22–26; *La Grande Encyclopédie,* XV, 150; Frank Monaghan, *French Travellers in the United States: a Bibliography* (New York, 1933), p. 38.

31. Borrett, pp. 205–6, 276–81, 288–89.

32. *The Diary of George T. Strong,* III, 573–79, 583–88.

33. Skinner, I, 50–51; *Dictionary of National Biography,* XVIII, 346–47.

34. Burn, pp. 14–15; Russell, pp. 15–17; Gerstäcker, pp. 8–9; Henry S. Commager, ed., *America in Perspective; the United States through Foreign Eyes* (New York, 1947), p. 186; Brockhaus, *Konversations-Lexikon,* VII, 230.

35. [Ferdinand (Frederick?) Longchamp], pp. 238–42, 244; Monaghan, p. 63; Morris, pp. 46–49; New York *Herald,* February 1, 1863, quoted in Fite, p. 268.

36. *Walt Whitman of the New York "Aurora,"* p. 19; Walt Whitman, articles written for *Life Illustrated,* in *New York Dissected* (New York, 1936), pp. 199–200; Walt Whitman, *Specimen Days & Collect* (Philadelphia, 1882–1883), pp. 117–18; Walt Whitman, *Democratic Vistas,* in *Complete Poetry and Prose,* Cowley ed., II, 215. See also "City of Ships," *ibid.*, I, 273–74.

37. *Mark Twain's Travels with Mr. Brown,* pp. 82–83, 259–61, 278. See also Walter Blair, "Mark Twain, New York Correspondent," in *American Literature,* XI (1939), 247–59.

38. Forster, II, 399, 401–3, 411–13.

CHAPTER 8

1. James Dabney McCabe, *New York by Sunlight and Gaslight. A Work Descriptive of the Great American Metropolis* (n.p., preface dated 1882), pp. 39, 153; Jacob A. Riis, *How the Other Half Lives: Studies among the Tenements of New York* (New York, 1890), *passim.*

2. U.S. Census, 1940, *Population,* I, 712; James Macaulay, "First Impressions of America and Its People," in *The Leisure Hour,* XX (1871), 74; William Dean Howells, "Letters of an Altrurian Traveller," in *Cosmopolitan,* XVI (1893–1894), 415.

3. McCabe, *New York by Sunlight and Gaslight,* pp. 40–49; W. E. Adams, *Our American Cousins* (London, 1883), pp. 206–7; Lady Duffus Hardy, *Through Cities and Prairie Lands* (New York, 1881), p. 67; von Hübner, in Handlin, p. 298; [T. Smith], *Rambling Recollections of a Trip to America* (Edinburgh, 1875), p. 20; Ephraim Turland, *Notes of a Visit to America* (Manchester, 1877), p. 140; John Leng, *America in 1876: Pencillings during a Tour in the Centennial Year* (Dundee, 1877), p. 219; Rev. John Kirkwood, *An Autumn Holiday in the United States and Canada* (Edinburgh, 1887), p. 47; G. W. Steevens, *The Land of the Dollar* (New York, 1897), p. 7; William Archer, *America Today* (New York, 1899), p. 21; *The Diary of George T. Strong,* IV, 535.

4. Stokes, *Iconography,* V, 1930, 1940; [Union History Co.], *History of Architecture and the Building Trades of Greater New York* (2 vols., New York, 1899), I, 56–57; Walter G. Marshall, *Through America; or, Nine Months in the United States* (London, 1882), pp. 11–12; Adams, p. 207.

5. Union History Co., I, 93, 96–97; Stokes, *New York Past and Present,* p. 83; Siegel-Cooper Co., *A Bird's-Eye View of Greater New York and Its Most Magnificent Store* (New York, 1898), p. 73.

6. David Macrae, *America Revisited* (Glasgow, 1908), p. 13; William D. Howells, *Impressions and Experiences* (New York, 1896), pp. 267, 271; Frederic Harrison, "Impressions of America," in *The Nineteenth Century,* XLIX (1901), 928; *Dictionary of National Biography,* 20th Century supplement, 1922–1930, pp. 406–8; Walt Whitman, *Specimen Days & Collect* (Philadelphia, 1882–1883), p. 117; *Complete Poetry and Prose,* Cowley ed., II, 518; Paul Bourget, *Outre-Mer: Impressions of America* (New York, 1895), pp. 28, 30.

7. McCabe, *New York by Sunlight and Gaslight,* pp. 54–55; Michael B. Buckley, *Diary of a Tour in America,* ed. by Kate Buckley (Dublin, 1886), p. 222 ["The pervading idea everywhere is the dollar above and beyond all things."]; James F. Hogan, *The Australian in London and America* (London, 1889), p. 78; T. Smith, p. 33; Maria Theresa Longworth [pseud., Thérèse Yelverton], *Teresina in America* (2 vols., London, 1875), I, 2; Edward A. Aveling, *An American Journey* (New York, 1887), p. 31; Henryk Sienkiewicz, *Briefe aus Amerika mit specialler Erlaubnis des Verfassers aus dem Polnischen,* tr. from the Polish by I. von Immendorf (Oldenburg and Leipzig, [1903?]), p. 97; Dario Papa and Ferdinando Fontana, *New-York* (Milan, 1884), p. 254; Princesse Souvoroff, *Quarante Jours à New-York: Impressions de Voyage* (Paris, 1878), p. 143 ["New Yorkers have dollars for hearts."]; Georges Sauvin, *Autour de Chicago: Notes sur les États-Unis* (Paris, 1893), pp. 9–12; Marie Dugard, *La Société Américaine* (Paris, 1896), pp. 20–21; Marius Bernard, *Au Pays des Dollars* (Paris, 1893), *passim;* C. B. Berry, *The Other Side: How It Struck Us* (New York, 1880), p. 29; Steevens, pp. 11–12; José Marti, *Los Estados Unidos* (Madrid, 1915), p. 143; Alexander Craib, *America and the Americans* (London, 1892), p. 170; W. C. Brownell, *French Traits* (New York, 1897), pp. 392–93, 401.

8. Leng, p. 218; J. W. Boddam-Whetham, *Western Wanderings: A Record of Travel in the Evening Land* (London, 1874), p. 11; Oscar Wilde, *Impressions of America* (Sunderland, 1906), p. 22; Herbert Spencer, "The Americans," in *Essays, Scientific, Political, and Speculative* (3 vols., New York, 1914), III, 482, 486; Bourget, pp. 21, 27; Le Comte Gabriel Louis de Turenne d'Aynac, *Quatorze Mois dans l'Amérique du Nord (1875–1876)* (2 vols., Paris, 1879), I, 15; Friedrich Ratzel, *Städte- und Culturbilder aus Nordamerika* (2 vols., Leipzig, 1876), I, 34–35; Dugard, p. 19; Craib, p. 161; Brownell, p. 384.

9. Macaulay, p. 75; William H. Charlton, *Four Months in North America* (Hexham, n.d.), p. 6; Ratzel, I, 50; Gustave Molinari, *Lettres sur les États-Unis et le Canada* (Paris, 1876), p. 25; Gaétan Desaché, *Souvenir de mon voyage aux États-Unis et au Canada* (Tours, [1878]), p. 29; Émile de Damseaux, *Voyage dans l'Amérique du Nord* (Paris, 1878), p. 23; McCabe, *New York by Sunlight and Gaslight,* p. 132; Adams, p. 137; Edward Money, *The Truth About America* (London, 1886), p. 20; Lady Duffus Hardy, p. 64; James F. Muirhead, *The Land of Contrasts, A Briton's View of his American Kin* (New York and London, 1898), p. 195; Marshall, p. 7; Edward A. Freeman, *Some Impressions of the United States* (Philadelphia, 1883), p. 226; Howells, *Impressions and Experiences,* p. 245; Rudyard Kipling, *Letters of Travel (1892–1913)* (London, 1920), p. 16; Howells, "Letters of an Altrurian Traveller," p. 415; Dugard, pp. 20–21.

10. Aveling, p. 26; Hogan, p. 73; Macaulay, p. 74; Émile Barbier, *Voyage au Pays des Dollars* (Paris, [1893]), p. 32; Souvoroff, p. 93; Sauvin, p. 9; Adams, p. 202; Joseph Hatton, *To-day in America. Studies for the Old World and the New* (2 vols., London, 1881), I, 56; Howells, *Impressions and Experiences,* p. 258; Howells, "Letters of an Altrurian Traveller," p. 559; Jacques Offenbach, *Offenbach in America, Notes of a Travelling Musician* (New York, 1877), pp. 124–25; Steevens, pp. 13–14.

11. Kirkwood, p. 53; Stokes, *Iconography,* V, 1975, 1985, 1998, 2019; Howells, "Letters of an Altrurian Traveller," p. 416.

12. Union History Co., I, 365; Stokes, *Iconography,* V, 1975; *Appleton's Dictionary, 1900,* p. 90; Adams, p. 202; McCabe, *New York by Sunlight and Gaslight,* p. 153; Le Vicomte d'Haussonville, *À travers les États-Unis: notes et impressions* (Paris, 1883), pp. 26–27; Sauvin, p. 9; Macrae, *America Revisited,* p. 8; Archer, p. 45.

13. Muirhead, p. 195; Marshall, p. 19; Lady Duffus Hardy, pp. 61–62; London *Times,* September 5, 1887; Molinari, p. 27; Walt Whitman, "Broadway," in *Complete Poetry and Prose,* Cowley ed., I, 442.

14. Harrison, pp. 927–28; Union History Co., I, 83, 125–26; Morris, pp. 204–7; Muirhead, pp. 196–97. The home of Cornelius Vanderbilt, built, 1880–1882, occupying the entire frontage on Fifth Avenue between West Fifty-seventh and West Fifty-eighth streets, was a red brick and gray stone structure done in the manner of Fontainebleau.

15. Iza Duffus Hardy, *Between Two Oceans: or, Sketches of American Travel* (London, 1884), p. 96.

16. Louis L. Simonin, *Le Monde Américain, souvenirs de mes voyages aux États-Unis* (Paris, 1877), p. 52; Adams, p. 300; Haussonville, pp. 280–81; le Baron Edmond de Mandat-Grancey, *En Visite chez l'Oncle Sam: New York et Chicago* (Paris, 1891), p. 49; Arthur Montefiore, "New York and New Yorkers," in *Temple Bar,* LXXXIV (1888), 347; Stokes, *New York Past and Present,* p. 83; Charlotte O'Brien, "The Emigrant in New York," in *The Nineteenth Century,* XVI (October 1884), 530; Arthur M. Schlesinger, *The Rise of the City, 1878–1898* (New York, 1933), p. 110.

17. Riis, *How the Other Half Lives,* pp. 2, 15–19, 55, 64–65, 87–88, 95–96, 105, 123–24; Howells, *Impressions and Experiences,* pp. 131, 134.

18. Howells, "Letters of an Altrurian Traveller," p. 699; Macrae, *America Revisited,* p. 10; Ratzel, I, 7; London *Times,* August 31, 1887; Archibald Porteous, *A Scamper through some Cities of America* (Glasgow, 1890), pp. 21–23; McCabe, *New York by Sunlight and Gaslight,* p. 48.

19. Ratzel, I, 7; Steevens, pp. 20–21, 25.

20. *Ibid.,* p. 27; McCabe, *New York by Sunlight and Gaslight,* pp. 54–55; Spencer, III, 473–74.

21. Fergus Ferguson, *From Glasgow to Missouri and Back* (Glasgow, 1878), p. 17; Allan Nevins and John A. Krout, eds., *The Greater City: New York, 1898–1948* (New York, 1948), pp. 41–60; Schlesinger, pp. 89–90; Charles Beadle, *A Trip to the United States in 1887* (privately printed, n.d.), pp. 13–14; Kirkwood, p. 62; Bourget, pp. 29–30; Charles Russell Russell, *Diary of a Visit to the United States of America in the year 1883,* ed. by Charles G. Herbermann (New York, 1910), p. 31; Charles Bigot, *De Paris au Niagara* (Paris, 1887), p. 31; James A. M'Dougal, *My Trip to America* (n.p., 1892), p. 43.

22. U.S. Census, 1900 (Washington, 1901), I, *Population,* pt. I, 800–3.

23. Theodore Dreiser, *The Color of a Great City* (New York, 1923), p. vii; Samuel Smith, *America Revisited* (Liverpool, 1896), p. 6; Iza Duffus Hardy, pp. 104–5; Kipling, p. 19; Sir Lepel Henry Griffin, *The Great Republic* (New York, 1884), p. 112; Leng, pp. 217–18; Turenne d'Aynac, I, 15; Molinari, p. 25; Paul Creuse, *Une Promenade autour du Monde* (Limoges, [1882]), p. 27; Bigot, p. 50; Longworth (Thérèse Yelverton), I, 5; *Alexandra Gripenberg's A Half Year in the New World . . .*, tr. and ed. by Ernest J. Moyne (Newark, Del., 1954), p. 2; Macaulay, p. 71; Sauvin, pp. 6, 21–22; Hamilton Aïdé, "Social Aspects of American Life," in *The Nineteenth Century,* XXIX (1891), 892; Hatton, *To-day in America,* I, 58; James Howard Bridge [pseud., Harold Brydges], *Uncle Sam at Home* (New York, 1888), p. 117; Paul de Rousiers, *American Life,* tr. by A. J. Herbertson (New York, 1892), pp. 242–44; Joseph Alexander, graf von Hübner, *A Ramble Round the World,* tr. by Lady Herbert (2 vols., London, 1874), I, 31.

24. Macaulay, pp. 37, 70–71; *Dictionary of National Biography, Supplement, 1901–1911,* vol. II, 501–2; Charlton, p. 31; O'Brien, pp. 530–31, 537; Riis, *How the Other Half Lives,* pp. 23, 25, 27; Sienkiewicz, p. 108; Haussonville, pp. 266, 278; Russell, p. 33; Buckley, pp. 211–17, 287; McCabe, *New York by Sunlight and Gaslight,* p. 133; Aïdé, p. 889; Craib, p. 170.

25. Macaulay, p. 71; [Frederick Duensing], *New-York—Cultur-historische Beschreibung: Ein Beitrag zur Länder- und Völker-Kunde* (Leipzig, 1872), pp. 27–30; Charles D. Shanly, "Germany in New York," in *The Atlantic Monthly,* XIX (January–June 1867), 555–56; Ernst Hohenwart, *Land und Leute in den Vereinigten Staaten* (Leipzig, 1886), pp. 34–35; Dr. Emil Deckert, *Die Neue Welt: Reiseskizzen aus dem Norden und Süden der Vereinigten Staaten* (Berlin, 1892), pp. 29–30; Max Bahr, *Reise-Berichte über Amerika* (Landsberg, 1906), pp. 29–30.

26. Haussonville, pp. 279–80; U.S. Census, 1880, *Compendium of the Tenth Census* (2 parts, Washington, 1883), I, 546–51; Carl Wittke, *We Who Built America* (New York, 1939), pp. 435–36; Riis, *How the Other Half Lives,* pp. 48–49.

27. Giuseppe Giacosa, *Impressioni d'America* (Milan, 1908), quoted in Handlin, pp. 402–4; Giuseppe Giacosa, "Gli Italiani a New York ed a Chicago," in *Nuova Antologia di Scienze, Lettere ed Arti,* XL, series 3 (August 16, 1892), 639–40; *Appleton's Dictionary of New York, 1879,* p. 114; Bourget, pp. 188–89.

28. Dreiser, p. vii; Montefiore, pp. 348–49; Riis, *How the Other Half Lives,* pp. 123–33; Bourget, pp. 192–93; Howells, *Impressions and Experiences,* pp. 130, 139–48.

29. Montefiore, p. 349; Riis, *How the Other Half Lives,* pp. 105, 112–13.

30. *Ibid.,* pp. 92–103, 149–56; Montefiore, pp. 349–50; Bourget, p. 190; Duensing, pp. 129–30; *The America of José Martí,* selected writings, tr. by Juan de Onís (New York, 1953), pp. 124–25.

31. Giacosa, quoted in Handlin, p. 399; U.S. Census, 1900, *Abstract of the Twelfth Census of the United States* (Washington, 1904), p. 357; Rousiers, pp. 239–40; Claudio Jannet, *Les États-Unis Contemporains ou les moeurs, les institutions et les idées depuis la guerre de la Sécession* (Paris, 1889), II, 152, 189; Wilde, p. 37; see also Comte Alexandre Zannini, *De l'Atlantique au Mississippi: souvenirs d'un diplomate* (Paris, 1884), pp. 83–84.

32. London *Times,* August 31, 1887; Iza Duffus Hardy, pp. 108–9.

33. Marshall, p. 14; Macaulay, p. 76; M'Dougal, p. 45; London *Times,* August 31, 1887.

34. Ratzel, I, 43–48; Macaulay, pp. 75, 107; Damseaux, p. 31; Sir George Campbell, *White and Black: the Outcome of a Visit to the United States* (London, 1879), p. 208; Samuel P. Day, *Life and Society in America* (2 vols., London, 1880), I, 114–15.

35. London *Times,* September 6, 1887; Stokes, *Iconography,* V, 1945; Schlesinger, p. 91; Rand McNally and Co., *Handy Guide to New York City* (New York, 1900), p. 25; Marshall, pp. 24–25; Lady Duffus Hardy, p. 63.

36. Campbell, p. 208; Freeman, p. 228; London *Times,* September 6, 1887; Joseph Hatton, *Henry Irving's Impressions of America narrated in a series of Sketches, Chronicles, and Conversations* (Boston, 1884), p. 110; Iza Duffus Hardy, pp. 97–98; Russell, p. 204.

37. Aveling, p. 26; Howells, *Impressions and Experiences,* pp. 257–63; William Hardman, *A Trip to America* (London, 1884), pp. 13–14; Griffin, pp. 116–17;

Money, p. 23; Kirkwood, pp. 51–53; Lady Duffus Hardy, p. 63; Campbell, pp. 208–9; Bourget, pp. 20–21; Steevens, pp. 16–17; Stokes, *Iconography,* V, 2023; Russell, p. 204; Gripenberg, p. 4.

38. Stephen Crane, "In the Broadway Cars. Panorama of a Day from the Down-Town Rush of the Morning to the Uninterrupted Whirr of the Cable at Night . . . ," in *Last Words* (London, 1902), pp. 173–80; Howells, "Letters of an Altrurian Traveller," pp. 559–60; Hogan, p. 73; Schlesinger, p. 92; Stokes, *Iconography,* V, 1987, 1991, 1996; M'Dougal, pp. 40–41; Rand McNally and Co., *Handy Guide to New York City, 1900,* p. 35; Howells, *Impressions and Experiences,* p. 259.

39. Lady Duffus Hardy, pp. 64, 70; Giacosa, in Handlin, p. 398; Longworth [Thérèse Yelverton], I, 5–6; Howells, *Impressions and Experiences,* pp. 236–42; Montefiore, p. 346.

40. E. Catherine Bates, *A Year in the Great Republic* (2 vols., London, 1887), I, 252; Zannini, p. 86; Stokes, *Iconography,* V, 1948, 2008. See also Morris, chap. XII; Day, I, 18–21.

41. Damseaux, p. 54; Joseph Hatton, *Henry Irving's Impressions of America,* p. 109; Day, I, 41–42; Beadle, pp. 14–16; Ferguson, *From Glasgow to Missouri and Back,* pp. 21–22; Offenbach, pp. 54–55. Day contended that if Brooklyn "be . . . termed, 'the City of Churches,'" New York might "not inappropriately be denominated 'the City of Hotels.'" *Op. cit.,* I, 41. Remarking that Madison Square was the center of the city, Georges Sauvin, a French visitor of 1892, was impressed by the fact that while "the heart of the city is in Rome, a church, in London, a railway station, in Paris, the Opéra," it was "in New York, a group of hotels." *Op. cit.,* p. 4.

42. George Augustus Sala, *America Revisited* (London, 1883), pp. 78–80; Sauvin, p. 17.

43. Stokes, *Iconography,* V, 2013, 2031; Rand McNally and Co., *Handy Guide to New York City, 1900,* pp. 18, 128; Day, I, 42.

44. Macaulay, pp. 109–10; Buckley, p. 257; Day, I, 73; Paul Blouet [pseud., Max O'Rell], *A Frenchman in America* (New York, 1891), pp. 342–43; Muirhead, p. 195; von Hübner, in Handlin, p. 299.

45. Leng, p. 217; Day, I, 15; Carlo Gardini, *Gli Stati Uniti ricordi con 76 illustrazioni e carte* (Bologna, 1891), quoted in Handlin, p. 343; Bates, I, 248–49; Hatton, *Henry Irving's Impressions of America,* p. 65; Robert Louis Stevenson, quoted in New York *Herald,* September 9, 1887, and cited in J. C. Furnas, *Voyage to Windward* (New York, 1951), p. 267. Joseph Hatton, Henry Irving's biographer, took a somewhat less expansive view than Irving. He wrote, after a visit in 1883, "New York is something like Paris with a touch of the backwoods, the latter represented by gaunt, untrimmed telegraph poles, the former by Madison Square, Union Square, and Fifth Avenue." Hatton, *To-day in America,* I, 56. W. T. Stead, an English visitor of 1893, professed to find a strong resemblance between New York and St. Petersburg: "The streets, the pavement, the ancient mouse-like smell, the clear blue sky, all reminded me of the Russian capital." "My First Visit to America," in *Review of Reviews,* IX (1894), 412.

46. *Appleton's Dictionary of New York, 1879,* p. 226; Siegel-Cooper Co., *A Bird's-Eye View of Greater New York,* pp. 55–58; Stokes, *New York Past and Present,* p. 83; Morris, p. 189; Rand McNally and Co., *Handy Guide to New York City, 1900,* p. 47; Schlesinger, p. 299; Stokes, *Iconography,* V, 2024–25.

47. James Burnley, *Two Sides of the Atlantic* (London, [1880?]), p. 93; Hatton, *Henry Irving's Impressions of America,* p. 124.

48. Gardini, in Handlin, pp. 344–45; Mary Ellis Peltz, *Behind the Gold Curtain* (New York, 1950), p. 9; Morris, p. 192.

49. *Ibid.,* pp. 182, 192; Gardini, in Handlin, p. 345; Stokes, *Iconography,* V, 1971.

50. Lady Duffus Hardy, p. 306; Leng, p. 224; Iza Duffus Hardy, pp. 112–13; Charlton, pp. 6, 47.

51. London *Times,* September 9, 1887; Iza Duffus Hardy, p. 106; Lady Duffus Hardy, p. 306; *The America of José Marti,* pp. 103–6.

52. Hogan, pp. 76–77; M'Dougal, p. 45; Stokes, *Iconography,* V, 2021; Lady Duffus Hardy, p. 67; Deckert, p. 49.

53. Morris, pp. 157–59; Montefiore, pp. 352–53; Turenne d'Aynac, I, 224; J. W.

C., "Social New York," from *Macmillan's Magazine,* quoted in *Eclectic Magazine,* n.s., XVI (1872), 204.

54. Montefiore, pp. 352–53; Bates, I, 251–52; William Dean Howells wrote in 1895: "Nothing seems so characteristic of this city, after its architectural shapelessness, as the eating and drinking constantly going on in the restaurants and hotels, of every quality, and the innumerable saloons." Howells, *Impressions and Experiences,* p. 271.

55. Capt. Willard Glazier, *Peculiarities of American Cities* (Philadelphia, 1885), p. 317; McCabe, *New York by Sunlight and Gaslight,* pp. 59, 474–75; J. A. Estlander, *Lettres d'Amérique* (Helsingfors, 1878), pp. 60–64; Hardman, pp. 39–40; Macaulay, p. 143; M'Dougal, p. 41; Money, pp. 24–25; Craib, p. 205. Following a characteristic Marxian line, Edward Aveling, Marx's son-in-law, described the New York police in 1886 as "a brutal looking, brutally-behaving set of men." *Op. cit.,* pp. 28, 37–38.

56. Dreiser, *The Color of a Great City,* p. v; Lady Duffus Hardy, p. 67; Muirhead, p. 193; Haussonville, p. 264; Sienkiewicz, p. 96; Craib, p. 158; James D. McCabe, Jr., *Lights and Shadows of New York Life; or the Sights and Sensations of the Great City* (Philadelphia, 1872), pp. 13–14; Simonin, pp. 30, 48–49. Simonin wrote, after a visit in 1876: "Washington is only the political capital of the United States. . . . The true capital of the Union is New York. The society of Boston is more literary and straightlaced; that of Baltimore, of Charleston, of Richmond, more distinguished, more aristocratic, in the strict sense of the word: it is well known how proud Virginians are of lineage; the society of Philadelphia is more delicate, more reserved; that of New Orleans, where one finds the descendants of the French Creoles, more agreeable, more chivalric—especially so before the War of Secession, the disastrous consequences of which ruined the South and made it the prey of the 'ignoble' carpetbaggers; but no American city can dispute New York's position for population, expanse, or magnificence, nor contest with her the figure for business which is transacted there, for the richness of its nabobs, the elegant dress of its women, the luxury and sparkle of its balls and receptions. It is in this sense that New York is the veritable capital of the United States, and no city, be it St. Louis, which the French founded a century ago on the Mississippi River and which has grown so astonishingly since, whether it be Chicago or San Francisco, the queen of the lakes or that of the Pacific, will ever henceforth be able to take away this crown from her." *Op. cit.,* pp. 48–49.

57. Steevens, p. 10; Glazier, p. 317; Archer, p. 21; London *Times,* August 31, 1887; Muirhead, p. 193.

58. Longworth [Thérèse Yelverton], I, 12–17; *Dictionary of National Biography,* XII, 126–27.

59. Marshall, pp. 7–9, 24–30.

60. Hardy, *Through Cities and Prairie Lands,* pp. 64–65, 302–6; Bessie L. Pierce, compiler and ed., *As Others See Chicago* (Chicago, 1933), p. 226. For reference to "air-conditioned" theatre, see Hardman, *A Trip to America,* p. 46.

61. Spencer, III, 472–74; *Dictionary of National Biography, Supplement, 1901–1911,* vol. III, 365; Nevins, *America Through British Eyes,* pp. 348–49.

62. Griffin, pp. 112–15, 117; *Dictionary of National Biography, Supplement, 1901–1911,* vol. II, 167–69.

63. London *Times,* September 5, 1887.

64. O'Brien, pp. 530–31, 536; *Dictionary of National Biography, Supplement, 1901–1911,* vol. III, 32; Stokes, *New York Past and Present,* pp. 83–84; Stokes, *Iconography,* V, 2038; Schlesinger, p. 110.

65. Riis, *How the Other Half Lives,* pp. 21, 24–27; *Dictionary of American Biography,* XV, 607–8.

66. Giacosa, pp. 634–36, 639–40; Torrielli, *Italian Opinion on America as Revealed by Italian Travellers, 1850–1900,* p. 31; Pierce, p. 275.

67. Kipling, pp. 16–19; Stanley J. Kunitz and Howard Haycraft, eds., *Twentieth-Century Authors* (New York, 1942), p. 765; *Dictionary of National Biography, 1931–1940,* pp. 513–14.

68. Bourget, pp. 28–30; Kunitz and Haycraft, p. 167; Handlin, p. 370.

69. Steevens, pp. 274–77, 284–94; Pierce, p. 95.

CHAPTER 9

1. Randall Blackshaw, "The New New York," in *Century Magazine,* LXIV (August 1902), 493–513; Sydney Brooks, "London and New York," in *Harper's Monthly Magazine,* CIV (January 1902), 295; John Corbin, "The Twentieth-Century City," in *Scribner's Magazine,* XXXIII (March 1903), 269; Sir Philip Burne-Jones, *Dollars and Democracy* (New York, 1904), p. 57; Charles Whibley, *American Sketches* (Edinburgh and London, 1908), pp. 13–24; Eugène d'Eichthal, *Quelques notes d'un voyage aux États-Unis,* excerpt from *Annales des Sciences Politiques* (March 15, 1906), p. 4; Claude Blanchard, *Voilà l'Amérique* (Paris, 1931), p. 20. Jesse Lynch Williams suggests the novelty of the "new" New York to its own residents at the opening of the twentieth century in his *New York Sketches* (New York, 1902), pp. 8, 38–39, 61.

2. Henry James, *The American Scene* (New York, 1946), p. 76; J. A. Spender, *Through British Eyes* (New York, 1928), p. 9; J. B. Atkins, "America after Thirty Years," in *Living Age,* CCCXXXIV (January–August 1928), 1044; André Chevrillon, "New York àpres trente ans," in *Revue des deux mondes,* septième période, XIV (March–April 1923), 355; Arthur Feiler, *America Seen through German Eyes* (New York, 1928), p. 27; Paul Achard, *A New Slant on America* (New York, 1931), pp. 10, 25, 34; F. de Martens, "A Russian's Impressions of America," in *The Independent,* LIV (1902), 2871; Bernard Faÿ, *The American Experiment* (New York, 1929), pp. 189–90; Arnaldo Fraccaroli, *New York Ciclone di Genti* (Milan, [1931]), p. 6; Philip Guedalla, *Conquistador: American Fantasia* (New York, 1928), pp. 15, 16; Salvador de Madariaga, "Americans Are Boys: A Spaniard Looks at Our Civilization," in *Harper's Magazine,* CLVII (July 1928), 239. ". . . the Skyline . . . is undoubtedly the finest aspect of New York. It is New York." Collinson Owen, *The American Illusion* (London, 1929), p. 213. "Skyscraper . . . New York, throbbing Philadelphia, diplomatic Washington, grimy Pittsburg, hustling Chicago." Dr. Sudhindra Bose, *Fifteen Years in America* (Calcutta, 1920), p. 39.

3. W. L. George, *Hail Columbia* (New York, 1921), pp. 159–60.

4. Chevrillon, p. 349; Burne-Jones, pp. 58, 60; H. G. Wells, *The Future in America* (New York, 1906), pp. 35, 36; Pierre Loti, "Impressions of New York," in *Century Magazine,* LXXXV (September 1912), 609, 759; Lazare Weiller, *Les Grandes Idées d'un Grand Peuple* (Paris, 1903), p. 24; Johannes V. Jensen, *Den Ny Verden* (Copenhagen, 1907), pp. 1–9; Paul H. B. d'Estournelles de Constant, *America and her Problems* (New York, 1915), p. 7; Maxim Gorky, "The City of Mammon," in *Appleton's Magazine,* VIII (August 1906), 178; Charles Wagner, *My Impressions of America* (New York, 1906), pp. 23, 24; William D. Howells, "Editor's Easy Chair," in *Harper's Monthly Magazine,* CXVIII (February 1909), 481; Jules Huret, *En Amérique: de New-York à la Nouvelle-Orléans* (Paris, 1904), p. 9.

5. Corbin, pp. 260–61; Charles Huard, *New York comme je l'ai vu* (Paris, 1906), p. 110; Camille Saint-Saëns, *Au Courant de la Vie* (Paris, 1914), pp. 100, 101; Ludwig Fulda, *Amerikanische eindrücke* (Berlin, 1914), p. 42; A. Maufroid, *Du Mexique au Canada* (Paris, 1907), p. 20; Karl Lamprecht, *Americana: Reiseeindrücke, Betrachtungen, geschichtliche Gesamtansicht* (Freiburg, 1906), p. 81; Paul Adam, *Vues d'Amérique* (Paris, 1906), p. 388; Albert Gobat, *Croquis et impressions d'Amérique* (Berne, 1906), pp. 40, 41; W. H. Mallock, "First Impressions of America," in *Outlook,* LXXXVI (June 1907), 465.

6. Harold Spender, *A Briton in America* (London, 1921), p. 39; Rupert Brooke, *Letters from America* (New York, 1916), pp. 7, 8; Frederick E. Smith, 1st Earl of Birkenhead, *America Revisited* (Boston, 1924), p. 2; Rebecca West, "Impressions of America," in *New Republic,* XLI (December 1924), 65, 66; André Maurois, *En Amérique,* ed. by Robert M. Waugh (New York, 1936), p. 17; Walter R. Hadwen, *First Impressions of America* (London, 1921), pp. 15–17; Margot Asquith, *My Impressions of America* (New York, *ca.* 1922), p. 24; Vicente Blasco-Ibáñez, *A Novelist's Tour of the World* (New York, 1926); Sisley Huddleston, *What's Right with America* (Philadelphia and

London, 1930), p. 46; Alfred Kerr, *New York und London: Zwanzig Kapitel nach dem Weltkrieg* (Berlin, 1929), p. 23.

7. Chevrillon, p. 356; Huret, p. 5; J. Nelson Fraser, *America Old and New: Impressions of Six Months in the States* (London, [1912]), pp. 119, 120; Loti, p. 611; New York *Daily Tribune,* September 22, 1906, in Stokes, *Iconography,* V, 2063; William G. Fitzgerald [pseud., Ignatius Phayre], *America's Day: Studies in Light and Shade* (New York, 1918), p. 75; J. A. Spender, p. 7; Frank Dilnot, *The New America* (New York, 1919), pp. 5, 6; Elijah Brown [pseud. Alan Raleigh], *The Real America* (London, 1913), pp. 46, 47; Brooke, pp. 29–33; Marion Balderston, "New York Nights," in *Outlook* (London), LIX (1927), 576; Philippe de Rothschild [pseud., Philippe], *Paris-Paris: Instantanés d'Amérique* (Paris, 1931), p. 28.

8. Wells, p. 40; Arnold Bennett, *Your United States: Impressions of a First Visit* (New York and London, 1912), pp. 27–29; William D. Howells, "Editor's Easy Chair," in *Harper's Monthly Magazine,* CXVIII (1909), 479; Collinson Owen, pp. 14, 198; Sarah Bernhardt, "Comparative Impressions of America," in *Appleton's Booklovers' Magazine,* VII (1906), 833. Alan Devereux, an Australian visitor of 1924, called Fifth Avenue an aristocrat "superbly clothed in its atmosphere of breeding, culture, and refinement"; Broadway "a prostitute, perfumed, powdered, and painted." "The Home," quoted in *Literary Digest,* LXXXIV (February 1925), 52, 54.

9. Collinson Owen, p. 14; Paul Morand, *New York,* tr. from the French by Hamish Miles (New York, 1930), p. 249; J. A. Spender, p. 10.

10. Collinson Owen, p. 14; Whibley, pp. 7–11; Morand, pp. 248–50.

11. Whitman, *Democratic Vistas,* in *Complete Poetry and Prose,* Cowley ed., II, 215; Huret, pp. 5–9; Burne-Jones, p. 22; Wells, p. 37; Whibley, p. 16; Jensen, pp. 1–9; Achard, p. 25; Balderston, p. 711; H. W. Horwill, "Leisurely America," in *The Monthly Review,* XXVII (April 1907), 149; Annette M. B. Meakin, *What America Is Doing* (Edinburgh and London, 1911), p. 265; Maurois, *En Amérique,* pp. 19, 20; G. K. Chesterton, *What I Saw in America* (New York, 1922), p. 63; Julio Camba, *Un año en el otro mundo* (Madrid, 1917), p. 93, and digest thereof in *Literary Digest,* February 24, 1924, p. 46; Fitzgerald, p. 73; J. O. Hannay [pseud., George A. Birmingham], *From Dublin to Chicago: Some Notes on a Tour in America* (New York, 1914), p. 66; E. Brown, pp. 39, 40; Yvon Lapaquellerie, *New York aux sept couleurs* (Paris, 1930), p. 28; Blanchard, p. 17; William D. Howells, "Editor's Easy Chair," in *Harper's Monthly Magazine,* CXXVIII (December 1913–May 1914), 472; Collinson Owen, p. 13. "Verticality and speed, that's New York." Devereux, p. 52.

12. Wells, p. 35; Hannay, p. 84; Thomas C. Cochran, "The City's Business," in Nevins and Krout, eds., *The Greater City,* p. 182; Ramsay Muir, *America the Golden* (London, 1927), pp. 6, 7; Henri Hauser, *L'Amérique Vivante* (Paris, 1924), p. 40; Ernest Gruening, "New York: I. The City—Work of Man," in *Nation,* CXV (November 1922), 575; Ernest Gruening, ed., *These United States: a Symposium,* 2d series (New York, 1924), p. 184; Sir Arthur Conan Doyle, *Our American Adventure* (New York, 1923), p. 21; Chevrillon, pp. 601, 603.

13. Hugo Munsterberg, *The Americans,* tr. from the German by Edwin B. Holt (New York, 1904), pp. 347–48; John C. Van Dyke, *The New New York* (New York, 1909), pp. vii, 14, 16; Hadwen, p. 5; Paul Adam, *Vues d'Amérique* (Paris, 1906), p. 409; André Lafond, *Impressions of America,* tr. from the French by Lawrence Riesner (Paris, New York, 1930), p. 16; Hannay, p. 80; Huard, p. 126; Alfred M. Low, *America at Home* (London, 1908), p. 99; Cochran, in Nevins and Krout, eds., *The Greater City,* pp. 129–34, 147–49; Charles A. Beard, "New York, the Metropolis of Today," in *Review of Reviews,* LXIX (January–June 1924), 617.

14. Fitzgerald, pp. 71, 72; Wu Tingfang, *America Through the Spectacles of an Oriental Diplomat* (New York, 1914), p. 77.

15. Comtesse Madeleine de Bryas and Mlle. Jacqueline de Bryas, *A Frenchwoman's Impressions of America* (New York, 1920), pp. ix, 24–31, 53–56; Abbé Félix Klein, *En Amérique à la fin de la guerre* (Paris, 1919), pp. 14, 15; Dilnot, pp. 111–16; Annie S. Swan [Mrs. A. Burnett-Smith], *America at Home: Impressions of a Visit in War Time* (London, 1920), pp. 23–39.

16. Harold Spender, p. 41; George, p. 153; Alderman Sir Charles Cheers Wakefield, *America To-day and To-morrow, a Tribute of Friendship* (London, 1924), p. 144; Chevrillon, p. 604.

17. Faÿ, pp. 190–92; Georges Duhamel, *Scènes de la vie future* (Paris, 1930), pp. xiii, 215, 216; Achard, pp. 24, 25, 34; C. H. Bretherton, *Midas or the United States and the Future* (New York, 1926), p. 91; Vera Brittain, *Thrice a Stranger* (New York, 1938), p. 84; Ford Madox Ford, *New York Is Not America* (New York, 1927), p. 49.

18. Cochran, in Nevins and Krout, eds., *The Greater City*, pp. 125, 178, 180.

19. Fitzgerald, p. 84; Cochran, in Nevins and Krout, eds., *The Greater City*, p. 182.

20. Philip Gibbs, *People of Destiny: Americans as I Saw Them at Home and Abroad* (New York, 1920), pp. 17–19.

21. Federal Writers' Project of the Works Progress Administration in New York City, *New York City Guide* (New York, 1939), p. 85; Morand, pp. 65–72.

22. Cochran, in Nevins and Krout, eds., *The Greater City*, p. 158; *U.S. Census, 1930, Manufactures*, pp. 1130–34; George, p. 154; *Abstract of the Twelfth Census, 1900*, p. 357; *U.S. Census, Fifteenth, Manufactures, 1929*, III, 378–80; Beard, p. 619; Morand, p. 299.

23. Egon E. Kisch, *Paradies Amerika* (Berlin, 1930), tr. in Handlin, *This Was America*, pp. 515, 520–22.

24. Harold Spender, pp. 225–26; Meakin, p. 265; Bennett, p. 187; Stephen Graham, *With Poor Immigrants to America* (New York, 1914), p. 76; Mrs. Alec-Tweedie [Edith B. Harley], *America As I Saw It or America Revisited* (New York, 1913), p. 22; George, p. 165; Gorky, p. 182; Cochran, in Nevins and Krout, eds., *The Greater City*, pp. 154, 155, 160, 174, 175.

25. Meakin, pp. 252–54; Bennett, pp. 187–91; Gibbs, pp. 20, 21.

26. Gruening, "New York," p. 574; Felix graf von Luckner, *Seeteufel erobert Amerika* (Leipzig, 1928), tr. in Handlin, *This Was America*, p. 493; Lafond, p. 21; George, p. 178; Fitzgerald, p. 76; Bretherton, p. 88; Dilnot, p. 93.

27. Burne-Jones, pp. 53–54; Corbin, p. 266; Bennett, p. 29; Dilnot, pp. 15, 93; Morand, pp. 141, 314; Huddleston, p. 59.

28. Chevrillon, p. 349; Atkins, p. 1046; Mallock, p. 464; Loti, p. 611; Lapaquellerie, p. 106; Javier Lara, *En la Metropoli del Dollar* (New York [1919?]), p. 5; Graham, p. 73; Abbé Félix Klein, *In the Land of the Strenuous Life*, the author's translation of his *Au pays de la vie intense* (Chicago, 1905), p. 40; Collinson Owen, p. 199; Clare Sheridan, *My American Diary* (New York, 1922), pp. 81–83; Alexander Francis, *Americans, an Impression* (London, 1909), p. 65; André Siegfried, *America Comes of Age*, tr. from the French by H. H. Hemming and Doris Hemming (New York, 1927), p. 16; Brown, p. 36; d'Eichthal, p. 9. See *U.S. Census, 1900*, I, 796–803; *U.S. Census, 1930, Population*, III, part 2, pp. 290, 300–3.

29. Huard, pp. 88–90; Adam, pp. 371–73; A. Maufroid, pp. 14, 15, 18, 19; Monsignor Count Vay de Vaya and Luskod, *The Inner Life of the United States* (New York, 1908), pp. 39–40; Bennett, pp. 184–85; George, pp. 164, 165; Brooke, p. 16; J. A. Spender, pp. 8, 9; Harold Spender, pp. 222–25; Fraccaroli, p. 210; Prince Baldassare Odescalchi, "An Italian Prince's Opinion of New York," in *Review of Reviews*, XXXII (July–December 1905), 236; Lapaquellerie, pp. 106, 120; Balderston, p. 711. "Wherever you turn in New York you are face to face with foreigners, or persons of foreign extraction." Hadwen, p. 77; Luigi Barzini, Jr., *Nuova York* (Milan, 1931), pp. 5, 218, 219, 250–75. See also Raffaele Calzini, *Trionfi e disfatte di Nuova York* (Milan, 1937), pp. 126, 127.

30. Whibley, p. 26; Konrad Bercovici, *Around the World in New York* (New York, 1938), p. 416; Loti, p. 1912; Vay de Vaya and Luskod, p. 31; Chevrillon, p. 623; James, p. 123; André Siegfried, *Deux Mois en Amérique du Nord à la Veille de la Guerre (Juin–Juillet, 1914)* (Paris, 1916), p. 4; Siegfried, *America Comes of Age*, p. 17; Collinson Owen, p. 199; J. A. Spender, pp. 8, 9; Chesterton, p. 35.

31. Harold Spender, p. 222; Meakin, p. 251; M. J. Bonn, *The American Experiment: A Study of Bourgeois Civilization*, translation by Mabel Brailsford of *Die Kultur der Vereinigten Staaten von Amerika* (German edition, Berlin, 1930; English edition, London, 1933), pp. 35, 36.

32. Klein, *In the Land of the Strenuous Life*, p. 37; Hadwen, p. 77; Atkins, p.

1046; Lapaquellerie, p. 120; Hilaire Belloc, *The Contrast* (New York, 1923), pp. 170, 171; Francis, p. 63; Collinson Owen, p. 199; Morand, pp. 96–99. A most prejudiced attitude is seen in Col. J. F. C. Fuller, *Atlantis: America and the Future* (New York, 1925), pp. 47–53.

33. Klein, *In the Land of the Strenuous Life,* p. 37; Collinson Owen, p. 200; Juvenal [pseud.], *An Englishman in New York* (London, 1911), p. 21; Ford, pp. 127–30.

34. Alec-Tweedie, pp. 13, 32; Loti, p. 611; Feiler, p. 30; Achard, p. 10; Lara, p. 5; Edward Hungerford, *The Personality of American Cities* (New York, 1913), p. 60; Lamprecht, p. 82; Adam, *Vues d'Amérique,* p. 386; Rhodes, pp. 57–60; Kerr, p. 59; Collinson Owen, pp. 197, 198; J. A. Spender, pp. 8, 9; Chevrillon, p. 351; Lapaquellerie, pp. 105, 106; Morand, p. 307; Hermann Alexander, Graf von Keyserling, *America Set Free* (New York, 1929), pp. 66, 67.

35. Brooks, p. 298; Munsterberg, p. 348; Burne-Jones, pp. 101, 102, 118, 119; William D. Howells, *Literature and Life* (New York, 1902), p. 179; Van Dyke, p. 15; Rhodes, p. 75; Édouard Herriot, *Impressions d'Amérique* (Lyon, 1923), pp. 92–94; Chevrillon, pp. 604–5; Ford, pp. 47, 126, 127; Guedalla, p. 20; André Maurois, *En Amérique,* "Deuxième partie. Sécond voyage aux États-Unis" (1931), p. 111; Saint-Saëns, p. 110; H. L. Mencken, "Metropolis," in *Prejudices, Sixth Series* (New York, 1927), p. 216; Edward Bliss Reed, ed., *The Commonwealth Fund Fellows and their Impressions of America* (New York, 1932), p. 25; Morand, p. 303; Chevrillon, pp. 604, 605; Henri Hauser, *L'Amérique Vivante* (Paris, 1924), p. 37; Beard, pp. 620–21.

36. Cochran, in Nevins and Krout, eds., *The Greater City,* p. 152; von Luckner, in Handlin, *This Was America,* pp. 494, 495; Maurois, *En Amérique,* p. 20.

37. James, pp. 99–102; Maufroid, pp. 38–41; Burne-Jones, pp. 92–95; Stokes, *Iconography,* V, 2067; Fitzgerald, p. 83; Brittain, pp. 74, 75; Gibbs, pp. 5, 6; Chesterton, pp. 23, 24.

38. Klein, *In the Land of the Strenuous Life,* pp. 22, 23; Juvenal, pp. 170–73; Hannay, pp. 80, 81; Lapaquellerie, p. 16.

39. Aldous L. Huxley, *Jesting Pilate, an Intellectual Holiday* (New York, [1926?]), p. 322; Ernst Toller, *Which World—Which Way?* tr. of his *Quer durch; Reisebilder und Reden* (Berlin, 1930), pp. 58, 59; Rebecca West, p. 68; Gerhard Venzmer, *New Yorker Spaziergänge; Eindrücke und Betrachtungen aus der Metropole der neuen Welt* (Hamburg, 1925), pp. 282–90; Theodor Findahl, *Manhattan Babylon: en bok om New York idag* (Oslo, 1928), *passim;* Fraccaroli, p. 66 ff.; Collinson Owen, pp. 17, 18; J. A. Spender, p. 7; Morand, p. 176; Guedalla, p. 19; Blanchard, *Voilà l'Amérique, passim;* Balderston, pp. 504, 506; Achard, p. 176.

40. William D. Howells, "Editor's Easy Chair," in *Harper's Monthly Magazine,* CXVI (1908), 472; *ibid.,* CXVIII (1909), 481; *ibid.,* CXXXII (1915–1916), 473–76; Fulda, p. 48; Dilnot, pp. 12, 13; Hadwen, p. 12; von Luckner, in Handlin, *This Was America,* p. 491; Smith [Birkenhead], pp. 47, 48; Achard, p. 25; Fraccaroli, p. 73.

41. Fulda, p. 45; von Luckner, in Handlin, *This Was America,* p. 491; Lafond, p. 49; Stokes, *Iconography,* V, 2040, 2046, 2047; Brooke, pp. 14, 15; Burne-Jones, 22, 26, 79; Cochran, in Nevins and Krout, eds., *The Greater City,* pp. 139–44; Maurois, *En Amérique,* pp. 17, 18; Atkins, p. 1045; Harold Spender, p. 42; Margaret Clapp, "The Social and Cultural Scene," in Nevins and Krout, eds., *The Greater City,* p. 202.

42. Lafond, p. 52; Morand, pp. 244, 245; James, p. 75; Julio Camba, *La Ciudad automática* (Madrid, 1932), *passim;* Camba, *Un año en el otro mundo,* pp. 11, 12, 71, 74, 94; Wells, pp. 38, 39; J. A. Spender, p. 10; d'Eichthal, p. 5; Hauser, p. 40.

43. Meakin, pp. 254, 255.

44. André Tardieu, *Notes sur les États-Unis: la société, la politique, la diplomatie* (Paris, 1908), pp. 36–44; Burne-Jones, pp. 111, 112; Ford, p. 131; Gruening, in *Nation,* 1922, p. 573.

45. George, p. 155; Huret, p. 9; Corbin, p. 263; Faÿ, pp. 190, 191; Hamilton Wright Mabie, "The Genius of the Cosmopolitan City," in *Outlook,* LXXVI (1904), 578, 593; "The Spectator," *ibid.,* XCIV (1910), 796; Wells, p. 42; Gorky, p. 178; Gustav Frenssen, *Briefe aus Amerika* (Berlin, 1923), pp. 22, 172; Achard, p. 24; Camba, *Un año en el otro mundo,* pp. 12, 13; Odescalchi, p. 236; Devereux, p. 52; Chevrillon, p. 351, 621; Camba, *La*

Ciudad automática, p. 14; Hauser, p. 40; Mallock, p. 465; d'Eichthal, p. 4; Harold Spender, p. 40; Atkins, p. 1045; West, p. 68; Gruening, p. 574; Morand, pp. 306, 307; Lara, p. 5; André Maurois, "Premier Voyage en Amérique, II, Contact," in *Les Annales Politiques et Littéraires,* XC (1928), 217; Blasco-Ibáñez, pp. 12, 13, 17; Mencken, pp. 211–12. The American critic James Huneker called the New York of 1914 "the New Cosmopolis, the most versatile city on our globe." "She may be enormously vulgar, and the genius of her is enormous, and never suggests mediocrity. You may hate her but you cannot pass her by." James Huneker, *New Cosmopolis* (New York, 1915), p. 148.

46. Wells, pp. 35, 37–43; Kunitz and Haycraft, pp. 1492–94.

47. Whibley, pp. 3, 4, 25–31; *Dictionary of National Biography, 1922–1930,* p. 906.

48. Bennett, pp. 27, 29–31; *Dictionary of National Biography, 1931–1940,* p. 67.

49. Fulda, pp. 43, 45–48; *Columbia Dictionary of Modern European Literature,* ed. by Horatio Smith (New York, 1947), p. 298; *Theatre,* VI (March 1906), 68.

50. Fitzgerald, pp. 114, 115, 72, 74, 75, 284, 91–93.

51. Dilnot, pp. 110–16; *Who Was Who, 1941–1950,* p. 317.

52. Gibbs, pp. 1–3, 5–6; Kunitz and Haycraft, pp. 529, 530.

53. George, pp. 154–56; Pierce, *As Others See Chicago,* p. 466; Harold Spender, p. 40.

54. Ford, pp. 47, 48, 126, 127, 129–30, 141, 145, 146; Kunitz and Haycraft, p. 474; Guedalla, p. 20.

55. Morand, pp. 174–77, 314–18, 320; Kunitz and Haycraft, pp. 982, 983.

56. Faÿ, pp. 190–92; Kunitz and Haycraft, p. 443.

CHAPTER 10

1. George Brandt, "Farewell Manhattan: New York in the Depths of Depression," in *Review of Reviews,* LXXXII (1932), 75–76; John Gunther, *Inside U.S.A.* (New York, 1947), p. 550.

2. Julian Green, *Personal Record, 1928–1939,* tr. from the French by Jocelyn Godefroi (New York, 1939), p. 27; Maurois, *En Amérique,* p. 99; Philippe Soupault, "La 'dépression' à New-York," in *L'Europe Nouvelle,* XIV (August 1931), 1083, 1084; Mary Agnes Hamilton, *In America Today* (London, 1932), pp. 10, 11, 19, 20; M. Philips Price, *America after Sixty Years* (London, 1936), pp. 92, 93; Brandt, p. 74; Harrison Brown, "New York and Chicago Today," in *Fortnightly Review,* CXL (September 1933), 270; S. P. B. Mais, *A Modern Columbus* (Philadelphia, 1934), p. 297.

3. Soupault, pp. 64, 1083, 1084; Price, pp. 95–97; Gibbons, p. 213; J. B. Priestley, *Midnight on the Desert, A Chapter of Autobiography* (London, 1937), pp. 37, 38; Paul Hazard, "À New-York pendant les élections," in *Revue des deux mondes,* 8me période, XII (1932), 839–43; Ivan Kashkin, ed., *New York (an Outline)* (Cooperative Publishing Society of Foreign Workers in the U.S.S.R., Moscow, 1933), p. 157.

4. Priestley, *Midnight on the Desert,* p. 36; Brittain, *Thrice a Stranger,* pp. 276, xiii, xiv.

5. Camba, *La Ciudad automática,* p. 14; Edmund Wilson, *Travels in Two Democracies* (New York, 1936), pp. 38, 43; John Cowper Powys, "Farewell to America," in *Scribner's Magazine,* XCVII (1935), 202; E. F. Iddon, comment in London *Daily Express,* quoted in *Living Age,* CCCLIII (1937), 78; Eric Newton, comment in Manchester *Guardian,* quoted *ibid.,* p. 79; Bernard De Voto, "On Moving from New York," in *Harper's Monthly Magazine,* CLXXVII (1938), 336; Hector Bolitho, *Haywire: An American Travel Diary* (New York, 1939), pp. 6, 7, 10, 174, 176; Felix Riesenberg and Alexander Alland, *Portrait of New York* (New York, 1939), pp. 28, 29, 72; Peter Quennell, "Manhattan Notebook," in *Cornhill Magazine,* CLIX (1939), 56; A. G. Macdonnell, *A Visit to America* (New York, 1935), pp. 18–20; Priestley, *Midnight on the Desert,* pp. 22, 24, 25, 39; J. E. Strachan, *New Zealand Observer: A Schoolmaster Looks at America* (New York, 1940), p. 115; L. P. Jacks, *My American Friends* (New York, 1933), pp. 34, 37, 38, 46, 47; William Saroyan, in Milton Bracker, "Three New Yorks," in *New York Times Magazine,* March 31, 1940, p. 19; Odette Keun, *I Think Aloud in America* (New

York, 1939), pp. 36, 37, 42, 48–50, 56, 79, 80; Ilya Ilf and Eugene Petrov, *Little Golden America* (London, 1946; first published, 1936), pp. 16, 18, 27; Henry Miller, *The Air-Conditioned Nightmare* (New York, 1945), p. 12; Sinclair Lewis, "Towers at Dawn," in *Newsweek*, XI (January 31, 1938), 28.

6. Cecil Roberts, *And So to America* (New York, 1947), p. 44; Maurice Dekobra, *Seven Years Among Free Men*, tr. from the French by Warre Bradley Welles (London, 1948), pp. 4, 16, 22; W. J. Brown, *I Meet America* (London, 1942), pp. 18, 19; Pierre de Lanux, *New York, 1939–1945* (Paris, 1947), p. 64.

7. *Ibid.*, pp. 40–45; André Maurois, *États-Unis 39: journal d'un voyage en Amérique* (Paris, 1939), pp. 123, 124.

8. Lanux, pp. 48–57, 79–81; W. J. Brown, pp. 123, 124, 128.

9. Bernard Newman, *American Journey* (London, 1943), p. 10; Victor Vinde, *America at War*, tr. by E. Classen (London, 1944), p. 8; Ward Morehouse, *American Reveille: The United States at War* (New York, 1942), pp. 240, 241; Lanux, pp. 86, 115, 121.

10. James L. Hodson, *And Yet I Like America* (London, 1945), pp. 18–20; Carlos P. Romulo, *My Brother Americans* (Garden City, New York, 1945), pp. 146–51; Lanux, p. 120; W. J. Brown, pp. 143–44.

11. Lanux, pp. 114–16, 119, 120; Morehouse, p. 242.

12. Lanux, pp. 161–66.

13. D. W. Brogan, *American Themes* (New York, n.d.), p. 115; D. W. Brogan, "New York, 1900–1950," in *History Today*, I (February 1951), 55, 56; Brooks Atkinson, "The Fabulous Port of New York," in *New York Times Magazine* (August 5, 1951), p. 16; Gunther, p. 553; John Joslin, "Our Incredible City," in *New York Times Magazine* (December 22, 1946), p. 11; Douglas Reed, *Far and Wide* (London, 1951), pp. 72, 74; Paul Bastid, *Quelques notes sur les Amériques* (Paris, 1948), pp. 12–14.

14. Richard Rovere, "The Decline of New York City," in *The American Mercury*, LVIII (May 1944), 526–32; Jean-Paul Sartre, "Manhattan: Great American Desert," quotation from *Town and Country*, in Alexander Klein, ed., *The Empire City* (New York, 1955), p. 456; Chamber of Commerce of the State of New York, *New York City Guide* (New York, 1950), p. 61; E. B. White, *Here Is New York* (New York, 1949), pp. 50, 51.

15. J. B. Priestley, "Priestley Appraises New York," in New York *Times*, January 4, 1948; unpublished figures supplied by Department of Commerce, Bureau of the Census, courtesy Howard G. Brunsman; Keun, p. 87; Reed, p. 66; Cecil Beaton, *Cecil Beaton's New York* (New York, 1938), p. 154; Dekobra, p. 22; Jules Romains, *Salsette Discovers America*, tr. from the French by Lewis Galantière (New York, 1942), *passim*. D. W. Brogan asserted in 1939 that since the curtailment of immigration the "native New Yorker" was becoming "more numerous proportionately than at any time for three generations past." Brogan, *American Themes*, p. 116. According to George S. Perry, the biggest immigrant group in the city, in 1947, was "the one composed of fugitives from America's small towns." George S. Perry, "New York," in *Cities of America* (New York, 1947), p. 17. The most numerous foreign-born groups in 1950 were Italians (344,115), Russians (314,603), Germans (185,467), and Poles (179,878).

16. Edward F. Frazier, *The Negro in the United States* (New York, 1949), p. 230; New York *Times*, October 1, 1952; Atkins, p. 1046; Mais, p. 295; Price, p. 94; Robert Waithman, *Report on America* (London, 1940), p. 59; E. M. Delafield, *The Provincial Lady in America* (London, 1934), pp. 223–25; Vinde, pp. 11, 12; Keun, pp. 100–4; Cecil Beaton, *Portrait of New York* (London, 1948), pp. 102–10; Hodson, p. 268; Gunther, pp. 574–76; Simone de Beauvoir, *America Day by Day*, tr. from the French by Patrick Dudley (New York, 1953), pp. 34–40, 59–61, 299–301; Lanux, p. 17.

17. Barzini, p. 219; Pierre Malo, *La Féerie Américaine: New-York et Washington* (Paris, 1936), p. 37; Keun, pp. 90, 91, 94–99, 104–6; J. B. Priestley, "Priestley Appraises New York"; Beaton, *Portrait of New York*, pp. 96–98; Vinde, p. 10; Lanux, pp. 15–17, 40–45; Paul Crowell and A. H. Raskin, "New York, 'Greatest City in the World,'" in Robert S. Allen, ed., *Our Fair City* (New York, 1947), pp. 39, 58. One exception is the generally critical attitude of Douglas Reed toward the Jewish element, which he blames for the nervous tension in New York society. *Op. cit.*, pp. 63–68. For appreciation of the Jewish contribution,

see Alistair Cooke, *One Man's America* (New York, 1952), p. 55; Beaton, *Portrait of New York*, p. 97.

18. Chiang Yee, *The Silent Traveller in New York* (New York, n.d.), p. 113; Waithman, pp. 54, 55; Beaton, *Cecil Beaton's New York*, p. 154; Johannes V. Jensen, *Fra Fristaterne; Rejsebreve, med et Tilbageblik* (Copenhagen, 1939), p. 37.

19. Luis Rosario-Nieves, "Puerto Ricans in New York City from 1910 to 1950," manuscript, in author's possession; Beaton, *Portrait of New York*, p. 98; Beaton, *Portrait of New York* (1948 ed.), pp. 98–100. For reactions of a Puerto Rican commentator, see Tomás de Jesús Castro, *Nueva York* (Santurce, P. R., 1950).

20. Strachan, p. 114; Chiang Yee, p. 18; Haruko (Mrs. Sanki) Ichikawa, *Japanese Lady in America* (Tokyo, 1939), pp. 74, 75; Ilf and Petrov, p. 14; Price, p. 92; Waithman, p. 129; August W. Fehling, *Die Vereinigten Staaten von Amerika: Land und Menschen unter dem Sternenbanner* (Berlin, 1933), pp. 106–10; "Le Corbusier Considers the New York Skyscraper" (excerpts from Le Corbusier [pseud. of Charles-Édouard Jeanneret], *Quand les Cathédrales étaient blanches*), in *Légion d'Honneur Magazine*, X (October 1939), 284; Le Corbusier [pseud. of Charles-Édouard Jeanneret], *When the Cathedrals Were White*, tr. by Francis E. Hyslop, Jr. (New York, 1947), pp. 36, 45; Enrico Visconti-Venosta, *Impressions of America* (Chicago, 1933), p. 7; Ambroise Vollard, "Mon Voyage en Amérique," in *Revue Bleue, Politique et littéraire*, LXXV (1937), 596–97; Lewis, p. 28; Clair Price, "An Older and Wiser New York," in *New York Times Magazine*, January 19, 1941, p. 10; Guy Mollat du Jourdain, ed., *L'âme des cités* (Paris, 1946), p. 173; Gaspar Tato Cumming, *Nueva York. Un Español entre Rascacielos* (Madrid, 1945), p. 47.

21. Le Corbusier, *When the Cathedrals Were White*, pp. 36, 70, 71; Macdonnell, pp. 18–21; Priestley, "Priestley Appraises New York"; Vinde, p. 8; Waithman, p. 125; Keun, pp. 37, 44; Reed, pp. 70, 71.

22. Le Corbusier, *When the Cathedrals Were White*, pp. 107, 108; Keun, pp. 56–59; Ilf and Petrov, pp. 15, 16; C. V. R. Thompson, *I Lost My English Accent* (New York, 1939), pp. 20–23; Jules Romains, *Visite aux Américains* ([Paris], 1936), pp. 38–48; Priestley, "Priestley Appraises New York"; Francis Marshall, *An Englishman in New York* (London, 1949), p. 13; Elmer Rice, quoted in Milton Bracker, "Three New Yorks," in *New York Times Magazine*, March 31, 1940, p. 6; Theodor Findahl, *Moskva og New York; tyve år etter* (Oslo, 1949), pp. 94, 95; Henri-Jean Duteil, *The Great American Parade*, tr. from the French by Fletcher Pratt (New York, 1953), p. 298.

23. Jacks, pp. 33, 34; Mais, p. 296; Macdonnell, p. 19; Hamilton, *In America Today*, pp. 22, 23; Thompson, p. 17; Beaton, *Portrait of New York*, pp. 9, 15, 16; Priestley, "Priestley Appraises New York"; Thomas Wolfe, *The Web and the Rock* (New York, 1937), pp. 231–32 (see also 248, 272, 325, 390, 391, 471–3, 680); Truman Capote, *Local Color* (New York, 1946), p. 13.

24. Arnold Palmer, "Arrived New York," London *Mercury*, XXXIX (1939), pp. 432–33; Strachan, p. 114; Jules Romains, *Salsette Discovers America*, pp. 53–56; Sartre, quoted in Klein, *The Empire City*, p. 453; Newman, p. 12; Perry, p. 18; Cyril Connolly, "American Interjection," in *Ideas and Places* (London, 1953), p. 176; David Scott, "New York in a Day—an English Impression," in London *Mercury*, XXXII (1935), 258–59; Duteil, pp. 291, 294. Le Corbusier employs this "lengthwise" figure in referring to Broadway as "stretched out like a tightrope on which there is an abundance of dancers." *When the Cathedrals Were White*, p. 107. Chiang Yee uses a similar idiom in referring to Fifth Avenue as "*The White Satin Rope Fastened at Both Ends*, with the idea that we humans are the rope-walkers," *The Silent Traveller in New York*, p. 93.

25. Rebecca Rankin, ed., *New York Advancing: Seven More Years of Progressive Administration in The City of New York, 1939–1945* (New York, 1945), p. 32; Newman, p. 13.

26. Rankin, ed., *New York Advancing: Seven More Years . . .*, p. 33; Keun, p. 50; Macdonnell, p. 20; Hodson, p. 268; Chiang Yee, p. 40; Ichikawa, p. 94.

27. Brittain, p. xvi; Romains, *Visite aux Américains*, p. 55; Keun, p. 92; Nevins and Krout, eds., *The Greater City*, pp. 23, 24; Rodgers and Rankin, pp. 291–92, 298, 300, 332–33; Rankin, ed., *New York*

Advancing: Seven More Years . . . , pp. xxi, 105.

28. Vinde, pp. 9, 10; Romulo, p. 162; Rankin, ed., *New York Advancing: Seven More Years . . . ,* pp. 122, 123, 139, 267–69; Cooke, p. 107.

29. Rice, p. 6; Clifford Odets, quoted in Milton Bracker, "Three New Yorks," in *New York Times Magazine,* March 31, 1940, p. 7; Findahl, *Moskva og New York,* p. 9; Gunther, pp. 549–50; Maurois, *États-Unis 39,* pp. 45–52.

30. Beaton, *Portrait of New York,* pp. 121–22; Beaton, *Cecil Beaton's New York,* pp. 103, 183. See Irwin Edman, "The Spirit Has Many Mansions," quoted from New York *Times* (1953), in Klein, *The Empire City,* pp. 386–88; Connolly, p. 176.

31. Jean Joseph-Renaud, *New-York Flamboie* (Paris, 1931), p. 30; Strachan, p. 116; Simone de Beauvoir, *L'Amérique au jour le jour* (Paris, 1949), p. 383; Ilf and Petrov, pp. 24–27; Roland Lebel, *Intimes New York* (Bern-Stuttgart, [1938?]), pp. 43–44; Mollat du Jourdain, p. 162; Camba, *La Ciudad automática,* p. 50; Ichikawa, p. 90; K. Natarajan, *Our Trip to America* (Bombay, 1934), p. 59; Marshall, *An Englishman in New York,* p. 49. For a description of night life in 1933, see Delafield, pp. 214–25.

32. Alexander Woollcott, *Going to Pieces* (1928), quoted in Klein, *The Empire City,* pp. 420-21; Alistair Cooke, *One Man's America* (New York, 1952), pp. 194–95; 200–2; Chiang Yee, p. 277; John Steinbeck, "The Making of a New Yorker" (1953), quoted in Klein, *The Empire City,* pp. 474–75; Robert Benchley, "The Typical New Yorker" (1928), *ibid.,* pp. 341–42; Marshall, *An Englishman in New York,* p. 12; André Maurois, *From My Journal,* tr. from the French by Joan Charles (New York, 1947), p. 4; E. B. White, p. 27; Perry, p. 16; Christopher Morley, "New York, One Way," in *Saturday Review of Literature,* XVI (June 26, 1937), 14.

33. Clair Price, pp. 10, 22; Brandt, pp. 74, 76; Odets, in Bracker, p. 7; Rebecca B. Rankin, ed., *New York Advancing: a Scientific Approach to Municipal Government* (New York, 1936), p. 1; Rovere, p. 532; Beauvoir, *America Day by Day,* p. 236. See also Keun, p. 93; Vinde, p. 9; Romulo, p. 162; Walter Citrine, *My American Diary* (London, 1941), pp. 108–11 (a La Guardia broadcast described).

34. Barzini, p. 33; Wolfe, *The Web and the Rock,* p. 391; Soupault, p. 1084; Calzini, p. 33; Waithman, p. 127; Brandt, p. 75; Harrison Brown, p. 273; Romains, p. 64; Keun, p. 85 ("an excrescence of America, but nevertheless a microcosm of America"); Newman, p. 12; Jacks, pp. 31–33; Lanux, pp. 25–28; James Pope-Hennessy, *America is an Atmosphere* (London, 1947), p. 14; Benchley, p. 342; Vilhelm Moberg, "Att upptäcka Amerika," in *Folket i Bild,* XVI (October 30, 1949), 4.

35. Waithman, pp. 117–23; Brittain, p. 258; Collinson Owen, pp. 197–98; Brogan, *American Themes,* p. 115; William Allen White, "Imperial City," in *Literary Digest,* CXXIV (October 1937), 13, 14; Romulo, p. 151; Gunther, pp. 549–50.

36. Le Corbusier, *When the Cathedrals Were White,* p. 84; Beaton, *Portrait of New York* (1938 ed.), p. 246; Crowell and Raskin, pp. 37–39; Gunther, p. 550 ("Actually the U N will serve to further its transformation from merely a national into a world metropolis."); Beverley Nichols, *Uncle Samson* (London, 1950), p. 21; Vinde, p. 13; Beauvoir, *America Day by Day,* p. 235; Priestley, "Priestley Appraises New York."

37. Connolly, p. 175; Findahl, *Moskva og New York,* p. 92; Priestley, "Priestley Appraises New York"; Nichols, pp. 9, 21, 22; Beauvoir, *America Day by Day,* pp. 17, 36; Francis Marshall, p. 11.

38. Quennell, p. 51; Saroyan, in Bracker, pp. 7, 19; Pope-Hennessy, p. 49; Perry, pp. 25, 26; W. J. Brown, pp. 143, 144; E. B. White, p. 49; Findahl, *Moskva og New York,* p. 9; John Steinbeck, "The Making of a New Yorker," quoted in Klein, *The Empire City,* p. 474; Beaton, *Portrait of New York* (1948 ed.), pp. 129–31; George Dorsey, quoted in Frances Rodman, compiler, "New York, New York," in *New York Times Magazine,* August 10, 1952, p. 41; Gunther, p. 549.

39. Connolly, p. 176; Nichols, pp. 9, 20; Vinde, p. 10; Waithman, pp. 97–100, 116, 127; Beaton, *Portrait of New York* (1948 ed.), p. 129; Beauvoir, *L'Amérique au jour le jour,* pp. 382, 383; Crowell and Raskin, p. 39; E. B. White, p. 53 ("capital of everything"); Romains, *Visite aux Américains,* pp. 64, 65 ("extreme expression of

the country," highest realization of its "potential qualities," "most extraordinary exhibit the United States has to show"); Connolly, p. 170 ("the supreme metropolis of the present"); William Allen White asserted in 1937 that New York was the symbol of American individualism. White, p. 14.

40. Vinde, p. 13.

41. Hamilton, pp. 9, 10, 19, 20, 22–24; Nevins, *America Through British Eyes,* p. 442.

42. Ilf and Petrov, pp. 24–27; *Columbia Dictionary of Modern European Literature,* pp. 403, 404, 623.

43. Keun, pp. 56–59; Handlin, *This Was America,* p. 535.

44. Waithman, pp. 53–55.

45. Romulo, pp. 146, 147, 150, 151; *Current Biography* (1943), p. 628.

46. Vinde, pp. 8–10.

47. Anthony Armstrong Willis [pseud., Anthony Armstrong], *Britisher on Broadway* (London, 1932), pp. 43–49; *Who's Who 1954,* p. 3171.

48. Le Corbusier, pp. 36, 40, 44, 45, 55, 62, 70, 71; *Current Biography* (1947), p. 383. See Chiang Yee, p. 278; Brittain, p. xv.

49. Gunther, pp. 574–76.

50. Beaton, *Portrait of New York,* p. 128; Beaton, *Cecil Beaton's New York,* p. 246; Rodgers and Rankin, pp. 351–56; Nichols, pp. 8, 9, 11, 19–21; Kunitz and Haycraft, eds., *Twentieth-Century Authors,* pp. 1021, 1022.

BIBLIOGRAPHY

CONTEMPORARY ACCOUNTS

Following is an alphabetical list, by author, of the commentaries on New York City to which reference has been made in the foregoing pages. Obviously, this is by no means a complete inventory of descriptions of the city by eyewitnesses. It does constitute, however, a representative selection, with respect both to chronological coverage and to the nature, insight, and national origins of the writers who described the local scene. The earliest descriptions of the community were primarily the work of officials and residents of the Dutch outpost from which the metropolis was to grow. These were soon supplemented by the reports of royal administrators, European travelers, and visitors from other British possessions along the Atlantic coast. After 1783, when the American experiment was of increasing interest to the outside world, descriptions of New York were almost invariably included in the rapidly augmenting literature describing and, in time, attempting to interpret the American scene. Until the twentieth century, few books of a descriptive or interpretive character, other than guidebooks or gazetteers, dealt with New York City alone. By the period of the Civil War, some American writers had begun, in books and articles, to unveil the mysteries of the emerging metropolis; but not until the third decade of the twentieth century did book-length works on New York City become numerous. Then the world-wide appeal of the postwar wonder city was reflected not only in the description of it in commentaries upon the United States in general, but in books, of the most diverse authorship, about New York City itself. Since the date of publication often gives no proper indication of the time at which the observations were made, this information is supplied in the bracket concluding each citation. In some instances, for lack of precise information this date has had to be an approximation.

Abbate e Migliore, Salvatore. *Viaggio nella America Settentrionale.* Palermo, 1853. [1845]

Abdy, E. S. *Journal of a Residence and Tour in the United States of North America, from April, 1833, to October, 1834.* 3 vols. London, 1835. [1833]

Achard, Paul. *A New Slant on America.* New York, 1931. [1929]

[Acton, John E. E. Dalberg, Lord]. "Lord Acton's American Diaries," pt. I, in *Fortnightly Review,* n.s., CX (1921), 727–42. [1853]

Adam, Paul. *Vues d'Amérique.* Paris, 1906. [1904]

Adamoli, Luigi. "Letters from America, I," in *The Living Age,* CCCXII (March 1922), 582–93. [1866–1867]

[Adams, John]. *The Works of John Adams.* Ed. by Charles F. Adams. 10 vols. Boston, 1850–1856. [1774]

[Adams, John Quincy]. *Diary of John Quincy Adams, 1794–1845.* Ed. by Allan Nevins. New York, 1951. [1835]

[Adams, John Quincy]. *Writings of John Quincy Adams*. Ed. by Worthington C. Ford. 7 vols. New York, 1913–1917. [1801, 1806]
Adams, W. E. *Our American Cousins*. London, 1883. [1882]
"A Few Weeks in New York, by a Returned Emigrant," in *The New Monthly Magazine and Humorist*, XLVIII, pt. 3 (1836), 352–59. [1835?]
Aïdé, Hamilton. "Social Aspects of American Life," in *The Nineteenth Century*, XXIX (1891), 888–903. [*ca.* 1890]
Alec-Tweedie, Mrs. [Edith B. Harley]. *America As I Saw It or America Revisited*. New York, 1913. [1912]
Ampère, Jean J. A. *Promenade en Amérique*. 2 vols. Paris, 1855. [1851]
[Anburey, Thomas]. *Travels through the Interior Parts of America. In a Series of Letters. By an Officer*. 2 vols. London, 1789. [1781]
[Anderson, Dr. Alexander]. "Diary of Dr. Alexander Anderson," in *Old New York*, I (1890), 46–55, 85–93, 197–204, 233–53; II (1890–1891), 88–105, 184–92, 217–26, 289–301, 428–36. [1795]
[Andros, Sir Edmund]. "Answers of Gov. Andros to Enquiries about New York; 1678." Quoted in O'Callaghan. *Documentary History . . . New York*, I, 60–62. [1678]
Archer, William. *America Today*. New York, 1899. [1899]
Arfwedson, C. F. *The United States and Canada, in 1832, 1833, and 1834*. 2 vols. London, 1834. [*ca.* 1832]
Asquith, Margot. *My Impressions of America*. New York, *ca.* 1922. [*ca.* 1922]
Atkins, J. B. "America after Thirty Years," in *Living Age*, CCCXXXIV (January–August 1928), 1043–49. [1928]
Atkinson, Brooks. "The Fabulous Port of New York," in *New York Times Magazine* (August 5, 1951), 16, 17, 38. [1951]
Audouard, Mme. Olympe. *À travers l'Amérique . . .* Paris, 1907. [*ca.* 1868]
Aveling, Edward A. *An American Journey*. New York, 1887. [1886]
Bacourt, Adolphe Fourier de. *Souvenirs of a Diplomat*. New York, 1885. [1840]
Bahr, Max. *Reise-Berichte über Amerika*. Landsberg, 1906. [1897]
Baily, Francis. *Journal of a Tour in Unsettled Parts of North America in 1796 and 1797*. London, 1856. [1796]
Balderston, Marion. "New York Nights," in *Outlook* (London), LIX (1927), 504–8; 576–78; "New York Days," *ibid.*, 666–68; 709–11. [*ca.* 1927]
[Bangs, Lieut. Isaac]. *Journal of Lieutenant Isaac Bangs, April 1 to July 29, 1776*. Ed. by Edward Bangs. Cambridge, Mass., 1890. [1776]
Barbier, Émile. *Voyage au Pays des Dollars*. Paris, [1893]. [*ca.* 1892]
Barzini, Luigi, Jr. *Nuova York*. Milan, 1931. [*ca.* 1930]
Bastid, Paul. *Quelques notes sur les Amériques*. Paris, 1948. [1947]
Bates, E. Catherine. *A Year in the Great Republic*. 2 vols. London, 1887. [*ca.* 1886]
Baxter, William E. *America and the Americans*. London, 1855. [1854]
Bayard, Ferdinand-M. *Voyage dans l'intérieur des États-Unis . . . pendant l'été de 1791*. Paris, 1798. [1791]
Beadle, Charles. *A Trip to the United States in 1887*. Privately printed, n.d. [1887]
Beard, Charles A. "New York, the Metropolis of Today," in *Review of Reviews*, LXIX (January–June 1924), 609–24. [1924]
Beaton, Cecil. *Cecil Beaton's New York*. New York, 1938. [1936–1938]
——. *Portrait of New York*. London, 1948. [1947]
Beaujour, Félix, baron de. *Sketch of the United States of North America at the*

Commencement of the Nineteenth Century, from 1800 to 1810. Tr. by William Walton. London, 1814. [1800–1810]

Beauvallet, Leon. *Rachel and the New World: a Trip to the United States and Canada*. New York, 1856. [1855]

Beauvoir, Simone de. *America Day by Day*. Tr. from the French by Patrick Dudley. New York, 1953. [1947]

———. *L'Amérique au jour le jour*. Paris, 1949. [1947]

Belden, Ezekiel P. *New York: Past, Present, and Future*. New York, 1849, 1851. [1849, 1851]

Bell, Andrew [pseud., A. Thomason]. *Men and Things in America*. London, 1838. [1835]

Belloc, Hilaire. *The Contrast*. New York, 1923. [1923]

Benchley, Robert. "The Typical New Yorker." New York, 1928. Quoted in Klein, ed. *The Empire City*, pp. 338–42. [*ca.* 1927]

Bennett, Arnold. *Your United States: Impressions of a First Visit*. New York and London, 1912. [1911]

Benwell, J. *An Englishman's Travels in America*. London, 1853. [late 1840's]

Bercovici, Konrad. *Around the World in New York*. New York, 1938. [*ca.* 1930]

Bernard, John. *Retrospections of America, 1797–1811*. Ed. by Mrs. Bayle Bernard. New York, 1887. [1797]

Bernard, Marius. *Au Pays des Dollars*. Paris, 1893. [*ca.* 1893]

Bernhard, Karl, Duke of Saxe-Weimar-Eisenach. *Travels through North America, during the years 1825 and 1826*. 2 vols. Philadelphia, 1828. [1825–1826]

Bernhardt, Sarah. "Comparative Impressions of America," in *Appleton's Booklovers' Magazine*, VII (1906), 833–37. [*ca.* 1905]

Berry, C. B. *The Other Side: How It Struck Us*. New York, 1880. [*ca.* 1879]

Bigelow, Timothy. *Diary of a Visit to Newport, New York, and Philadelphia, during the Summer of 1815*. Ed. by Abbott Lawrence. Boston, 1880. [1815]

Bigot, Charles. *De Paris au Niagara*. Paris, 1887. [1886]

Bill, John. "Extracts from the Journal of Philo-Jocundus." Manuscript in New-York Historical Society. [1828]

Birket, James. *Some Cursory Remarks Made by James Birket in his Voyage to North America 1750–1751*. New Haven, 1916. [1750–1751]

Bishop, Isabella Lucy Bird. *The Englishwoman in America*. 2d ed. London, 1856. [1854]

Blackshaw, Randall. "The New New York," in *Century Magazine*, LXIV (August 1902), 493–513. [1902]

Blanchard, Claude. *Voilà l'Amérique*. Paris, 1931. [*ca.* 1930]

Blane, William N. *An Excursion through the United States and Canada during the Years 1822–23*. London, 1824. [1822]

Blasco-Ibáñez, Vicente. *A Novelist's Tour of the World*. New York, 1926. [1923]

Blouet, Paul [pseud., Max O'Rell]. *A Frenchman in America*. New York, 1891. [1890]

[Blunt, Edmund M.]. *The Picture of New-York and Stranger's Guide to the Commercial Metropolis of the United States*. New York, 1828. [1827]

Boardman, James. *America and the Americans*. London, 1833. [1829–1831]

[Bobo, William N.]. *Glimpses of New York by a South Carolinian (who had nothing else to do)*. Charleston, 1852. [1850–1851]

Boddam-Whetham, J. W. *Western Wanderings: A Record of Travel in the Evening Land*. London, 1874. [1872?]

Bolitho, Hector. *Haywire: An American Travel Diary*. New York, 1939. [1938]

Bonn, M. J. *The American Experiment: A Study of Bourgeois Civilization.* Translation by Mabel Brailsford of *Die Kultur der Vereinigten Staaten von Amerika.* German edition, Berlin, 1930; English edition, London, 1933. [*ca.* 1930]

Bonnet, J. E. *États-Unis de l'Amérique à la fin du XVIIIe siècle.* 2 vols. Paris, [1802?]. [*ca.* 1790]

Borrett, George T. *Letters from Canada and the United States.* London, 1865. [1864]

Bose, Dr. Sudhindra. *Fifteen Years in America.* Calcutta, 1920. [1910–1915?]

Boudinot, Elias. Letter to his wife, April 24, 1789. Excerpted in Stokes, *Iconography,* V, 1240. [1789]

[Bourgeois, Nicolas L.]. *Voyages intéressans dans Différentes Colonies Françaises, Espagnoles, Anglaises* . . . par M. N. . . . Paris, 1788. [1787]

Bourget, Paul. *Outre-Mer: Impressions of America.* New York, 1895. [1893]

Brandt, George. "Farewell Manhattan: New York in the Depths of Depression," in *Review of Reviews,* LXXXII (1932), 72–76. [1932]

Bremer, Fredrika. *The Homes of the New World; Impressions of America.* Tr. by Mary Howitt. 2 vols. New York, 1853. [1849–1851]

Bretherton, C. H. *Midas or the United States and the Future.* New York, 1926. [1925]

Bridge, James H. [pseud., Harold Brydges]. *Uncle Sam at Home.* New York, 1888. [1887]

Bridge, Samuel S. "Diary." Printed in "New York A Hundred Years Ago," in *Munsey's Magazine,* XL (November 1908), 196–205. [1809]

Brissot de Warville, J. P. *New Travels in the United States of America, Performed in 1788.* 2 vols. London, 1792. [1788]

Brittain, Vera. *Thrice a Stranger.* New York, 1938. [1925–1927, 1934, 1937]

Brogan, D. W. *American Themes.* New York, n.d. [1939]

——. "New York, 1900–1950," in *History Today,* I (February 1951), 46–56. [1950]

Bromme, Traugott. *Reisen durch die Vereinigten Staaten und Ober-Canada.* 2 vols. Baltimore, 1834. [*ca.* 1830's?]

Brooke, Rupert. *Letters from America.* New York, 1916. [1913–1914]

Brookes, Joshua. "Journal." Manuscript in New York Public Library. [1798]

Brooks, Sydney. "London and New York," in *Harper's Monthly Magazine,* CIV (January 1902), 295–303. [1901]

Brown, Harrison. "New York and Chicago Today," in *Fortnightly Review,* CXL (September 1933), 269–79. [1933]

Brown, Elijah [pseud., Alan Raleigh]. *The Real America.* London, 1913. [1912]

Brown, W. J. *I Meet America.* London, 1942. [1941]

Brown, William. *America: a Four Years' Residence in the United States and Canada.* Leeds, 1849. [*ca.* 1842]

Brownell, W. C. *French Traits.* New York, 1897. [1896]

Bryas, Madeleine, comtesse de, and Jacqueline de Bryas. *A Frenchwoman's Impressions of America.* New York, 1920. [1918]

Bryce, James. "America Revisited: the Changes of a Quarter-Century," in *Outlook,* LXXIX (1905), 733–40; 846–55. [1870, 1883, 1905]

Buckingham, James S. *America, Historical, Statistic, and Descriptive.* 3 vols. London, 1841. [1837–1840]

Buckley, Michael B. *Diary of a Tour in America.* Ed. by Kate Buckley. Dublin, 1886. [1870–1871]

Bullivant, Dr. Benjamin. "A Journall with observations on my travail from Boston in N. E. to N. Y. New-Jersies & Philadelphia in Pensilvania. A. D. 1697." Edited as "A Glance at New York in 1697: The Travel Diary of Dr. Benjamin Bullivant," by Wayne Andrews, in *The New-York Historical Society Quarterly,* XL (January 1956), 55–73. [1697]

Burn, James D. *Three Years Among the Working-Classes in the United States during the War.* London, 1865. [1864]

Burnaby, Rev. Andrew. *Travels Through the Middle Settlements in North America in the Years 1759 and 1760.* London, 1798. Ed. by Rufus R. Wilson. New York, 1904. [1759]

Burne-Jones, Sir Philip. *Dollars and Democracy.* New York, 1904. [1902–1903]

Burnley, James. *Two Sides of the Atlantic.* London, [1880?]. [*ca.* 1879?]

Burroughs, John. "From London to New York," in *Galaxy,* XV (January–June 1873), 188–98. [*ca.* 1872]

[Byrd, William]. "Capt. Byrd's Letters," in *The Virginia Historical Register, and Literary Advertiser,* II (1849), 203–9. [1685]

C——, J. and A. *The United States and Canada, as Seen by Two Brothers in 1858 and 1861.* London, 1862. [1858, 1861]

C., J. W. "Social New York," from *Macmillan's Magazine.* Quoted in *Eclectic Magazine,* n.s., XVI (1872), 204–11. [*ca.* 1872]

Cabral, Oswaldo R. *Terra da Liberdade.* Rio, São Paulo, 1944. [*ca.* 1943]

Cadillac, Antoine de la Mothe. "Memoir." Excerpted in Stokes. *Iconography,* IV, 373. [1692]

Calzini, Raffaele. *Trionfi e disfatte di Nuova York.* Milan, 1937. [early 1930's]

Camba, Julio. *La Ciudad automática.* Madrid, 1932. [1931]

——. *Un año en el otro mundo.* Madrid, 1917. [1916]

Campbell, Sir George. *White and Black: the Outcome of a Visit to the United States.* London, 1879. [1878]

Candler, Isaac. *A Summary View of America: comprising a description of the face of the country, and of several of the principal cities; and remarks on the social, moral, and political character of the people.* London, 1824. [1822–1823]

Capote, Truman. *Local Color.* New York, 1946. [*ca.* 1945]

Carlisle, George William Frederick Howard, seventh earl of. *Travels in America.* New York, 1851. [1841]

Carr, Lieut. George Kirwan. "Journal." Ed. by Deoch Fulton, as *A Short Tour Through the United States & Canadas, October 10th to December 31st, 1832.* New York, 1937. [1832]

Castiglioni, Luigi. *Viaggio negli Stati Uniti dell' America Settentrionale, fatto negli anni 1785, 1786 e 1787.* 2 vols., Milan, 1790. [1785]

Castro, Tomás de Jesús. *Nueva York.* Santurce, P. R., 1950. [*ca.* 1949]

Chambers, William. *Things as They Are in America.* London and Edinburgh, 1857. [1853]

Charlton, William H. *Four Months in North America.* Hexham, n.d. [1872]

Chateaubriand, François Auguste, viscount de. *Travels in America and Italy.* 2 vols. London, 1828. [1791]

Chesterton, G. K. *What I Saw in America.* New York, 1922. [1921]

Chevalier, Michel. *Lettres sur l'Amérique du Nord.* 2 vols. Brussels, 1837. [1833–1835]

——. *Society, Manners, and Politics in the United States.* Boston, 1839. [1833–1835]

Chevrillon, André. "New York après trente ans," in *Revue des deux mondes,* septième période, XIV (March–April 1923), 345–64; 601–25. [*ca.* 1922]

Chiang, Yee. *The Silent Traveller in New York.* New York, n.d. [1946]

"Citizen" to editor. *Loudon's New-York Packet,* December 16, 1784. [1784]

Citrine, Walter. *My American Diary.* London, 1941. [1940]

Clemens, Samuel L. [Mark Twain]. *Mark Twain's Travels with Mr. Brown, . . . sketches written by Mark Twain for the San Francisco "Alta California" in 1866 & 1867, . . .* Collected and edited with an introduction by Franklin Walker and G. Ezra Dane. New York, 1940. [1867]

[Clitherall, Dr. James]. "Extracts from the Diary of Dr. James Clitherall, 1776," in *Pennsylvania Magazine,* XX (1898), 468–74. [1776]

[Cobden, Richard]. *The American Diaries of Richard Cobden.* Ed. by Elizabeth H. Cawley. Princeton, 1952. [1835, 1859]

Coke, E. T. *A Subaltern's Furlough: descriptive of scenes in various parts of the United States . . . during the summer and autumn of 1832.* New York, 1833. [1832]

[Colden, Cadwallader]. "Cadwallader Colden on the Trade of New York; 1723." Quoted in O'Callaghan. *Documentary History . . . New York,* I, 487–91. [1723]

[——]. Letter to Lord Dartmouth, July 6, 1774. Excerpted in Stokes. *Iconography,* IV, 859. [1774]

Collyer, Robert H. *Lights and Shadows of American Life.* Boston, [1844?]. [1836–1842]

Combe, George. *Notes on the United States of North America, during a Phrenological Visit in 1838–9–40.* 3 vols. Edinburgh, 1841. [1838–1839]

"Concerning New Netherland, or Manhattan," in "The Clarendon Papers," in New-York Historical Society, *Collections,* II (1869), 1–14. [*ca.* 1660]

Connolly, Cyril. "American Interjection," in *Ideas and Places.* London, 1953. [*ca.* 1947]

Cooke, Alistair. *One Man's America.* New York, 1952. [1948–1950]

Cooke, Henry. "Notes of a Loiterer in New York," in *Bentley's Miscellany,* XVI (1844), 596–602. [1843]

Cooper, James Fenimore. *America and the Americans.* 2d ed. 2 vols. London, 1836. [1826–1827]

Cooper, Thomas. *Some Information Respecting America collected by Thomas Cooper, late of Manchester.* London, 1795. [1793–1794]

Corbin, John. "The Twentieth-Century City," in *Scribner's Magazine,* XXXIII (March 1903), 259–72. [1903]

Craib, Alexander. *America and the Americans.* London, 1892. [1892?]

Crane, Stephen. "In the Broadway Cars. Panorama of a Day from the Down-Town Rush of the Morning to the Uninterrupted Whirr of the Cable at Night . . . ," in *Last Words* (London, 1902), pp. 173–80. [*ca.* 1894]

Crapsey, Edward. "The Nether Side of New York," in *Galaxy,* XI (January–June 1871), 188–97; 401–9; 559–67; 652–60; 827–35, XII (July–December 1871), 57–65; 170–78; 355–63, XIII (1872), 314–23; 489–97. [1871–1872]

[Cresswell, Nicholas]. *The Journal of Nicholas Cresswell, 1774–1777.* New York, 1924. [1776]

Creuse, Paul. *Une Promenade autour du Monde.* Limoges, [1882]. [*ca.* 1881]

Crèvecoeur, Michel Guillaume Jean de. *Lettres d'un Cultivateur Américain, écrites à W. S.* [William Seton], *écuyer, depuis l'Année 1770, jusqu'à 1781* (2 vols., Paris, 1784), as excerpted in *Magazine of American History,* II (1878), 748–51. [1772]

Crowell, Paul and A. H. Raskin. "New York, 'Greatest City in the World,'" in Robert S. Allen, ed. *Our Fair City* (New York, 1947), pp. 37–58. [1947]

Curtis, George W. "Editor's Easy Chair," in *Harper's New Monthly Magazine,* XXIV (February 1862), 409. [1862]

[Cutler, Rev. Manasseh]. *Life, Journals and Correspondence of Rev. Manasseh Cutler, LL.D.* Ed. by William P. Cutler and Julia P. Cutler. 2 vols. Cincinnati, 1888. [1787]

Dalton, William. *Travels in the United States of America and Parts of Upper Canada.* Appleby, 1821. [1819]

Damseaux, Émile de. *Voyage dans l'Amérique du Nord.* Paris, 1878. [1877]

Danckaerts, Jasper. *Journal of Jasper Danckaerts, 1679–1680.* Ed. by Bartlett B. James and J. Franklin Jameson. New York, 1913. [1679]

Daubeny, Charles G. B. *Journal of a Tour through the United States and in Canada, made during the years 1837–38.* Oxford, 1843. [1837]

[Davis, John]. *Travels of John Davis in the United States of America, 1798–1802.* Ed. by John V. Cheney. 2 vols. Boston, 1910 [?]. [1798–1802]

Davis, Samuel. "Journal of a Tour to Connecticut—Autumn of 1789," in Massachusetts Historical Society, *Proceedings,* XI (1869–1870), 9–32. [1789]

Day, Samuel P. *Life and Society in America.* 2 vols. London, 1880. [1878]

Deckert, Dr. Emil. *Die Neue Welt: Reiseskizzen aus dem Norden und Süden der Vereinigten Staaten.* Berlin, 1892. [*ca.* 1890]

Dekobra, Maurice. *Seven Years Among Free Men.* Tr. by Warre B. Welles. London, 1948. [1939–1940]

Delafield, E. M. *The Provincial Lady in America.* London, 1934. [1933]

Denton, Daniel. *A Brief Description of New-York: Formerly Called New-Netherlands. With the Places thereunto Adjoyning.* London, 1670. (Facsimile Text Society edition, ed. by Victor H. Paltsits.) [1670]

De Roos, Lieut. Frederick F. *Personal Narrative of Travels in the United States and Canada.* London, 1827. [1826]

Desaché, Gaétan. *Souvenir de mon voyage aux États-Unis et au Canada.* Tours, [1878]. [1876–1877]

"Description of the Towne of Mannadens, 1661." Reprinted in Jameson, ed. *Narratives of New Netherland,* pp. 421–24. [1661]

De Sille, Nicasius. Letter from Nicasius de Sille to Maximiliaen van Beeckerke, May 23, 1654, in "Letters of Nicasius de Sille, 1654." New York State Historical Association, *Quarterly Journal,* I (1920), 98–108. [1653–1654]

Devereux, Alan. "The Home." Quoted in *Literary Digest,* LXXXIV (February 1925), 52–54. [*ca.* 1924]

Devereux, John W. "My Journal of one of my trips to New York," in *Georgia Historical Quarterly,* XV (1931), 46–80. [1799]

De Voto, Bernard. "On Moving from New York," in *Harper's Monthly Magazine* CLXXVII (1938), 333–36. [1938]

Dicey, Edward. *Six Months in the Federal States.* 2 vols. London and Cambridge, 1863. [1862]

Dickens, Charles. *American Notes for General Circulation.* London, 1892. [1842]

[———]. Letters. Excerpted in John Forster. *The Life of Charles Dickens.* 2 vols. New York, 1907. [1867–1868]

Dilke, Charles W. *Greater Britain: a record of travel in English-speaking countries during 1866 and 1867.* 2 vols. London, 1868. [1866]

Dilnot, Frank. *The New America.* New York, 1919. [1917]

[Dongan, Thomas]. "Gov. Dongan's Report to the Committee of Trade on the Province of New-York, dated 22d February, 1687." Quoted in O'Callaghan *Documentary History . . . New York,* I, 95–118. [1687]

Doyle, Sir Arthur Conan. *Our American Adventure.* New York, 1923. [1922]

Drayton, John. *Letters Written During a Tour through the Northern and Eastern States of America.* Charleston, S. C., 1794. [1793]

Dreiser, Theodore. *The Color of a Great City.* New York, 1923. [1894]

[Drisius, Rev. Samuel]. Letter to the Classis of Amsterdam, September 15, 1664. Excerpted in Jameson, ed. *Narratives of New Netherland,* pp. 414–15. [1664]

[Duensing, Frederick]. *New York—Cultur-historische Beschreibung: Ein Beitrag zur Länder- und Völker-Kunde.* Leipzig, 1872. [*ca.* 1871]

Dugard, Marie. *La Société Américaine.* Paris, 1896. [1893]

Duhamel, Georges. *Scènes de la vie future.* Paris, 1930. [*ca.* 1929]

Duncan, John M. *Travels Through Part of the United States and Canada.* 2 vols. Glasgow, 1823. [1818]

[Dunlap, William]. *Diary of William Dunlap, 1766–1839.* 3 vols. New York, 1930. [1788–1797]

Duteil, Henri-Jean. *The Great American Parade.* Tr. from the French by Fletcher Pratt. New York, 1953. [late 1940's]

Duvergier de Hauranne, Ernest. *Lettres et Notes de Voyage 1864–1865.* 2 vols. Paris, 1866. [1864]

Dwight, Theodore. *Things As They Are; or, Notes of a Traveller through Some of the Middle and Northern States.* New York, 1834. [*ca.* 1833]

Dwight, Timothy. *Travels; in New-England and New-York.* 4 vols. New Haven, 1821. [1811]

Eddis, William. *Letters from America, Historical and Descriptive, comprising Occurrences from 1769, to 1777, Inclusive.* London, 1792. [1777]

Edman, Irwin. "The Spirit Has Many Mansions." Quoted from New York *Times,* 1953, in Klein, ed. *The Empire City,* pp. 385–89. [*ca.* 1953]

Eichthal, Eugène d'. *Quelques notes d'un voyage aux États-Unis.* Excerpt from *Annales des Sciences Politiques* (March 15, 1906). [1905]

Estlander, J. A. *Lettres d'Amérique.* Helsingfors, 1878. [1876]

Estournelles de Constant, Paul H. B., baron d'. *America and her Problems.* New York, 1915. [1902, 1907, 1911]

Faux, William. *Memorable Days in America: Being a Journal of a Tour to the United States.* London, 1823. [1819–1820]

Faÿ, Bernard. *The American Experiment.* New York, 1929. [1928?]

Fearon, Henry B. *Sketches of America.* London, 1819. [1817]

Fehling, August W. *Die Vereinigten Staaten von Amerika: Land und Menschen unter dem Sternenbanner.* Berlin, 1933. [early 1930's]

Feiler, Arthur. *America Seen through German Eyes.* New York, 1928. [*ca.* 1925]

Felton, Mrs. *Life in America: A Narrative of two years city and country residence in the United States.* Hull, 1838. [*ca.* 1836]

Ferguson, Fergus. *From Glasgow to Missouri and Back.* Glasgow, 1878. [1874]

Ferguson, Robert. *America during and after the War.* London, 1866. [1864]

Ferguson, William. *America by River and Rail; or, Notes by the Way on the New World and its People.* London, 1856. [1855]

Ferrall, S. A. *A Ramble of Six Thousand Miles through the United States of America.* London, 1832. [1830]

Ferri-Pisani, Lieut. Col. Camille. *Lettres sur les États-Unis d'Amérique.* Paris, 1862. [1861]

Fidler, Rev. Isaac. *Observations on Professions, Literature, Manners, and Emigration, in the United States and Canada, Made During a Residence There in 1832.* New York, 1833. [1832]

Finch, I. *Travels in the United States of America and Canada*. London, 1833. [1823–1825]

Findahl, Theodor. *Manhattan Babylon: en bok om New York idag*. Oslo, 1928. [*ca.* 1927]

——. *Moskva og New York; tyve år etter*. Oslo, 1949. [*ca.* 1946]

Fisch, Rev. Georges. *Nine Months in the United States during the Crisis*. London, 1863. [1860–1861]

Fitzgerald, William G. [pseud., Ignatius Phayre]. *America's Day: Studies in Light and Shade*. New York, 1918. [1915?–1918]

Flint, James. *Letters from America*. Edinburgh, 1822. Reprinted in R. G. Thwaites, ed. *Early Western Travels*, IX. [1818]

[Fontaine, John]. "Journal of John Fontaine." Quoted in Ann Maury, *Memoirs of a Huguenot Family*. New York, 1853. [1716]

Ford, Ford Madox. *New York Is Not America*. New York, 1927. [1926]

[Foster, Sir Augustus John, Bart.]. *Jeffersonian America: Notes on the United States of America Collected in the Years 1805–6–7 and 11–12 by Sir Augustus John Foster, Bart.* Ed. by Richard B. Davis. San Marino, Cal., 1954. [1807]

[Foster, George G.]. *New York in Slices by an experienced carver: being the original slices published in the New York Tribune*. New York, 1849. [1848?]

——. *New York by Gas-light: with here and there a streak of sunshine*. New York, 1850. [1849?]

Fowler, John. *Journal of a Tour in the State of New York in the year 1830. . . .* London, 1831. [1830]

Fraccaroli, Arnaldo. *New York Ciclone di Genti*. Milan, [1931]. [late 1920's]

Franchère, Gabriel. *Narrative of a Voyage to the Northwest Coast of America in the Years 1811, 1812, 1813, and 1814. . . .* Tr. by J. V. Huntington. New York, 1854. Reprinted in R. G. Thwaites, ed. *Early Western Travels*, VI, 173–410. [1810]

Francis, Alexander. *Americans, an Impression*. London, 1909. [1905]

Fraser, J. Nelson. *America Old and New: Impressions of Six Months in the States*. London, [1912]. [1910]

Freeman, Edward A. *Some Impressions of the United States*. Philadelphia, 1883. [1881–1882]

Frenssen, Gustav. *Briefe aus Amerika*. Berlin, 1923. [1922]

Fulda, Ludwig. *Amerikanische eindrücke*. Berlin, 1914. [1906, 1913]

Fuller, Col. J. F. C. *Atlantis: America and the Future*. New York, 1925. [1924]

"The Future of New York," in *Galaxy*, IX (January–July 1870), 545–53. [*ca.* 1870]

[Gage, John]. "Diary of John Gage," in *Vineland Historical Magazine*, IX (1924), 188–91, 216–20; X (1925), 229–32, 29–31, 47–51, 66–68. [1835]

Gardini, Carlo. *Gli Stati Uniti ricordi con 76 illustrazioni e carte*. Bologna, 1891. [1882–1883]

[Garry, Nicholas]. "Diary of Nicholas Garry." Ed. by F. N. A. Garry, in Royal Society of Canada, *Proceedings and Transactions*, 2d series, VI (1900), section II, 73–204. [1821]

Gasparin, Agénor E. de. *The Uprising of a Great People. The United States in 1861*. Tr. from the French by Mary Booth. New York, 1861. [1861]

"General Description of the City of New York," in *The American Magazine* (March 1788), 224–27. [1788]

George, W. L. *Hail Columbia*. New York, 1921. [1920]

Gerstäcker, Friedrich. *Zwischen Wildnis und Kultur: Reisen und Abenteuer in der neuen Welt*. Berlin, 1943. [1867]

Giacosa, Giuseppe. "Gli Italiani a New York ed a Chicago," in *Nuova Antologia di Scienze, Lettere ed Arti,* XL, series 3 (August 16, 1892), 619–40. [1891]

——. *Impressioni d'America.* Milan, 1908. [1891]

Gibbons, John. *Is This America?* New York, 1935. [1934?]

Gibbs, Philip. *People of Destiny: Americans as I Saw Them at Home and Abroad.* New York, 1920. [1918–1919]

[Gilmor, Robert]. "The Diary of Robert Gilmor, 1774–1848," in *Maryland Historical Magazine,* XVII (1922), 231–68; 319–47. [1827]

Glazier, Capt. Willard. *Peculiarities of American Cities.* Philadelphia, 1885. [1883]

Gobat, Albert. *Croquis et impressions d'Amérique.* Berne, 1906. [*ca.* 1906]

Godley, John R. *Letters from America.* 2 vols. London, 1844. [1842]

Golovin, Ivan. *Stars and Stripes, or American Impressions.* London, New York, 1856. [1855]

[Gordon, Lord Adam]. "Journal of an Officer Who Travelled in America and the West Indies in 1764 and 1765." Reprinted in Newton D. Mereness, ed. *Travels in the American Colonies, 1690–1783* (New York, 1916), pp. 365–453. [1765]

Gorky, Maxim. "The City of Mammon," in *Appleton's Magazine,* VIII (August 1906), 177–82. [1906]

Gosselman, Carl A. *Resa i Norra Amerika.* 2 vols. Nyköping, 1835. [1826]

Graham, Stephen. *With Poor Immigrants to America.* New York, 1914. [1913]

Grandfort, Marie Fontenay [Mme. Manoel] de. *The New World.* Tr. by Edward C. Wharton. New Orleans, 1855. [1852?]

Grattan, Thomas Colley. *Civilized America.* 2 vols. London, 1859. [1840's]

Green, Julian. *Personal Record, 1928–1939.* Tr. from the French by Jocelyn Godefroi. New York, 1939. [1930–1933]

[Greene, Asa]. *A Glance at New York.* New York, 1837. [*ca.* 1836]

Griesinger, Karl Theodor. *Land und Leute in Amerika: Skizzen aus dem amerikanischen Leben.* 2d ed. 2 vols. Stuttgart, 1863. [1852–1857]

Griffin, Sir Lepel Henry. *The Great Republic.* New York, 1884. [1881?]

[Gripenberg, Alexandra]. *Alexandra Gripenberg's A Half Year in the New World.* . . . Tr. and ed. by Ernest J. Moyne. Newark, Del., 1954. [1888]

Gruening, Ernest. "New York: I. The City—Work of Man," in *Nation,* CXV (November 1922), 571–75. [1922]

Gruening, Ernest, ed. *These United States: a Symposium.* 2d series. New York, 1924. [1922]

Grund, Francis J. *The Americans in Their Moral, Social, and Political Relations.* 2 vols. London, 1837. [1836?]

Guedalla, Philip. *Conquistador: American Fantasia.* New York, 1928. [1927]

Gunther, John. *Inside U.S.A.* New York, 1947. [mid-1940's]

Gurowski, Adam G. de. *America and Europe.* New York, 1857. [1856]

Hadwen, Walter R. *First Impressions of America.* London, 1921. [1921]

Haecker, Ludwig. *Amerikanische Reise-Skizzen aus dem Gebiete der Technik, Landwirthschaft und des socialen Lebens.* Braunschweig, 1867. [1862–1863]

Hall, Capt. Basil. *Travels in North America in the Years 1827 and 1828.* 3 vols. Edinburgh, 1829. [1827]

[Hall, Mrs. Basil]. *The Aristocratic Journey, Being the Outspoken Letters of Mrs. Basil Hall. Written during a Fourteen Months' Sojourn in America 1827–1828.* Ed. by Una Pope-Hennessy. New York, 1931. [1827]

Hall, Lieut. Francis. *Travels in Canada and the United States in 1816 and 1817.* 2d ed. London, 1819. [1816]

Hall, Maj. H. Byng. "New York As It Is," in *St. James's Magazine*, VIII (August–November 1853), 62–68. [1853?]

[Hamilton, Dr. Alexander]. *Gentleman's Progress: the Itinerarium of Dr. Alexander Hamilton, 1744*. Ed. by Carl Bridenbaugh. Chapel Hill, 1948. [1744]

Hamilton, Mary Agnes. *In America Today*. London, 1932. [1931–1932]

Hamilton, Thomas. *Men and Manners in America*. 2 vols. London, 1833. [1831–1832]

Hannay, James O. [pseud., George A. Birmingham]. *From Dublin to Chicago: Some Notes on a Tour in America*. New York, 1914. [1913]

Hardie, James. *The Description of the City of New-York; containing its population, institutions, commerce, manufactures, public buildings, courts of justice, places of amusement, etc.* New York, 1827. [1827]

Hardman, William. *A Trip to America*. London, 1884. [1883]

Hardy, Iza Duffus. *Between Two Oceans: or, Sketches of American Travel*. London, 1884. [1881]

Hardy, Mary (McDowell) Duffus, lady. *Through Cities and Prairie Lands*. New York, 1881. [1879–1880]

Harriott, Lieut. John. *Struggles through Life, Exemplified in the Various Travels and Adventures in Europe, Asia, Africa, and America of Lieut. John Harriott*. 2d ed. London, 1808. Excerpted in Stokes. *Iconography*, V, 1295. [1795?]

Harrison, Frederic. "Impressions of America," in *The Nineteenth Century*, XLIX (1901), 913–30. [*ca.* 1900]

Hatton, Joseph. *Henry Irving's Impressions of America narrated in a series of Sketches, Chronicles, and Conversations*. Boston, 1884. [1883]

———. *To-day in America. Studies for the Old World and the New*. 2 vols. London, 1881. [1876–1880]

Hauser, Henri. *L'Amérique Vivante*. Paris, 1924. [1923]

Hausmann, Manfred. *Kleine Liebe zu Amerika*. Berlin, 1931. [*ca.* 1930]

Haussonville, Gabriel P. O. de C., vicomte d'. *À travers les États-Unis: notes et impressions*. Paris, 1883. [1882]

Hauswolff, Carl. *Teckningar utur sällskapslifvet i Nordamerikas förenta stater*. Norrköping, 1835.

Hauterive, Alexandre Maurice Blanc de la Naulte, comte d'. "Journal." Manuscript in New-York Historical Society. [1793]

Hawley, Zerah. *A Journal of a Tour through Connecticut, Massachusetts, New-York, the North Part of Pennsylvania and Ohio. . . .* New Haven, 1822. [1820]

Hazard, Paul. "À New-York pendant les élections," in *Revue des deux mondes*, huitzième période, XII (1932), 837–52. [1932]

Hedderwick, Mr. Comment in Glasgow *Chronicle*, May 24, 1823. Excerpted in Stokes. *Iconography*, V, 1630. [1823]

Herriot, Édouard. *Impressions d'Amérique*. Lyon, 1923. [*ca.* 1920]

Herz, Henri. *Mes Voyages en Amérique*. Paris, 1866. [1846]

Heywood, Robert. *A Journey to America in 1834*. Cambridge, England, 1919. [1834]

Hidalgo, Diego. *Nueva York: Impresiones de un español del siglo XIX que no sabe inglés*. Madrid, 1947. [1947]

Hodson, James L. *And Yet I Like America*. London, 1945. [1943–1944]

Hogan, James F. *The Australian in London and America*. London, 1889. [*ca.* 1888]

Hohenwart, Ernst. *Land und Leute in den Vereinigten Staaten*. Leipzig, 1886. [1885–1886]

Holmes, Isaac. *An Account of the United States of America derived from actual observation, during a residence of four years in that republic.* London, 1823. [1822]

Hone, Philip. "Commerce and Commercial Character," in *Hunt's Merchants' Magazine,* IV (1841), 129–46. [1841]

[——]. *The Diary of Philip Hone.* Ed. by Allan Nevins. 2 vols. New York, 1927. [1828–1851]

[Honyman, Dr. Robert]. *Colonial Panorama, 1775: Dr. Robert Honyman's Journal for March and April.* Ed. by Philip Padelford. San Marino, Cal., 1939. [1775]

Horwill, H. W. "Leisurely America," in *The Monthly Review,* XXVII (April 1907), 149. [1906]

Howells, William D. "Editor's Easy Chair," in *Harper's Monthly Magazine,* CXVI (1908), 471–74; CXVIII (1909), 479–82; CXXVIII (1913–1914), 472–75; CXXXII (1915–1916), 473–76. [1908–1916]

——. *Impressions and Experiences.* New York, 1896. [1895]

——. "Letters of an Altrurian Traveller," in *Cosmopolitan,* XVI (1893–1894), 110–16; 218–32; 259–77; 415–25; 558–69; 697–704. [1893]

——. *Literature and Life.* New York, 1902. [1902]

Huard, Charles. *New York comme je l'ai vu.* Paris, 1906. [1905]

Huddleston, Sisley. *What's Right with America.* Philadelphia and London, 1930. [1929]

Huneker, James. *New Cosmopolis.* New York, 1915.

Hungerford, Edward. *The Personality of American Cities.* New York, 1913. [*ca.* 1912]

[Hunter, Robert]. "Gov. Hunter to the Board of Trade. 12 Novr 1715." Quoted in O'Callaghan. *Documentary History . . . New York,* I, 486. [1715]

[Hunter, Robert, Jr.] *Quebec to Carolina in 1785–1786, Being the Travel Diary and Observations of Robert Hunter, Jr., a Young Merchant of London.* Ed. by Louis B. Wright and Marian Tinling. San Marino, Cal., 1943. [1785–1786]

Huret, Jules. *En Amérique: de New-York à la Nouvelle-Orléans.* Paris, 1904. [1903]

Hurt-Binet, Marc-Gabriel. *Neuf Mois aux États-Unis d'Amérique.* Geneva, 1862. [*ca.* 1862]

Huxley, Aldous L. *Jesting Pilate, an Intellectual Holiday.* New York, 1926. [*ca.* 1926]

Ichikawa, Haruko [Mrs. Sanki]. *Japanese Lady in America.* Tokyo, 1939. [1937–1938]

Iddon, E. F. Comment in London *Daily Express.* Quoted in *Living Age,* CCCLIII (1937), 78. [1937]

Ilf, Ilya and Eugene Petrov. *Little Golden America.* London, 1946; first published, 1936. [1935–1936]

Jacks, L. P. *My American Friends.* New York, 1933. [1931–1932]

James, Henry. *The American Scene.* New York, 1946. [1904–1905]

James, Thomas Horton [Rubio]. *Rambles in the United States and Canada during the year 1845.* London, 1846. [1845]

Jannet, Claudio. *Les États-Unis Contemporains, ou les moeurs, les institutions et les idées depuis la guerre de la Sécession.* 2 vols. Paris, 1889. [1875]

Janson, Charles W. *The Stranger in America, 1793–1806.* Reprinted from the London edition of 1807 with introduction and notes by Carl S. Driver. New York, 1935. [*ca.* 1805]

Jensen, Johannes V. *Den Ny Verden.* Copenhagen, 1907. [*ca.* 1903]

Jensen, Johannes V. *Fra Fristaterne; Rejsebreve, med et Tilbageblik.* Copenhagen, 1939. [*ca.* 1938]

Jogues, Father Isaac. "Novum Belgium, 1646." Reprinted in Jameson, ed. *Narratives of New Netherland,* pp. 259–63. [1643]

[Johnson, William]. "A Young Man's Journal of 1800–1813 [William Johnson of Newton, N. J.]," in New Jersey Historical Society, *Proceedings,* n.s., VII (1922), 49–59; 122–34; 211–16; 305–14; VIII (1923), 150–54; 219–25; 313–20. [1805–1806]

Johnston, James F. W. *Notes on North America, Agricultural, Economical, and Social.* 2 vols. Boston, 1850. [1850]

Joseph-Renaud, Jean. *New-York Flamboie.* Paris, 1931. [*ca.* 1931]

Joslin, John. "Our Incredible City," in *New York Times Magazine* (December 22, 1946), 10, 11 ff. [1946]

"Journal of a French Traveller in the Colonies, 1765, II," in *American Historical Review,* XXVII (October 1921), 70–89. [1765]

"Journal of an Irishman in New York at the Close of the American Revolution." Ed. by Victor H. Paltsits, in *Bulletin of the New York Public Library,* XXVII (November 1923), 891–95. [1782]

Juet, Robert. "The Third Voyage of Master Henry Hudson." Excerpted in Jameson, ed. *Narratives of New Netherland,* pp. 16–28. [1609]

Juvenal [pseud.]. *An Englishman in New York.* London, 1911. [1910–1911]

Kalm, Peter. *Travels into North America.* Tr. by John R. Forster. 2 vols. London, 1772. [1748]

Kashkin, Ivan, ed. *New York (an Outline).* Cooperative Publishing Society of Foreign Workers in the U.S.S.R. Moscow, 1933. [1931–1932]

Kemble, Frances A. [Mrs. Pierce Butler]. *Journal.* 2 vols. Philadelphia, 1835. [1832]

Kerr, Alfred. *New York und London: Zwanzig Kapitel nach dem Weltkrieg.* Berlin, 1929. [*ca.* 1922]

Keun, Odette. *I Think Aloud in America.* New York, 1939. [late 1938]

Kipling, Rudyard. *Letters of Travel (1892–1913).* London, 1920. [1892]

Kirkwood, Rev. John. *An Autumn Holiday in the United States and Canada.* Edinburgh, 1887. [1886]

Kisch, Egon E. *Paradies Amerika.* Berlin, 1930. [1928?]

Klein, Abbé Félix. *En Amérique à la fin de la guerre.* Paris, 1919. [1918]

———. *In the Land of the Strenuous Life.* The author's translation of his *Au pays de la vie intense.* Chicago, 1905. [1903]

[Klinkowström, Baron Axel]. *Baron Klinkowström's America.* Ed. by Franklin D. Scott. Evanston, Ill., 1952. [1818–1820]

Knight, Sarah Kemble. *The Private Journal of a Journey from Boston to New York in the Year 1704.* Albany, 1865. [1704]

Kowalski, Henri. *À travers l'Amérique: Impressions d'un musicien.* Paris, 1872. [1869]

Lafond, André. *Impressions of America.* Tr. from the French by Lawrence Riesner. Paris, New York, 1930. [1928]

Lambert, John. *Travels through Canada, and the United States of North America in the Years 1806, 1807, & 1808.* 2 vols. London, 1814. [1807–1808]

Lamprecht, Karl. *Americana: Reiseeindrücke, Betrachtungen, geschichtliche Gesamtansicht.* Freiburg, 1906. [*ca.* 1904]

Lanux, Pierre de. *New York, 1939–1945.* Paris, 1947. [1939–1945]

Lapaquellerie, Yvon. *New York aux sept couleurs.* Paris, 1930. [1929]

Lara, Javier. *En la Metropoli del Dollar.* New York, [1919?]. [*ca.* 1916]

La Rochefoucauld-Liancourt, François Alexandre Frédéric, duc de. *Travels through the United States of North America, the Country of the Iroquois, and Upper Canada in the Years 1795, 1796, and 1797; with an Authentic Account of Lower Canada.* 2 vols. London, 1799. [1797]

Latham, Henry. *Black and White, a Journal of a Three Months' Tour in the United States.* London, 1867. [1866]

Latrobe, Charles J. *The Rambler in North America.* 2 vols. New York, 1835. [1832]

Lebel, Roland. *Intimes New York.* Bern-Stuttgart, [1938?]. [mid-1930's]

[Le Corbusier [pseud. of Charles-Édouard Jeanneret]]. "Le Corbusier Considers the New York Skyscraper." Excerpts from *Quand les Cathédrales étaient blanches,* in *Légion d'Honneur Magazine,* X (October 1939), 283–86. [1936, 1946]

——. *When the Cathedrals Were White.* Tr. by Francis E. Hyslop, Jr. New York, 1947. [1936, 1946]

Leng, John. *America in 1876; Pencillings during a Tour in the Centennial Year.* Dundee, 1877. [1876]

"Letter from an Officer at New-York to a Friend in London [1777]." Excerpted in Stokes. *Iconography,* V, 1041–42. [1777]

Letter from New York, April 12, 1776. Reprinted in *Historical Magazine,* 1st series, X, pt. 2, p. 111. [1776]

Letter to *Cymro America,* June 1, 1832. Tr. and ed. as "A Disillusioned Welshman in New York," by Rowland T. Berthoff, in *New York History,* XXXVII (January 1956), 80–84. [1832]

Letters from America, 1776–1779. Tr. by Ray W. Pettengill. Cambridge, Mass., 1924. [1777, 1780]

"Letters from New York," in *Southern Literary Messenger,* XVI (1850), 315–20; 450–53; 512–16; 588–92; 669–72; 755–57; XVII (1851), 180–84. [1850–1851]

Levasseur, Auguste. *Lafayette in America in 1824 and 1825; or Journal of a Voyage to the United States.* Tr. by John D. Godman. 2 vols. Philadelphia, 1829. [1824]

Lewis, Sinclair. "Towers at Dawn," in *Newsweek,* XI (January 31, 1938), 28. [1938]

Lieber, Francis. *The Stranger in America . . . a series of letters to a friend in Europe.* 2 vols. London, 1835. [1834]

——. *The Stranger in America, or Letters to a Gentleman in Germany.* Philadelphia, 1835. [1834]

Lin Yutang. *On the Wisdom of America.* New York, 1950. [1940's]

Lodwick, Charles. Letter to Francis Lodwick, May 20, 1692. Excerpted in Stokes. *Iconography,* IV, 375. See also New-York Historical Society, *Collections,* 3d series (1849), II:241–50. [1692]

Löher, Franz von. *Geschichte und Zustände der Deutschen in Amerika.* Cincinnati, 1847; Göttingen, 1855. [1847?]

"London, Paris, and New-York." Reprinted from the American edition of *Bentley's Miscellany* for July 1851, in *The International Monthly Magazine of Literature, Science, and Art,* IV (August–December 1851), 101–10. [*ca.* 1850]

[Longacre, James B.] "Extracts from the Diary of James B. Longacre," in *Pennsylvania Magazine of History and Biography,* XXIX (1905), 134–42. [1825]

[Longchamp, Ferdinand (Frederick?)]. *Asmodeus in New York.* New York, 1868. [1867]

Longworth, Maria Theresa [Thérèse Yelverton]. *Teresina in America.* 2 vols. London, 1875. [*ca.* 1874]

Loti, Pierre. "Impressions of New York," in *Century Magazine,* LXXXV (1912–1913), 609–13; 758–62. [1912]

Low, Alfred M. *America at Home.* London, 1908. [1906–1907]

Loyalist letter, September 23, 1776. Quoted from *St. James's Chronicle,* in Stokes, *Iconography,* V, 1020. [1776]

Ludlow, Fitz-Hugh. "The American Metropolis," in *The Atlantic Monthly,* XV (1865), 73–88. [1864]

Lumsden, James. *American Memoranda, by a Mercantile Man, during a short tour in the summer of 1843.* Glasgow, 1844. [1843]

Lyell, Sir Charles. *A Second Visit to the United States of North America.* 2 vols. New York, 1849. [1841, 1845–1846]

Mabie, Hamilton W. "The Genius of the Cosmopolitan City," in *Outlook,* LXXVI (1904), 577–93. [1903]

Macaulay, James. "First Impressions of America and Its People," in *The Leisure Hour,* XX (1871), 36–40; 70–76; 107–11; 143–44; 170–73; 205–8; 234–37; 278–83; 311–16; 344–46; 374–79; 442–46; 458–60; 503–8; 535–41; 616–21; 676–79; 746–51; 804–7. [1870]

Macdonnell, A. G. *A Visit to America.* New York, 1935. [1934]

Mackay, Alexander. *The Western World.* 3 vols. London, 1850. [1846]

Mackay, Charles. *Life and Liberty in America: or Sketches of a Tour in the United States and Canada, in 1857–8.* 2 vols. London, 1859. [1857]

[Maclay, William]. *The Journal of William Maclay.* New York, 1927. [1789]

Macrae, David. *America Revisited.* Glasgow, 1908. [1898]

——. *The Americans at Home: Pen and Ink Sketches of American Men, Manners, and Institutions.* 2 vols. Edinburgh, 1870. [1867]

Madariaga, Salvador de. "Americans Are Boys: A Spaniard Looks at Our Civilization," in *Harper's Magazine,* CLVII (July 1928), 239–45. [*ca.* 1928]

Mair, John. "Journal of John Mair, 1791," in *American Historical Review,* XII (1906), 77–94. [1791]

Mais, S. P. B. *A Modern Columbus.* Philadelphia, 1934. [1933]

Malézieux, Émile. *Souvenirs d'une Mission aux États-Unis d'Amérique.* Paris, 1874. [1870]

Mallock, W. H. "First Impressions of America," in *Outlook,* LXXXVI (June 1907), 462–67. [1907]

Malo, Pierre. *La Féerie Américaine: New-York et Washington.* Paris, 1936. [1935]

Mandat-Grancey, Edmond, baron de. *En Visite chez l'Oncle Sam: New York et Chicago.* Paris, 1891. [*ca.* 1883]

Mandrillon, Joseph. *Précis sur l'Amérique Septentrionale & la République des Treize-États-Unis,* appendix to [Alexander Cluny], *Le voyageur américain.* Amsterdam, 1782. [*ca.* 1769]

Marjoribanks, Alexander. *Travels in South and North America.* London, 1853. [1850]

Marmier, M. Xavier. *Les États-Unis et le Canada.* Tours, 1875. [*ca.* 1850]

Marryat, Capt. Frederick. *Diary in America, with remarks on its institutions.* New York, 1839. [1837]

Marshall, Francis. *An Englishman in New York.* London, 1949. [*ca.* 1948]

Marshall, Walter G. *Through America; or, Nine Months in the United States.* London, 1882. [1879]

Martens, F. de. "A Russian's Impressions of America," in *The Independent,* LIV (1902), 2871–74. [1901?]

[Marti, José]. *The America of José Marti.* Tr. by Juan de Onís. New York, 1953. [1888–1889?]
——. *Los Estados Unidos.* Madrid, 1915. [1888–1889?]
Martineau, Harriet. *Retrospect of Western Travel.* 3 vols. London, 1838. [1834]
[Mason, Jonathan]. "Diary of the Honorable Jonathan Mason," in Massachusetts Historical Society, *Proceedings,* 2d series, II (1885–1886), 5–34. [1804]
Massie, James W. *America: the Origin of her present conflict, her prospect for the slave, and her claim for anti-slavery sympathy; illustrated by incidents of travel, during a tour in the summer of 1863, throughout the United States, from the eastern boundaries of Maine to the Mississippi.* London, 1864. [1863]
Matthews, Brander. *Vignettes of New York.* New York, 1894. [early 1890's]
Maufroid, A. *Du Mexique au Canada.* Paris, 1907. [1906]
Maulevrier, Édouard Charles Victurnien Colbert, comte de. *Voyage dans l'intérieur des États-Unis et au Canada.* Ed. by Gilbert Chinard. Baltimore, 1935. [1798]
Maurois, André. *En Amérique.* Ed. by Robert M. Waugh. New York, 1936. [1927]
——. *En Amérique,* "Deuxième partie. Sécond voyage aux États-Unis," in Maurois, *En Amérique* (Paris, 1933), pp. 70–113. [1931]
——. *États-Unis 39: journal d'un voyage en Amérique.* Paris, 1939. [1939]
——. *From My Journal.* Tr. from the French by Joan Charles. New York, 1947. [1946]
——. "Premier Voyage en Amérique, II, Contact," in *Les Annales Politiques et Littéraires,* XC (1928), 217–23. [1927]
Maury, Sarah M. *An Englishwoman in America.* London, 1848. [1845]
Maximilian, Prince of Wied. *Travels in the Interior of North America.* London, 1843. Reprinted in R. G. Thwaites, ed. *Early Western Travels,* XXII, XXIII, XXIV. [1832]
McCabe, James D., Jr. *Lights and Shadows of New York Life; or the Sights and Sensations of the Great City.* Philadelphia, 1872. [1872]
McCabe, James D. [pseud., Edward W. Martin]. *The Secrets of the Great City.* Philadelphia, 1868. [1868]
McCabe, James Dabney. *New York by Sunlight and Gaslight. A Work Descriptive of the Great American Metropolis.* No place, preface dated 1882. [1882]
M'Dougal, James A. *My Trip to America.* No place, 1892. [1891]
Meakin, Annette M. B. *What America Is Doing.* Edinburgh and London, 1911. [1907]
Melish, John. *Travels through the United States of America, in the Years 1806 & 1807, and 1809, 1810, & 1811. . . .* London, 1818. [1806]
Melville, Herman. *Moby-Dick, or the Whale.* New York, 1950. [1850]
Mencken, H. L. "Metropolis," in *Prejudices, Sixth Series.* New York, 1927. [*ca.* 1927]
Merlin, María de las Mercedes, comtesse de. *La Havane.* 3 vols., Paris, 1844. [1840]
Michaëlius, Rev. Jonas. Letter from Jonas Michaëlius to Adrianus Smoutius, 1628. Reprinted in Jameson, ed. *Narratives of New Netherland,* pp. 122–33. [1628]
Michaux, François A. *Travels to the West of the Allegheny Mountains.* London, 1805. Reprinted in R. G. Thwaites, ed. *Early Western Travels,* III. [1802]
Miller, Henry. *The Air-Conditioned Nightmare.* New York, 1945. [1935]
Miller, Rev. John. *A Description of the Province and City of New York; with Plans of the City and Several Forts as they existed in the year 1695.* London, 1843. [1695]
[Miranda, Francisco de]. *The Diary of Francisco de Miranda: Tour of the United*

States, 1783–1784. Spanish text. Ed. by William S. Robertson. New York, 1928. [1784]

Mitchell, David W. *Ten Years in the United States: Being an Englishman's Views of Men and Things in the North and South*. London, 1862. [*ca.* 1857]

[Mitchill, Samuel L.]. *The Picture of New-York; or the Traveller's Guide, through the Commercial Metropolis of the United States*. By a Gentleman residing in this City. New York, 1807. [*ca.* 1807]

Moberg, Vilhelm. "Att upptäcka Amerika," in *Folket i Bild,* XVI (October 30, 1949), 3–5, 39.

Molinari, Gustave de. *Lettres sur les États-Unis et le Canada*. Paris, 1876. [1876]

Mollat du Jourdain, Guy, ed. *L'âme des cités*. Paris, 1946. [*ca.* 1940's]

Money, Edward. *The Truth About America*. London, 1886. [1885]

Montefiore, Arthur. "New York and New Yorkers," in *Temple Bar,* LXXXIV (1888), 343–57. [1888]

[Montlezun, Barthélemi Sernin du Moulin de la Barthelle, baron de]. *Souvenirs des Antilles: voyage en 1815 et 1816, aux États-Unis, et dans l'archipel Caraïbe; aperçu de Philadelphie et New-Yorck. . . . Par M. . . .* 2 vols. Paris, 1818. [1815]

[——]. *Voyage fait dans les années 1816 et 1817, de New-Yorck à la Nouvelle-Orléans . . . par l'auteur des souvenirs des Antilles*. 2 vols. Paris, 1818. [1816–1817]

Montulé, Édouard de. *Travels in America*. Tr. by Edward D. Seeber. Indiana University Publications. Social Science Series, no. 9 (1950). [1816]

Moor, Rev. A. P. *Letters from North America written during the Summer of 1853*. Canterbury, 1855. [1853]

[Moore, Sir Henry]. "Gov. Moore to the Lords of Trade," January 12, 1767. Quoted in O'Callaghan. *Documentary History . . . New York,* I, 498–99. [1767]

Morand, Paul. *New York*. Tr. from the French by Hamish Miles. New York, 1930. [1925–1929]

[Moravian Congregation]. "Diary," in "Occupation of New York City by the British, 1776," in *Pennsylvania Magazine of History and Biography,* I (1877), 133–48, 250–62, 467–68. [1776]

[Moreau de St. Méry, Médéric-Louis-Élie]. *Moreau de St. Méry's American Journey [1793–1798]*. Tr. and ed. by Kenneth Roberts and Anna M. Roberts. New York, 1947. [1794, 1799, 1814]

Morehouse, Ward. *American Reveille: The United States at War*. New York, 1942. [1942]

Morley, Christopher. "New York, One Way," in *Saturday Review of Literature,* XVI (June 26, 1937), 13–14. [1937]

M'Robert, Patrick. *A Tour through Part of the North Provinces of America: Being A Series of Letters wrote on the Spot, in the Years 1774 & 1775*. Edinburgh, 1776. [1774]

Muir, Ramsay. *America the Golden*. London, 1927. [1926]

Muirhead, James F. *The Land of Contrasts, A Briton's View of his American Kin*. New York and London, 1898. [1893]

Munsterberg, Hugo. *The Americans*. Tr. from the German by Edwin B. Holt. New York, 1904. [1904]

Murat, Achille. *America and the Americans*. New York, 1849. [1829–1830]

Natarajan, K. *Our Trip to America*. Bombay, 1934. [1933]

Neilson, Peter. *Recollections of a Six Years' Residence in the United States of America*. Glasgow, 1833. [1822–1828]

Nevinson, Henry W. "Good-bye, America!" Reprinted in Allan Nevins, ed. *America Through British Eyes* (New York, 1948), 395–98.

Newman, Bernard. *American Journey*. London, 1943. [1942]

Newton, Eric. Comment in Manchester *Guardian*. Quoted in *Living Age*, CCCLIII (1937), 78–79. [1937]

"New York in America." Quoted in O'Callaghan. *Documentary History . . . New York*, I, 494–95. [1749]

New York *Independent*, June 25, 1864. Quoted in E. D. Fite, *Social and Industrial Conditions in the North During the Civil War*. New York, 1910. [1864]

New York *Evening Post*. August 20, 1814. Quoted in Stokes. *Iconography*, V, 1574. [1814]

Nichols, Beverley. *Uncle Samson*. London, 1950. [1949]

O'Brien, Charlotte. "The Emigrant in New York," in *The Nineteenth Century*, XVI (October 1884), 530–49. [1881]

Odescalchi, Prince Baldassare. "An Italian Prince's Opinion of New York," in *Review of Reviews*, XXXII (July–December 1905), 236–37. [1905]

Odets, Clifford. Quoted in Milton Bracker. "Three New Yorks," in *New York Times Magazine* (March 31, 1940), 6–7. [1940]

Offenbach, Jacques. *Offenbach in America, Notes of a Travelling Musician*. New York, 1877. [1875]

Oldmixon, Capt. John W. *Transatlantic Wanderings*. London, 1855. [1854?]

Owen, Collinson. *The American Illusion*. London, 1929. [1928]

Owen, Capt. William. "Narrative of American Voyages and Travels. . . ." Ed. by Victor H. Paltsits, in *Bulletin of the New York Public Library*, XXXV (February 1931), 71–98; (March 1931), 139–62; (April 1931), 263–300; (September 1931), 659–85; (October 1931), 705–58. Much of the material on New York is clearly copied from Burnaby (*supra*) and hence cannot be properly regarded as describing the city at the date of Owen's visit, 1767. [1767]

Pairpont, Alfred. *Uncle Sam and His Country, or Sketches of America, in 1854–55–56*. London, 1857. [1854]

Palmer, Arnold. "Arrived New York," in London *Mercury*, XXXIX (1939), 432–35. [1938–1939]

Palmer, John. *Journal of Travels in the United States of North America and in Lower Canada, Performed in 1817*. London, 1818. Excerpted in Stokes. *Iconography*, V, 1592. [1817]

Papa, Dario and Ferdinando Fontana. *New-York*. Milan, 1884. [1882]

Pavie, Théodore. *Souvenirs Atlantiques. . . .* 2 vols. Paris, 1833. [1832]

Perrin du Lac, François Marie. *Voyage dans les deux Louisianes et chez les nations sauvages du Missouri, par les États-Unis, l'Ohio et les provinces qui le bordent, en 1801, 1802, et 1803*. Lyon, 1805. [1801]

Perry, George S. "New York," in *Cities of America*. New York, 1947. [1947]

Pfeiffer, Ida. *A Lady's Second Journey Round the World*. 2 vols. London, 1855. [1854]

Pinochet Le-Brun, Tancredo. *Viaje de Esfuerzo*. Santiago de Chile, 1914. [*ca.* 1911]

[Pintard, John]. *Letters from John Pintard to his Daughter Eliza Noel Pintard Davidson, 1816–1833*. New-York Historical Society, *Collections*, LXX–LXXIII (1937–1940). [1816–1833]

[Pitou, Louis Ange]. "The Travels of Louis Ange Pitou in the United States, 1801." Tr. by Sylvia H. Monaghan, in *Légion d'Honneur*, IV (April 1934), 239–50. [1801]

Pope-Hennessy, James. *America is an Atmosphere.* London, 1947. [1945?]
Porteous, Archibald. *A Scamper through some Cities of America.* Glasgow, 1890. [1889?]
Power, Tyrone. *Impressions of America, during the Years 1833, 1834, and 1835.* 2 vols. London, 1836. [1833]
Pownall, Thomas. *A Topographical Description of the Dominions of the United States of America.* Ed. by Lois Mulkearn. Pittsburgh, 1949. [1753–1755]
Powys, John Cowper. "Farewell to America," in *Scribner's Magazine,* XCVII (1935), 201–07. [1934]
Prentice, Archibald. *A Tour in the United States.* 7th ed. London, 1850. [1848]
Price, Clair. "An Older and Wiser New York," in *New York Times Magazine* (January 19, 1941), 10 ff. [1940]
Price, M. Philips. *America after Sixty Years.* London, 1936. [1934]
Priest, William. *Travels in the United States of America; Commencing in the Year 1793 and Ending in 1797.* London, 1802. [1797]
Priestley, J. B. *Midnight on the Desert, A Chapter of Autobiography.* London, 1937. [1935]
———. "Priestley Appraises New York," in New York *Times,* January 4, 1948. [1947]
Pulszky, Francis and Theresa. *White, Red, Black: Sketches of American Society in the United States.* 2 vols. New York, 1853. [1851–1852]
Quennell, Peter. "Manhattan Notebook," in *Cornhill Magazine,* CLIX (1939), 51–57. [1938]
[Quincy, Josiah, Jr.]. "Journal of Josiah Quincy, Junior, 1773," in Massachusetts Historical Society, *Proceedings,* XLIX (1915–1916), 424–81. [1773]
[Raeder, Ole M.]. *America in the Forties: the Letters of Ole Munch Raeder.* Tr. and ed. by Gunnar J. Malmin. Minneapolis, 1929. [1848]
Rasière, Isaack de. Letter from Isaack de Rasière to the Amsterdam Chamber of the West India Company, September 23, 1626. Reprinted in A. J. F. van Laer, tr. and ed. *Documents Relating to New Netherland 1624–1626 in the Henry E. Huntington Library.* San Marino, Cal., 1924. [1626]
Ratzel, Friedrich. *Städte- und Culturbilder aus Nordamerika.* 2 vols. Leipzig, 1876. [1873–1874]
Reed, Douglas. *Far and Wide.* London, 1951. [1949]
Reed, Edward Bliss, ed. *The Commonwealth Fund Fellows and their Impressions of America.* New York, 1932. [1928–1930]
Reiss, N. *Excursion à New-York.* Brussels, 1851. [*ca.* 1850]
Rhinelander, Frederick. Letter to Peter Van Schaack, February 23, 1776. Quoted in Henry C. Van Schaack. *The Life of Peter Van Schaack.* New York, 1842. [1776]
Rhodes, Harrison. *American Towns and People.* New York, 1920. [*ca.* 1920]
Rice, Elmer. Quoted in Milton Bracker. "Three New Yorks," in *New York Times Magazine* (March 31, 1940), 6–7. [1940]
Riedesel, Frederika. *Letters and Journals Relating to the War of the American Revolution, and the Capture of the German Troops at Saratoga.* Tr. by William L. Stone. Albany, 1867. [1779–1781]
Riesenberg, Felix and Alexander Alland. *Portrait of New York.* New York, 1939. [1938]
Riis, Jacob A. *How the Other Half Lives: Studies among the Tenements of New York.* New York, 1890. [1888]
[Rivington, —— and —— Harris] [pseud., Two Englishmen]. *Reminiscences of America in 1869.* London, 1870. [1869]

Roberts, Cecil. *And So to America.* New York, 1947. [1939]

[Robertson, Archibald]. *Archibald Robertson, His Diaries and Sketches in America.* Ed. by Harry M. Lydenberg. New York, 1930. [1776]

Robertson, James. *A Few Months in America: containing remarks on some of its Industrial and Commercial Interests.* London, n.d. [1853–1854]

Robertson, William and W. F. *Our American Tour.* Edinburgh, 1871. [1869]

Rogers, Robert. *A Concise Account of North America.* Dublin, 1770. [*ca.* 1765]

Romains, Jules. *Salsette Discovers America.* Tr. from the French by Lewis Galantière. New York, 1942. [1941]

——. *Visite aux Américains.* [Paris], 1936. [1935]

Romulo, Carlos P. *My Brother Americans.* Garden City, N. Y., 1945. [1943]

Rose, George [pseud., Arthur Sketchley]. *The Great Country; or, Impressions of America.* London, 1868. [*ca.* 1867?]

Rothschild, Philippe de [pseud., Philippe]. *Paris-Paris: Instantanés d'Amérique.* Paris, 1931. [*ca.* 1930]

Rousiers, Paul de. *American Life.* Tr. by A. J. Herbertson. Paris, 1892. [1890]

Rovere, Richard. "The Decline of New York City," in *The American Mercury,* LVIII (May 1944), 526–32. [1944]

[Royall, Anne]. *Sketches of History, Life, and Manners in the United States, By a Traveller.* New Haven, 1826. [1824–1825]

——. *The Black Book; or, a Continuation of Travels in the United States.* 3 vols. Washington, 1828, 1829. [1827]

[Ruggles, Edward]. *A Picture of New-York in 1846; with a Short Account of Places in Its Vicinity designed as a Guide to Citizens and Strangers.* New York, 1846. [1846]

[Russell, Charles Russell]. *Diary of a Visit to the United States of America in the year 1883* by Charles lord Russell, of Killowen. Ed. by Charles G. Herbermann. New York, 1910. [1883]

Russell, William H. *My Diary North and South.* Boston, New York, 1863. [1861]

Sagra, Ramon de la. *Cinq Mois aux États-Unis de l'Amérique du Nord. . . .* Tr. de l'espagnol par M. René Baïssas. Brussels, 1837. [1835]

Saint-Saëns, Camille. *Au Courant de la Vie.* Paris, 1914. [1906]

Saint-Victor, Jacques Benj. Maximilien Bins, comte de. *Lettres sur les États-Unis d'Amérique, écrites en 1832 et 1833.* 2 vols. Paris, 1835. [1832]

Sala, George Augustus. *America Revisited.* London, 1883. [1879]

——. *My Diary in America in the Midst of War.* 2 vols. London, 1865. [1864]

[Sarmiento, Domingo F.]. *A Sarmiento Anthology.* Tr. from the Spanish by Stuart E. Grummon. Princeton, 1948. [1847, 1865–66]

Saroyan, William. Quoted in Milton Bracker. "Three New Yorks," in *New York Times Magazine* (March 31, 1940), 6–7. [1940]

Sartre, Jean-Paul. "Manhattan: Great American Desert." Excerpted from *Town and Country* (1946), in Klein, ed. *The Empire City,* 451–57. [1945]

Sauvin, Georges. *Autour de Chicago: Notes sur les États-Unis.* Paris, 1893. [1892]

[Schaukirk, Rev. Ewald G.]. "Diary." Published as *Occupation of New York City by the British,* a reprint from *Pennsylvania Magazine of History and Biography,* I (January 1877). [1775–1783]

[Schliemann, Heinrich]. *Schliemann's First Visit to America, 1850–1851.* Ed. by Shirley H. Weber. Cambridge, Mass., 1942. [1850, 1852]

Scott, David. "New York in a Day—an English Impression," in London *Mercury,* XXXII (1935), 253–61. [*ca.* 1935]

[Serle, Ambrose]. *The American Journal of Ambrose Serle.* Ed. by Edward H. Tatum, Jr. San Marino, Cal., 1940. [1776–1777]

Shanly, Charles D. "Germany in New York," in *The Atlantic Monthly,* XIX (January–June 1867), 555–64. [*ca.* 1867]

Sheridan, Clare. *My American Diary.* New York, 1922. [1921]

Shirreff, Patrick. *A Tour through North America; together with a Comprehensive View of the Canadas and the United States as adapted for agricultural emigration.* Edinburgh, 1835. [1833]

Siegfried, André. *America Comes of Age.* Tr. from the French by H. H. Hemming and Doris Hemming. New York, 1927. [1925]

———. *Deux Mois en Amérique du Nord à la Veille de la Guerre (Juin–Juillet, 1914).* Paris, 1916. [1914]

Sienkiewicz, Henryk. *Briefe aus Amerika mit specialler Erlaubnis des Verfassers aus dem Polnischen.* Tr. from the Polish by I. von Immendorf. Oldenburg and Leipzig, [1903?]. [1876]

Simoneschi, Ottavio. *Il mio viaggio negli Stati Uniti d'America.* Livorno, 1937. [1937]

Simonin, Louis L. *Le Monde Américain, souvenirs de mes voyages aux États-Unis.* Paris, 1877. [1876]

Skinner, John E. Hilary. *After the Storm; or, Jonathan and his neighbours in 1865–66.* 2 vols. London, 1866. [1865]

Smith, Frederick E., 1st Earl of Birkenhead. *America Revisited.* Boston, 1924. [1923]

Smith, Matthew Hale. *Sunshine and Shadow in New York.* Hartford, 1868. [1868]

Smith, Samuel. *America Revisited.* Liverpool, 1896. [1896]

[Smith, T.]. *Rambling Recollections of a Trip to America.* Edinburgh, 1875. [1874]

Smith, William. "Diary." Excerpted in Stokes. *Iconography,* IV, V, *passim.* [1756]

Smyth, J. F. D. *A Tour in the United States of America.* 2 vols. London, 1784. [1777?]

Soissons, G. J. R., comte de. *A Parisian in America.* Boston, 1896. [1895?]

Soupault, Philippe. "La 'dépression' à New-York," in *L'Europe Nouvelle,* XIV (August 1931), 1083–84. [1931]

Souvoroff, Princesse. *Quarante Jours à New-York: Impressions de Voyage.* Paris, 1878. [1878]

[Sparks, Jared]. Herbert Adams. *The Life and Writings of Jared Sparks.* 2 vols. Boston, 1893. [1826]

Spectator, The. Comment in *Outlook,* XCIV (1910), 795–96. [1910]

Spencer, Herbert. "The Americans," in *Essays, Scientific, Political, and Speculative.* 3 vols. New York, 1914. [1882]

Spender, Harold. *A Briton in America.* London, 1921. [1920–1921]

Spender, J. A. *Through British Eyes.* New York, 1928. [1927–1928]

Stead, W. T. "My First Visit to America," in *Review of Reviews,* IX (1894), 410–17. [1893]

Steevens, G. W. *The Land of the Dollar.* New York, 1897. [1896]

Steinbeck, John. "The Making of a New Yorker" (1953). Quoted in Klein, ed. *The Empire City,* pp. 469–75. [*ca.* 1953]

Stevenson, Robert L. Quoted in J. C. Furnas. *Voyage to Windward.* New York, 1951. [1879–80, 1887]

———. *The Travels and Essays of Robert L. Stevenson.* New York, 1911. [1887]

[Stiles, Ezra]. "Diary of Ezra Stiles," in Massachusetts Historical Society, *Proceedings,* 2d series, VII (1891–1892), 338–44. [1754]

Strachan, J. E. *New Zealand Observer: A Schoolmaster Looks at America.* New York, 1940. [1938]

[Strong, George T.]. *The Diary of George Templeton Strong.* Ed. by Allan Nevins and Milton Halsey Thomas. 4 vols. New York, 1952. [1837–1874]

Strunsky, Simeon. *No Mean City.* New York, 1944. [1944]

Stuart, James. *Three Years in America.* 2 vols. Edinburgh, 1833. [1828]

Stuart-Wortley, Lady Emmeline. *Travels in the United States, etc. during 1849 and 1850.* 3 vols. London, 1851. [1849]

Sutcliff, Robert. *Travels in Some Parts of North America in the Years 1804, 1805, & 1806.* Philadelphia, 1812. [1804, 1805]

Swan, Annie S. [Mrs. A. Burnett-Smith]. *America at Home: Impressions of a Visit in War Time.* London, 1920. [1917–1918]

[Talleyrand-Périgord, Charles Maurice de]. *Talleyrand in America as a Financial Promoter, 1794–1796.* Tr. and ed. by Hans Huth and Wilma J. Pugh, in American Historical Association, *Annual Report, 1941.* [1795]

Tappan, Henry P. *The Growth of Cities: a Discourse delivered before the New York Geographical Society, on the evening of March 15th, 1855.* New York, 1855. [1855]

Tardieu, André. *Notes sur les États-Unis: la société, la politique, la diplomatie.* Paris, 1908. [1908]

Tato Cumming, Gaspar. *Nueva York. Un Español entre Rascacielos.* Madrid, 1945. [1945]

Techla, Georg. *Drei Jahre in New-York: eine Skizze, für das Volk nach der Natur gezeichnet.* Zwichau, 1862. [*ca.* 1858–1859]

[Thackeray, William M.] James Grant Wilson. *Thackeray in the United States, 1852–53, 1855–56.* 2 vols. New York, 1904. [1852–1853]

Thompson, C. V. R. *I Lost My English Accent.* New York, 1939. [1933]

Times, The (London). *A Visit to the States.* 2 vols. London, 1888. [1887]

Tingfang, Wu. See Wu Tingfang.

Tocqueville, Alexis de. *Democracy in America.* Ed. by Phillips Bradley. 2 vols. New York, 1945. [1831]

Toller, Ernst. *Which World—Which Way?* Tr. of his *Quer durch; Reisebilder und Reden.* Berlin, 1930. [1929]

Trollope, Anthony. *North America.* 2 vols. London, 1862. [1861]

Trollope, Frances. *Domestic Manners of the Americans.* Ed. by Michael Sadleir. Reprinted from 5th ed. New York, 1927. [1831]

Tudor, Henry. *Narrative of a Tour in North America* . . . 2 vols. London, 1834. [1831]

Tudor, William. *Letters on the Eastern States.* Boston, 1821. [1819]

Turenne d'Aynac, Gabriel Louis, comte de. *Quatorze Mois dans l'Amérique du Nord (1875–1876).* 2 vols. Paris, 1879. [1875–1876]

Turland, Ephraim. *Notes of a Visit to America.* Manchester, 1877. [1876]

Unonius, Gustav E. M. *A Pioneer in Northwest America.* Minneapolis, 1950. Translation by Jonas O. Backlund of Unonius, *Minnen från en sjuttonårig vistelse i nordvestra Amerika.* Upsala, 1861–1862. [1841, 1853, 1858]

Van Dyke, John C. *The New New York.* New York, 1909. [*ca.* 1908]

Vanéechout, Édouard Polydore [pseud., L. du Hailly]. *Campagnes et Stations sur les côtes de l'Amérique du Nord.* Paris, 1864. [1861]

van Wassenaer, Nicolaes Janzoon. *Historisch Verhael,* pt. XII (November 1626).

Excerpted in Jameson, ed. *Narratives of New Netherland,* pp. 67–96. [1626]
Vay, Péter, count Vay de Vaya and Luskod. *The Inner Life of the United States.* New York, 1908. [1905]
Venzmer, Gerhard. *New Yorker Spaziergänge; Eindrücke und Betrachtungen aus der Metropole der neuen Welt.* Hamburg, 1925. [*ca.* 1923]
Verrazano, Giovanni da. *Cèllere Codex.* Quoted in Jacques Habert. *When New York Was Called Angoulême.* New York, 1949. [1524]
Vetter, Christoph. *Zwei Jahre in New-York: Schilderung einer Seereise von Havre nach New-York und Charakteristik des New-Yorker politischen und socialen Lebens.* Hof, 1849. [1847–1848]
Vigne, Godfrey T. *Six Months in America.* Philadelphia, 1833. [1831]
Vinde, Victor. *America at War.* Tr. by E. Classen. London, 1944. [1942]
Visconti-Venosta, Enrico. *Impressions of America.* Chicago, 1933. [1932?]
Vollard, Ambroise. "Mon Voyage en Amérique," in *Revue Bleue, Politique et littéraire,* LXXV (1937), 595–97. [1937]
Volney, Constantin F. Chasseboeuf, comte de. *View of the Climate and Soil of the United States of America.* London, 1804. [*ca.* 1795]
von Bülow, Adam Heinrich Dietrich. *Der Freistaat von Nordamerika in seinem neuesten Zustand.* 2 vols. Berlin, 1797. [1795–1796]
von Gerstner, Clara. *Beschreibung einer Reise durch die Vereinigten Staaten von Nordamerica in den Jahren 1838 bis 1840.* Leipzig, 1842. [1838]
von Hübner, graf Joseph Alexander. *A Ramble Round the World.* Tr. by Lady Herbert. 2 vols. London, 1874. [1871]
——. *Promenade autour du monde, 1871.* Paris, 1873. [1871]
von Keyserling, graf Hermann Alexander. *America Set Free.* New York, 1929. [1928]
——. *The Travel Diary of a Philosopher.* 2 vols. New York, 1925. [1912]
von Koeller, Joseph. *Nordamerikanische Schilderungen (1855–65).* Hilpoltstein, 1880. [1855–1865]
von Krafft, Lieut. John Charles Philip. "Journal," in New-York Historical Society, *Collections,* XV (1882). [1778, 1779]
von Luckner, graf Felix. *Seeteufel erobert Amerika.* Leipzig, 1928. [1926–1927]
von Raumer, Friedrich L. G. *America and the Americans.* Tr. by William Turner. New York, 1846. [1844]
Vries, David P. De. *Short Historical and Journal-Notes of various Voyages performed in the Four Quarters of the Globe, . . .* Excerpted in Jameson, ed. *Narratives of New Netherland,* pp. 186–234. [1642]
Wagner, Charles. *My Impressions of America.* New York, 1906. [1904]
Waithman, Robert. *Report on America.* London, 1940. [1937–1939]
Wakefield, Sir Charles Cheers. *America To-day and To-morrow, a Tribute of Friendship.* London, 1924. [1922]
Walter, J[ohn]. *First Impressions of America.* London, 1867. [1866]
Wansey, Henry. *An Excursion to the United States of North America in the Summer of 1794.* Salisbury, 1798. [1794]
Watkin, Edward W. *A Trip to the United States and Canada: in a series of letters.* London, 1852. [1851]
Weiller, Lazare. *Les Grandes Idées d'un Grand Peuple.* Paris, 1903. [*ca.* 1902]
Weld, Isaac, Jr. *Travels through the States of North America and Provinces of Upper and Lower Canada during the Years 1795, 1796, and 1797.* London, 1800. [1795–1796]

Wells, H. G. *The Future in America*. New York, 1906. [1906]

West, Rebecca. "Impressions of America," in *New Republic,* XLI (December 1924), 65–68. [*ca.* 1924]

Whibley, Charles. *American Sketches*. Edinburgh and London, 1908. [*ca.* 1907?]

White, E. B. *Here Is New York*. New York, 1949. [1948]

White, William Allen. "Imperial City," in *Literary Digest,* CXXIV (October 1937), 13–14. [1937]

[Whitman, Walt]. Articles written by Whitman as editor of New York *Aurora*. Excerpted in *Walt Whitman of the New York "Aurora."* Ed. by Joseph J. Rubin and Charles H. Brown. State College, Pa., 1950. [1842]

——. "A Broadway Pageant," in *Complete Poetry and Prose*. Ed. by Malcolm Cowley (2 vols., New York, 1948), I, 234–37; "Broadway," *ibid.,* I, 442; "City of Ships," *ibid.,* I, 273–74; "Crossing Brooklyn Ferry," *ibid.,* I, 166–72; "Give Me the Splendid Silent Sun," *ibid.,* I, 287–88; "Mannahatta," I, 409–10; "Song of Myself," *ibid.,* I, 62–114. [1860–1888]

——. *Democratic Vistas. Ibid.,* II, 208–63. [1870]

——. Articles written for *Life Illustrated*. Reprinted in *New York Dissected*. New York, 1936. [1856]

——. *Specimen Days & Collect*. Philadelphia, 1882–1883. [1878–1879]

Wilde, Oscar. *Impressions of America*. Sunderland, 1906. [1882]

Williams, Jesse L. *New York Sketches*. New York, 1902.

Willis, Anthony A. [pseud., Anthony Armstrong]. *Britisher on Broadway*. London, 1932. [1932]

Willis, Nathaniel P. *The Complete Works*. New York, 1846. [1843–1844]

Wilson, Charles H. *The Wanderer in America, or Truth at Home*. 2d ed. Thirsk, 1822. [1819]

Wilson, Edmund. *Travels in Two Democracies*. New York, 1936. [1932–1934]

Wilson, James G. *Thackeray in the United States, 1852–53, 1855–56*. 2 vols. New York, 1904. [1850's]

Wolfe, Thomas. *The Web and the Rock*. New York, 1937. [1930's]

Wolley, Charles. *A Two Years' Journal in New York*. Ed. by Edward G. Bourne. Cleveland, 1902. [1679]

Woollcott, Alexander. *Going to Pieces*. New York, 1928. Quoted in Klein, ed. *The Empire City,* pp. 420–21. [*ca.* 1927]

Wright, Frances. [Mrs. Darusmont]. *Views of Society and Manners in America; in a series of letters from that country to a friend in England, during the years 1818, 1819 & 1820, By an Englishwoman*. London, 1821. [1818–1820]

Wu Tingfang. *America Through the Spectacles of an Oriental Diplomat*. New York, 1914. [*ca.* 1913]

[Yanagawa, Masakiyo]. *The First Japanese Mission to America (1860), Being a Diary Kept by a Member of the Embassy*. Tr. by Junichi Fukuyama and Roderick H. Jackson and ed. by M. G. Mori. Kobe, Japan, 1937. [1860]

Yee Chiang. See Chiang, Yee.

Yutang, Lin. See Lin Yutang.

Zannini, Alexandre, comte. *De l'Atlantique au Mississippi: souvenirs d'un diplomate*. Paris, 1884. [*ca.* 1882]

Zavala, D. Lorenzo de. *Viage a los Estados-Unidos del Norte de América*. Paris, 1834. [1830]

Zincke, Foster B. *Last Winter in the United States*. London, 1868. [1867–1868]

SECONDARY WORKS

The following titles, to which reference has been made in footnotes, will be found useful in amplifying the picture of New York City which is presented in the foregoing pages.

Albion, Robert G. *The Rise of the New York Port [1815–1860]*. New York, 1939.

Andrews, Charles M. *The Colonial Period of American History*. 4 vols. New Haven, 1934–1938.

Bakeless, John. *Eyes of Discovery*. Philadelphia, 1950.

Barck, Oscar T., Jr. *New York City during the War for Independence*. New York, 1931.

Bell, Whitfield L. "Thomas Anburey's 'Travels through America': a note on eighteenth-century plagiarism," in Bibliographical Society of America, *Papers*, XXXVII (1943), 23–36.

Berger, Max. *The British Traveller in America, 1836–1860*. New York, 1943.

Blair, Walter. "Mark Twain, New York Correspondent," in *American Literature*, XI (1939), 247–59.

Blake, Nelson M. *Water for the Cities*. Syracuse, N. Y., 1956.

Bridenbaugh, Carl. *Cities in the Wilderness*. New York, 1938.

Chamber of Commerce of the State of New York. *New York City Guide*. New York, 1950.

Channing, Edward. *History of the United States*. 6 vols. New York, 1905–1930.

Childs, Frances S. *French Refugee Life in the United States*. Baltimore, 1940.

Clapp, Margaret. "The Social and Cultural Scene," in Nevins and Krout, eds. *The Greater City* (New York, 1948), 187–260.

Cochran, Thomas C. "The City's Business," in Nevins and Krout, eds. *The Greater City* (New York, 1948), 125–85.

Cole, Arthur C. *The Irrepressible Conflict, 1850–1865*. New York, 1934.

Commager, Henry S., ed. *America in Perspective; the United States through Foreign Eyes*. New York, 1947.

Edwards, George W. *New York as an Eighteenth Century Municipality, 1731–1776*. New York, 1917.

Ernst, Robert. *Immigrant Life in New York City, 1825–1863*. New York, 1949.

Evans, Meryle R. "Knickerbocker Hotels and Restaurants, 1800–1850," in *The New-York Historical Society Quarterly*, XXXVI (October 1952), 377–409.

Federal Writers' Project of the Works Progress Administration in New York City. *New York City Guide*. New York, 1939.

Fite, E. D. *Social and Industrial Conditions in the North During the Civil War*. New York, 1910.

Flick, Alexander, ed. *History of the State of New York*. 10 vols. New York, 1933–1937.

Foner, Philip S. *Business and Slavery: The New York Merchants and the Irrepressible Conflict*. Chapel Hill, 1941.

Forster, John. *The Life of Charles Dickens*. 2 vols. New York, 1907.

Frazier, Edward F. *The Negro in the United States*. New York, 1949.

Gibson, Florence E. *The Attitudes of the New York Irish Toward State and National Affairs, 1848–1892*. New York, 1951.

Greene, Evarts B. and Virginia D. Harrington. *American Population before the Federal Census of 1790*. New York, 1932.

Griffith, Ernest S. *History of American City Government: The Colonial Period.* New York, 1938.

Grout, Donald J. *A Short History of Opera*. New York, 1947.

Guernsey, R. S. *New York City and Vicinity during the War of 1812–1815*. 2 vols. New York, 1895.

Handlin, Oscar. *This Was America*. Cambridge, 1949.

Hartnoll, Phyllis, ed. *The Oxford Companion to the Theatre*. New York, 1951.

Jameson, J. Franklin, ed. *Narratives of New Netherland, 1609–1664*. New York, 1909.

Janvier, Thomas A. *In Old New York*. New York, 1894.

King, Moses, ed. *King's Handbook of New York City*. Buffalo, 1893.

Klein, Alexander, ed. *The Empire City*. New York, 1955.

Kunitz, Stanley J. and Howard Haycraft, eds. *Twentieth-Century Authors*. New York, 1942.

Marraro, Howard R. "Count Luigi Castiglioni, an early traveller to Virginia," in *Virginia Magazine of History and Biography,* LVIII (1950), 473–91.

Mease, James. *The Picture of Philadelphia*. Philadelphia, 1811.

Monaghan, Frank. *French Travellers in the United States: a Bibliography*. New York, 1933.

Morris, Lloyd. *Incredible New York*. New York, 1951.

Musical U.S.A. Ed. by Quaintance Eaton. New York, 1949.

Nevins, Allan, compiler and ed. *America Through British Eyes*. New York, 1948.

Nevins, Allan. *The Emergence of Modern America*. New York, 1927.

Nevins, Allan and John A. Krout, eds. *The Greater City: New York, 1898–1948*. New York, 1948.

Odell, George C. D. *Annals of the New York Stage*. 14 vols. New York, 1927–1945.

O'Callaghan, E. B., ed. *The Documentary History of the State of New-York.* 4 vols. Albany, 1950–1951.

Paltsits, Victor H. "The Founding of New Amsterdam in 1626." *Proceedings of the American Antiquarian Society,* n.s. XXXIV (April 1924), 39–65.

Peltz, Mary Ellis. *Behind the Gold Curtain*. New York, 1950.

Pierce, Bessie L., compiler and ed. *As Others See Chicago*. Chicago, 1933.

Pierson, George W. *Tocqueville and Beaumont in America*. New York, 1938.

Pleasants, Samuel A. *Fernando Wood of New York*. New York, 1948.

Pomerantz, Sidney I. *New York an American City, 1783–1803*. New York, 1938.

Raesly, Ellis L. *Portrait of New Netherland*. New York, 1945.

Rankin, Rebecca B., ed. *New York Advancing: Seven More Years of Progressive Administration in the City of New York, 1939–1945*. New York, 1945.

——, ed. *New York Advancing: a Scientific Approach to Municipal Government*. New York, 1936.

Rezneck, Samuel. "Social History of an American Depression, 1837–1843," in *American Historical Review,* XL (July 1935), 662–87.

——. "The Influence of Depression upon American Opinion, 1857–1859," in *Journal of Economic History,* II (May 1942), 1–23.

Rodgers, Cleveland and Rebecca B. Rankin. *New York: The World's Capital City*. New York, 1948.

Rosario-Nieves, Luis. "Puerto Ricans in New York City from 1910 to 1950." Manuscript, in author's possession.

Schlesinger, Arthur M. *The Rise of the City, 1878–1898.* New York, 1933.

Shepherd, William R. *The Story of New Amsterdam.* New York, 1926.

Siegel-Cooper Company. *A Bird's-Eye View of Greater New York and Its Most Magnificent Store.* New York, 1898.

Singleton, Esther. "History of the Opera in New York from 1750 to 1898," in *Musical Courier,* December 8, 1898, unpaged.

Stokes, I. N. Phelps. *New York Past and Present.* New York, 1939.

———, ed. *The Iconography of Manhattan Island, 1498–1909, compiled from original sources and illustrated by photo-intaglio reproductions. . . .* 6 vols. New York, 1915–1928.

Thwaites, Reuben G., ed. *Early Western Travels, 1748–1846.* 32 vols. Cleveland, 1904–1907.

Torrielli, Andrew J. *Italian Opinion on America As Revealed by Italian Travelers, 1850–1900.* Cambridge, Mass., 1941.

[Union History Co.]. *History of Architecture and the Building Trades of Greater New York.* 2 vols. New York, 1899.

Van Schaack, Henry C. *The Life of Peter Van Schaack.* New York, 1842.

Walt Whitman of the New York "Aurora." Ed. by Joseph J. Rubin and Charles H. Brown. State College, Pa., 1950.

Wertenbaker, Thomas J. *Father Knickerbocker Rebels.* New York, 1948.

———. *The Golden Age of Colonial Culture.* New York, 1949.

Wilson, James G., ed. *The Memorial History of the City of New York.* 4 vols. New York, 1892–1893.

Wittke, Carl. *We Who Built America.* New York, 1939.

INDEX

(Excerpt pages are in italic.)